Microsoft® Official Academic Course

Installation, Storage, and Compute with Windows Server 2016 Exam 70-740

VP & PUBLISHER	Barry Pruett
SENIOR EXECUTIVE EDITOR	Jim Minatel
MICROSOFT PRODUCT MANAGER	Microsoft Learning
PRODUCT DATA MAINTENANCE COORDINATOR	Devon Lewis
TECHNICAL EDITOR	Ron Handlon
CHANNEL MARKETING MANAGER	Michele Szczesniak
CONTENT MANAGEMENT DIRECTOR	Lisa Wojcik
CONTENT MANAGER	Nichole Urban
PRODUCTION COORDINATOR	Nicole Repasky
PRODUCTION EDITOR	Umamaheswari Gnanamani
COVER DESIGNER	Tom Nery

COVER PHOTO: © shutterstock/wavebreakmedia

This book was set in Garamond by SPi Global and printed and bound by Quad/Graphics. The covers were printed by Quad/Graphics.

Microsoft, Active Directory, AppLocker, Bing, BitLocker, Hyper-V, Internet Explorer, Microsoft Intune, Microsoft Office 365, SQL Server, Visual Studio, Windows Azure, Windows, Windows PowerShell, and Windows Server are either registered trademarks or trademarks of Microsoft Corporation in the United States and/or other countries. Other product and company names mentioned herein may be the trademarks of their respective owners.

The example companies, organizations, products, domain names, e-mail addresses, logos, people, places, and events depicted herein are fictitious. No association with any real company, organization, product, domain name, e-mail address, logo, person, place, or event is intended or should be inferred.

The book expresses the author's views and opinions. The information contained in this book is provided without any express, statutory, or implied warranties. Neither the authors, John Wiley & Sons, Inc., Microsoft Corporation, nor their resellers or distributors will be held liable for any damages caused or alleged to be caused either directly or indirectly by this book.

Evaluation copies are provided to qualified academics and professionals for review purposes only, for use in their courses during the next academic year. These copies are licensed and may not be sold or transferred to a third party. Upon completion of the review period, please return the evaluation copy to Wiley. Return instructions and a free-of-charge return mailing label are available at: www.wiley.com/go/returnlabel. If you have chosen to adopt this textbook for use in your course, please accept this book as your complimentary desk copy. Outside of the United States, please contact your local sales representative.

ISBN: 9781119126683 (PBK)
ISBN: 9781119298656 (EVAL)

The inside back cover will contain printing identification and country of origin if omitted from this page. In addition, if the ISBN on the back cover differs from the ISBN on this page, the one on the back cover is correct.

V10002536_071718

Welcome to the Microsoft Official Academic Course (MOAC) program for becoming a Microsoft Certified Solutions Associate for Windows 10. MOAC represents the collaboration between Microsoft Learning and John Wiley & Sons, Inc. publishing company. Microsoft and Wiley teamed up to produce a series of textbooks that deliver compelling and innovative teaching solutions to instructors and superior learning experiences for students. Infused and informed by in-depth knowledge from the creators of Windows 10, and crafted by a publisher known worldwide for the pedagogical quality of its products, these textbooks maximize skills transfer in minimum time. Students are challenged to reach their potential by using their new technical skills as highly productive members of the workforce.

Because this knowledgebase comes directly from Microsoft, architect of the Windows operating system and creator of the Microsoft Certified Solutions Associate exams, you are sure to receive the topical coverage that is most relevant to students' personal and professional success. Microsoft's direct participation not only assures you that MOAC textbook content is accurate and current; it also means that students will receive the best instruction possible to enable their success on certification exams and in the workplace.

■ The Microsoft Official Academic Course Program

The Microsoft Official Academic Course series is a complete program for instructors and institutions to prepare and deliver great courses on Microsoft software technologies. With MOAC, we recognize that because of the rapid pace of change in the technology and curriculum developed by Microsoft, there is an ongoing set of needs beyond classroom instruction tools for an instructor to be ready to teach the course. The MOAC program endeavors to provide solutions for all these needs in a systematic manner in order to ensure a successful and rewarding course experience for both instructor and student—technical and curriculum training for instructor readiness with new software releases; the software itself for student use at home for building hands-on skills, assessment, and validation of skill development; and a great set of tools for delivering instruction in the classroom and lab. All are important to the smooth delivery of an interesting course on Microsoft software, and all are provided with the MOAC program. We think about the model below as a gauge for ensuring that we completely support you in your goal of teaching a great course. As you evaluate your instructional materials options, you may wish to use the model for comparison purposes with available products.

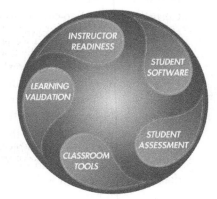

■ Textbook Organization

This textbook is organized in twenty-one lessons, with each lesson corresponding to a particular exam objective for the 70-740 Windows Server 2016 Microsoft Certified Solutions Associate (MCSA) exam. This MOAC textbook covers all the learning objectives for the 70-740 MCSA certification exam. The exam objectives are highlighted throughout the textbook.

■ Pedagogical Features

Many pedagogical features have been developed specifically for Microsoft Official Academic Course programs.

Presenting the extensive procedural information and technical concepts woven throughout the textbook raises challenges for the student and instructor alike. The Illustrated Book Tour that follows provides a guide to the rich features contributing to Microsoft Official Academic Course program's pedagogical plan. Following is a list of key features in each lesson designed to prepare students for success on the certification exams and in the workplace:

- Each lesson begins with an overview of the skills covered in the lesson. More than a standard list of learning objectives, the overview correlates skills to the certification exam objective.

- Illustrations: Screen images provide visual feedback as students work through the exercises. The images reinforce key concepts, provide visual clues about the steps, and allow students to check their progress.

- Key Terms: Important technical vocabulary is listed at the beginning of the lesson. When these terms are used later in the lesson, they appear in bold italic type and are defined.

- Engaging point-of-use reader aids, located throughout the lessons, tell students why this topic is relevant (*The Bottom Line*), provide students with helpful hints (*Take Note*), or show cross-references to where content is covered in greater detail. Reader aids also provide additional relevant or background information that adds value to the lesson.

- Certification Ready features throughout the text signal students where a specific certification objective is covered. They provide students with a chance to check their understanding of that particular exam objective and, if necessary, review the section of the lesson where it is covered.

- Knowledge Assessments provide lesson-ending activities that test students' comprehension and retention of the material taught, presented using some of the question types that they'll see on the certification exam.

- An important supplement to this textbook is the accompanying lab work. Labs are available via a Lab Manual, and also by MOAC Labs Online. MOAC Labs Online provides students with the ability to work on the actual software simply by connecting through their Internet Explorer web browser. Either way, the labs use real-world scenarios to help students learn workplace skills associated with configuring a Windows infrastructure in an enterprise environment.

■ Lesson Features

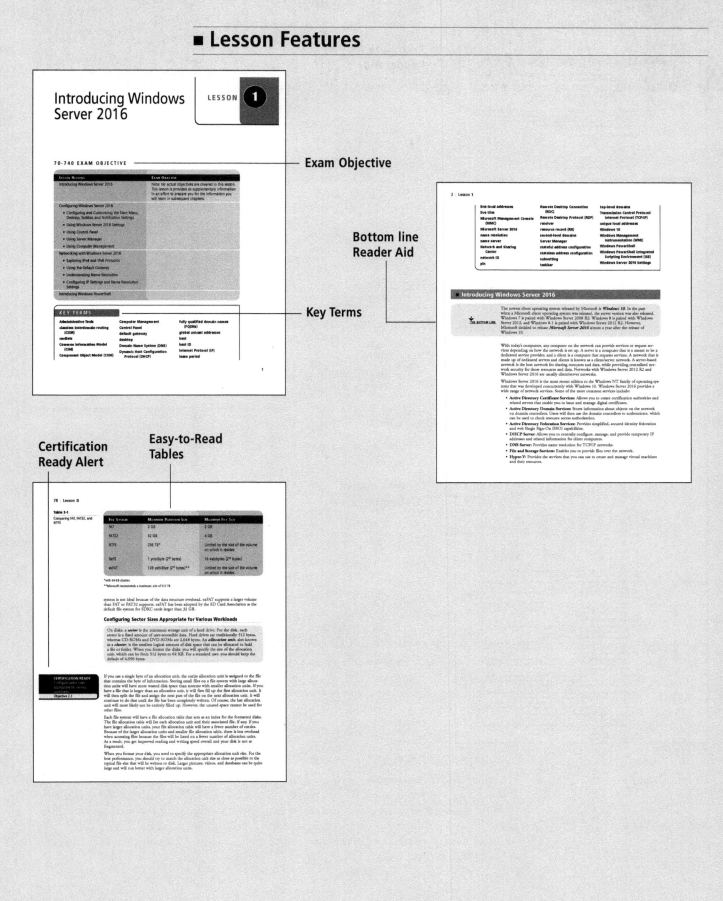

Exam Objective

Bottom line
Reader Aid

Key Terms

Certification
Ready Alert

Easy-to-Read
Tables

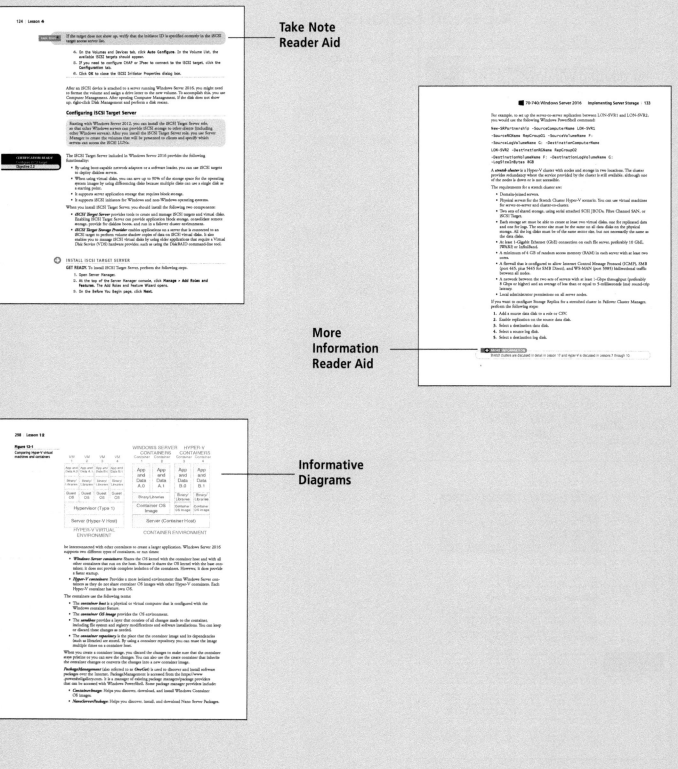

Take Note
Reader Aid

More
Information
Reader Aid

Informative
Diagrams

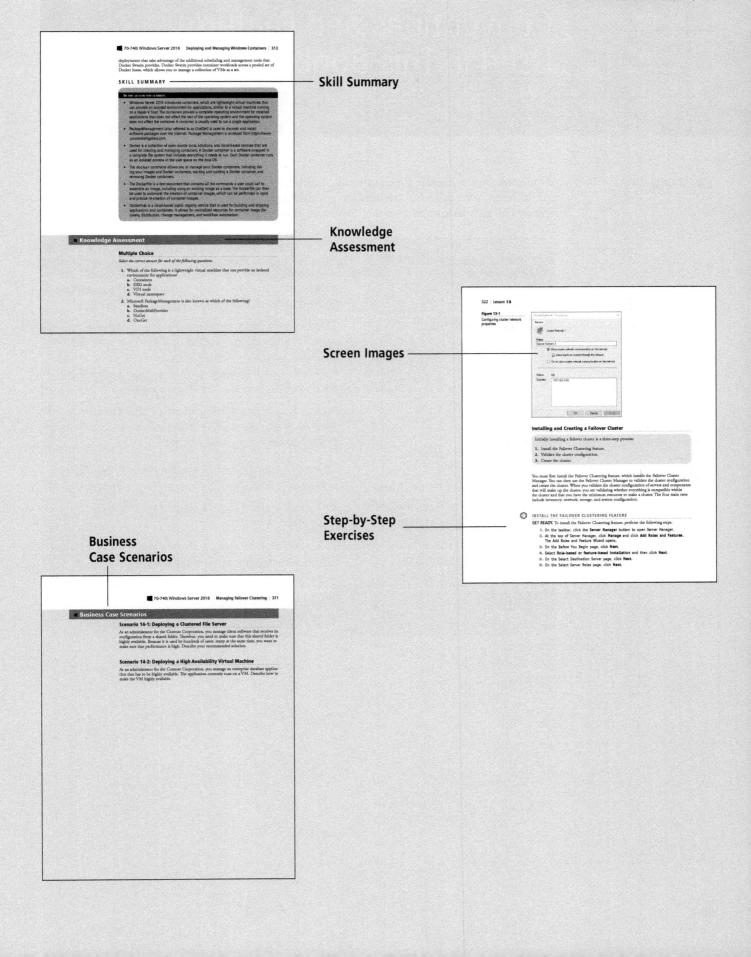

Skill Summary

Knowledge Assessment

Screen Images

Step-by-Step Exercises

Business Case Scenarios

Conventions and Features Used in This Book

This book uses particular fonts, symbols, and heading conventions to highlight important information or to call your attention to special steps. For more information about the features in each lesson, refer to the Illustrated Book Tour section.

CONVENTION	MEANING
↓ THE BOTTOM LINE	This feature provides a brief summary of the material to be covered in the section that follows.
CERTIFICATION READY	This feature signals the point in the text where a specific certification objective is covered. It provides you with a chance to check your understanding of that particular exam objective and, if necessary, review the section of the lesson where it is covered.
TAKE NOTE* ✚ MORE INFORMATION	Reader aids appear in shaded boxes found in your text. *Take Note and More Information* provide helpful hints related to particular tasks or topics.
⚠ WARNING	*Warning* points out instances when error or misuse could cause damage to the computer or network.
A *shared printer* can be used by many individuals on a network.	Key terms appear in bold italic.
cd\windows\system32\ ServerMigrationTools	Commands that are to be typed are shown in a special font.
Click **Install Now**.	Any button on the screen you are supposed to click on or select will appear in bold.

The Microsoft Official Academic Course programs are accompanied by a rich array of resources that incorporate the extensive textbook visuals to form a pedagogically cohesive package. These resources provide all the materials instructors need to deploy and deliver their courses. Instructor resources available at www.wiley.com/ includes:

- **Instructor's Guide.** The Instructor's Guide contains solutions to all the textbook exercises as well as chapter summaries and lecture notes. The Instructor's Guide and Syllabi for various term lengths are available from the Instructor's Book Companion site.

- **Test Bank.** The Test Bank contains hundreds of questions organized by lesson in multiple-choice, best answer, build list, and essay formats and is available to download from the Instructor's Book Companion site. A complete answer key is provided.

- **PowerPoint Presentations.** A complete set of PowerPoint presentations is available on the Instructor's Book Companion site to enhance classroom presentations. Tailored to the text's topical coverage, these presentations are designed to convey key Windows Server 2012 concepts addressed in the text.

- **Available Textbook Figures.** All figures from the text are on the Instructor's Book Companion site. By using these visuals in class discussions, you can help focus students' attention on key elements of Windows 8 and help them understand how to use it effectively in the workplace.

- **MOAC Labs Online.** MOAC Labs Online is a cloud-based environment that enables students to conduct exercises using real Microsoft products. These are not simulations but instead are live virtual machines where faculty and students can perform any activities they would on a local virtual machine. MOAC Labs Online relieves the need for local setup, configuration, and most troubleshooting tasks. This represents an opportunity to lower costs, eliminate the hassle of lab setup, and support and improve student access and portability. MOAC Labs Online are available for students at an additional cost. Contact your Wiley rep about including MOAC Labs Online with your course offering.

- **Lab Answer Keys.** Answer keys for review questions found in the lab manuals and MOAC Labs Online are available on the Instructor's Book Companion site.

- **Lab Worksheets.** The review questions found in the lab manuals and MOAC Labs Online are gathered in Microsoft Word documents for students to use. These are available on the Instructor's Book Companion site.

Book Companion Web Site (www.wiley.com)

The students' book companion site for the MOAC series includes any resources, exercise files, and Web links that will be used in conjunction with this course and any errata.

■ Microsoft Certification

Microsoft Certification has many benefits and enables you to keep your skills relevant, applicable, and competitive. In addition, Microsoft Certification is an industry standard that is recognized worldwide—which helps open doors to potential job opportunities. After you earn your Microsoft Certification, you have access to a number of benefits, which can be found on the Microsoft Certified Professional member site.

Microsoft Learning has reinvented the Microsoft Certification Program by building cloud-related skills validation into the industry's most recognized certification program. Microsoft Certified Solutions Expert (MCSE) and Microsoft Certified Solutions Developer (MCSD) are Microsoft's flagship certifications for professionals who want to lead their IT organization's journey to the cloud. These certifications recognize IT professionals with broad and deep skill sets across Microsoft solutions. The Microsoft Certified Solutions Associate (MCSA) is the certification for aspiring IT professionals and is also the prerequisite certification necessary to earn an MCSE. These new certifications integrate cloud-related and on-premise skills validation in order to support organizations and recognize individuals who have the skills required to be productive using Microsoft technologies.

On-premise or in the cloud, Microsoft training and certification empowers technology professionals to expand their skills and gain knowledge directly from the source. Securing these essential skills will allow you to grow your career and make yourself indispensable as the industry shifts to the cloud. Cloud computing ultimately enables IT to focus on more mission-critical activities, raising the bar of required expertise for IT professionals and developers. These reinvented certifications test on a deeper set of skills that map to real-world business context. Rather than testing only on a feature of a technology, Microsoft Certifications now validate more advanced skills and a deeper understanding of the platform.

Preparing to Take an Exam

Unless you are a very experienced user, you will need to use test preparation materials to prepare to complete the test correctly and within the time allowed. The Microsoft Official Academic Course series is designed to prepare you with a strong knowledge of all exam topics, and with some additional review and practice on your own, you should feel confident in your ability to pass the appropriate exam.

After you decide which exam to take, review the list of objectives for the exam. You can easily identify tasks that are included in the objective list by locating the exam objective overview at the start of each lesson and the Certification Ready sidebars in the margin of the lessons in this book.

To register for the MCSA exam, visit the Microsoft Certifications webpage for directions on how to register with Pearson VUE, the company that delivers the MCSA exams. Keep in mind these important items about the testing procedure:

- **What to expect.** Microsoft Certification testing labs typically have multiple workstations, which may or may not be occupied by other candidates. Test center administrators strive to provide a quiet and comfortable environment for all test takers.

- **Plan to arrive early.** It is recommended that you arrive at the test center at least 30 minutes before the test is scheduled to begin.

- **Bring your identification.** To take your exam, you must bring the identification (ID) that was specified when you registered for the exam. If you are unclear about which forms of ID are required, contact the exam sponsor identified in your registration information. Although requirements vary, you typically must show two valid forms of ID, one with a photo, both with your signature.

- **Leave personal items at home.** The only item allowed into the testing area is your identification, so leave any backpacks, laptops, briefcases, and other personal items at home. If you have items that cannot be left behind (such as purses), the testing center might have small lockers available for use.

- **Nondisclosure agreement.** At the testing center, Microsoft requires that you accept the terms of a nondisclosure agreement (NDA) and complete a brief demographic survey before taking your certification exam.

We thank the MOAC faculty and instructors who have assisted us in building the Microsoft Official Academic Course courseware. These elite educators have acted as our sounding board on key pedagogical and design decisions leading to the development of the MOAC courseware for future Information Technology workers. They have provided invaluable advice in the service of quality instructional materials, and we truly appreciate their dedication to technology education.

Brian Bridson, Baker College of Flint

David Chaulk, Baker College Online

Ron Handlon, Remington College – Tampa Campus

Katherine James, Seneca College of Applied Arts & Technology

Wen Liu, ITT Educational Services

Zeshan Sattar, Pearson in Practice

Jared Spencer, Westwood College Online

David Vallerga, MTI College

Bonny Willy, Ivy Tech State College

We also thank Microsoft Learning's Heidi Johnson, Larry Kaye, Rob Linsky, Colin Lyth, Paul Pardi, Merrick Van Dongen, Liberty Munson, Keith Loeber, Natasha Chornesky, Briana Roberts, Jim Clark, Anne Hamilton, Erika Cravens, and Jim Cochran, for their encouragement and support in making the Microsoft Official Academic Course programs the finest academic materials for mastering the newest Microsoft technologies for both students and instructors.

Patrick Regan has been a PC technician, network administrator/engineer, design architect, and security analyst for the past 23 years. He has taught computer and network classes at Sacramento local colleges (Heald Colleges and MTI Colleges) and participated in and led many projects (Heald Colleges, Intel Corporation, Miles Consulting Corporation, and Pacific Coast Companies). For his teaching accomplishments, he received the Teacher of the Year award from Heald Colleges and he has received several recognition awards from Intel. As a senior system administrator, he supports approximately 120 servers and 1,500 users spread over 5 subsidiaries and 70 sites. He has authored a number of textbooks, including books on SharePoint 2010, Windows 7, Windows 8.1, and Windows Server 2012 for John Wiley & Sons.

Contents

Introducing Windows Server 2016

70-740 EXAM OBJECTIVE

LESSON HEADING	EXAM OBJECTIVE
Introducing Windows Server 2016	Note: No actual objectives are covered in this lesson. This lesson is provided as supplementary information in an effort to prepare you for the information you will learn in subsequent chapters.
Configuring Windows Server 2016 • Configuring and Customizing the Start Menu, Desktop, Taskbar, and Notification Settings • Using Windows Server 2016 Settings • Using Control Panel • Using Server Manager • Using Computer Management	
Networking with Windows Server 2016 • Exploring IPv4 and IPv6 Protocols • Using the Default Gateway • Understanding Name Resolution • Configuring IP Settings and Name Resolution Settings	
Introducing Windows PowerShell	

KEY TERMS

Administrative Tools

classless interdomain routing (CIDR)

cmdlets

Common Information Model (CIM)

Component Object Model (COM)

Computer Management

Control Panel

default gateway

desktop

Domain Name System (DNS)

Dynamic Host Configuration Protocol (DHCP)

fully qualified domain names (FQDNs)

global unicast addresses

host

host ID

Internet Protocol (IP)

lease period

link-local addresses	Remote Desktop Connection (RDC)	top-level domains
live tiles	Remote Desktop Protocol (RDP)	Transmission Control Protocol/Internet Protocol (TCP/IP)
Microsoft Management Console (MMC)	resolver	unique local addresses
Microsoft Server 2016	resource record (RR)	Windows 10
name resolution	second-level domains	Windows Management Instrumentation (WMI)
name server	Server Manager	Windows PowerShell
Network and Sharing Center	stateful address configuration	Windows PowerShell Integrated Scripting Environment (ISE)
network ID	stateless address configuration	Windows Server 2016 Settings
pin	subnetting	
	taskbar	

■ Introducing Windows Server 2016

THE BOTTOM LINE

The newest client operating system released by Microsoft is *Windows 10*. In the past when a Microsoft client operating system was released, the server version was also released. Windows 7 is paired with Windows Server 2008 R2. Windows 8 is paired with Windows Server 2012, and Windows 8.1 is paired with Windows Server 2012 R2. However, Microsoft decided to release *Microsoft Server 2016* almost a year after the release of Windows 10.

With today's computers, any computer on the network can provide services or request services depending on how the network is set up. A server is a computer that is a meant to be a dedicated service provider, and a client is a computer that requests services. A network that is made up of dedicated servers and clients is known as a client/server network. A server-based network is the best network for sharing resources and data, while providing centralized network security for those resources and data. Networks with Windows Server 2012 R2 and Windows Server 2016 are usually client/server networks.

Windows Server 2016 is the most recent edition to the Windows NT family of operating systems that was developed concurrently with Windows 10. Windows Server 2016 provides a wide range of network services. Some of the more common services include:

- **Active Directory Certificate Services:** Allows you to create certification authorities and related servers that enable you to issue and manage digital certificates.
- **Active Directory Domain Services:** Stores information about objects on the network on domain controllers. Users will then use the domain controllers to authenticate, which can be used to check resource access authorization.
- **Active Directory Federation Services:** Provides simplified, secured identity federation and web Single Sign-On (SSO) capabilities.
- **DHCP Server:** Allows you to centrally configure, manage, and provide temporary IP addresses and related information for client computers.
- **DNS Server:** Provides name resolution for TCP/IP networks.
- **File and Storage Services:** Enables you to provide files over the network.
- **Hyper-V:** Provides the services that you can use to create and manage virtual machines and their resources.

- **Print and Document Services:** Enables you to centralize print server and network printer management tasks.
- **Remote Access:** Provides connectivity via DirectAccess, VPN, and Web Application Proxy.
- **Remote Desktop Services:** Enables users to access virtual desktops, session-based desktops, and RemoteApp programs.
- **Web Server/Internet Information Services (IIS):** Provides a reliable, manageable, and scalable Web Application infrastructure.
- **Windows Deployment Services:** Provides a simplified, secure means of rapidly and remotely deploying Windows operating systems to computers over the network.
- **Windows Server Update Services:** Allows network administrators to specify the Microsoft updates that should be installed and to create separate groups of computers for different sets of updates.

■ Configuring Windows Server 2016

THE BOTTOM LINE

Windows Server 2016 is a robust and flexible system that is made to work on and support a wide range of hardware. Although it was designed for larger computers, it can work on laptops and desktop computers. In addition, it can also be executed as a virtual machine.

Because Windows Server 2016 contains a graphical user interface, the primary tools to configure Windows are Windows Server 2016 Settings and Control Panel, which are also graphical tools.

Configuring and Customizing the Start Menu, Desktop, Taskbar, and Notification Settings

The **desktop** is the main screen that you see when you first start the computer and log on to Windows. Like the top of an actual desktop, it is where you perform your work by opening and running one or more applications. It also includes the Recycle Bin, which is used to recover files that have been previously deleted.

At the bottom of the desktop, you will find the **taskbar**, which shows you the programs that are running and allows you to navigate between those programs. On the taskbar, the Start button is shown at the lower-left corner. When you click the Start button, you open the Windows Server 2016 Start menu (as shown in Figure 1-1), which is a blend of the Windows 7 Start menu and the Windows 8 Start screen.

The left side of the Windows Server 2016 Start menu shows the most used programs and provides you with access to File Explorer, Settings, Power, and All apps. When you click All programs, all installed programs are shown in alphabetical order. When you right-click an installed application, you can choose Pin to Start or Pin to taskbar.

When you **pin** a program, the icon for that program displays on the taskbar even when the program isn't running. This provides you with quick access to your frequently used programs. Shortcuts for Task View, Microsoft Edge, File Explorer, and Store appear there by default. You can unpin programs from the taskbar as well. You'll learn about shortcuts later in this lesson.

The right side of the Windows Server 2016 Start menu displays tiles, which are larger than the icons found on the Windows desktop. Unlike the static icons, tiles can contain dynamic

Figure 1-1

Viewing the Windows Server 2016 desktop with the Start menu open

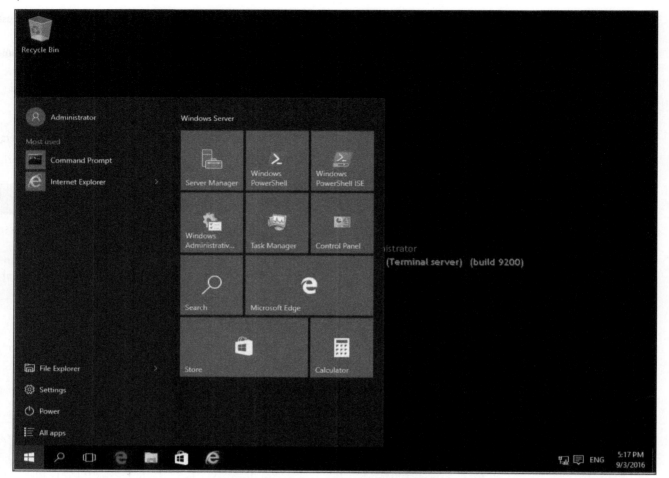

content provided by the software they represent. For example, the tile for a web browser can contain a thumbnail of the currently open website, while the Messaging tile can display part of your latest incoming email. Tiles in Windows Server 2016 that contain this type of dynamic content are called *live tiles*.

The tiles on the Start menu are configurable in a number of ways. You can move the tiles around, change their size, change their groupings, and control whether they display live content. It is also possible to remove seldom-used tiles and add new tiles for applications, files, and shortcuts on the computer.

Using Windows Server 2016 Settings

The *Windows Server 2016 Settings* is a modern interface for common configuration settings that would have been found in Control Panel on older versions of Windows. In addition, you will find additional settings such as touch screen, tablet, and privacy settings that are geared toward phones and tablets that you will not find in Control Panel.

To open settings, click the Start button and then click Settings, which opens the Settings page (see Figure 1-2). These settings are organized as follows:

- **System:** Allows you to configure the display, notifications & actions, apps and features, multitasking, tablet mode, power & sleep options, and default apps
- **Devices:** Provides quick access to hardware devices, such as printers, which you can use with the currently selected app
- **Network & Internet:** Keeps track of Wi-Fi connections and allows you to configure VPN, dial-up connections, Ethernet connections, and proxy settings
- **Personalization:** Provides settings for the background, colors, lock screen, themes, and Start menu
- **Accounts:** Allows you to change the profile picture and add accounts
- **Time & language:** Allows you to configure Date & time, Region & language, and Speech
- **Ease of Access:** Provides settings for Narrator, Magnifier, high contrast, closed captions, keyboard, and mouse settings
- **Privacy:** Allows you to configure camera, microphone, speech, account information, contacts, calendar, messaging, and application radios control for Wi-Fi/Bluetooth connection
- **Update and security:** Allows you to configure Windows Update, activate Windows, perform backups and recoveries, and configure Windows Defender

Figure 1-2

Accessing Windows Server 2016 Settings

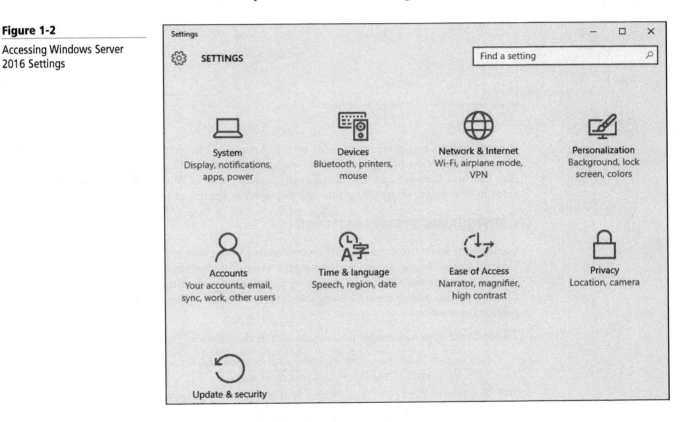

Using Control Panel

With previous versions of Windows, *Control Panel* was a primary graphical utility to configure the Windows environment and hardware devices. It can be accessed in Windows Server 2016 by right-clicking the Start button and choosing Control Panel. See Figure 1-3.

Each category includes a top-level link, and under each top-level link are several of the most frequently performed tasks for the category.

Figure 1-3

Opening Control Panel

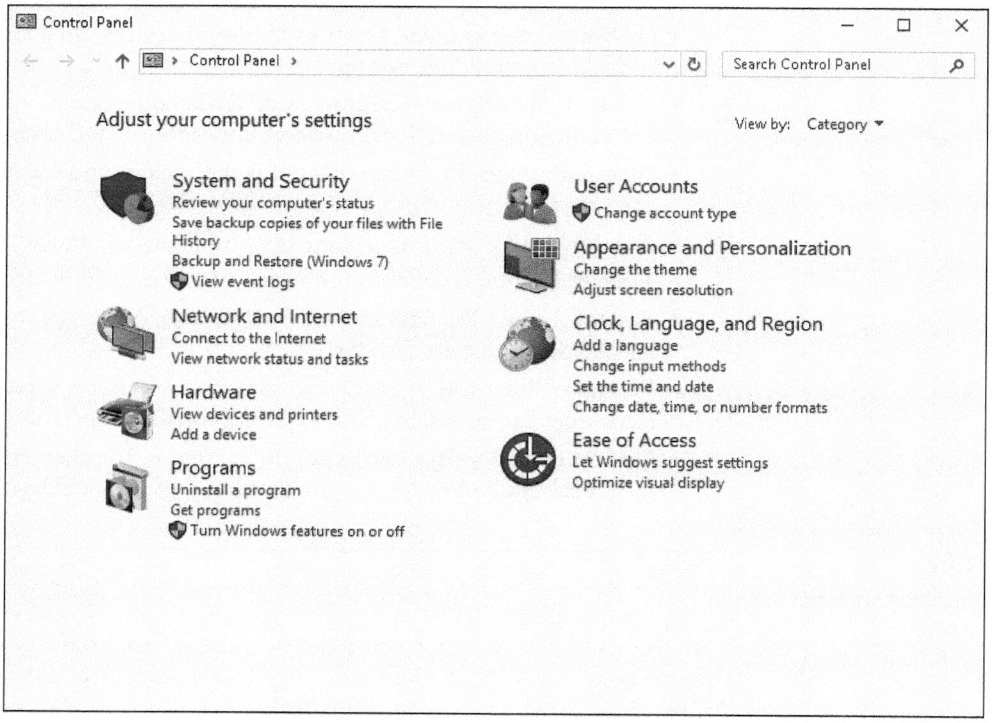

As with current and previous versions of Windows, you can change from the default Category view to Classic view (a large icon view or a small icon view). Icon view is an alternative view that provides the look and functionality of Control Panel in Windows 2000 and earlier versions of Windows, where all options are displayed as applets or icons.

CONFIGURING SYSTEM SETTINGS

Some of the most important configuration settings for a user are the system settings within Control Panel. These include gathering generation information about your system, changing the computer name, adding the computer to a domain, accessing the device manager, configuring remote settings, configuring startup and recovery options, and configuring overall performance settings.

To access the system settings, you can do one of the following:

- In Control Panel, in Category view, click System and Security and then click System or click View amount of RAM and processor speed.
- In Control Panel, in Classic view, double-click the System applet.
- Right-click Computer and choose Properties.
- Right-click the Start button and choose System.

In Windows, there are often several ways to perform a task.

At the top of the screen, your Windows edition and system type are shown. If Windows comes in 64-bit, it will show 64-bit Operating System in the middle of the screen. Toward the bottom of the screen, you will see the computer name and domain (if any) if Windows is activated and the Product ID. See Figure 1-4.

Figure 1-4

Displaying System settings

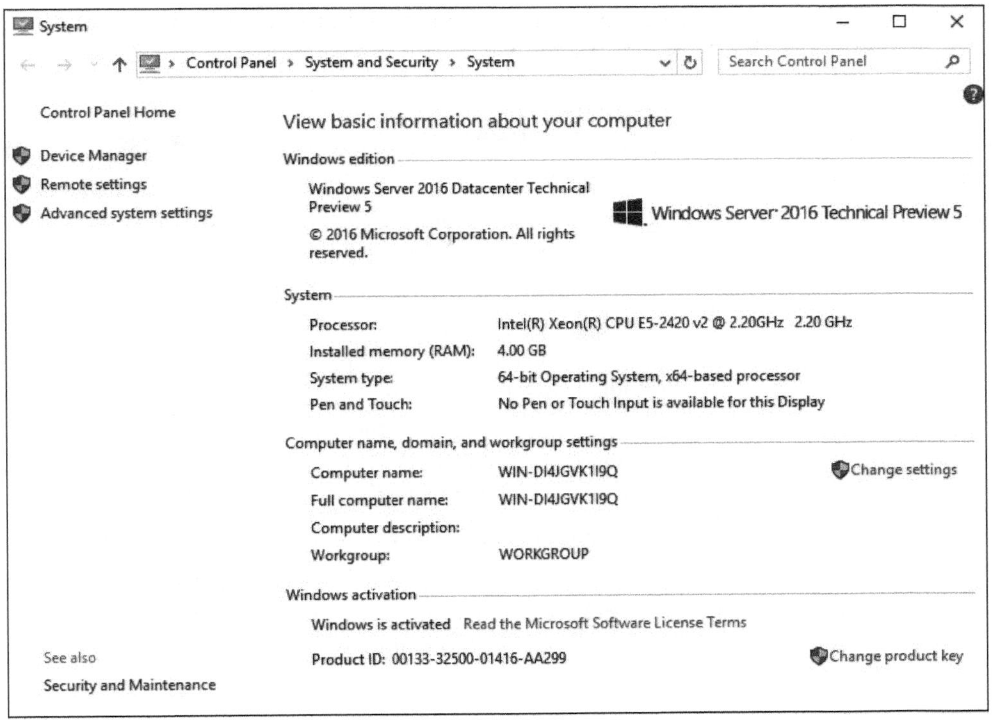

To help identify computers, you should name each computer with a meaningful name. This can be done within the System settings within Control Panel. You can also add a computer to a domain or workgroup.

Every computer must have a unique computer name assigned to a network. If two computers have the same name, one or both of the computers will have trouble communicating on the network. To change the computer name, open System from Control Panel. Then click the Change Settings option in the Computer name, domain, and workgroup settings. In the System Properties dialog box, with the Computer Name tab selected, click the Change button. See Figure 1-5. Any changes to the computer name or workgroup/domain name will require a reboot.

Figure 1-5

Displaying System Properties

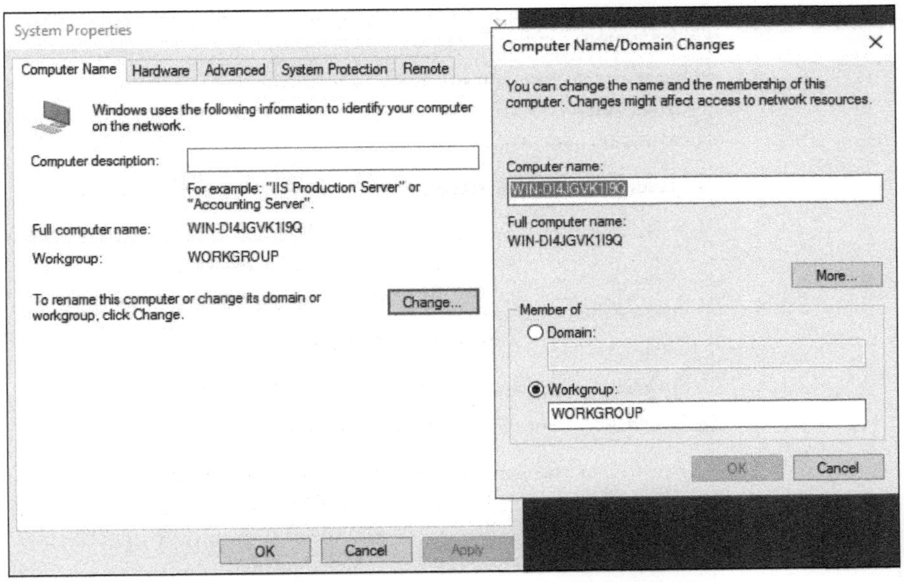

→ **ADD A COMPUTER TO THE DOMAIN**

GET READY. To add a computer running Windows Server 2016 to the domain, perform the following steps.

1. On a computer that is running Windows Server 2016, log on as a local administrator.

2. Right-click the **Start** button and choose **System**.

3. When the Control Panel System page opens, in the Computer name, domain, and workgroup settings option, click the **Change settings** option.

4. When the System Properties dialog box opens, the Computer Name tab is already selected. Click the **Change** button.

5. When the Computer Name/Domain Changes dialog box opens, select the **Domain** option. Then type in the name of the domain, such as **Adatum.com**, and click **OK**.

6. When the Windows Security dialog box opens, log on as **administrator** with the password of **Pa$$w0rd**, and click **OK**.

7. When you receive a welcome to the domain message, click **OK**.

8. When you are prompted to restart your computer to apply these changes, click **OK**.

9. Back at the System Properties dialog box, click **Close**.

10. When you are prompted to restart your computer to apply these changes, click **Restart Now**.

The *Remote Desktop Protocol (RDP)* is a proprietary protocol that was developed by Microsoft to connect to another computer over a network connection using the same graphical interface that you would use if you were sitting in front of the physical server. RDP uses TCP port 3389. Typically, you would access computers remotely using the *Remote Desktop Connection (RDC)*, which would allow you to connect to a Remote Desktop Session Host or to a Remote Application.

To enable either or both of these technologies, open the System Properties (open Control Panel, click System and Security, click Security, and then click Remote settings), as shown in Figure 1-6. By default, the Remote Assistance feature is not installed on Windows Server 2016. By default, Remote Desktop is installed, but it is not enabled.

Figure 1-6

Enabling Remote Desktop

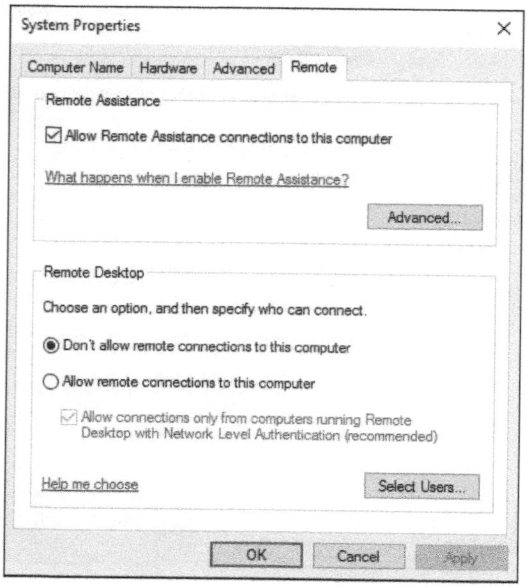

INSTALL THE REMOTE ASSISTANCE FEATURE

GET READY. To install the Remote Assistance feature, perform the following steps.

1. Open Server Manager.
2. At the top of the Server Manager console, click **Manage > Add Roles and Features**. The Add Roles and Feature Wizard opens.
3. On the Before You Begin page, click **Next**.
4. Select **Role-based or feature-based installation** and then click **Next**.
5. On the Select Destination Server page, select the server that you are installing to and click **Next**.
6. On the Select Server Roles page, click **Next**.
7. On the Select Features page, select the **Remote Assistance** feature and click **Next**.
8. On the Confirm Installation Selections page, click **Install**.
9. When the installation is complete, click **Close**.

Click the Advanced button in the Remote Assistance section to specify the maximum amount of time an invitation can remain open (the default is 6 hours) and whether the computer can be controlled remotely or not. You can also specify whether you can create invitations that can only be used from computers running Windows Vista or later, which will encrypt the IP address, which, in turn, cannot be read by Windows XP.

For Remote Desktop, the Allow connections only from computers running Remote Desktop with Network Level Authentication (recommended) option is used to require the user to be authenticated before the session is created, which helps protect the remote computer from malicious users and software. To use Network Level Authentication, the client computer must be using at least Remote Desktop Connection 6.0 and operating systems such as Windows XP with Service Pack 3 or Windows Vista and newer.

The Select Users button is used to specify which users can connect to the system using the RDP. These users are added to the local computer Remote Desktop Users group. The Administrators group already has access even though they are not listed in the Remote Desktop Users list.

To connect to a computer, you use the *Remote Desktop Connections (RDC),* which is the mstsc.exe program, which is found in the Windows Accessories folder. When the program opens, specify a server name or IP address, and click Connect.

CHANGING DATE AND TIME

One of your easiest but most essential tasks is making sure that the computer has the correct date and time, which is essential for logging purposes and for security. If a secure packet is sent with the wrong date or time, the packet might be automatically denied because the date and time is used to determine if the packet is legit.

To access the date and time settings, perform one of the following steps:

- In Category view in Control Panel, click Clock, Language, and Region and then click Set the time and date.
- In Icon view, double-click Date and Time.
- If the date and time is shown in the notification area, double-click the date and time.

To set the clock:

1. Click the Date and Time tab and then click Change date and time.
2. Double-click the hour, minutes, or seconds and then click the arrows to increase or decrease the value.
3. Click OK.

To change the time zone, click Change time zone and then click your current time zone in the drop-down list. Then click OK.

If you are part of a domain, the computer should be synchronized with the domain controllers. When you have a computer that is not part of a domain, you can synchronize with an Internet time server by clicking the Internet Time tab and then selecting the check box next to Synchronize with an Internet time server. Then select a time server and click OK.

Using Server Manager

When managing Windows Server 2016, one of the primary tools you will use is Server Manager. As mentioned earlier, *Server Manager* is used to install, configure, and manage Windows Server 2016 server roles and features. It can also be used to manage local and remote servers without using the Remote Desktop Protocol connections.

Server Manager (as shown in Figure 1-7) provides a single tool so that you can perform the following:

- View, add, remove, and modify server roles and features installed on the server.
- Perform common local server management tasks (as shown in Figure 1-8), such as enabling or disabling Windows Firewall, Remote management, Remote Desktop, NIC teaming, Windows Defender, and IE Enhanced Security Configuration. It can also configure Windows updates and the computer time zone.
- Perform management tasks associated with the installed server role.
- Determine server and server role status, identify critical events, and analyze and troubleshoot configuration issues or failures.
- Access Best Practices Analyzer, which is used to reduce best practice violations for specific server roles.

By default, Server Manager is pinned to the Start menu.

Figure 1-7

Accessing Server Manager

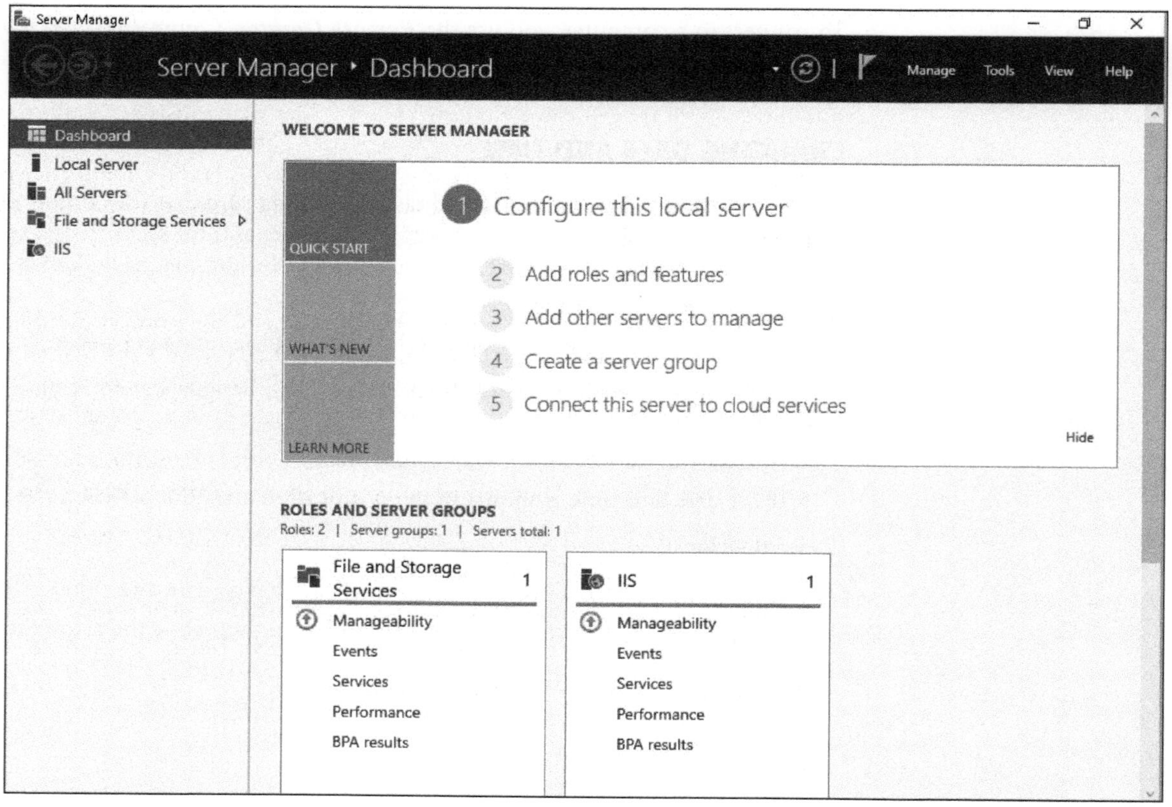

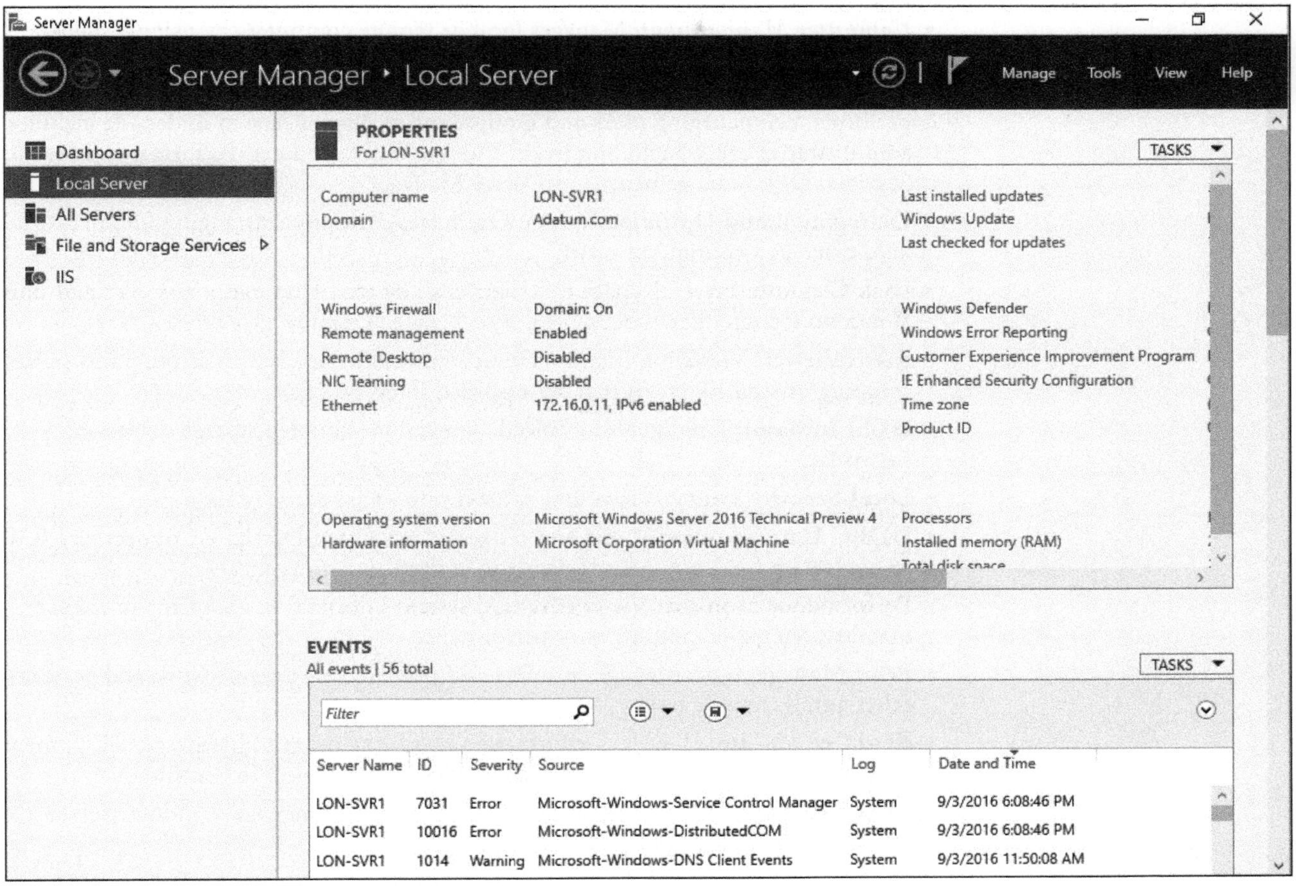

Figure 1-8

Accessing Server Manager
Local Server settings

Using Computer Management

> Windows includes an Administrative Tools folder that consists of multiple tools that will be used to configure Windows Server 2016. One of the more useful tools when managing a computer running Windows Server 2016 is the Computer Management console, which allows you to view events, configure disks, manage users and groups, and manage shared folders.

The *Microsoft Management Console (MMC)* is one of the primary administrative tools used to manage Windows and many of the network services provided by Windows. It provides a standard method to create, save, and open the various administrative tools provided by Windows. When you open Administrative Tools, most of these programs are MMCs.

Administrative Tools is a folder in Control Panel that contains tools for system administrators and advanced users. There are four ways to access Administrative Tools:

- Open Control Panel and then click Start > Control Panel > System and Security > Administrative Tools while in Category view.
- Double-click the Administrative Tools applet while in Icon view.
- Click the Start button > Windows Administrative Tools.
- Open the Tools menu in Server Manager.

Some common administrative tools in this folder include:

- **Component Services:** Configures and administers Component Object Model (COM) components. Component Services is designed for use by developers and administrators.
- *Computer Management:* Manages local or remote computers by using a single, consolidated desktop tool. Using Computer Management, you can perform many tasks, such as monitoring system events, configuring hard disks, managing system performance, managing users and groups, and managing shared folders. It includes other administrative tools, including Event Viewer, Task Scheduler, Performance Monitor, Services, Disk Management, and Device Manager.
- **Defragment and Optimize Drives:** Optimizes drives by rearranging files of a specific hard drive in a contiguous order.
- **Disk Cleanup:** Frees up space on a hard disk by removing temporary files and unneeded Windows Update files.
- **Event Viewer:** Views information about significant events, such as programs starting or stopping or security errors that are recorded in event logs.
- **iSCSI Initiator:** Configures advanced connections between storage devices on a network.
- **Local Security Policy:** Views and edits Group Policy security settings.
- **ODBC Data Sources (32-bit and 64-bit):** Uses Open Database Connectivity (ODBC) to move data from one type of database (a data source) to another.
- **Performance Monitor:** Views advanced system information about the processor, memory, hard disk, and network performance.
- **Print Management:** Manages printers and print servers on a network and performs other administrative tasks.
- **Resource Monitor:** Displays information about the usage of hardware (CPU, memory, disk, and network) and software (file handles and modules) in real time.
- **Server Manager:** Allows you to install, configure, and manage Windows Server 2016 server roles and features.
- **Services:** Manages the different services that run in the background on your computer.
- **System Configuration:** Identifies problems that might be preventing Windows from running correctly.
- **System Information:** Shows details about your computer's hardware configuration, computer components, and software, including drivers.
- **Task Scheduler:** Schedules programs or other tasks to run automatically.
- **Windows Firewall with Advanced Security:** Manages the host-based firewall, including enabling/disabling Windows Firewall and creating exceptions.
- **Windows Memory Diagnostic:** Checks your computer's memory to see whether it is functioning properly.
- **Windows PowerShell:** Provides a task-based command-line shell and scripting language designed especially for system administration.

When many of the Windows Server 2016 server roles are installed, an MMC console is added to Administrative Tools.

You might assume that these tools are used only to manage the local computer. However, many of them can be used to manage remote computers as well. For example, you can use the Computer Management console to connect to and manage other computers, assuming you have administrative rights to the computer.

You can access the Computer Management console with one of the following methods:

- Right-click the Start button and choose Computer Management.
- Using Server Manager, open the Tools menu and click Computer Management.
- Open the Administrative Tools folder and double-click Computer Management.

Local user accounts allow a user to log on directly to a computer running Windows 10 for which the local account is created on. However, if a remote computer has a local account with the same user name and password, the user can access resources on the remote computer. Local user accounts can be managed using the Windows 10 Settings or using Computer Management.

⊙ **CREATE A WINDOWS SERVER 2016 LOCAL ACCOUNT USING COMPUTER MANAGEMENT**

GET READY. To create a Windows Server 2016 local account using Computer Management, perform the following steps.

1. On LON-SVR1, right-click the **Start** button and choose **Computer Management**.
2. When the Computer Management console opens, expand **Local Users and Groups** and click **Users**, as shown in Figure 1-9.

Figure 1-9

Managing users with Computer Management

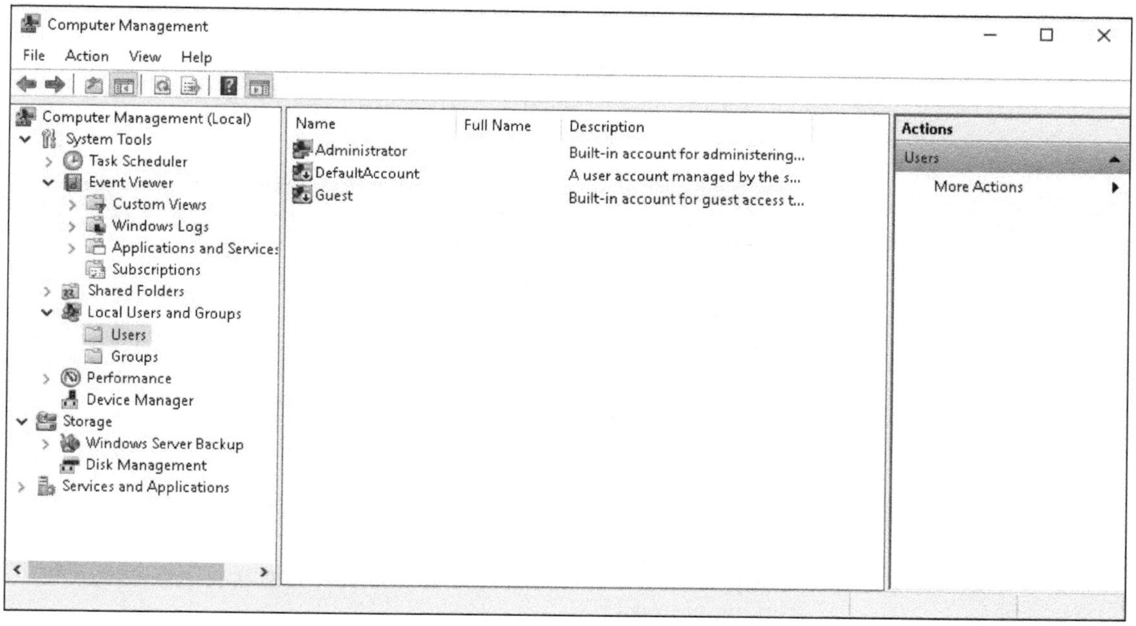

3. Right-click the **Users** node and choose **New User**.
4. In the User name text box, type a name such as **User2**. In the Full name text box, type **User 2**.
5. In the Password and Confirm password text boxes, type a password such as **Pa$$w0rd**.
6. Click the **Create** button.
7. To close the New User dialog box, click **Close**.

You can then double-click the user to manage the properties of the user. For example, to add a user to a group, you can use the Member Of tab. To specify the location of the profile path or the home folder, you can use the Profile tab.

By default, the administrator is a built-in local user found in Windows that has full control of the specified system. To give administrative access to a computer, you just need to add the local or domain user account to the Administrators group.

⊕ ADD A USER ACCOUNT TO THE ADMINISTRATOR ACCOUNT

GET READY. To create a Windows 10 local account using Computer Management, perform the following steps.

1. On LON-SVR1, right-click the **Start** button and choose **Computer Management.**
2. When the Computer Management console opens, expand **Local Users and Groups** and click **Groups.**
3. Double-click the **Administrators** group.
4. When the Administrators Properties dialog box opens, click **Add.**
5. If the computer is not part of a domain, the location will be set to the local computer. If the computer is part of a domain, the location will be set to the domain. If you need to change the domain to a local computer so that you can add a local user account, click the **Locations** button to open the Locations dialog box. Then select the domain (such as **Adatum.com**), and click **OK.**
6. When the Select Users dialog box opens, in the Enter the object names to select text box, type the name of the user that you want to add, such as **user2**, and click **OK.**

■ Networking with Windows Server 2016

↓
THE BOTTOM LINE

When accessing computers on a network, you typically communicate by using their host names. If you are accessing a website, you enter a friendly name such as www.microsoft.com. Every device that connects to your network or the Internet must have an Internet Protocol (IP) address. You also need a way to associate these names to their assigned IP address.

Internet Protocol (IP) is the key protocol in the TCP/IP suite. It is responsible for adding addressing information to the packets for the sender and the receiver, as well as adding data to help route and deliver the packet. Windows Server 2016 uses TCP/IP as its default networking protocol.

Transmission Control Protocol/Internet Protocol (TCP/IP) is a set of protocols that allows computers to exchange data within a network and between networks. These protocols (or rules) manage the content, format, timing, sequencing, and error control of the messages that are exchanged between the devices. Every device that communicates over TCP/IP must have a unique IP address. Windows Server 2016 uses a dual-layer architecture that enables it to implement both IPv4 and IPv6 address schemes. Both share the common TCP Transport layer protocol.

Before configuring TCP/IP on your network, take time to plan the implementation. For example, how big do you expect your network to be? How will your network be designed from a physical and logical standpoint?

Exploring IPv4 and IPv6 Protocols

Microsoft, along with other industry leaders, is working hard to make IPv6 the next standard for IP addressing. In the meantime, you have a mixture of IPv4 and IPv6 devices on your network, so you need to understand how these devices are configured and how they interact with each other.

During the 1960s, several universities and research centers needed a network to share information. To address this need, a U.S. government agency called the Advanced Research Projects Agency (ARPA) developed the ARPANET, which initially used the Network Control Protocol (NCP) to handle file transfers, remote logon, and email needs. NCP, the predecessor to TCP/IP, was first used in 1972. By 1973, the protocol no longer met the needs of its users, and research was done to find a better solution. TCP/IPv4 was introduced and standardized in 1981 and is still in use today. Microsoft and other industry leaders have been working for years to roll out a newer version: IPv6.

TAKE NOTE*

IPv6 is not backward compatible with IPv4. An IPv6-only device cannot talk to an IPv4 device. Your current transition strategy should be to use both in the short-term.

The goal of IPv6 is to address the exhaustion of the IPv4 address space, which supports about 4 billion addresses. At the time IPv4 was created, no one considered that anything other than computers would be connected. As more computers, smartphones, tablets, and home appliances are being attached to the Internet, the IPv4 address space is quickly being exhausted.

Over the years, engineers have found ways to reduce the number of addresses needed through a process called Network Address Translation (NAT). Instead of assigning an IPv4 public address to every device on your network, you can purchase a single IPv4 address and allow all devices behind your router to share the same address. Still, as each year passes and the number of devices connected to the Internet continues to grow exponentially, IPv6 will need to eventually take over as the main addressing scheme. In the meantime, let's take a closer look at each of the protocols.

UNDERSTANDING IPv4

An IPv4 address is a 32-bit-long number assigned to a host on the network. These addresses are broken into four different sections called octets, which are 8 bits long. For example, the number 192.160.10.2 in binary is 11000000.10100000.00001010.00000010 (see Figure 1-10).

Figure 1-10

Converting binary to decimal

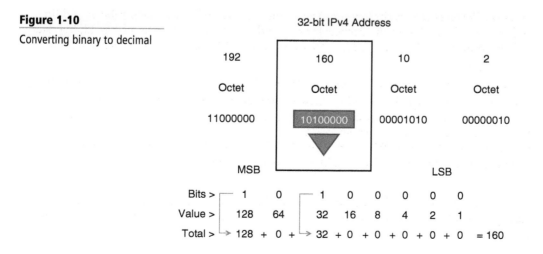

A portion of the 32 bits is associated with the network on which the computer is physically located. This portion of bits is called the **network ID**. The remaining bits, allocated to the host, are called the **host ID**. All computers on the same local network/subnet share the same network ID, but each computer within the local network/subnet has its own unique host ID.

A subnet mask, also 32 bits long, is used to determine which of the 32 bits represent the network ID and which represent the host ID (see Table 1-1). The class of IP address you are using determines the default subnet mask. IPv4 addresses are divided into classes based on the number in the first octet of the IP address. These classes were originally designed to support different organizational sizes. However, classful IP addressing is very wasteful and has mostly been discarded.

There are five classes of IP addresses (see Table 1-1).

Table 1-1

TCP/IP v4 Address Classes

Class	Range	Network ID (Octet)	Host ID (Octet)	Number of Networks	Number of Hosts
A	1–127*	First octet	Second, third, and fourth octets	126	16,777,214
B	128–191	First and second octets	Third and fourth octets	16,384	65,534
C	192–223	First, second, and third octets	Fourth octet	2,097,152	254
D	224–239	N/A	N/A	N/A	N/A
E	240–254	N/A	N/A	MA	N/A

*0, 127, and 255 are reserved and cannot be used for a specific host. An IP address with all 0s in the host ID describes the network, whereas 127 in the first octet is reserved for loopback testing and handling traffic to the local host. An IP address using 255s in the host ID is a broadcast transmitting to all interfaces on the specified network.

Table 1-2 shows the default subnet masks for each class along with its binary and decimal values.

Table 1-2

Default Subnet Masks for IPv4 Address Classes

Class	Binary	Decimal
A	11111111.00000000.00000000.00000000	255.0.0.0
B	11111111.11111111.00000000.00000000	255.255.0.0
C	11111111.11111111.11111111.00000000	255.255.255.0

Subnetting is the process used to break a larger network into smaller segments. For example, a Class B IP address has more than 65,000 host addresses for a single, logical segment. Adding that many computers to a single network isn't feasible. If you break the larger network into smaller segments (for example, 254 subnetworks), each can host up to 254 hosts. You accomplish subnetting by stealing bits from the host portion of an address to create a new subnet section.

UNDERSTANDING CLASSLESS INTERDOMAIN ROUTING (CIDR)

In practical use, the IP address classes proved to be wasteful, and when the Internet first experienced a massive period of growth in the 1990s, it was feared that there might at some time be a shortage of addresses. To avoid assigning entire addresses of a particular class to networks that didn't have that many hosts, the IETF eventually published a new standard for assigning IP addresses called *classless interdomain routing (CIDR)*.

CIDR differs from traditional addressing (now called *classful addressing*) by allowing the division between the network identifier and the host identifier to fall anywhere in an IPv4 address; it does not have to fall on one of the 8-bit boundaries. For example, a subnet mask of 255.255.240.0 translates into a binary value of 11111111 11111111 11110000 00000000, meaning that the network identifier is 20 bits long and the host identifier is 12 bits. This falls between a Class B and a Class C address, and enables ISPs to assign clients only the number of addresses they need, which conserves the IP address space.

CIDR also introduced a new syntax for IP network address references. In classful notation, an address like 172.23.0.0 was assumed to be a Class B address and used the standard 255.255.0.0 Class B subnet mask. In CIDR notation, the network address is followed by a slash and the number of bits in the network identifier. Therefore, 172.23.0.0/16 would be the CIDR equivalent of a Class B address. An address that used the 255.255.240.0 subnet mask described earlier would, therefore, look something like 172.23.0.0/20.

UNDERSTANDING IPv6 AND IPv6 ADDRESSING

As mentioned earlier, available public IPv4 addresses are running low. To overcome this problem as well as a few others, IPv6 was developed as the next-generation Internet Protocol version.

IPv6 provides a number of benefits for TCP/IP-based networking connectivity, including:

- A 128-bit address space to provide addressing for every device on the Internet with a globally unique address
- More efficient routing than IPv4
- Support for automatic configuration
- Enhanced security to protect against address and port scanning attacks and utilization of IPsec to protect IPv6 traffic

Because IPv6 uses 128 bits, the addresses are usually divided into groups of 16 bits, written as 4 hex digits. Hex digits include 0, 1, 2, 3, 4, 5, 6, 7, 8, 9, A, B, C, D, E, and F. The groups are separated by colons. Here is an example of an address:

FE80:0000:0000:0000:02C3:B2DF:FEA5:E4F1

Similar to the IPv4 addresses, IPv6 is divided into network bits and host bits. However, the first 64 bits define the network address and the second 64 bits define the host address. Therefore, for our sample address, FE80:0000:0000:0000 defines the network bits and 02C3:B2DF:FEA5:E4F1 defines the host bits. The network bits are also further divided where a block of 48 bits is used as the network prefix and the next 16 bits are used for subnetting.

To facilitate simplified automatic addressing, the IPv6 subnet size has been standardized and fixed to 64 bits, and the MAC address is used to generate the host bits within the unicast network address or link-local address when stateless autoconfiguration is used.

If a block is set to 0 and is followed by another block set to 0, it can be written as ::, but the substitution may only be applied once in the address. Using this notation, FE80:0:AC4A:AA04:E713A:0:0:CE2B would be written as FE80:0:AC4A:AA04:E713A::CE2B.

When a network card is configured in Windows Server 2016, it automatically has both an IPv4 and IPv6 address by default. This is called a dual stack.

With IPv6, you still have unicast and multicast addressing. However, unicast addressing can be divided into:

- *Global unicast addresses*: Public addresses that are globally routable and reachable on the IPv6 portion of the Internet.
- *Link-local addresses*: Private nonroutable addresses confined to a single subnet. They are used by hosts when communicating with neighboring hosts on the same link, but can also be used to create temporary networks for conferences or meetings, or to set up permanent, small LANs. Routers process packets destined for a link-local address, but they will not forward them to other links.
- *Unique local addresses*: Meant for private addressing, with the addition of being unique, so that joining two subnets does not cause address collisions.

You might also have an anycast address, which is an address that is assigned to multiple computers. When IPv6 addresses communicate with an anycast address, only the closest host responds. You typically use this for locating services or the nearest router.

The transition from IPv4 to IPv6 is expected to take several more years. In the meantime, expect to see a mix of IPv4, IPv4/IPv6 (dual stack), and IPv6-only networks. To help with the transition from IPv4 to IPv6, several methods were developed, including 6 to 4, Teredo, and Intra-Site Automatic Tunnel Addressing Protocol (IPv6).

Using the Default Gateway

A *default gateway* is a device, usually a router, which connects the local network to other networks. When you need to communicate with a host on another subnet, you forward all packets to the default gateway.

The default gateway allows a host to communicate with remote hosts. Every time a host needs to send packets to another host, it first determines if the destination host is local (same subnet) or if it is remote (where it has to go through a router to get to it). The router determines the best way to get to the remote host, and then it forwards the packets to the remote subnet.

To determine if the destination address is local or remote, the router looks at the network bits of both the sending and destination hosts. If the network bits are the same, it assumes the destination host is local and sends the packets directly to the local host. If the network bits are different, it assumes the destination host is remote and sends the packets to the default gateway.

For example, you have the following:

Sending host address: 10.10.57.3

Sending host subnet mask: 255.255.255.0

Destination host address: 10.10.89.37

By isolating the network address from the sending host, you have 10.10.57.0. By isolating the network address for the destination host address, you have 10.10.89.0. Because they are different, the packet is sent to the default gateway, and the router determines the best way to get to its final destination.

Of course, if the subnet mask is wrong, the host might misidentify a host as being local or remote. If the default gateway is wrong, packets might not be able to leave the local subnet.

Understanding Name Resolution

Name resolution is the process of associating host names to IP addresses. The Windows operating system supports multiple name resolution systems. The most common is the Domain Name System (DNS).

Domain Name System (DNS) is a naming service used by the TCP/IP network, is an essential service used by the Internet, and can be integrated with other services, such as WINS, DHCP, and Active Directory. DNS servers are used to associate a computer name, such as Server01.Support.contoso.com, to an IP address.

Every time a user accesses a web page, the user must type a URL, usually a name. Before the client communicates with the web server, the client computer needs to use DNS to retrieve the IP address of the web server, similar to someone using a phone book to find a phone number. When an enterprise client needs to communicate with a corporate server, the enterprise client also uses DNS to find the IP address of the corporate service. The DNS servers are often referred to as name servers.

DNS uses *fully qualified domain names (FQDNs)* to map a host name to an IP address. An FQDN describes the exact relationship between a host and its DNS domain. For example, computer1.sales.microsoft.com represents an FQDN; the computer1 host is located in the sales domain, which is located in the Microsoft second-level domain, which is located in the .com top-level domain.

DNS is a hierarchical distributed naming system used to locate computers and services on a TCP/IP network. DNS clients send queries to a DNS server and the Domain Name System receives and resolves queries such as translating a host or domain name to an IP address. Because it is so closely tied to the Internet and TCP/IP network, it is an essential service that enables the Internet and network to function and it is required by many network services, including Active Directory.

DNS is known as a distributed naming system because the information stored with DNS is not found on only a single DNS server. Instead, the information is distributed among multiple DNS servers, all of which are linked into a hierarchical structure.

The DNS is a hierarchical system consisting of a tree of domain names/DNS namespaces. At the top of the tree is the root zone (see Figure 1-11). The tree can then be divided into zones, each served by a name (DNS) server. Each zone can contain one domain or many domains. The administrative responsibility over any zone can be delegated or divided by creating a subdomain, which can be assigned to a different name server and administrative entity.

Figure 1-11

Exploring the DNS namespace

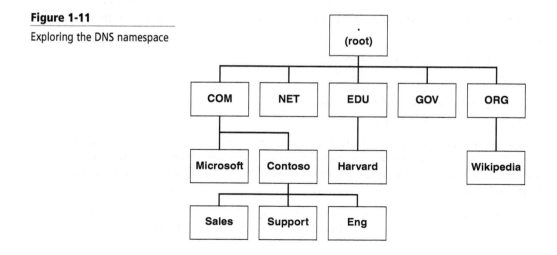

A domain name consists of one or more labels. Each label can be up to 63 characters. The full domain name cannot exceed a total length of 253 characters.

The root domain is managed by the Internet Corporation for Assigned Names and Numbers (ICANN) under the authority of the U.S. Department of Commerce. It is essential for the function of the Internet; without the root domain, services that depend upon DNS (email, browsing the Internet, and so on) would not function. Although the root domain is represented by a single period, it is supported by several hundred root servers spread across the world (to see where they are located, visit the root servers' website). The root servers have a file (zone file) that lists the names and IP addresses of the authoritative DNS servers for all top-level domains.

The rightmost label designates the top-level domain. For example, *microsoft.com* consists of two labels. The top-level domain is .com. The hierarchy of domains descends from right to left. Each label to the left specifies a subdomain of the domain or label on the right. Therefore, in our example, *microsoft* is a subdomain of the *.com* domain.

Traditionally, ***top-level domains*** consist of generic, top-level domains and international country codes (such as *us* for United States, *uk* for United Kingdom, *de* for Germany, and *jp* for Japan). Traditional, generic top-level domains include the following:

.com	Commercial
.org	Organization (originally intended for nonprofit organizations)
.edu	Educational
.gov	U.S. governmental entities
.net	Network (originally intended for the portal to a set of smaller websites)

Over the years, many other generic domains have been added, such as .aero, .biz, .coop, .info, .int, .jobs, .name, and .pro. More recently, organizations can purchase their own top-level domains.

Second-level domains are registered to individuals or organizations. Examples include:

microsoft.com	Microsoft Corporation domain
contoso.com	A fictional company used by Microsoft for examples, training, and support
mit.edu	Massachusetts Institute of Technology
wikipedia.org	Free encyclopedia
gov.au	Australian government

Second-level DNS domains can have many subdomains, and any domain can have hosts.

Second-level domains, also called parent domains, can be divided into subdomains (child domains). When registering a second-level domain for an organization, it is common to register multiple second-level domains (microsoft.com, microsoft.org, microsoft.net) to ensure that users can reach them regardless of whether they type .com, .net, or .org at the end of the address. An organization could then divide their second-level domains to subdomains, such as Sales, Support, or Eng.

A ***host*** is a specific computer or other network device in a domain. For example, *computer1 .sales.contoso.com* is the host called *computer1* in the sales subdomain of the *contoso.com* domain. A host has at least one IP address associated with it. For example, www.microsoft .com represents a particular address.

If you have *server1.corporate.contoso.com*, *.com* is the top-level domain. *contoso* is a subdomain of .com, and corporate is a subdomain of *contoso*. In the *corporate* domain, you find one or more addresses assigned to *server1*, such as 192.168.1.53. So as a result, when you type *server1.corporate.contoso.com* into your browser, the client sends a query to a DNS server asking what the IP address is for *server1.corporate.contoso.com*. The DNS server responds back with the 192.168.1.53 address. The client then communicates with the server with the address of 192.168.1.53.

Each node or leaf in the DNS tree is a ***resource record (RR)***, which holds information associated with the domain name. The most common resource record is the host address (A or AAA), which lists a host name and the associated IP address.

Here are a few of the record types you will find in a zone database file:

- Start of Authority (SOA) records are the first records added to a zone. They define parameters for the zone and include the name of the primary name server.
- Name Server (NS) records list any additional name servers for the zone.
- Address (host name) (A) records associate a host name to an IP4 address.
- Address (host name) (AAAA) records associate a host name to its IPv6 address.
- Pointer (PTR) records associate an IP address to a host name.
- Mail Exchange (MX) records identify the mail host(s) for the domain.

Active Directory domains utilize DNS when implementing their hierarchy and naming structure. When you install the first domain controller on a network, you are asked to install DNS automatically. When fully integrated with DNS, all domain controllers can access the data, replicate changes throughout the domain, and register clients into their zone. A zone is a scope of names that are served by a specific DNS name server. The part of the namespace that a zone is responsible for is known as the zone of authority. A zone must contain at least one domain, called the root domain of that zone. All the information about each zone is stored in a file called the zone database file. Inside the zone database file are the resource records that DNS uses to resolve host names to IP addresses.

The DNS server that creates and modifies a locally stored zone file is called the primary name server. A secondary name server is often used and holds a copy of the zone file that it gets from the primary name server. Updates to the primary name server are automatically replicated to the secondary name server. This process, called a zone transfer, provides redundancy for name resolution if one of the servers fails.

To identify a DNS host in the namespace, you use its fully qualified domain name (FQDN). The FQDN includes the host name in addition to the domain name where it is located. For example, the server (Support) in Figure 1-11 has an FQDN of support.contoso.com.

Understanding the DNS hierarchy can help you understand how name resolution works. DNS uses two components to resolve names to IP addresses:

- ***Resolver:*** An application that provides address information about other network hosts for the client. During the name resolution process, if a client cannot resolve the destination's host name to an IP address, the resolver sends a query to DNS servers, including root servers, to look up the records on its behalf.
- ***Name server:*** A server that performs recursive and iterative queries to contact other DNS servers in an attempt to resolve a host name to an IP address if the DNS server cannot resolve it using its own records. When a computer uses a recursive query, it is putting the entire responsibility on the other computer to find the IP address. An iterative query is a call to a name server to reply with the requested data or tell it who else to talk to in order to find an answer to its request.

Configuring IP Settings and Name Resolution Settings

> Network settings can be configured either manually or automatically using DHCP. Using manual settings can introduce configuration issues that could affect communications. Using a centralized approach to IP address management requires you to have a solid understanding of DHCP.

In Windows Server 2016, the **Network and Sharing Center** (as shown in Figure 1-12) is the primary tool that can view, create, and modify local area network (LAN), wireless local area network (WLAN), virtual private network (VPN), dial-up, and Broadband connections. It can also be used to configure connections and advanced sharing settings.

Figure 1-12

Using the Network and Sharing Center

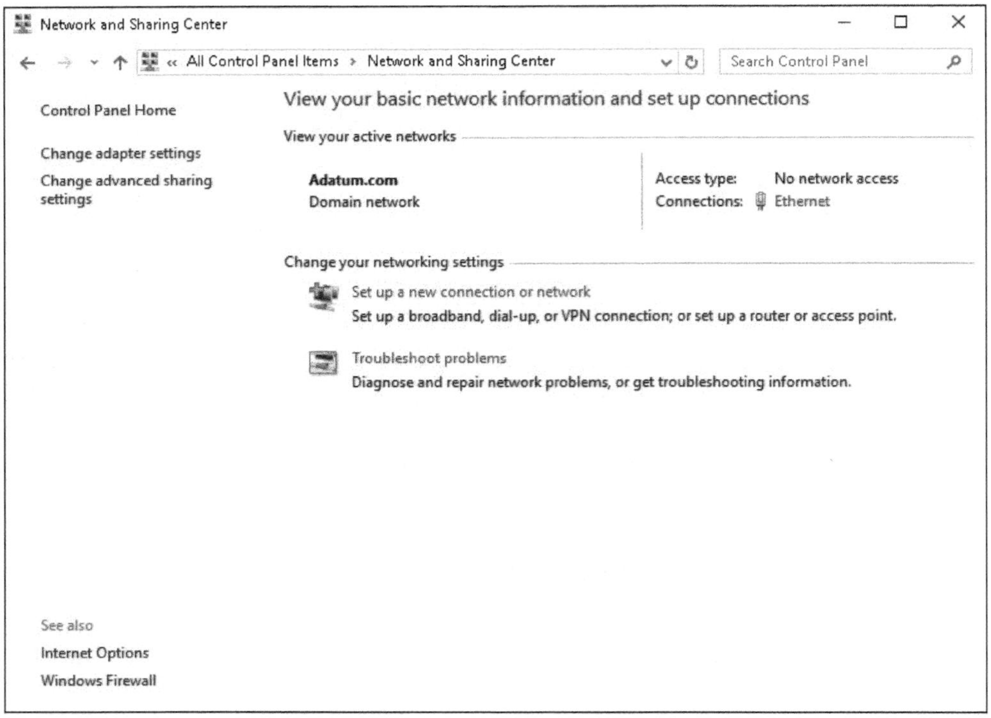

Configuring TCP/IP on a Windows Server 2016 computer can be done manually or automatically. Setting up TCP/IP manually involves configuring it to use a static IP address. This involves entering an IP address, a subnet mask, and (if you need to access computers outside of the local network segment) a default gateway address. To resolve friendly names to IP addresses, you also need to configure at least one IP address for a DNS on your network.

DEFINE A STATIC IPv4 ADDRESS

GET READY. To define a static IPv4 address, perform the following steps.

1. On LON-SVR1, on the taskbar, right-click the **network status** icon and choose **Open Network and Sharing Center**.
2. Click **Change adapter settings**.
3. Right-click a network adapter, such as **Ethernet**, and choose **Properties**.
4. When the Ethernet Properties dialog box opens, as shown in Figure 1-13, click **Internet Protocol Version 4 (TCP/IPv4)** and then click **Properties**.

Figure 1-13

Configuring the properties
of an Ethernet adapter

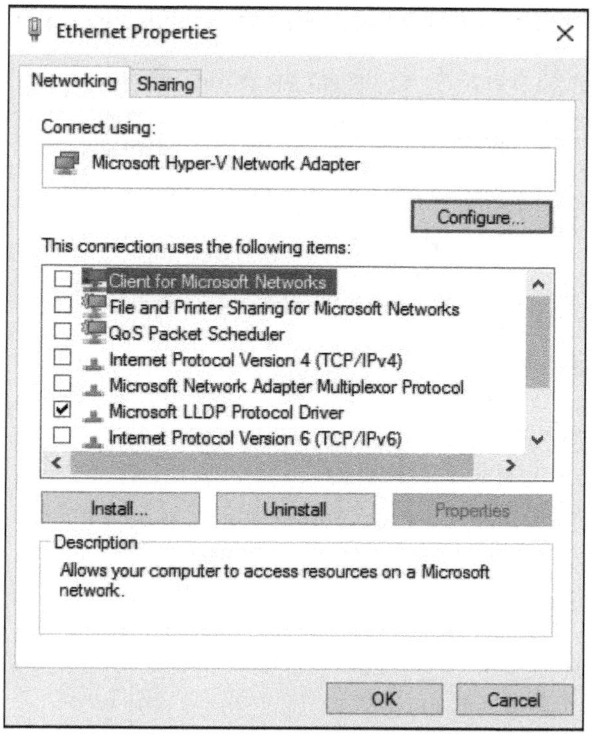

5. Select **Use the following IP address** and then type the IPv4 address, subnet mask, and default gateway you want to use, as shown in Figure 1-14.

Figure 1-14

Entering a static IPv4 address

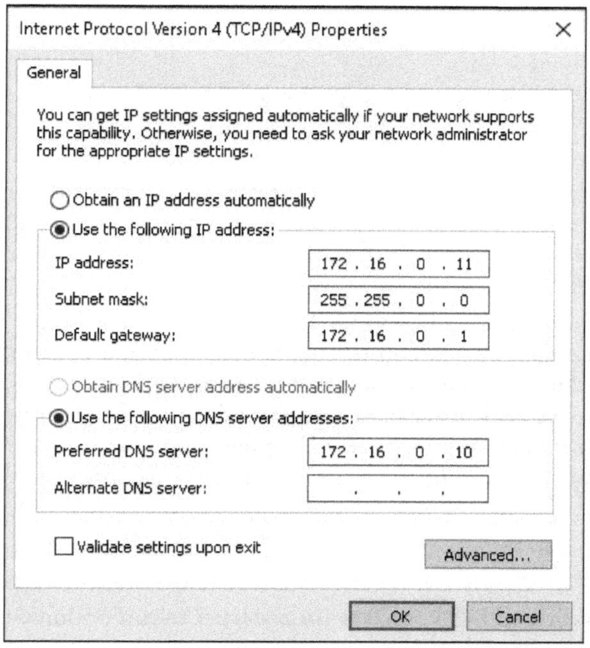

6. Select **Use the following DNS server addresses** and then type an IP address for a preferred DNS server and an alternate DNS server.

7. Click **OK** to accept your settings and to close the Internet Protocol Version 4 (TCP/IPv4) Properties dialog box.

8. Click **Close** to close the Ethernet Properties dialog box.

If you selected the Validate settings upon exit option after configuring IP settings, Windows Server 2016 performs a network diagnostics test to check your settings for any problems and offers to help fix them. If you clicked the Advanced button, you could make additional configurations to your TCP/IP configuration. For example, in Windows Server 2016, you can configure multiple gateways. When you do this, a metric is used to determine which gateway to use. Multiple gateways are used to provide fault tolerance so if one router goes down, the computer defaults to the other gateway. You can configure additional gateways and DNS settings in the Advanced TCP/IP Settings dialog box (see Figure 1-15):

Figure 1-15

Reviewing advanced TCP/IP setting options

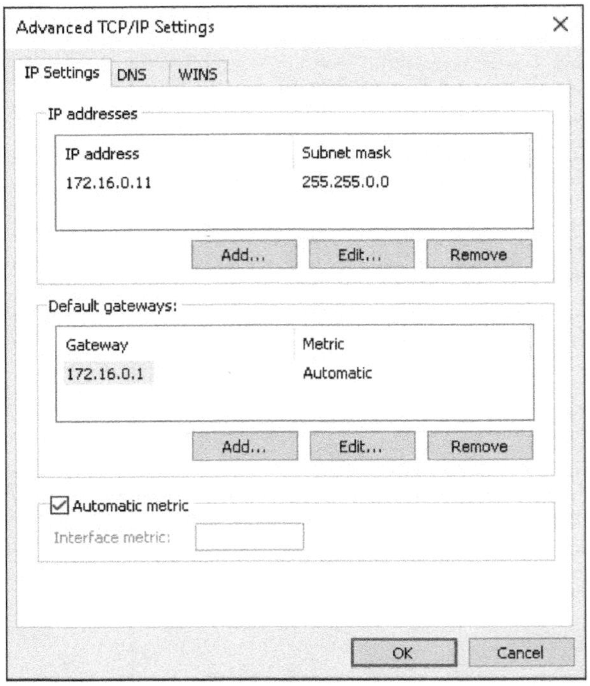

- **DNS server addresses, in order of use:** You can specify multiple DNS servers to use for name resolution. The order listed determines the sequence in which your client attempts to resolve host names. If the first server does not respond to a name resolution request, the client contacts the next one in the list.
- **Append primary and connection specific DNS suffixes:** This is selected by default. If you attempt to access a computer named FileServer1, and the parent name is contoso .com, the name resolves to FileServer1.contoso.com. If the FQDN does not exist in the domain, the query fails. The parent name used (contoso.com) is configured on the System Properties/Computer Name tab.
- **Append parent suffixes of the primary DNS suffix:** This is selected by default. It works as follows: If the computer FS2 is in the eastcoast.contoso.com domain, DNS attempts to resolve the name to FS2.eastcoast.contoso.com. If this doesn't work, it tries FS2.contoso.com.
- **Append these DNS suffixes (in order):** Use this option when you want to specify DNS suffixes to use other than resolving names through your parent domain.
- **DNS suffix for this connection:** This setting overrides DNS names that are already configured for this connection. This is typically configured through the System Properties/Computer Name tab by clicking the More button.

- **Register this connection's addresses in DNS:** This option, selected by default, automatically enters the FQDN in DNS records.
- **Use this connection's DNS suffix in DNS registration:** If this option is selected, all IP addresses for this connection are registered in DNS at the parent domain.

→ **DEFINE A STATIC IPv6 ADDRESS**

GET READY. To define a static IPv6 address, perform the following steps.

1. On the taskbar, right-click the **network status** icon and choose **Open Network and Sharing Center.**
2. Click **Change adapter settings.**
3. Right-click a network adapter, such as **Ethernet**, and choose **Properties.**
4. When the Ethernet Properties dialog box opens, click **Internet Protocol Version 6 (TCP/IPv6)** and then click **Properties.**
5. Select **Use the following IPv6 address** (as shown in Figure 1-16) and then type the IPv6 address, subnet prefix length, and default gateway you want to use.

Figure 1-16

Entering a static IPv6 address

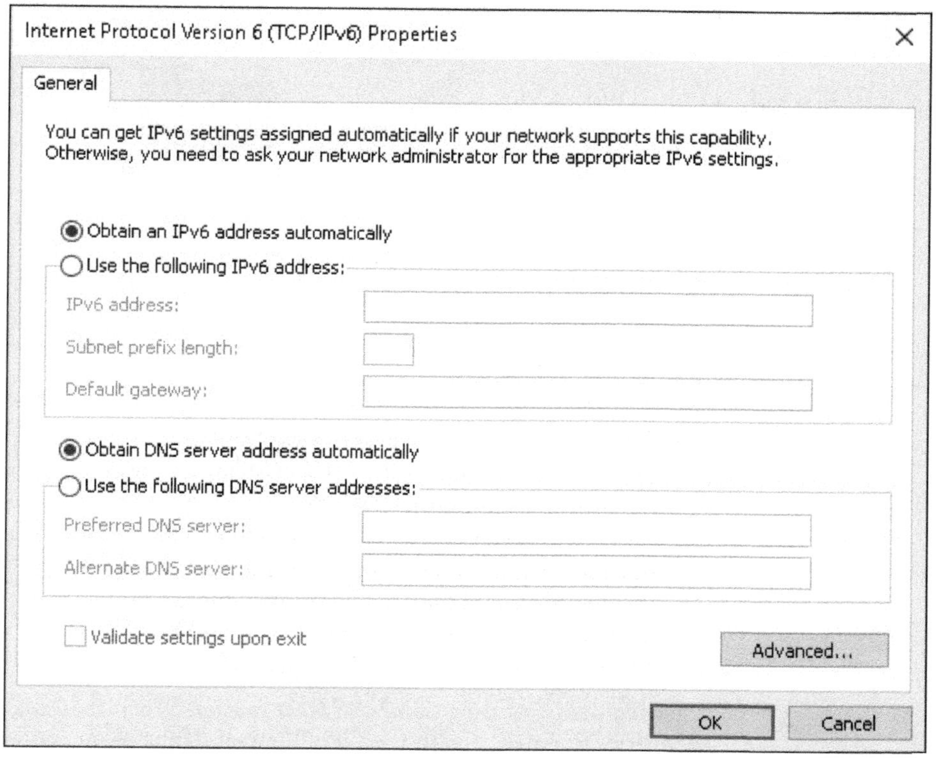

Internet Protocol Version 6 (TCP/IPv6) Properties   ✕

General

You can get IPv6 settings assigned automatically if your network supports this capability.
Otherwise, you need to ask your network administrator for the appropriate IPv6 settings.

◉ Obtain an IPv6 address automatically
○ Use the following IPv6 address:

IPv6 address:

Subnet prefix length:

Default gateway:

◉ Obtain DNS server address automatically
○ Use the following DNS server addresses:

Preferred DNS server:

Alternate DNS server:

☐ Validate settings upon exit   Advanced...

OK   Cancel

6. Select **Use the following DNS server addresses** and then type an IP address for a preferred DNS server and an alternate DNS server.
7. Click **OK** to accept your settings and to close the Internet Protocol Version 6 (TCP/IPv6) Properties dialog box.
8. Click **Close** to close the Ethernet Properties dialog box.

UNDERSTANDING AUTOMATIC IP ADDRESS ASSIGNMENT

When you assign static IP addresses (IPv4 or IPv6) to your clients, you run the risk of duplicating IP addresses on your network or misconfiguring the settings, which can result in communication problems. A better approach is to dynamically assign your TCP/IP configurations from a central pool of IP addresses. This is done by using the *Dynamic Host Configuration Protocol (DHCP)* server. The DHCP server can also be configured to provide the default gateway, primary, and secondary DNS information; WINS server; and DNS domain name.

Figure 1-17 shows how DHCP communications work.

Figure 1-17

Understanding DHCP communications

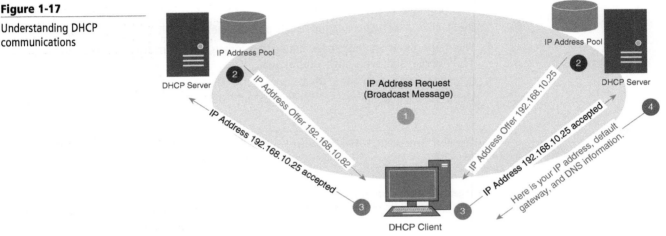

Here is a high-level overview of what happens with DHCP-enabled clients:

1. The DHCP-enabled client starts and broadcasts a request for an IP address over the network.

2. Any DHCP servers that receive the request review their pool of IP addresses (DHCP scope) and select one to offer to the client.

3. The client reviews the offers and broadcasts a message to the servers, letting them know which IP address it has accepted.

4. All DHCP servers see the message. Those whose offers are not accepted place the IP address back into their pool for a future client request. The server the client accepted acknowledges and provides additional information to complete the client configuration (default gateway, DNS information, and so on).

After a client receives an IP address and additional configuration information, it has it for a specific period of time called the *lease period*. When the lease is 50 percent expired, the client tries to renew it with the DHCP server. If the client cannot renew the lease, it tries again at 75 percent and 87.5 percent expired before the lease expires. At this point, if it cannot renew the lease, it tries to contact an alternate DHCP server. If all attempts fail, and the client cannot obtain a new IP address, it autoconfigures with a Microsoft Class B subnet (169.254.0.0/255.255.0.0). If it cannot find a DHCP server and does not have an active lease, it will keep trying to find another DHCP server every 5 minutes.

Before it chooses an IP address in this network, the client checks to make sure no other client is using the address it wants to assign. After it has an address assigned, it attempts to make contact with a DHCP server every five minutes. Once found, it is reconfigured to use an address assigned from the DHCP pool.

TAKE NOTE*   You can use DHCP to assign IPv6 addresses through either DHCPv6 stateful mode or stateless mode. If DHCPv6 is used, you need to make sure your routers are configured to support it.

USING STATEFUL DHCP AND STATELESS DHCP

There are two ways to configure DHCP when using it for IPv6 implementations: *stateless address configuration* and *stateful address configuration*.

If you are using DHCP to assign IPv6 addresses to stateful mode clients, they work similarly to the IPv4 when obtaining their IP addresses. When a client is configured to use DHCP in stateful mode, it first uses a link-local address (IPv6). After it is autoconfigured with the link-local address, it seeks out a DHCP server on the network by multicasting (sending data across to multiple nodes at the same time with a single transmission) to the link-local all nodes multicast group a message every five minutes. When the client finally reaches a DHCP server, it configures itself with the assigned IP parameters.

DHCP servers running in stateful mode centrally manage the IPv6 addresses and configuration parameters and provide addresses to stateful clients.

TAKE NOTE*   Link-local addresses are equivalent to Automatic Private IP Addressing (APIPA) IPv4 addresses using the 169.254.0.0/255.255.0.0 prefix. These address always begin with FE80::/64.

Stateless mode clients work a little differently; they assign both a link-local address and additional non-link-local addresses by exchanging messages with neighboring routers. When a DHCP server is set up to serve stateless clients, the DHCP clients autoconfigure using router advertisements. These clients do not use the DHCP server to obtain an IP address, but instead use it to only obtain additional configuration information such as DNS recursive name servers and a DNS search list (domains to be searched during name resolution). If a DHCP server has been configured to service stateless clients, it does not respond to clients asking for IP addresses.

■ Introducing Windows Powershell

↓

THE BOTTOM LINE   ***Windows PowerShell*** is a command-line interface used mainly by IT professionals to run cmdlets (pronounced command-lets), complete background jobs (processes or programs that run in the background without a user interface), and run scripts to perform administrative tasks.

The Windows PowerShell environment is built on the .NET Framework, which allows administrators to use many more tools and commands than the MS-DOS command window environment. PowerShell and the MS-DOS command environment are compatible. For example, you can run Windows command-line programs in Windows PowerShell and also start Windows programs like Calculator and Notepad at the Windows PowerShell prompt. Windows PowerShell providers enable you to access other data stores, such as the registry and the digital signature certificate stores, as easily as you access the file system. PowerShell also provides full access to COM and WMI, which enables administrators to perform tasks on both local and remote Windows systems and with some remote Linux systems.

Component Object Model (COM) provides a platform-independent, distributed, object-oriented system for creating software components. Software can call these components at will. For example, File Explorer is an empty shell that links to multiple COM interfaces that allow you to navigate and display the file structure and related objects such as This PC/My Computer, drives, folders, and files. Other programs such as Microsoft Office can call up the same COM objects so that you can browse, store, and access documents on disks.

Windows Management Instrumentation (WMI) is the Microsoft implementation of Web-Based Enterprise Management (WBEM) that allows accessing management information in an enterprise environment. WMI uses the *Common Information Model (CIM)* industry standard to represent systems, applications, networks, devices, and other managed components. With WMI, you can retrieve the status of local and remote computers and their components. Some of the things you can do with WMI is configure security settings, configure system properties, change permissions of users and groups, manage processes, and view and configure error logging.

Cmdlets (pronounced *command-lets*) are native commands available in Windows PowerShell. Cmdlets follow a verb-noun naming pattern, such as get-process, get-service, get-help, set-date, or stop-process. Common verbs include:

- **Add:** Add a resource to a container, or attach an item to another item.
- **Get:** Retrieve data from a resource.
- **New:** Create a new resource.
- **Remove:** Delete a resource from a container.
- **Set:** Modify a resource, such as data or system parameters.
- **Start:** Begin an operation, such as a process or a program.

Knowing the legal verbs and remembering the singular noun rule really helps guessing cmdlet names.

Windows PowerShell includes more than one hundred basic core cmdlets, and additional cmdlets will be added when you install additional software components such as Microsoft Exchange. You can even write your own cmdlets and share them with other users.

To get help on a cmdlet, you can use the get-help cmdlet. For example, to get help for the ps cmdlet, you would type the following command:

```
Get-Help ps
```

To get more detailed help, add a –full at the end of the command.

 RUN A CMDLET IN WINDOWS POWERSHELL

GET READY. To run a cmdlet in Windows PowerShell, perform the following steps.

1. Click the **Start** button and type **PowerShell.** From the results, click **Windows PowerShell.**

2. A commonly used command is ps (or get-process). The ps command lists the currently running processes and their details, such as the process ID, process name, and percentage of processor usage (CPU). Type **ps** and press **Enter**, as shown in Figure 1-18.

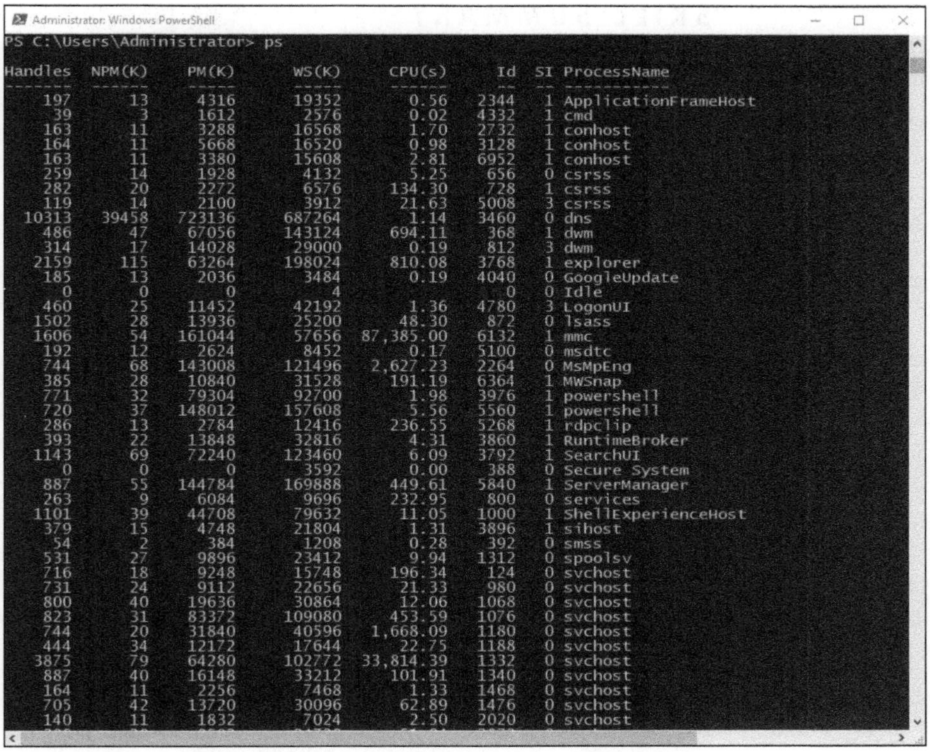

Figure 1-18

Running the ps command
in Windows PowerShell

```
Administrator: Windows PowerShell                                        —   □   ×
PS C:\Users\Administrator> ps

Handles  NPM(K)     PM(K)      WS(K)     CPU(s)      Id  SI ProcessName
-------  ------     -----      -----     ------      --  -- -----------
    197      13      4316      19352       0.56    2344   1 ApplicationFrameHost
     39       3      1612       2576       0.02    4332   1 cmd
    163      11      3288      16568       1.70    2732   1 conhost
    164      11      5668      16520       0.98    3128   1 conhost
    163      11      3380      15608       2.81    6952   1 conhost
    259      14      1928       4132       5.25     656   0 csrss
    282      20      2272       6576     134.30     728   1 csrss
    119      14      2100       3912      21.63    5008   3 csrss
  10313   39458    723136     687264       1.14    3460   0 dns
    486      47     67056     143124     694.11     368   1 dwm
    314      17     14028      29000       0.19     812   3 dwm
   2159     115     63264     198024     810.08    3768   1 explorer
    185      13      2036       3484       0.19    4040   0 GoogleUpdate
      0       0         0          4                  0   0 Idle
    460      25     11452      42192       1.36    4780   3 LogonUI
   1502      28     13936      25200      48.30     872   0 lsass
   1606      54    161044      57656  87,385.00    6132   1 mmc
    192      12      2624       8452       0.17    5100   0 msdtc
    744      68    143008     121496   2,627.23    2264   0 MsMpEng
    385      28     10840      31528     191.19    6364   1 MWSnap
    771      32     79304      92700       1.98    3976   1 powershell
    720      37    148012     157608       5.56    5560   1 powershell
    286      13      2784      12416     236.55    5268   1 rdpclip
    393      22     13848      32816       4.31    3860   1 RuntimeBroker
   1143      69     72240     123460       6.09    3792   1 SearchUI
      0       0         0       3592       0.00     388   0 Secure System
    887      55    144784     169888     449.61    5840   1 ServerManager
    263       9      6084       9696     232.95     800   0 services
   1101      39     44708      79632      11.05    1000   1 ShellExperienceHost
    379      15      4748      21804       1.31    3896   1 sihost
     54       2       384       1208       0.28     392   0 smss
    531      27      9896      23412       9.94    1312   0 spoolsv
    716      18      9248      15748     196.34     124   0 svchost
    731      24      9112      22656      21.33     980   0 svchost
    800      40     19636      30864      12.06    1068   0 svchost
    823      31     83372     109080     453.59    1076   0 svchost
    744      20     31840      40596   1,668.09    1180   0 svchost
    444      34     12172      17644      22.75    1188   0 svchost
   3875      79     64280     102772  33,814.39    1332   0 svchost
    887      40     16148      33212     101.91    1340   0 svchost
    164      11      2256       7468       1.33    1468   0 svchost
    705      42     13720      30096      62.89    1476   0 svchost
    140      11      1832       7024       2.50    2020   0 svchost
```

3. To get help with the ps command, type **get-help ps** and press **Enter**.

4. To view running services, type **get-service** and then press **Enter**. A list of services displays along with their status (Running or Stopped).

5. To exit the Window PowerShell window, type **exit** and then press **Enter**.

Besides most cmdlets having multiple parameters, Windows PowerShell commands can get very complicated by combining cmdlets. A pipe (|)uses the output of one command as the input to another command. For example, *Get-VM* will list VMs on a Hyper-V host. The get-vmmemory server01 will display the memory settings of one VM called server01. However, if you combine the two with a pipe:

```
Get-vm | Get-vmmemory
```

you will get the memory settings for all of the servers in a list.

Windows PowerShell allows you to create scripts, which can be created and executed as needed. Scripts are text files that contain a list of cmdlets. Scripts will have an extension .ps1. To assist in writing more complex scripts, Windows includes the ***Windows PowerShell Integrated Scripting Environment (ISE)***, which provides command-completion functionality, and enables you to see all available commands and the parameters that you can use with those commands. Although you can use a text editor to create a PowerShell script, the Windows PowerShell ISE makes it easier because you can view cmdlet parameters, which helps you create syntactically correct Windows PowerShell commands.

SKILL SUMMARY

IN THIS LESSON YOU LEARNED:

- The desktop is the main screen that you see when you first start the computer and log on to Windows. Like the top of an actual desktop, it is where you perform your work by opening and running one or more applications. It also includes the Recycle Bin, which is used to recover files that have been previously deleted.

- The Windows Server 2016 Settings is a modern interface for common configuration settings that would have been found in Control Panel on older versions of Windows. In addition, you will find additional settings such as touch screen, tablet, and privacy settings that are geared toward phones and tablets that you will not find in Control Panel.

- When managing Windows Server 2016, one of the primary tools you will use is Server Manager. As mentioned earlier, Server Manager is used to install, configure, and manage Windows Server 2016 server roles and features. It can also be used to manage local and remote servers without using the Remote Desktop Protocol connections.

- Windows includes an Administrative Tools folder that consists of multiple tools that will be used to configure Windows Server 2016. One of the more useful tools when managing a computer running Windows Server 2016 is the Computer Management console, which allows you to view events, configure disks, manage users and groups, and manage shared folders.

- When accessing computers on a network, you typically communicate by using their host names. If you are accessing a website, you enter a friendly name such as www.microsoft .com. Every device that connects to your network or the Internet must have an Internet Protocol (IP) address. You also need a way to associate these names to their assigned IP address.

- Available public IPv4 addresses are running low. To overcome this problem as well as a few others, IPv6 was developed as the next-generation Internet Protocol version.

- Name resolution is the process of associating host names to IP addresses. The Windows operating system supports multiple name resolution systems. The most common is the Domain Name System (DNS).

- Windows PowerShell is a command-line interface used mainly by IT professionals to run cmdlets (pronounced command-lets), complete background jobs (processes or programs that run in the background without a user interface), and run scripts to perform administrative tasks.

■ Knowledge Assessment

Multiple Choice

Select the correct answer for each of the following questions.

1. Which of the following is the primary tool to add or remove server roles?
   a. Computer Management
   b. Server Manager
   c. Add/Remove Programs
   d. Programs

2. Which of the following is used to view the Windows logs?
   a. Performance Monitor
   b. Reliability Monitor
   c. System Viewer
   d. Event Viewer

3. Which of the following allows users to connect to virtual desktops and applications that are hosted on a remote computer?
   a. App-V
   b. RD Connection Broker
   c. RD Gateway
   d. Remote Desktop Services

4. Which of the following statements are true regarding IPv4?
   a. IPv4 uses 32-bit addresses
   b. IPv4 uses 128-bit addresses.
   c. IPv4 consists of a network ID and MAC address.
   d. IPv4 consists of a host ID and MAC address.

5. How many bits does a standard IPv6 unicast address use to represent the network ID?
   a. 32
   b. 64
   c. 128
   d. 10

6. When communicating with a server on another subnet, which of the following settings are used to determine which direction it needs to go to get to its final destination?
   a. Subnet mask
   b. Default gateway
   c. DNS
   d. IP address

7. IPv4 networks are based on a(n) _____-bit address.
   a. 8
   b. 24
   c. 32
   d. 48

8. The default subnet mask in a classful network for a host with the IP address of 132.75.3.5 is _____.
   a. 255.0.0.0
   b. 255.255.0.0
   c. 255.255.255.0
   d. 255.255.255.255

9. In an address of 183.23.54.2/24, which of the following types of IP addresses does this host use?
   a. Classful
   b. CIDR
   c. NAT
   d. Multicasting

10. Which of the following tools allows you to see the edition and version of Windows 10 as well as how much memory is used by Windows 10?
    a. System Configuration
    b. Event Viewer
    c. Windows Memory Diagnostic
    d. System

Best Answer

Choose the letter that corresponds to the best answer. More than one answer choice may achieve the goal. Select the BEST answer.

1. Which of the following programs should be used to make items larger on the desktop?
   a. Settings
   b. Control Panel
   c. Device Manager
   d. System Configuration

2. When communicating with a server on another subnet, which setting is used to determine which direction it needs to go to get to its final destination?
   a. Subnet mask
   b. Default gateway
   c. DNS
   d. IP address

3. Which configuration can a DHCPv6 server setup running in stateless mode provide to clients?
   a. IP address
   b. Subnet mask
   c. Default gateway
   d. DNS recursive name servers

4. Which TCP/IP setting should be configured when you want to specify DNS suffixes to use other than resolving names through your parent domain?
   a. DNS suffix for this connection
   b. Append these DNS suffixes (in order)
   c. Append primary and connection specific DNS suffixes
   d. DNS server address, in order of use

5. Which of the following Windows tools allows you to manage and configure local and remote systems and can be used with scripts?
   a. Command Prompt
   b. Task Manager
   c. Computer Management
   d. Windows PowerShell

Matching and Identification

1. Match the following terms with the related description or usage.
   _____ a. AAAA record
   _____ b. DNS server
   _____ c. LLMNR
   _____ d. Subnet mask
   _____ e. ANDing
   _____ f. Stateful

   1. The process a computer uses to determine whether another computer is on the same network
   2. Used to associate a computer name to an IP address; stores host-to-IP address mappings in a zone file
   3. Used to determine the bits associated with the network ID and host ID

4. An IPv6 address (host name) mapping to its IP address

5. A fallback name resolution technique when DNS and WINS are not available

6. One of the ways you can configure a DHCP IPv6 server; provides IP address configuration to DHCP clients

Build a List

1. Specify the correct order of the steps that must be completed for a DHCP-enabled client to obtain IPv4 addressing information.

_____ Client receives offers of an IP address from a DHCP server.

_____ DHCP server selects an IP address from the available address pool.

_____ Client broadcasts request for an IP address.

_____ Client sends broadcast message letting other DHCP servers know it has accepted an IP address offer.

_____ Client requests additional IP configuration from a selected DHCP server (DNS, default gateway).

■ Business Case Scenarios

Scenario 1-1: Implementing the Correct Class Network

A client wants you to design a single IP network that can support 84,576 computers. Complete Table 1-3, and state which IP class is the correct one to use.

Table 1-3

IPv4 Class Analysis

CLASS	IP RANGE (1ST OCTET)	DEFAULT SUBNET MASK	NETWORK/ NODE PORTIONS	TOTAL NUMBER OF NETWORKS	TOTAL NUMBER OF USABLE ADDRESSES
A					
B					
C					
D	224–239	N/A	N/A	N/A	N/A
E	240–255	N/A	N/A	N/A	N/A

Scenario 1-2: Configuring Name Resolution

As the administrator of the Contoso Corporation, you manage an internal website that is often used by most users with the company. You try to connect to an internal website but cannot open the web page. You soon discover that the website is now hosted on another server. Describe how to enable users to connect to the new server.

2 LESSON

Installing, Upgrading, and Migrating Servers and Workloads

70-740 EXAM OBJECTIVE

Objective 1.1 – Install, upgrade, and migrate servers and workloads. This objective may include but is not limited to the following: Determine Windows Server 2016 installation requirements; determine appropriate Windows Server 2016 editions per workloads; install Windows Server 2016; install Windows Server 2016 features and roles; install and configure Windows Server Core; manage Windows Server Core installations using Windows PowerShell, command line, and remote management capabilities; implement Windows PowerShell Desired State Configuration (DSC) to install and maintain integrity of installed environments; perform upgrades and migrations of servers and core workloads from Windows Server 2008 and Windows Server 2012 to Windows Server 2016; determine the appropriate activation model for server installation, such as Automatic Virtual Machine Activation (AVMA), Key Management Service (KMS), and Active Directory–based Activation.

LESSON HEADING	EXAM OBJECTIVE
Installing Windows Server 2016 • Determining Windows Server 2016 Installation Requirements • Determining the Appropriate Windows Server 2016 Editions Per Workloads • Installing Windows Server 2016—Full Version • Performing Post-Installation Configuration Settings • Installing Windows Server 2016 Features and Roles	Determine Windows Server 2016 installation requirements Determine appropriate Windows Server 2016 editions per workloads Install Windows Server 2016 Install Windows Server 2016 features and roles
Installing and Configuring Windows Server Core • Installing Windows Server Core • Managing Windows Server Core Installations • Installing Windows Server 2016 Features and Roles on Windows Server Core	Install and configure Windows Server Core Manage Windows Server Core installations using Windows PowerShell, command line, and remote management capabilities
Performing a Windows Server 2016 Upgrade • Understanding Upgrade Paths • Preparing to Upgrade • Performing an Upgrade Installation	Perform upgrades from Windows Server 2008 and Windows Server 2012 to Windows Server 2016
Migrating Server and Core Workloads to Windows Server 2016	Perform migrations of servers and core workloads from Windows Server 2008 and Windows Server 2012 to Windows Server 2016

LESSON HEADING	EXAM OBJECTIVE
Activating Windows Server 2016 • Implementing Volume Activation Using a Key Management Service (KMS) • Implementing Active Directory–Based Activation • Implementing Automatic Virtual Machine Activation • Querying and Configuring Activation States Using the Command Line	Determine the appropriate activation model for server installation, such as Automatic Virtual Machine Activation (AVMA), Key Management Service (KMS), and Active Directory–Based Activation
Implementing Windows PowerShell Desired State Configuration	Implement Windows PowerShell Desired State Configuration (DSC) to install and maintain integrity of installed environments

KEY TERMS

activation

Active Directory–Based Activation (ADBA)

Active Directory Migration Tool (ADMT)

Automatic Virtual Machine Activation (AVMA)

feature

Generic Volume License Key (GVLK)

in-place upgrade

interforest migration

intraforest migration

Key Management Service (KMS)

Local Configuration Manager (LCM)

multiple activation key (MAK)

Nano Server

Original Equipment Manufacturer (OEM) keys

PowerShell Desired State Configuration (DSC)

PowerShell Remoting

role services

server role

slmgr.vbs

Software Licensing Manager (SLMgr) module

virtual disk

Web Services for Management

Windows Remote Management (WinRM)

Windows Server 2016 Datacenter edition

Windows Server 2016 Desktop Experience

Windows Server 2016 Essentials edition

Windows Server 2016 Server Core

Windows Server 2016 Standard edition

WinRS.exe

■ Installing Windows Server 2016

↓
THE BOTTOM LINE

Installing Windows Server 2016 on a server-class computer is relatively easy. However, before you actually install Windows Server 2016, you should first understand the capabilities of Windows Server 2016. Then, you need to look at the desired purpose and workload the server must perform. Some of the server roles were discussed in Lesson 1.

When you install Windows Server 2016, you can select one of three installation options:

• *Windows Server 2016 with Desktop Experience*: Previously known as Server with a GUI installation, a full installation with the GUI interface that you would expect on a Windows operating system. This installation option supports all Windows Server roles.

- ***Windows Server 2016 Server Core***: The Server Core installation that provides a command-line management interface. Because the installation does not include the GUI interface, the Server Core installation has a reduced hardware footprint and a reduced security footprint/attack surface. Unfortunately, it does not support all Windows Server roles.
- ***Nano Server***: A new installation option that was not available in Windows Server 2012 R2 or earlier. Nano Server is administered remotely and optimized for hosting in private clouds and data centers. The Nano Server runs from a VHD, either from within Hyper-V or you can boot directly from the VHD at startup.

A ***virtual disk*** (also known as virtual hard disk [VHD]) is a file that represents a physical disk drive to a guest operating system running on a virtual machine. The user can install a new operating system onto the virtual disk without repartitioning the physical disk or rebooting the host machine.

TAKE NOTE* You cannot convert from Server Core to Server with Desktop Experience, or from Server with Desktop Experience to Server Core.

The first two options can be selected by starting the Windows 2016 installation program and selecting the appropriate option. However, the Nano Server is installed as a VHD or as a Windows Imaging (WIM) file that is built using Windows PowerShell cmdlets.

Determining Windows Server 2016 Installation Requirements

Before installing Windows Server 2016, you need to first determine the minimum hardware requirements so that you can ensure that you have the correct hardware. The minimum hardware can then be used to gauge what is needed to carry the necessary load.

CERTIFICATION READY
Determine Windows Server 2016 installation requirements
Objective 1.1

Although the hardware requirements to support Windows Server 2016 will depend on the servers that the server is hosting, the load on the server, and how responsive you want your server to be, the following is the minimum to install Server Core on a physical machine:

- **Processor:** A 64-bit processor running 1.4 GHz
- **RAM:** 512 MB
- **Free hard drive space:** 32 GB

If you want to run the Desktop Experience, you should increase the requirements even more. Although Microsoft states that you would need an additional 4 GB of free disk space, you should consider two core processors running at 1.4 GHz, 2 GB of memory, and 50 GB free as the minimum if you desire fair performance. Then based on the server roles and applications the server will run, you will increase the requirements even further. You should also add additional disk space if you are to perform a network installation or for computers with more than 16 GB of RAM.

In addition, storage and network adapters must be PCI Express compliant. Ethernet adapters should be at least gigabit throughput. The graphics device and monitor should be capable of Super VGA (1024 × 768). If you need to install Windows Server 2016, you may need a DVD drive, USB drive, or network drive.

The requirements for Nano Server will depend on the features and roles installed. The smallest Nano Server VHD will be approximately 440 MB. But after installing IIS or commonly used drivers, the VHD with IIS will be just over 500 MB.

Determining the Appropriate Windows Server 2016 Editions Per Workloads

> Similar to previous Windows Server operating systems, you have multiple editions to choose from. These editions allow you to select the edition that you need rather than paying for all features, some of which you do not need.

<table>
<tr><td>CERTIFICATION READY
Determine appropriate
Windows Server 2016
editions per workloads
Objective 1.1</td></tr>
</table>

The editions of Windows Server 2016 include:

- *Windows Server 2016 Essentials edition*: This edition corresponds to the Windows Small Business Server from earlier versions of Windows Server, and it is designed for small businesses. It allows up to 25 users and 50 devices. It supports two processor cores and up to 64 gigabytes (GB) of random access memory (RAM). It does not support many of the features of Windows Server 2016, including virtualization.

- *Windows Server 2016 Standard edition*: This edition is designed for physical server environments with little or no virtualization. It provides many of the roles and features available for the Windows Server 2016 operating system and it supports up to 64 processor sockets and up to 4 terabytes (TB) of RAM. It includes licenses for up to two virtual machines and supports Nano Server installation. Licensing is processor core based.

- *Windows Server 2016 Datacenter edition*: Because it includes unlimited Windows Server–based virtual machine licenses for unlimited Windows Server–based virtual machines that run on the same physical server, this edition is ideal for highly virtualized infrastructures, including private cloud and hybrid cloud environments. It provides all of the roles and features available for the Windows Server 2016 operating system and it supports up to 64 processor sockets, up to 640 processor cores, and up to 4 TB of RAM. It also includes new features such as Storage Spaces Direct and Storage Replica, along with new Shielded Virtual Machines and features for software-defined data center scenarios. Licensing is processor core based.

- **Microsoft Hyper-V Server 2016:** This edition acts as a stand-alone virtualization server for virtual machines. It includes all new features around virtualization in Windows Server 2016. Although it supports limited file server features, it does not support other Windows server roles. Although the host operating system has no licensing cost, the virtual machines must be licensed separately. It supports up to 64 processor sockets and up to 4 TB of RAM. It supports domain joining. Different from the Standard and Datacenter editions, Hyper-V Server edition does not have a GUI, but it does have a user interface that displays a menu of configuration tasks.

- **Windows Storage Server 2016 Workgroup edition:** This edition is meant as an entry-level unified storage appliance. It allows 50 users, one processor core, and 32 GB of RAM.

- **Windows Storage Server 2016 Standard edition:** This edition is meant as a unified storage appliance that supports up to 64 sockets but is licensed on a two-socket, incrementing basis. It supports up to 4 TB of RAM and it includes two virtual machine licenses. It includes Domain Name System (DNS) and Dynamic Host Configuration Protocol (DHCP) server roles, but does not support others, including Active Directory Domain Services (AD DS), Active Directory Certificate Services (AD CS), and Active Directory Federation Services (AD FS). Licensing is processor core based.

For small data centers that only consist of a few servers, you should consider Windows Server 2016 Standard edition. For large data centers that will use powerful physical servers or blades, you should consider purchasing a Datacenter edition for each physical server or blade. However, both are licensed based on the number of cores within the physical processors.

> Besides licensing the core processors, each user and/or device accessing a licensed Windows Server Standard or Datacenter edition requires a Windows Server CAL. Each Window Server CAL allows access to multiple licenses of Windows Server, including any edition of Windows Server of the same or earlier version.

Windows Server 2016 users the 5+5 service and support model, which means that there will be five years of mainstream support and five years of extended support. Customers who choose to install full Windows Server 2016 with a Desktop GUI or Server Core will maintain the same servicing experience, which is known as Long-Term Servicing Branch (LTSB), whereas the Windows server will be updated every couple of years with new or updated features. However, normal critical and security packs will be made available as with all Windows operating systems.

Installing Windows Server 2016—Full Version

Installing Windows Server 2016 is a relatively easy process. You typically boot from the Windows Server 2016 installation disk and go through the installation wizard.

CERTIFICATION READY
Install Windows
Server 2016
Objective 1.1

Based on the key that you specify, you will then be asked to install Server Core or Server with Desktop Experience. Selecting the Server with Desktop Experience option provides a Server Graphical Shell, including Server Manager, and selecting Server Core provides a command prompt.

To boot from a DVD drive, you insert the DVD into your DVD/Blu-ray drive and turn on the computer. If the system does not boot from the DVD, you might need to configure the BIOS Setup program to boot from the DVD/Blu-ray drive and you might need to configure the boot order so that the DVD/Blu-ray drive booting will occur before any other boot drives.

 INSTALL WINDOWS SERVER 2016 WITH DESKTOP EXPERIENCE

GET READY. To install Windows Server 2016 with Desktop Experience, perform the following steps.

1. Insert the Windows Server 2016 disc into the DVD drive and turn on the computer. Press any key to boot from the DVD (if necessary).
2. The computer switches to the Windows graphical interface and the Windows Setup page appears, as shown in Figure 2-1. Using the drop-down lists provided, select the appropriate language to install, the time and currency format, and the keyboard or input method. Then, click **Next**.

Figure 2-1

The Windows Setup page

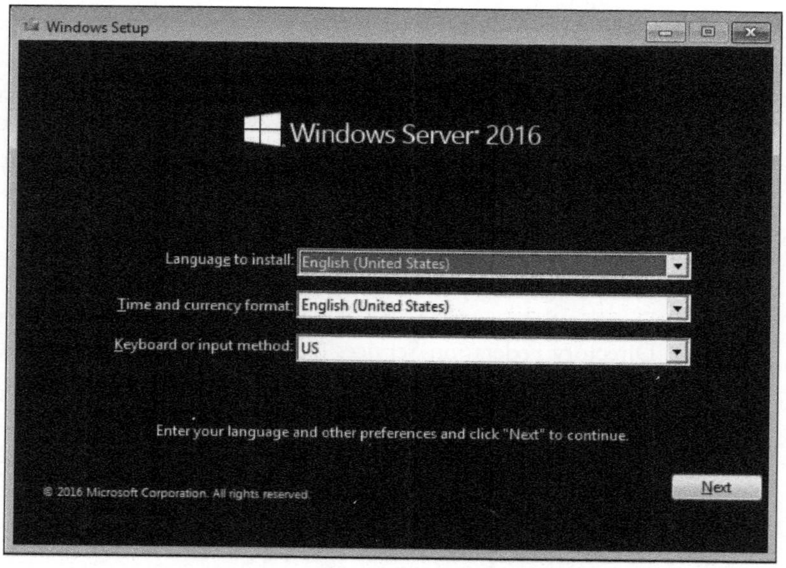

![The Windows Setup page showing Windows Server 2016 with fields for Language to install: English (United States), Time and currency format: English (United States), Keyboard or input method: US, and a Next button. Text reads "Enter your language and other preferences and click 'Next' to continue." © 2016 Microsoft Corporation. All rights reserved.]

3. On the Windows Server 2016 Install Now page, click **Install now**.
4. When the Activate Windows page appears, in the text box, type the Windows Server 2016 activation key and then click **Next**.

5. On the Select the Operating System to Install page (as shown in Figure 2-2), select **Windows Server 2016 Datacenter (Desktop Experience).** Click **Next.**

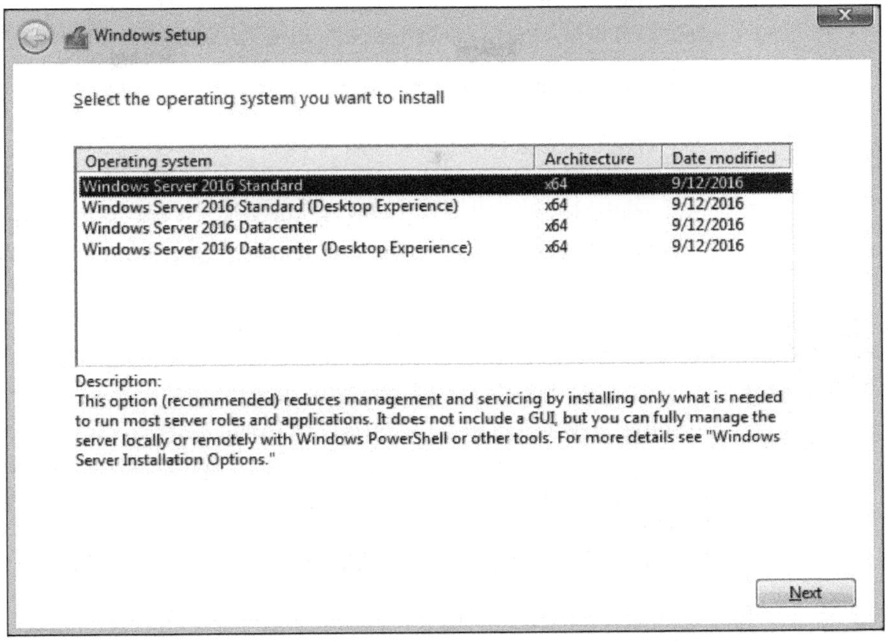

Figure 2-2

Selecting which operating system to install

6. On the License Terms page, select the **I accept the license terms** option and then click **Next.**

7. Click the **Custom: Install Windows only (advanced)** option.

8. The Where Do You Want to Install Windows? page appears, as shown in Figure 2-3. From the list provided, select the partition on which you want to install Windows Server 2016, or select an area of unallocated disk space where the Setup program can create a new partition. Then click **Next.**

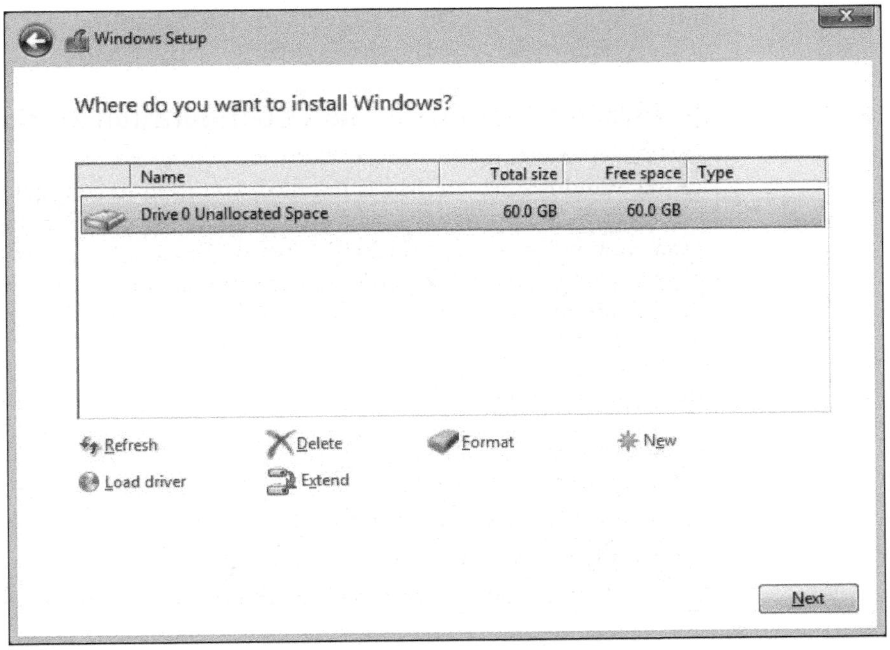

Figure 2-3

The Where Do You Want to Install Windows? page

9. After several minutes, during which the Setup program installs Windows Server 2016, the computer reboots. When the Customize Settings page appears, in the Password and Reenter password text boxes, type **Pa$$w0rd.** Click **Finish.**

The Where Do You Want to Install Windows? page enables you to create, manage, and delete the partitions on your disks. It also allows you to load specialized storage drivers.

Clicking the Drive options (advanced) button on the page causes four additional buttons to appear. These buttons have the following functions:

- Delete removes an existing partition from a disk, permanently erasing all its data. You might want to delete partitions to consolidate unallocated disk space, enabling you to create a new, larger partition.

- Extend enables you to make an existing partition larger, as long as unallocated space is available immediately following the selected partition on the disk.

- Format enables you to format an existing partition on a disk, thereby erasing all its data. You do not need to format any new partitions you create for the install, but you might want to format an existing partition to eliminate unwanted files before installing Windows Server 2016 on it.

- New creates a new partition of a user-specified size in the selected area of unallocated space.

In some cases, it might be necessary to install a driver supplied by a hardware manufacturer before the disks (for example, RAID drivers) in the computer appear in the Setup program. During the Windows Server 2016 installation procedure, the Setup program enables you to select the partition or area of unallocated disk space where you want to install the operating system. The Where Do You Want to Install Windows? page lists the partitions on all the computer's disk drives that the Setup program can detect with its default drivers. In most cases, all the computer's drives should appear in the list; if they do not, it is probably because Windows does not include a driver for the computer's drive controller.

If the computer's hard drives are connected to a third-party controller, rather than the one integrated into most motherboards, the list of partitions might appear empty, and you might need to supply a driver for the Setup program to see the drives. Check the controller manufacturer's website for a driver supporting Windows Server 2016, or another recent version of Windows Server.

To load the disk driver, on the Where Do You Want to Install Windows? page, click the Load driver button. You will then be prompted to insert the storage medium that contains the drivers (CD, DVD, or USB flash drive). You can then browse to the location of the driver and click OK. Then, select the driver and click Next. You would then continue with the rest of the Windows Server 2016 installation.

Performing Post-Installation Configuration Settings

After Windows Server 2016 is installed, you need to configure Windows before it is ready for use. For example, you need to configure the IP configuration so that the server can communicate over a TCP/IP network. You need to name the server, and you most likely need to add the server to an Active Directory domain. You then need to install and configure any roles and features, and install and configure any applications.

After you have installed Windows Server 2016, you typically should complete the following:

- Configure the IP address.
- Set the computer name.
- Join an Active Directory domain.
- Configure the time zone.
- Load additional drivers that were not installed during installation.
- Activate Windows.

- Enable automatic updates.
- Download and install updates.
- Add and configure roles and features.
- Enable the Remote Desktop feature.
- Configure Windows Firewall settings.
- Install and configure additional applications.
- Grant access to the server.

Installing Windows Server 2016 Features and Roles

A *server role* is a set of software programs that perform a specific function as a network service for multiple users. *Role services* are made up of one or more role services that provide the functionality of the server role. A *feature* is a software program that is not directly part of a server role, but can support or augment the functionality of a server role. To add, remove, or manage server roles and features, you use Server Manager.

CERTIFICATION READY
Install Windows Server
2016 features and roles
Objective 1.1

For example, the File and iSCSI Services consists of a server role that provides technologies that help you manage file servers and storage. It can be used to reduce disk space utilization, replicate data, cache files, or share files with Server Message Block (SMB) or Network File System (NFS) protocol. It consists of the following role services:

- **File Server:** Provides basic access to shared folders.
- **BranchCache for Network Files:** Allows the caching of network shares so that you don't always have to access recently accessed files over a slow WAN link.
- **Data Deduplication:** Reduces disk utilization by storing a single copy of data on a volume. Therefore, if files contain the same sets of data, it will only store the one set of data, and the files will point to the single set of data.
- **DFS Namespace:** Allows you to create DFS namespaces so that you can organize your shared folders into a hierarchy.
- **DFS Replication:** Allows you to synchronize files between servers or across branch offices.
- **File Server Resource Manager:** Allows you to create file screens, manage folder-level quotas, create file classifications, and generate storage reports.
- **File Server VSS Agent Service:** Allows applications that store data on the file server to create Volume Shadow Copy Service (VSS) snapshots, which can be used with several types of applications such as backups.
- **iSCSI Target Server:** Allows the server to function as an iSCSI target that provides iSCSI disks for other systems.
- **iSCSI Target Storage Provider (VDS and VSS):** Allows applications connected to an iSCSI target on the local server to create VSS snapshots.
- **Server for NFS:** Allows the server to function as an NFS server, which is primarily used by UNIX and Linux clients.
- **Work Folders:** Allows users to provide a consistent way for users to access their work files from their PCs and personal devices.
- **Storage Services:** Provides storage-management functionality.

The File Server role and the Storage Services role are enabled by default in Windows Server 2016, although the File Server role does not always show as enabled in Server Manager.

Two examples of features are Failover Clustering and Network Load Balancing. Although these two features do not provide network services for users, they can be used to make the server roles fault tolerant. Some other features include:

- **.NET Framework 3.5 Features:** Provides older .NET Framework application programming interfaces (APIs) that are required for some programs to function properly.
- **.NET Framework 4.6 Features:** Provides a consistent programming model and APIs that are required for some programs to function.
- **Background Intelligent Transfer Service (BITS):** Provides asynchronous transfer of files in the foreground and background, and controls the flow of traffic so that responsiveness of other network applications is not seriously degraded. It will also resume file transfers after network disconnects and computer restarts.
- **BitLocker Drive Encryption:** Allows you to encrypt a drive, which can be used to protect the contents of a drive if the drive or system is stolen.
- **Containers:** Provides services and tools to create and manage Windows Server Containers and their resources. Containers are isolated, resource-controlled and portable operating environments that can be moved from server to server as needed.
- **Failover Clustering:** Allows multiple servers to work together to provide high availability of server roles.
- **Network Load Balancing:** Distributes web traffic across several servers so that it can provide scalability and fault tolerance for web services.
- **Remote Differential Compression:** Minimizes network traffic by only transferring the differences of two objects rather than sending both objects.
- **Remote Server Administration Tools:** Provides administrative tools for the various server roles and features so that you can manage those server roles and features on local and remote systems.
- **SMB Bandwidth Limit:** Allows you to limit the amount of traffic allowed for a defined category, such as Default, Hyper-V, or Live Migration.
- **SNMP Service:** Enables the use of Simple Network Management Protocol (SNMP) so that you can monitor the activity of network devices.
- **Telnet Client:** Allows you to connect to a remote Telnet server and run applications on that server via a command prompt. It can also be used to test TCP applications.
- **TFTP Client:** Provides the ability to read files from and write files to a remote Trivial File Transfer Protocol (TFTP).
- **Windows Defender Features:** Helps protect your machine against malware.
- **Windows Search Service:** Provides fast file searches by creating and maintaining file indexes.
- **Windows Server Backup:** Allows you to back up and recover your operating system, applications, and data.

Although you could install and configure all server roles and features, it is never recommended for several reasons. First, it would consume a large amount of resources. Second, by not running all roles and features, you are minimizing your security footprint by only using the necessary role services.

 INSTALL WINDOWS SERVER 2016 SERVER ROLES AND FEATURES

GET READY. To install Windows Server 2016 server roles and features, perform the following steps.

1. Log on to **LON-SVR1** as **adatum\administrator** with the password of **Pa$$w0rd**.
2. On LON-SVR1, to open Server Manager, click **Start** and then click the **Server Manager** tile.
3. When Server Manager opens, open the **Manage** menu and click **Add Roles and Features**.

4. When the Add Roles and Features Wizard opens, on the Before You Begin page, click **Next**.

5. On the Select Installation Type page, Role-based or feature-based installation is already selected. Click **Next**.

6. On the Server Selection page, select the desired server. Most of the time, the local server will already be selected. Click **Next**.

7. On the Select Server Roles page (as shown in Figure 2-4), select the desired server role. If the server role is already installed, expand the server role to select specific role services. If you are prompted to add or remove any features, click the **Add Features** button. Click **Next**.

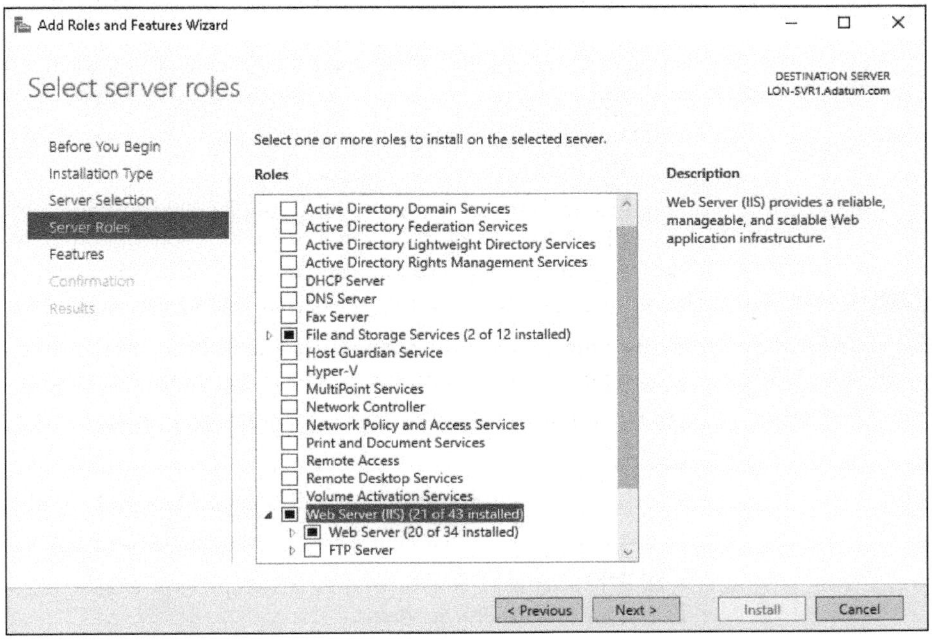

Figure 2-4

Selecting server roles

8. On the Select Features page (as shown in Figure 2-5), select the appropriate features and then click **Next**.

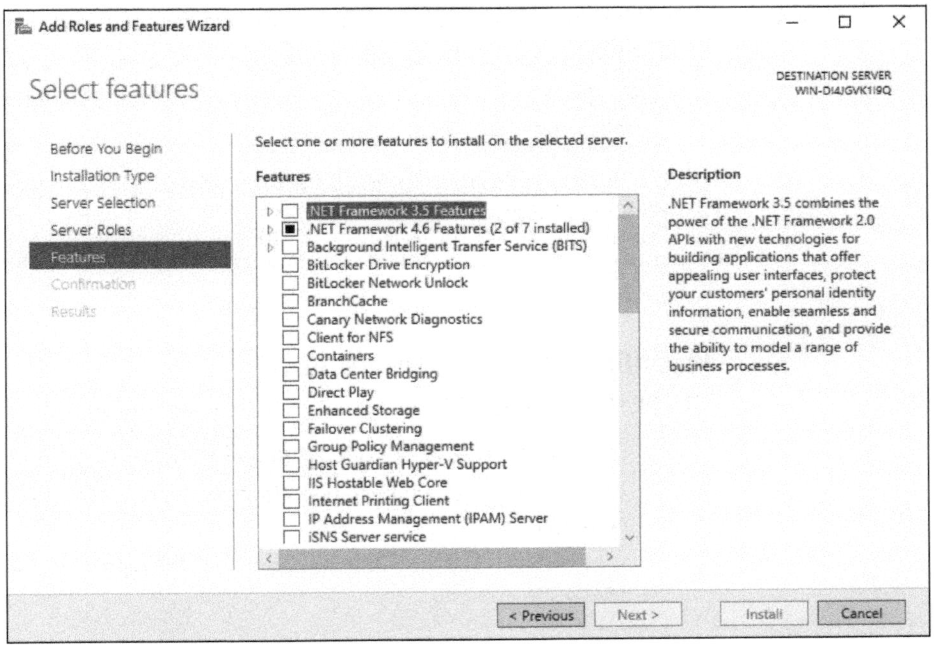

Figure 2-5

Selecting server features

9. On the Confirmation page, you can select the **Restart the destination server automatically if required** option, if desired. In either case, click **Install**.

10. When the feature or role is installed, click **Close**.

Depending on which server role or feature you install, you might need to use Server Manager or an administrative tool to further configure the server role or feature. The administrative tools are accessible from the Tools menu.

■ Installing and Configuring Windows Server Core

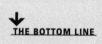
THE BOTTOM LINE

It was already mentioned that Server Core is the Windows Server 2016 installation option that provides a command-line management interface. Because it does not have a GUI interface, it uses fewer hardware resources. In addition, because it has fewer running components, there are fewer components that can be compromised and it requires fewer updates. When you install Windows Server 2016, the Server Core is the default installation.

CERTIFICATION READY
Install and configure
Windows Server Core
Objective 1.1

The following server roles are available on Server Core deployments:

- Active Directory Certificate Services (AD CS)
- Active Directory Domain Services (AD DS)
- Dynamic Host Configuration Protocol (DHCP) Server
- Domain Name System (DNS) Server
- File Services (including File Server Resource Manager)
- Active Directory Lightweight Directory Services (AD LDS)
- Hyper-V
- Print and Document Services
- Streaming Media Services
- Web Server (including a subset of ASP.NET)
- Windows Server Update Server
- Active Directory Rights Management Server
- Routing and Remote Access Server and the following subroles:
  - Remote Desktop Connection Broker
  - Licensing
  - Virtualization

Because Server Core does not have a GUI interface, you will have to manage it with one of the following methods:

- Locally with Windows PowerShell or a command-line interface
- Remotely with a remote management option

Installing Windows Server Core

Installing Server Core is very similar to installing Windows Server 2016 with Desktop Experience. You can insert a Windows Server 2016 installation DVD into the DVD drive and boot from the installation disk.

If you decide to use Windows Server Core, be sure to plan how you are going to manage the server. Determine if you will have direct access to the console anytime you need to perform local commands and set up remote tools so that you can access it remotely.

➡ INSTALL WINDOWS SERVER 2016 SERVER CORE

GET READY. To install Windows Server 2016 Server Core, perform the following steps.

1. Insert the Windows Server 2016 disc into the DVD drive and turn on the computer. Press any key to boot from the DVD (if necessary).
2. The computer switches to the Windows graphical interface and the Windows Setup page appears. Using the drop-down lists provided, select the appropriate language to install, the time and currency format, and the keyboard or input method. Then, click **Next.**
3. On the Windows Server 2016 Install Now page, click **Install now.**
4. When the Activate Windows page appears, in the text box, type the Windows Server 2016 activation key and then click **Next.**
5. On the Select the Operating System to Install page, select **Windows Server 2016 Datacenter.** Click **Next.**
6. On the License Terms page, select the **I accept the license terms** option and then click **Next.**
7. Click the **Custom: Install Windows only (advanced)** option.
8. The Where Do You Want to Install Windows? page appears. From the list provided, select the partition on which you want to install Windows Server 2016, or select an area of unallocated disk space where the Setup program can create a new partition. Then, click **Next.**
9. After several minutes, during which the Setup program installs Windows Server 2016, the computer reboots. When the Customize Settings page appears, in the Password and Reenter password text boxes, type **Pa$$w0rd.** Click **Finish.**

Managing Windows Server Core Installations

> After you install Server Core, you need to configure Server Core by connecting locally to execute traditional command-line tools using cmd.exe. From there, you can start PowerShell.exe and other programs to configure Windows. You can also configure Server Core remotely by using remote commands or MMC programs that can manage roles, features, or other programs remotely.

CERTIFICATION READY
Manage Windows Server Core installations using Windows PowerShell, command line, and remote management capabilities
Objective 1.1

When you are connected to the system locally, you can use the following tools:

- **Cmd.exe:** Allows you to run traditional command-line tools, such as ping.exe, ipconfig .exe, and netsh.exe. Figure 2-6 shows executing the ipconfig command from the cmd.exe prompt and opening the Registry Editor.
- **PowerShell.exe:** Opens a Windows PowerShell session so that you can execute Windows PowerShell commands. Windows Server 2016 comes with Windows PowerShell version 5.0 installed.
- **Sconfig.cmd:** Functions as a command-line, menu-driven administrative tool (as shown in Figure 2-7) that enables you to perform most common server administrative tasks, such as configuring networking, workgroups, and domains and configuring Windows Firewall.
- **Regedt32.exe:** Opens the Registry Editor to change registry settings.
- **Msinfo32.exe:** Allows you to view system information for the system.
- **Taskmgr.exe:** Launches Task Manager.

Figure 2-6

Executing commands at the
Server Core cmd.exe prompt

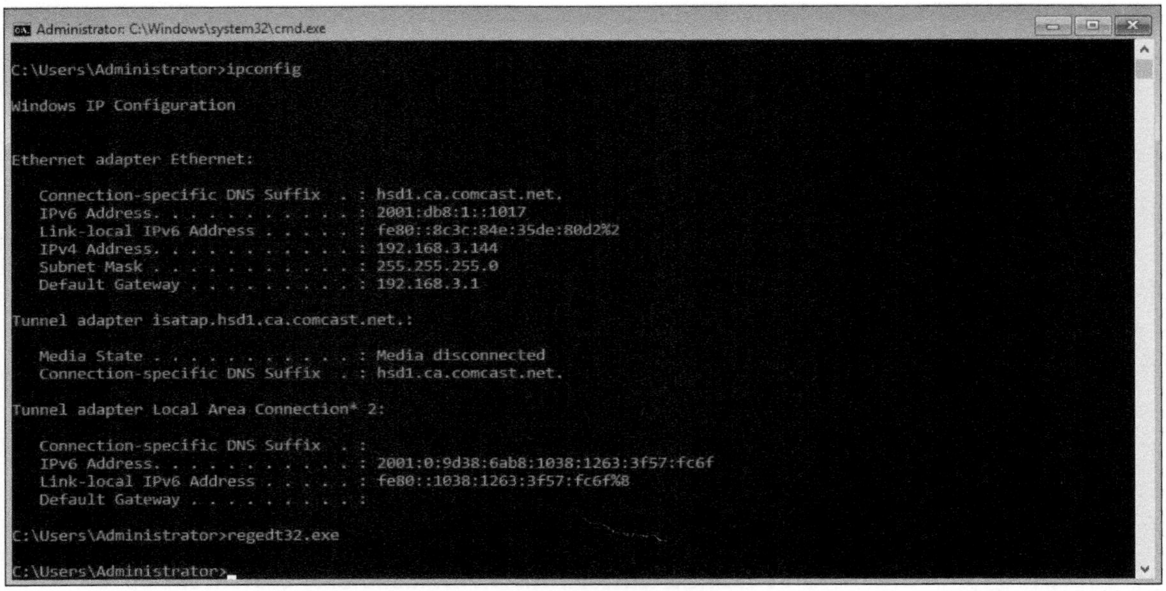

Figure 2-7

Using sconfig.cmd to configure
Server Core

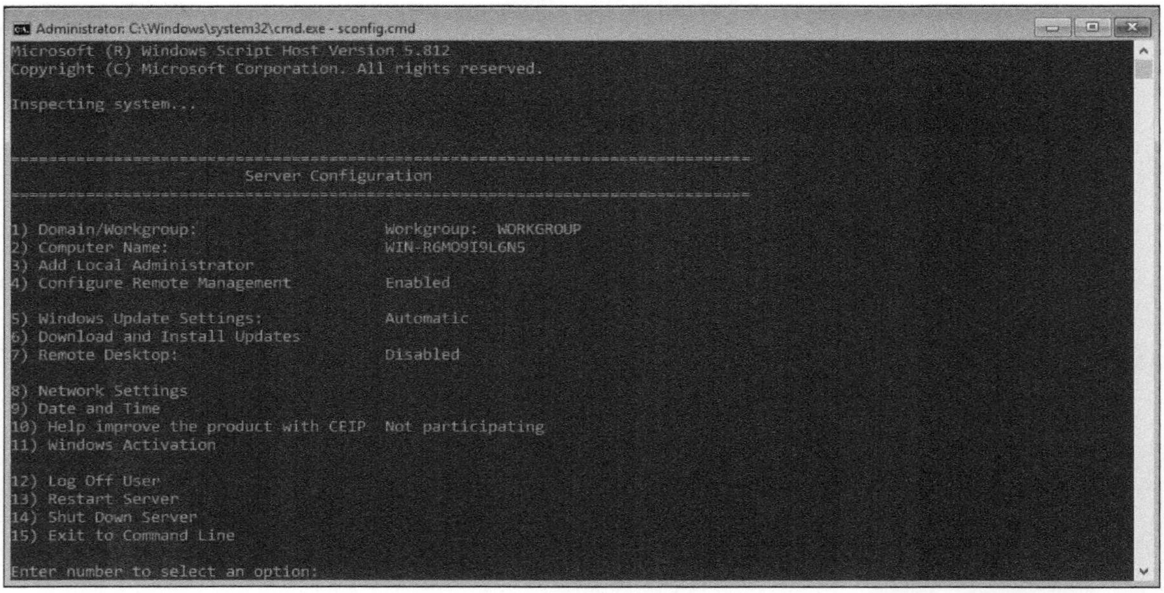

USING REMOTE DESKTOP CONNECTIONS TO MANAGE A SERVER

The Remote Desktop Protocol (RDP) and Remote Desktop was covered in Lesson 1. You can use the Remote Desktop Connection program to connect to computers running Server with Desktop Experience and Server Core. For Server Core, you need to enable Remote Desktop by using sconfig.cmd.

TAKE NOTE*

You cannot use
Remote Desktop to
remotely manage
Nano Server.

MANAGING COMPUTERS REMOTELY WITH ADMINISTRATIVE TOOLS

Many of the snap-ins supplied with Windows Server 2016 enable you to manage other Windows computers on the network as well. There are two ways to access a remote computer using a Microsoft Management Console (MMC) snap-in:

- Redirect an existing snap-in to another system.
- Create a custom console with snap-ins directed to other systems.

To connect to and manage another system (Server with Desktop Experience or Server Core) using an MMC snap-in, you must launch the console with an account that has administrative credentials on the remote computer. You then click, then right-click the snap-in, then choose Connect to another computer. The Select Computer dialog box shown in Figure 2-8 opens. If your credentials do not provide the proper permissions on the target computer, you will be able to load the snap-in, but you will not be able to read information from or modify settings on the target computer.

TAKE NOTE*

You can also manage the systems running Windows Server 2016 remotely from a computer running Windows 10 by installing Remote Server Administration Tools on the computer running Windows 10.

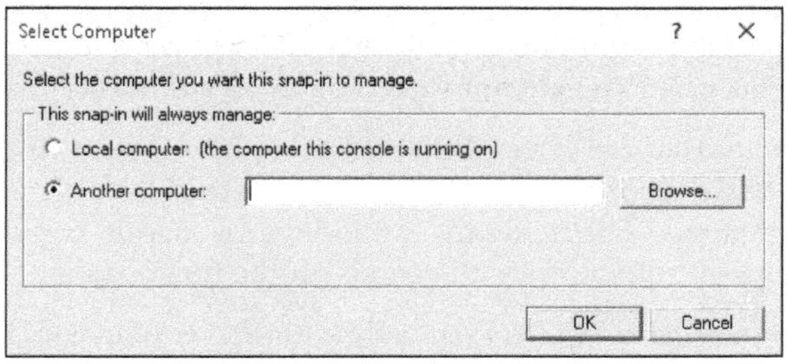

Figure 2-8

The Select Computer dialog box in an MMC console

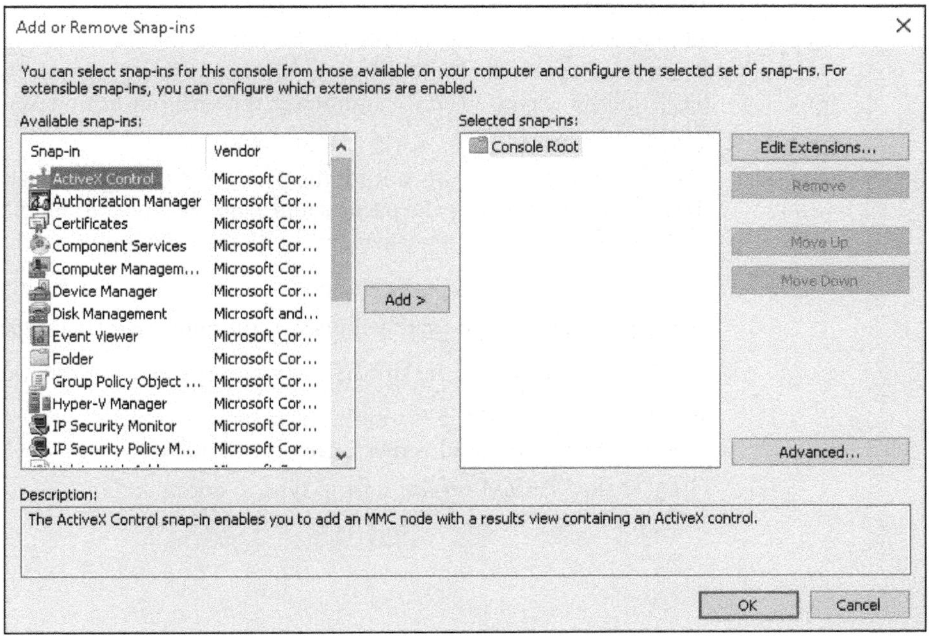

Figure 2-9

Selecting snap-ins for a custom MMC

CREATE A CUSTOM MMC AND MODIFY SETTINGS REMOTELY

GET READY. To create a custom MMC and then modify settings remotely, perform the following steps.

1. Right-click **Start** and type **mmc** in the Run text box. Click **Yes** to open the MMC Console.
2. In the MMC Console window, click **File > Add/Remove Snap-in**. The Add or Remove Snap-ins dialog box opens (as shown in Figure 2-9).

3. In the Available snap-ins list on the left, select a snap-in of your choice, such as **Computer Management.** In the middle of the dialog box, click **Add.** In the dialog box that opens, leave **Local computer** selected (unless the computer you want to manage is one other than the current computer).

4. Click **Finish.** The snap-in is added to the Selected snap-ins pane on the right.

5. You can then repeat Steps 2 through 4 for each snap-in you want to include in the custom MMC.

6. When done adding snap-ins, click **OK.**

7. Click **File > Save As.** In the File name text box, type a name for the custom MMC and then click **Save.**

8. If you loaded the Computer Management MMC, expand **System Tools > Event Viewer > Windows logs** and click **System.**

9. View the logs on the remote computer.

10. Expand the **Services and Applications** node and click **Services.**

11. Right-click the **Computer Browser** service and choose **Restart.**

12. Close the MMC console.

To avoid exposing a computer to malicious attacks, Microsoft recommends that you use MMC snap-ins when you are not logged on as an administrator.

The other factor that can affect the ability of an MMC snap-in to connect to a remote computer is the existence of Windows Firewall rules that block the necessary network traffic between the computers. The traffic that an individual snap-in requires and whether the default Windows Firewall rules restrict it depends on the functions that the snap-in performs.

You can also manage computers remotely with Server Manager, including installing server roles and features. However, to manage other remote computers, you need to add the computer to Server Manager. This can be done by opening the Manage menu and selecting the Add Servers option.

USING WINDOWS REMOTE MANAGEMENT

Using Windows Remote Management, administrators can execute programs from the command line on remote computers (Server with Desktop Experience and Server Core) without having to open a Remote Desktop session.

Windows Remote Management (WinRM) is a Windows Server 2016 service that enables administrators to execute commands on remote computers using Windows PowerShell or the Windows Remote Shell (WinRS.exe) command-line program. By default, WinRM is enabled on Windows Server 2012 R2 and newer systems, but not on Windows 8.1 or Windows 10 clients.

WinRM is responsible for routing the packets to the right location, while *Web Services for Management* structures the packets and requires a port to be made accessible via your firewall. To enable remote management for a target computer, you can do one of the following:

- Open a command prompt and execute the `winrm quickconfig` command.
- Open Windows PowerShell on the computer, and then type `Enable-PSRemoting`.

The following tasks are performed when you run `winrm quickconfig` or `Enable-PSRemoting`:

- Start or restart (if already started) the WinRM service.
- Set the WinRM service startup type to automatic.

- Create a listener to accept requests on any IP address.
- Enable Windows Firewall inbound rule exceptions for WS-Management traffic (for http only). This inbound rule is listed as Windows Remote Management via WS-Management (TCP port 5985) in the inbound rules of your Windows Firewall.

 CONFIGURE REMOTE MANAGEMENT WITH THE WinRM COMMAND

GET READY. To configure remote management with the WinRM command, log on to Windows Server 2016 using an account with administrative privileges and then perform the following steps.

1. Open a command prompt with administrator privileges. If the User Account Control dialog box opens prompting you to continue, click **Yes**.

2. Execute the following command:

   winrm quickconfig

   The command prompts you to start the WinRM service.

3. When it notifies you that it will start the WinRM service and set the WinRM service to delayed auto start, type **y** and then press **Enter** to continue.

4. When you are asked to create a WinRM listener, enable the WinRM firewall exception, type **y**, and then press **Enter** to continue.

5. Close the Administrator: Command Prompt window.

 The WinRM.exe program will fail to configure the required firewall exception if the computer's network location is set to Public. The computer must use either the Private or Domain location settings for the remote management configuration process to succeed.

WinRM can be enabled for all computers within a domain via a Group Policy Object. To help keep the use of WinRM secure, you can enable the Computer Configuration\Policies\ Administrative Templates\Windows Components\Windows Remote Management (WinRM)\ WinRM Service\Allow remote server management through WinRM setting and specify the IP address ranges from which the service will accept connections.

After you have configured the Remote Management service, you can execute commands on other computers that have been similarly configured. To execute a command from the Windows Server 2016 command prompt, you must use the *WinRS.exe* program.

To use WinRS.exe, you frame the command you want to execute on the remote computer as follows:

winrs –r:*computer* [-u:*user*] [-p:*password*] command

- **–r:*computer***: Specifies the name of the computer on which you want to execute the command, using a NetBIOS name or a fully qualified domain name (FQDN).
- **-u:*user***: Specifies the account on the remote computer that you want to use to execute the command.
- **-p:*password***: Specifies the password associated with the account specified in the –u parameter. If you do not specify a password on the command line, WinRS.exe prompts you for one before executing the command.
- ***command***: Specifies the command (with arguments) that you want to execute on the remote computer.

USING REMOTE WINDOWS POWERSHELL

PowerShell Remoting is a server-client application that allows you to securely connect to a remote PowerShell host and run script interactively. It allows you to run commands on a remote system as though you were sitting physically at its console. PowerShell Remoting is built upon the Web Services for Management protocol and uses Windows Remote Management service to handle the authentication and communication elements.

There are two types of remoting:

- **One-to-one remoting:** Allows you to bring up the PowerShell prompt on a remote computer. The credentials you use are delegated to the remote computer. Any commands you run will run under those credentials.
- **One-to-many remoting:** Allows you to send one or more commands, in parallel, to multiple computers. Each of these computers runs the command, produces the results into an XML file, and then returns the results to your computer over the network. When the results are returned, they include the computer name.

 USE POWERSHELL (ONE-TO-ONE REMOTING)

GET READY. To connect to a target Windows Server 2016 computer using PowerShell and one-to-one remoting, perform the following steps.

First, you need to enable PSRemoting on a target computer:

1. Log on with administrative privileges to a computer running Windows 10 or Windows Server 2016.
2. Click **Start** and type **PowerShell**. From the results, click **Windows PowerShell**.
3. From the Windows PowerShell window, type **Enable-PSRemoting** and then press **Enter** (see Figure 2-10).

Figure 2-10

Enabling PS Remoting

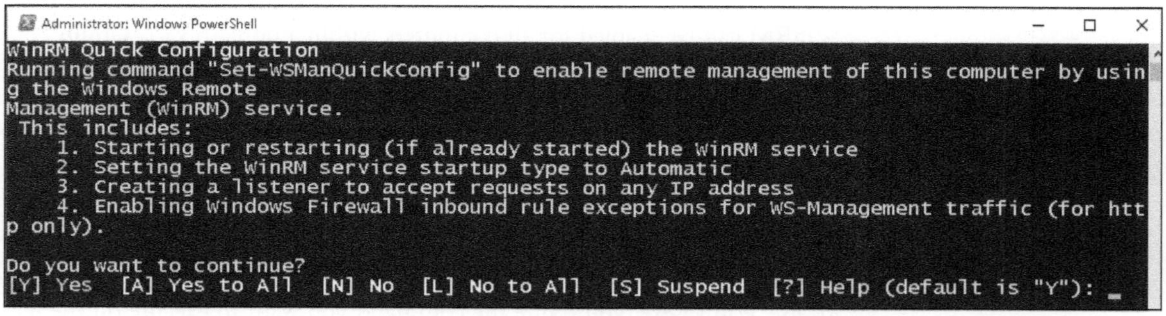

```
Administrator: Windows PowerShell                                    —   □   ×
WinRM Quick Configuration
Running command "Set-WSManQuickConfig" to enable remote management of this computer by usin
g the Windows Remote
Management (WinRM) service.
 This includes:
    1. Starting or restarting (if already started) the WinRM service
    2. Setting the WinRM service startup type to Automatic
    3. Creating a listener to accept requests on any IP address
    4. Enabling Windows Firewall inbound rule exceptions for WS-Management traffic (for htt
p only).

Do you want to continue?
[Y] Yes  [A] Yes to All  [N] No  [L] No to All  [S] Suspend  [?] Help (default is "Y"): _
```

4. If any necessary tasks need to be done, read the tasks that will be performed, type **A**, and then press **Enter**.

NEXT, from the source Windows Server 2016 computer, log on with administrative privileges to the domain and perform the following steps.

1. Press the **Windows logo key + r**, type **Powershell** in the Run text box, and then click **OK**.
2. From the Windows PowerShell window, type the following and press **Enter**:
   enter-pssession –ComputerName <computername>
   Replace *<computername>* with your domain controller's name. Once connected, the PowerShell prompt should include the name of the computer you are currently connected to remotely.

3. Type **get-service** and press **Enter** to see the services running on the domain controller.

4. Type **get-process** and press **Enter** to see a list of all processes running on the domain controller.

5. Type **get-acl c:** and press **Enter** to see the access control list applied via NTFS for the C drive.

6. Type **exit-pssession** and press **Enter** to exit PowerShell.

Some Windows PowerShell cmdlets are not available in the default Windows PowerShell library. When you install certain components such as Microsoft Exchange, Windows PowerShell cmdlets are added to the systems. When you enable some Windows features or you want to administer particular environments, you must obtain and import additional Windows PowerShell functions.

For example, to manage Nano Server remotely, you must import the NanoServerImage Generator.psm1 module using the `Import-Module` command:

```
Import-Module NanoServerImageGenerator.psm1
```

Installing Windows Server 2016 Features and Roles on Windows Server Core

> Because Server Core does not have a GUI interface, the GUI-based management tools and snap-ins cannot be installed on servers that are running the Server Core installation options of Windows Server 2016. Therefore, to install roles and features to Windows Server 2016 Server Core, you must use the Windows PowerShell `Install-WindowsFeature` cmdlet.

The `Install-WindowsFeature` cmdlet uses the following syntax:

```
Install-WindowsFeature –Name <feature_name>
-IncludeManagementTools -Restart
```

The Management tools and snap-ins are added by using the `IncludeManagementTools` parameter. The `Restart` command will restart the computer after the server role or feature is installed.

 INSTALL ROLES AND FEATURES USING THE INSTALL-WINDOWSFEATURE CMDLET

GET READY. To install roles and features using the `Install-WindowsFeature` cmdlet on a computer running Windows Server 2016 Server Core, perform the following steps.

1. Log on with administrative privileges to a computer running Windows Server 2016 Server Core.

2. To open Windows PowerShell, from the command prompt, type PowerShell.exe.

3. To view the roles and features, execute the following command (as shown in Figure 2-11):

Get-WindowsFeature

Figure 2-11

Executing the Get-Windows
Feature command

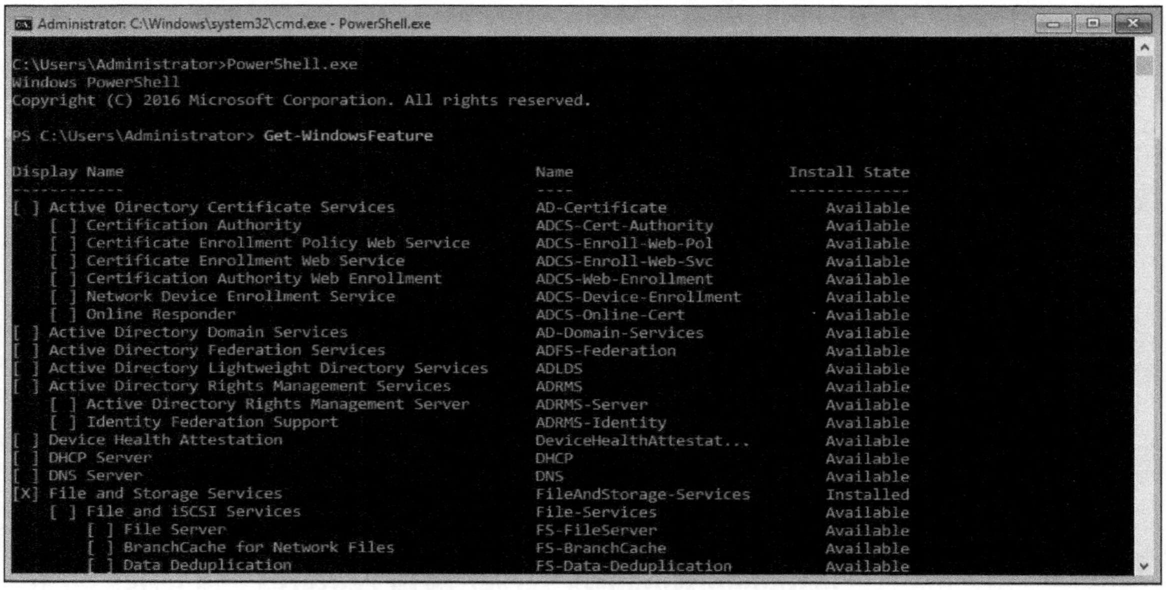

```
Administrator: C:\Windows\system32\cmd.exe - PowerShell.exe

C:\Users\Administrator>PowerShell.exe
Windows PowerShell
Copyright (C) 2016 Microsoft Corporation. All rights reserved.

PS C:\Users\Administrator> Get-WindowsFeature

Display Name                                      Name                      Install State
------------                                      ----                      -------------
[ ] Active Directory Certificate Services         AD-Certificate            Available
    [ ] Certification Authority                   ADCS-Cert-Authority       Available
    [ ] Certificate Enrollment Policy Web Service ADCS-Enroll-Web-Pol       Available
    [ ] Certificate Enrollment Web Service        ADCS-Enroll-Web-Svc       Available
    [ ] Certification Authority Web Enrollment    ADCS-Web-Enrollment       Available
    [ ] Network Device Enrollment Service         ADCS-Device-Enrollment    Available
    [ ] Online Responder                          ADCS-Online-Cert          Available
[ ] Active Directory Domain Services              AD-Domain-Services        Available
[ ] Active Directory Federation Services          ADFS-Federation           Available
[ ] Active Directory Lightweight Directory Services ADLDS                   Available
[ ] Active Directory Rights Management Services   ADRMS                     Available
    [ ] Active Directory Rights Management Server ADRMS-Server              Available
    [ ] Identity Federation Support               ADRMS-Identity            Available
[ ] Device Health Attestation                     DeviceHealthAttestat...   Available
[ ] DHCP Server                                   DHCP                      Available
[ ] DNS Server                                    DNS                       Available
[X] File and Storage Services                     FileAndStorage-Services   Installed
    [ ] File and iSCSI Services                   File-Services             Available
        [ ] File Server                           FS-FileServer             Available
        [ ] BranchCache for Network Files         FS-BranchCache            Available
        [ ] Data Deduplication                    FS-Data-Deduplication     Available
```

4. To install the Active Directory Domain Services role and the Group Policy Management feature on a remote server, execute the following command:

```
Install-WindowsFeature –Name AD-Domain-Services, GPMC –
IncludeManagementTools -Restart
```

■ Performing a Windows Server 2016 Upgrade

↓
THE BOTTOM LINE

An *in-place upgrade* is the most complicated form of Windows Server 2016 installation. It is also the lengthiest and the most likely to cause problems during its execution. Whenever possible, Microsoft recommends that administrators perform a clean installation, or migrate required applications and settings instead.

CERTIFICATION READY
Perform upgrades from
Windows Server 2008
and Windows Server 2012
to Windows Server 2016
Objective 1.1

During an in-place upgrade, the Setup program creates a new Windows folder and installs the Windows Server 2016 operating system files into it. This is only half of the process, however. The program must then migrate the applications, files, and settings from the old OS. This calls for a variety of procedures, such as importing the user profiles, copying all pertinent settings from the old registry to the new one, locating applications and data files, and updating device drivers with new versions.

While in-place upgrades often proceed smoothly, the complexity of the upgrade process and the large number of variables involved means that many things can potentially go wrong. To minimize the risks involved, you must take the upgrade process seriously, prepare the system beforehand, and be able to troubleshoot any problems that might arise. The following sections discuss these subjects in detail.

Understanding Upgrade Paths

> If you want to upgrade or move an older server operating system to Windows Server 2016, you can use existing hardware and upgrade to Windows Server 2016 or you can install Windows Server 2016 on new hardware and migrate the roles, features, settings, and data from the older servers to the new server. You can upgrade from Windows Server 2008 R2 with Service Pack 1, Windows Server 2012, or Windows Server 2012 R2 to Windows Server 2016.

If you have a 64-bit computer running Windows Server 2008 R2, Windows Server 2012, or Windows Server 2012 R2, you can upgrade it to Windows Server 2016 based on the following paths:

- Windows Server 2008 R2 Standard (with Service Pack 1) or Windows Server 2008 R2 Enterprise (with Service Pack 1) to Windows Server 2016 Standard or Windows Server 2016 Datacenter
- Windows Server 2008 R2 Datacenter (with Service Pack 1) to Windows Server 2016 Datacenter
- Windows Web Server 2008 R2 (with Service Pack 1) to Windows Server 2016 Standard
- Windows Server 2008 R2 Datacenter (with Service Pack 1) to Windows Server 2016 Datacenter
- Windows Server 2008 R2 Enterprise (with Service Pack 1) to Windows Server 2016 Standard or Windows Server 2016 Datacenter
- Windows Server 2008 R2 Standard (with Service Pack 1) to Windows Server 2016 Standard or Windows Server 2016 Datacenter
- Windows Web Server 2008 R2 (with Service Pack 1) to Windows Server 2016 Standard
- Windows Server 2012 Datacenter or Windows Server 2012 R2 Datacenter to Windows Server 2016 Datacenter
- Windows Server 2012 Standard or Windows Server 2012 R2 Standard to Windows Server 2016 Standard or Windows Server 2016 Datacenter

TAKE NOTE*

You cannot perform an upgrade that includes one language to another with a different language.

If you want to run Windows Server 2016 on a new machine, or you are not using one of the previous upgrade paths, you must perform a migration.

Preparing to Upgrade

> Before you begin an in-place upgrade to Windows Server 2016, you should perform a number of preliminary procedures to ensure that the process goes smoothly and that server data is protected.

Consider the following before you perform any upgrade to Windows Server 2016:

- Check hardware compatibility. Make sure that the server meets the minimum hardware requirements for Windows Server 2016.
- Check disk space. Make sure that sufficient free disk space is on the partition where the old operating system is installed. During the upgrade procedure, sufficient disk space is needed to hold both operating systems simultaneously. After the upgrade is complete, you can remove the old files, freeing up some additional space.
- Confirm that software is signed. All kernel-mode software on the server, including device drivers, must be digitally signed, or the upgrade will not proceed. If you cannot locate a software update for any signed application or driver, you must uninstall the application or driver before you proceed with the installation.

- Check application compatibility. The Setup program displays a Compatibility Report page that can point out possible application compatibility problems. You can sometimes solve these problems by updating or upgrading the applications. Create an inventory of the software products installed on the server and check the manufacturers' websites for updates, availability of upgrades, and announcements regarding support for Windows Server 2016. In an enterprise environment, you should test all applications for Windows Server 2016 compatibility, no matter what the manufacturer says, before you perform any operating system upgrades.

- Ensure computer functionality. Make sure that Windows Server 2012 or Windows Server 2012 R2 is running properly on the computer before you begin the upgrade process. Check the Event Viewer console for warnings and errors. You must start an in-place upgrade from within the existing operating system, so you cannot count on Windows Server 2016 to correct any problems that prevent the computer from starting or running the Setup program.

- Perform a full backup. Before you perform any upgrade procedure, you should back up the entire system, or at the very least the essential data files. Removable hard drives make this a simple process, even if the computer does not have a suitable backup device.

- Purchase Windows Server 2016. Be sure to purchase the appropriate Windows Server 2016 edition for the upgrade, and have the installation disc and product key handy.

Performing an Upgrade Installation

Windows Server 2016 permits you to perform an upgrade installation only after you have met the prerequisites described in the previous section.

To perform a Windows Server 2016 upgrade installation from Windows Server 2012 or Windows Server 2012 R2, use the following procedure.

PERFORM AN UPGRADE TO WINDOWS SERVER 2016

GET READY. To upgrade Windows Server 2012 R2 to Windows Server 2016, perform the following steps.

1. Log on to a server running Windows Server 2012 R2 as **adatum\administrator** with the password of **Pa$$w0rd**.

2. Insert the Windows Server 2016 installation disc into the DVD drive. Then open the DVD drive, and double-click the **Setup** program. The Windows Setup window opens.

3. On the Get Important Updates page, the Download and install updates (recommended) option is already selected. Click **Next**.

4. On the Product Key page, in the Enter Product key text box, type the product key and then click **Next**.

5. Select the desired Windows version, **Windows Server 2016** or **Windows Server 2016 (Desktop Experience)**. Click **Next**.

6. On the License Terms page, click the **Accept** button.

7. On the Choose What to Keep page, you can select the **Keep personal files and apps**, or **Nothing**. The Keep personal files and apps option will be grayed out if you are installing an edition of Windows that is different from the one you're currently using. Click **Next**. If you are prompted to indicate whether you want to continue using this selection, click the **Yes** button.

8. On the Ready to Install page, click the **Install** button.

9. After several minutes, during which the Setup program upgrades Windows Server 2012 or Windows Server 2012 R2 to Windows Server 2016 and restarts the computer several times, the system finalizes the installation and the Windows sign-on screen appears.

■ Migrating Server and Core Workloads to Windows Server 2016

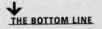
THE BOTTOM LINE

Many roles included with Windows Server 2016 involve a lot of configuring. A particular role might require policies, security, or other settings that you must configure before it can be used. Therefore, when you want to migrate such roles, you want to find a way that can migrate them and all their configuration settings to another server quickly and easily without having to install and configure the role from the beginning. If you search for *Migrating Roles and Features in Windows Server*, you should find a list of available migration guides, including how to use the Windows Server Migration Tools (WSMT) and how to migrate individual roles from one server to another.

CERTIFICATION READY
Perform migrations of servers and core workloads from Windows Server 2008 and Windows Server 2012 to Windows Server 2016
Objective 1.1

You can migrate the following roles by using the WSMT from earlier versions of Windows to Windows Server 2016 or from a Windows Server 2016 server to another Windows Server 2016 server:

- Active Directory Certificate Services
- Active Directory Federation Services (AD FS) Role Services
- File and Storage Services
- DHCP
- DNS
- Hyper-V
- Network Policy Server
- Print and Document Services
- Remote Access
- Remote Desktop Services
- Cluster Role Services

Windows Server Migration Tools installation and preparation can be divided into the following stages:

1. Identify the source and destination servers.
2. Install WSMT on destination servers that run Windows Server 2016.
3. Install all critical updates to the source server.
4. Prepare a migration store file location that source and destination servers can both access.
5. Register WSMT on source servers.
6. Perform the actual migration.

The Windows Server Migration Tools role is installed like any other role, by using Server Manager. You can also load the WSMT by using the following Windows PowerShell command:

```
Add-PSSnapin Microsoft.Windows.ServerManager.Migration
```

When you perform the actual migration, you export the configuration to the migration store by using the Windows PowerShell cmdlet Export-SmigServerSettings, and import the configuration from the migration store by using the cmdlet Import-SmigServerSettings.

→ **USE WINDOWS SERVER MIGRATION TOOLS**

GET READY. To migrate the DHCP server from one server to another, perform the following steps.

1. On the source server, using Server Manager, open the **Tools** menu and click **Services**.

2. Right-click the **DHCP Server** service and choose **Stop**.

3. On the source server, using Server Manager, open the **Tools** menu and then click **Windows Server Migration Tools > Windows Server Migration Tools**.

4. In the Windows Server Migration Tools window, execute the following command:

   ```
   Export-SmigServerSetting -featureID DHCP -User All -Group -
   IPConfig -path \\rwdc01\software -Verbose
   ```

5. When prompted for a password, type **Pa$$wOrd** and press **Enter**.

6. On the target server, using Server Manager, open the **Tools** menu and click **Services**.

7. Right-click the **DHCP Server** and choose **Stop**.

8. On the target server, using Server Manager, open the **Tools** menu and then click **Windows Server Migration Tools > Windows Server Migration Tools**.

9. From the Windows Server Migration Tools window, execute the following command:

   ```
   Import-SmigServerSetting -featureID DHCP -User All -Group
   -IPConfig -SourcePhysicalAddress "00-15-5D-01-32-24" -
   TargetPhysicalAddress "00-15-5D-01-32-1F" -path \\rwdc01\
   software -Verbose
   ```

   The MAC addresses used in this command will vary from system to system.

10. Back on the Services console, right-click the **DHCP Server** service and choose **Start**.

If you think about it, not all servers have to be migrated with the WSMT. For example, instead of migrating an Active Directory domain controller, you can install a system with Windows Server 2016, install the Active Directory Domain Services role, and promote the server to a domain controller. When the server is promoted to a domain controller, all Active Directory information is replicated to the server. You can then demote the old domain controller and remove it from the domain.

Although it is uncommon, server migration can occur across domains and forests, as long as the roles do not depend on Active Directory Domain Services. For example, if your company purchases another company, you will need to migrate the resources from the purchased company into the organization's forest. Migrating objects between forests is known as an *interforest migration*, whereas migrating objects between domains within the same forest is known as *intraforest migration*.

To perform these migrations, you must have a trust between the two domains. After the trust is enabled, you can use tools such as *Active Directory Migration Tool (ADMT)* to migrate resources between domains. Interforest trusts are called forest trusts and can be a one-way trust or a two-way transitive trust.

ADMT version 3.2 simplifies the process of restructuring Active Directory resources such as users, groups, and computers between domains. ADMT also performs security translation for Active Directory domains in different forests. After you migrate a computer between domains and forests, you must restart the computer.

■ Activating Windows Server 2016

↓
THE BOTTOM LINE

Activation helps verify that your copy of Windows is genuine and that it has not been used on more computers than the Microsoft Software Terms allow. Windows Server 2016 requires product activation, which validates each Windows Server 2016 license through an online activation service at Microsoft by phone, through KMS, or through Active Directory Domain Services, in order to be fully functional. During the activation step, you install the proper license key for Windows.

TAKE NOTE*

There are no activation grace periods. If you do not activate Windows Server 2016, you cannot use the personalization settings or customize the operating system.

TAKE NOTE*

As part of the planning, you must ensure that you have the correct number of licenses for your Windows operating systems, including Windows Server 2016. Windows Server 2016 is licensed by physical processor core, not by server. You can purchase additional licenses for two physical processor cores at a time.

CERTIFICATION READY
Determine the appropriate activation model for server installation, such as Automatic Virtual Machine Activation (AVMA), Key Management Service (KMS), and Active Directory–Based Activation
Objective 1.1

You can activate Windows in two ways: manually or automatically. With manual activation, you must enter the product key and activate over the Internet to the special clearinghouse website, or over the phone by using a retail product key or a *multiple activation key (MAK)*. To activate over the Internet, you open Settings, click Update & Security, and click Activation, as shown in Figure 2-12. When you use a MAK, you can activate multiple computers, up to a set activation limit.

You can also use *Original Equipment Manufacturer (OEM) keys* with computers. Manufacturers provide OEM keys, which are typically tied to specific computers. OEM keys are usually distributed with systems running Windows 7 or higher, but can also be found on systems running Windows Server operating systems.

If you have many clients and servers, consider setting up a Volume Activation Services server. When you install the Volume Activation Services server role, you can choose Key Management Service or Active Directory–Based Activation. After adding the Volume Activation Services role, you can use the Volume Activation Tools GUI to configure activation. When you use Volume Activation Services, each activated computer must contact the KMS server periodically to renew its activation status. To report on activated licenses, you can use the Volume Activation Management Tool (VAMT), which is part of the Windows Assessment and Deployment Kit (ADK).

Implementing Volume Activation Using a Key Management Service (KMS)

Key Management Service (KMS) is a service that activates Volume License versions of Windows Vista and later as well as Office 2010 and later. To activate operating systems, you need at least 25 client operating systems or 5 server operating systems. When you use Volume Activation Services, each activated computer must contact the KMS server periodically to renew its activation status. Activation lasts for 180 days and attempts to renew with the KMS host every 7 days by default. The KMS host is found by referencing an SRV record in DNS.

Figure 2-12

Activating Windows Server
2016

To enable KMS functionality, you install a KMS host key on the KMS host and then activate it on the phone or by using an online web service at Microsoft. After you initialize KMS, the KMS activation infrastructure is self-maintaining. A single KMS host can support an almost unlimited number of KMS clients. Most organizations can operate with just two KMS hosts for their entire infrastructure: one main KMS host and a backup host for redundancy.

INSTALL AND CONFIGURE A KEY MANAGEMENT SERVICE

GET READY. On a server running Windows Server 2016, to install and configure a Key Management Service (KMS), perform the following steps.

1. Log on to LON-SVR1 as **Adatum\administrator** with the password of **Pa$$Word**. If Server Manager does not open, click **Start** and click **Server Manager.**

2. When Server Manager opens, open the **Manage** menu and click **Add Roles and Features.**

3. When the Add Roles and Features Wizard opens, on the Before You Begin page, click **Next.**

4. On the Installation Type page, the Role-based or feature-based installation option is selected. Click **Next.**

5. On the Server Selection page, click **Next.**

6. On the Server Roles page, select the **Volume Activation Services** option. When you are prompted to add additional features, click **Add Features.** Click **Next.**

7. On the Features page, click **Next.**

8. On the Volume Activation Services page, click **Next.**

9. On the Confirmation page, click **Install.**

10. When the Volume Activation Tool is installed, click **Close.**

11. In Server Manager, click the **Tools** menu and then click **Volume Activation Tools.**

12. When the Volume Activation Tools Wizard opens, on the Introduction page, click **Next.**

13. On the Select Volume Activation Method page (as shown in Figure 2-13), select the **Key Management Service (KMS)** option.

Figure 2-13

Selecting the Volume Activation Method

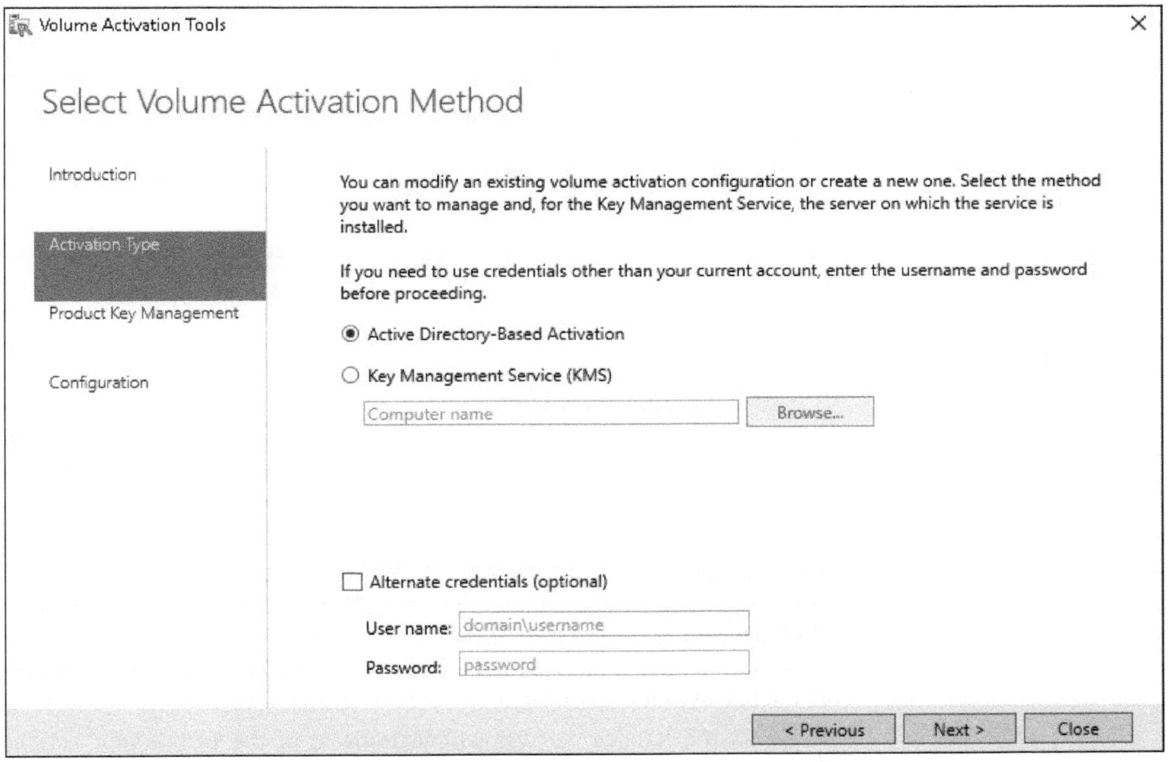

14. Then in the Key Management Service (KMS) text box, type **LON-SVR1.** Click **Next.**

15. On the Manage KMS Host page, in the Install your KMS host key text box, type your key. Click **Commit.**

16. On the Product Key Management page, the Activate Product option is already selected. Click **Next.**

17. On the Activate Product page, the Activate online option is already selected. Click **Commit.**

Once your KMS is configured, you can configure DNS so clients can automatically locate the KMS. If the DNS record has not been automatically created, create the following DNS SRV record:

Service _VLMCS

Protocol _TCP.<your domain>

Port 1688

<The host that has the KMS service>

Implementing Active Directory–Based Activation

Active Directory–Based Activation (ADBA) is a new feature for Windows 8 and higher, and Windows Server 2012 and higher, which enables enterprises to activate computers when a computer is joined to the domain, as long as the computer has a *Generic Volume License Key (GVLK)* installed. No single physical computer is required to act as the activation object because it is distributed throughout the domain. To activate an ADBA forest online, you need to specify a KMS host key, and optionally specify an Active Directory–Based Activation Object display name.

To use ADBA, you need to extend the domain to Windows Server 2012 or higher. You then:

1. Install the Volume Activation Services server role on a domain controller.
2. Add a KMS host key by using the Volume Activation Tools Wizard.
3. Microsoft verifies the KMS host key, and an activation object is created.

Client computers are activated by receiving the activation object from a domain controller during startup.

→ INSTALL AND CONFIGURE ACTIVE DIRECTORY–BASED ACTIVATION

GET READY. On a server running Windows Server 2016, to install and configure the Active Directory-Based Activation, perform the following steps.

1. Log on to LON-SVR1 as **Adatum\administrator** with the password of **Pa$$Word**.
2. In Server Manager, click the **Tools** menu and click **Volume Activation Tools**.
3. When the Volume Activation Tools Wizard opens, on the Introduction page, click **Next**.
4. On the Select Volume Activation Method page, select **Active Directory–Based Activation**. Click **Next**.
5. On the Manage Activation Objects page, in the Install your KMS host key text box, type in your key and click **Next**.
6. On the Product Key Management page, the Activate Product option is already selected. Click **Next**.
7. On the Activate Product page, the Activate online option is already selected. Click **Commit**.

Implementing Automatic Virtual Machine Activation

Automatic Virtual Machine Activation (AVMA) was introduced with Windows Server 2016 and allows you to activate your Windows virtual machines without using a KMS server or even a network connection. Different from a KMS, the activation will only last seven days, after which it would need to be renewed again.

To use AVMA, you need to have a server running Windows Server 2012 R2 Datacenter or Windows Server 2016 Datacenter with Hyper-V. The virtual machines need to be running Hyper-V. Windows Server 2016 AVMA can activate guests that run the Datacenter, Standard, or Essentials editions of Windows Server 2012 R2 or Windows Server 2016.

The basic steps to set up AVMA are:

1. Install Windows Server 2012 R2 or Windows Server 2016 Datacenter.
2. Activate Windows Server 2012 R2 or Windows Server 2016 Datacenter.
3. Install Hyper-V on a Windows Server 2012 R2 or Windows Server 2016 server.
4. Create a virtual machine and install a supported server operating system on it.
5. Install the AVMA key in the virtual machine by opening an elevated command prompt and run the following command:

```
slmgr /ipk <AVMA_key>
```

AVMA uses the following keys:

- **Windows Server 2012 R2 Datacenter:** Y4TGP-NPTV9-HTC2H-7MGQ3-DV4TW
- **Windows Server 2012 R2 Standard:** DBGBW-NPF86-BJVTX-K3WKJ-MTB6V
- **Windows Server 2012 R2 Essentials:** K2XGM-NMBT3-2R6Q8-WF2FK-P36R2
- **Windows Server 2016 Datacenter:** TMJ3Y-NTRTM-FJYXT-T22BY-CWG3J
- **Windows Server 2016 Standard:** C3RCX-M6NRP-6CXC9-TW2F2-4RHYD
- **Windows Server 2016 Essentials:** B4YNW-62DX9-W8V6M-82649-MHBKQ

➕ MORE INFORMATION

For more information about how to configure Hyper-V and Hyper-V virtual machines, refer to Lesson 7.

The virtual machine will automatically activate the license against the virtualization server. To check the status of a VM activated through AVMA, run the following command:

```
slmgr.vbs /dlv
```

Querying and Configuring Activation States Using the Command Line

The Windows activation process is handled by the *Software Licensing Manager (SLMgr) module*, also known as the Windows Software Licensing Management Tool. A VBScript called *slmgr.vbs* keeps track of licensing details.

Slmgr.vbs allows users to query the current installation and see details about the Windows installation and its activation and licensing status. For example, to display very basic license and activation information about the current system, run the following command:

```
slmgr.vbs /dli
```

To display more detailed license information—including the activation ID, installation ID, and other details, run the following command:

```
slmgr.vbs /dlv
```

To display the expiration date of the current license, run the following command:

```
slmgr.vbs /xpr
```

You can change the product key by executing the following command:

```
slmgr.vbs /ipk #####-#####-#####-#####-#####
```

where #####-#####-#####-#####-##### is the actual product key.

To uninstall the current product key, run the following command and then restart your computer:

```
slmgr.vbs /upk
```

To force Windows to attempt an online activation, run the following command:

```
slmgr.vbs /ato
```

If you need to activate Windows offline, first run the following command:

```
slmgr.vbs /dti
```

You then need to get a confirmation ID to activate the system over the phone by calling the Microsoft Product Activation Center and providing the installation ID you received. After obtaining an activation ID, execute the following command:

```
slmgr.vbs /atp <ACTIVATIONID>
```

Once you're done, you can use the `slmgr.vbs /dli` or `slmgr.vbs /dlv` commands to confirm you're activated.

■ Implementing Windows Powershell Desired State Configuration

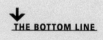

THE BOTTOM LINE

When you manage several servers in a data center, configuring all of those servers requires a lot of work. The burden of managing several is eased when those servers share a common configuration. To reduce the time necessary to configure all your data center servers, you can use Windows *PowerShell Desired State Configuration (DSC)* to manage and maintain systems based on your declared configuration.

CERTIFICATION READY
Implement Windows PowerShell Desired State Configuration (DSC) to install and maintain integrity of installed environments
Objective 1.1

Windows PowerShell DSC (Desired State Configuration) is an extension of Windows PowerShell and the Windows Management Framework. Instead of creating and executing scripts, you can define the configuration, and the configuration will be reapplied based on a specified interval. If a configuration on a system has drifted, it will correct the configuration drift. DSC can be deployed in centralized and decentralized environments, and the systems do not have to belong to an Active Directory domain. It can also be used to manage any operating system with an OMI-compliant Common Information Model (CIM) server, such as CentOS, or other varieties of Linux.

TAKE NOTE*

Although DSC takes some time and effort to establish, its benefits can be seen if you have hundreds of systems (virtual or physical) for which you need to maintain the system configuration.

Some of the configurations that you can apply include:
- Enabling or disabling server roles and features
- Managing registry settings
- Managing files and directories
- Starting, stopping, and managing processes and services
- Managing groups and user accounts
- Deploying new software

- Managing environment variables
- Running Windows PowerShell scripts

The **Local Configuration Manager (LCM)** is the Windows PowerShell Desired State Configuration (DSC) engine. It will periodically check whether the configuration is still valid or if drift has occurred. When you configure the LCM, you will either push the configuration to a server, or you will establish an HTTP server or SMB share, from which the systems will pull the configuration. You will then specify how often it will retrieve the configuration and how often it will check and apply the specified configuration.

The LCM-specific parameters include:

- **RefreshMode:** By default, RefreshMode is set to *Push*, which runs the Start-DscConfiguration cmdlet on the system. When the RefreshMode is set to *Pull*, the LCM agent regularly checks a remote HTTP server or Server Message Block (SMB) share for configurations. If the RefreshMode is set to *Disabled*, the LCM does not apply any configurations. Configuring a pull server is not required to use DSC. However, pull servers can be beneficial in large, distributed environments.
- **RefreshFrequencyMins:** This parameter indicates the time intervals, in minutes, at which the LCM polls the remote HTTP server or SMB share for configurations. When configured in Push mode, this value is ignored. The default value is 30 minutes.
- **ConfigurationMode:** This mode indicates the action that the LCM agent takes when applying configurations. By default, the LCM agent is configured to *ApplyAndMonitor*, meaning that the initial configuration is applied. If changes to the configuration occur, they are logged but are not corrected automatically. The *ApplyAndAutoCorrect* configuration mode applies the initial configuration and will automatically apply the deviation during future checks. *ApplyOnly* mode applies the configuration, but does not do anything further after the initial configuration.
- **ConfigurationModeFreqencyMins:** This parameter indicates the time interval, in minutes, at which the LCM checks and, if necessary, reapplies the configurations. By default, this value is every 15 minutes.

To view the available DSC functions and cmdlets available, execute the following command at the Windows PowerShell prompt:

```
Get-Command –Module PSDesiredStateConfiguration
```

USING POWERSHELL

You can manage DSC using Windows PowerShell by using the following cmdlets and functions:

Functions:
- **Configuration:** Names the configuration.
- **Disable-DscDebug:** Stops debugging of DSC resources.
- **Enable-DscDebug:** Starts debugging of all DSC resources, which will be used for troubleshooting.
- **Get-DscConfiguration:** Gets the current configuration of the DSC nodes. If you do not specify a target computer, the cmdlet will get the configuration for the local computer.
- **Get-DscConfigurationStatus:** Retrieves detailed information about completed configuration runs.
- **Get-DscLocalConfigurationManager:** Gets LCM settings and states of LCM for the node.
- **Get-DscResource:** Retrieves the Windows PowerShell Desired State Configuration (DSC) resources present on the computer.
- **New-DscChecksum:** Creates checksum files for DSC documents and DSC resources. This is used when systems are in pull mode to ensure that the correct configuration and resources exist on the target node.
- **Remove-DscConfigurationDocument:** Removes a configuration document (.mof file) from the DSC configuration store.
- **Restore-DscConfiguration:** Reapplies the previous configuration for the node.

> **Cmdlets:**
> - **Invoke-DscResource:** Runs a method of a specified DSC resource
> - **Publish-DscConfiguration:** Publishes a DSC configuration to a set of computers
> - **Set-DscLocalConfigurationManager:** Applies LCM settings to nodes
> - **Start-DscConfiguration:** Applies configuration to nodes
> - **Test-DscConfiguration:** Tests whether the actual configuration on the nodes matches the desired configuration
> - **Update-DscConfiguration:** Checks the pull server for an updated configuration and applies it

To use DSC, you must first create an .mof file using a Windows PowerShell script. The .mof file is a text file that contains the configuration information. The .mof file does not enforce the desired state, but is used to specify what the desired state would be.

To retrieve a list of the DSC managed elements that can be used in configuration files, you can execute the following Windows PowerShell command:

```
Get-DscResource | Select-Object -Property Name, Properties
```

The DSC managed elements include the following:

- **File:** Manages files and folders on a node
- **Archive:** Decompresses an archive in the .zip format
- **Environment:** Manages system environment variables
- **Group:** Allows you to manage local user groups on a node
- **Log:** Writes a message in the DSC event log
- **Package:** Installs or removes a package
- **Registry:** Manages registry key of a node (except HKEY Users)
- **Script:** Executes several PowerShell commands on a node
- **Service:** Manages Windows services (State, Startup Type)
- **User:** Manages local users on a node
- **WindowsFeature:** Adds or removes a role/feature on a node
- **WindowsOptionalFeature:** Adds or removes an optional role/feature
- **WindowsProcess:** Manages a Windows process

You can also use the `Get-DscResource` cmdlet with the `-Syntax` option to get the syntax of the managed elements. For example, to get the syntax for Service, you would execute the following command:

```
Get-DscResource -Name Service -Syntax
```

which responds with:

```
PS C:\Users\PatPC> Get-DscResource -Name Service -Syntax

Service [String] #ResourceName
{
    Name = [string]
    [BuiltInAccount = [string]{ LocalService | LocalSystem |
    NetworkService }]
    [Credential = [PSCredential]]
    [Dependencies = [string[]]]
```

```
        [DependsOn = [string[]]]
        [Description = [string]]
        [DisplayName = [string]]
        [Ensure = [string]{ Absent | Present }]
        [Path = [string]]
        [PsDscRunAsCredential = [PSCredential]]
        [StartupType = [string]{ Automatic | Disabled | Manual }]
        [State = [string]{ Running | Stopped }]
}
```

The configuration script that will create the .mof file would be saved with a .ps1 extension. For example, if the following script was saved as Config.ps1 and is executed from a Windows PowerShell prompt as .\config.ps1, a folder called MyFileServerConfig folder will be created with a localhost.mof file. The localhost.mof file will specify to install the Windows features called snmp and DSCServiceFeature, set the service called Spooler to Manual, and stop the Spooler service.

```
configuration MyFirstServerConfig

{

        WindowsFeature snmp

          {

                Name = "SNMP-Service";

                Ensure = "Present"

          }

        WindowsFeature DSCServiceFeature

          {

                Name = "DSCServiceFeature";

                Ensure = "Present"

          }

        Service Spooler

          {

              Name = "Spooler"

              StartupType = "Manual"

              State = "Stopped"

          }

}

MyFirstServerConfig
```

Each configuration can have one or more node blocks and each node block can have one or more resource blocks. You can even use the same resource more than once in the same node block. When typing your configuration script, you have a lot of freedom of how you space the braces. However, because braces are used as pairs (opening and closing braces), it is best to line up opening and closing braces so that you can easily see when a block begins and ends.

The main part of this example has a function called MyFirstServerConfig, which is marked by an opening and closing brace. A function doesn't do anything by itself until the function is called. Therefore, the last line, MyFirstServerConfig, calls up the function MyFirstServerConfig.

To configure the system with the .mof file that was just created, you would execute the following command:

```
Start-DscConfiguration –Wait –Verbose –Path C:\MyFirstServerConfig
```

The –Wait parameter tells Windows that you want to run the command interactively, while the –Verbose switch allows you to see a detailed output of what is happening when the configuration is being applied. The path specifies the folder where the .mof file is stored.

CONFIGURE A SYSTEM WITH WINDOWS POWERSHELL DESIRED STATE CONFIGURATION

GET READY. To configure a system with Windows PowerShell Desired State Configuration, perform the following steps.

1. Log on to LON-SVR1 as **adatum\administrator** with the password of **Pa$$w0rd**.
2. If Server Manager does not open, click **Start** and click **Server Manager**.
3. Open the **Tools** menu and click **Windows PowerShell ISE**.
4. When Windows PowerShell ISE opens, in the top white pane, type the following text, as shown in Figure 2-14.

```
configuration MyFirstServerConfig
{

    WindowsFeature snmp
        {
            Name = "SNMP-Service";
         Ensure = "Present"
        }

    WindowsFeature DSCServiceFeature
        {
            Name = "DSCServiceFeature";
         Ensure = "Present"
        }

    Service Spooler
      {
            Name = "Spooler"
            StartupType = "Manual"
            State = "Stopped"
        }
}

MyFirstServerConfig
```

Figure 2-14

Creating a Windows
PowerShell script with
Windows PowerShell ISE

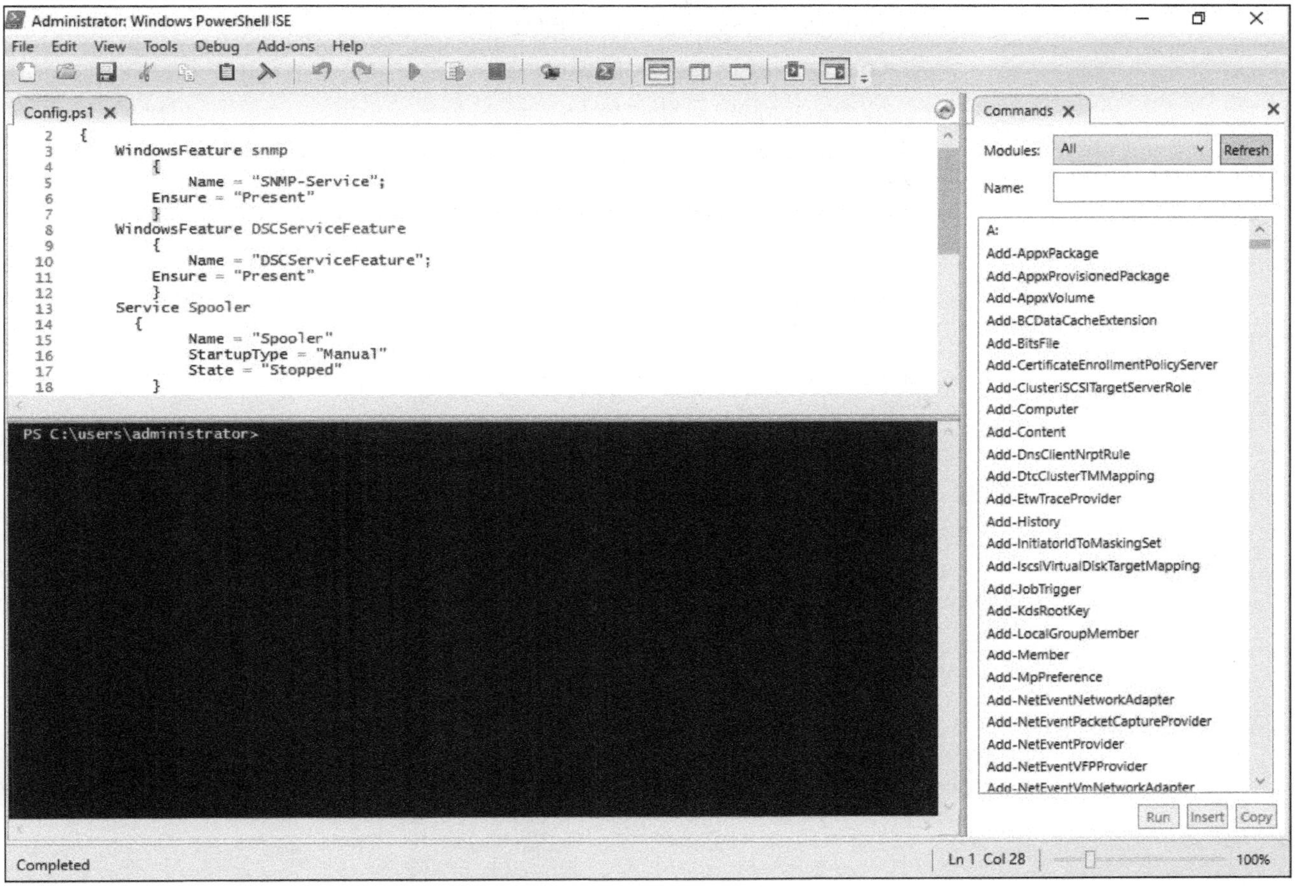

5. Open the **File** menu and click **Save As**. When the Save As dialog box opens, in the File name text box, type **C:\Config.ps1** and click the **Save** button.

6. Click the blue, bottom pane. Then in the blue, bottom pane, type **CD** and press **Enter**.

7. To create the .mof file, from the Windows PowerShell command prompt, execute the following command:

```
.\config1.ps1
```

8. At the Windows PowerShell command prompt, execute the following command:

```
Start-DscConfiguration –Wait –Verbose –Path C:\MyFirstServerConfig
```

In order to provision the pull server with configuration files, you need to:

- Run the script that generates node configuration MOFs.
- Use the New-DSCChecksum cmdlet to generate checksum files.
- Copy all MOFs and associated checksum files to the pull server.

Of course, each node must be able to contact the specified pull server. The following script configures the mode to Pull and specifies the pull server.

```
Configuration SimplePullConfiguration
```

```
{
LocalConfigurationManager
 {
     ConfigurationMode = 'ApplyOnly'
     ConfigurationID = $guid
     RefreshMode = 'Pull'
     DownloadManagerName = 'WebDownloadManager'
     DownloadManagerCustomData = @
     {
     ServerUrl = 'http://LON-SVR1.adatum.com:80/PSDSCPullServer.svc';
     AllowUnsecureConnection = 'true'
     }
 }
}
```

Then, to configure the system for pull mode, you need to configure the LCM by running the `Set-DscLocalConfigurationManager` cmdlet on each of the pull clients. For example, you may execute the following command:

`Set-DscLocalConfigurationManager –ComputerName localhost –Path . –Verbose`

If you have any problems with DSC, you should open Event Viewer and navigate to the Applications and Services Logs/Microsoft/Windows/Desired State Configuration. You can also use the `Test-DscConfiguration` and `Get-DscConfiguration` cmdlets to test your current configuration and to view the current configuration.

SKILL SUMMARY

IN THIS LESSON YOU LEARNED:

- Before installing Windows Server 2016, you need to first determine the minimum hardware requirements so that you can ensure you have the correct hardware. The minimum hardware can then be used to gauge what is needed to carry the necessary load.

- Similar to previous Windows Server operating systems, you have multiple editions to choose from. These editions allow you to select the edition that you need rather than paying for all features, some of which you do not need.

- Server Core is a Windows Server 2016 installation option that provides a command-line management interface. Because it does not have a GUI interface, it uses fewer hardware resources. In addition, because it has fewer running components, there are fewer components that can be compromised and it requires fewer updates. When you install Windows Server 2016, Server Core is the default installation.

- You can use Remote Desktop Connections and the Windows Server 2016 Administrative Tools to manage remote servers. In addition, you can use PowerShell Remoting, which allows you to securely connect to a remote PowerShell host and run scripts interactively.

- An in-place upgrade is the most complicated form of Windows Server 2016 installation. It is also the lengthiest and the most likely to cause problems during its execution. Whenever possible, Microsoft recommends that administrators perform a clean installation, or migrate required applications and settings instead.

- Many roles included with Windows Server 2016 involve a lot of configuring. A role might require policies, security, or other settings that you must configure before it can be used. Therefore, when you want to migrate such roles, you want to find a way that can migrate them and all their configuration settings to another server quickly and easily without having to install and configure the role from the beginning.

- Activation helps verify that your copy of Windows is genuine and that it has not been used on more computers than the Microsoft Software Terms allow. Windows Server 2016 requires product activation, which validates each Windows Server 2016 license through an online activation service at Microsoft by phone, through KMS, or through Active Directory Domain Services, to be fully functional. During the activation step, you install the proper license key for Windows.

■ Knowledge Assessment

Multiple Choice

Select the correct answer for each of the following questions.

1. Which of the following is the minimum processor specification needed for Windows Server 2016?
   - **a.** x32 or x64 processor running at 1.4 GHz
   - **b.** x64 processor running at 1.4 GHz
   - **c.** x64 dual-core processor running at 1.4 GHz
   - **d.** x64 processor running at 1.8 GHz

2. Which of the following are reasons to perform a migration instead of an in-place upgrade to Windows Server 2016? (Choose all that apply.)
   - **a.** The hardware is not sufficient to run Windows Server 2016.
   - **b.** You do not have all the correct drivers of Windows Server 2016.
   - **c.** You do not have an upgrade path to Windows Server 2016.
   - **d.** You want to run in a virtualized environment.

3. Which of the following describes how to perform an in-place upgrade?
   - **a.** Start from a Windows Server 2016 installation disk and choose Upgrade.
   - **b.** Insert the Windows Server 2016 installation disk into the computer while Windows is running and choose Upgrade.
   - **c.** Perform a startup over the network and choose Upgrade.
   - **d.** Open the Windows Update site and select Upgrade.

4. Which command is used to attempt an online activation?
   - **a.** slmgr.vbs /ato
   - **b.** slmgr.vbs /xpr
   - **c.** slmgr.vbs /dti
   - **d.** slmgr.vbs /ipk

5. Which of the following programs are used to change the password of a user in Active Directory? (Choose two answers.)
   - **a.** Active Directory Users and Computers
   - **b.** Active Directory Domains and Trusts
   - **c.** Active Directory Sites and Services
   - **d.** Active Directory Administrative Center

6. Which of the following stores the Active Directory database?
   a. SQL server
   b. Domain controller
   c. Oracle server
   d. Jet server

7. Which of the following tasks is *not* one of the volume activation options for Windows operating systems provided by Microsoft?
   a. Key Management Services (KMS)
   b. DNS-based activation
   c. Multiple Activation Key (MAK)
   d. Active Directory–Based Activation (ADBA)

8. Which of the following operating systems can be activated using Active Directory-Based Activation? (Choose all that apply.)
   a. Windows 8.1
   b. Windows 10
   c. Windows 7
   d. Windows Vista
   e. Windows Server 2016

9. Which of the following types of product key should be installed on client computers when using Active Directory–Based Activation?
   a. GVLK
   b. MAK
   c. KMS host
   d. Retail

10. Which of the following is the activation validity interval for KMS clients?
    a. 2 hours
    b. 7 days
    c. 180 days
    d. 365 days

11. Which Windows PowerShell cmdlet is used with the Windows Server Migration Tools to export a role?
    a. ExportServerRole
    b. Export-Role
    c. Export-SmigServerSettings
    d. Export-RoleService

12. Which of the following tools can be used to migrate Print and Document Services and Remote Access running on Windows Server 2008 R2 to another server running Windows Server 2012 R2?
    a. Application Compatibility Toolkit
    b. Roles Migration Tools
    c. Server Manager
    d. Windows Server Migration Tools

Best Answer

Choose the letter that corresponds to the best answer. More than one answer choice may achieve the goal. Select the BEST answer.

1. Which type of key should be used for an organization that has more than 250 servers and 1,000 client computers?
   a. KMS
   b. OEM
   c. MAK
   d. Retail

2. Which of the following is the best volume activation method for a network of 40 computers?
   a. Active Directory–Based Activation
   b. MAK activation
   c. KMS activation
   d. Retail license activation

3. Which of the following is the best way to perform an online volume activation with the least amount of traffic to the Internet?
   a. MAK Independent
   b. MAK Proxy
   c. KMS
   d. Retail product keys

4. A server is currently acting as a print server with the following requirements:
   - x64 Processor running at 1.8 GHz
   - 256 MB of RAM
   - 120 GB drive
   - 10/100 MHz network card

   Which of the above requirements is preventing administrators from running Windows Server 2016?
   a. The processor does not support Windows Server 2016.
   b. The memory does not support Windows Server 2016.
   c. The hard drive does not support Windows Server 2016.
   d. The network card does not support Windows Server 2016.

5. An extremely busy file server is running Windows Server 2012 and holding 1.5 TB of data. As they administrator, you want to migrate the file server to a new server running Windows Server 2016 with the following hardware:
   - x64 Processor running at 1.4 GHz
   - 512 MB of RAM
   - 2-TB drive
   - 1-Gbps network card

   Which of the following describes the recommended course of action?
   a. You should increase the processor and memory.
   b. You should increase the disk space.
   c. You should increase the network card speed.
   d. You do not migrate to Windows Server 2016. Instead, you should install Windows Server 2012 R2.

Build a List

1. Specify the correct order of steps necessary to installing a KMS host.

   __3__ Select KMS as the volume activation method.

   __1__ Add the Volume Activation Services role.

   __5__ Activate the KMS host key.

   __4__ Type your KMS host key.

   __2__ Run the Volume Activation Tools Wizard.

2. Specify the correct order of steps necessary when migrating roles from one server to another using the Windows Server Migration Tools (WSMT).

___4___ Prepare a migration store location that the source and destination servers can both access.

___1___ Identify the source and destination servers.

___6___ Perform the actual migration.

___2___ Install WSMT on destination servers on a server running Windows Server 2016.

___5___ Register WSMT on the source server.

___3___ Install all critical updates to the source server.

■ Business Case Scenarios

Scenario 2-1: Selecting the Windows Server 2016 Edition

You administer nine virtual file servers on a single Hyper-V physical host that contains two 8-core processors. Currently, each server is running Windows Server 2012 Standard edition on one host. You are thinking of migrating these servers to Windows Server 2016. Over a three-day period, you discover the following load for the virtual file servers:

	Avg Proc	95% CPU utilization
Server 1	25	5%
Server 2	25	3%
Server 3	35	6%
Server 4	15	5%
Server 5	15	3%
Server 6	10	6%
Server 7	25	5%
Server 8	20	3%
Server 9	30	6%

Which type of license should be purchased? Why purchase this license if you upgrade these servers to Windows Server 2016?

Scenario 2-2: Deploying and Configuring Windows Server 2016

You administer 250 servers running Windows Server 2016 and you need to deploy another 140 servers over the next six months. You want to ensure that each computer has the following configuration performed:

- Certain server roles and features need to be installed.
- A set of default users and groups needs to be created on each server.
- Diagnostic and malware software need to be deployed.
- Several environment variables need to be set.

Describe how to ensure that your current servers and any servers that you install will have this base configuration. Also, describe how to ensure that when these settings are changed, the system is automatically reconfigured.

Configuring Disks and Volumes

70-740 EXAM OBJECTIVE

Objective 2.1 – Configure disks and volumes. This objective may include but is not limited to the following: Configure sector sizes appropriate for various workloads; configure GUID partition table (GPT) disks; create VHD and VHDX files using Server Manager or Windows PowerShell; mount virtual hard disks; determine when to use NTFS and ReFS file systems; configure NFS and SMB shares using Server Manager; configure SMB share and session settings using Windows PowerShell; configure SMB server and SMB client configuration settings using Windows PowerShell; configure file and folder permissions.

Objective 1.3 – Create, manage, and maintain images for deployment. Manage and maintain VHDs using Windows PowerShell. *Other Objective 1.3 topics are covered in Lesson 6.*

LESSON HEADING	EXAM OBJECTIVE
Configuring Disks and Volumes	Configure GUID partition table (GPT) disks
– Configuring Disks and Drive Types, Including MBR and GUID Partition Tables Disks	Determine when to use NTFS and ReFS file systems
– Determining When to Use NTFS and ReFS File Systems	Configure sector sizes appropriate for various workloads
	Configure GUID partition table (GPT) disks
– Configuring Sector Sizes Appropriate for Various Workloads	Create VHD and VHDX files using Server Manager or Windows PowerShell
– Using Disk Management to Configure Disks, Volumes, and File Systems	Mount virtual hard disks
– Using Windows PowerShell to Configure Disks, Volumes, and File Systems	Manage and maintain VHDs using Windows PowerShell
– Creating, Configuring, and Mounting VHDs	
Configuring File Sharing	Configure SMB shares using Server Manager
– Creating a Shared Folder Using Basic and Advanced Sharing	Configure SMB share and session settings using Windows PowerShell
– Configuring SMB Shares Using Server Manager	Configure SMB server and SMB client configuration settings using Windows PowerShell
– Creating and Configuring SMB Shares by Using Windows PowerShell	

(continued)

LESSON HEADING	EXAM OBJECTIVE
Configuring File and Folder Permissions	Configure file and folder permissions
– Configuring File System Permissions	
– Understanding Effective NTFS Permissions	
– Viewing Effective Permissions on a Resource	
– Combining NTFS and Share Permissions	
Configuring NFS Shares	Configure NFS shares using Server Manager

KEY TERMS

advanced sharing	FAT	Server Message Block (SMB) 3.0
allocation unit	FAT32	Server Message Block (SMB)
basic disks	file system	share permissions
basic sharing	inherited permissions	shared folder
cluster	mirrored volume	simple volume
Common Internet File System (CIFS)	Network File System (NFS)	Small Computer System Interface (SCSI)
Disk Management	NTFS	spanned volume
dynamic disks	NTFS permissions	striped volume
effective permissions	partition	Universal Naming Convention (UNC)
explicit permissions	Resilient File System (ReFS)	Universal Serial Bus (USB)
Extended File Allocation Table (exFAT)	sector	volume
external SATA (eSATA)	Serial Advanced Technology Attachment (SATA)	
	Server for NFS	

■ Configuring Disks and Volumes

THE BOTTOM LINE

Although the average disk capacity of storage devices has increased dramatically over the years, there is one thing you can count on: Users will always find a way to store enormous amounts of data on volumes they have access to. Therefore, you will need to know how to configure, manage, and support storage on the Windows clients.

User data typically includes multiple versions of their documents, copies of other users' documents, high-definition videos downloaded from the Internet, or just about anything else the user is not ready to delete. As users' appetites for more storage continue to increase, administrators find themselves purchasing and using a wide variety of drives with different capacities (1 TB, 2 TB, 4 TB, or larger) and different drive interfaces to fit their data storage needs.

The type of interface you select depends a lot on the connections available with your motherboard and the performance you need from the drive. Examples of drive interfaces include:

- **Small Computer System Interface (SCSI)**: A set of standards for interfaces designed to connect and transfer information between high-speed hardware devices and a motherboard. Devices are connected in a chain. Each device in the chain gets a SCSI ID and the last device in the chain must be terminated. SATA has replaced SCSI on most modern computers.

- **Serial Advanced Technology Attachment (SATA)**: A serial interface that transfers data in bursts instead of in parallel. It comes in three varieties: 1.5 Gbps (SATA-1.0), 3 Gbps (SATA-2.0), and 6 Gbps (SATA 3.0). These have maximum throughputs of 150 Mbps, 300 Mbps, and 600 Mbps, respectively. **External SATA (eSATA)** extends the SATA bus to external devices.

- **Universal Serial Bus (USB)**: A serial interface that is used to connect keyboards, mice, printers, scanners, and removable media drives. Up to 127 peripherals can be connected to a single USB port. USB 2.0 has a maximum transfer rate of 480 Mbps, whereas USB 3.0, released in 2008, claims a theoretical maximum transmission speed of up to 5 Gbps.

Configuring Disks and Drive Types, Including MBR and GUID Partition Tables Disks

Windows Server 2016 supports two partition styles—Master Boot Record (MBR) and GUID partition table (GPT)—and two primary types of disks—basic and dynamic. In addition, the operating system supports simple, spanned, striped, and mirrored volumes. You use the Disk Management tool in the Computer Management snap-in to manage disks, partitions, and volumes.

CERTIFICATION READY
Configure GUID partition table (GPT) disks
Objective 2.1

In Windows Server 2016, a physical hard drive can be designated as a basic disk or a dynamic disk. **Basic disks** contain only simple volumes. **Dynamic disks** can contain simple, spanned, striped, and mirrored volumes.

TAKE NOTE*

You cannot use Windows PowerShell to manage dynamic disks. The storage cmdlets will not recognize dynamic disks.

Traditionally, basic disks use partitions and logical drives. A **partition** is a defined storage space on a hard disk. To be usable, a hard disk needs to have at least one partition. A **volume** is a partition that has been formatted into a file system.

The MBR partition style has been around for quite a while and all Windows operating systems support MBR partitions. The MBR is stored at a consistent location on a physical disk, enabling a computer's BIOS to reference it. After the computer examines the MBR to determine the active partition, it then loads the operating system startup files from the active partition.

But as with most legacy technologies, MBR partitions have their limitations, including the following:

- MBR partitions are limited to four basic partitions and each partition is limited to 2 terabytes (TBs) in size.
- You can have up to four primary partitions, or up to three primary partitions with one extended partition, which can be further divided into multiple logical partitions.
- The MBR is a single point of failure. If it becomes corrupted or damaged, it could prevent the computer from starting.

A GPT partition style allows for more partitions and larger volume sizes. Features of GPT disks include:

- A disk initialized as a GPT partition style may contain up to 128 primary partitions.
- Each partition can be as large as 9.4 zetabytes (ZB) with 512-byte sectors. One zetabyte is equal to one billion terabytes. However, the maximum raw GPT partition size is 18 exabytes.

TAKE NOTE * You can implement GPT disks on Windows Server 2008 and newer versions, and Windows Vista and newer versions. You cannot use the GPT partition style on removable disks.

You can typically convert a basic disk to a dynamic disk without losing any data; however, you should back up all data before attempting the conversion just to be safe. If you have software or hardware that does not work with dynamic disks, you may need to convert a dynamic disk to basic.

When you initialize a disk, you specify if the disk will be MBR or GPT. To convert an MBR partition style to GPT, you can open Disk Management, right-click the disk, and choose Convert to GPT Disk. However, if the Convert to GPT Disk option is grayed out, you will need to back up the data, delete all partitions, and then convert MBR to GPT.

With dynamic disks, free space on a hard drive is divided into volumes instead of partitions. Dynamic disks are not limited by partition styles like basic disks are. You can configure dynamic disk volumes as simple, spanned, mirrored, or striped:

- *Simple volume*: Uses free space available on a single disk.
- *Spanned volume*: Extends a simple volume across multiple disks, up to a maximum of 32.
- *Mirrored volume*: Duplicates data from one disk to a second disk for redundancy and fault tolerance; if one disk fails, data can be accessed from the second disk. You cannot span a mirrored volume; a mirrored volume must reside on a single disk. Mirroring is also referred to as RAID-1.
- *Striped volume*: Stores data across two or more physical disks. Data on a striped volume is written evenly to each of the physical disks in the volume. You cannot mirror or span a striped volume. Striping is often referred to as RAID-0.

Disks, volumes, and file systems can be managed with the following Windows Server 2016 tools:

- *Disk Management*: A GUI tool based on the MMC for managing disks and volumes locally and remotely. Disk Management is located in the Administrative Tools, and is part of the Computer Management console.
- **Windows PowerShell 5.0:** A scripting language/and command environment that accomplishes many of these tasks in Disk Management. You can execute these commands as stand-alone commands or as part of a script.
- **DiskPart:** A scriptable command-line tool that has similar functionality as Disk Management. You can create scripts to automate disk-related tasks, such as creating volumes or converting disks to dynamic. This tool can only be executed locally.

➕ MORE INFORMATION

To see how to create a partition (MBR or GPT), refer to the "Using Disk Management to Configure Disks, Volumes, and File Systems" section and the "Using Windows PowerShell to Configure Disks, Volumes, and File Systems" section in this lesson.

Determining When to Use NTFS and ReFS File Systems

> A *file system* is the overall structure your computer uses to name, store, and organize files and folders on a hard disk or partition. The file system provides a map of the clusters (the basic units of logical storage on a hard disk) that a file has been stored in. When you install a hard disk in a computer, you must format it with a file system.

CERTIFICATION READY
Determine when to use NTFS and ReFS file systems
Objective 2.1

Today, the primary file system choices for a computer that will run Windows are New Technology File System (NTFS), File Allocation Table (FAT), and FAT32. In Windows Server 2016, you can use the Disk Management Microsoft Management Console (MMC) snap-in, which is available from the Computer Management console, to view the file systems in use on your computer.

When a disk or volume is added to Windows Server 2016, you have to partition and format the drive. The three primary types of file systems for Windows are FAT, FAT32, and NTFS. *FAT32* and *FAT* (which is seldom used today) were popular in earlier versions of Windows (such as Windows 95, Windows 98, Windows Millennium Edition, Windows NT, and Windows 2000). The limitations of FAT32 make it less desirable than NTFS:

- A FAT32 partition is limited to a maximum size of 32 gigabytes (GB).
- The maximum size of a file that can be stored on a FAT32 volume is 4 GB.

NTFS is the preferred file system that supports much larger hard disks and a higher level of reliability than FAT-based file systems. In addition, NTFS offers better security through permissions and encryption.

 TAKE NOTE*   You can view all available disks or volumes that have been formatted with a file system in the *This PC* folder in its *Devices and drives* section.

Resilient File System (ReFS) was introduced as an enhanced NTFS file system by offering larger volume sizes and files. ReFS also offers greater resiliency, meaning better data verification, error correction, and scalability. It is recommended that you should use ReFS for very large volumes and file shares. However, you cannot use ReFS for the boot volume. For maximum file name length, NTFS only supports 256 characters, whereas ReFS supports up to 32,000 characters.

Because ReFS uses a subset of NTFS features, it maintains backward compatibility with NTFS that can be accessed directly by Windows Server 2012 or higher, or Windows 8.1 or higher. Different from NTFS, ReFS has a fixed allocation unit size of 64 KB, and ReFS does not support Encrypting File System (EFS) for files.

When deciding which file system to use, you should always consider NTFS or ReFS. It is recommended to use ReFS for the following situations:

- Microsoft Hyper-V workloads. (ReFS has performance advantages when using both .vhd and .vhdx files.)
- Storage Spaces Direct when using shared direct attached storage. ReFS supports larger volumes and improved throughput.
- Archive data that you want to retain for long periods. Archived data can benefit from ReFS resiliency.

Table 3-1 compares the attributes of FAT, FAT32, and NTFS.

Another file system worth mentioning is the *Extended File Allocation Table (exFAT)*, which is a Microsoft file system optimized for flash drives. It is typically used where the NTFS file

Table 3-1

Comparing FAT, FAT32, and NTFS

FILE SYSTEM	MAXIMUM PARTITION SIZE	MAXIMUM FILE SIZE
FAT	2 GB	2 GB
FAT32	32 GB	4 GB
NTFS	256 TB*	Limited by the size of the volume on which it resides
ReFS	1 yobiByte (2^{80} bytes)	16 exbibytes (2^{64} bytes)
exFAT	128 pebiBtye (2^{50} bytes)**	Limited by the size of the volume on which it resides

*with 64-KB clusters

**Microsoft recommends a maximum size of 512 TB

system is not ideal because of the data structure overhead. exFAT supports a larger volume than FAT or FAT32 supports. exFAT has been adopted by the SD Card Association as the default file system for SDXC cards larger than 32 GB.

Configuring Sector Sizes Appropriate for Various Workloads

On disks, a *sector* is the minimum storage unit of a hard drive. For the disk, each sector is a fixed amount of user-accessible data. Hard drives are traditionally 512 bytes, whereas CD-ROMs and DVD-ROMs are 2,048 bytes. An *allocation unit*, also known as a *cluster*, is the smallest logical amount of disk space that can be allocated to hold a file or folder. When you format the disks, you will specify the size of the allocation unit, which can be from 512 bytes to 64 KB. For a standard user, you should keep the default of 4,096 bytes.

If you use a single byte of an allocation unit, the entire allocation unit is assigned to the file that contains the byte of information. Storing small files on a file system with large allocation units will have more wasted disk space than systems with smaller allocation units. If you have a file that is larger than an allocation unit, it will first fill up the first allocation unit. It will then split the file and assign the next part of the file on the next allocation unit. It will continue to do that until the file has been completely written. Of course, the last allocation unit will most likely not be entirely filled up. However, the unused space cannot be used for other files.

Each file system will have a file allocation table that acts as an index for the formatted disks. The file allocation table will list each allocation unit and their associated file, if any. If you have larger allocation units, your file allocation table will have a fewer number of entries. Because of the larger allocation units and smaller file allocation table, there is less overhead when accessing files because the files will be listed on a fewer number of allocation units. As a result, you get improved reading and writing speed overall and your disk is not as fragmented.

When you format your disk, you need to specify the appropriate allocation unit size. For the best performance, you should try to match the allocation unit size as close as possible to the typical file size that will be written to disk. Larger pictures, videos, and databases can be quite large and will run better with larger allocation units.

Using Disk Management to Configure Disks, Volumes, and File Systems

When you add a new hard drive to a computer, there are a few steps you need to take to introduce a new drive to the operating system. You need to initialize the disk and then choose a drive type and a partition style (for basic disks). You can perform all of these steps in the Disk Management tool, which is part of the Computer Management MMC snap-in.

CERTIFICATION READY
Configure GUID partition table (GPT) disks
Objective 2.1

To open Computer Management, click Start, type computer, and then select Computer Management from the resulting list. Alternatively, you can right-click Start and choose Computer Management. After Computer Management is open, click the Disk Management node. To open just the Disk Management snap-in, you can right-click the Start button and choose Disk Management. Figure 3-1 shows the Disk Management snap-in.

Figure 3-1
The Disk Management snap-in

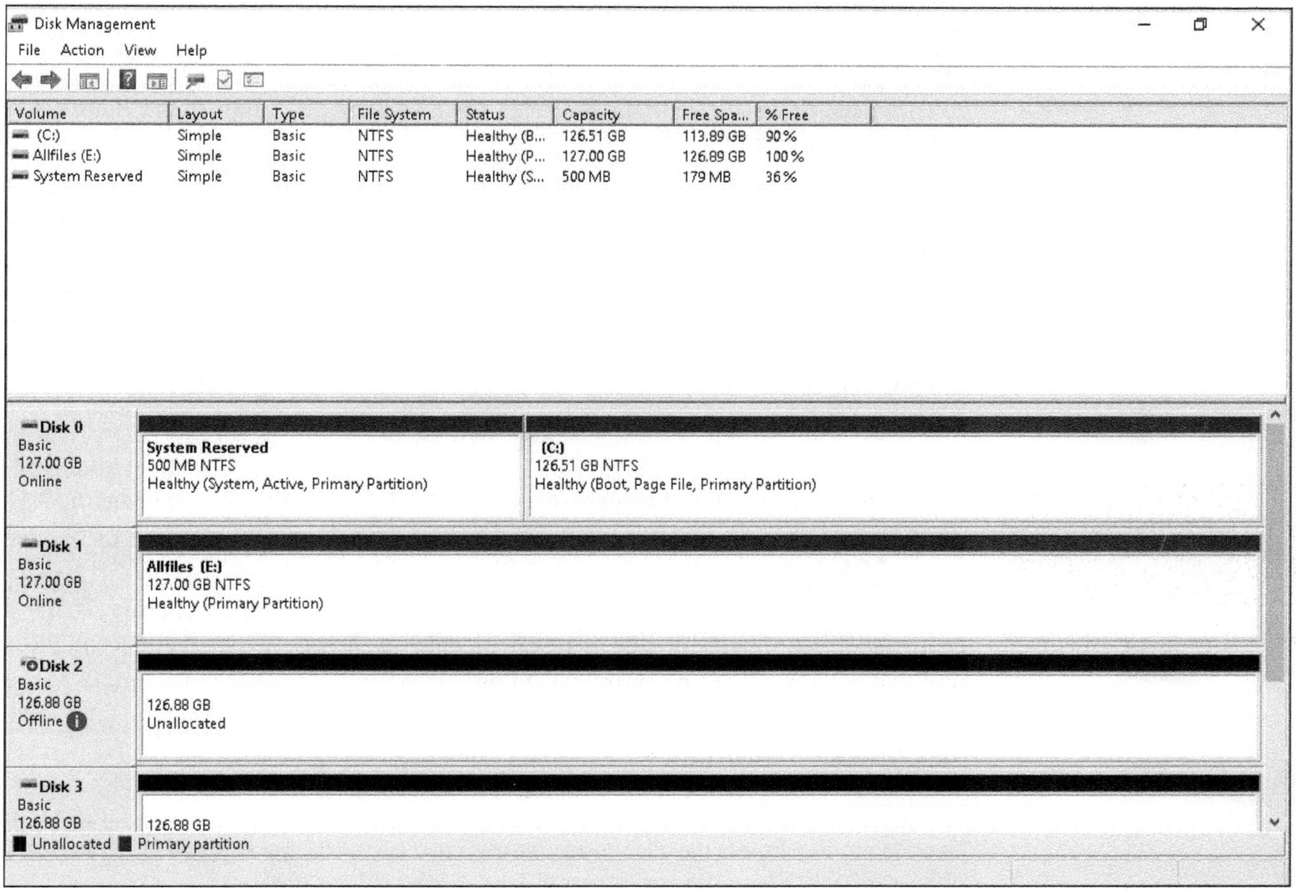

If you just installed a new hard disk and the disk is not initialized, right-click the disk and choose Initialize Disk. When the Initialize Disk window opens, you are prompted to select a partition style, as shown in Figure 3-2.

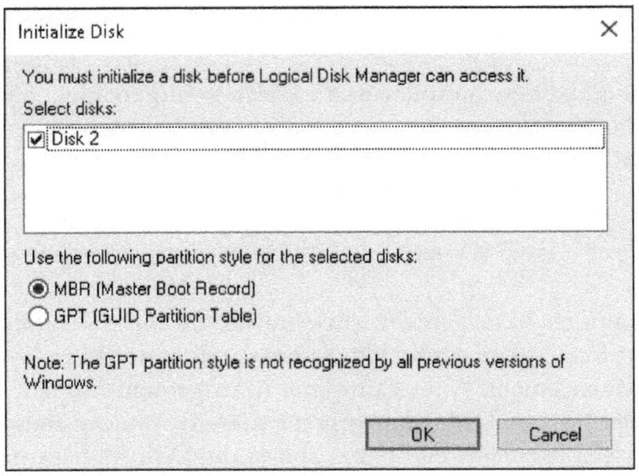

Figure 3-2

The Initialize Disk dialog box

The first choice you need to make is to choose the partition style of the disk. Be sure you select the correct partition style because this is not something you can easily change later. The two partition styles are MBR and GPT.

You can change your partition style as long as you have not created any partitions. If you have created partitions that contain data and want to change the partition style, you need to back up your data, delete all partitions, and then right-click the disk number and choose to convert to the new partition style.

Next, you need to choose the type of disk: basic or dynamic. Basic disks contain only simple partitions. The partition style you choose dictates the number of partitions you can create and their sizes. Dynamic disks can contain simple, spanned, striped, and mirrored volumes.

CONVERT A DISK FROM BASIC TO DYNAMIC

GET READY. To convert a disk from basic to dynamic, perform the following steps.

1. Back up all data on the disk you want to convert.
2. Open Disk Management in the Computer Management console. Right-click **Start**, choose **Computer Management**, and then click the **Disk Management** node.
3. Right-click the basic disk you want to convert and choose **Convert to Dynamic Disk**.
4. If the disk is currently MBR, the Convert to GPT Disk option appears. If the disk is GPT, the Convert to MBR Disk option appears. Select the appropriate option.

After you convert the partition style, you can create partitions again and restore the data that you previously backed up.

➕ MORE INFORMATION

The conversion from basic to dynamic can occur automatically based on the type of volume you create. You'll see this in action in the step-by-step exercise named "Create a Spanned Volume" in Lesson 4.

In the next example, a second disk is added to the computer, so two disks have been initialized as MBR. However, you will create a simple volume on only one of the dynamic disks. Spanning, striping, and mirroring, which you will do in subsequent step-by-step exercises, involve two or more disks.

CREATE A SIMPLE VOLUME

GET READY. To create a simple volume, perform the following steps.

1. Open Disk Management in the Computer Management console. Right-click **Start**, choose **Computer Management**, and then click the **Disk Management** node.
2. Right-click an empty area (unallocated space) of a dynamic disk. The New Volume menu displays, similar to Figure 3-3. Choose **New Simple Volume**.

Figure 3-3

The New Volume menu

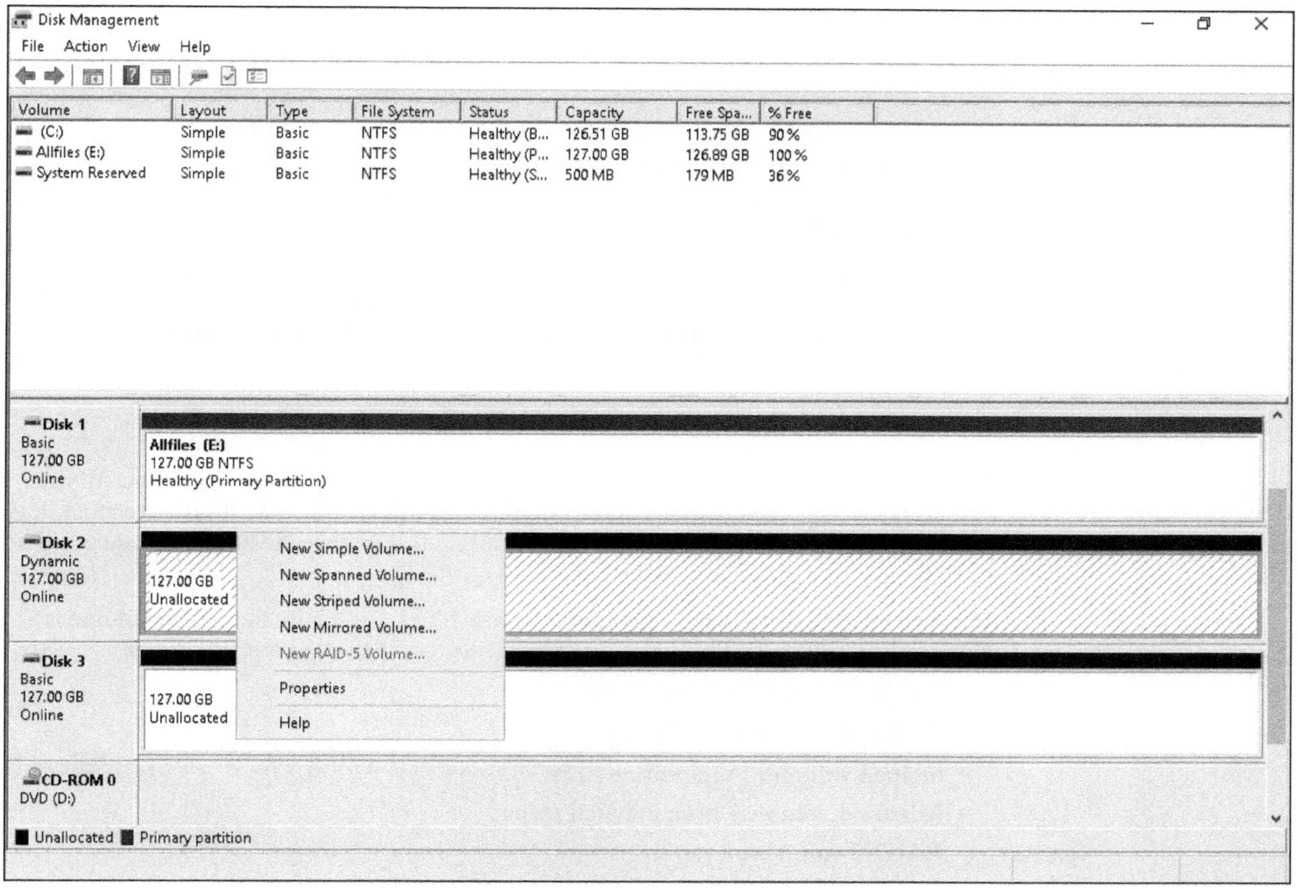

```
Disk Management                                                                          —   □   ×
File   Action   View   Help

Volume          Layout    Type    File System   Status        Capacity    Free Spa...   % Free
(C:)            Simple    Basic   NTFS          Healthy (B...  126.51 GB   113.75 GB    90 %
Allfiles (E:)   Simple    Basic   NTFS          Healthy (P...  127.00 GB   126.89 GB    100 %
System Reserved Simple    Basic   NTFS          Healthy (S...  500 MB      179 MB       36 %


Disk 1
Basic           Allfiles (E:)
127.00 GB       127.00 GB NTFS
Online          Healthy (Primary Partition)

Disk 2              New Simple Volume...
Dynamic             New Spanned Volume...
127.00 GB       127.00 GB
Online          Unallocated  New Striped Volume...
                    New Mirrored Volume...
Disk 3              New RAID-5 Volume...
Basic
127.00 GB       127.00 GB   Properties
Online          Unallocated
                    Help

CD-ROM 0
DVD (D:)

■ Unallocated  ■ Primary partition
```

3. The New Simple Volume Wizard starts. Click **Next** on the welcome page. Click **Next** to accept the default volume size.
4. On the Assign Drive Letter or Path page, assign a drive letter or path and then click **Next**.
5. On the Format Partition page (as shown in Figure 3-4), you can specify the file system, allocation unit size, and volume label. The file system choices (FAT, FAT32, NTFS, exFAT, or ReFS) are based on the size of the volume. There are two other options you can set: Perform a quick format (selected by default, which is a good idea) and Enable file and folder compression, which is not selected by default. Click **Next**.

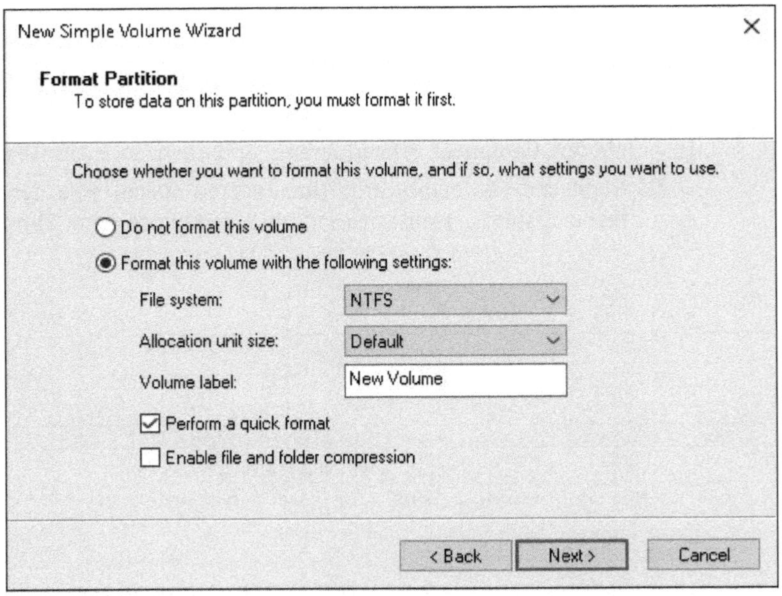

Figure 3-4

Formatting a partition

6. On the Completing the New Simple Volume Wizard page, click **Finish**.

You now have a new partition on the dynamic disk on which you can store data. All the other volume types—spanned, striped, and mirrored—require two or more disks. Therefore, if you have only one disk, the options to create spanned volumes, striped volumes, or mirrored volumes are grayed out and cannot be selected.

After you create a few different types of volumes, it's easy to figure out which volume is which—they're identified by a strip of color at the top of the volume, as follows:

- **Simple volumes:** Dark blue strips
- **Spanned volumes:** Purple strips
- **Striped volumes:** Aquamarine strips
- **Mirrored volumes:** Burgundy red strips
- **RAID-5 volumes:** Cyan strips

Using Windows PowerShell to Configure Disks, Volumes, and File Systems

Just as you can manage disks, volumes, and file systems with Disk Management, you can also use Windows PowerShell. Windows PowerShell allows for task automation and configuration management that consist of a command-line shell and associated scripting language.

In Windows PowerShell, administrative tasks are generally performed with cmdlets. However, when executing many of these commands to manage a system, you will have to run the Windows PowerShell cmdlets as an administrator.

You can perform Windows storage management with Windows PowerShell by using the following cmdlets:

- **Clear-Disk:** Removes all partition information and uninitializes the disk. As a result, all data is erased from the disk.
- **Format-Volume:** Formats an existing volume.
- **Get-Disk:** Displays available disks as seen by the operating system.
- **Get-Partition:** Displays all partitions on a disk.
- **Get-PartitionSupportedSize:** Displays a list of partitions on a disk.
- **Get-PhysicalDisk:** Displays a list all PhysicalDisk objects.
- **Get-ResiliencySetting:** Displays Windows-based resiliency settings (also known as storage layouts) for the specified storage subsystem.
- **Initialize-Disk:** Initializes a RAW disk for first time use, enabling the disk to be formatted and used to store data.
- **Mount-DiskImage:** Mounts a disk image (virtual hard disk or ISO), so that it appears as a normal disk.
- **New-Partition:** Creates a new partition on an existing Disk object.
- **New-Volume:** Creates a volume with the specified file system.
- **Remove-Partition:** Deletes the specified Partition object and any underlying Volume objects.
- **Repair-Volume:** Attempts to repair a volume.
- **Resize-Partition:** Resizes a partition and the associated file system.
- **Set-Partition:** Sets attributes of a partition, such as active, read-only, and offline states.
- **Set-PhysicalDisk:** Sets attributes on a specific physical disk.
- **Set-ResiliencySetting:** Modifies the resiliency setting of a storage system.
- **Set-Volume:** Sets or changes the file system label of a volume.

When using Windows PowerShell to manage disks, you have to organize your commands just like you would if you were using Disk Management. To list all disks in the system, perform the following Windows PowerShell command:

```
Get-Disk
```

To initialize a disk to allow creation of a partition and volume, type the following Windows PowerShell command, where <DiskNumber> is the number of the disk to initialize:

```
Initialize-Disk <DiskNumber>
```

All disks are initialized as GPT by default unless otherwise specified.

To initialize a disk as MBR, use the –PartitionStyle parameter. For example, to initialize disk 1, execute the following Windows PowerShell command:

```
Initialize-Disk 1 –PartitionStyle MBR
```

To list all disks that are currently offline, type the following command:

```
Get-Disk | Where-Object IsOffline –Eq $True
```

To bring all offline disks online, execute the Windows PowerShell command:

```
Get-Disk | Where-Object IsOffline –Eq $True | Set-Disk –IsOffline
$False
```

To list all partitions on all disks, type the following Windows PowerShell command:

```
Get-Partition
```

To create a new partition on a blank initialized disk, use the following command:

```
New-Partition –DiskNumber <DiskNumber>

–UseMaximumSize –AssignDriveLetter
```

To list all of the volumes that have been formatted with a file system, execute the following Windows PowerShell command:

```
Get-Volume
```

To format a volume with the NTFS file system, type the following, replacing *<DriveLetter>* with the letter of the drive you want to format:

```
Format-Volume -DriveLetter <DriveLetter>
```

To resize a volume to 3 GB, execute the following Windows PowerShell command:

```
Resize-Partition -DiskNumber 1 -PartitionNumber 1
-Size 3GB
```

To resize a volume to the maximum size, execute the following Windows PowerShell command:

```
Resize-Partition -DiskNumber 1 -PartitionNumber 1
-Size $size.SizeMax
```

To clear all of the partitions and volumes from a disk, perform the following Windows PowerShell command:

```
Clear-Disk 1 -RemoveData
```

If the specified disk contains an OEM partition, for system recovery, for example, you should also specify the **-RemoveOEM** switch when using the **clear-disk** cmdlet.

Creating, Configuring, and Mounting VHDs

Because virtual disks are associated with virtual machines, it would make sense that you would use Hyper-V to manage and create virtual disks. However, you can also create VHD/VHDX files with the Disk Management snap-in or Windows PowerShell. The Disk Management console can be accessed directly or from the Computer Management console. Of course, the Computer Management console can be accessed from Server Manager.

CERTIFICATION READY
Create VHD and VHDX files using Server Manager or Windows PowerShell
Objective 2.1

With Disk Management and Server Manager, you can create a new .vhd/.vhdx file by using the available disk space on the computer and saving it to the location that you specify. If you have a .vhd/vhdx file, you can mount the drive to your system running Windows Server 2016.

CREATE A VHD USING DISK MANAGER

CERTIFICATION READY
Mount virtual hard disks
Objective 2.1

GET READY. To create a VHD using Disk Management, perform the following steps.

1. Open Disk Management in the Computer Management console. Right-click **Start**, choose **Computer Management**, and then click the **Disk Management** node. Alternatively, you can use Server Manager to open Computer Management.

CERTIFICATION READY
Manage and maintain VHDs using Windows PowerShell
Objective 1.3

2. Right-click the **Disk Management** node and choose **Create VHD**.
3. When the Create and Attach Virtual Hard Disk dialog box opens (as shown in Figure 3-5), specify the location of the virtual hard drive, such as **C:\VDisk.vhdx**. Alternatively, you can use the Browse button to navigate to the folder and specify the file name.
4. In the Virtual hard disk size text box, type **5**, and change **MB** to **GB**.

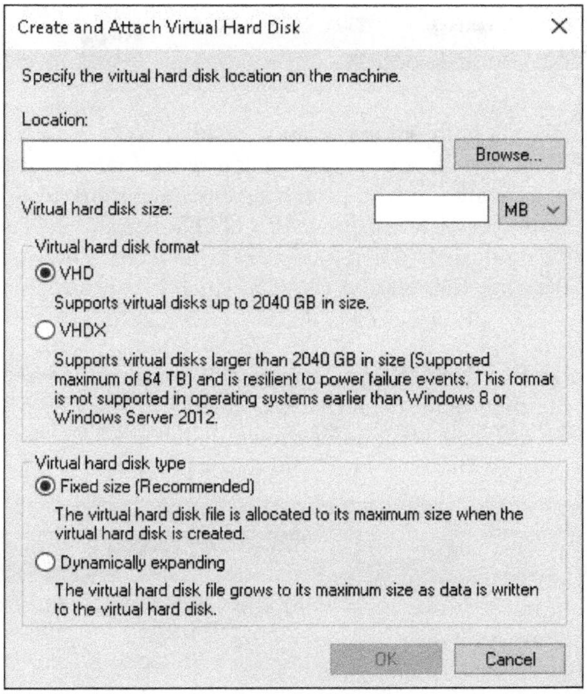

Figure 3-5

Creating and attaching a virtual hard disk

5. To create a .vhdx file, select **VHDX**.
6. With the Fixed size (Recommended) option already selected, click **OK**. The disk will be created.
7. To initialize the disk, right-click the new disk and choose **Initialize Disk**.
8. When the Initialize Disk dialog box opens, click **OK**.
9. Right-click the unallocated space and choose **New Simple Volume**.
10. When the New Simple Volume Wizard opens, on the Welcome page, click **Next**.
11. On the Specify Volume Size page, click **Next**.
12. On the Assign Drive Letter or Path page, click **Next**.
13. On the Format Partition page, for the Volume label, type **VDisk** and click **Next**.
14. When the wizard is complete, click **Finish**.

To mount or attach a .vhd or .vhdx file, right-click the Disk Management node and choose Attach VHD. You then specify the location of the .vhd or .vhdx file, and click OK. To detach a .vhd or .vhdx file, right-click the virtual disk and choose Detach VHD.

➕ MORE INFORMATION

Detaching a .vhd or .vhdx file does not delete the file from the disk. If you want to free up the disk space the file is taking, you have to manually delete the file.

To create a VHD with Windows PowerShell using the Storage module cmdlets, you would use the New-VHD cmdlet. To create a 10-GB VHDX file, you would use the following command:

```
New-VHD –Path C:\Base.vhdx –SizeBytes 10GB
```

To mount the new VHD disk, use the following command:

```
Mount-VHD -Passthru C:\base.vhdx
```

You will then have to use other Windows PowerShell commands to initialize the disk, partition the disk, and format the volume.

■ Configuring File Sharing

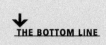

THE BOTTOM LINE

Most users are not going to log on to a server directly to access their data files. Instead, a drive or folder will be shared (known as a *shared folder*), and they will access the data files over the network. To help protect against unauthorized drive or folder access, you should use share permissions along with NTFS permissions (assuming the shared folder is on an NTFS volume). When a user needs to access a network share, she will use the *Universal Naming Convention (UNC)*, which is \\servername\sharename.

Server Message Block (SMB), also known as *Common Internet File System (CIFS)*, is a client/server file-sharing protocol that was created in 1984 by Microsoft. Through the years, there have been different versions, as shown in Table 3-2.

Table 3-2

SMB Versions

SMB VERSION	OPERATING SYSTEM
SMB 3.1.1	Windows 10 and Windows Server 2016
SMB 3.0.2	Windows 8.1 and Windows Server 2012 R2
SMB 3.0	Windows 8 and Windows Server 2012
SMB 2.1	Windows 7 and Windows Server 2008 R2
SMB 1.x	Windows Vista and Windows Server 2008

Server Message Block (SMB) 3.0 was introduced with Windows 8 and Windows Server 2012. It brings significant changes to add functionality and improve performance, particularly in virtualized data centers.

SMB 3.0 has the following additional features:

- **SMB Transparent Failover:** Provides Continuously Available properties that allow SMB 3 clients to not lose an SMB session when failover occurs. Both the SMB client and SMB server must support SMB 3.0 to take advantage of the SMB Transparent Failover functionality.

- **SMB Scale Out:** Allows users to scale shared bandwidth by adding cluster nodes. Both the SMB client and SMB server must support SMB 3.0 to take advantage of the SMB Scale Out feature. SMB 1.0 clients do not contain the required client functionality to access SMB scale-out file shares and will receive an "Access Denied" error message when they try to connect to a scale-out file share. SMB 2.x clients will be able to connect to SMB scale-out file shares but will not benefit from the SMB Transparent Failover functionality.

- **SMB Multichannel:** Uses multiple network interfaces to provide both high performance through bandwidth aggregation and network fault tolerance through the use of multiple network paths to data on an SMB share. SMB 1.0 and SMB 2.x clients will use a single SMB connection.

- **SMB Direct (SMB over Remote Direct Memory Access [RDMA]):** Enables direct memory-to-memory data transfers between servers, with minimal CPU utilization and low latency, using standard RDMA-capable network adapters (iWARP, InfiniBand, and RoCE). It also minimizes the processor utilization when performing large file I/O operations. SMB Direct Functionality requires that the SMB client and SMB server support SMB 3.0.

- **SMB Encryption:** Performs encryption by selecting a check box. Both the SMB client and SMB server must support SMB 3.0 to take advantage of the SMB Encryption functionality.
- **VSS for SMB file shares:** Extends the Windows Volume Shadow Copy Service infrastructure to enable application-consistent shadow copies of server application data stored on SMB file shares, for backup and restore purposes. Both the SMB client and SMB server must support SMB 3.0 to take advantage of the Volume Shadow Copy Service (VSS) for SMB file shares functionality.
- **SMB Directory Leasing:** Reduces the latency when accessing files over slow WAN links by caching directory and file metadata for longer periods, which reduces the associated round-trips to fetch the metadata from the server. Both the SMB client and SMB server must support SMB 3.0 to take advantage of the SMB Directory Leasing functionality.
- **SMB PowerShell:** Adds SMB PowerShell management cmdlets that were introduced in Windows Server 2012 and in Windows 8.

SMB 3.1.1 has the following new features:

- **Pre-authentication integrity:** This feature protects from man-in-the-middle attacks by using a Secure Hash Algorithm 512 (SHA-512) hash to verify packet contents during session setup.
- **SMB encryption improvements:** SMB encryption now defaults to the AES-128-GCM encryption algorithm, which has better performance than AES-128-CCM, which was used in SMB 3.0.2.
- **Cluster dialect fencing:** This feature supports rolling upgrades of Scale-Out File Server clusters.

➕ MORE INFORMATION

For more information about clustering, refer to Lesson 15.

Creating a Shared Folder Using Basic and Advanced Sharing

Traditional Windows file sharing allows you to restrict access to shared specific files and folders, and choose which users have access. *Basic sharing* allows you to share a file or folder with a specific user and restrict the user to Read or Read/Write actions.

When using Basic Sharing, there are basic configuration options. It does not provide you with fine control of the share permissions. The following exercise shows you how to set up a basic share.

➡ SET UP A BASIC SHARE

GET READY. To set up a basic share for a specific user, perform the following steps.

1. Using File Explorer, navigate to the file or folder you want to share.
2. Right-click the file or folder, choose **Properties**, click the **Sharing** tab in the Properties dialog box, and then click the **Share** button to open the File Sharing dialog box (see Figure 3-6). Alternately, right-click the file or folder, choose **Share with**, and then click **Specific people**.
3. Click the arrow next to the text box, click a name from the list, and then click **Add**. Alternately, if you know the user name of the person you want to add, type it in the text box and click **Add**.
4. In the Permission Level column, click the down arrow for the new user and select **Read** or **Read/Write**. Read allows the user to open and view items but not make changes or delete them. Read/Write allows users to open, modify, and delete items. You can also remove the user by clicking **Remove**.

Figure 3-6

Windows Server 2016 basic sharing

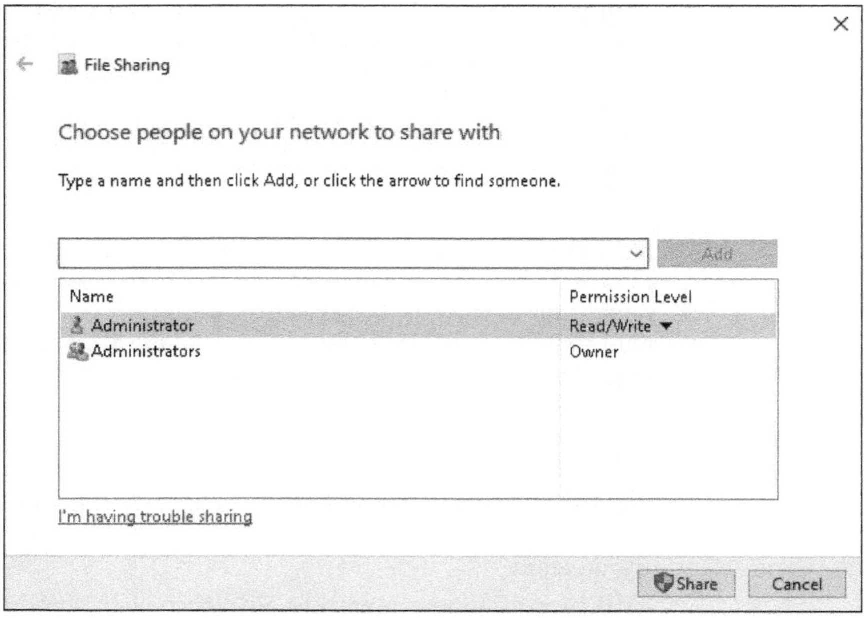

5. When you're finished, click **Share**. If you're prompted for an administrator password or confirmation, type the password or provide confirmation.

6. After you set up a basic share for a user, Windows lets you send a confirmation to that user via email, or you can copy and paste a link to the shared item and send it to the user via email or instant messaging, for example.

7. When you're finished, click **Done**.

Advanced sharing offers the greatest amount of control; you can:

- Share files, folders, or an entire drive
- Choose users or groups with which to share files and folders
- Limit the number of users who may use a file or folder at the same time, mainly for security purposes
- Set permissions on shared files and folders, such as allowing users Read, Change, or Full Control
- Choose which files are available to users offline

➕ **MORE INFORMATION**

You'll learn about permissions later in this lesson.

To set up basic or advanced shares, you must make sure file sharing and network discovery are turned on. A best practice is to also turn on password-protected sharing for security purposes. File sharing, network discovery, and password-protected sharing is enabled by default from the Network and Sharing Center, Advanced Sharing Settings page.

➡ **SET UP AN ADVANCED SHARE**

GET READY. To set up an advanced share, perform the following steps.

1. In File Explorer, navigate to the folder or drive you want to share. This exercise assumes you are not working with Public folders.

2. Right-click the item to be shared, choose **Properties**, click the **Sharing** tab in the Properties dialog box, and then click the **Advanced Sharing** button. If you're prompted for an administrator password or confirmation, type the password or provide confirmation.

3. In the Advanced Sharing dialog box, select the **Share this folder** check box (see Figure 3-7).

Figure 3-7

The Advanced Sharing dialog box

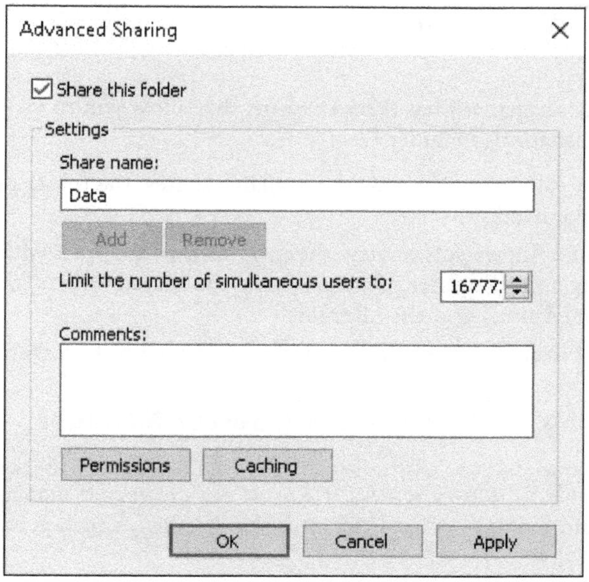

4. Use the **Limit the number of simultaneous users to** spin box to select the number of users who may access the item simultaneously.

5. In the Comments text box, type a description of the shared item (if desired).

6. To specify users or groups, or change permissions, click the **Permissions** button. The Permissions dialog box opens (see Figure 3-8).

Figure 3-8

The Permissions dialog box

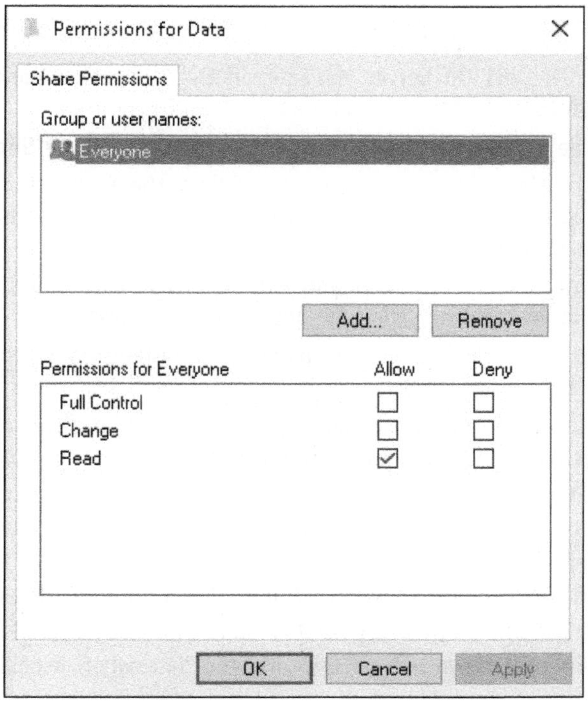

7. Click **Add** to add a user or group. (You can also click **Remove** to remove a user or group from the share.) The Select Users or Groups dialog box opens.

8. Type a user or group name in the text box or click **Locations** to find a user or group to add. When you're finished, click **OK**.

9. In the Permissions dialog box, select a user or group, select the check boxes for the permissions you want to assign, and then click **OK**.

10. When you're finished, click **OK** to close the Advanced Sharing dialog box.

Computer Management has three snap-ins that allow you to view the usage of your share folders. The snap-ins include:

- **Shares:** Allows you to view the available shares, the folder path, and the number of client connections
- **Sessions:** Allows you to view the sessions that are open with shared folders, including the user and computer name accessing the shared folders, the number of open files, the connected time, and the idle time
- **Open Files:** Shows which files are open and who is accessing the files

Configuring SMB Shares Using Server Manager

Starting with Windows Server 2012, you can create and manage share folders. Of course, the File and Storage Services role must be installed, which is installed by default.

CERTIFICATION READY
Configure SMB shares
using Server Manager
Objective 2.1

File and Storage Services allows you to create volumes and create shares. It also allows you to manage iSCSI connections and create and manage storage pools. Storage pools and iSCSI are discussed in Lesson 4.

CREATE AN SMB SHARE USING SERVER MANAGER

GET READY. To create an SMB share using Server Manager, perform the following steps.

1. On LON-SVR1, in Server Manager, in the navigation pane, click **File and Storage Services** and then click **Shares**.

2. In the Shares area, click **TASKS** and then click **New Share**.

3. In the New Share Wizard, on the Select the Profile for This Share page, in the File share profile box (as shown in Figure 3-9), click **SMB Share – Quick** and then click **Next**.

4. On the Select the Server and Path for this Share page, select **LON-SVR1**, click **Select by volume**, click **E:**, and then click **Next**.

5. On the Specify Share Name page, in the Share name box, type **ServerManagerShare** and then click **Next**.

6. On the Configure Share Settings page, select or deselect the configure share settings as needed and then click **Next**:

   a. **Enable access-based enumeration:** Displays only the files and folders that a user has permissions to access. Therefore, if the user does not have Read permissions for a folder, Windows will hide the folder from the user's view.

   b. **Allow caching of share:** Makes the content of the share available to offline users. This option is enabled by default.

   c. **Encrypt data access:** Encrypts the data when accessed as a shared folder.

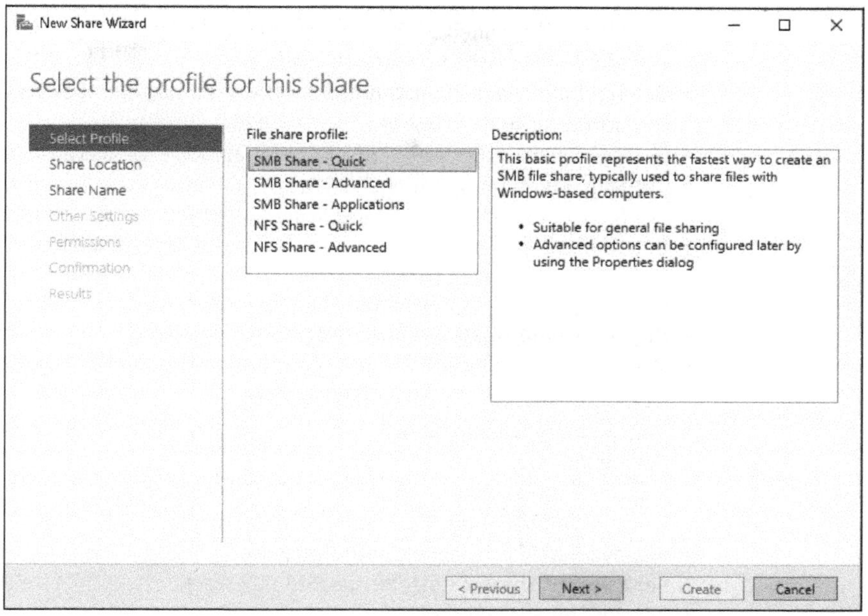

Figure 3-9

Selecting a profile to share

7. On the Specify Permissions to Control Access page, click **Next**.
8. On the Confirm Selections page, click **Create**.
9. When creation of the share is complete, click **Close**.

Creating and Configuring SMB Shares by Using Windows PowerShell

The SmbShare module for Windows PowerShell contains 35 cmdlets that allow you to create and manage SMB shares. In fact, there are some options that are available through Windows PowerShell that are not available through Server Manager.

To create an SMB share, you use the `New-SmbShare` cmdlet. To identify the shares that exist on a server and view the properties of those shares, you can use the `Get-SmbShare` cmdlet. You can also use `Get-SmbSession` to identify users who are connected to SMB shares. You can use `Get-SmbOpenFile` to identify open files.

USING WINDOWS POWERSHELL

You can perform SMB management with Windows PowerShell by using the following cmdlets:

- **Block-SmbShareAccess:** Adds a deny access control entry (ACE) for a user or group of the SMB share
- **Close-SmbOpenFile:** Closes a file that is open by one of the clients of the SMB server
- **Close-SmbSession:** Forcibly ends the SMB session
- **Disable-SmbDelegation:** Disables a constrained delegation authorization for an SMB client and server
- **Enable-SmbDelegation:** Enables a constrained delegation authorization for an SMB client and server
- **Get-SmbBandwidthLimit:** Gets the list of SMB bandwidth caps for each traffic category
- **Get-SmbClientConfiguration:** Retrieves the SMB client configuration
- **Get-SmbClientNetworkInterface:** Retrieves the network interfaces used by the SMB client
- **Get-SmbConnection:** Retrieves the connections established from the SMB client to the SMB servers
- **Get-SmbDelegation:** Gets the constrained delegation authorizations for an SMB client
- **Get-SmbMapping:** Retrieves the SMB client directory mappings created for a server

(continued)

- **Get-SmbMultichannelConnection:** Retrieves the SMB connections made between the SMB client network interfaces and the SMB server network interfaces
- **Get-SmbMultichannelConstraint:** Retrieves the constraints that define how the SMB client uses network interfaces to connect to the servers
- **Get-SmbOpenFile:** Retrieves basic information about the files that are open on an SMB server by SMB clients
- **Get-SmbServerConfiguration:** Retrieves the SMB server configuration
- **Get-SmbServerNetworkInterface:** Retrieves the network interfaces used by the SMB server
- **Get-SmbSession:** Retrieves information about the SMB sessions that are currently established between the SMB server and the associated clients
- **Get-SmbShare:** Retrieves the SMB shares on the computer
- **Get-SmbShareAccess:** Retrieves the ACL of the SMB share
- **Grant-SmbShareAccess:** Adds an allow ACE for a trustee to the security descriptor of the SMB share
- **New-SmbMapping:** Creates an SMB mapping
- **New-SmbMultichannelConstraint:** Creates an SMB multichannel constraint for the specified server
- **New-SmbShare:** Creates an SMB share
- **Remove-SmbBandwidthLimit:** Removes SMB bandwidth caps
- **Remove-SmbMapping:** Removes the SMB mapping to an SMB share
- **Remove-SmbMultichannelConstraint:** Removes SMB multichannel constraints
- **Remove-SmbShare:** Deletes the specified SMB shares
- **Revoke-SmbShareAccess:** Removes all of the allow ACEs for a trustee from the security descriptor of the SMB share
- **Set-SmbBandwidthLimit:** Adds an SMB bandwidth cap
- **Set-SmbClientConfiguration:** Sets the SMB client configuration
- **Set-SmbPathAcl:** Sets the ACL for the file system folder to match the ACL used by an SMB share
- **Set-SmbServerConfiguration:** Sets the SMB Service configuration
- **Set-SmbShare:** Modifies the properties of the SMB share
- **Unblock-SmbShareAccess:** Removes all of the deny ACEs for the trustee from the security descriptor of the SMB share
- **Update-SmbMultichannelConnection:** Forces the SMB client to update the multichannel-related information

 CREATE AN SMB SHARE USING WINDOWS POWERSHELL

GET READY. To create an SMB share using Server Manager, perform the following steps.

1. Right-click **Start** and choose **Windows PowerShell (Admin).**
2. At the Windows PowerShell prompt, type the following command and then press **Enter:**

   Mkdir E:\Shares\DemoShare2

3. To create an SMB share, type the following command and then press **Enter:**

   New-SmbShare -Name DemoShare2 -Path E:\Shares\DemoShare2 -FolderEnumerationMode AccessBased

4. To show the SMB shares, type the following command and then press **Enter:**

   Get-SmbShare

5. To view detailed information about the DemoShare2 shared folder, type the following command and then press **Enter:**

   Get-SmbShare DemoShare2 | FL *

6. To show the SMB sessions, type the following command and then press **Enter:**

   Get-SmbSession

7. To see the open SMB files, type the following command and then press **Enter:**

   Get-SmbOpenFile

Microsoft recommends that unless you have clients running Windows XP, Windows Server 2003, or earlier and you have no applications that require SMB 1.0, you should disable SMB 1.0.

To disable SMB 1.x, use the following Windows PowerShell command:

```
Set-SMBServerConfiguration -EnableSMB1Protocol $false
```

To view the current SMB client configuration settings, execute the following Windows PowerShell command:

```
Get-SMBClientConfiguration
```

To view the current SMB server configuration settings, use the following Windows PowerShell command:

```
Get-SmbServerConfiguration
```

To change an SMB client configuration setting, like SMB Signing, use the following Windows PowerShell command:

```
Set-SmbClientConfiguration -RequireSecuritySignature $true
```

To change an SMB server configuration setting, like SMB Signing, use the following Windows PowerShell command:

```
Set-SmbServerConfiguration -RequireSecuritySignature $true
```

■ Configuring File and Folder Permissions

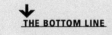
THE BOTTOM LINE

Anytime a file is accessed from an NTFS or ReFS file system, NTFS permissions are used to secure the system. In addition, if you access a file remotely through a UNC, shared permissions are also applied.

CERTIFICATION READY
Configure file and folder permissions
Objective 2.1

Share permissions are set for folders when they are shared in workgroups and domain-based networks and are only associated with the folder. They determine the type of access that others will have to the folder when they connect to it over the network.

Share permissions only apply when you are accessing a shared folder via the UNC. If you log on locally and access the files directly without using the UNC, these permissions will not apply. Share permissions are not granular; therefore, the permission you assign to the share will automatically apply to the files and subfolders within the share itself.

In Windows Server 2016, you will create and manage shares and share permissions from the folder properties Sharing tab. To see the permissions, you must click Advanced Sharing and click the Permissions button. Table 3-3 shows the available permissions.

Table 3-3

Understanding Share Permissions

PERMISSION	DESCRIPTION
Read	Enables user/group to view file and subfolder names, view data in files, and run programs
Change	Enables user/group to add files and subfolders to the shared folder, change data in files, delete subfolders and files, and change any permission associated with Read
Full Control	Enables user/group to change file permissions (NTFS only), take ownership of files (NTFS only), and perform tasks associated with Change/Read

Configuring File System Permissions

> NTFS file permissions is a powerful tool that enables you to control access to your files and folders whether they are accessed across the network or by someone logging on to the computer locally.

In addition to the permissions you set when sharing a folder, Windows offers a more comprehensive set of permissions called *NTFS permissions*. These permissions are available on volumes formatted with the NTFS file system.

NTFS permissions differ from share permissions in two ways:

- They apply to files and folders on NTFS volumes.
- They apply whether the user attempts to access them over the network or locally.

In Figure 3-10, an additional Security tab is present because the folder is located on an NTFS volume. As you can see, a number of different permissions are available for selected users and groups (see Table 3-4).

Figure 3-10

Managing NTFS permissions

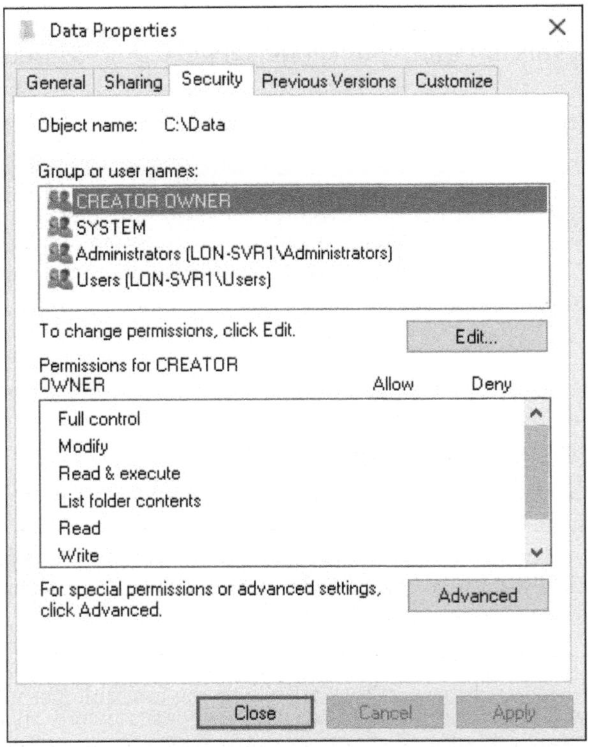

Table 3-4

NTFS Permissions

Permission	Description
Read	**Folder**: Enables user/group to read the contents of the folder/view file and folder listings.
	File: Enables user/group to read the contents of the file.
Read & Execute	**Folder**: Enables user/group to read the contents of the folder and execute programs in the folder.
	File: Enables user/group to read the contents of the file and execute the program.

Permission	Description
Write	**Folder**: Enables user/group to create files and folders. **File**: Enables changing or writing to a file
Modify	**Folder**: Enables user/group to read and write permissions. User can delete files within the folder and view the contents of subfolders. **File**: Enables user/group to read and write permissions. User can modify the contents of the file.
List Folder Contents	**Folder**: Enables user/group to view a list of files in the selected folder; user is not allowed to read the contents of a file or execute a file. **File**: There is no equivalent permission for files.
Full Control	**Folder**: Enables user/group to add, change, move, and delete items. User can also add and remove permissions on the folder and its subfolders. **File**: Enables user/group to change, move, delete, and manage permissions. User can also add, change, and remove permissions on the file.

Groups or users who are granted full control permission on a folder can delete any files in that folder regardless of the permissions protecting the file. In addition, the List folder contents permission is inherited by folders but not files, and it should only appear when you view folder permissions. In Windows Server 2016, the Everyone group does not include the Anonymous Logon group by default, so permissions applied to the Everyone group do not affect the Anonymous Logon group.

Each of the standard permissions consists of a logical group of special permissions. The available special permissions are as follows:

- **Traverse folder/Execute file:** Traverse folder allows or denies moving through folders to reach other files or folders, even if the user has no permissions for the traversed folders. By default, the Everyone group is granted the Bypass traverse checking user right. (This applies to folders only.) Execute file allows or denies running program files. (This applies to files only.) Setting the Traverse folder permission on a folder does not automatically set the Execute file permission on all files within that folder.

- **List folder/Read data:** List folder allows or denies viewing file names and subfolder names within a folder. List folder affects the contents of that folder only and does not affect whether the folder you are setting the permission on will be listed. (This applies to folders only.) Read data allows or denies viewing data in files. (This applies to files only.)

- **Read attributes:** Read attributes allows or denies viewing the attributes of a file or folder, such as read-only and hidden.

- **Read extended attributes:** This permission allows or denies viewing the extended attributes of a file or folder. Extended attributes are defined by programs and may vary by program.

- **Create files/Write data:** Create files allows or denies creating files within a folder. (This applies to folders only.) Write data allows or denies making changes to a file and over-writing existing content. (This applies to files only.)

- **Create folders/Append data:** Create folders allows or denies creating folders within a folder. (This applies to folders only.) Append data allows or denies making changes to the end of a file but not changing, deleting, or overwriting existing data. (This applies to files only.)

- **Write attributes:** Write attributes allows or denies changing the attributes of a file or folder, such as read-only or hidden. The Write attributes permission does not imply creating or deleting files or folders; it only includes the permission to make changes to the attributes of a file or folder. To allow (or deny) create or delete operations, see Create files/Write data, Create folders/Append data, Delete subfolders and files, and Delete.

- **Write extended attributes:** This permission allows or denies changing the extended attributes of a file or folder. Extended attributes are defined by programs and may vary by program. The Write extended attributes permission does not imply creating or deleting files or folders; it only includes the permission to make changes to the attributes of a file or folder. To allow (or deny) create or delete operations, see Create folders/Append data, Delete subfolders and files, and Delete.

- **Delete subfolders and files:** This permission allows or denies deleting subfolders and files, even if the Delete permission has not been granted on the subfolder or file.

- **Delete:** Delete allows or denies deleting the file or folder. If you do not have Delete permission on a file or folder, you can still delete it if you have been granted Delete subfolders and files permission on the parent folder.

- **Read permissions:** This allows or denies reading the permissions of a file or folder, such as Full Control, Read, and Write.

- **Change permissions:** This allows or denies changing the permissions of a file or folder, such as Full Control, Read, and Write.

- **Take ownership:** This permission allows or denies taking ownership of a file or folder. The owner of a file or folder can always change permissions on it, regardless of any existing permissions on the file or folder.

- **Synchronize:** Synchronize allows or denies different threads to wait on the handle for a file or folder and synchronize with another thread that may signal it. This permission applies only to multi-threaded, multi-process programs.

To simplify administration, you can grant permissions using groups. By assigning NTFS permissions to a group, you are granting permissions to one or more people simultaneously, reducing the number of entries in each access list, as well as the amount of effort required to grant multiple people access to certain files or folders.

Understanding Effective NTFS Permissions

The folder/file structure on an NTFS drive can be complicated, with many folders and nested folders. In addition, because you can assign permissions to groups and at different levels on an NTFS volume, determining the effective permissions of a particular folder or file for a particular user can be tricky.

There are two types of permissions used in NTFS:

- *Explicit permissions*: Permissions granted directly to a file or folder
- *Inherited permissions*: Permissions that are granted to a folder (parent object or container) that flow into child objects (subfolders or files inside the parent folder)

In a file system, a folder with subfolders is considered the parent folder. The subfolders are considered child folders. After you set permissions on a parent folder, new files and subfolders that are created in the folder inherit these permissions.

To stop permissions from being inherited, you can select the "Replace all existing inheritable permissions on all descendants with inheritable permissions from this object" check box in the Advanced Security Settings dialog box. You will then be prompted to determine whether you are sure you want to proceed. You can also clear the "Allow inheritable permissions from parent to propagate to this object" check box. When this check box is clear, Windows will respond with a Security dialog box. When you click on the Copy button, the explicit permission will be copied from the parent folder to the subfolder or file. You can then change the subfolder's or file's explicit permissions. If you click the Remove button, you will remove the inherited permission altogether.

By default, any objects within a folder inherit the permissions from that folder when they are created (see Table 3-5). However, explicit permissions take precedence over inherited permissions (see Table 3-6). So, if you grant different permissions at a lower level, the lower-level permissions take precedence.

For example, suppose you have a folder called Data. Within the Data folder, you have Folder1, and within Folder1, you have Folder2. If you grant Allow full control to a user account, the Allow full control permission will flow down to the subfolders and files within the Data folder.

Table 3-5

Inherited Permissions

Object	NTFS Permissions
Data	Grant Allow full control (explicit)
Folder1	Allow full control (inherited)
Folder2	Allow full control (inherited)
File1	Allow full control (inherited)

In comparison, if you grant Allow full control on the Data folder to a user account and you grant Allow read permission to Folder1, the Allow read permission will overwrite the inherited permissions and will then flow down to Folder2 and File1.

Table 3-6

Explicit Permissions Overwrite Inherited Permissions

Object	NTFS Permissions
Data	Grant Allow full control (explicit)
Folder1	Allow read (explicit)
Folder2	Allow read (inherited)
File1	Allow read (inherited)

If a user has access to a file, he will still be able to gain access to the file even if he does not have access to the folder containing the file. Of course, because the user doesn't have access to the folder, the user cannot navigate or browse through the folder to get to the file. Therefore, the user will have to use the Universal Naming Convention (UNC) or local path to open the file.

When you view permissions, they will be one of the following:

- **Checked:** Here, permissions are explicitly assigned.
- **Cleared (unchecked):** Here, no permissions are assigned.
- **Shaded:** Here, permissions are granted through inheritance from a parent folder.

Besides granting the Allow permissions, you can also grant the Deny permission. The Deny permission overrides other permissions that have been granted, including when a user or group has been given Full Control. For example, if a group has been granted Read and Write permission yet one person within the group has been denied the Write permission, the user's effective rights would be the Read permission.

When you combine applying Deny versus Allowed with explicit versus inherited permissions, the hierarchy of precedence of permission is as follows:

1. Explicit Deny
2. Explicit Allow
3. Inherited Deny
4. Inherited Allow

Because users can be members of several groups, it is possible for them to have several sets of explicit permissions for a particular folder or file. When this occurs, the permissions are combined to form the *effective permissions*, which are the actual permissions when logging on and accessing a file or folder. These consist of explicit permissions plus any inherited permissions.

When you calculate effective permissions, you must first calculate the explicit and inherited permissions for an individual or group and then combine them. When combining user and group permissions for NTFS security, the effective permission is the cumulative permission. The only exception is that Deny permissions always apply.

For example, suppose you have a folder called Data. Within the Data folder, you have Folder1, and within Folder1, you have Folder2. If User 1 is a member of Group 1 and Group 2 and you assign the Allow write permission to the Data folder to User 1, the Allow read permission to Folder1 to Group 1, and the Allow modify permission to Folder2 to Group 2, then User 1's effective permissions would be as shown in Table 3-7.

Table 3-7

Calculating Effective Permissions

OBJECT	USER 1 NTFS PERMISSIONS	GROUP 1 PERMISSIONS	GROUP 2 PERMISSIONS	EFFECTIVE PERMISSIONS
Data	Allow write (explicit)			Allow write
Folder1	Allow write (inherited)	Allow read (explicit)		Allow read and write
Folder2	Allow write (inherited)	Allow read (inherited)	Allow modify* (explicit)	Allow modify*
File1	Allow write (inherited)	Allow read (inherited)	Allow modify* (inherited)	Allow modify*

*The Modify permission includes the Read and Write permissions.

As another example, suppose you have a folder called Data. Within the Data folder, you have Folder1, and within Folder1, you have Folder2. If User 1 is a member of Group 1 and Group 2 and you assign the Allow write permission to the Data folder to User 1, the Allow read permission to Folder1 to Group 1, and the Deny modify permission to Folder2 to Group 2, User 1's effective permissions would be as shown in Table 3-8.

Table 3-8

Effective Permissions Affected
by Deny Permissions

OBJECT	USER 1 NTFS PERMISSIONS	GROUP 1 PERMISSIONS	GROUP 2 PERMISSIONS	EFFECTIVE PERMISSIONS
Data	Allow write (explicit)			Allow write
Folder1	Allow write (inherited)	Allow read (explicit)		Allow read and write
Folder2	Allow write (inherited)	Allow read (inherited)	Deny modify (explicit)	Deny modify
File1	Allow write (inherited)	Allow read (inherited)	Deny modify (inherited)	Deny modify

The concept of inheritance is important to keep in mind when setting NTFS permissions. When users:

- Copy files and folders, the files and folders inherit permissions of the destination folder
- Move files and folders within the same volume, they retain their permissions
- Move files and folders to a different volume, they inherit the permissions of the destination folder

Effective permissions for an object, such as a folder, are permissions granted to a user or group based on the permissions granted through group membership and any permissions inherited from the parent object. Windows does not include share permissions as part of the effective permissions.

NTFS permissions are cumulative. For example, if you give a user in the sales group Read permissions to a folder and its contents, and the user is also a member of the marketing group, which has been given the Write permission to the same folder, the user will have Read + Write permissions. In this type of situation, if you do not want the user to be able to write to the folder, you can use the Deny permission and select the specific user account. The Deny permission overrides the Allow permission.

Viewing Effective Permissions on a Resource

In Windows Server 2016, the Effective Access tab has been added to enable you to view the effective NTFS permissions for a user, group, or device account on a resource. You can access this tab by right-clicking the file or folder, choosing Properties, clicking the Security tab, and then clicking Advanced.

For example, let's say you create a folder called *Data* and then share the folder, allowing the Sales group Full Control. Larry is a member of the Sales group. You also configure the NTFS permissions for Larry, with the following settings: Read & Execute, List Folder Contents, and Read. What would Larry's effective permissions be?

To determine Larry's effective permissions, you would right-click the Data folder and choose Properties. You can then click the Security tab and then click Advanced. Once you are in the Advanced Security Settings for Data dialog box, select the Effective Access tab. Then, click

Select a user and then search for Larry's account. Once it's located, click View effective access to see what permissions he has for the folder.

As shown in Figure 3-11, even though Larry has Full Control to the share due to his membership in the Sales group, NTFS permissions are restricting him to only reading, listing folder contents, and executing files within the folder. He cannot create files or folders, or make any changes to the documents.

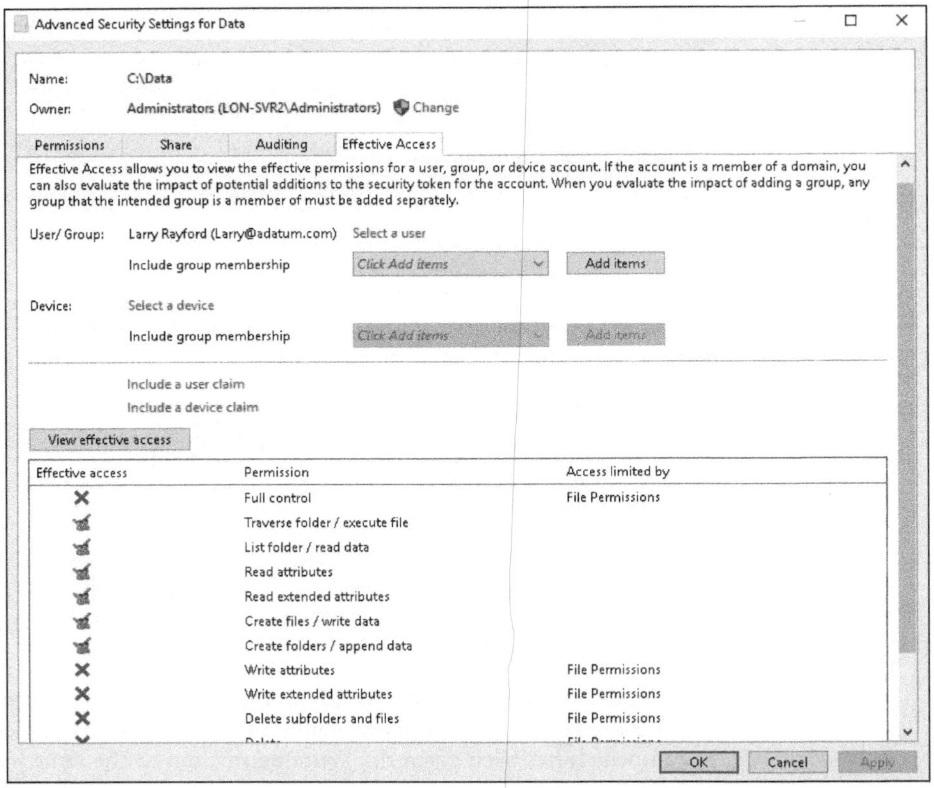

Figure 3-11

Viewing a user's effective permissions

Advanced Security Settings for Data			— ☐ ✕

Name: C:\Data

Owner: Administrators (LON-SVR2\Administrators) 🛡 Change

Permissions	Share	Auditing	Effective Access

Effective Access allows you to view the effective permissions for a user, group, or device account. If the account is a member of a domain, you can also evaluate the impact of potential additions to the security token for the account. When you evaluate the impact of adding a group, any group that the intended group is a member of must be added separately.

User/ Group: Larry Rayford (Larry@adatum.com)   Select a user

Include group membership   Click Add items   ∨   Add items

Device: Select a device

Include group membership   Click Add items   ∨   Add items

Include a user claim
Include a device claim

View effective access

Effective access	Permission	Access limited by
✕	Full control	File Permissions
🐾	Traverse folder / execute file	
🐾	List folder / read data	
🐾	Read attributes	
🐾	Read extended attributes	
🐾	Create files / write data	
🐾	Create folders / append data	
✕	Write attributes	File Permissions
✕	Write extended attributes	File Permissions
✕	Delete subfolders and files	File Permissions
✓	Delete	File Permissions

		OK	Cancel	Apply

 REVIEW PERMISSIONS USING THE EFFECTIVE ACCESS TAB

GET READY. To view the effective permissions for the local Administrator account, log on to your computer with administrative credentials and then perform the following steps.

1. To open File Explorer, click the **File Explorer** icon on the taskbar.
2. Click **Local Disk (C:)**.
3. Right-click the **Windows** folder and choose **Properties**.
4. Click the **Security** tab and then click **Advanced**.
5. Click the **Effective Access** tab.
6. Click **Select a user**.
7. In the Enter the object name to select field, type **Administrator** and then click **OK**.
8. Click **View effective access**.
9. Review the current permissions for the local Administrator account on C:\Windows and then click **OK**.
10. Click **OK** to accept your changes and to close the Windows Properties dialog box.

When planning your NTFS/Share permissions on storage spaces or any volumes in which files/folders are shared, the best approach is to set the Share permissions to provide Full Control to the appropriate user group and then use NTFS permissions to further lock down access to the resource. This process ensures that resources are secured regardless of how they are accessed (remotely or locally).

Combining NTFS and Share Permissions

It is very common to combine share and NTFS permissions when providing access to resources on NTFS volumes. When this happens, you must have a good understanding of the cumulative effects to ensure that your resources remain protected. Now that you have a better understanding of NTFS permissions and share permissions, you need to understand what happens when you combine the two on the same resource.

For example, let's say you create and share a folder with the following settings:

- Share permission (Share tab)—Sales group: Read
- NTFS permission (Security tab)—Sales group: Full Control

When users connect to the share over the network, both the share and NTFS permissions combine, and the most restrictive set is applied. In the preceding example, the share permission of Read is more restrictive than the NTFS permission, so users could read the folder and its contents. If the same users were to log on locally to the computer in which this share is located, they would bypass the share permissions, and their level of access would be based on the NTFS permission. In this example, they would have Full Control.

■ Configuring NFS Shares

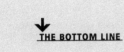

THE BOTTOM LINE

Network File System (NFS) is a distributed file system protocol that is used to access files over a network, similar to accessing a file using a shared folder in Windows that uses Server Message Block (SMB). It is used with UNIX and Linux file server clients and VMware. Therefore, to support these clients, Windows Server 2016 supports NFS.

CERTIFICATION READY
Configure NFS shares
using Server Manager
Objective 2.1

NFS was originally developed by Sun Microsystems in the 1980s. NFS was later released to the public, and by 1995, the Internet Engineering Task Force (IETF) standardized it as RFC 1813, "NFS Version 3 Protocol Specification." Virtually all UNIX and Linux distributions available today include both NFS client and server support.

By installing the ***Server for NFS*** role service, you can provide NFS Server and NFS Client capabilities. Different from using a Universal Naming Convention (UNC), which uses a \\ servername\sharename, or mounting a UNC to a drive letter, NFS takes part of a remote file system and mounts it or connects to a local file system. The client can then access the server's files as if they were a local resource.

 INSTALL THE SERVER AND CLIENT FOR NFS

GET READY. To install the Server for NFS and Client for NFS, perform the following steps.

1. On the task bar, click the **Server Manager** button to open Server Manager.
2. At the top of Server Manager, click **Manage** and click **Add Roles and Features**. The Add Roles and Feature Wizard opens.
3. On the Before You Begin page, click **Next.**

4. Select **Role-based or feature-based installation** and then click **Next**.

5. On the Select Destination Server page, click **Next**.

6. On the Select Server Roles page, expand **File and Storage Services**, expand **File and iSCSI Services**, and click to select **Server for NFS**. Click **Next**.

7. When you are prompted to add features required for Server for NFS, click **Add Features**.

8. On the Select Features page, click to select **Client for NFS** and click **Next**.

9. Back on the Select Features page, click **Next**.

10. On the Confirm Installation Selections page, click **Install**.

11. When the installation is complete, click **Close**.

CONFIGURE ACCOUNT LOOKUPS

GET READY. To configure Account Lookup for NFS, perform the following steps.

1. Using Server Manager, open the **Tools** menu and click **Services for Network File System (NFS)**. The Services for Network File System Server for NFS node is shown in Figure 3-12.

Figure 3-12

Opening the Services for Network File System console

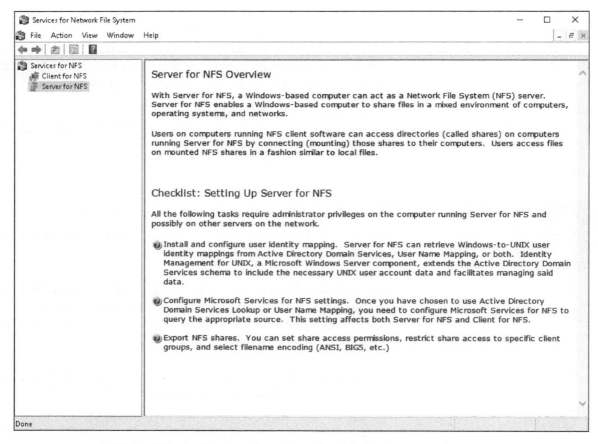

2. Right-click the **Services for NFS** node and choose **Properties**. The Services for NFS Properties dialog box opens (see Figure 3-13).

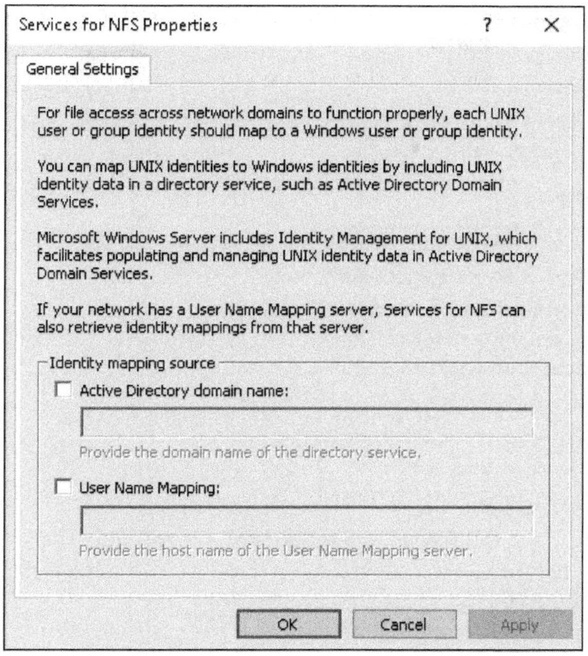

Figure 3-13

Configuring the identity mapping source

Services for NFS Properties   ?   ✕

┌─ General Settings ──┐

For file access across network domains to function properly, each UNIX
user or group identity should map to a Windows user or group identity.

You can map UNIX identities to Windows identities by including UNIX
identity data in a directory service, such as Active Directory Domain
Services.

Microsoft Windows Server includes Identity Management for UNIX, which
facilitates populating and managing UNIX identity data in Active Directory
Domain Services.

If your network has a User Name Mapping server, Services for NFS can
also retrieve identity mappings from that server.

┌─ Identity mapping source ─────────────────────────────────┐
│ ☐ Active Directory domain name: │
│   ┌──┐   │
│   └──┘   │
│   Provide the domain name of the directory service.   │
│   │
│ ☐ User Name Mapping: │
│   ┌──┐   │
│   └──┘   │
│   Provide the host name of the User Name Mapping server. │
└───┘

                    [OK   ]   [Cancel]   [Apply]

3. Select one of the following check boxes to choose an identity mapping source:
   - **Active Directory domain name:** Specify the name of the domain that Services for NFS should use to look up user UIDs and GIDs.
   - **User Name Mapping:** Specify the name or IP address of the User Name Mapping server that Services for NFS should use to look up user UIDs and GIDs.

4. Click **OK** to close the Server for NFS Properties dialog box.

When you install the Services for NFS role service, an NFS Sharing tab is added to the properties of every volume and folder on the computer's drives.

 CREATE AN NFS SHARE

GET READY. To create an NFS share, perform the following steps.

1. Browse to a volume or folder on a local NTFS drive, right-click it, and choose **Properties**. The Properties dialog box opens.

2. Click the **NFS Sharing** tab.

3. Click **Manage NFS Sharing**. The NFS Advanced Sharing dialog box opens.

4. Select the **Share this folder** check box, as shown in Figure 3-14.

5. In the Share Name text box, type the name that you want NFS clients to use when accessing the folder and select one of the encoding schemes from the Encoding drop-down list.

6. If you want NFS clients to be able to access the share without authenticating, click to select the **Allow anonymous access**, and modify the Anonymous UID and Anonymous GID values, if necessary.

7. Click **Permissions**. The NFS Share Permissions dialog box opens (see Figure 3-15).

Figure 3-14

Sharing an NFS folder

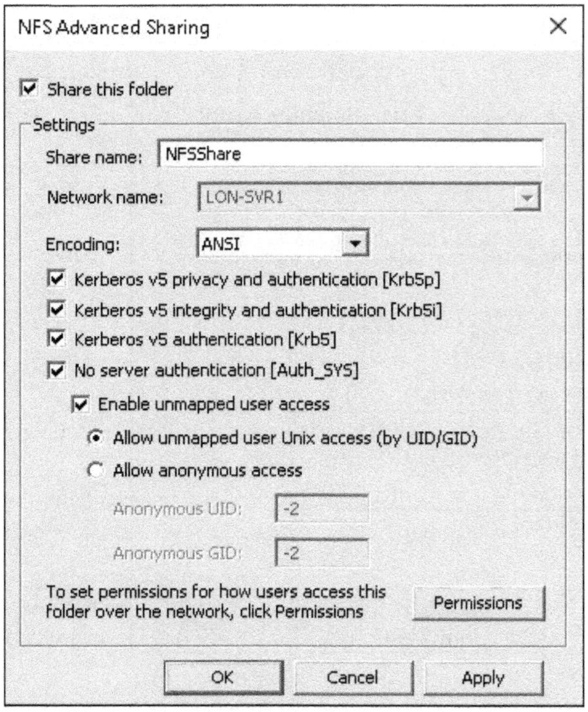

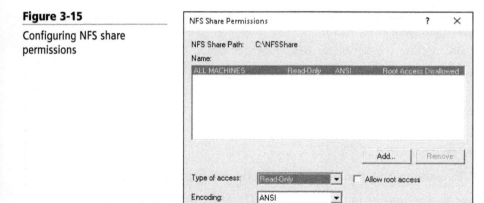

Figure 3-15

Configuring NFS share
permissions

8. By default, all NFS clients have read-only access to the share. If you want clients to have Read-Write, change the type of access. You can also grant root access by clicking the **Allow root access** option.

9. You can click **Add** to select users or groups and create new permission assignments.

10. Click **OK** to close the NFS Share Permissions dialog box.

11. Click **OK** to close the NFS Advanced Sharing dialog box.

12. Click **Close** to close the Properties dialog box.

CREATE AN NFS SHARE WITH SERVER MANAGER

GET READY. To create an NFS share with Server Manager, perform the following steps.

1. On LON-SVR1, if Server Manager is not open, click **Start** and then click **Server Manager.**

2. In Server Manager, in the navigation pane, click **File and Storage Services** and then click **Shares.**

3. In the Shares section, click **TASKS** and then click **New Share.**

4. When the New Share Wizard opens, on the Select the Profile for This Share page, in the File share profile box, click **NFS Share - Quick** and then click **Next.**

5. On the Select the Server and Path for This Share page, click **LON-SVR1**, click **Select by volume**, click **E:**, and then click **Next.**

6. On the Specify Share Name page, in the Share name text box, type **NFSShare2** and then click **Next.**

7. If you did not specify an authentication method previously, on the Specify Authentication Methods page, select **Kerberos v5 authentication(Krb5)** and then click **Next.**

8. On the Specify the Share Permissions page, click **Add.**

9. In the Add Permissions window (as shown in Figure 3-16) click **All Machines.**

Figure 3-16

Specifying NFS permissions
with Server Manager

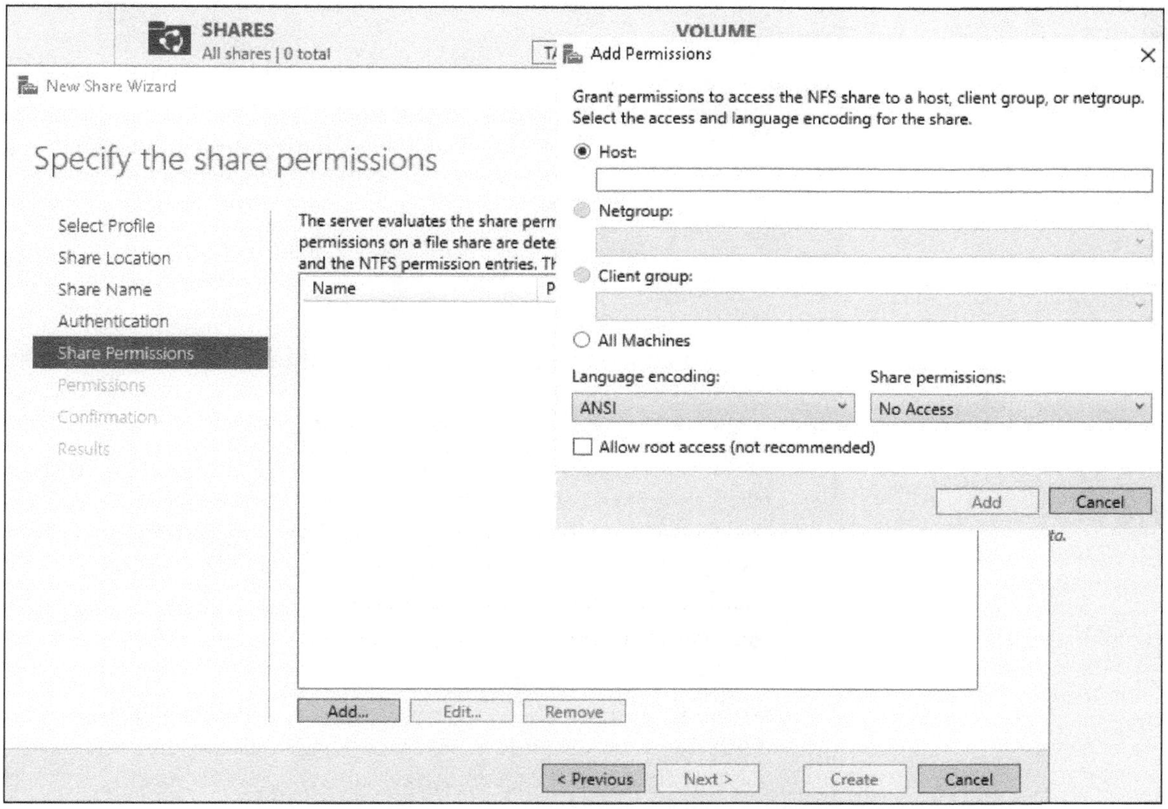

10. In the Share permissions box, select **Read/Write** and then click **Add**.
11. On the Specify the Share Permissions page, click **Next**.
12. On the Specify Permissions to Control Access page, click **Next**.
13. On the Confirm Selections page, click **Create**.
14. On the View Results page, click **Close**.

SKILL SUMMARY

IN THIS LESSON YOU LEARNED:

- Windows Server 2016 supports two partition styles—Master Boot Record (MBR) and GUID partition table (GPT)—and two primary types of disks—basic and dynamic. In addition, the operating system supports simple, spanned, striped, and mirrored volumes. You use the Disk Management tool in the Computer Management snap-in to manage disks, partitions, and volumes.

- A file system is the overall structure your computer uses to name, store, and organize files and folders on a hard disk or partition. The file system provides a map of the clusters (the basic units of logical storage on a hard disk) that a file has been stored in. When you install a hard disk in a computer, you must format it with a file system.

- Because virtual disks are associated with virtual machines, it would make sense that you would use Hyper-V to manage and create virtual disks. However, you can also create VHD/VHDX files with the Disk Management snap-in or Windows PowerShell. The Disk Management console can be accessed directly or from the Computer Management console. Of course, the Computer Management console can be accessed from Server Manager.

- Most users are not going to log on to a server directly to access their data files. Instead, a drive or folder will be shared (known as a shared folder), and they will access the data files over the network. To help protect against unauthorized drive or folder access, you should use share permissions along with NTFS permissions (assuming the shared folder is on an NTFS volume). When a user needs to access a network share, she will use the Universal Naming Convention (UNC), which is \\servername\sharename.

- Traditional Windows file sharing allows you to restrict access to shared specific files and folders, and choose which users have access. Basic sharing allows you to share a file or folder with a specific user and restrict the user to Read or Read/Write actions.

- Share permissions are set for folders when they are shared in workgroups and domain-based networks and are only associated with the folder. They determine the type of access that others will have to the folder when they connect to it over the network.

- When planning your NTFS/Share permissions on storage spaces or any volumes in which files/folders are shared, the best approach is to set the Share permissions to provide Full Control to the appropriate user group and then use NTFS permissions to further lock down access to the resource.

- When users connect to the share over the network, both the share and NTFS permissions combine, and the most restrictive set is applied.

- Network File System (NFS) is a distributed file system protocol that is used to access files over a network, similar to accessing a file using a shared folder in Windows that uses Server Message Block (SMB). It is used with UNIX and Linux file server clients and VMware. Therefore, to support these clients, Windows Server 2012 supports NFS.

Multiple Choice

Select the correct answer for each of the following questions.

1. Which of the following statements are true of striped volumes? (Choose all that apply.)
   a. Striped volumes provide enhanced performance over simple volumes.
   b. Striped volumes provide greater fault tolerance than simple volumes.
   c. You can extend striped volumes after creation.
   d. If a single physical disk in the striped volume fails, all of the data in the entire volume is lost.

2. Which of the following are requirements for extending a volume on a dynamic disk? (Choose all that apply.)
   a. When extending a simple volume, you can use only the available space on the same disk, if the volume is to remain simple.
   b. The volume must have a file system before you can extend a simple or spanned volume.
   c. You can extend a simple or spanned volume if you formatted it using the FAT or FAT32 file systems.
   d. You can extend a simple volume across additional disks if it is not a system volume or a boot volume.

3. Which of the following volume types supported by Windows Server 2016 does *not* provide fault tolerance? (Choose all that apply.)
   a. Striped
   b. Spanned
   c. Mirrored
   d. RAID-5

4. Which of the following is the next step after creating a virtual hard disk (VHD)?
   a. Mounting it either through Server Manager or the Disk Management snap-in
   b. Initializing the disk and creating volumes on it, just as you would a physical disk
   c. Using the VHD (creation of the VHD file readies the disk for storage)
   d. Mounting the VHD file to a Hyper-V virtual machine

5. Which of the following is the maximum size of an NTFS volume with 64-KB clusters?
   a. 2 GB
   b. 32 GB
   c. 4 TB
   d. 256 TB
   e. 512 TB

6. Which of the following share permissions on a FAT32 volume enable adding files and folders to a shared folder? (Choose all that apply.)
   a. Read
   b. Write
   c. Change
   d. Full Control

7. Which of the following NTFS permissions is needed to change attributes and permissions?
   a. Full Control
   b. Modify
   c. Read and Execute
   d. Write

8. Which type of permission is granted directly to a file or folder?
   a. Explicit
   b. Inherited
   c. Effective
   d. Share

9. Which of the following is *not* a share permission?
   a. Full Control
   b. Write
   c. Change
   d. Read

10. Which method of file sharing is used with UNIX and Linux machines?
    a. SMB
    b. CIFS
    c. NTFS
    d. NFS

11. When using NFS, how do you connect to the shared folder?
    a. You mount the volume to a local folder.
    b. You mount the volume to a remote folder.
    c. You access the shared folder using a UNC.
    d. You access the shared folder using a URL.

12. When defining access to NFS, which two items must be included? (Choose two answers.)
    a. Domain name
    b. GID
    c. Admin access
    d. UID

Best Answer

Choose the letter that corresponds to the best answer. More than one answer choice may achieve the goal. Select the BEST answer.

1. Which of the following can be used to extend the Active Directory schema to store UNIX attributes?
   a. NFS Management console
   b. Server for NFS role
   c. Computer Management console
   d. Identity Management for UNIX

Matching and Identification

1. Identify the correct minimum standard NTFS permission, for the task that needs to be done.

   _____ a. To open a file

   _____ b. To make changes to a file

   _____ c. To change NTFS permissions

   _____ d. Delete a file

   _____ e. To view the contents of a folder

Build a List

1. Specify the correct order of steps necessary to creating and mounting a VHD.

   _____ Select the virtual hard disk format option (VHD or VHDX).

   _____ Log on with administrative privileges and open Server Manager.

   _____ Click Tools > Computer Management.

   _____ Click OK for the system to create and attach the VHD file. The VHD appears as a disk in the Disk Management snap-in.

   _____ Click Disk Management and then click Create VHD from the Action menu.

   _____ Specify the Location path and name for the new VHD file and then specify the maximum size of the disk.

   _____ Select one of the following VHD types (Fixed size or Dynamically expanding).

■ Business Case Scenarios

Scenario 3-1: Configuring Permissions

You have set up a shared folder on a FAT32 volume that is set with the following permissions:

Share name: **MyDocs**

Share Permission: **Read**

Group: **Everyone**

After configuring the share, you notice that multiple people have added files to it. What is the problem and how should you address it?

Scenario 3-2: Working with UNIX Machines

You are an administrator for a large organization with a group of web developers that works on UNIX machines. You need to come with a solution that enables the web developers to save their files on the Windows system so that those files can be backed up with all of your other data. Because the web servers are critical to the company, you must ensure that the data is available and backed up regularly. Describe your proposed solution.

4 LESSON

Implementing Server Storage

70-740 EXAM

Objective 2.2 – Implement server storage. This objective may include but is not limited to the following: Configure storage pools; implement simple, mirror, and parity storage layout options for disks or enclosures; expand storage pools; configure Tiered Storage; configure iSCSI target and initiator; configure iSNS; configure Datacenter Bridging (DCB); configure multi-path I/O (MPIO); determine usage scenarios for Storage Replica; implement Storage Replica for server-to-server, cluster-to-cluster, and stretch cluster scenarios.

Objective 5.2 – Implement Failover clustering. This objective may include but is not limited to the following: Implement Storage Replica. *Other Objective 5.2 topics are covered in Lessons 13 and 14.*

LESSON HEADING	EXAM OBJECTIVE
Implementing Simple, Mirror, and Parity Storage Layout Options	Implement simple, mirror, and parity storage layout options for disks or enclosures
Configuring Storage Pools and Storage Spaces	Configure storage pools
– Creating Storage Pools	Expand storage pools
– Creating and Configuring Storage Spaces	Configure Tiered Storage
– Expanding Storage Pools	
– Configuring Tiered Storage	
Implementing ISCSI Storage	Configure iSCSI initiator
– Implementing iSCSI SAN	Configure iSCSI target
– Configuring the iSCSI Initiator	Configure multi-path I/O (MPIO)
– Configuring iSCSI Target Server	Configure iSNS
– Configuring Multi-Path I/O (MPIO)	Configure Data Center Bridging (DCB)
– Configuring Internet Storage Name Service (iSNS)	
– Using iSCSI Best Practices	
– Configuring Data Center Bridging (DCB)	
Implementing Storage Replica	Determine usage scenarios for Storage Replica
– Determining Usage Scenarios for Storage Replica	Implement Storage Replica for server-to-server, cluster-to-cluster, and stretch cluster scenarios
– Implementing Storage Replica	Implement Storage Replica

KEY TERMS

cluster-to-cluster replication

converged network

Data Center Bridging (DCB)

Discovery Domain (DD)

fill and spill

Internet Small Computer
System Interface (iSCSI)

Internet Storage Name Service
(iSNS)

iSCSI initiators

iSCSI qualified names (IQNs)

iSCSI Target Server

iSCSI Target Storage Provider

iSCSI targets

logical unit number (LUN)

mirrored volumes

multi-path I/O (MPIO)

multiple connected session (MCS)

network attached storage (NAS)

parity

RAID-5 volume

server-to-server replication

shared storage

simple (no resiliency)

spanned volume

storage area network (SAN)

storage pool

Storage Replica

Storage Spaces

stretch cluster

striped volume

thin provisioning

three-way mirror

tiered storage

two-way mirror

■ Implementing Simple, Mirror, and Parity Storage Layout Options

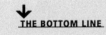 **THE BOTTOM LINE**

In Lesson 3, you learned how to create a simple volume, including partitioning and formatting the volume. This section expands the number of storage layout options to include spanned, mirror, and parity.

CERTIFICATION READY
Implement simple, mirror, and parity storage layout options for disks or enclosures
Objective 2.2

If you have an additional disk with unused space, you can create a *spanned volume*. Spanned volumes include two or more disks (up to 32) that are represented in Windows Explorer as a single drive letter. They are sometimes referred to as *fill and spill* because all of the storage space on the first disk must be filled before data is stored on the second and subsequent disks.

 CREATE A SPANNED VOLUME

GET READY. To create a spanned volume, perform the following steps.

1. Open Disk Management in the Computer Management console. Right-click **Start**, choose **Computer Management**, and then click the **Disk Management** node.
2. Right-click an empty area of a dynamic disk and choose **New Spanned Volume**.
3. Click **Next** on the Welcome to the New Spanned Volume Wizard page.
4. Highlight the desired disk in the Available box, as shown in Figure 4-1. Click **Add.** (You can also double-click the available disk to add it to the selected box.)

Figure 4-1

The Select Disks page

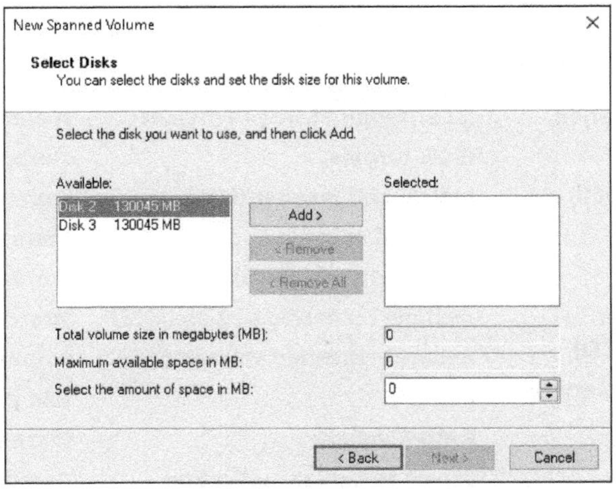

New Spanned Volume   ×

Select Disks
You can select the disks and set the disk size for this volume.

Select the disk you want to use, and then click Add.

Available:

Disk 2 130045 MB
Disk 3 130045 MB

[Add >]
[< Remove]
[< Remove All]

Selected:

Total volume size in megabytes (MB):   0
Maximum available space in MB: 0
Select the amount of space in MB: 0

[< Back] [Next >] [Cancel]

5. When you add disks to the Selected box, the Total volume size in megabytes (MB) box displays the combined size of all disks. When you highlight one of the disks in the Selected box, the Maximum available space in MB box and the Select the amount of space in MB box show what you have selected for that specific disk. You can select a different amount of space for each disk you add. You can continue to add as many disks as you would like included in your spanned volume. After you have selected the disks, click **Next**.

6. On the Assign Drive Letter or Path page, select a drive letter and click **Next**.

7. The Format Volume page is the same as creating a simple volume. Set your format volume options and click **Next**.

8. Click **Finish** on the Completing the New Spanned Volume Wizard page.

9. A warning message appears letting you know that to create a spanned volume, the basic disk will be converted to a dynamic disk. If you convert the disk to a dynamic disk, you will not be able to start installed operating systems from any volume on the disk. Click **Yes** to continue or **No** to cancel the operation.

Do not plan to use spanned volumes for fault tolerance. If one disk in the spanned volume fails, all data in the spanned volume is lost unless you have a backup.

Creating a ***striped volume*** is similar to creating a spanned volume in that almost all of the steps are the same. However, the way data is stored on a striped volume is different from a spanned volume. As with a spanned volume, striped volumes must contain at least 2 disks and can contain up to 32 disks. But when the data is stored, it is separated into 64-kilobyte (KB) chunks. The first 64 KB is stored on Disk 1 in the striped volume, the second 64-KB chunk is stored on Disk 2, and so on. Figure 4-2 shows a striped volume. The data is literally striped across multiple drives.

Figure 4-2

A striped volume

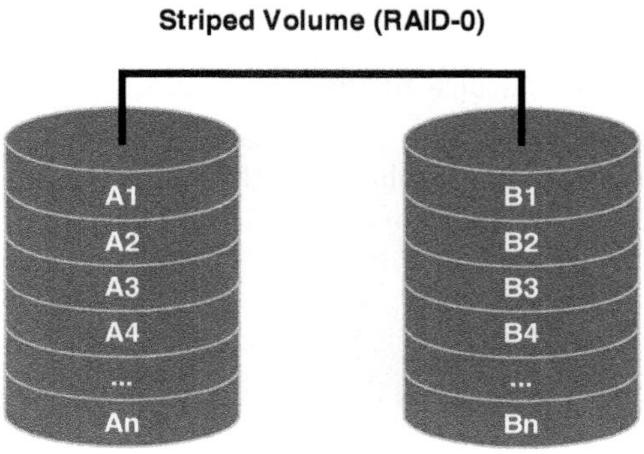

Striped Volume (RAID-0)

Accessing data on a striped volume is faster than accessing data on a spanned volume because a striped volume has multiple sets of read/write heads working simultaneously when reading and writing data. In this regard, spanned volumes are good for high capacity, whereas striped volumes are better for performance.

 CREATE A STRIPED VOLUME

GET READY. To create a striped volume, perform the following steps.

1. Open Disk Management in the Computer Management console. Right-click **Start**, choose **Computer Management**, and then click the **Disk Management** node.

2. In Disk Management, right-click an empty disk and choose **New Striped Volume**. Click **Next** on the Welcome to the New Striped Volume Wizard page.

3. Highlight the second disk from the Available box and then click **Add**.

   When you add disks to the Selected box, the Total volume size in megabytes (MB) box displays the combined size of all disks. This is where one of the big differences between spanned volumes and striped volumes takes place: On spanned volumes, you could take different amounts of hard drive space from each disk—you cannot do this with striped volumes. Striped volumes must use the same amount of disk space from each disk you take to the striped volume. So after you add two or more disks to the Selected box, if you change the Select the amount of space in MB setting (regardless of which disk is highlighted in the Selected box), the size difference will be reflected on both (or all) disks that you added.

4. After you have selected the disks, click **Next**.

5. On the Assign Drive Letter or Path page, select your drive letter and then click **Next**. The Format Volume page appears. Set your format volume options and then click **Next**. Click **Finish**.

6. A warning appears alerting you that to create a striped volume, the basic disk will be converted to a dynamic disk. If you convert the disk to dynamic, you will not be able to start installed operating systems from any volume on the disk. Click **Yes** to continue or **No** to cancel.

Striped volumes do not offer fault tolerance. Just as with spanned volumes, if one disk in the striped volume fails, all data from the entire striped volume is lost. You will have to retrieve the data from a previous backup.

Mirrored volumes require only two disks. In Traditional RAID, you cannot mirror to a third or fourth disk. Mirrored volumes store an exact copy of data from the first member of the mirrored volume to the second member. Because the data is written across both drives, you do get fault tolerance with mirrored volumes. Figure 4-3 shows an example of a mirrored volume.

Figure 4-3

A mirrored volume

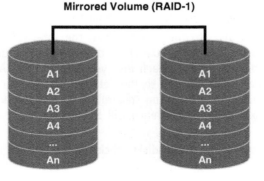

Mirrored Volume (RAID-1)

CREATE A MIRRORED VOLUME

GET READY. To create a mirrored volume, perform the following steps.

1. Open Disk Management in the Computer Management console. Right-click **Start**, choose **Computer Management**, and then click the **Disk Management** node.

2. In Disk Management, right-click an empty disk and choose **New Mirrored Volume**. Click **Next** on the Welcome to the New Mirrored Volume Wizard screen.

3. Highlight the second disk from the Available box. Mirrored volumes require the same amount of disk space from each disk. When you add a disk to the Selected box, the Total volume size in megabytes (MB) box displays the most available free space from the disk with the smallest amount. You can reduce the amount of space, but it will be reduced on both disks. This makes sense because you're creating an exact copy of data stored on the source disk, so you don't need the destination disk to have additional free space that you will never use. After you have selected the disks, click **Next**.

4. On the Assign Drive Letter or Path screen, select a drive letter and then click **Next**. The Format Volume screen is the same as the previous Format Volume screens. Set your format volume options and then click **Next**. Click **Finish**.

5. A warning message appears, informing you that the basic disk will be converted to a dynamic disk. If you convert the disk to a dynamic disk, you will not be able to start installed operating systems from any volume on the disk. Click **Yes**.

A ***RAID-5 volume*** is a fault-tolerant volume where data is interleaved across three or more disks much in the same way as in a striped volume, but with additional information known as parity. Essentially, it is striped disks with parity. If one disk in a RAID-5 volume fails, the data contained on the failed disk can be rebuilt using the parity information stored on the disks in the rest of the volume. A RAID-5 volume can be created using a minimum of three disks and a maximum of 32 disks.

If you have three disks, each disk being 1 TB, you will have 2 TB of usable disk space and the third TB is used to store the parity information. If you have five disks, each disk being 1 TB, you will have 4 TB of usable disk space. The fifth TB is to store the parity information.

 CREATE A RAID-5 VOLUME

GET READY. To create a striped volume, perform the following steps.

1. Open Disk Management in the Computer Management console. Right-click **Start**, choose **Computer Management**, and then click the **Disk Management** node.

2. In Disk Management, right-click an empty disk and choose **New RAID-5 Volume**. Click **Next** on the Welcome to the New RAID-5 Volume Wizard page.

3. Highlight the second and third disk from the Available box and then click **Add**.

4. When you add disks to the Selected box, the Total volume size in megabytes (MB) box displays the combined size of all disks. Striped volumes must use the same amount of disk space from each disk you take to the RAID-5 volume. So after you add three or more disks to the Selected box, if you change the Select the amount of space in MB setting (regardless of which disk is highlighted in the Selected box), the size difference will be reflected on both (or all) disks that you added.

5. After you have selected the disks, click **Next**.

6. On the Assign Drive Letter or Path page, select your drive letter and then click **Next**. The Format Volume page appears. Set your format volume options and then click **Next**. Click **Finish**.

7. A warning appears alerting you that to create a striped volume, the basic disk will be converted to a dynamic disk. If you convert the disk to dynamic, you will not be able to start installed operating systems from any volume on the disk. Click **Yes** to continue or **No** to cancel.

If one disk within a RAID-5 volume is intermittently failing, you can attempt to reactivate it by right-clicking the disk and choosing Reactivate Disk. In addition, if one disk within a RAID-5 volume appears to have permanently failed, you can replace the failed disk with another dynamic disk attached to the computer, or you can install a new disk. To regenerate the RAID-5 volume, right-click the RAID-5 volume on the failed disk and choose Repair Volume. The replacement disk must contain at least as much unallocated space as that used by the failed disk for the RAID-5 volume.

■ Configuring Storage Pools and Storage Spaces

↓ THE BOTTOM LINE

Storage Spaces is a feature in Windows Server 2016 that allows you to combine multiple disks into a single logical volume that can be mirrored to protect against one or more drive failures.

CERTIFICATION READY
Configure storage pools
Objective 2.2

The Storage Spaces feature in Windows Server 2016 allows you to combine several physical drives, which the operating system will see as one large drive. The drives can be any capacity and can consist of a variety of different drive interfaces, such as Small Computer System Interface (SCSI), Universal Serial Bus (USB), and Serial ATA (SATA).

When the drives are combined, Windows places them into a ***storage pool***. These storage pools can then be segmented into multiple storage spaces, which are then formatted with a file system and can be used just like any other regular disk on your computer. New disks (internal/external) can be added to the storage pool as space requirements increase over time.

Although data can be stored on the drives, you cannot use storage spaces to host the Windows operating system files.

Storage spaces offer two key benefits:

- By spreading data across multiple disks, you achieve data resiliency, which can protect your data against hard disk failure.
- Volume sizes can be larger than the actual physical size of your drives in the storage pool. This is accomplished through a process called thin provisioning.

Creating Storage Pools

Creating a storage pool allows you to combine multiple smaller drives that you might not otherwise be able to use by themselves into a larger, single logical volume.

To create a storage pool on a Windows Server 2016, you use the Manage Storage Spaces tool found in Control Panel. The wizard prompts you to select the disks that you want to use and then adds them to the storage pool. For example, if you have two physical disks with capacities of 200 GB and 300 GB, it creates a pool that has a total capacity of 500 GB (as shown in Figure 4-4).

Figure 4-4

Creating a storage pool with two disks

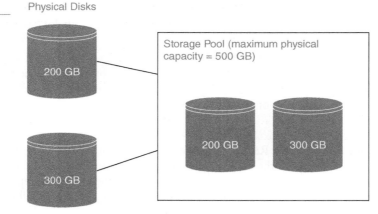

Creating and Configuring Storage Spaces

After selecting the drives to include in your storage pool, you are prompted to create the storage space. This involves entering a name, selecting a drive letter, identifying the type of resiliency you want to configure, and setting the maximum size that you want to assign to the storage space.

When creating storage spaces, there are four resiliency types to select from. Only three of them provide real fault tolerance, as shown in the following list:

- **_Simple (no resiliency)_**: Writes one copy of your data but doesn't protect against drive failures; requires at least one drive
- **_Two-way mirror_**: Writes two copies of your data to protect against a single drive failure; requires at least two drives
- **_Three-way mirror_**: Writes three copies of your data to protect against two simultaneous drive failures; requires at least five drives
- **_Parity_**: Writes data with parity information to protect against single drive failures; requires at least three drives

You also need to decide how much of the total storage pool capacity you want to use for your new storage space. By using a process called **_thin provisioning_** (see Figure 4-5), you can create a storage space that is larger than the available capacity of the storage pool. After setting the size, the wizard will create the storage space based on the parameters you provided.

Figure 4-5

An example of thin provisioning

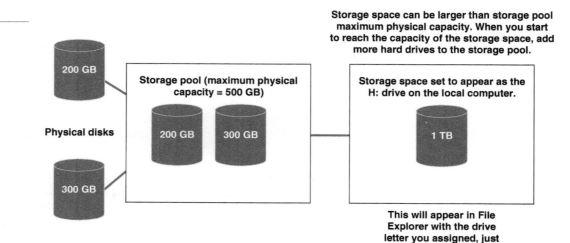

Thin provisioning reserves the space for future use. For example, in Figure 4-5, there are two physical drives being added to the storage pool to create a total capacity of 500 GB. Even though you have a total capacity of only 500 GB, you can configure the storage space that uses this pool to be 1 TB or greater capacity. When the storage pool approaches capacity, you will receive a warning and you will need to add more disks to the pool. This approach works well in situations in which you expect your data storage needs will grow, but you don't want to purchase additional disks immediately.

After the storage space is created, it will appear as a drive in File Explorer. The drive can be protected using BitLocker and NTFS permissions—just like any other drive in Windows Server 2016.

CREATE A STORAGE POOL AND A STORAGE SPACE IN WINDOWS SERVER 2016

GET READY. To create a storage pool and storage space, perform the following steps.

1. Connect the drives you want to use to your computer.
2. On LON-SVR1, log on with administrative credentials.
3. Right-click **Start** and choose **Control Panel.**
4. When Control Panel opens, in the Search Control Panel text box, type **Storage Spaces.** Then, from the results, click **Storage Spaces.**
5. When the Manage Storage Spaces window opens (as shown in Figure 4-6), click **Create a new pool and storage space.**

Figure 4-6

Managing Storage Spaces

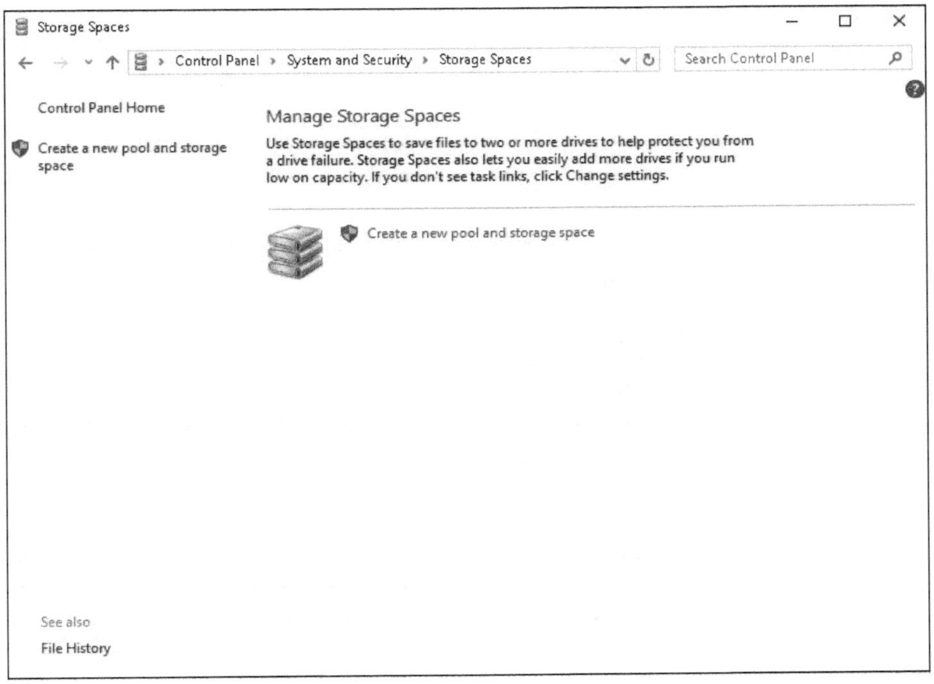

6. Select the drive(s) you want to include in the new storage pool. (Warning: Any data on these drives will be deleted.)
7. Click **Create pool.**

Once the pool is created, you will be taken automatically to the Create a storage space page shown in Figure 4-7.

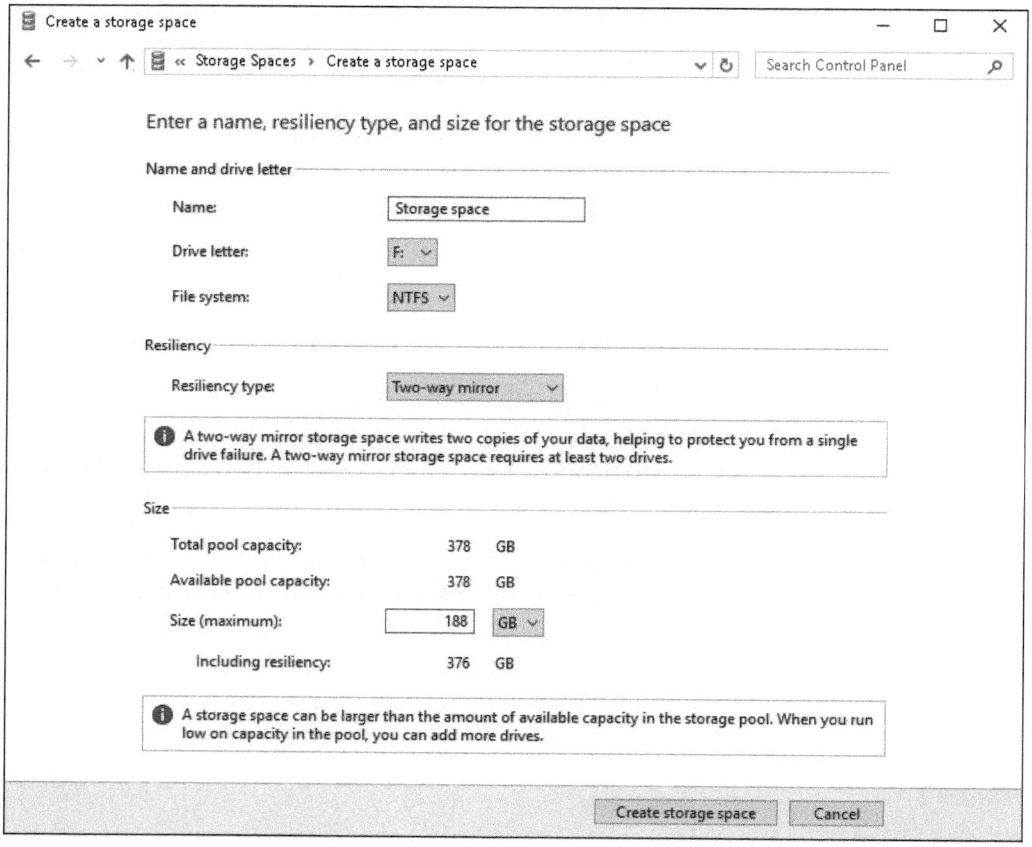

Figure 4-7

Creating a storage space

8. In the Name field, type a name for your storage space.

9. In the Drive letter field, click the down arrow and then choose a drive letter for the storage space.

10. In the Resiliency type field, click the down arrow and then choose the resiliency type.

11. In the Size (maximum) field, type the maximum size that you want for your storage space.

12. Click **Create storage space**.

13. Open File Explorer and confirm that the new storage space appears under the drive letter you assigned in Step 9.

After completing the setup of your storage space, you can continue to monitor and manage it from the Manage Storage Spaces tool. You can perform the following tasks:

- View your storage pool(s).
- View the storage spaces in the pools.
- View the physical drives included in the pool(s).

- Identify how much pool capacity is currently being used.
- Add more drives to the pool.
- Rename the pool.
- Change the size of storage spaces.
- View files stored in storage spaces.
- Delete storage spaces.

USING POWERSHELL

You can manage storage pools using Windows PowerShell by using the following cmdlets:

- **Get-StoragePool:** Lists storage pools
- **Get-VirtualDisk:** Lists virtual disks
- **Repair-VirtualDisk:** Repairs a virtual disk
- **Get-PhysicalDisk | Where {$_.HealthStatus -ne "Healthy"}:** Lists unhealthy physical disks
- **Reset-PhysicalDisk:** Removes a physical disk from a storage pool
- **Get-VirtualDisk | Get-PhysicalDisk:** Lists physical disks that are used for a virtual disk
- **Optimize-Volume:** Optimizes a volume, performing such tasks on supported volumes and system SKUs as defragmentation, trim, slab consolidation, and storage tier processing

---

Expanding Storage Pools

Storage pools allow you to combine several smaller disks to create a larger disk. However, there will be times when a storage pool fills up and you need to have a larger storage pool. Fortunately, you can expand a storage pool by adding additional disks or expanding the current disks that make up the storage pool.

CERTIFICATION READY
Expand storage pools
Objective 2.2

After you connect and configure a new disk, the disks should appear in Disk Management and Server Manager storage pools. However, those disks must be undefined before you can add them to the storage pools.

 CREATE A STORAGE POOL AND A STORAGE SPACE IN WINDOWS SERVER 2016

GET READY. To create a storage pool and a storage space, perform the following steps.

1. On LON-SVR1, log on with administrative credentials.
2. On LON-SVR1, if Server Manager is not open, click **Start** and click **Server Manager.**
3. On the Dashboard page, click **File and Storage Services.** Then, on the File and Storage Services page, under Volumes, click **Storage Pools.**
4. In the Storage Pools section, right-click the **Storage Pools** and choose **Add Physical Disk.** When the Add Physical Disk dialog box opens, select the disk that you want to add to the storage pool, as shown in Figure 4-8.

Figure 4-8

Selecting a disk

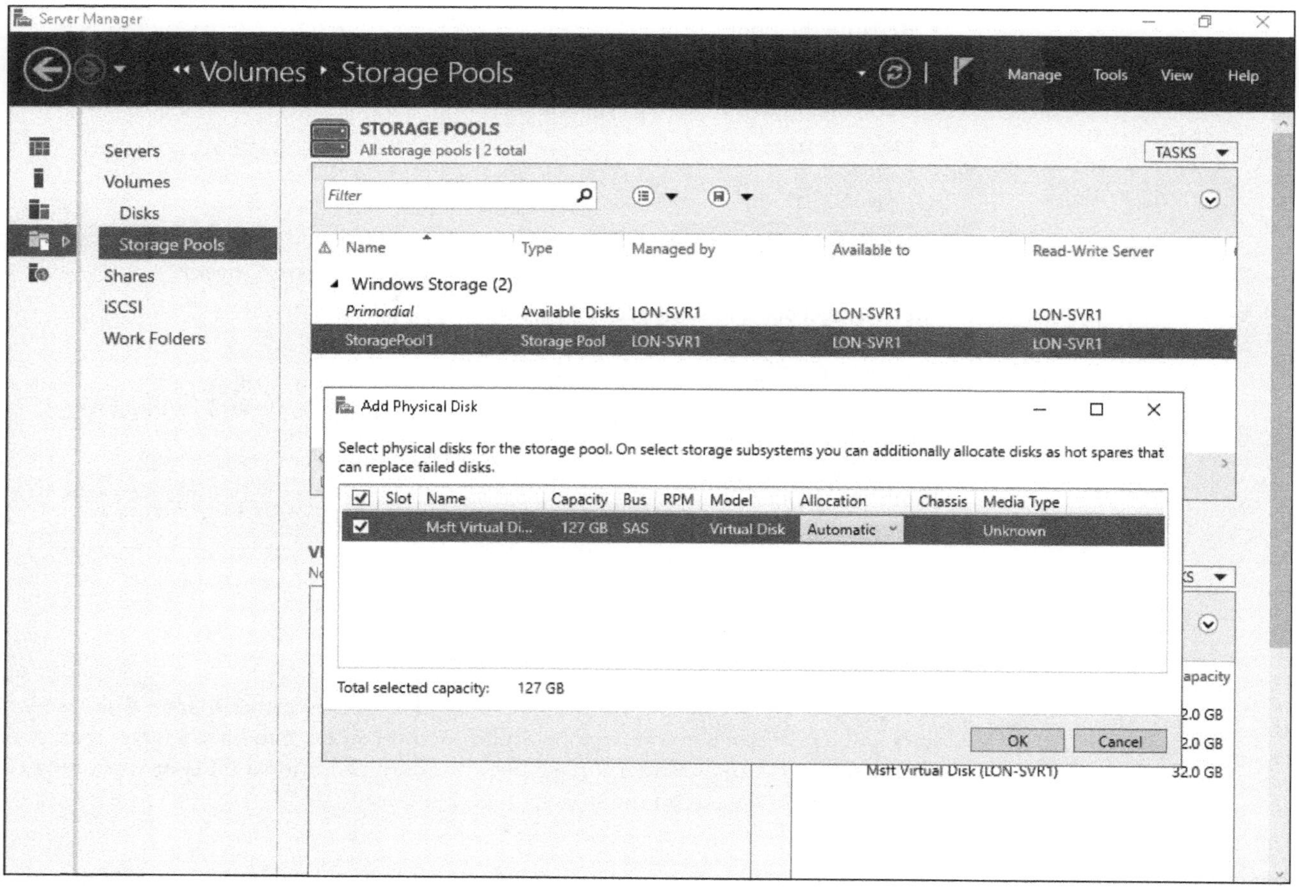

5. For Allocation, Automatic is already selected. If you wanted to use the drive as a hot spare, select the **Hot Spare** option.
6. To close the Add Physical Disk dialog box, click **OK.**

Configuring Tiered Storage

If you use disks of different types, architecture, or speed, and you combine those disks into a single pool, you might not achieve the best throughput for the virtual disks provisioned in your pool. Therefore, when you create a pool, you should use the same type of physical disks. However, with storage pools, you can combine traditional disks/hard disk drives (HHDs) with solid-state disks (SSDs) using tiered storage, so that you can increase performance while minimizing costs.

CERTIFICATION READY
Configure Tiered Storage
Objective 2.2

Typically, faster disk space costs more than slower disk space. So although you would always want faster disk space, using all SSDs might not make economic sense. However, if you use the faster disk for often-used programs and access, you can achieve better performance while keeping costs down. Windows Server 2012 R2 offers ***tiered storage***, in which you can combine the two types of disks into one virtual disk and volume. Keep in mind that you cannot remove storage tiers from a virtual disk after it is created. Storage tiers also require fixed provisioning.

With Windows Server 2016, you can manually create the pools based on the type of the physical disks. In addition, you can create storage tiers within the same storage pool. When the operating system recognizes that different types of disks are used within the same pool, you can create tiered virtual disks via the New Virtual Disk Wizard by selecting *Create storage tiers on this virtual disk*. When you enable storage tiers, the operating system moves files that are more frequently accessed to faster media. If the disks do not recognize the disk type, you can change the media type by using Windows PowerShell.

During the day, Storage Spaces creates a map of how often users and applications access each data block. Then at 1:00 AM, a Storage Tiers Optimization task runs that moves the most frequently accessed (hot) data blocks to the SSD tier and moves the less frequently accessed (cold) data blocks to the slower HDD tier.

■ Implementing iSCSI Storage

↓
THE BOTTOM LINE

Many servers used in an organization require large amounts of disk space to provide services and resources. For example, file servers need to store data files, and mail servers and database servers need to store large databases. Therefore, these servers typically need many hard drives connected directly to the machine, or the servers connect to shared storage. *Shared storage* devices have many hard drives to provide huge amounts of disk space.

Two network storage solutions are used in networking:

- *Network attached storage (NAS)* is a file-level data storage device that is connected to the server over a computer network to provide shared drives or folders, usually using Server Message Block (SMB) or Network File System (NFS).
- *Storage area network (SAN)* is a storage architecture that allows systems to attach to the storage in the SAN and presents the drives to the server just as if the drives were locally attached.

Accessing the shared files on a NAS is like accessing a shared folder on a server. To provide fault tolerance and better performance, most NAS devices use Redundant Array of Independent Disks (RAID). NAS devices can be managed with a web interface, and some enterprise NAS devices include a command-line interface accessible with Secure Shell (SSH).

If a server fails, the data is still stored in the SAN. You can then bring up another server, present the same storage to the server, and have all your data intact. Typically, when you use clustering in a production environment and for a virtual environment such as Hyper-V, using a SAN is common and recommended. Of course, robust SANs usually have a higher level of RAID such as RAID 10, spare drives, redundant power supplies, redundant network connections, and built-in monitoring tools.

Most SANs use the SCSI command for communication between servers and disk drive devices. By using the SCSI commands, you can connect disks to a server using copper Ethernet cables or fiber-optic cables. The two standards used in SANs are Fibre Channel and iSCSI. Both technologies use a fabric, which is a network topology in which devices are connected to each other through one or more high-efficient data paths. In addition to allowing multiple servers to access the SAN, both technologies allow the SAN to be in a different rack in the server room, a separate room, or even a separate building. Of course, deciding on what is an acceptable performance always comes down to bandwidth and latency.

A *logical unit number (LUN)* is a logical reference to a portion of a storage subsystem. The LUN can be a disk, part of a disk, an entire disk array, or part of the disk array. So when configuring servers to attach to a SAN, you usually configure the SAN to assign a LUN to a specific server. In other words, the LUN allows the administrator to break the SAN storage into manageable pieces. If the LUN is not mapped to a specific server, the server cannot see or access the LUN.

Implementing iSCSI SAN

Internet Small Computer System Interface (iSCSI) is a protocol that enables clients to send SCSI commands over a TCP/IP network using TCP port 3260. Unlike with Fibre Channel, you use standard Ethernet cabling and switches to connect servers to the SAN. Because you connect to the SAN over the network, you should use a minimum of two network adapters on the server, one for the SAN communications and one for standard network communications. Currently, the fastest network connection is capable of 10 gigabits per second or more.

Unlike standard local SCSI drives, iSCSI allows data transfers over intranets and can be used over long distances. iSCSI allows clients (called *iSCSI initiators*) to send SCSI commands to iSCSI storage devices (*iSCSI targets*).

Storage devices provided by iSCSI are often used as storage devices that contain sensitive or critical data. Therefore, you need to protect the iSCSI infrastructure. The best approach for security is to use a defense-in-depth security strategy consisting of the following:

- Implementing policies, procedures, and awareness that include security best practices, enforcement of a strong user password policy and strong administrator password policy for accessing iSCSI storage devices, and computers that have iSCSI management software installed.
- Implementing physical security that protects servers and iSCSI storage devices that can be accessed by authorized personnel only.
- Establishing perimeter security that includes firewalls to protect attacks from outside the organization and prevent attacks on the iSCSI devices.
- Using network protection, including authentication such as target access lists, Challenge-Handshake Authentication Protocol (CHAP), virtual LANs (VLANs), and physical isolation. You might also consider using Internet Protocol security (IPsec).
- Keeping your servers updated with the latest security updates.
- Protecting the data stored on the iSCSI storage devices, including encryption (using BitLocker and Encrypting File System [EFS]) and Access Control Lists (ACLs).
- Performing backups regularly and storing the backups in a safe place.

Of these, iSCSI targets and initiators have the following security features built in:

- They limit which iSCSI initiators can connect to an iSCSI target.
- They use CHAP to provide authentication between an iSCSI initiator and an iSCSI target.
- For encryption of traffic between an iSCSI initiator and an iSCSI target, you can use IPsec.

iSCSI qualified names (IQNs) are unique identifiers used to address initiators and targets on an iSCSI network. An IQN uses the following format:

- Literal IQN
- Date (yyyy-mm) that the naming authority took ownership of the domain
- Reversed domain name of the authority
- Optional : (colon) prefixing a storage target name specified by the naming authority

An example of an IQN is as follows:

`iqn.1991-05.com.contoso:storage01-target1-target`

When you configure an iSCSI target, you define which iSCSI initiators can connect to an iSCSI LUN by the client's IQN. You can also specify which servers can connect to the iSCSI target based on MAC address, IP address, and DNS name. iSCSI initiators use IQNs to connect to iSCSI targets. If name resolution is possible, you can also use IP addresses to identify initiators and targets.

Configuring the iSCSI Initiator

To connect to an iSCSI target, you use an iSCSI initiator. As mentioned previously, the iSCSI initiator is already included with Windows.

CERTIFICATION READY
Configure iSCSI initiator
Objective 2.2

After the targets are configured and registered, you open the iSCSI initiator, as discussed in the following procedure.

⊖ CONFIGURE THE iSCSI INITIATOR

GET READY. To configure the iSCSI initiator, perform the following steps.

1. In Server Manager, click **Tools > iSCSI Initiator**. The iSCSI Initiator Properties dialog box opens. If it is the first time launching, Microsoft iSCSI will not be running. Therefore, when it prompts you to determine whether to start automatically each time the computer restarts, click **Yes**.

2. The Targets tab is shown in Figure 4-9. If you just created an iSCSI target, and it does not show up, click **Refresh**. If it still does not show up, in the Target text box, type the address of the iSCSI Target Server or SAN and click **Quick Connect**. When the Quick Connect dialog box opens, click **Done**.

Figure 4-9

Connecting to a target

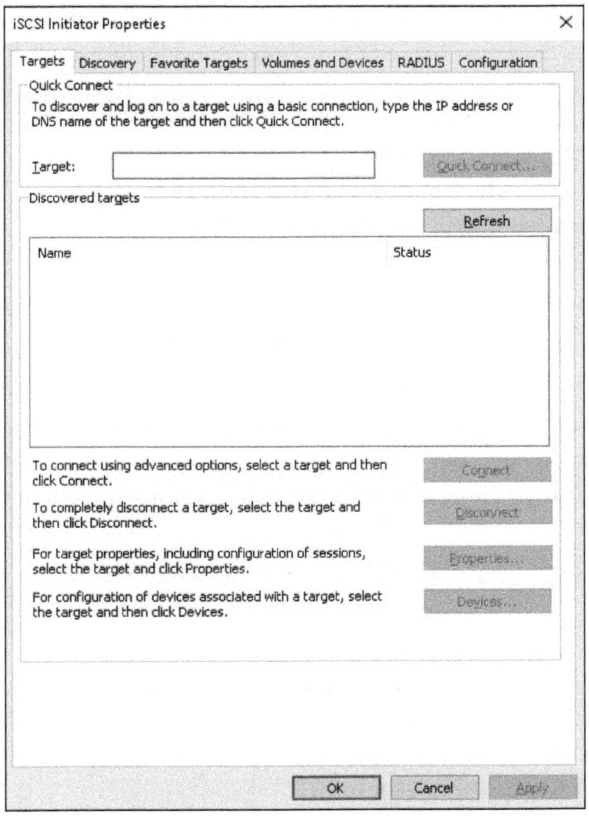

3. If the target is not connected, select it and click **Connect**. In the Connect to Target dialog box, if you need to specify the target portal IP address or a CHAP user name, click **Advanced** to open the Advanced Settings dialog box. When you click **OK** to close the Advanced Settings dialog box and Connect to Target dialog box, the status should show Connected.

TAKE NOTE＊ If the target does not show up, verify that the initiator ID is specified correctly in the iSCSI target access server list.

4. On the Volumes and Devices tab, click **Auto Configure**. In the Volume List, the available iSCSI targets should appear.

5. If you need to configure CHAP or IPsec to connect to the iSCSI target, click the **Configuration** tab.

6. Click **OK** to close the iSCSI Initiator Properties dialog box.

After an iSCSI device is attached to a server running Windows Server 2016, you might need to format the volume and assign a drive letter to the new volume. To accomplish this, you use Computer Management. After opening Computer Management, if the disk does not show up, right-click Disk Management and perform a disk rescan.

Configuring iSCSI Target Server

Starting with Windows Server 2012, you can install the iSCSI Target Server role, so that other Windows servers can provide iSCSI storage to other clients (including other Windows servers). After you install the iSCSI Target Server role, you use Server Manager to create the volumes that will be presented to clients and specify which servers can access the iSCSI LUNs.

The iSCSI Target Server included in Windows Server 2016 provides the following functionality:

• By using boot-capable network adapters or a software loader, you can use iSCSI targets to deploy diskless servers.

• When using virtual disks, you can save up to 90% of the storage space for the operating system images by using differencing disks because multiple disks can use a single disk as a starting point.

• It supports server application storage that requires block storage.

• It supports iSCSI initiators for Windows and non-Windows operating systems.

When you install iSCSI Target Server, you should install the following two components:

• *iSCSI Target Server* provides tools to create and manage iSCSI targets and virtual disks. Enabling iSCSI Target Server can provide application block storage, consolidate remote storage, provide for diskless boots, and run in a failover cluster environment.

• *iSCSI Target Storage Provider* enables applications on a server that is connected to an iSCSI target to perform volume shadow copies of data on iSCSI virtual disks. It also enables you to manage iSCSI virtual disks by using older applications that require a Virtual Disk Service (VDS) hardware provider, such as using the DiskRAID command-line tool.

⊙ INSTALL iSCSI TARGET SERVER

GET READY. To install iSCSI Target Server, perform the following steps.

1. Open Server Manager.

2. At the top of the Server Manager console, click **Manage > Add Roles and Features**. The Add Roles and Feature Wizard opens.

3. On the Before You Begin page, click **Next**.

4. Select **Role-based or feature-based installation** and then click **Next**.

5. On the Select Destination Server page, select the server that you are installing to and click **Next**.

6. On the Select Server Roles page, expand **File and Storage Services**, expand **File and iSCSI Services**, and click **iSCSI Target Server** and **iSCSI Target Storage Provider (VDS and VSS hardware providers)**. Click **Next**.

7. On the Select Features page, click **Next**.

8. On the Confirm Installation Selections page, click **Install**.

9. When the installation is complete, click **Close**.

Virtual disks or targets are created on an iSCSI disk storage subsystem that is not directly assigned to a server. Targets are created to manage the connections between an iSCSI device and the servers that need to access it. Rather than having its own console, iSCSI manages iSCSI virtual disks and iSCSI targets through Server Manager.

⊕ CREATE AN iSCSI VIRTUAL DISK

GET READY. To create an iSCSI virtual disk, perform the following steps.

1. In Server Manager, click **File and Storage Services** and then click **iSCSI**. The iSCSI page is displayed as shown in Figure 4-10.

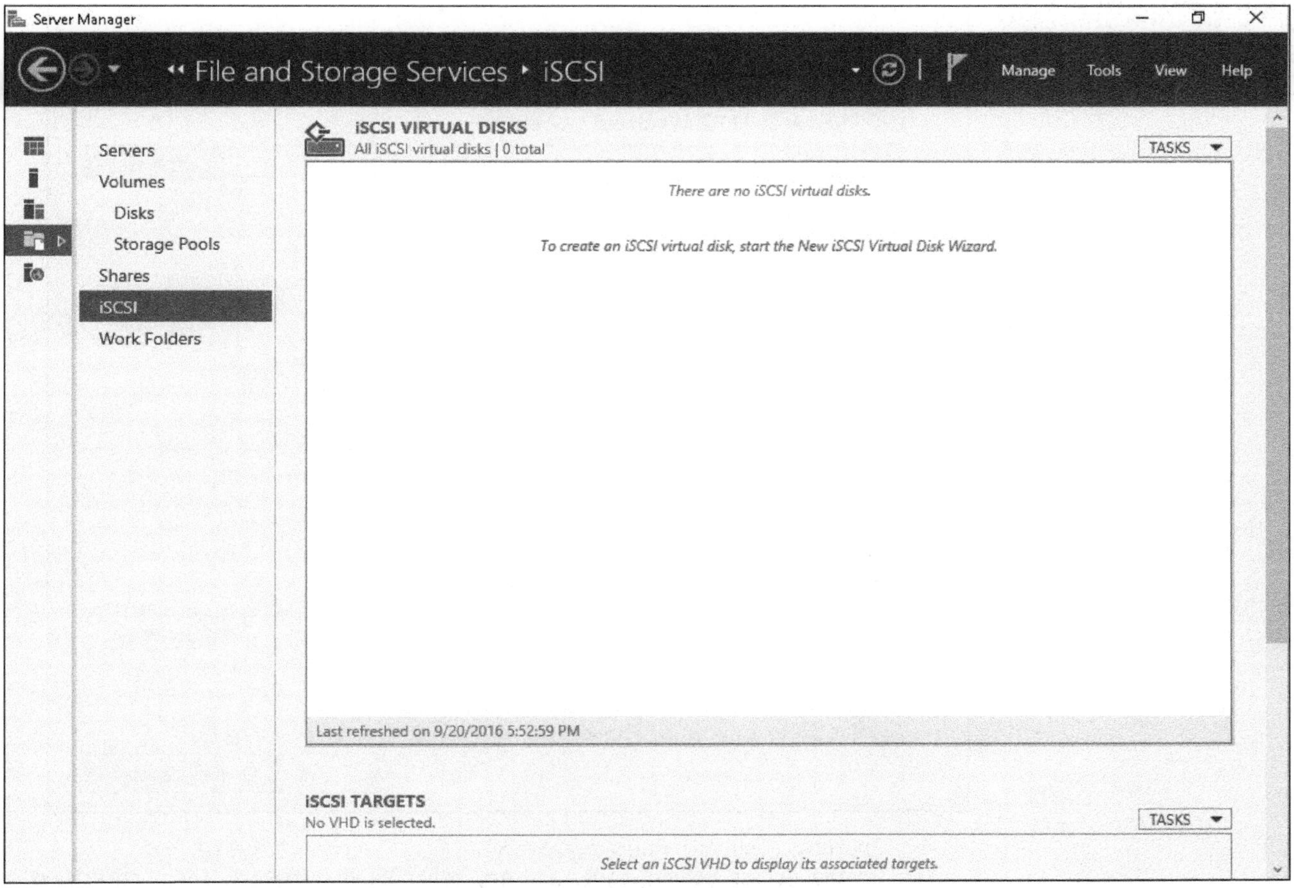

Figure 4-10

Managing iSCSI virtual disks

2. Click **To create an iSCSI virtual disk, start the New iSCSI Virtual Disk Wizard.** Alternatively, in the iSCSI Virtual Disks section, you can open the **Tasks** menu and click **New iSCSI Virtual Disk.**

3. On the Select Virtual Disk Location page, click a drive to store the iSCSI virtual disk and then click **Next.**

4. On the iSCSI Virtual Disk Name page, in the Name text box, type the name of the iSCSI virtual disk, such as **ISCSIDRIVEA.** Click **Next.**

5. On the iSCSI Virtual Disk Size page, specify the size in gigabytes (GB) of the iSCSI virtual disk, such as **5 GB.** Click **Next.**

6. On the iSCSI Target page, if targets have been defined previously, you can click a target and then click **Next.** To create a new target, click **New iSCSI target** and then click **Next.**

7. If you chose the New iSCSI target, on the Target Name and Access page, type the name of the target, such as **ISCSITarget1.** Click **Next.**

8. On the Access Servers page, click **Add.**

9. On the Add Initiator ID page (as shown in Figure 4-11), for the type, select **IQN,** **DNS Name, IP Address,** or **MAC address.** Then, in the Value text box, type the corresponding value for the initiator that matches the type. For example, specify IP Address, and the address of LON-SVR2, which is 172.16.0.12. Click **OK.**

Figure 4-11

Specifying the iSCSI initiators that can connect to the target

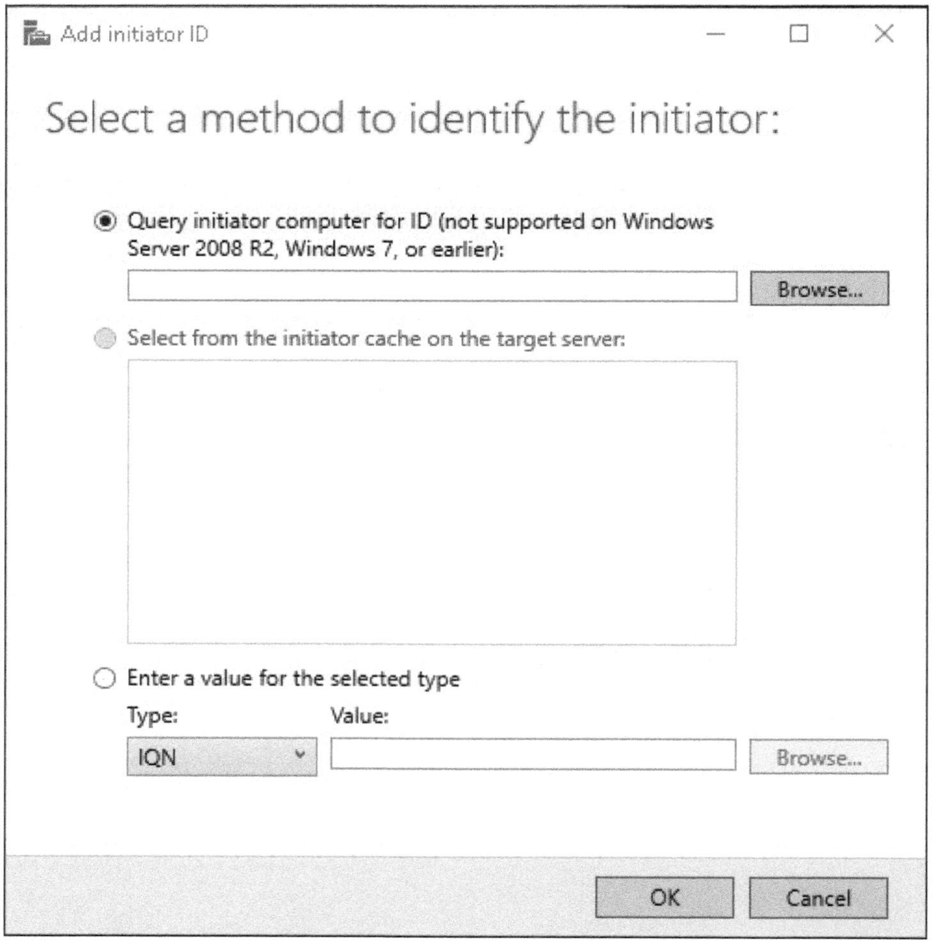

10. On the Access Servers page, add any other iSCSI initiators. Then, click **Next.**

11. On the Enable Authentication page, if you want to use authentication, select **Enable CHAP.** Then, type a user name and password. When done, click **Next.**

12. On the Confirmation page, click **Create**.

13. When the iSCSI virtual disk is created, click **Close**.

You can assign a current iSCSI virtual disk to an initiator by right-clicking the virtual disk and choosing Assign iSCSI Virtual Disk. You can modify the iSCSI targets by right-clicking an iSCSI target and choosing Properties.

Configuring Multi-Path I/O (MPIO)

A single connection to an iSCSI storage device makes the storage available, but it does not make the storage connections highly available. If the network connection or a switch fails, the server connecting to the iSCSI storage will lose access to its storage. Because many servers require high availability, you need to use high-availability technologies, such as multiple connected session (MCS) and multi-path I/O (MPIO).

CERTIFICATION READY
Configure Multi-Path
I/O (MPIO)
Objective 2.2

Multiple connected session (MCS) enables multiple TCP/IP connections from the initiator to the target for the same iSCSI session. If a failure occurs, all outstanding commands are reassigned to another connection automatically. Typically, MCS has better failover recovery and better performance than MPIO.

→ **ENABLE A MULTIPLE CONNECTED SESSION**

GET READY. To enable multiple connected sessions on Windows Server 2016, perform the following steps.

1. In Server Manager, click **Tools > iSCSI Initiator**. The iSCSI Initiator Properties dialog box opens.

2. On the Targets tab, click **Properties**. The Properties dialog box opens.

3. On the Sessions tab, under the Configure Multiple Connected Session (MCS) section, click **MCS**. The Multiple Connected Session (MCS) dialog box opens (see Figure 4-12).

Figure 4-12

Configuring MCS

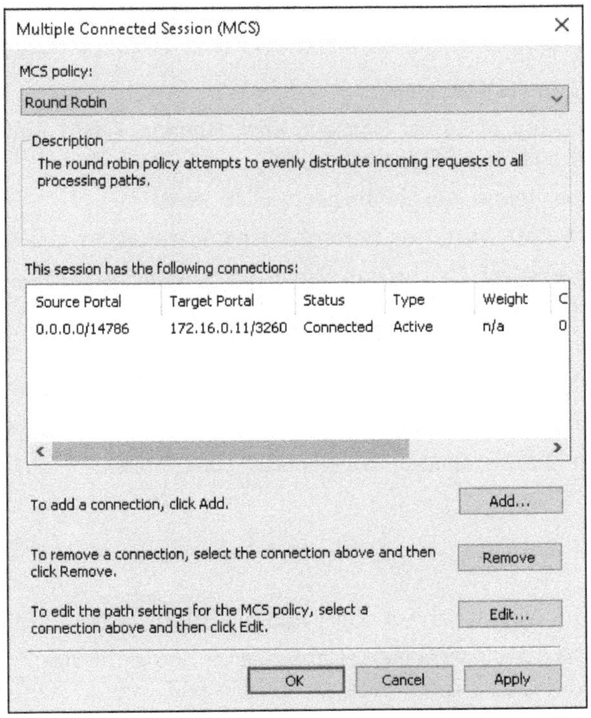

4. To add a second connection, click **Add** and click **Connect**.

5. In the Advanced dialog box, in the Initiator IP text box, specify an IP address for a second local network card. In the iSCSI target text box, specify the second remote target portal.

6. Click **OK** to close the Multiple Connected Session (MCS) dialog box and click **OK** to close the Properties dialog box.

7. Click **OK** to close the iSCSI Initiator Properties dialog box.

Often organizations need to have redundancy to provide high availability. Because a SAN can provide central storage to be used by multiple servers, the entire SAN infrastructure needs to be highly available, including disks and connections. *Multi-path I/O (MPIO)* is a multi-path solution that supports iSCSI, Fibre Channel, and serial attached storage (SAS) SAN connectivity by establishing multiple sessions or connections to the storage array. Multi-path solutions use redundancy path components, such as adapters, cables, and switches to create logical paths between the server and the storage device. To use MPIO, you can install multi-path I/O as a feature.

Configuring Internet Storage Name Service (iSNS)

The *Internet Storage Name Service (iSNS)* protocol is used to discover, manage, and configure iSCSI devices automatically on a TCP/IP network. iSNS is used to emulate Fibre Channel fabric services to provide a consolidated configuration point for an entire storage network.

CERTIFICATION READY
Configure iSNS
Objective 2.2

You can install iSNS as a feature. iSNS provides a registration function to enable entities in a storage network to register a query in the iSNS database. Both targets and initiators can register in the iSNS database. After information is entered in the database, targets and initiators can query information about other initiators and targets. For information to be entered into the database, you specify the iSNS server on the iSCSI Initiator's Discovery tab.

→ **INSTALL ISNS**

GET READY. To install iSNS on Windows Server 2016, perform the following steps.

1. Open Server Manager.

2. At the top of Server Manager, click **Manage > Add Roles and Features**. The Add Roles and Feature Wizard opens.

3. On the Before You Begin page, click **Next**.

4. Select **Role-based or feature-based installation** and then click **Next**.

5. On the Select Destination Server page, select the server that you are installing to and click **Next**.

6. On the Select Server Roles page, click **Next**.

7. On the Select Features page, click to select **iSNS Server service** and click **Next**.

8. On the Confirm Installation Selections page, click **Install**.

9. When the installation is complete, click **Close**.

You can start the iSNS Server from Administrative Tools or the Server Manager Tools menu. Registered iSCSI initiators and targets are listed in the iSNS Server Properties dialog box (see Figure 4-13). For more information about the initiator or target, click the iSCSI initiator or target and click Details.

Figure 4-13

Viewing registered iSCSI initiators and targets

Initiator Details   ×

iSCSI Name:

iqn.1991-05.com.microsoft:lon-svr2.adatum.com

Alias

<MS SW iSCSI Initiator>

Entity

LON-SVR2.Adatum.com

Portals

Portal IP Address   Portal Port

172.16.0.12   49724

Discovery Domains

Discovery Domain

Default DD

OK

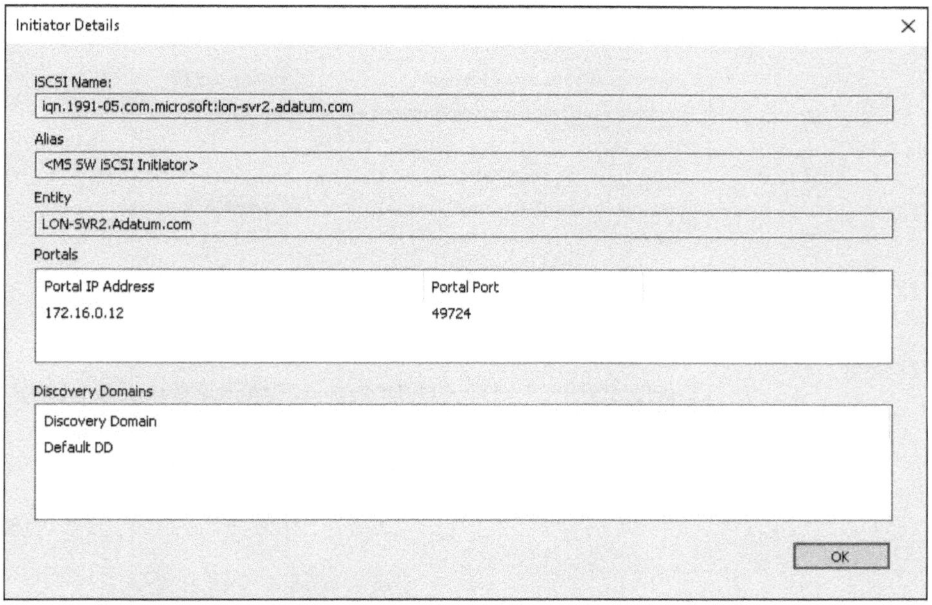

The ***Discovery Domain (DD)*** service allows the partitioning of storage nodes into management groupings (called *discovery domains*) for administrative and logon control purposes. The iSNS Server Properties start with the Default DD. You can create a new discovery domain by clicking Creating and typing the name of the discovery domain. Then click Add to add members.

You will need to connect your iSCSI initiators to the iSNS server to take advantage of the discovery functionality. This can be done on the Discovery tab in the iSNS server.

 ADDING iSNS SERVERS

GET READY. To install iSNS on Windows Server 2016, perform the following steps.

1. Open Server Manager.
2. Open the **Tools** menu and click **iSCSI Initiator.**
3. When the iSCSI Initiator Properties dialog box opens, click the **Discovery** tab, as shown in Figure 4-14.

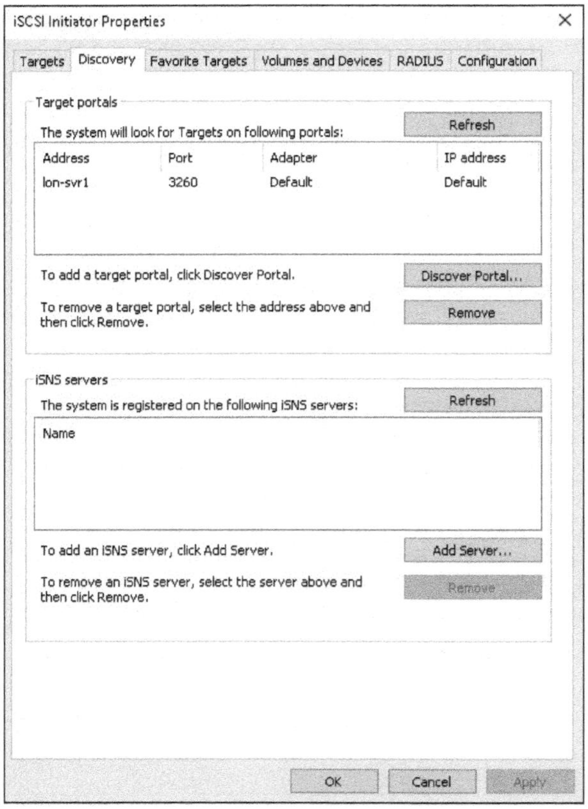

Figure 4-14

The Discovery tab

4. In the iSNS servers section, click the **Add Server** button.
5. When the iSCSI Initiator Properties dialog box opens, in the Enter the IP address or DNS name of the server, specify the name or address of the iSNS server.
6. To close the iSCSI Initiator Properties dialog box, click **OK.**

Using iSCSI Best Practices

When designing and implementing iSCSI, you need to follow the iSCSI best practices that are outlined in this section.

When designing your iSCSI storage solution, you should consider following best practices:

- You should deploy iSCSI on at least one 1-Gbps (gigabits per second) dedicated network.
- For production, you should design high availability, including redundant adapters, switches, and paths.
- Implement a security strategy for the iSCSI storage solution.
- For larger organizations, to ensure required performance levels, optimization, and security, be sure to engage various areas of specialization, including Windows administrators, network administrators, storage administrators, and security administrators. Also consider engaging administrators for specific applications, such as Microsoft Exchange Server and Microsoft SQL Server.

- Be sure to review vendor-specific best practices for all network devices and adapters.
- Be sure to review best practices for specific applications such as Exchange Server and SQL Server.

Configuring Data Center Bridging (DCB)

A ***converged network*** shares a single network infrastructure that handles storage, data, voice, video, cluster, and management traffic. ***Data Center Bridging (DCB)*** is a suite of Institute of Electrical and Electronics Engineers (IEEE) standards that supports converged networks so network traffic can get sufficient bandwidth allocation, while maintaining reliability.

CERTIFICATION READY
Configure Datacenter Bridging (DCB)
Objective 2.2

For you to use DCB, the converged network adapters, dedicated iSCSI host bus adapters (HBA), and related switches must support hardware-based Quality of Service (QoS) and other features of DCB. The feature of DCB include:

- **Congestion notification:** Manages congestion for protocols that do not have built-in control mechanisms
- **Priority-based flow control:** Controls the flow of data
- **Enhanced transmission selection:** Enables the system to reserve bandwidth for iSCSI and other network protocols
- **Data Center Bridging Capabilities eXchange (DCBX) protocol:** Enables devices such as the network adapters and switches to communicate and share capabilities and configuration information

When establishing QoS enforced by DCB, you first configure the switches and then create the QoS rules using Windows PowerShell. The four steps in configuring the QoS rules include:

1. Install the DCB feature with the `Install-WindowsFeature` cmdlet or Server Manager.
2. Create QoS rules using the `New-NetQoSPolicy` cmdlet that will classify protocols.
3. Create traffic classes for DCB using the `New-NetQoSTrafficClass` cmdlet.
4. Enable DCB on the NICs using the `Set-NetQosDcbxSetting` and `Enable-NetAdapterQos` cmdlets.

To create the QoS rules, you would use the `New-NetQoSPolicy` cmdlet. The priorities can range from 0 through 7. For example, the following command will classify SMB Direct that uses port 445:

```
New-NetQoSPolicy "SMB Direct" -NetDirect 445 -Priority 2

New-NetQosPolicy "Live Migration" -LiveMigration -Priority 5
```

The `New-NetQoSTrafficClass` cmdlet will create a class that matches the higher-level QoS rule. The command requires that you name the class, use a priority to pair the QoS rule, specify the fair ETS algorithm, and specify the minimum bandwidth weight. Enhanced Transmission Selection (ETS) is a transmission selection algorithm (TSA) that is specified by the IEEE 802.1Qaz draft standard.

```
New-NetQosTrafficClass "Live Migration" -Priority 5 -Algorithm ETS -Bandwidth 30

New-NetQosTrafficClass "SMB Direct" -Priority 2 -Algorithm ETS -Bandwidth 40
```

Lastly, on each server, enable the DCB settings with the following command:

```
Set-NetQosDcbxSetting -Willing $false
```

and enable DCB on the RDMA-capable NICs (rNICs). For example, to enable rNIC1, you would use the following command:

```
Enable-NetAdapterQos "rNIC1"
```

■ Implementing Storage Replica

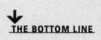 **THE BOTTOM LINE**

Storage Replica is new in Windows Server 2016 and can be used to synchronize data on a block level on two independent storage units. As a result, you can have multiple systems located at different sites access the same data.

Storage Replica offers both synchronous and asynchronous replication. Synchronous replication writes data to the primary and secondary sites at the same time so that the data remains current between sites. Asynchronous replication takes a store-and-forward approach that first writes data to the primary storage, and then copies the data to the replica. Asynchronous replication may occur in near-real-time or it may occur on a scheduled basis. Typically, synchronous is more expensive than asynchronous replication. If there is high latency between the two systems, you would use asynchronous replication.

Determining Usage Scenarios for Storage Replica

You can configure Storage Replica to replicate storage among servers and clusters, and clusters in different data centers. Storage Replica supports three scenarios: server-to-server, stretch cluster, and cluster-to-cluster.

Server-to-server replication is one of the simplest uses of storage replication where it replicates storage from one server to another server's storage. The requirements for server-to-server replication is:

- Both servers must be joined to a domain.
- You must have two sets of storage, using DAS, serial-attached SCSI JBODs, Fibre Channel SAN, or iSCSI Target.
- Each storage set must have at least two volumes, one for replicated data and one for logs. The sector size and volume size must be the same on all data disks on the physical storage and all the log disks also need to be the same sector size.
- At least 1-GbE connections on each file server, preferably 10 GbE, Internet Wide Area RDMA Protocol (iWARP), or InfiniBand.
- A network between the servers that has at least 1-Gbps throughput (preferably 8 Gbps or higher) and an average of less than or equal to 5-ms round-trip latency.
- A minimum of 4 GB of RAM in each server with at least two cores.
- A firewall that is configured to allow ICMP, SMB (port 445, plus 5445 for SMB Direct), and WS-MAN (port 5985) bidirectional traffic between all nodes.
- Local administrator permissions on all server nodes.

For example, to set up the server-to-server replication between LON-SVR1 and LON-SVR2, you would use the following Windows PowerShell command:

```
New-SRPartnership -SourceComputerName LON-SVR1

-SourceRGName RepGroup01 -SourceVolumeName F:

-SourceLogVolumeName G: -DestinationComputerName

LON-SVR2 -DestinationRGName RepGroup02

-DestinationVolumeName F: -DestinationLogVolumeName G:
-LogSizeInBytes 8GB
```

A *stretch cluster* is a Hyper-V cluster with nodes and storage in two locations. The cluster provides redundancy where the service provided by the cluster is still available, although one of the nodes is down or is not accessible.

The requirements for a stretch cluster are:

- Domain-joined servers.
- Physical servers for the Stretch Cluster Hyper-V scenario. You can use virtual machines for server-to-server and cluster-to-cluster.
- Two sets of shared storage, using serial attached SCSI JBODs, Fibre Channel SAN, or iSCSI Target.
- Each storage set must be able to create at least two virtual disks, one for replicated data and one for logs. The sector size must be the same on all data disks on the physical storage. All the log disks must be of the same sector size, but not necessarily the same as the data disks.
- At least 1-Gigabit Ethernet (GbE) connection on each file server, preferably 10 GbE, iWARP, or InfiniBand.
- A minimum of 4 GB of random access memory (RAM) in each server with at least two cores.
- A firewall that is configured to allow Internet Control Message Protocol (ICMP), SMB (port 445, plus 5445 for SMB Direct), and WS-MAN (port 5985) bidirectional traffic between all nodes.
- A network between the two sets of servers with at least 1-Gbps throughput (preferably 8 Gbps or higher) and an average of less than or equal to 5-milliseconds (ms) round-trip latency.
- Local administrator permissions on all server nodes.

If you want to configure Storage Replica for a stretched cluster in Failover Cluster Manager, perform the following steps:

1. Add a source data disk to a role or CSV.
2. Enable replication on the source data disk.
3. Select a destination data disk.
4. Select a source log disk.
5. Select a destination log disk.

➕ MORE INFORMATION

Stretch clusters are discussed in detail in Lesson 17 and Hyper-V is discussed in Lessons 7 through 10.

A *cluster-to-cluster replication* is when one failover cluster replicates its storage to another cluster. Different from a stretch cluster, the cluster-to-cluster does not require Hyper-V and the clusters can be next to each other or far apart. You configure and manage cluster-to-cluster replication similar to how you configure and manage server-to-server replication.

The requirements for cluster-to-cluster are as follows:

- Both servers must be joined to a domain.
- Two sets of shared storage, using Storage Spaces Direct, serial attached SCSI JBODs, Fibre Channel SAN, or iSCSI Target.
- Each storage set must be able to create at least two virtual disks, one for replicated data and one for logs. The sector size must be the same on all data disks on the physical storage. All the log disks must be of the same sector size, but not necessarily the same as the data disks.
- At least 1-GbE connections on each file server, preferably 10 GbE, iWARP, or InfiniBand.
- A minimum of 4 GB of RAM in each server with at least two cores.
- A firewall that is configured to allow ICMP, SMB (port 445, plus 5445 for SMB Direct), and WS-MAN (port 5985) bidirectional traffic between all nodes.
- A network between the two sets of servers that has at least 1-Gbps throughput (preferably 8 Gbps or higher) and an average of less than or equal to 5-ms round-trip latency.
- Local administrator permissions on all server nodes.

+ **MORE INFORMATION**

Clustering is discussed in detail in Lesson 15.

Implementing Storage Replica

CERTIFICATION READY
Implement Storage Replica for server-to-server, cluster-to-cluster, and stretch cluster scenarios
Objective 2.2

As mentioned before, the simplest storage replica is the server-to-server replica. Storage Replica can only do a one-to-one replication. In addition, Storage Replica is not suited for branch office replication because of higher latency and lower bandwidth. All Storage Replica scenarios require the Windows Server 2016 Datacenter Edition and GPT-initialized disks.

CERTIFICATION READY
Implement Storage Replica
Objective 5.2

To implement server-to-server replica, you need to first install the File Server service role. You will then use Windows PowerShell to configure the replica.

→ INSTALL THE FILE SERVER SERVICE ROLE

GET READY. To install the File Server service role on Windows Server 2016, perform the following steps on LON-SVR1 and LON-SVR2.

1. Open Server Manager.
2. In Server Manager, open the **Manage** menu and then click **Add Roles and Features.**
3. In the Add Roles and Features Wizard, on the Before You Begin page, click **Next.**
4. On the Select Installation Type page, click **Next.**

5. On the Select Destination Server page, select the appropriate server and click **Next**.

6. On the Select Server Roles page, expand **File and Storage Services (Installed)**, expand **File and iSCSI services**, and then click **File Server**.

7. Click **Next** two times.

8. On the Confirmation page, click **Install**.

9. When the Installation succeeded message appears, click **Close**.

➡ **CONFIGURE THE SERVER-TO-SERVER REPLICA'**

GET READY. To configure the server-to-server replica on Windows Server 2016, perform the following steps on LON-SVR1 and LON-SVR2.

1. Open the Windows PowerShell window.

2. Type the following two commands, pressing **Enter** after each command:

   ```
   MD c:\temp

   Test-SRTopology -SourceComputerName LON-SVR1

   -SourceVolumeName f: -SourceLogVolumeName g:

   -DestinationComputerName LON-SVR2

   -DestinationVolumeName f:

   -DestinationLogVolumeName g: -DurationInMinutes 5
   -ResultPath c:\temp
   ```

3. Open the report file TestSrTopologyReport.html and verify that you meet the Storage Replica requirements.

4. To configure server-to-server replication, at the Windows PowerShell command prompt, type the following command and then press **Enter**:

   ```
   New-SRPartnership -SourceComputerName LON-SVR1

   -SourceRGName rg01 -SourceVolumeName f:

   -SourceLogVolumeName g: -DestinationComputerName
   LON-SVR2 -DestinationRGName rg02

   -DestinationVolumeName f:

   -DestinationLogVolumeName g:
   ```

5. To verify the replication source and destination state, at the Windows PowerShell command prompt, type the following three commands pressing **Enter** after each command:

   ```
   Get-SRGroup

   Get-SRPartnership

   (Get-SRGroup).replicas
   ```

6. To verify the number of the remaining bytes to be replicated on the destination server, at the Windows PowerShell command prompt, type the following command and then press **Enter**:

   ```
   (Get-SRGroup).Replicas | Select-Object numofbytesremaining
   ```

SKILL SUMMARY

IN THIS LESSON YOU LEARNED:

- You can combine disks to create larger disks. In addition, based on the storage layout (spanned, mirror, and RAID-5), you can allow for better performance and fault tolerance.

- Storage Spaces is a feature in Windows Server 2016 that allows you to combine multiple disks into a single logical volume that can be mirrored to protect against one or more drive failures.

- Internet Small Computer System Interface (iSCSI) is a protocol that enables clients to send SCSI commands over a TCP/IP network using TCP port 3260. Unlike with Fibre Channel, you use standard Ethernet cabling and switches to connect servers to the SAN. Because you connect to the SAN over the network, you should use a minimum of two network adapters on the server, one for the SAN communications and one for standard network communications.

- Starting with Windows Server 2012, you can install the iSCSI Target Server role, so that other Windows servers can provide iSCSI storage to other clients (including other Windows servers). After you install the iSCSI Target Server role, you use Server Manager to create the volumes that will be presented to clients and specify which servers can access the iSCSI LUNs. To connect to an iSCSI target, you use an iSCSI initiator.

- Storage Replica is new in Windows Server 2016 and can be used to synchronize data on a block level on two independent storage units. As a result, you can have multiple systems located at different sites access the same data.

■ Knowledge Assessment

Multiple Choice

Select the correct answer for each of the following questions.

1. Which of the following drives can be added to a storage pool? (Choose all that apply.)
   a. SATA
   b. eSATA
   c. USB
   d. SCSI

2. When creating a storage space, which of the following resiliency settings requires at least five drives?
   a. Parity
   b. Three-way mirror
   c. Two-way mirror
   d. Simple

3. Which of the following processes reserves space for future use when working with storage spaces/storage pools?
   a. Partitions
   b. Thin provisioning
   c. SMB blocks
   d. Provisioned storage blocks

4. When creating a storage space, how many disks are needed when setting up parity for resiliency settings in a storage pool?
   a. 2
   b. 3
   c. 5
   d. 4

5. Which of the following statements are true of striped volumes? (Choose all that apply.)
   a. Striped volumes provide enhanced performance over simple volumes.
   b. Striped volumes provide greater fault tolerance than simple volumes.
   c. You can extend striped volumes after creation.
   d. If a single physical disk in the striped volume fails, all of the data in the entire volume is lost.

6. When creating storage spaces, which of the following types of resiliency works best for protection against two drives failing simultaneously while setting up storage spaces?
   a. Three-way mirror
   b. Two-way mirror
   c. Parity
   d. Simple

7. Which of the following approaches is best when reserving at least 500 GB of space for a new storage space when there is only 100 GB of actual physical disk space?
   a. Wait until there is enough physical disk capacity to create the 500-GB storage space.
   b. Purchase new drives before creating the space.
   c. Use thin provisioning and create the larger space. Drives can be purchased later when needed.
   d. Configure one pool now and another when the drives are available.

8. Which protocol allows a server to connect to a SAN by sending SCSI commands over a TCP/IP network?
   a. Fibre Channel
   b. iSCSI
   c. SATA
   d. MPIO

9. Which port is used by iSCSI?
   a. 1080
   b. 8080
   c. 3260
   d. 4800

10. Which client connects to an iSCSI SAN?
    a. iSCSI target
    b. iSCSI source
    c. iSCSI receiver
    d. iSCSI initiator

11. Which of the following can be installed so that Windows Server 2016 can be used to present iSCSI volumes to Windows servers?
    a. iSCSI target
    b. iSCSI source
    c. iSCSI receiver
    d. iSCSI initiator

12. Which of the following is a unique identifier that is used to identify iSCSI initiators and targets?
    a. iSNS
    b. IQN
    c. MPIO
    d. MPC

13. Which protocol is used for authentication for iSCSI?
    a. PAP
    b. CHAP
    c. MS-CHAPv2
    d. SPAP

14. Which of the following can be used to encrypt iSCSI traffic?
    a. CHAP
    b. IPsec
    c. BitLocker
    d. EFS

15. Which technologies can help make iSCSI highly available? (Choose two answers.)
    a. MCS
    b. EFS
    c. LUNX
    d. MPIO

16. Which of the following is used to automatically discover, manage, and configure iSCSI devices?
    a. LUN
    b. IQN
    c. MPIP
    d. iSNS

Best Answer

Choose the letter that corresponds to the best answer. More than one answer choice may achieve the goal. Select the BEST answer.

1. A company uses nearly 30 servers, all running Windows Server 2016 and each using iSCSI storage. The small team of administrators is complaining that it is becoming difficult to locate the available iSCSI resources on the network. Which of the following can be used to help the administrators quickly locate iSCSI resources?
    a. DNS
    b. iSNS
    c. iSCSI Target Storage Provider
    d. Windows Standard-Based Storage Management feature

2. Which PowerShell cmdlet should be used to view the iSCSI initiator connections?
    a. Get-IscsiConnection
    b. Get-IscsiSession
    c. Get-IscsiTarget
    d. Connect-IscsiTarget

3. As an administrator, you are configuring an iSCSI Target Server role and multiple volumes that will be assigned to multiple servers using iSCSI initiators. Because these servers contain confidential information, you want to make sure that they are not accessed by other servers using an iSCSI initiator. Which of the following statements best describes the recommended course of action?

    a. You should specify the initiator ID that can connect when creating the iSCSI virtual disk.

    b. You should specify the initiator ID that can connect when creating the iSCSI target.

    c. You should enable IPsec.

    d. You should configure the iSCSI ACL list when he configures the iSCSI initiator.

Matching and Identification

1. Specify the correct order of steps necessary to creating an iSCSI virtual disk. Not all steps will be used.

    _____ Specify the access servers.

    _____ Specify the IP address of the iSCSI volumes.

    _____ Specify the size of the virtual disk.

    _____ Specify the location of the iSCSI virtual disk.

    _____ Specify the IPsec password.

    _____ Specify the name of the iSCSI virtual disk.

    _____ Specify the type of volume.

2. Specify the correct order of the IQN components that make up an IQN string.

    _____ `microsoft`

    _____ `1992-03`

    _____ `iqn`

    _____ `:storage01-targetnew-target`

    _____ `com`

Build a List

1. Specify the correct order of steps necessary to creating a storage pool.

    _____ Click Create pool.

    _____ Log on with administrative credentials.

    _____ Select the drive(s) you want to include in the new storage pool.

    _____ Click Create a new pool and storage space.

    _____ Connect the drives to your computer.

    _____ Press the Windows logo key + r, type Storage Spaces, and then select it from the Results list.

    _____ From the Results list, click Storage Spaces.

■ Business Case Scenarios

Scenario 4-1: Creating a Large Volume

You have a new desktop running Windows Server 2016. However, you try to copy your file repository and find out that you do not have enough disk space. You have 400 GB of free disk space on your C drive and you have three smaller 500-GB drives. Describe the recommended course of action.

Scenario 4-2: Using iSCSI Devices

As an administrator for the Contoso Corporation, you manage a large server that is running Windows Server 2016 and that has about 8 TB of disk space that you can allocate to be used by other servers. Describe how to configure the servers such that the two other servers running Windows Server 2016 can use the disk space just as if the disk space was local?

Implementing Data Deduplication

70-740 EXAM OBJECTIVE

Objective 2.3 – Implement data deduplication. This objective may include but is not limited to the following: Implement and configure deduplication; determine appropriate usage scenarios for deduplication; monitor deduplication; implement a backup and restore solution with deduplication.

LESSON HEADING	EXAM OBJECTIVE
Implementing Data Deduplication	Determine appropriate usage scenarios for deduplication
– Determining Appropriate Usage Scenarios for Deduplication	
– Implementing and Configuring Deduplication	Implement and configure deduplication
– Monitoring Deduplication	Monitor deduplication
– Implementing a Backup and Restore Solution with Deduplication	Implement a backup and restore solution with deduplication

KEY TERMS

data deduplication   Deduplication Evaluation Tool (DDPEVAL.exe)

Implementing Data Deduplication

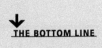

THE BOTTOM LINE

Data deduplication was introduced with Windows Server 2012 to reduce disk space by removing duplicate data to preserve storage capacity. Data deduplication breaks data into small chunks, identifies the duplicates, and maintains a single copy of each chunk. Data deduplication is ideal for general shared folders, such as public and home folders, offline folders, images, software deployment shares, and VHD libraries that store VHD files.

As server administrator, you will find many situations where you have to deal with large repositories of data. Because servers are being consolidated into a virtual environment, you need to plan your server storage to be scalable and optimized for data.

Data deduplication can provide the following:

- **Capacity optimization:** Data deduplication stores more data in less physical space, even more efficient than NTFS compression. It can deliver optimization ratios of 2:1 for general file servers and up to 20:1 for virtualization data.

- **Scale and performance:** Data deduplication is highly scalable, resource efficient, and nonintrusive. Although Windows Server 2012 R2 can process about 50 MB per second, Windows Server 2016 has an improved Deduplication Processing Pipeline to provide even better performance. To minimize the effect of deduplication on a server, Windows Server 2016 deduplication throttles the processor and memory processors. You can also schedule data deduplication jobs to periods when the server is not being heavily used and you can establish file selection policies.

- **Reliability and data integrity:** When data deduplication is applied to a volume on a server, the integrity of the data is maintained. Data deduplication uses checksum results, consistency, and identity validation to ensure data integrity. Data deduplication maintains redundancy, for all metadata and the most frequently referenced data, to ensure that the data is repaired, or at least recoverable, in the event of data corruption.

- **Optimization over the site links:** BranchCache is a WAN acceleration/bandwidth optimization technology that caches data for branch offices so that remote data does not always have to be accessed over the slower WAN links. When you combine data deduplication with BranchCache, the same optimization techniques are applied to data transferred over the WAN to a branch office, which results in faster file download times and reduced bandwidth consumption.

- **Supporting large volumes and file sizes:** Windows Server 2016 data deduplication supports volume sizes up to 64 TB and support for file sizes up to 1 TB. In addition, the Deduplication Processing Pipeline is now multithreaded and able to utilize multiple CPUs per volume to increase optimization throughput.

- **Supporting Nano Severs and failover cluster:** Windows Server 2016 deduplication supports Nano Servers and failover clustering. In addition, data deduplication in Windows Server 2016 allows you to efficiently store, transfer, and back up fewer bits.

Data deduplication potentially can process all of the data on a selected volume, except for files that are less than 32 KB in size and files in folders that are excluded. You must carefully determine if a server and its attached volumes are suitable candidates for deduplication prior to enabling the feature. You should also consider backing up important data regularly during the deduplication process.

Determining Appropriate Usage Scenarios for Deduplication

Data deduplication can be used for almost any situation where you need to reduce disk space usage. You can use data deduplication for user documents, software deployment shares, virtualization libraries, and general file shares.

CERTIFICATION READY
Determine appropriate
usage scenarios for
deduplication
Objective 2.3

The data storage savings will vary by data type, the mix of the data, the size of the volume, and the size of the files. The following list shows you the type of savings you might see with data deduplication:

- **User documents:** Stores documents, photos, music, and videos; saves up to 30% to 50% of your system's storage space
- **Software deployment shares:** Stores software binaries, cab files, and symbols files; saves up to 70% to 80% of your system's storage space
- **Virtualization libraries:** Stores virtual hard disk files; saves up to 80% to 95% of your system's storage space
- **General file share:** Stores a mix of user documents, software deployment shares, and virtualization libraries; saves up to 50% to 60% of your system's storage space

Ideal candidates for data deduplication include:

- Folder redirection servers and user home folders
- Virtualization depots or provisioning libraries
- Software deployment shares
- SQL Server and Exchange Server backup volumes
- Scale-out File Servers (SoFS) CSVs
- Virtualized disk backups
- Virtual desktop infrastructure (VDI) virtual hard disks

Implementing and Configuring Deduplication

To implement data deduplication in Windows Server 2016, you just have to install the Data Deduplication role service. After the service role is installed, you then configure each volume for data deduplication.

CERTIFICATION READY
Implement and configure
deduplication
Objective 2.3

The Data Deduplication role service consists of the following components:

- **Filter driver:** Monitors local or remote I/O and handles the chunks of data on the file system by interacting with the various jobs. There is one filter driver for every volume.
- **Deduplication service:** Manages optimization by managing multiple jobs that perform deduplication and compression of files. It performs garbage collection, removing data chunks that are no longer being referenced, and it scrubs the volume by checking and maintaining data integrity. In addition, deduplication keeps backup copies of popular chunks when they are referenced over 100 times in an area called the hotspot.
- **Unoptimization:** Undoes deduplication on all the optimized files on the volume, such as when you are decommissioning a server with volumes enabled for data deduplication, troubleshooting issues with deduplicated data, or migrating data to another system that doesn't support data deduplication.

By default, data deduplication does not attempt to deduplicate a file until after three days. Data deduplication runs garbage collection once an hour. You can also define an exclusion list, which will specify which files to exclude from deduplication.

Data deduplication can be implemented on nonremovable NTFS or ReFS drives but not on system or boot volumes or Cluster Share Volumes (CSVs). Lastly, files smaller than 32 KB or those that are encrypted aren't processed.

→ INSTALL AND ENABLE DATA DEDUPLICATION

GET READY. To install and enable data deduplication, perform the following steps.

1. Using Server Manager, open the **Manage** menu and select **Add Roles and Features.**
2. When the Add Roles and Features Wizard opens, on the Before You Begin page, click **Next.**
3. On the Installation Type page, Role-based or features-based installation is selected. Click **Next.**
4. On the Select Destination Server page, click **Next.**
5. On the Select Server Roles page, expand **File and Storage Services**, expand **File and iSCSI Services**, and select **Data Deduplication.** Click **Next.**
6. On the Select Features page, click **Next.**
7. On the Confirmation page, click **Install.**
8. When data deduplication is installed, click **Close.**
9. On Server Manager, click **File and Storage Services** and then click **Volumes.**
10. Right-click a volume and choose **Configure Data Deduplication.**
11. When the New Volume Deduplication Settings dialog box opens, click the down arrow for the Data deduplication option and select **General purpose file server** (as shown in Figure 5-1).

Figure 5-1

Configuring deduplication

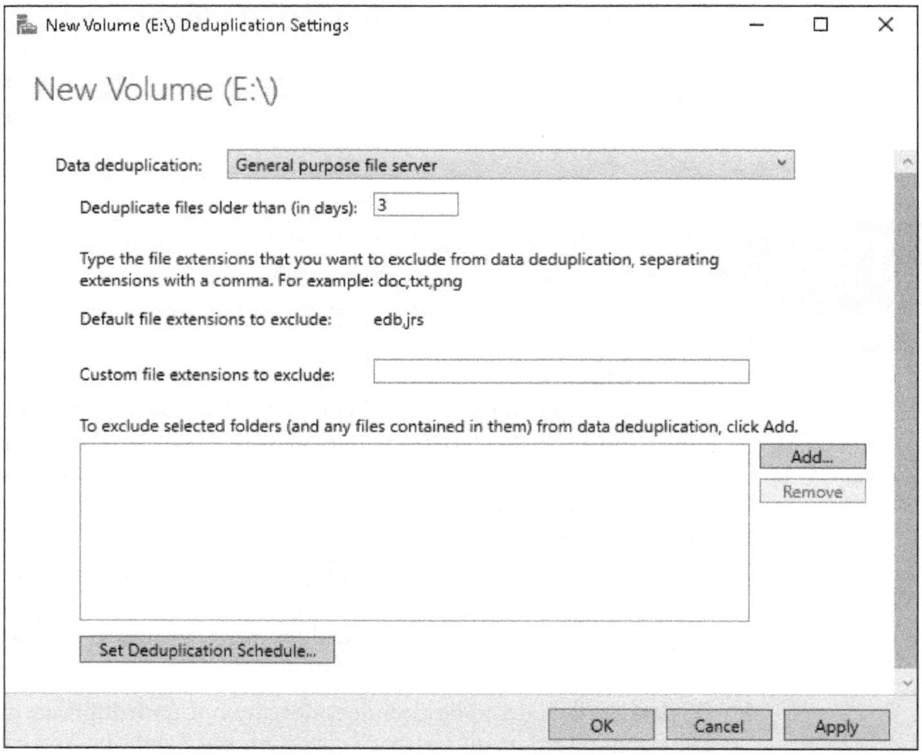

New Volume (E:\) Deduplication Settings — □ ×

New Volume (E:\)

Data deduplication: General purpose file server ⌄

Deduplicate files older than (in days): 3

Type the file extensions that you want to exclude from data deduplication, separating extensions with a comma. For example: doc,txt,png

Default file extensions to exclude: edb,jrs

Custom file extensions to exclude: _____

To exclude selected folders (and any files contained in them) from data deduplication, click Add.

[   ] Add...
                        Remove

Set Deduplication Schedule...

OK   Cancel   Apply

12. Click **OK.**

Monitoring Deduplication

> After you deploy data deduplication, you need to monitor and maintain the systems that are enabled for data deduplication to ensure optimal performance. After data deduplication is installed, you can use the ***Deduplication Evaluation Tool (DDPEVAL.exe)*** command-line tool to estimate capacity savings on Windows. The Windows PowerShell `Measure-DedupFileMetaData` cmdlet determines the amount of disk that can be reclaimed by using deduplication.

CERTIFICATION READY
Monitor deduplication
Objective 2.3

In most deployments, deduplication operates in the background. However, you can change the deduplication to occur on a daily schedule as long as deduplication is able to optimize all of the data churned on a daily basis. However, if the data cannot be processed on a daily basis, or you are experiencing low optimization rates, you might need to use smaller volumes and/or increase the number of processors.

To monitor deduplication in your environment and to report on its health, you use the following Windows PowerShell cmdlets:

- **Get-DedupStatus:** Returns the deduplication status for volumes that have data deduplication metadata, which includes the deduplication rate, the number/sizes of optimized files, the last run time of the deduplication jobs, and the amount of space saved on the volume.

- **Get-DedupVolume:** Returns the deduplication status for volumes that have data deduplication metadata. The metadata includes the deduplication rate, the number/sizes of optimized files, and deduplication settings such as minimum file age, minimum file size, excluded files/folders, compression-excluded file types, and the chunk redundancy threshold.

- **Get-DedupMetadata:** Returns status information of the deduplicated data store for volumes that have data deduplication metadata, which includes the number of data chunks in a container, the number of containers in the data store, the number of data streams in a container, the number of containers in the stream map store, the number of hotspots in a container, the number of hotspots in the stream map store, and the number of corruptions on the volume.

- **Get-DedupJob:** Returns the deduplication status and information for currently running or queued deduplication jobs.

So when you execute the `Get-DedupStatus` cmdlet, you can compare the number of optimized files with the number of in-policy files. If the number of in-policy files is continuously rising faster than the number of optimized files, you should consider upgrading your hardware. However, if the output value from the cmdlet for `LastOptimizationResult` is 0x00000000, the entire data set was processed successfully during the previous optimization job.

Lastly, if you suspect problems with data deduplication, you should check the Event Viewer logs, specifically Applications and Services Logs > Microsoft > Windows > Deduplication. Event ID 6153 will provide you with the elapsed time of a deduplication job and the throughput rate.

After data has been deduplicated, you can use the following Windows PowerShell cmdlets to ensure deduplication is running efficiently:

- **Update-DedupStatus:** Because some of the storage cmdlets, such as `Get-DedupStatus` and `Get-DedupVolume`, retrieve information from the cached metadata, the `Update-DedupStatus` cmdlet scans volumes to compute new data deduplication information for updating the metadata.

- **Start-DedupJob:** This cmdlet is used to launch ad hoc deduplication jobs, such as optimization, garbage collection, scrubbing, and unoptimization.

- **Measure-DedupFileMetadata:** This cmdlet is used to measure potential disk space on a volume after files have been deduplicated.

- **Expand-DedupFile:** This cmdlet expands an optimized file into its original location, which might be needed for application compatibility problems.

Note: While allowing deduplication to manage memory allocation automatically is recommended, you might need to adjust the maximum percentage in some scenarios. For most of these scenarios, you should consider a maximum percentage within a range of 15 to 50, and a higher memory consumption for jobs that you schedule to run when you specify the `StopWhenSystemBusy` parameter. For garbage collection and scrubbing deduplication jobs, which you typically schedule to run after business hours, you can consider using a higher memory consumption, such as 50.

Implementing a Backup and Restore Solution with Deduplication

By using data deduplication, you can perform backup and restore operations faster if you are performing a block-based backup because you have less data to back up. File-based backup operations would not benefit from data deduplication because it would copy the files in their original format.

The following backup and restore scenarios are supported with deduplication in Windows Server 2016:

- Individual file backup/restore
- Full volume backup/restore
- Optimized file-level backup/restore using VSS writer

On the other hand, the following backup and restore scenarios are not supported with deduplication in Windows Server 2016:

- Backup or restore of only the reparse points
- Backup or restore of only the chunk store

In addition, a backup application can perform an incremental optimized backup as follows:

- Back up only the changed files created, modified, or deleted since your last backup.
- Back up the changed chunk store container files.
- Perform an incremental backup at the sub-file level.

When using third-party backup software, you should always confirm with the software vendor whether the backup solution supports data deduplication in Windows Server 2016 to avoid corruption after a restore.

SKILL SUMMARY

IN THIS LESSON YOU LEARNED:

- Data deduplication was introduced with Windows Server 2012 that reduces disk space by removing duplicate data to preserve storage capacity. Data deduplication breaks data into small chunks, identifies the duplicates, and maintains a single copy of each chunk. Data deduplication is ideal for general shared folders, such as public and home folders, offline folders, images, software deployment shares, and VHD libraries that store VHD files.

- Data deduplication can be used for almost any situation where you need to reduce disk space usage. You can use data deduplication for user documents, software deployment shares, virtualization libraries, and general file shares.

- To implement data deduplication in Windows Server 2016, you just have to install the Data Deduplication role service. After the service role is installed, you then configure each volume for data deduplication.

- After you deploy data deduplication, you need to monitor and maintain the systems that are enabled for data deduplication to ensure optimal performance.

- By using data deduplication, you can perform backup and restore operations faster if you are performing a block-based backup because you have less data to back up. File-based backup operations would not benefit from data deduplication because it would simply copy the files in their original format.

■ Knowledge Assessment

Multiple Choice

Select the correct answer for each of the following questions.

1. Which technology is used to reduce disk space usage by eliminating blocks of data that are repeated among files?
   a. Compression
   b. Deduplication
   c. Encryption
   d. Search and Destroy

2. When using deduplication, which of the following ratios would be expected for general files?
   a. 1:1
   b. 2:1
   c. 3:1
   d. 4:1
   e. 20:1

3. Which of the following is the maximum size file supported by Windows Deduplication?
   a. 100 MB
   b. 256 MB
   c. 10 GB
   d. 1 TB
   e. 10 TB

4. Which tool is used to estimate the deduplication capacity savings on Windows?
   a. Server Manager
   b. Repadmin
   c. Deduplication Estimation Tool
   d. Deduplication Evaluation Tool

5. Which type of backup would benefit from Windows deduplication?
   a. Block-based backups
   b. File-based backups
   c. Chunk store backups
   d. Reparse point backups

6. Which command can be used to view the status of a volume that is configured to use Windows deduplication?
   a. `Get-DedupStatus`
   b. `Get-DedupVolume`
   c. `Get-DedupJob`
   d. `Get-DedupVolumeStatus`

Best Answer

Choose the letter that corresponds to the best answer. More than one answer choice may achieve the goal. Select the BEST answer.

1. You are the administrator for an organization that provides 70 sites in which users store their home and shared public folders. These sites use DFS to replicate files to four subsidiary servers. Which of the following can be used to significantly reduce the file size while maintaining performance?
   a. EFS
   b. NTFS encryption
   c. Data deduplication
   d. Disk Cleanup

Matching and Identification

1. Match the PowerShell command with the appropriate description.
   ___ a. Get-DedupJob
   ___ b. Measure-DedupFileMetadata
   ___ c. Update-DedupStatus
   ___ d. Measure-DedupFileMetadata
   ___ e. Get-DedupVolume
   1. Returns the deduplication status for volumes that have data deduplication metadata
   2. Measures potential disk space on a volume after files have been deduplicated.
   3. Returns the deduplication status and information for currently running or queued deduplication jobs
   4. Scans volumes to compute new data deduplication information for updating the metadata
   5. Measures potential disk space on volumes after files have been deduplicated

Build a List

1. Specify the correct order of the steps necessary to installing and configuring Windows Server 2016 data deduplication.

   _____ Select General purpose file server.

   _____ Click Install.

   _____ Click Add Roles and Features.

   _____ Click File and Storage Services > Volumes.

   _____ Open Server Manager.

   _____ Select File and Storage Services > File and iSCSI Services > Data Deduplication.

   _____ Click Configure Data Deduplication.

■ Business Case Scenarios

Scenario 5-1: Reducing Disk Space

As an administrator for the Contoso Corporation, you manage a server that uses three data drives; each data drive is 4 TB, combined as a single drive letter. There is about 11 TB of data and you need to add 3 TB of data. Describe your solution.

Creating, Managing, and Maintaining Images for Deployment

70-740 EXAM OBJECTIVE

Objective 1.3 – Create, manage, and maintain images for deployment. This objective may include but is not limited to the following: Plan for Windows Server virtualization; plan for Linux and FreeBSD deployments; assess virtualization workloads using the Microsoft Assessment and Planning (MAP) Toolkit; determine considerations for deploying workloads into virtualized environments; update images with patches, hotfixes, and drivers; install roles and features in offline images; manage and maintain Windows Server Core, Nano Server images, and VHDs using Windows PowerShell. *Manage and maintain VHDs using Windows PowerShell is also covered in Lesson 3.*

LESSON HEADING	EXAM OBJECTIVE
Understanding Images	Update images with patches, hotfixes, and drivers
– Selecting Image Characteristics	
– Selecting Image Types	Manage and maintain Windows Server Core, Nano Server images, and VHDs using Windows PowerShell
– Determining the Number of Images	
– Updating Images with Patches, Hotfixes, and Drivers	Install roles and features in offline images
– Managing and Maintaining Images with Windows PowerShell	
– Installing Features for Offline Images	
Implementing a Server Deployment Infrastructure with WDS	
– Deploying WDS	
– Configuring and Managing Boot, Install, and Discover Images	
Designing a Server Implementation Using Windows Assessment and Deployment Kit (ADK)	
– Using Windows PE	
– Creating and Configuring a Reference Computer and Image	
– Creating and Using Answer Files with Windows SIM	
– Using Sysprep to Prepare the Reference Computer	
– Capturing a Reference Image Using DISM	
– Performing an Unattended Installation Using WDS	

(continued)

LESSON HEADING	EXAM OBJECTIVE
Introducing Microsoft Deployment Toolkit (MDT)	
– Understanding the MDT Deployment Process	
– Installing MDT 2013	
– Configuring MDT 2013	
Planning for Windows Server Virtualizations	Plan for Windows Server virtualization
– Determining Considerations for Deploying Workloads into Virtualized Environments	Determine considerations for deploying workloads into virtualized environments
– Using the Microsoft Assessment and Planning (MAP) Toolkit	
– Accessing Virtualization Workloads	Assess virtualization workloads using the Microsoft Assessment and Planning (MAP) Toolkit
Planning for Linux and FreeBSD Deployments	Plan for Linux and FreeBSD deployments

KEY TERMS

answer file

boot image

capture image

Deployment Image Servicing and Management (dism.exe)

Deployment Server

discover image

DISM cmdlets

features

file-based disk image

hybrid images

image

image file

image group

install image

Lite-Touch Installation (LTI)

Microsoft Assessment and Planning (MAP) Toolkit

Microsoft Deployment Toolkit (MDT) 2013

Preboot eXecution Environment (PXE)

reference computer

sector-based image

System Image Manager (SIM)

System Preparation Utility (sysprep.exe)

task sequences

thick images

thin images

Transport Server

User-Driven Installation (UDI)

virtual hard disk (VHD)

virtual machines (VMs)

Windows Assessment and Deployment Kit (ADK)

Windows Deployment Services (WDS)

Windows Deployment Services Capture Utility

Windows Imaging Format (WIM)

Windows Preinstallation Environment (Windows PE)

Zero-Touch Installation (ZTI)

■ Understanding Images

Images are a key component used to deploy Windows to server and client computers. Without images, you would have to install Windows and all applications, update Windows and the applications, and configure Windows and the applications each time you wanted to deploy a server. Installing, updating, and configuring the computer might take several hours. When you must install many servers within a relatively short period of time, you can either hire several people to perform these tasks or develop a faster way to deploy the servers. Images can reduce the time it takes to deploy a computer.

An *image* is a single file or other storage device that contains the complete contents and structures of a disk or other data storage device used with computers and other computing devices. The image has all the necessary information install a copy of Windows onto another machine. Often, the images can contain additional software packages, drivers, and features, which also are deployed as a single complete package.

In the simplest method, an image is created from a reference or master computer. On the *reference computer*, you install Windows, install any necessary drivers, configure Windows, install additional software, and configure the additional software. You also should update and patch Windows and any applications that run on the computer. When you are done, the reference computer becomes a pristine computer that you can hand to a user, ready to use. Instead of giving the computer to a user, capture the content of the system by copying the drive's content to an image file. You can store and access this image from a central location so that you can copy it to other computers.

When creating the reference computer, you want to take time and care to ensure that it is properly installed and configured, that Windows and the applications are running properly, and that the desktop environment is clean and ready for any user to use. You also need to ensure that the computer follows any policies established within your organization and that it fits into the security model established by the organization. By taking extra time to configure the reference computer and create the image, you save lots of time and effort in the future as you deploy that image to a hundred or more computers.

Sometimes, a system becomes corrupted or badly misconfigured, causing the system to become unreliable or unresponsive. You can use images to refresh computers. So rather than wasting hours working on one computer that a technician might or might not be able to fix, you can use a new image to overwrite the computer drive, essentially making the computer new again. Of course, doing so would not fix a hardware failure unless that failure is caused by a corrupted driver. Remember that the hard device is a physical component; the driver is a software component that controls the devices.

Selecting Image Characteristics

As explained earlier, a disk image is a single file that contains a disk's complete contents and structure. However, a disk image is just one of several different types of images. Before you choose a specific image type, you need to understand the various types of images.

When selecting the image type, you need to understand the following:

- Thin, thick, and hybrid images
- Sector-based and file-based formats
- Image type (boot, install, capture, or discover)
- Image format (VHD or WIM)

SELECTING THICK IMAGES, THIN IMAGES, AND HYBRID IMAGES

During the planning phase of a deployment project or as a standard procedure when deploying servers, you need to determine whether to create a thick image, thin image, or hybrid image. How you deploy applications varies, depending on the type of image you select.

Thick images are monolithic images that contain the operating system, all core applications, language packs, and other files. In this case, monolithic indicates massive or huge. Thick images have the following advantages over thin images:

- Because they include all applications, they are simple to deploy.
- After a thick image is deployed, applications and language packs are available immediately to the end user.

Thick images also have the following disadvantages:

- Each image file is large.
- Creating and testing an image requires a lot of work.
- Updating a thick image (such as adding an application, adding a patch or update, or upgrading a new version of an application) requires rebuilding, retesting, and redistributing the image.
- Either all computers receive all applications whether they are needed or not, or many different thick images must be developed and maintained.

Thin images, as you can surmise, are the opposite of thick images. They contain the operating system and software updates. Typically, they contain no or few core applications but no language packs. When a new computer is deployed, the thin image is deployed first. Then, after the thin image is successfully deployed, the system and software installation is customized, usually over the network. Thin images have the following advantages over thick images:

- Thin images cost less to build, maintain, and test.
- Storage costs are lower because the image size is smaller.
- Thin images are more flexible than thick images.

Thin images have the following disadvantages:

- The initial deployment of thin images, followed by applications and language packs, is a more complex process than deploying thick images.
- Thin images usually require scripting and/or a software distribution infrastructure to deploy the additional software packages and language packs.
- Fully deploying a system takes longer because it is done in multiple parts back to back.
- Core applications and language packs are not available when end users first start their computers.
- More traffic is generated over the network.

Hybrid images mix thin and thick image strategies, which include applications that everyone uses or needs (such as the operating system, VPN software, antivirus software, and Microsoft Office). Therefore, as a hybrid image is deployed, users can quickly have the necessary applications to perform their jobs. Hybrid images still require a longer install time than a thick image, but not as long as a thin image. Using hybrid images takes advantage of the single instancing in a Windows image by combining multiple hybrid images into a single WIM file.

SELECTING SECTOR-BASED IMAGES OR FILE-BASED IMAGES

Some system image programs use sector-based images, whereas others use file-based images. A *sector-based image* copies each sector to a file. One well-known example of a sector-based image is ISO images, which are images of a CD or DVD disk. Other well-known examples of sector-based images are Norton/Symantec Ghost and Acronis True Image. One problem with using sector-based images is that you need to take additional steps to rename a computer and to regenerate the security identifier (SID), which uniquely identifies a computer running Windows on a network. Sector-based images might not work on other computers that run on different hardware.

A *file-based disk image* captures images based on files on the disk. Because a file-based image is hardware independent, it can be deployed to different computers. It uses single-instance storage, which keeps a single copy of a file that might be referenced multiple times in a file system tree. When a file-based image is applied, it is nondestructive, which means that data files still exist after the image is applied. Examples of file-based images include virtual hard disk (.vhd) and Windows Imaging Format (.wim).

SELECTING IMAGE FORMATS

The *virtual hard disk (VHD)* format, traditionally used with virtual machines, represents a virtual hard disk drive. It can be found with Microsoft Virtual PC and Hyper-V. Starting with Windows 7, a computer can mount and start from an operating system stored within the .vhd file. Windows 8 Enterprise introduced Windows To Go, which allows Windows to start and run from a storage device such as a USB flash drive or an external hard disk drive. VHD images are limited to a maximum size of 2 terabytes (2 TB) and are compatible with all versions of Hyper-V, as well as Microsoft Type 2 hypervisor products, such as Virtual Server and Virtual PC.

Windows 8 and Windows Server 2012 introduced an updated version of the virtual hard disk file called VHDX, whose specification is publicly available through the Microsoft Open Source Promise initiative. The VHDX format supports up to 64 TB. It can support a 4-KB logical sector size to provide compatibility with new 4-KB native drives. VHDX files can also use larger block sizes, up to 256 MB, to allow you to fine-tune the performance of a virtual storage subsystem based on the specific application and data types. To protect against data corruption during power failures, it logs updates to the VHDX metadata structures. Finally, VHDX files can add custom metadata to the file. Unfortunately, the VHDX format is not backward compatible and can be read only by Windows 8/8.1 and higher and Windows Server 2012 and higher.

Windows Imaging Format (WIM) is a file-based image format developed by Microsoft that allows a file structure (folders and files) to be stored inside a single WIM database. WIM files have the following features:

- They incorporate compression.
- A single WIM file allows multiple images.
- WIM files use single instancing of files when multiple WIM files are appended.
- Because the WIM image format is a file-based image, it can be used on different hardware platforms and various size disks.
- WIM file format supports offline servicing, which allows you to open a WIM file in Windows and directly add or remove folders, files, drivers, and operating system components.

A WIM file structure contains up to six components:

- The WIM header defines the content of the WIM file, including file attributes (such as version, size, and compression type). It also acts as an index to locate the other components.
- File resources are packages that contain the captured data.
- The metadata resource contains information about captured files, including directory structure and file attributes. Each image in a WIM file has one metadata resource.
- The lookup table defines the memory location of resource files.
- XML data contains additional data about the image.
- The integrity table contains security hash (one-way encryption) information to verify integrity when the image is being applied.

A single WIM file can address many hardware configurations. It does not require that the destination hardware match the source hardware. This helps you greatly reduce the number of images, and gives you the advantage of having only one image to address the many hardware configurations.

One WIM file can store multiple images. This is useful because you can store images, with or without core applications, in a single image file. Another benefit is that you can mark one image as bootable, which means you can start a machine from a disk image that a WIM file contains.

By using WIM files for imaging, you can perform maintenance so that when the image is deployed to a new system, it will also include the updates (operating system updates, application updates, and driver updates) and changes without creating a new image from scratch and without deploying and recapturing the image.

If you will be imaging computers with Microsoft tools, you will most likely work with WIM files. You need to know how to update or modify a WIM file by using Deployment Image Servicing and Management (DISM). As you recall from previous exams, DISM is a command-line tool that you can use to service and deploy WIM, VHD, and VHDX files. You also can use DISM to prepare Windows PE images.

Selecting Image Types

To deploy Windows, you must create or use two types of images: a boot image (boot .wim) and an install image (install.wim). The Windows installation disc already includes basic copies of both images.

Like the name implies, the *boot image* starts the computer and can be used to start the operating system installation. Boot images are built with Windows PE, which is a lightweight version of Windows used to deploy client computers and servers and troubleshoot offline operating systems. Windows PE 10 is built with the Windows 10 code base and is included with the Windows Assessment and Deployment Kit (ADK).

Most of the time, an installation can be done by performing a *Preboot eXecution Environment (PXE)* boot, where the computer loads the operating system directly from a boot image over the network. If you have a computer that does not support a PXE boot, you can start the computer from disc by using a *discover image*. You can burn a discover image to a CD-ROM or another startup medium and then start the computer. You can use a discover image to connect directly to a Windows Deployment Services (WDS) server or to Microsoft System Center Configuration Manager and then start the operating system installation process. You can also deploy an image by using the Microsoft Deployment Toolkit (MDT).

You can configure discover images to use the following:

- **Static discovery:** An image that connects to a specific deployment server
- **Dynamic discovery:** An image file that emulates the PXE boot process to find a deployment server

An *install image* contains the operating systems you will deploy to client computers. Although the Windows installation disc has a default install.wim file, you would typically create your own installation images by building a reference computer, modifying the reference computer, and then capturing the system to an install image.

To capture a reference computer, you restart the reference computer and boot the computer using a mobile device (such as an optical disc or USB device) or a *capture image*. The mobile device or capture images contain the files necessary to load an operating system and the tools to capture an image (such as the DISM tools or the Windows Deployment Server Image Capture Wizard).

By using WIM files for imaging, you can perform maintenance on the image so that when it is deployed to a new system, it will also include the updates (operating system updates, application updates, and driver updates) and changes without creating a new image from scratch and without deploying and recapturing the image.

Determining the Number of Images

When you plan the images, you need to determine the number of images based on the operating system, hardware platform, drivers, and operating features. As mentioned earlier, sector-based and file-based images each have their own advantages and disadvantages.

Sector-based images can be deployed faster than file-based images and work well with identical computers. So if you use sector-based images, you need at least one image for each computer type. If you have one set of applications on some computers and another set of applications on others, you need two images for each computer type you are installing to. If you want to make changes to the sector-based image, you need to deploy the sector-based image, make the necessary changes, and recapture the image.

File-based images are hardware independent, can contain multiple images in a single file, can offer offline servicing, and can provide nondestructive deployment. So by using file-based images, you can use one image for several different computers, with different applications. Thus, you use less space when storing the file-based images.

You can include device drivers in captured images, or you can install them after the image is deployed. Of course, critical drivers, such as storage and network drivers, need to be included within the image.

Updating Images with Patches, Hotfixes, and Drivers

When you create an image file, you install Windows on a master computer, update and configure the computer, and then install any applications—all of which can take many hours to get everything just right. When Microsoft releases updates that you want to include in the new image, instead of going through the entire process of creating and setting up a new master computer, you can update the image file using Deployment Image Servicing and Management (dism.exe) or the PowerShell DISM cmdlets.

CERTIFICATION READY
Update images with
patches, hotfixes,
and drivers
Objective 1.3

Deployment Image Servicing and Management (dism.exe) is a command-line tool that can be used to service a Windows image or to prepare a Windows PE image. With DISM, you can mount an image offline and then add, remove, update, or list the features, packages, drivers, or international settings stored on that image. Dism.exe is not included with Windows.

To make changes to an image, you must mount the Windows image in the Windows file structure using the `Mount-Wim` option. To mount the *D:\RemoteInstall\install.wim* file to the *C:\Offline* folder, use the following command:

```
Dism /Mount-Wim /WimFile: D:\RemoteInstall\install.wim /index:1 /
MountDir:C:\Offline
```

After you make changes to the image, you need to commit the changes by using the `/Commit-Wim` option:

```
Dism /Commit-Wim /MountDir:C:\Offline
```

To unmount the image, use the /Unmount-Wim option. If you want to commit the changes while you unmount the image, add the /Commit option. To discard the changes, use the /Discard option. For example, to unmount the image mounted to the *C:\Offline* folder while saving the changes, execute the following command:

```
Dism /Unmount-Wim /MountDir:C:\offline /commit
```

To get information about an image or WIM file, use the /Get-WimInfo option. For example, in the previous WIM file, execute the following command:

```
Dism /Get-WimInfo /WimFile:C:\offline\install.wim /index:1
```

Packages are used by Microsoft to distribute software patches, hotfixes, service packs, language packages, and Windows features. If a Windows package is provided as a cabinet (.cab) file or as a Windows Update Stand-alone Installer (.msu) file, you can add the package using the /Add-Package command. For example, to add the *C:\Update\Update.cab* file, execute the following command:

```
Dism /image:C:\offline /Add-Package /Packagepath:C:\Update\Update.cab
```

To remove a package, use the /Remove-Package option. For example, to remove the *update .cab* file, execute the following command:

```
Dism /image:C:\offline /Remove-Package /PackagePath:C:\Update\
Update.cab
```

You can use the /Add-Driver option to add third-party driver packages that include a valid INF file. For example, to add *mydriver* to the Windows image, execute the following command:

```
Dism /image:C:\offline /Add-Driver /driver:C:\Drivers\mydriver.INF
```

If you point to a path and use /Recurse, all subfolders will be checked for valid drivers. For example, to add drivers from the *C:\Drivers* folder, execute the following command:

```
Dism /image:C:\offline /Add-Driver /driver:C:\drivers /recurse
```

To remove a third-party device driver, use the /Remove-Driver option to specify the name of a device driver (such as *oem0.inf*, *oem1.inf*, and so on). For example, to remove the second third-party driver (*oem1.inf*) that has been added to the system, execute the following command:

```
Dism /image:C:\offline /Remove-Driver /driver:oem1.inf
```

Managing and Maintaining Images with Windows PowerShell

Windows 10 and Windows Server 2016 include **DISM cmdlets** in the DISM PowerShell module that can be used to manage and maintain images. The DISM cmdlets are similar to using the dism.exe command, which can be used to manage .wim or VHD files.

CERTIFICATION READY
Manage and maintain Windows Server Core, Nano Server images, and VHDs using Windows PowerShell
Objective 1.3

USING POWERSHELL

You can manage images, including Windows Server Core, Nano Server images, and VHDs, using Windows PowerShell by using the following cmdlets:

- **Add-AppxProvisionedPackage:** Adds an app package (.appx) that will install for each new user to a Windows image
- **Add-WindowsCapability:** Installs a Windows capability package on the specified operating system image
- **Add-WindowsDriver:** Adds a driver to an offline Windows image
- **Add-WindowsImage:** Adds an additional image to an existing image (.wim) file

(continued)

- **Add-WindowsPackage:** Adds a single .cab or .msu file to a Windows image
- **Clear-WindowsCorruptMountPoint:** Removes all of the resources that are associated with a mounted image that has been corrupted
- **Disable-WindowsOptionalFeature:** Disables a feature in a Windows image
- **Dismount-WindowsImage:** Dismounts a Windows image from the directory that it is mapped to
- **Enable-WindowsOptionalFeature:** Enables a feature in a Windows image
- **Expand-WindowsCustomDataImage:** Expands a custom data image
- **Expand-WindowsImage:** Expands an image to a specified location
- **Export-WindowsImage:** Exports a copy of the specified image to another file
- **Get-AppxProvisionedPackage:** Gets information about app packages (.appx) that are set to install for each new user in an image
- **Get-WindowsCapability:** Displays Windows capabilities for an image or a running operating system
- **Get-WindowsDriver:** Displays information about drivers in a Windows image
- **Get-WindowsEdition:** Displays edition information about a Windows image
- **Get-WindowsImage:** Displays information about a Windows image in a WIM or VHD file
- **Get-WindowsImageContent:** Displays a list of the files and folders in a specified image
- **Get-WindowsOptionalFeature:** Displays information about optional features in a Windows image
- **Get-WindowsPackage:** Displays information about packages in a Windows image
- **Mount-WindowsImage:** Mounts a Windows image in a WIM or VHD file to a directory on the local computer
- **New-WindowsImage:** Captures an image of a drive to a new WIM file
- **Remove-AppxProvisionedPackage:** Removes app packages (.appx) from a Windows image
- **Remove-WindowsCapability:** Uninstalls a Windows capability package from an image
- **Remove-WindowsDriver:** Removes a driver from an offline Windows image
- **Remove-WindowsImage:** Removes the specified volume image from a WIM file that has multiple volume images
- **Remove-WindowsPackage:** Removes a package from a Windows image
- **Repair-WindowsImage:** Repairs a Windows image in a WIM or VHD file
- **Save-WindowsImage:** Applies changes made to a mounted image to its WIM or VHD file
- **Set-AppXProvisionedDataFile:** Adds custom data into the specified app (.appx) package that has been provisioned in a Windows image
- **Set-WindowsEdition:** Changes a Windows image to a higher edition
- **Set-WindowsProductKey:** Configures the product key for the Windows image
- **Split-WindowsImage:** Splits an existing .wim file into multiple read-only split .wim files
- **Use-WindowsUnattend:** Applies an unattended answer file to a Windows image

To make changes to an image, you must mount the Windows image using the Mount-WindowsImage cmdlet. To mount the *D:\RemoteInstall\install.wim* file to the *C:\Offline* folder, use the following command:

```
Mount-WindowsImage ImagePath "D:\RemoteInstall\install.wim" -Index:1
Path "C:\Offline"
```

After you make changes to the image, you need to commit the changes by using the Save-WindowsImage cmdlet:

```
Save-WindowsImage -Path "c:\offline"
```

To unmount the image, use the Dismount-WindowsImage cmdlet. If you want to commit the changes while you unmount the image, add the /Commit option. To discard the changes, use the -Discard option. For example, to unmount the image mounted to the *C:\Offline* folder while saving the changes, execute the following command:

```
Dismount-WindowsImage -Path "c:\offline" -Save
```

This command gets information, including mount path, about all of the Windows images mounted on the local computer:

```
Get-WindowsImage -Mounted
```

To get information about an image or WIM file, use the `Get-WindowsImage` cmdlet. For example, in the previous WIM file, execute the following command:

```
Get-WindowsImage -ImagePath "c:\offline\install.wim" -Name Ultimate
```

Packages are used by Microsoft to distribute software patches, hotfixes, service packs, language packages, and Windows features. If a Windows package is provided as a cabinet (.cab) file or as a Windows Update Stand-alone Installer (.msu) file, you can add the package using the `-Add-Package` command. For example, to add the *C:\Update\Update.cab* file, execute the following command:

```
Add-WindowsPackage -Online -PackagePath "c:\update\package.cab"
```

You can use the `Add-Driver` cmdlet to add third-party driver packages that include a valid INF file. For example, to add *mydriver* to the Windows image, execute the following command:

```
Add-WindowsDriver -Path "c:\offline" -Driver "C:\Drivers\mydriver.INF"
-ForceUnsigned
```

If the driver is unsigned, you need to use the `-ForceUnsigned` option.

If you point to a path and use `-Recurse`, all subfolders will be checked for valid drivers. For example, to add drivers from the *C:\Drivers* folder, execute the following command:

```
Add-WindowsDriver -Path "c:\offline" -Driver "c:\drivers\drivers"
-Recurse
```

To remove a third-party device driver, use the `Remove-WindowsDriver` cmdlet option to specify the name of a device driver (such as *oem0.inf, oem1.inf,* and so on). For example, to remove the second third-party driver (*oem1.inf*) that has been added to the system, execute the following command:

```
Remove-WindowsDriver -Path "c:\offline" -Driver "OEM1.inf"
```

Installing Features for Offline Images

Features are a set of Windows programs that can be enabled or disabled by an administrator and are included with Windows. Examples of features include FreeCell, Hearts, Solitaire, FTP Server, World Wide Web Service, and Microsoft .NET Framework 3.5. To add or remove features in Windows Server 2016, you use Server Manager. To add or remove features in Windows 10, you use Control Panel > Programs and Features. Similarly, you can use dism.exe to add to or remove features from an offline image.

CERTIFICATION READY
Install roles and features
in offline images
Objective 1.3

Similar to adding or removing packages, you can use dism.exe to mount an image offline and then use dism.exe to add, remove, update, or list the Windows feature. For example, to list the features, execute the following command:

```
Dism /image:C:\offline /Get-Features
```

To enable a feature, use the `/Enable-Feature` option. For example, to install the Hearts game, execute the following command:

```
Dism /image:C:\offline /Enable-Feature /FeatureName:Hearts
```

To remove the Hearts game, use the `/Disable-Features` option. For example, to remove the Hearts game, execute the following command:

```
Dism /Image:C:\offline /Disable-Feature /FeatureName:Hearts
```

Of course, after you add or remove features, remember to commit the changes with the Dism /Commit-Wim command that was discussed previously.

Implementing a Server Deployment Infrastructure with WDS

THE BOTTOM LINE

Windows Deployment Services (WDS) is a Windows server role used to deploy Windows over the network with little or no user intervention. If the client can perform a PXE boot, you perform an installation over a network with no local operating system or local startup device on it. The WDS server stores and helps administrators manage the boot and operating system image files used in the network installations.

WDS supports deploying .vhd images and .wim files. If WDS deploys a .vhd file, it copies that file to the local hard drive, and then configures the local Boot Configuration Data (BCD) so that the file is used to start the computer.

Deploying WDS

WDS is a server role that is included with Windows Server 2016. Therefore, before you can use WDS, you must install the WDS role and configure the services. Then, you need to create and add the images that you want to deploy.

To use WDS with Active Directory, you need the following:

- The WDS server as a member of an Active Directory Domain Services (AD DS) domain, or as a domain controller for an AD DS domain
- An active DHCP server on the network
- An active DNS server on your network
- An NTFS file system partition on the server to store images

Starting with Windows Server 2012, you can deploy WDS in stand-alone mode, which means no dependency on Active Directory. To use WDS in stand-alone mode, you need the following:

- An active DHCP server on the network
- An active DNS server on your network
- An NTFS file system partition on the server to store images

In either case, you must be a member of the Local Administrators group to install WDS.

WDS is a Windows server role that can be installed using the Server Manager console. WDS includes the following two role services:

- ***Deployment Server:*** Deployment Server provides full functionality of WDS, including providing an image repository (such as boot images, install images, and other files necessary for remote installation over a network), a PXE server for remote computers to start, and a Trivial File Transfer Protocol (TFTP) server to transfer files over the network. Deployment Server also includes tools to create and customize images.
- ***Transport Server:*** Although required by Deployment Server, the Transport role is a subset of WDS functionality, but can also be used for custom solutions. Transport Server can also use multicasting.

Most likely, you will need Deployment Server.

INSTALL WDS

GET READY. To install WDS on a computer running Windows Server 2016, perform the following steps.

1. In Windows Server 2016, click **Start** and click **Server Manager.**

2. At the top of the Server Manager console, select **Manage** and then click **Add Roles and Features.**

3. After the Add Roles and Feature Wizard opens, on the Before You Begin page, click **Next.**

4. On the Select Installation Type page, select **Role-based or feature-based installation** and then click **Next.**

5. Click **Select a server from the server pool**, click the name of the server to install WDS to, and then click **Next.**

6. On the Select Server Roles page, scroll down and select **Windows Deployment Services.** In the Add Roles and Features Wizard dialog box, select **Add Features.**

7. Back on the Select Server Roles page, click **Next.**

8. On the Select Features page, click **Next.**

9. On the WDS page, click **Next.**

10. On the Select Role Services page, ensure that the **Deployment Server** and **Transport Server** options are selected and then click **Next.**

11. On the Confirm Installation Selections page, click the **Install** button.

12. When the installation is done, click **Close.**

After WDS is installed, you need to run the Windows Deployment Services Configuration Wizard to perform the initial configuration.

 CONFIGURE WDS

GET READY. To configure WDS on a computer running Windows Server 2016, perform the following steps.

1. In Server Manager, open the **Tools** menu and then click **Windows Deployment Services.**

2. In the Windows Deployment Services console, expand **Servers**, right-click the **WDS server**, and choose **Configure Server.**

3. On the Before You Begin page, click **Next.**

4. On the Install Options page, click **Integrated with Active Directory** for an Active Directory–integrated WDS. (For a stand-alone installation, select **Standalone server.**) Click **Next.**

5. On the Remote Installation Folder Location page, specify the location of the remote installation folder. The default is *C:\RemoteInstall*. Using the system drive (C drive) is not recommended. Click **Next.**

   If you use the C drive, you should receive a warning that you have selected the Windows system volume and that you should use a separate volume. To continue, click **Yes.** Of course, in a production environment, for performance and system reliability, you should create a separate volume to store the WDS images.

6. If your WDS server is also a DHCP server, an additional page appears that allows you to configure the server so that no port conflicts occur:

   - By default, when a DHCP client is looking for a DHCP server, it performs a broadcast, using UDP port 67. If your WDS server is also the DHCP server, you must tell WDS not to listen on port 67 so that DHCP can function properly. Select the **Do not listen on DHCP and DHCPv6 ports** option.

   - If the local DHCP server is a Microsoft DHCP server, you should select the **Configure DHCP options for Proxy DHCP** option so that the DHCP server is automatically configured to forward the PXE requests to the WDS server. If the local DHCP server is not a Microsoft DHCP server, you need to configure the DHCP server manually to forward the request to the WDS server.

   Click **Next**.

7. On the PXE Server Initial Settings page, select the appropriate options:

   - **Do not respond to any client computers:** If you select this option, WDS cannot perform installations. You typically would use this option to keep WDS disabled until you are ready to use it.

   - **Respond only to known client computers:** A known computer has an account prestaged or created in Active Directory before you perform the installation. By prestaging a computer, WDS responds to only computers you specify and not to unstaged or rogue systems.

   - **Respond to all client computers (known and unknown):** This least secure option allows WDS to respond to any client system that makes an installation request.

   Click **Next**.

8. When the task is completed, the Add images to the server now option is already selected. If you do not want to load images, clear that option. Click **Finish**. When done, Windows Deployment Services appears, as shown in Figure 6-1.

Figure 6-1

Opening a configured Windows Deployment Services console

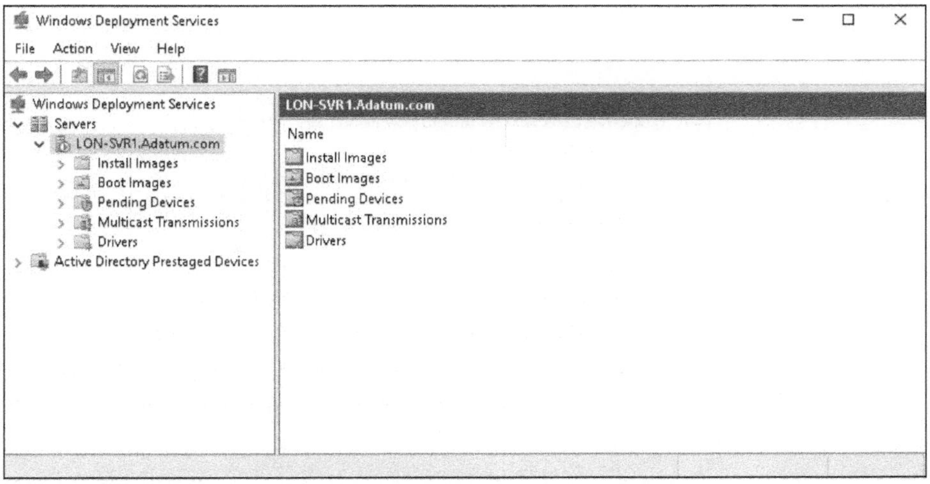

To further configure WDS, right-click the server in the Windows Deployment Services console and choose Properties. The WDS server properties include the following tabs:

- **General:** Displays the server name, mode, and location of the remote installation folder where images are stored.

- **PXE Response:** Enables you to specify which types of computers (known or unknown) can download and install images from the server. You also can specify the PXE boot delay in seconds (0 by default).

- **AD DS:** Allows you to determine the automatic naming format for WDS clients in AD DS that are not prestaged. It also allows you to specify where the computer account will be created in Active Directory.

- **Boot:** Specifies the default network boot image for each architecture type (x86, x64, and ia64) and the PXE Boot Policy settings for known and unknown clients. It also allows you to specify whether a user must press F12 to continue the PXE boot.

- **Client:** Allows you to enable and configure an unattended installation of the WDS clients. If you do not want to add a computer to the domain, select the Do not join the client to a domain after an installation option.

- **DHCP:** Allows you to enable or disable whether a server listens on the DHCP ports (port 67) and to configure DHCP option 60 automatically on a DHCP server.

- **Multicast:** Allows you to use one set of packets to install operating systems on multiple computers simultaneously. As a result, you minimize network traffic. The Multicast tab allows you to configure multicast transfer settings, as shown in Figure 6-2.

Figure 6-2

The Windows Deployment Services Multicast tab

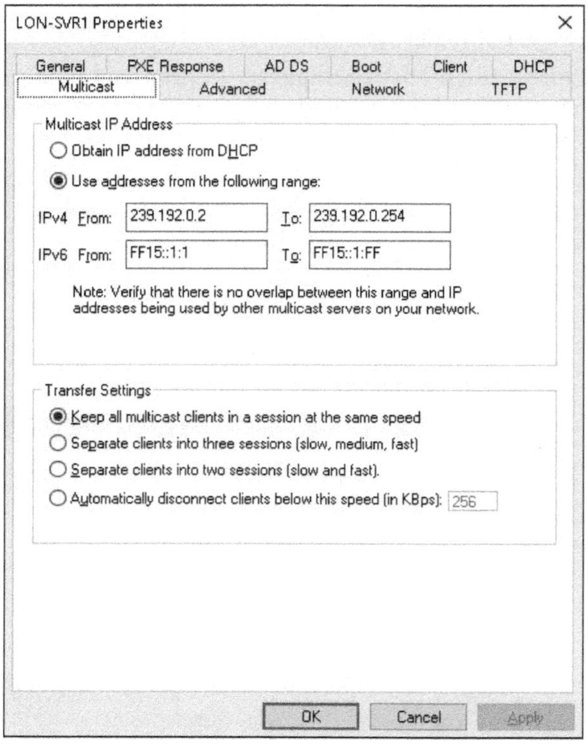

- **Advanced:** Allows you to authorize your WDS server in DHCP. It also allows you to specify a domain controller and global catalog or to enable WDS to discover them on its own.

- **Network:** Allows you to specify the UDP port ranges WDS uses. Typically, you would keep the default option, Obtain dynamic ports from Winsock. Note that the Network profile option is grayed out in Windows Server 2016, which would allow you to specify the bandwidth of your network. Instead, the bandwidth is determined automatically.

- **TFTP:** Allows you to configure the maximum block size used for FTP transfers.

Configuring and Managing Boot, Install, and Discover Images

To deploy Windows, you must create two types of images: a boot image and an install image. Just as the name implies, the boot image boots the computer. In addition, the boot image starts the operating system installation. The install image contains the operating system that WDS installs.

The Windows Server 2016 installation DVD includes a boot image file named *boot.wim*, located in the *sources* folder, which loads Windows PE 10 on the client computer. Because it is used to boot the computer and start the installation of an operating system, it can be used for virtually any operating system deployment without modification.

 ADD A BOOT IMAGE

GET READY. To add a boot image file to WDS, perform the following steps.

1. Open Server Manager.
2. Click **Tools > Windows Deployment Services.** The Windows Deployment Services console opens.
3. Expand **Servers** and then expand the server so that you can see the Install Images folder and the Boot Images folder.
4. To add a boot image, right-click the **Boot Images** folder and choose **Add Boot Image.** The Add Image Wizard opens.
5. Browse to the location of the image file (such as the **Sources** folder located on the installation DVD), click the **boot.wim** file, and then click **Open.**
6. On the Image File page, click **Next.**
7. On the Image Metadata page, type a name and description of the image and then click **Next.** Most of the time, you can use the default values shown.
8. On the Summary page, click **Next.**
9. When the image is added to the server, click **Finish.** The Boot image appears, as shown in Figure 6-3.

Figure 6-3

Showing the Windows Deployment Services boot images

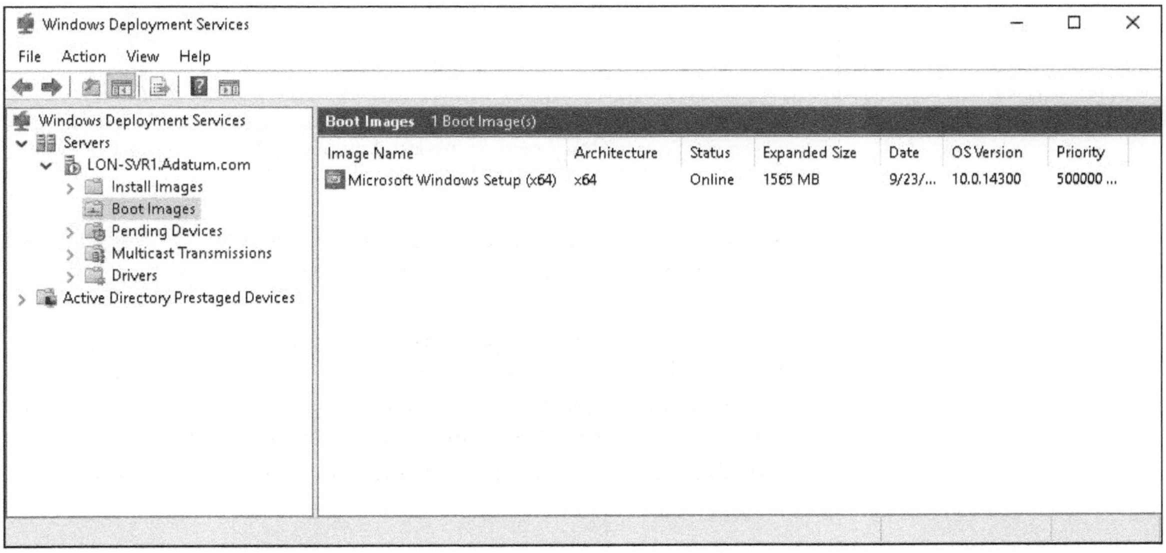

Windows Deployment Services							
File Action View Help							
Boot Images 1 Boot Image(s)							
Image Name	Architecture	Status	Expanded Size	Date	OS Version	Priority	
Microsoft Windows Setup (x64)	x64	Online	1565 MB	9/23/...	10.0.14300	500000 ...	

Tree:
- Windows Deployment Services
  - Servers
    - LON-SVR1.Adatum.com
      - Install Images
      - Boot Images
      - Pending Devices
      - Multicast Transmissions
      - Drivers
  - Active Directory Prestaged Devices

The image file contains the operating system that WDS will install on the client computer. Included in the Sources folder on the Windows Server 2016 installation disc is an install.wim file for Windows Server 2016 that allows you to perform a standard Windows Server 2016 installation similar to performing a manual installation from disc.

When you create image files, you place the image file in an image group. An *image group* is a folder within the image repository of WDS that shares security options and file resources. The image group consists of the following two components:

- The resource *.wim* file (*Res.rwm*). This contains the file resources for all of the images in an image group. Although the file name seems to indicate otherwise, the .rwm file is actually a .wim file.
- The *<imagename>.wim* files. Each *.wim* image file contains the metadata that describes the image, but the actual file resources for the image reside in *Res.rwm*.

Any permission assigned to an image group is inherited by all the images in the group. By default, authenticated users are granted read access to image groups and images, whereas administrators have full control. You can control who can receive specific images by modifying the permissions of the images or by placing the images in image groups and modifying the permissions of the groups.

 ADD AN INSTALL IMAGE FILE

GET READY. To add an install image file to WDS, perform the following steps.

1. Open Server Manager.
2. Click **Tools > Windows Deployment Services**. The Windows Deployment Services console opens.
3. Expand **Servers** and then expand the server so that you can see the Install Images folder and the Boot Images folder.
4. Right-click the **Install Images** folder and choose **Add Install Image**. The Add Image Wizard page opens (see Figure 6-4).

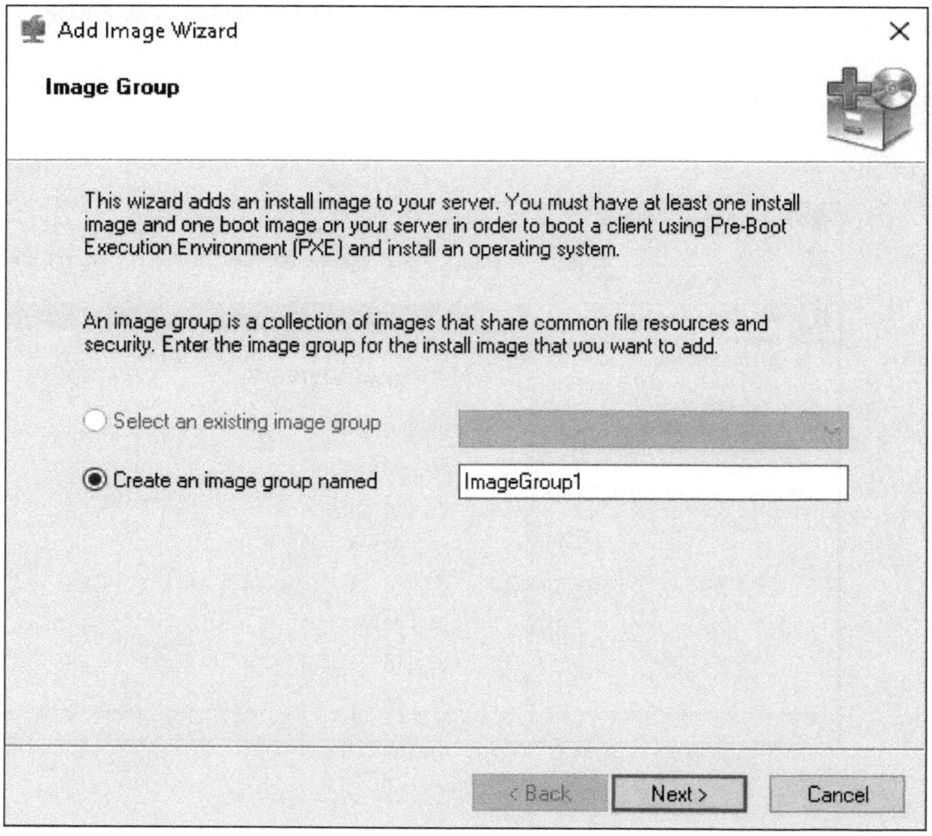

Figure 6-4

Creating an image group

Add Image Wizard

Image Group

This wizard adds an install image to your server. You must have at least one install image and one boot image on your server in order to boot a client using Pre-Boot Execution Environment (PXE) and install an operating system.

An image group is a collection of images that share common file resources and security. Enter the image group for the install image that you want to add.

○ Select an existing image group

◉ Create an image group named   ImageGroup1

< Back   Next >   Cancel

5. On the Image Group page, the Create an image group named option is selected. If desired, type a different name of the image group and then click **Next.**

6. Browse to the location of the image file (such as the **Sources** folder located on the installation DVD), select the **install.wim** file, and then click **Open.**

7. On the Image File page, click **Next.**

8. On the Available Images page, select the images you want to include (see Figure 6-5) and then click **Next.**

Figure 6-5

Specifying the images you want to include

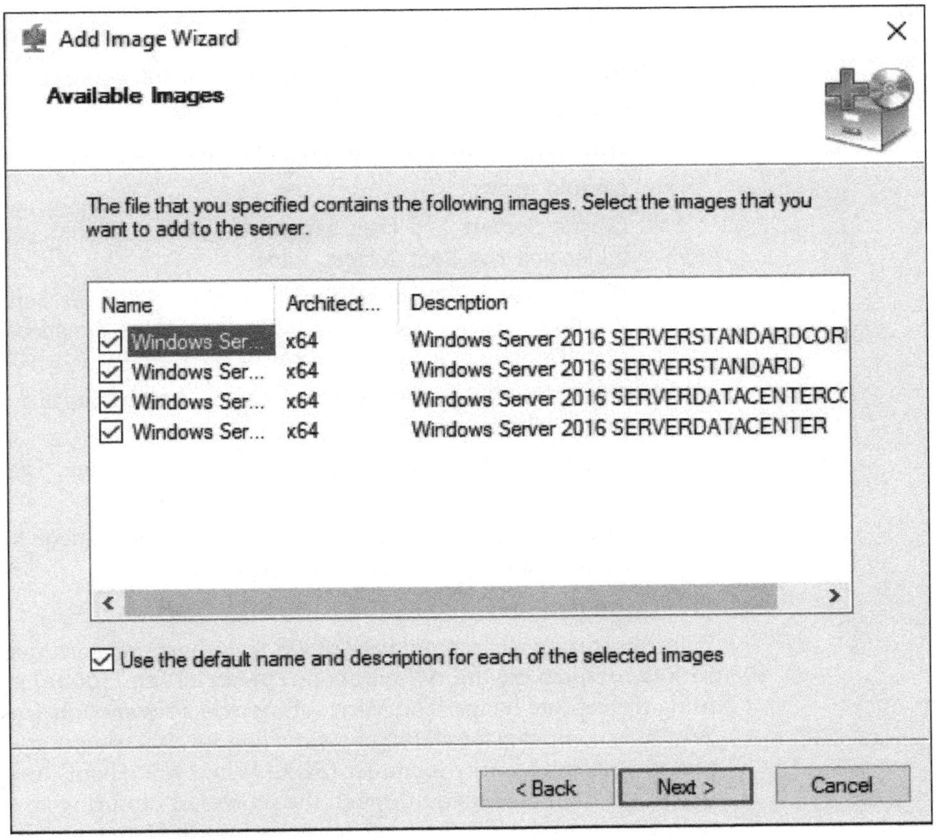

9. On the Summary page, click **Next.**

10. When the images are added to the server, click **Finish.**

CREATING AN IMAGE FILE WITH WDS

An *image file* is basically a snapshot of a computer's hard drive taken at a particular moment in time. The image file is sometimes referred to as an install image and is used to install an operating system. It contains the following:

- All of the operating system files on the computer
- Any updates and drives that have been applied
- Any applications that have been installed
- Any configuration changes that have been made

The install images that are included on a Windows installation disc are images of a basic Windows installation, with no patches, updates, or additional drivers. If you would like to create your own image files, you must first set up a master computer with all the patches, drivers, applications, and configurations applied. Then, use WDS to create your own image file by modifying an existing boot image, booting the master computer with the modified boot image, and running the *Windows Deployment Services Capture Utility*. The Windows Deployment Services Capture Utility will create an image file and write it to the computer's drive, which will eventually be copied to the WDS server. You can then use it to be deployed to other computers.

CREATE AN IMAGE FILE

GET READY. To create an image file, perform the following steps.

1. Open Server Manager.

2. Click **Tools > Windows Deployment Services**. The Windows Deployment Services console opens.

3. Expand **Servers** and then expand the server so that you can see the Install Images folder and the Boot Images folder.

4. If you have not done so already, add the Windows Server 2016 boot.wim image to the Boot Images store by following the steps provided in the "Add a Boot Image" exercise.

5. Right-click the boot image and choose **Create Capture Image.** The Create Capture Image Wizard opens.

6. Specify a name and description for the new image. Then, specify the location and file name for the new image file. Click **Next**.

7. When the task is complete, you can select **Add image to the Windows Deployment Server now** (if desired). Then, click **Finish**.

Before capturing a computer with WDS, you must prepare a master or reference computer with the sysprep.exe utility (`sysprep /generalize /oobe`) and reboot the computer using the capture image. The Microsoft *System Preparation Utility (sysprep.exe)* prepares a Windows computer for cloning by removing specific computer information, such as the computer name and security identifier (SID). When you reboot the computer with the capture image, a wizard guides you through the process of capturing an image of the computer and uploading it to the WDS server. For more information, go to the "Using Sysprep to Prepare the Reference Computer" section in this lesson.

CREATING A DISCOVER IMAGE

If you have a computer that does not support a PXE boot, you can boot the computer from a disc using a discover image. A discover image is an image file that you can burn to a CD-ROM or other boot medium. When you boot the client computer using the discover image disc, the computer loads Windows PE, connects to a specified WDS server, and proceeds with the operating system installation process.

CREATE A DISCOVER IMAGE

GET READY. To create a discover image file, perform the following steps.

1. Open Server Manager.

2. Click **Tools > Windows Deployment Services**. The Windows Deployment Services console opens.

3. Expand **Servers** and then expand the server so that you can see the Install Images folder and the Boot Images folder.

4. To create a discover boot image, right-click a boot image in the Windows Deployment Services console and choose **Create Discover Image**.

5. On the Metadata and Location page, leave the default Image name and Image description fields as is. Then, specify where you want to store the discover image file. In addition, in the *Enter the name of the Windows Deployment Services server. . .* text box, type the name of the WDS server (see Figure 6-6). Click **Next**.

Figure 6-6

Specifying the image name, the image description, and where to store the discover image file

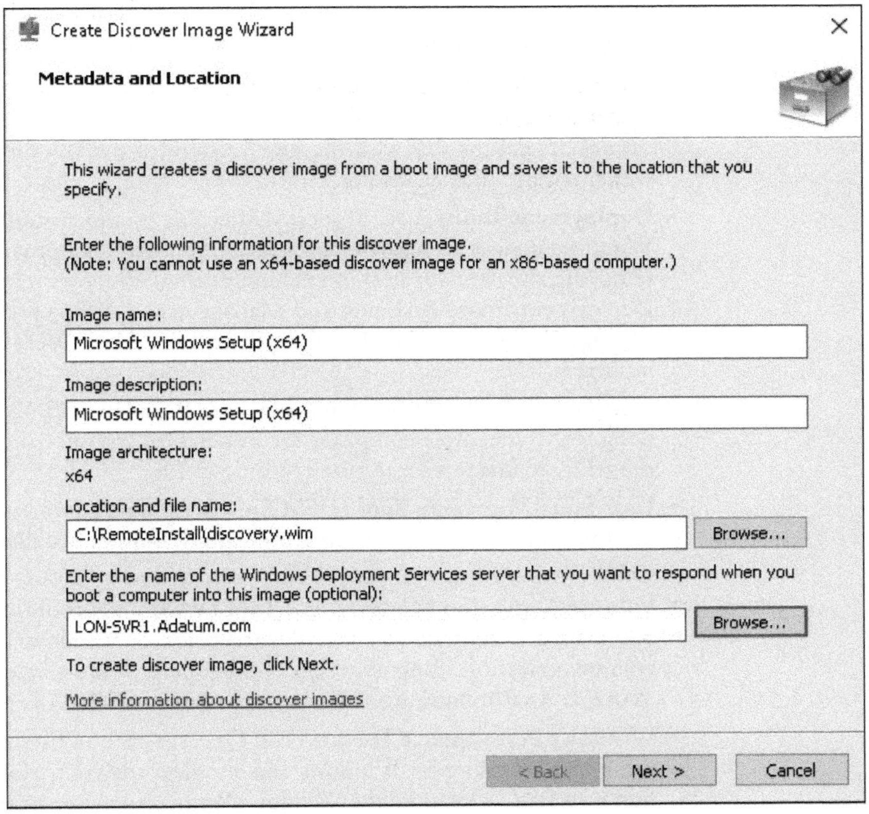

6. On the Summary page, click **Next**.

7. When the images are added to the server, click **Finish**.

To convert the discover image to a bootable .iso image, you first must download and install the Windows Assessment and Deployment Kit (ADK) for Windows 10. ADM is a set of tools provided by Microsoft to customize, assess, and deploy a Windows operating system to new computers. The `oscdimg.exe` command will create the .iso image.

■ Designing a Server Implementation Using Windows Assessment and Deployment Kit (ADK)

THE BOTTOM LINE

Windows Assessment and Deployment Kit (ADK) is a collection of tools and documentation designed to help IT professionals deploy Windows operating systems. Windows ADK is ideal for use with highly customized environments because the tools in Windows ADK can be used to configure many deployment options. Depending on your business needs, you can choose to use all or part of the resources available in Windows ADK.

By default, Windows ADK is installed to the C:\Program Files (x86)\Windows Kits directory. This directory contains all the tools and documentation included in the Windows ADK. The ADK includes the following tools:

- **Application Compatibility Toolkit (ACT):** A toolkit that helps to identify which applications are compatible with the new versions of the Windows operating system and which require further testing.

- **Deployment Tools:** A set of tools that enable you to customize, manage, and deploy Windows images. Deployment tools can be used to automate Windows deployments, removing the need for user interaction during Windows setup. These tools include the Deployment Image Servicing and Management (DISM) tool, Windows System Image Manager (SIM), OSCDIMG, BCDBoot, DISMAPI, WIMGAPI, and other tools and interfaces.

- *Windows Preinstallation Environment (Windows PE):* A minimal operating system designed to prepare a computer for installation and servicing of Windows. You can use the ADK to create a customized Windows PE.

- **User State Migration Tool (USMT):** A scriptable command-line tool that can be used to migrate user data from a previous Windows installation to a new Windows installation.

- **Volume Activation Management Tool (VAMT):** A tool that enables administrators to automate and centrally manage the activation of Windows. The VAMT can manage volume activation using retail keys (or single activation keys), multiple activation keys (MAKs), or Windows Key Management Service (KMS) keys.

- **Windows Performance Toolkit (WPT):** A set of tools used to record system events by using Event Tracing for Windows and a tool to analyze performance data in a graphical user interface. It includes the Windows Performance Recorder, Windows Performance Analyzer, and Xperf.

- **Windows Assessment Toolkit:** A set of tools to discover and run assessments on a single computer, so that you can determine how to improve performance.

⊕ **INSTALL THE WINDOWS ASSESSMENT AND DEPLOYMENT KIT**

GET READY. To install the Windows Assessment and Deployment Kit (ADK), perform the following steps.

1. On LON-SVR1, open the *\\LON-DC1\software\Windows Kits\10\ADK* folder and double-click **adksetup**. When you are prompted to confirm that you want to run the file, click **Run**.
2. On the Specify Location page, click **Next**.
3. On the Join the Customer Experience Improvement Program (CEIP) page, click **Next**.
4. On the License Agreement page, click **Accept**.
5. On the Select the Features You Want to Install page (as shown in Figure 6-7), select and deselect the desired features. Click **Install**.

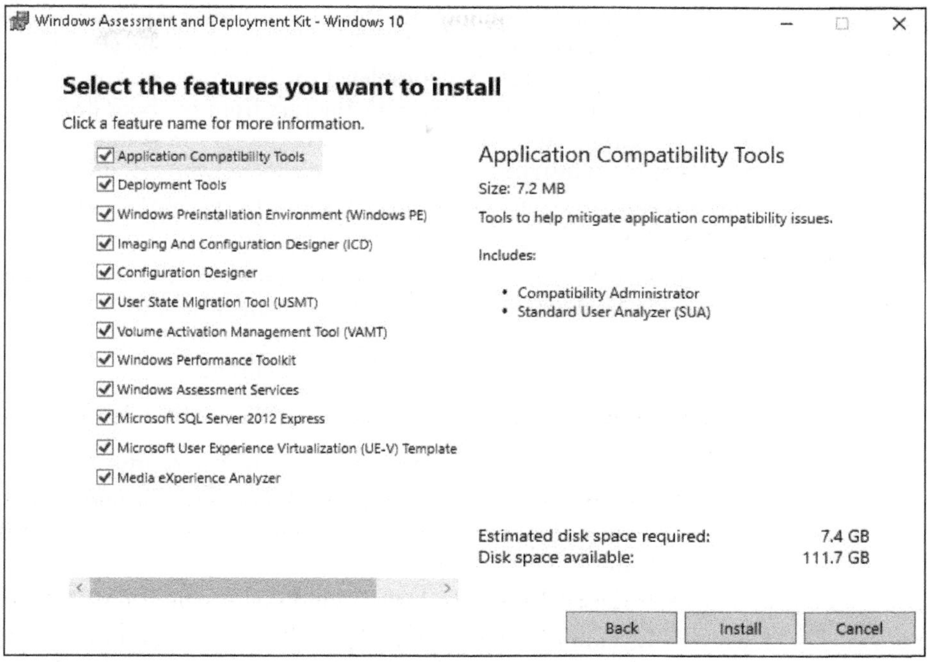

Figure 6-7

Selecting ADK features

Windows Assessment and Deployment Kit - Windows 10   — □ ✕

Select the features you want to install

Click a feature name for more information.

☑ Application Compatibility Tools
☑ Deployment Tools
☑ Windows Preinstallation Environment (Windows PE)
☑ Imaging And Configuration Designer (ICD)
☑ Configuration Designer
☑ User State Migration Tool (USMT)
☑ Volume Activation Management Tool (VAMT)
☑ Windows Performance Toolkit
☑ Windows Assessment Services
☑ Microsoft SQL Server 2012 Express
☑ Microsoft User Experience Virtualization (UE-V) Template
☑ Media eXperience Analyzer

Application Compatibility Tools

Size: 7.2 MB

Tools to help mitigate application compatibility issues.

Includes:

• Compatibility Administrator
• Standard User Analyzer (SUA)

Estimated disk space required: 7.4 GB
Disk space available: 111.7 GB

[Back]   [Install]   [Cancel]

6. When the installation is complete, click **Close**.

Using Windows PE

Windows PE is the core deployment foundation for Windows 10 and Windows Server 2016. Windows PE is a compact, special-purpose Windows operating system that prepares and initiates a computer for Windows operating system setup, maintenance, or imaging tasks, and recovers Windows operating systems such as Windows 10.

Windows PE is a lightweight, bootable version of the Windows operating system. Typically, when you boot Windows PE, you are booting to a command prompt; however, some GUI-based tools run in Windows PE. Windows PE is used for:

• Installing Windows, including preparing the system for the Windows install, such as creating partitions and formatting drives
• Troubleshooting Windows, including starting a computer and running diagnostic tools such as the Startup Repair feature
• Recovery, including building customized boot disks to automate recovery and rebuilding of the Windows operating system

Windows PE 10 can be started from almost any boot device, including CDs, DVDs, and USB boot devices. It supports both 32-bit and 64-bit hardware and supports installing both 32-bit and 64-bit versions of Windows. Unlike DOS, Windows supports the NTFS file system. It also supports network connections, where you can configure IP settings and connect to a network share. Because it is a disk image, Windows PE supports offline sessions, which even allow the servicing of the image. Lastly, Windows supports some Windows-based applications and includes add-in modules for additional Windows-based components.

When you boot Windows PE, the boot process creates a RAM disk (part of the RAM that is used as a disk) to store the Windows PE files and allows you to remove the Windows PE boot disk after the system has completed the boot process. You can also configure Windows PE to perform a flat boot, which reads the files from the boot device and requires the boot disk to remain in the boot device. If you decide to run Windows PE as a flat boot, Windows PE needs to be installed on a FAT32 file system, which is limited to a 32-GB partition. To run Windows PE, you need a minimum of 512 megabytes (MB) of RAM. By default, the RAM disk is assigned the letter X.

Windows PE has a limited set of built-in device drivers. Therefore, if you need to support specific hardware, you might need to create or modify a Windows PE image so that you can add additional storage or network drivers. To modify a Windows PE image, you can use DISM or the Windows ADK Drvload command.

Remember that Windows PE is only a minimal Windows operating system. Therefore,

- It will automatically stop running and restart after 72 hours of continuous use.
- It cannot be used as a server; it cannot create or host shared folders or terminal service connections. It can be used to connect to TCP/IP and NetBIOS over TCP/IP (NetBT) connections to file servers.
- It cannot be used to install Windows Installer (.msi) file packages.
- It cannot be started from a path that contains non-English characters.
- You cannot convert a disk to a dynamic disk using Diskpart and have the Windows Setup process recognize the volumes on the dynamic disk.
- 64-bit Windows PE does not include Windows 32-bit on Windows 64-bit (WOW64). In addition, you must use 32-bit of Windows PE to run 32-bit Windows Setup and you need to use 64-bit Windows PE to run 64-bit Windows Setup.
- If you are using a Unified Extensible Firmware Interface (UEFI)–based motherboard, you must install a 64-bit version of the Windows operating system. Therefore, you cannot install Windows using a 32-bit Windows PE.

The following Windows ADK command-line tools can be used to help deploy Windows using WinPE:

- **BCDboot:** Initializes the Boot Configuration Data (BCD) store and copies the necessary boot environment files to the system partition so that it can boot Windows
- **Bootsect:** Updates the master boot code so that it can support the Windows Boot Manager (bootmgr.exe) and Windows NT Loader (NTLDR)
- **Copype:** Creates and populates a directory structure for Windows PE files
- **Drvload:** Adds third-party drivers to Windows PE
- **Expand:** Expands one or more .cab files
- **Lpksetup:** Installs language packs and configures international settings
- **Makewinpemedia:** Creates bootable Windows PE media
- **Oscdimg:** Creates an .iso image file of a Windows PE image
- **Powercfg:** Controls power settings, including the hibernate and standby settings
- **Tzutil:** Manages available time zones
- **Wpeinit:** Initializes Windows PE every time that it boots and installs Plug and Play devices, processes Unattend.xml settings, and loads network resources when Windows PE is loaded
- **Wpeutil:** Enables you to run commands during a Windows PE session, including shutting down or restarting Windows PE, enabling or disabling a firewall, or initializing a network

Additional components can be added to Windows PE. For example, you can add language packs, third-party drivers, third-party components, and Windows PE updates.

➔ CONFIGURE A CUSTOM WINDOWS PE ENVIRONMENT

GET READY. To configure a custom Windows PE environment, perform the following steps.

1. Open the Start screen, right-click **Deployment and Imaging Tools Environment** and choose **Run as administrator.**

2. In the Administrator: Deployment and Imaging Tools Environment window, type the following command and then press **Enter:**

   Copype amd64 C:\WinPE_X64

   When complete, the Administrator: Deployment and Imaging Tools Environment window should display a *Success* message.

3. To mount a boot.wim file to the C:\winpe_x64\mount folder, in the Administrator: Deployment and Imaging Tools Environment window, type the following command and then press **Enter:**

   DISM /mount-image /imagefile:C:\winpe_x64\media\sources\boot.wim /index:1 /mountdir:C:\winpe_x64\mount

   When complete, the Administrator: Deployment and Imaging Tools Environment window should display *The operation completed successfully*.

4. To add drivers to the Windows PE image, assuming that drivers are in the C:\Drivers folder, type the following command and then press **Enter:**

   DISM /image:C:\winpe_x64\mount /add-Driver /driver:C:\Drivers /recurse /forceunsigned

   When complete, the Administrator: Deployment and Imaging Tools Environment window should show that drivers have been installed, and you should have a message that *The operation completed successfully*.

5. To add support for Windows PowerShell 3.0 to the Windows PE image, execute each of the following commands:

   CD "C:\Program Files (x86)\Windows Kits\8.1\Assessment and deployment kit\Windows preInstallation Environment\amd64\ WinPE_OCs"

   DISM /image:C:\winpe_x64\mount /Add-Package /PackagePath:.\ WinPE-NetFX4.cab

   DISM /image:C:\winpe_x64\mount /Add-Package /PackagePath:.\ WinPE-Scripting.cab

   DISM /image:C:\winpe_x64\mount /Add-Package /PackagePath:.\ WinPE-WMI.cab

   DISM /image:C:\winpe_x64\mount /Add-Package /PackagePath:.\ WinPE-PowerShell3.cab

   CD C:\winpe_x64

6. To save the changes and unmount the image, type the following command:

   DISM /unmount-image /mountdir:C:\winpe_x64\mount /commit

7. When complete, the Administrator: Deployment and Imaging Tools Environment window should display *The operation completed successfully*.

8. To create an ISO image that can be used to boot media, run the following command:

```
Makewinpemedia /iso C:\winpe_x64 C:\winpe_x64\media\sources
\winpe_x64.iso
```

9. Close File Explorer and the Administrator: Deployment and Imaging Tools Environment.

Creating and Configuring a Reference Computer and Image

The reference computer is a pristine computer that is ready to be deployed. Windows ADK has several tools that will help you create a reference image of the reference computer. You can install from the image stored on a Windows DVD, USB flash drive, or network drive.

The following general steps include how to use a USB and a Windows installation disc to create a reference computer and retrieve an image:

1. Install and customize Windows PE. You need to copy a Windows PE image and add the drivers and packages necessary for Windows PE to function on the reference computer. If you are using a USB device, you can use the `MakeWinPEMedia /UFD` command to create the bootable USB device.

2. Create and modify answer files, which will be used to install Windows based on your organization's environment. To create and edit the answer file, use Windows SIM. When done, copy the answer file to the root directory of the USB device with the name autounattend.xml. Create a profile that includes the CopyProfile setting, so that you can customize the default user profile and copy the answer file profile to the root directory of the USB device as CopyProfile.xml.

3. Plug the USB device and boot the computer with the Windows installation disc. The Setup process will use the Autounattend.xml file to complete the installation. You will then customize the administrator profile.

4. To capture the image, use the `sysprep.exe` command to generalize the system and to use the CopyProfile.xml file:

```
C:\Windows\System32\Sysprep\Sysprep.exe /generalize /oobe /shutdown
/unattend:D:\CopyProfile.xml
```

Then, start up the computer with the Windows PE USB device and use the DISM tool to copy the Windows partition to a network location or external hard drive.

1. Next, deploy the image to a test computer by starting the test system with the Windows PE USB device, use Diskpart to configure the hard drive, and use the `Applyimage` command to apply the previously captured image.

2. Verify and test that the computer image and profile settings are correct.

Starting with Windows Vista, Windows Setup uses a process called image-based (IBS) to provide a single, unified process to install all versions of Windows using the install.wim file. Setup.exe used in the installation process supports the following command-line options:

• **/installfrom:<path>:** Enables you to specify a custom .wim file to use for installation.

• **/m:<folder_name>:** Causes Windows Setup to copy files from an alternate location. This option does not support a UNC path. The folder has a prescribed structure that is described in the Windows ADK.

- **/noreboot:** Instructs Windows Setup not to restart the computer after the first phase of the Setup process completes.
- **/tempdrive:<drive_letter>:** Instructs Windows Setup to create the temporary installation files on the partition specified with this option.
- **/unattend:<answer_file>:** Instructs Windows Setup to use the specified answer file to complete the installation.

During the installation, Windows Setup goes through several different configuration passes. Unattended installation settings can be applied in one or more configuration settings. The configuration passes include:

1. **windowsPE:** Configures the Windows PE and basic Windows setup, including partitioning and formatting a disk, specifying networking parameters, specifying the Windows image to use for the deployment, and specifying any critical drivers needed to access the disk systems or network interfaces. This is done as Windows PE is used to boot a computer to perform Windows installations and troubleshooting.

2. **offlineServicing:** Updates a Windows image using dism.exe, including software fixes, language packs, and other security updates.

3. **generalize:** Removes system-specific information, such as computer name and security ID.

4. **specialize:** Creates and applies system-specific information, such as network settings, international settings, and domain information (including joining a computer to the domain). During this pass, unique security IDs (SIDs) are created.

5. **auditSystem:** Applies settings to the system if the computer is started in audit mode. Audit mode allows you to install and test additional device drivers, applications, and updates to an image. Audit mode can be specified with the sysprep command.

6. **auditUser:** Applies settings to the user if the computer is started in audit mode as specified with the sysprep command.

7. **oobeSystem:** Applies settings to Windows before Windows Welcome starts. It is used to configure Windows Shell options, create user accounts, and specify language and locale settings.

Creating and Using Answer Files with Windows SIM

To streamline the installation process, you can automate the installation of Windows using an *answer file* that is used to provide responses to the prompts that would normally appear during the Windows installation. For example, the answer file can also be used to partition and format disks, install additional device drivers, and specify the Windows features to install and the install language.

Because an answer file is just a text file based on XML, you create an answer file with a text editor or XML editor. However, Microsoft recommends that you use the *System Image Manager (SIM)*, which is part of the Windows ADK. SIM is a tool used to create and manage unattended Windows Setup answer files using a graphical interface and to check answer files.

You can perform the following with the answer file:

- **Partition the hard disk:** Create and format one partition or create and format multiple partitions.
- **Install additional device drivers:** By installing additional drivers that are not included with Windows, you can ensure that the computers are ready to use immediately after installing the Windows operating system. Drivers can be installed by scripting

the installation of an executable file that installs the device driver into the Windows installation disc.

- **Install applications:** Adding applications during installation can be automated by executing a file from a local disk, or even the network.

- **Apply updates:** Critical updates and security updates can be installed by running an executable file much like you would automatically install an application.

- **Configure settings:** By using the answer file, you can customize hundreds of settings during deployment, including defining the computer, adding the computer to the domain, and defining the Internet Explorer home page.

- **Enable or disable features:** Using scripts or answer files, you can easily and automatically add or remove Windows features.

- **Minimize user interaction:** By using an answer file, you can limit or reduce the amount of user interaction. In fact, you could use the answer file to avoid all user interaction during Windows installation. By reducing user interaction, you decrease the time to install Windows, while minimizing user error.

To add a configuration setting to the answer file, browse through the available settings in the Windows Image pane, right-click the setting you want to add and choose the configuration pass specifying when you want the Setup program to configure the setting. The setting then displays in the Answer File pane and the properties specific to that setting appear in the adjacent Properties pane. After the setting has been added, you modify the values in the properties. If you need clarification on a setting, press F1 while a property or setting is highlighted to open the Unattended Windows Setup Reference Guide.

CREATE AN ANSWER FILE

GET READY. To create an answer file, log on to the computer where you installed the ADK and then perform the following steps.

1. Open File Explorer from the taskbar.
2. Create a folder called **C:\DistFold**.
3. Create a folder called **C:\Images**.
4. Copy the **\sources\install.wim** from the Windows installation disc to the **C:\Images** folder.
5. Copy the **\\LON-DC1\Software\unattend.xml** folder to the **C:\Images** folder.
6. Open the Start screen and click **Windows Kits > Windows System Image Manager**.
7. When the Windows System Image Manager console opens, click **Tools** and then click **Create Distribution Share**.
8. When the Create Distribution Share dialog box opens, in the Folder name text box, type **C:\DistFold** and click **Open**.
9. Click **File** and click **Select Windows Image**.
10. When the Select a Windows Image dialog box opens, in the File name text box, type **C:\Images\install.wim** and click **Open**.
11. When the Select an Image dialog box opens, select one of the following and then click **OK:**
    - Windows Server 2016 SERVERSSTANDARDCORE
    - Windows Server 2016 SERVERSSTANDARD
    - Windows Server 2016 SERVERSDATACENTERCORE
    - Windows Server 2016 SERVERSDATACENTER

12. The first time you load the image, it will need to create a catalog file. Click **Yes**. This might take a couple of minutes.

13. Click **File** and click **Open Answer File**. Navigate to and click **C:\Images\unattend .xml** and click **Open**. If you are prompted to associate the answer file with the Windows Server 2016 Windows image, click **Yes**. The answer file elements display in the Answer File pane, as shown in Figure 6-8. To create a new answer file, open the **File** menu and select **New Answer File**.

Figure 6-8

Opening an answer file with
Windows System Image
Manager

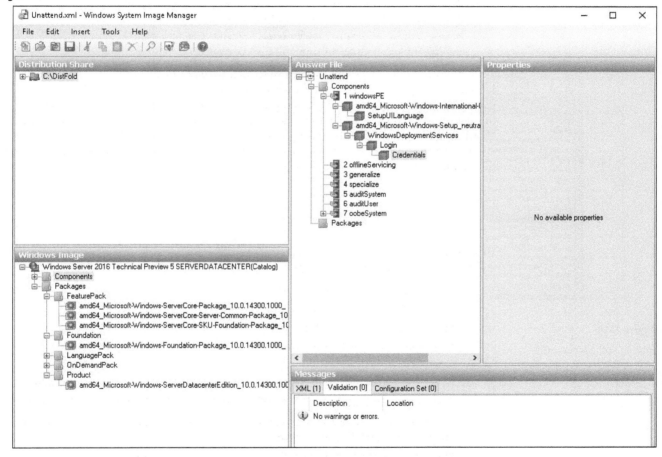

As you can see in the answer file, you can see the seven configuration passes starting with WindowsPE and ending with oobeSystem. To add settings to the configuration pass, go to the Windows Image pane, right-click the component that you want to add, and choose the configuration pass that you want to add the setting to, as shown in Figure 6-9.

The setting then displays in the Answer File pane and the properties specific to that setting appear in the adjacent Properties pane, as shown in Figure 6-10. After the setting has been added, you modify the values in the properties. If you need clarification on a setting, press F1 while a property or setting is highlighted to open the Unattended Windows Setup Reference Guide.

Figure 6-9

Adding settings to a
specialize pass

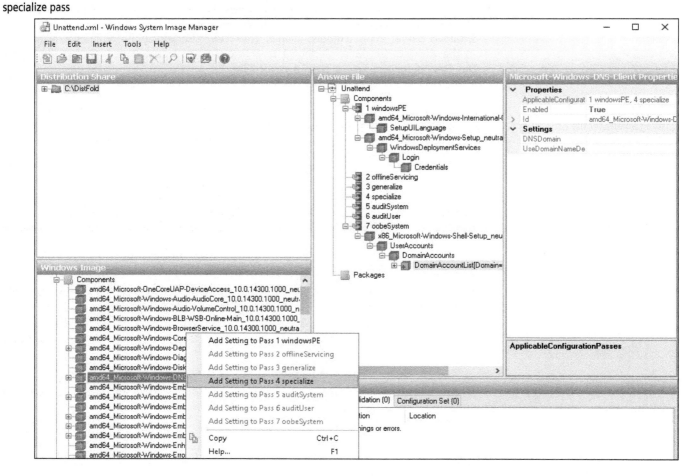

Figure 6-10

Looking at the Answer File
pane and adjacent properties

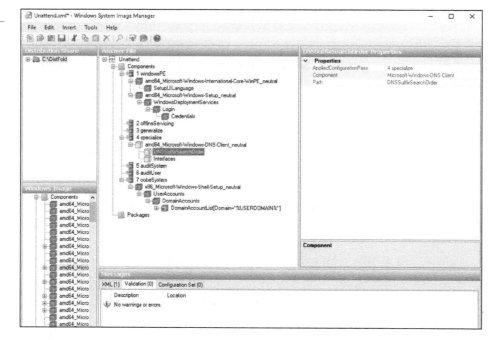

Although you can create the answer file by downloading and installing the Windows Automated Installation Kit (AIK) and running the System Image Manager (SIM), there are a number of non-Microsoft websites that provide unattend.xml files. However, if you download one of these answer files, you need to review the file using a text editor such as Notepad to provide the proper product key and to use your own company information.

Using Sysprep to Prepare the Reference Computer

Before capturing a reference computer, you need to prepare the reference computer with the sysprep.exe utility. The Microsoft System Preparation Utility (sysprep.exe) prepares a Windows computer for cloning by removing specific computer information, such as the computer name and security identifier (SID).

On Windows 10 and Windows Server 2016, sysprep.exe is located in the C:\Windows\System32\Sysprep folder. When you reboot the computer with the capture image, a wizard will then guide you through the process of capturing an image of the computer and uploading it to the WDS server.

The `sysprep.exe` command supports the following options:

- **/generalize:** Instructs sysprep to remove system-specific data, such as event logs, the computer name, and unique SIDs from the Windows operating system installation.
- **/oobe:** Instructs Windows to present the Windows Welcome Wizard when the computer starts next time. The Windows Welcome Wizard allows you to name the computer and generate a SID and any other required unique information.
- **/shutdown:** Instructs the computer to shut down and not to restart.
- **/audit:** Instructs the Windows operating system installation to run in audit mode the next time the computer starts.
- **/reboot:** Instructs the computer to restart. You use this option if you want to verify that the OOBE phase runs correctly.
- **/quiet:** Runs sysprep without displaying on-screen confirmation messages. If you automate sysprep, use this option in conjunction with an answer file.
- **/unattend:answerfile:** Applies settings in an answer file to sysprep.

Therefore, the basic command to prepare a computer for imaging is:

```
sysprep /generalize /oobe /shutdown
```

Capturing a Reference Image Using DISM

After you have configured the reference computer, used the `sysprep` command to prepare a computer for imaging, and shut down the computer, you are ready to manually capture the image of a partition.

To manually capture the image using DISM, you need to perform the following steps:

1. Boot the computer using Windows PE.
2. Map a drive to a network share.
3. Use Diskpart to assign a drive letter to any partitions that you need to capture that do not have any drive letters assigned. Unless you customized the system partition, you will not have to create an image of it because it will automatically be re-created.
4. Use DISM to capture the system partition (if the system partition has been customized).
5. Use DISM to capture the primary partitions and any logical partitions.

When you boot the computer using Windows PE, and if for some reason, you accidently boot the computer to Windows, the OOBE will start. If this happens, the computer will no longer be generalized. Therefore, you should finish the OOBE wizard, let the computer finish booting, and then run the `sysprep` command again.

If you want to capture the system partition (or any volume that does not have a drive letter assigned to it), you need to assign a drive letter to the volume. After you boot to Windows PE, you start at the X: drive. Then, execute the following commands:

```
Diskpart
Select disk 0
List partition
Select partition=1
Assign letter=s
Exit
```

The `List partition` command displays the partitions defined on the hard disk. Typically, the system partition will be partition 1. The `Assign letter` command assigns the drive letter. The `Exit` command closes the `Diskpart` command environment.

To capture the images using the `DISM` command and save the .wim files to the C drive, use the following commands:

```
DISM /Capture-Image /ImageFile:c:\windows-partition.wim /
CaptureDir:C:\ /Name:"Windows partition"
```

```
DISM /Capture-Image /ImageFile:s:\system-partition.wim /CaptureDir:C:\
/Name:"System partition"
```

It should be noted that you could have also saved the image directly to a network shared folder.

When you use the `/Capture-Image` option, you can use the following options:

- **/ConfigFile:** Specifies the location of a configuration file that lists exclusions for image capture and compress commands.
- **/Compress:** Specifies the type of compression (maximum, fast, none) used for the initial capture operation.
- **/Bootable:** Marks a volume image as being a bootable image. This option can only be used with Windows PE images, and only one volume image can be marked as bootable in a .wim file.
- **/CheckIntegrity:** Detects and tracks .wim file corruption when used with `capture`, `unmount`, `export`, and `commit` operations.
- **/Verify:** Checks for errors and file duplication.
- **/NoRpFix:** Disables the reparse point tag fix. A reparse point is a file that contains a link to another file on the file system.

When you capture the image, you need a place to store the image. Therefore, you need to share a folder so that it can be accessed over the network. After you boot the reference computer with Windows PE, execute the following commands:

```
Net Use G: \\Server01\Images
```

You will then be prompted to enter a user name and password. Then, use the following two commands to copy the image files to the network share.

```
copy C:\windows-partition.wim G:\Images\
```

```
copy c:\system-partition.wim G:\Images\
```

Performing an Unattended Installation Using WDS

If you load the standard Windows image files and boot files, and you connect to **Windows Deployment Services (WDS)**, you would still be doing a manual installation where you need to go through the Installation Wizard. If you have hundreds of installations, you probably want to perform an unattended installation where you boot the computer and it automatically starts and completes the installation.

To perform an unattended installation using WDS, you need to upload two unattend files. The two unattend files are:

- **WDS client unattend file:** The unattend file automates the WDS client procedure that begins when the client computer loads the boot image file. It is loaded from the Properties of the server on the Client tab.
- **Operating system unattend file:** The unattend file for a standard operating system installation contains responses to all the prompts that appear after the client computer loads the install image file. It is specified within the Properties of the image.

■ Introducing Microsoft Deployment Toolkit (MDT)

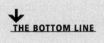
THE BOTTOM LINE

Although WDS can deploy an operating system image and even supports adding some drivers, you are limited to what you can do with WDS. However, when you combine WDS with Microsoft Deployment Toolkit (or combine Configuration Manager with MDT), you get a much more robust deployment solution.

The *Microsoft Deployment Toolkit (MDT)* Build 8443 or higher provides end-to-end guidance for the planning, building, and deploying of Windows 10 and Windows Server 2016. It allows you to deploy Windows by using a Lite-Touch Installation (LTI) or Zero-Touch Installation (ZTI). MDT allows you to create a deployment share, which contains additional scripts and task sequences to customize the Windows installation process.

The latest version of MDT, as of this writing, is Microsoft Deployment Toolkit Build 8443, which is available as a free download from the Microsoft Download Center. Be sure to get the latest update to support Windows 10 and Windows Server 2016.

An MDT deployment is controlled by customized scripts called *task sequences*, which automate the various tasks required to install operating systems, applications, and other software on a computer. You create and manage task sequences using the Deployment Workbench application included in MDT.

In addition to performing the actual OS installation, task sequences can control the installation of additional drivers, service packs, and other updates. You can also use task sequences to automate the process of migrating user data from an existing workstation to a new installation.

MDT supports three types of deployments, which differ primarily in the amount of interaction required at the client and the tools they use at the server end. These deployment types are as follows:

- *Lite-Touch Installation (LTI):* Stores images on an MDT deployment share and typically requires some interaction from a user at the client computer during the deployment.
- *Zero-Touch Installation (ZTI):* Requires System Center Configuration Manager (SCCM) for image storage and deployment. No interaction is required or allowed at the client.

- **User-Driven Installation (UDI):** Requires System Center Configuration Manager for image storage and deployment. A variable amount of interaction is required from a user at the client computer.

From an infrastructure perspective, the main difference between these deployment types is that ZTI and UDI require SCCM to be installed on the network. This is no small undertaking, as SCCM is a complex and expensive product.

Few administrators would find it worthwhile to purchase and install SCCM solely for the purpose of server and workstation deployment. SCCM, along with the other System Center components, provides a comprehensive management solution that can extend far beyond the deployment process, so its adoption is likely to be a departmental decision. However, in situations where administrators must deploy servers and workstations at remote sites, where no client interaction is possible, a ZTI might be the best solution.

You can perform an LTI deployment, on the other hand, with only free tools, such as MDT, so it requires only a minimal investment in infrastructure.

Understanding the MDT Deployment Process

The high-level process of installing servers and workstations using MDT is the same whether you are using an LTI, ZTI, or UDI deployment.

Essentially, you deploy the software needed for your workstation configuration to a reference computer, capture an image of the reference computer, and then deploy that image to your target computers. This reference computer is, therefore, the model for your mass deployment.

Preparing to use the LTI method involves the following basic steps:

1. Plan the MDT imaging strategy, including how you will build the MDT management computer and how you will store images and related files.
2. Install the prerequisites and MDT.
3. Create the deployment share.
4. Create and customize the task sequences. Task sequences are used to automate the deployment process.
5. Start the reference computer with the MDT media. This transfers the task sequence files, the task sequence, and the boot image to the reference computer.
6. Run the deployment wizard to install the operating system on the reference computer and capture an image of the reference computer.
7. Copy the captured image to the management computer.
8. Create the boot image and task sequence to deploy the captured image to target computers.
9. Update the deployment share.
10. Start the target computer with the MDT media. This transfers the task sequence files, the task sequence, and the boot image to the reference computer.
11. Run the deployment wizard to install the operating system on the target computer.

How you initiate the installations, get the necessary files to the target computers, and interact with the Setup process are all issues that depend on the deployment type you are using and the planning decisions you make before you begin the deployment. For example, you can choose to initiate the deployment process for an individual workstation by having it perform a network boot and download the necessary files from a WDS server, or you can create boot disks for the workstations—DVDs or flash drives—and have the computers download the installation files from a network share after booting, or you could place all of the required installation files on a bootable disk and run the installation with no network access at all. Finally, you can use SCCM to push the files onto the target computers and initiate the installation.

You can install MDT on any workstation running Windows 7 or later, or on any server running Windows Server 2008 R2 or later. There are also some software prerequisites for MDT deployment scenarios, as follows:

- **Windows Assessment and Deployment Toolkit (ADK) for Windows 10:** Another free download, the Windows ADK contains a variety of tools used during the MDT planning and deployment processes, including the User State Migration Tool, Windows PE, Deployment Image Servicing and Management, Windows System Image Manager, and sysprep.
- **System Center Configuration Manager:** SCCM 2012 R2 or 2016 is required for ZTI deployments.
- **SQL Server:** To store configuration settings in an MDT database, you must have access to a SQL Server installation. You can use the SCCM SQL Server or any other SQL Server installed on the network, or you can install one (such as the free SQL Server Express) on the MDT computer.
- **Microsoft Word:** Microsoft Word is required to view the MDT documentation files. You can also use the free Word Viewer, available from the Microsoft Download Center.

INSTALL MDT

GET READY. Log on to the computer where you will install MDT using an account with administrative privileges and download the MDT files from the Microsoft Download Center. Then, to install MDT, perform the following steps.

1. Open File Explorer, browse to the location of your download, and launch the **MicrosoftDeploymentToolkit_x64.msi** or **MicrosoftDeploymentToolkit_x86.msi** file. If you are prompted to determine whether you want to run this file, click **Run**. The Microsoft Deployment Toolkit Setup Wizard appears.
2. Click **Next** to bypass the Welcome page. The End User License Agreement page appears.
3. Select the **I accept the terms in the license agreement** check box and click **Next**. The Custom Setup page appears.
4. Modify the features to be installed (if needed) and click **Next**. The Customer Experience Improvement Program page appears.
5. Select one of the options and click **Next**. The Ready to Install Microsoft Deployment Toolkit page appears.
6. Click **Install**. The wizard installs MDT and the Completed the Microsoft Deployment Toolkit Setup Wizard page appears.
7. Click **Finish**.

Configuring MDT

> Once you have installed MDT, you must configure it before you can start assembling the components needed for your deployments.

During the configuration, you will create a deployment share, which will be used to hold images, applications, drivers, and packages.

⊖ CONFIGURE MDT

GET READY. Log on to the computer where you installed MDT using an account with administrative privileges. To configure MDT, perform the following steps.

1. Click **Start**, click **Microsoft Deployment Toolkit > Deployment Workbench**. Open the Deployment Workbench console, as shown in Figure 6-11.

Figure 6-11

The Deployment Workbench console

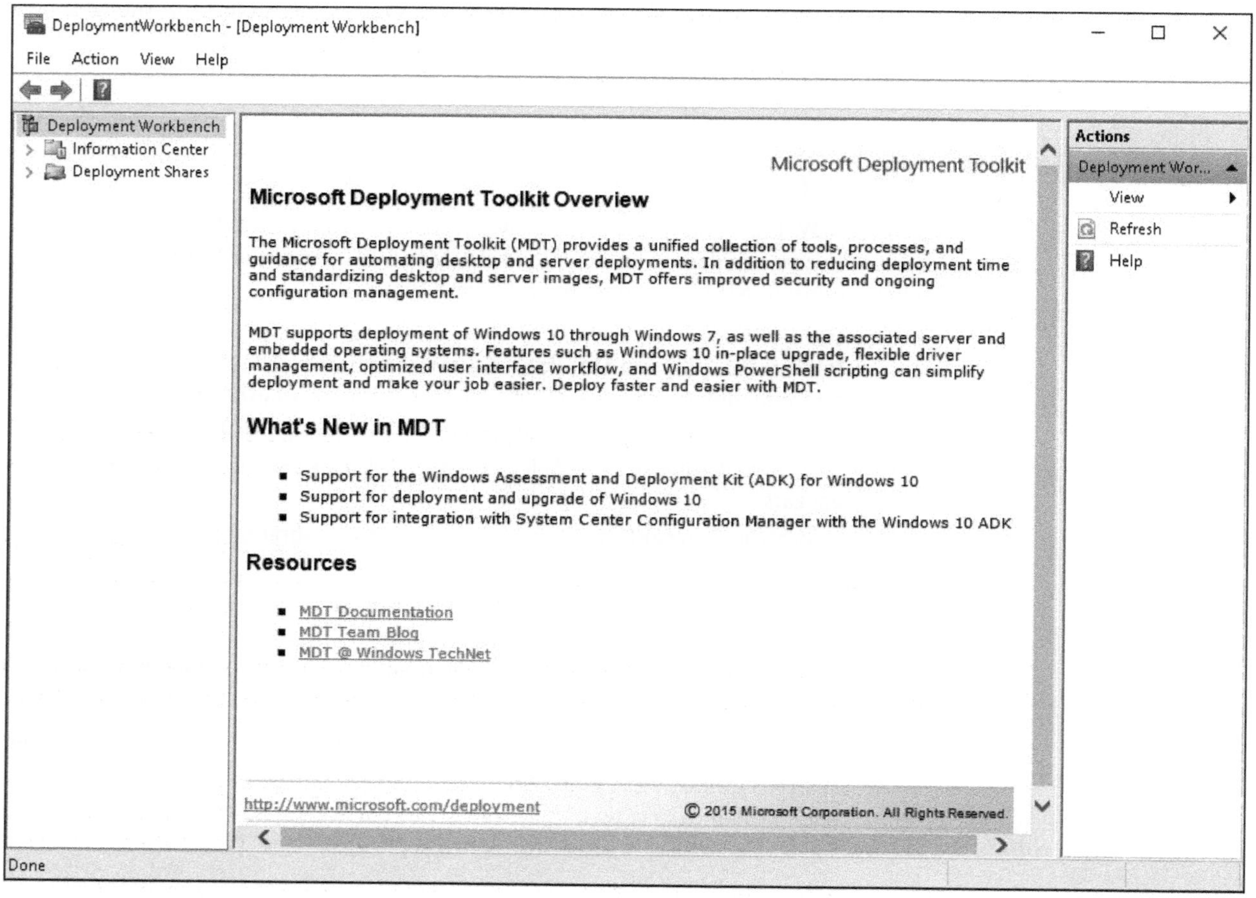

2. Right-click the **Deployment Shares** folder and, choose **New Deployment Share.** The New Deployment Share Wizard appears, displaying the Path page.

3. In the Deployment share path text box, type the location where you want to create the deployment share and click **Next**. The Share page appears.

4. In the Share name text box, type the name you want to assign to the network share and click **Next**. The Descriptive Name page appears.

5. Type a descriptive name for the share and click **Next**. The Options page appears, as shown as Figure 6-12.

Figure 6-12

The Options page of the New Deployment Share Wizard

New Deployment Share Wizard   ✕

Options

Path
Share
Descriptive Name
Options
Summary
Progress
Confirmation

When performing deployments, the behavior of the Deployment Wizard can be customized by turning various wizard panes on or off. For those that are not desired, modify the defaults below as appropriate.

☑ Ask if a computer backup should be performed.

☐ Ask for a product key.

☐ Ask to set the local Administrator password.

☑ Ask if an image should be captured.

☑ Ask if BitLocker should be enabled.

These settings can be changed later by modifying the rules defined for the deployment share.

Previous   Next   Cancel

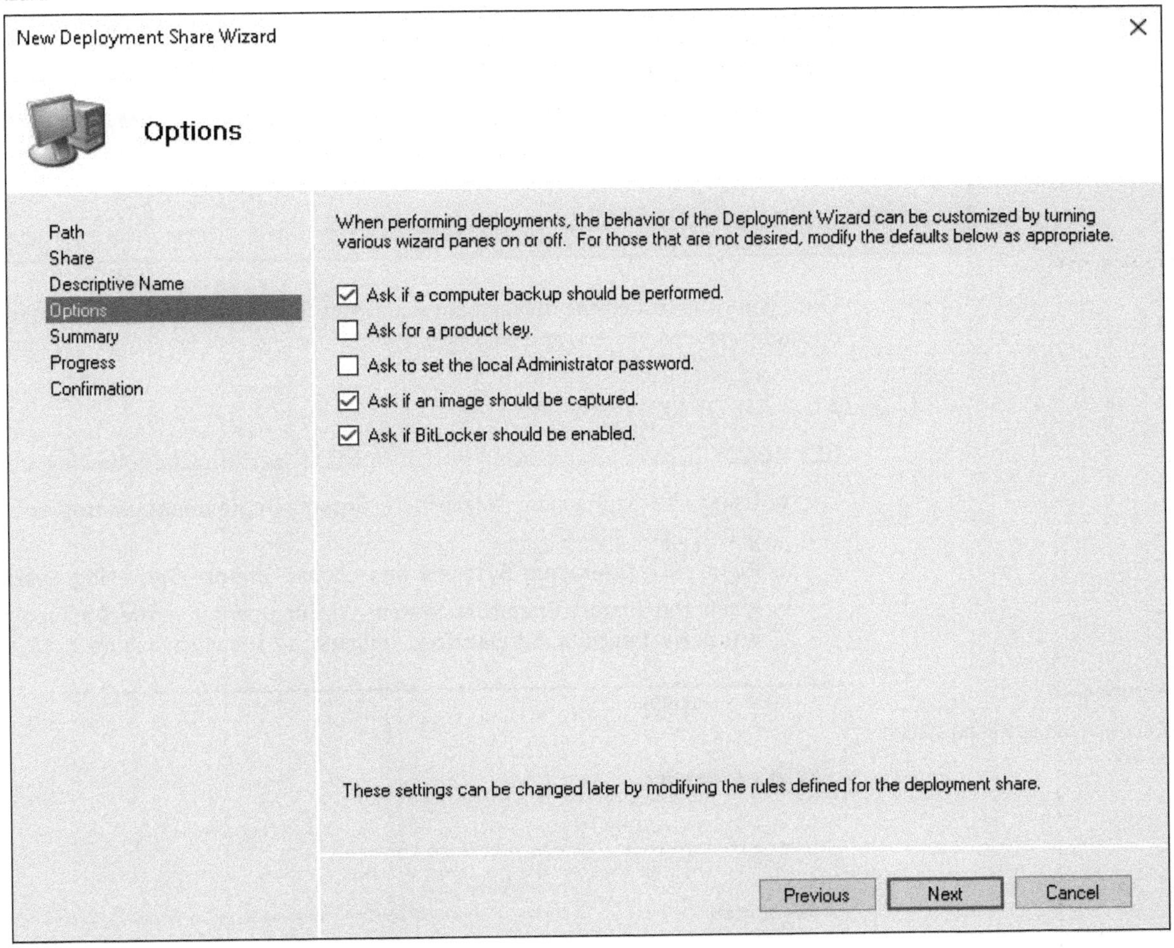

TAKE NOTE* Placing a dollar sign ("$") at the end of a share name renders it invisible to users browsing the network. However, the share is still accessible to people and processes that know the name.

6. Select or clear the check boxes to specify which panes should appear in the Deployment Wizard and click **Next**. The Summary page appears. Click **Next** to continue. The wizard creates the deployment share and the Confirmation page appears.

7. Click **Finish**. The deployment share appears in the Deployment Workbench console, as shown in Figure 6-13.

Figure 6-13

The Deployment Workbench console with a new deployment share

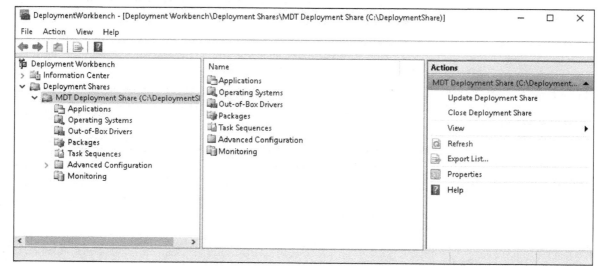

Once you have created the deployment share, you can begin to populate it by adding applications, operating systems, drivers, and packages, and by creating task sequences and configuration settings.

→ ADD AN OPERATING SYSTEM

GET READY. To add an operating system in MDT, perform the following steps.

1. Using the Deployment Workbench, expand **Deployment Shares** and expand a deployment share.

2. Right-click **Operating Systems** and choose **Import Operating System**.

3. When the Import Operating System Wizard opens, on the OS Type page, select **Windows Deployment Services images**, as shown in Figure 6-14, and click **Next**.

Figure 6-14

Choosing the operating system to add

Import Operating System Wizard

OS Type

OS Type
Source
Image
Setup
WDS Server
Destination
Summary
Progress
Confirmation

Choose the type of operating system to add.

○ Full set of source files
The operating system being added consists of source files from a Windows DVD, CD, or equivalent.

○ Custom image file
Add a captured image (WIM file) that you wish to deploy.

◉ Windows Deployment Services images
Add the images available on a specific Windows Deployment Services server.

Previous   Next   Cancel

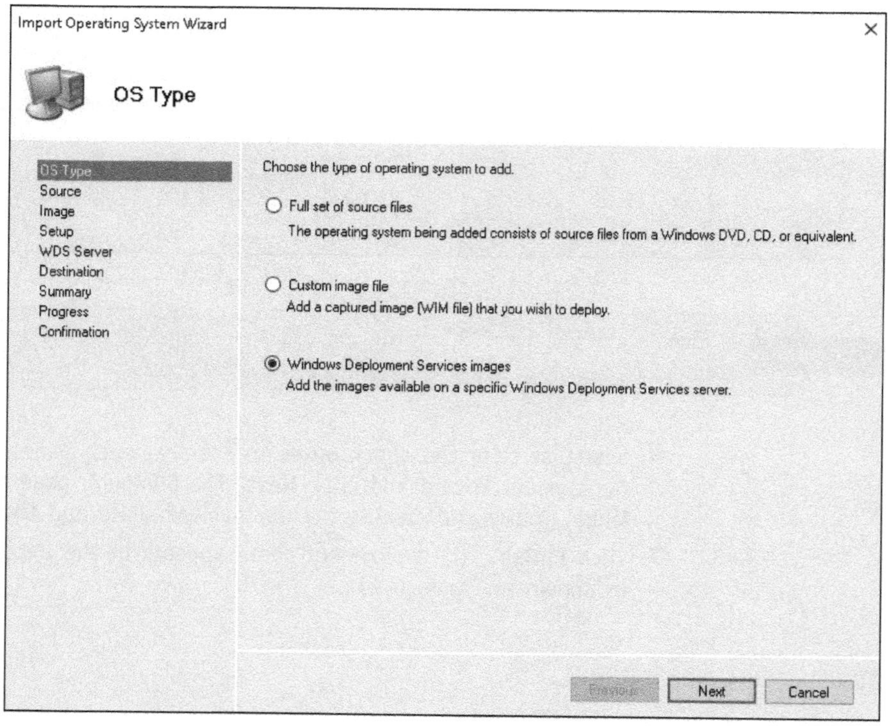

4. On the WDS Server page, in the Server name text box, type **LON-SVR1** and click **Next**.

5. On the Summary page, click **Next**.

6. When the operating systems are imported, click **Finish**.

CREATE A TASK SEQUENCE

GET READY. To create a task sequence in MDT, perform the following steps.

1. Using the Deployment Workbench, expand the **Deployment Shares** and expand a deployment share.

2. Right-click **Task Sequences** and choose **New Task Sequence**.

3. When the New Task Sequence Wizard starts, as shown in Figure 6-15, in the Task Sequence ID text box, type an ID for the task sequence, such as **DEP2016**. In the Task Sequence name text box, type **Deploy Windows Server 2016**. Click **Next**.

Figure 6-15

Creating a new task sequence

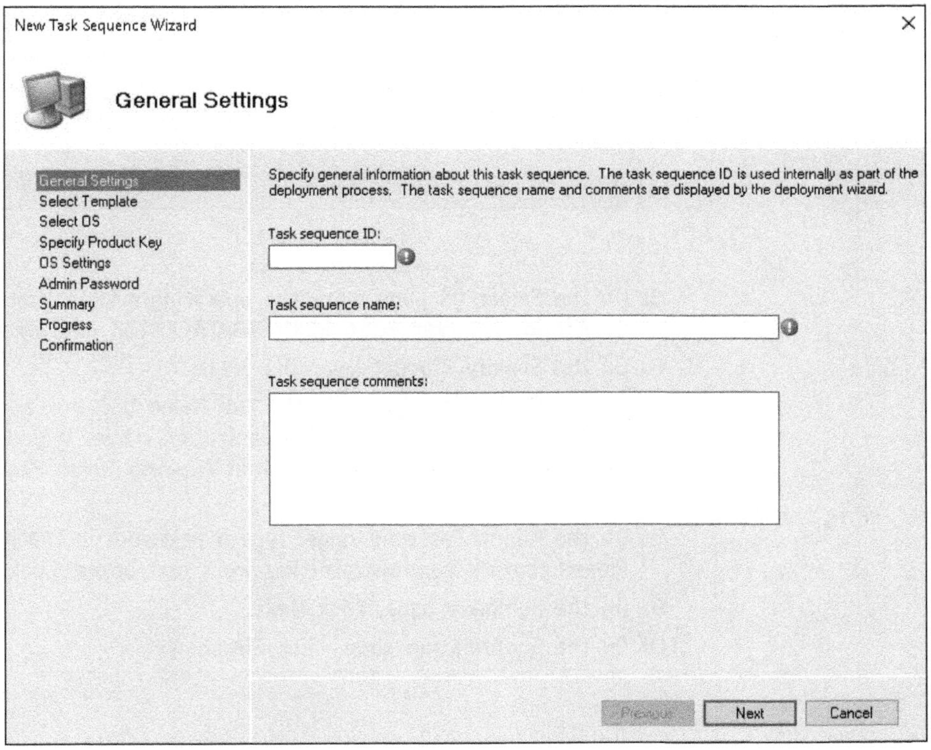

4. Figure 6-16 shows the available task sequence templates. On the Select Template page, select the **Standard Client Task Sequence**. Click **Next**.

Figure 6-16

Selecting a template

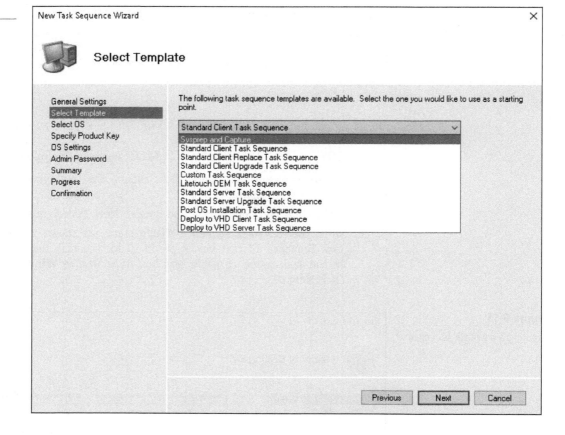

5. On the Select OS page, click the operating system that you want to deploy, such as **Windows Server 2016 SERVERDATACENTER**, and click **Next**.

6. On the Specify Product key, click **Next**.

7. On the OS Settings page, in the Full Name text box and the Organization text box, type the Full Name and Organization name. If you want an Internet Explorer home page, in the Internet Explorer Home Page text box, type an URL. Click **Next**.

8. On the Admin Password page, type a password in the Administrator Password and Please confirm Administrator Password text boxes. Click **Next**.

9. On the Summary page, click **Next**.

10. On the Confirmation page, click **Finish**.

You can modify a task sequence by right-clicking the task sequence and choosing Properties. On the General tab, you can modify the task sequence name, comments, and task sequence version. You can also specify which platform the task can run on, and if the task is hidden or enabled.

On the Task Sequence tab (as shown in Figure 6-17), you can specify what occurs during the task sequence, including injecting or adding the drivers that you added to the Deployment Workbench earlier. To help organize these tasks, the tasks are divided into groups, such as State Capture, State Restore, Preinstall, Install, and Postinstall.

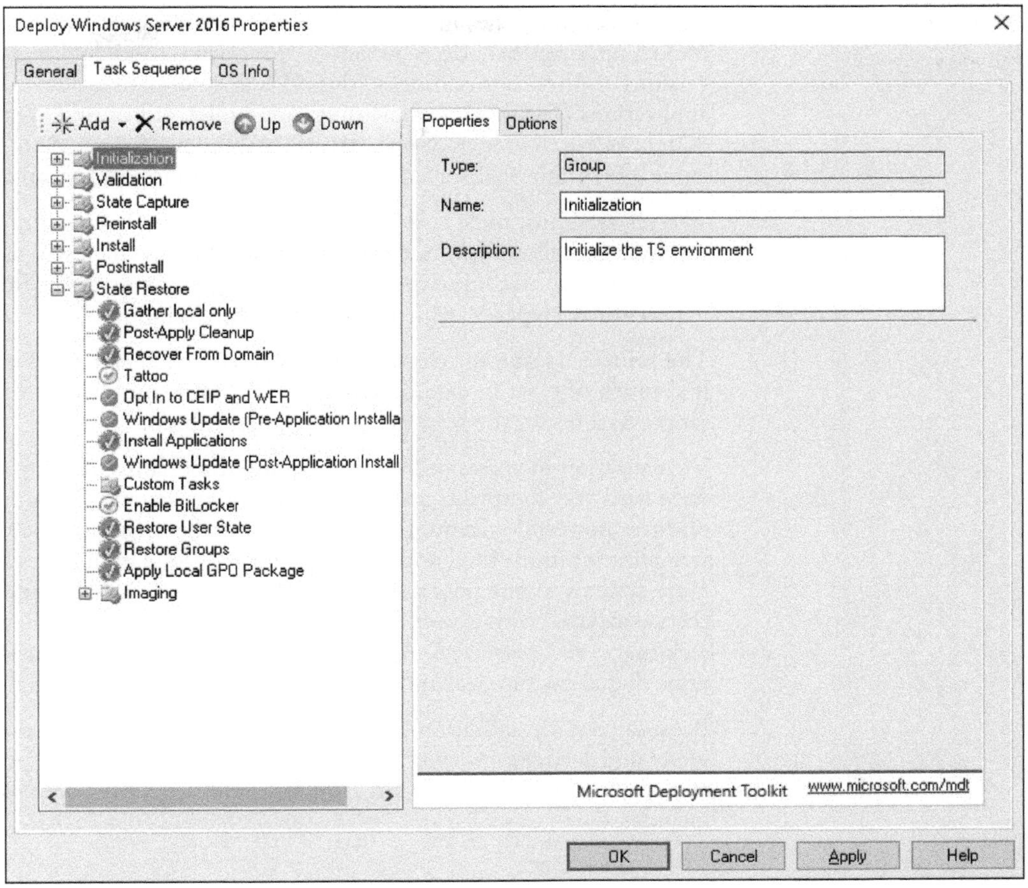

Figure 6-17

Configuring the task sequence

■ Planning for Windows Server Virtualizations

THE BOTTOM LINE

Early data centers could consist of hundreds of physical servers, with each server being assigned a workload (such as a specific application or service). Unfortunately, most of the resources on an individual server were often wasted. Eventually, data centers started to consolidate many physical servers to a single server running multiple virtual machines or virtual servers using Microsoft Hyper-V or VMware ESX/ESXi. As a result, there was a significant increase in resource use while reducing overall cost and power consumption. Since virtualization was introduced, virtualization has matured into an efficient and dependable system and architecture.

CERTIFICATION READY
Plan for Windows Server virtualization
Objective 1.3

When you first learned about computers and Windows, you mostly learned by running Windows on a desktop or mobile computer running on a physical system. Also, if you have a home computer, it likely consists of Windows running on a physical system (a desktop or mobile computer).

When you run Windows servers on a physical system in a production environment, Windows is the primary operating system on the server and the hardware is dedicated to Windows and the applications that are running on Windows.

When you use virtualization for a server environment, you use a few very powerful host systems onto which you install guest systems, known as *virtual machines (VMs)*. VMs behave like physical machines in almost every conceivable way. They must be patched, restarted, backed up, upgraded, decommissioned, replaced, fixed, and maintained. They are virtual versions of physical machines with CPUs, memory, disk, network, an operating system, and applications. Today, almost any operating system (including Windows 7, Windows 8/8.1, Windows 10, Windows Server 2012 R2, Windows Server 2016, Linux, and FreeBSD just to name a few) can be installed into a virtual machine and run on a host system.

The physical host must run hypervisor software that manages the resources of the physical machine and allows you to create virtual machines, which will use portions of the resources of the physical machine, while isolating the operating systems from each other. The Microsoft hypervisor is Hyper-V, which is included with Windows Server 2016.

The primary reason for virtualization is efficiency. Server hardware has become so powerful that much of it sat in data centers with utilization numbers hovering in the 5% to 10% range. As a result, the server is grossly underutilized.

Virtualization increases utilization of computing hardware with server consolidation to minimize hardware footprints and to save money by "stacking" multiple, complementary services on these powerful systems. As server hardware became more powerful, with hardware-assisted virtualization from Intel and AMD, having consolidation ratios in the range of 20, 30, or more systems to one host system is common. With virtualization, you have lower computing costs associated with power, cooling, hardware expenditures, maintenance, rented data center rack space, and personnel. Also, virtualization vendors and third parties have created applications that allow physical and virtual systems to be managed in a single application.

Because your virtualization infrastructure will most likely run the bulk of your organization server and services, in which you want to maintain acceptable performance while minimizing cost, you need to plan your virtualization infrastructure. Some of the evaluation factors would include:

- Project scope
- Resources and performance
- Compatibility
- Application and services
- Supportability
- Licensing
- Availability

As a general guideline, each virtualization project should include the following steps:

1. Determine the virtualization scope.
2. Determine the workloads.
3. Determine the backup and fault-tolerance requirements.
4. Design the host infrastructure.
5. Map workloads to host.

Any time you start a project, you need to define the scope of the project. In other words, determine what needs to be accomplished with the project. Many projects tend to have scope creep where items keep getting added to the project. As a result, you miss deadlines of when the project was supposed to be done, which can cause cost overruns.

When determining the virtualization scope, you need to determine the milestones and goals of the project. The scope determination might not be as easy as it sounds because a virtualization environment could run the applications and services for an entire company and you want to make sure you do it right.

When you determine the workload, you are basically taking an inventory of all current machines and their applications. You should also ask which machines and applications need to be added or upgraded during the foreseeable future. You want to make sure that you do not outgrow the selected hardware before you get started, or shortly after you complete the project. Luckily, there are applications that can help you determine your current workload such as Microsoft Assessment and Planning (MAP) Toolkit.

Before you start moving to a virtual environment, list your fault-tolerance requirements and how you are going to back up each system, applications, or pools of data. You can then determine the fault-tolerance mechanism and technology that you are already using. At this point, you can still look at your vulnerabilities to see what additional fault-tolerance mechanisms and technology that you will still need.

The next logical step is to figure out which VMs should go on which hosts. You would like your design to be flexible so that if you lose a host or you need to do maintenance on a host, you can move the affected VMs to another host. You need to make sure that you have enough resources so that you can still run all your hosts if you lose a host, or even an entire chassis, which might contain multiple physical servers.

Because VMs can be moved from host to host, you might take another approach and look at which VMs need to be running on different hosts, such as those used in a failover cluster. That way, if you lose a host with one of the failover cluster nodes, the node will be on another host, and the applications running on the cluster will continue to function. In any case, you should create a standard design for all virtualization hosts.

When you map workloads to hosts, you need to consider the following:

- What is the host server capacity, including how many virtual machines you can place on a host?
- How much resource buffer do you want to implement on each host computer?
- What performance characteristics and resource utilization do you want for the virtual machines, including network, processor, disk, and memory?

To help you determine which VMs should run on each host, MAP has the MAP Server Virtualization and Consolidation Wizard, which assists in the design of the host server infrastructure. Lastly, the project should be well-documented and you should consider creating a proof of concept (POC) that you can use as a test before implementing the infrastructure into production. The POC can also be used for training purposes.

Determining Considerations for Deploying Workloads into Virtualized Environments

> While you are trying to determine your scope, you can take a look at the required resources to run the virtualization infrastructure. You can start with how many virtual computers you need to run. You then need to know how much memory and processing these servers use.

CERTIFICATION READY
Determine considerations for deploying workloads into virtualized environments
Objective 1.3

If a virtual machine needs to use half of the processors or memory of a host computer, or requires most of the I/O compatibility of a host, the virtual machine might not be a good candidate for virtualization. It should go without saying that your hosts need to have sufficient resources to run all the virtual machines at the same time.

You also need to look at your storage and network requirements. Larger virtual environments require large amounts of central storage to run many virtual machines. You also need to look at how the physical hosts will communicate with the central storage and if the communication links will be sufficient to support adequate disk performance, as well as normal network performance.

You also need to look at your operating systems, applications, and services to determine if they can run on a virtual machine. Some applications might need direct access to the system hardware, or to hardware items that are not available in a virtual machine. You also need to evaluate if your applications are licensed to run in a virtual environment.

Lastly, when looking at your applications and services, determine which applications require high availability and which high-availability options you have. It is very easy to move a virtual machine from one host to another if a host fails. In addition, you can configure a failover cluster, which uses two servers to run an application or service. One server is actively doing the work, while the other is waiting passively. If the active server fails, the passive server can take over the workload.

The goal in most organizations is to utilize all servers adequately, whether they are physical or virtual. You can fully utilize some server roles such as SQL Server or Exchange Server Mailbox servers, by deploying additional SQL Server instances or moving more mailboxes to the server. In some cases, you can virtualize server workloads in one scenario, but not in other scenarios. For example, in a very large domain with thousands of users logging on simultaneously, it might not be practical to virtualize a domain controller. However, in a smaller domain or in a branch office deployment, virtualizing domain controllers might be your best option.

Using the Microsoft Assessment and Planning (MAP) Toolkit

The *Microsoft Assessment and Planning (MAP) Toolkit* is a free, comprehensive agentless tool that can inventory, assess, and report on an organization's environment. You can install it on any system running Windows Vista and higher or Windows Server 2008 and higher.

CERTIFICATION READY
Assess virtualization workloads using the Microsoft Assessment and Planning (MAP) Toolkit
Objective 1.3

The MAP Toolkit analyzes the inventory of an organization's server infrastructure, performs an assessment, and then creates reports used for upgrade and migration plans. MAP is available for Windows 10, Windows Server 2012 R2, and Windows Server 2016, as well as for other products, such as SQL Server 2016. It can also determine the movement to cloud-based software, including Office 365 and Microsoft Azure.

You can use MAP to perform the following tasks:

- Perform an inventory of your organization's IT infrastructure and provide a detailed report about which machines can run Windows XP or higher and Windows 2000 Server or higher. It can also inventory Linux, HP-UX, VMware ESX, VMWare ESXi, and VMWare Server v2. MAP can also recommend specific upgrades that you can do to ensure that a computer can run Windows 10, Windows Server 2012 R2, and Windows Server 2016.
- Capture the performance metrics of the current IT infrastructure, which can be used to plan consolidation, server virtualization, or scaling of servers. Based on the metrics, you can estimate server usage before and after virtualization, determine which servers are the best candidates to be virtualized, and determine the hosts on which those virtual machines should be placed.

INSTALL MAP

GET READY. To install MAP on a computer running Windows Server 2016, perform the following steps.

1. In Windows Server 2016, double-click **MapSetup.exe**. If you are prompted to run this file, click **Run**.

2. When the Microsoft Assessment and Planning Toolkit Wizard opens, on the Welcome page, click **Next**.

3. On the License Agreement page, select **I accept the terms in the License Agreement** and click **Next**.

4. On the Installation Folder page, click **Next**.

5. On the Customer Experience Improvement Program page, select **Do not join the program at this time**. Click **Next**.

6. On the Begin the Installation page, click **Install**.

7. When the installation is complete, click **Finish**.

8. Open the **Start** menu and click **All Apps**. Then, under the Microsoft Assessment and Planning Toolkit section, click **Microsoft Assessment and Planning Toolkit**.

9. When the Microsoft Assessment and Planning Toolkit initially opens, the Microsoft Assessment and Planning Toolkit dialog box opens. In the *Create an inventory database* section, in the Name text box, type **MAP**. Click **OK**. Figure 6-18 shows the Microsoft Assessment and Planning Toolkit.

Figure 6-18

The Microsoft Assessment and Planning Toolkit

Accessing Virtualization Workloads

> After you install the Microsoft Assessment and Planning Toolkit, you can use the MAP Toolkit to perform a complete inventory of all your servers and to collect performance metrics for those servers. You can then analyze data to determine which servers should be virtualized and where you should place the virtual machines.

When you use MAP, you should consider the following six phases:

1. Choose goals.
2. Gather data collection requirements.
3. Prepare the environment.
4. Install MAP.
5. Collect data.
6. Review reports.

MAP can be used in several inventory, assessment, and capacity planning and software usage tracking scenarios. Therefore, before you start using the tool, as part of Phase 1, you should determine what information you must gather. To help you perform data collection and organize the data, MAP uses wizards.

In phase 2, you determine what is needed for MAP to communicate with the machine. This includes determining a user name and password that can connect to and inventory the machines. You also might need to determine whether you need to configure any firewall and antivirus software settings so that MAP can connect to the computer and perform the inventory.

In phase 3, you configure MAP's communication protocols, including Windows Management Instrumentation (WMI), Active Directory Domain Services (AD DS), SQL Server commands, VMware Web services, and Secure Shell with remote shell commands. During this phase, you also configure the firewalls and antivirus software packages.

- MAP contains several helpful wizards to assist in the inventory process:
- Inventory and Assessment Wizard
- Performance Metrics Wizard
- Hardware Library Wizard
- Server Virtualization and Consolidation Wizard
- Prepare New Reports and Proposals Wizard

In phase 4, you install MAP. You can use either a Microsoft SQL Server 2012 Express database, or you can use a dedicated SQL server that is running SQL Server 2008 or higher. If you use a full database server, you must create a nondefault instance named MAPS before running the MAP installer. Note that you cannot load MAP on a domain controller.

During phase 5, you collect data by selecting the inventory scenario, selecting the discovery method, and providing the credentials that will connect to and inventory the target machine. You can also use the Performance Metrics Wizard to collect specific performance-related information, such as the processor, memory, and network and disk usage for Windows and Linux-based servers. As MAP runs, it shows the number of computers found, the number of machines inventoried, and the number of machines that still need to be inventoried.

In phase 6, you review the reports. If you click Desktop > Server > Desktop Virtualization, you can view information specific to a scenario such as Windows 10 Readiness or Windows Server 2016 Readiness.

Before you deploy MAP, you should ensure the following:

- That the firewall allows WMI traffic from the inventory subnet
- That Remote Administration and File and Printer Sharing are allowed through firewalls
- If you are using network access policy, that local accounts are set to Classic mode

→ **PERFORM AN INVENTORY BY USING MAP**

GET READY. To perform an inventory using MAP on a computer running Windows Server 2016, perform the following steps.

1. Click **Start** to open the Start menu and then click **All Programs.** Then, under the Microsoft Assessment and Planning Toolkit section, click **Microsoft Assessment and Planning Toolkit.**

2. From Overview, click **Perform an inventory.**

3. When the Inventory and Assessment Wizard opens, on the Inventory Scenarios page (see Figure 6-19), select the desired inventory, such as **Windows computers.** Click **Next.**

Figure 6-19

Specifying an inventory scenario

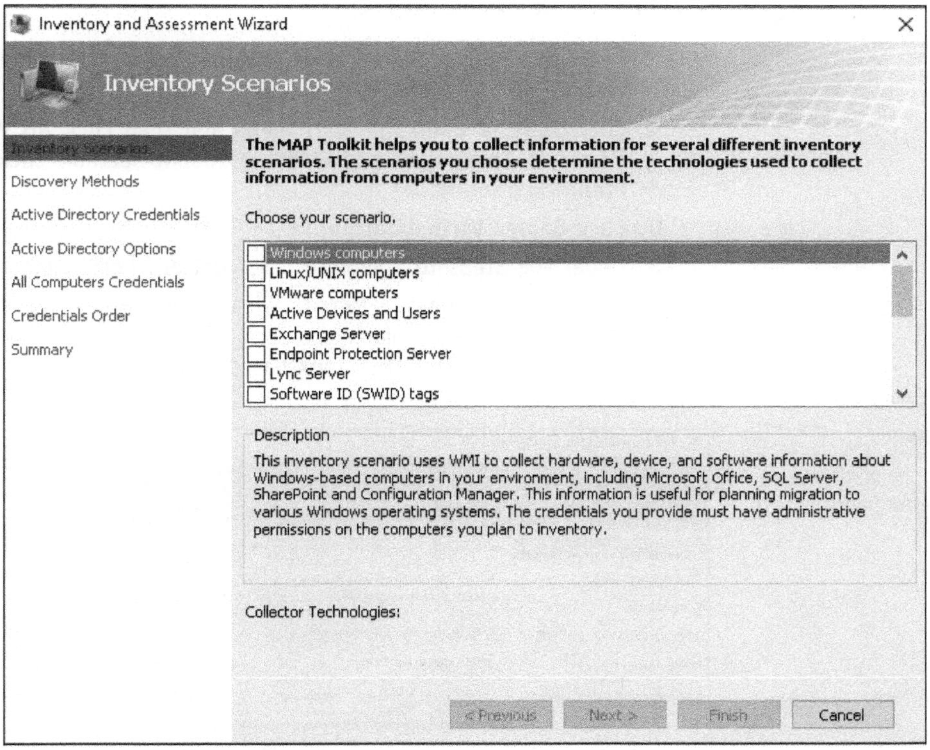

4. On the Discovery Methods page, select which methods you want to use to discover computers, such as **Use Active Directory Domain Services (AD DS)** or **Use Windows networking protocols.** Click **Next.**

5. On the Active Directory Credentials page, in the Domain text box, type the name of the domain. In the Domain account text box, type a user account, using the *domain\user* format.

6. In the Password text box, type the password for the domain account. Click **Next.**

7. On the Active Directory Options page, click **Next.**

8. On the All Computers Credentials page, click **Create.**

9. On the Account Entry page, in the Account name text box, type a user name, using the *domain\user* format.

10. In the Password and Confirm password text boxes, type the password for the account.

11. In the Technology section, WMI and Active Directory are already selected. Click **Save.**

12. Back on the All Computers Credentials page, click **Next.**

13. On the Credentials Orders page, click **Next.**

14. On the Summary page, click **Finish.** After some time, the Overview page shows the number of machines found and inventoried.

After the servers have been inventoried, the next step is to collect performance metrics for the servers. MAP is configured to monitor physical and logical disk, memory, network, and processor performance counters on the set of inventoried servers.

COLLECT PERFORMANCE DATA

GET READY. To collect performance data using MAP on a computer running Windows Server 2016, perform the following steps.

1. Click **Start** to open the Start menu and then click **All Programs.** Then, under the Microsoft Assessment and Planning Toolkit section, click **Microsoft Assessment and Planning Toolkit.**

2. Click **Server Virtualization.**

3. Under the Steps to complete, click **Collect performance data.**

4. When the Performance Metrics Wizard opens, on the Collection Configuration page, the Windows-based machines option is already selected, as shown in Figure 6-20. If necessary, select the Linux-based machines.

Figure 6-20

Configuring the platforms to collect performance metrics from

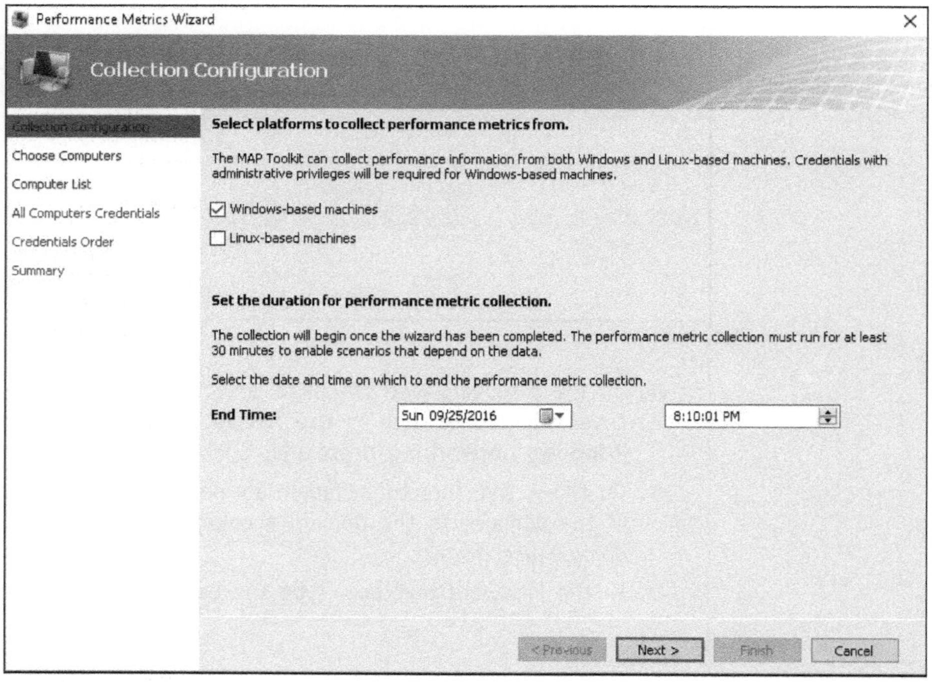

5. Specify the end time that the collection will stop. Click **Next**.

6. On the Choose Computers page, the Choose the computers from a list on the next step of the wizard option is already selected. Click **Next**.

7. On the Computer list page, select the servers that you want to collect data from and click **Next**.

8. On the All Computers Credentials page, click **Next**.

9. If you have more than one credential, specify the credentials to try first. Click **Next**.

10. On the Summary page, click **Finish**.

To analyze the data that you have collected, run the Server Consolidation Wizard. You can specify your host specifications and the utilization settings, such as processing and memory. The MAP Toolkit will then specify the expected CPU utilization, memory utilization, IOPs, disk utilization, and network throughput for the physical host.

 RUN THE SERVER CONSOLIDATION WIZARD

GET READY. To run the Server Consolidation Wizard on a computer running Windows Server 2016, perform the following steps.

1. Click **Start** to open the Start menu and then click **All Programs**. Then, under the Microsoft Assessment and Planning Toolkit section, click **Microsoft Assessment and Planning Toolkit**.

2. Click **Server Virtualization**.

3. Click the **Run the Server Consolidation Wizard** option.

4. When the Server Virtualization and Consolidation Wizard opens, on the Virtualization Technology page, select the version of Hyper-V that you would like to see recommendations for, such as **Windows Server 2016 Hyper-V**. Click **Next**.

5. On the Hardware Configuration page, select **Sample host** and click **Next**.

6. On the Utilization Settings page (as shown in Figure 6-21), specify the utilization settings that you would like to use. Click **Next**.

Figure 6-21

Specifying utilization settings to use when consolidating

Server Virtualization and Consolidation Wizard ✕

Utilization Settings

Virtualization Technology

Hardware Configuration

Utilization Settings

Choose Computers

Computer List

Summary

Specify the utilization settings to use when consolidating.

This defines a ceiling on resources of the infrastructure or the host in which the virtual machines will be placed. Defining a reasonable ceiling limit on the resources allows for periodic spikes in performance.

Processor	100	(50 - 100) %
Memory	100	(50 - 100) %
Storage Capacity	100	(50 - 100) %
Storage IOPS	100	(50 - 100) %
Network Throughput	100	(50 - 100) %

< Previous   Next >   Finish   Cancel

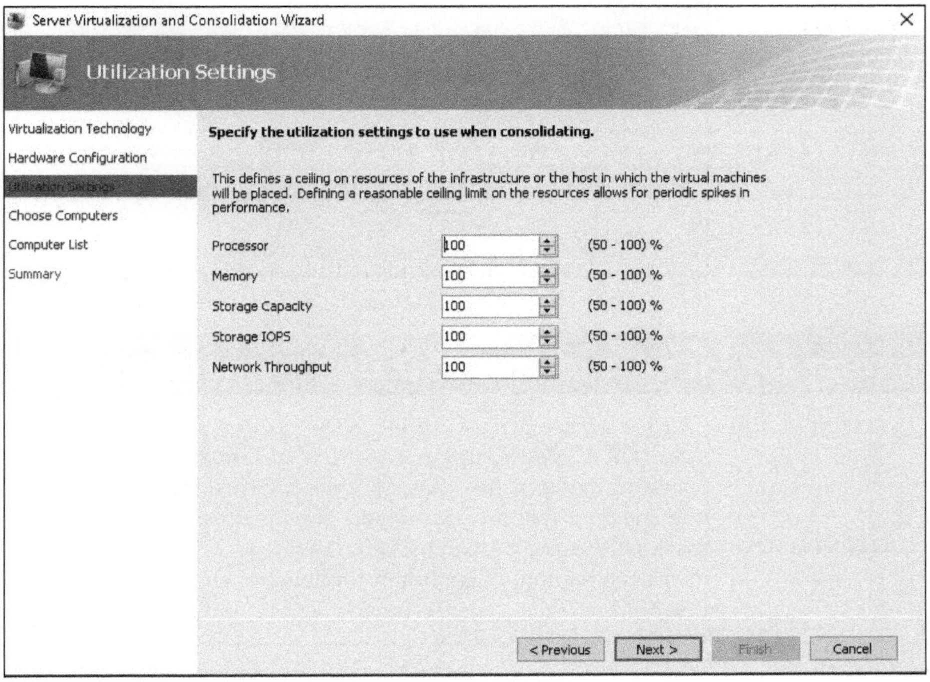

7. On the Computer list page, select the servers that you want to collect data from and click **Next.**

8. On the All Computers Credentials page, click **Next.**

9. On the Summary page, click **Finish.**

10. When the assessment is complete, click **Close.**

The Server Consolidation page will then show the virtualization summary, as shown in Figure 6-22. To see a more detailed report, click the Server Virtualization Report option.

Figure 6-22

Viewing the Server Consolidation report

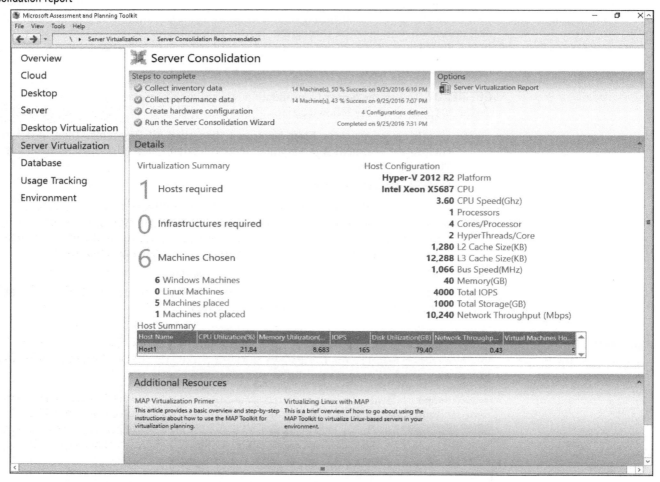

Planning for Linux and FreeBSD Deployments

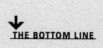

THE BOTTOM LINE

Microsoft Hyper-V supports a variety of Linux distributions and FreeBSD as guest operating systems. Just like a Windows virtual machine, specify how much virtual memory, how many virtual processors, and how much storage you want to assign to the virtual machine. Instead of loading Windows, load Linux or FreeBSD. Much of what was stated in the last section, "Planning for Windows Server Virtualization," applies to Linux and FreeBSD.

CERTIFICATION READY
Plan for Linux and
FreeBSD deployments
Objective 1.3

Hyper-V supports both emulated and Hyper-V-specific devices for Linux and FreeBSD virtual machines. Typically, for best performance and for better management, you want to use the specific drivers that come with Hyper-V. Like Windows Integration Services, the collection of drivers that are required to run Hyper-V-specific devices are known as Linux Integration Services (LIS) or FreeBSD Integration Services (BIS).

Starting with Windows Server 2016, Hyper-V supports secure boot for Linux and FreeBSD. Secure Boot is a security standard that makes sure the PC boots using only software that is trusted by the PC manufacturer.

When you are planning your virtualization infrastructure, you need to verify that your virtual environment supports the specific Linux and FreeBSD distribution and version. You need to make sure you assign sufficient resources, and you need to look at how you are going to back up the Linux and FreeBSD virtual machines, and what fault-tolerant mechanism you want to use with those machines.

SKILL SUMMARY

IN THIS LESSON YOU LEARNED:

- An image is a single file or other storage device that contains the complete contents and structures of a disk or other data storage device used with computers and other computing devices. The image has the necessary information to be installed as a copy of Windows onto another machine.

- In the simplest method, an image is created from a reference or master computer. On the reference computer, you install Windows, install any necessary drivers, configure Windows, install additional software, and configure the additional software. You also should update and patch Windows and any applications that run on the computer.

- Windows Imaging Format (WIM) is a file-based image format developed by Microsoft that allows a file structure (folders and files) to be stored inside a single WIM database.

- Windows 10 and Windows Server 2016 include DISM cmdlets in the DISM PowerShell module that can be used to manage and maintain images. The DISM cmdlets are like using the `dism.exe` command.

- Windows Deployment Services (WDS) is a Windows server role used to deploy Windows over the network with little or no user intervention. If the client can perform a PXE boot, you perform an installation over a network with no local operating system or local startup device on it. The WDS server stores and helps administrators manage the boot and operating system image files used in the network installations.

- Data centers consolidate many physical servers to a single server running multiple virtual machines or virtual servers using Microsoft Hyper-V or VMware ESX/ESXi. Thus, there was a significant increase in resource use while reducing overall cost and power consumption. Since virtualization was introduced, virtualization has matured into an efficient and dependable system and architecture.

- The Microsoft Assessment and Planning (MAP) Toolkit is a free, comprehensive agentless tool that can inventory, assess, and report on an organization's environment. You can install it on any system running Windows Vista higher or Windows Server 2008 and higher.

Multiple Choice

Select the correct answer for each of the following questions.

1. An organization's 250 computers use several different motherboards and processors. To deploy Windows 10 to all 250 computers, which type of image should be used?
   a. Disk-based image
   b. File-based image
   c. Sector-based image
   d. Folder-based image

2. Which of the following are advantages of using WIM files to deploy Windows 10? (Choose all that apply.)
   a. Supports offline servicing
   b. Uses file-based servicing
   c. Offers conditional images
   d. Uses compression

3. Which of the following statements best describes the advantage of VHDX over VHD files?
   a. VHDX enables multiple images in a single VHDX file.
   b. VHDX supports up to 256 TB.
   c. VHDX enables master-child updating.
   d. VHDX uses larger block sizes up to 256 MB.

4. As an administrator, you manage a server named Server01 running Windows Server 2016 that is part of an Active Directory domain. You want to deploy Windows 10 to 500 client computers. Which image types should be used to deploy Windows? (Choose two.)
   a. Boot image
   b. Capture image
   c. Discover image
   d. Install image

5. As an administrator, you manage a remote site with many computers that are not PXE-capable. However, you need to use WDS to deploy Windows to these computers. Which type of image must be created to overcome this problem?
   a. Boot image
   b. Capture image
   c. Discover image
   d. Install image

6. Which program is used to create and validate an answer file, which is used in the deployment of Windows?
   a. Windows SIM
   b. WDS
   c. VDI
   d. Sysprep.exe

7. Where is Windows SIM located?
   a. WDS
   b. VDI
   c. Configuration Manager
   d. Windows ADK

8. Which of the following is used to start a computer over the network?
   a. Multicast transmitter
   b. System Preparation utility
   c. PXE
   d. Answer file

9. Which of the following are necessary for deploying WDS for stand-alone mode? (Choose all that apply.)
   a. AD DS
   b. FAT32 or NTFS
   c. DHCP
   d. DNS

10. The answer file is made as a(n) _____ file.
    a. XLS
    b. SIM
    c. XML
    d. RTF

Best Answer

Choose the letter that corresponds to the best answer. More than one answer choice may achieve the goal. Select the BEST answer.

1. When preparing 300 computers for classroom instruction, which of the following is the quickest way to redeploy all 300 computers?
   a. Use WDS to deploy each computer one at a time.
   b. Use WDS to deploy all the computers at the same time while using unicast transmissions.
   c. Use WDS to deploy all the computers while using multicasting.
   d. Use TFTP to copy the image to each computer manually.

2. When administering a computer that does not support PXE start, which action should be taken to start the computer and install an image using WDS?
   a. Use a boot image.
   b. Use an install image.
   c. Use a discover image.
   d. Start with a DOS floppy disk.

3. Over the next three months, you need to deploy hundreds of computers running Windows 10. Which of the following deployment strategies should be used?
   a. You should use High Touch with Retail Media
   b. You should use High Touch with Standard Image
   c. You should use Lite-Touch, High-Volume Deployment
   d. You should use Zero-Touch, High-Volume Deployment

4. As the administrator for a small company that supports 50 client computers, you need to deploy Windows 10 to 20 of the older computers. Which of the following deployment strategies should be used?
   a. You should use High Touch with Retail Media
   b. You should use High Touch with Standard Image
   c. You should use Lite-Touch, High-Volume Deployment
   d. You should use Zero-Touch, High-Volume Deployment

Matching and Identification

1. Identify the appropriate DISM PowerShell cmdlet.

Get-WindowsImage	Displays information about a Windows image (a WIM or VHD file)
Mount-WindowsImage	Mounts a Windows image in a WIM or VHD file to a directory on the local computer
New-WindowsImage	Captures an image of a drive to a new WIM file
Disable-WindowsOptionalFeature	Disables a feature in the Windows image
Remove-WindowsPackage	Removes a package from a Windows image

Build a List

1. Specify the correct order of steps necessary to creating a new reference computer and retrieving an image from the reference computer:

_____ Use DISM to capture the reference computer.

_____ Create and modify the answer file. Copy the answer file to the USB startup device.

_____ Prepare the computer by running sysprep.

_____ Install and customize Windows PE.

_____ Plug in the USB device and start the computer with the Windows installation disc.

■ Business Case Scenarios

Scenario 6-1: Determining the Images to Use

You are an administrator responsible for deploying 340 clients running Windows 10. These clients contain a mix of mobile computers and desktop computers, 32-bit computers, and 64-bit computers. They will be distributed throughout a campus of three buildings and five subnets. Each subnet starts from a single DHCP server located on the server subnet. You manage a newly installed WDS server (located on the server subnet) that is used to deploy Windows. You also administer several older computers that do not support PXE. How many images do you need to deploy Windows to these clients and why do you need each of these images?

Scenario 6-2: Creating Images

As an administrator, you must deploy Windows to 300 clients by using Windows Server 2016 with Windows Deployment Services. You decide to create a master image. What would you need and how would you prepare the master image? After the image is created, which steps are used to prepare the WDS server to use the image.

Installing and Configuring Hyper-V

70-740 EXAM OBJECTIVE

Objective 3.1 – Install and configure Hyper-V. This objective may include but is not limited to the following: Determine hardware and compatibility requirements for installing Hyper-V; install Hyper-V; install management tools; upgrade from existing versions of Hyper-V; delegate virtual machine management; perform remote management of Hyper-V hosts; configure virtual machines using Windows PowerShell Direct; implement nested virtualization.

Objective 3.2 – Configure virtual machine (VM) settings; move and convert VMs from previous versions of Hyper-V to Windows Server 2016 Hyper-V. *Other Objective 3.2 topics are covered in Lesson 8.*

Lesson Heading	Exam Objective
Installing and Configuring Hyper-V	Determine hardware and compatibility requirements for installing Hyper-V
– Determining Hardware and Compatibility Requirements for Installing Hyper-V	• Install Hyper-V
– Installing Hyper-V	• Install management tools
– Installing Management Tools	• Perform remote management of Hyper-V hosts
– Performing Remote Management of Hyper-V Hosts	• Upgrade from existing versions of Hyper-V
– Upgrading from Existing Versions of Hyper-V	• Move and convert VMs from previous versions of Hyper-V to Windows Server 2016 Hyper-V
– Configuring Virtual Machines Using Windows PowerShell Direct	• Configure virtual machines using Windows PowerShell Direct
– Implementing Nested Virtualization	• Implement nested virtualization
– Delegating Virtual Machine Management	• Delegate virtual machine management

KEY TERMS

Data Execution Prevention (DEP)	**partition**	**virtual machine**
host	**PowerShell Direct**	**Virtual Machine Monitor (VMM)**
Hyper-V	**second level address translation (SLAT)**	**VM configuration version**
hypervisor		**VMBus**

■ Installing and Configuring Hyper-V

THE BOTTOM LINE

Virtualization has become quite popular during the last few years. By using *virtual machine* technology, you can run multiple operating systems concurrently on a single machine, which allows separation of services while keeping cost to a minimum. It can also be used to create Windows test systems in a safe, self-contained environment. Microsoft Hyper-V is a hypervisor-based virtualization system for x64 computers starting with Windows Server 2008. The *hypervisor* is installed between the hardware and the operating system and is the main component that manages the virtual computers.

Hyper-V is a hardware virtualization server role that enables you to create and manage virtual machines (VMs). By using hardware virtualization, you can subdivide the single physical computer to be subdivided, and allocated, to multiple virtual machines. Like a physical computer, the virtual machine will have its virtual processors, virtual memory, virtual disks, and an operating system that will run independently and be isolated from the Hyper-V host and the other virtual machines. These VMs can be used to test your applications for compatibility with new operating systems, allow you to run applications written for older versions of Windows, or isolate an application. The physical machine that Hyper-V and the virtual machines run on are often referred to as the *host*.

Server virtualization in Windows Server 2016 is based on a module called a hypervisor. Sometimes called a *Virtual Machine Monitor (VMM)*, the hypervisor is responsible for abstracting the computer's physical hardware and creating multiple virtualized hardware environments, called virtual machines (VMs). Each VM has its own (virtual) hardware configuration and can run a separate copy of an operating system. Therefore, with sufficient physical hardware and the correct licensing, a single computer running Windows Server 2016 with the Hyper-V role installed can support multiple VMs, which you can manage as though they were stand-alone computers.

TAKE NOTE*

VMM is usually associated with older virtual machine technology. Don't confuse VMM with System Center Virtual Machine Manager (VMM), which is a software package that is used to manage a virtual machine environment based on Microsoft Hyper-V, VMWare ESX/ESXi, and Citrix XenServer.

To run several virtual machines on a single computer, you need to have sufficient processing power and memory to handle the load. However, because most servers often sit idle, virtualization utilizes the server's hardware more efficiently.

To keep each virtual server secure and reliable, each server is placed in its own logical partition that isolates processing and memory. A *partition* is a logical unit of storage in which operating systems are hosted. The partition is not to be confused with a disk partition or a volume that divides a storage area. Each virtual machine accesses the hypervisor, which handles interrupts to the processor and redirects them to the respective partition.

The *VMBus* is a high-speed memory bus that was developed specifically for Hyper-V. I/O traffic between the physical host and the virtual machine and request for access to physical devices occur over the VMBus.

By using Hyper-V Manager, you can create new virtual machines and define the hardware resources that the system should allocate to them. In the settings for a particular virtual machine, depending on the physical hardware available in the computer and the limitations of the guest operating system, you can specify the number of processors and the amount of

memory a virtual machine should use, install virtual network adapters, and create virtual disks using various technologies, including storage area networks (SANs).

By default, Hyper-V stores the files that make up virtual machines in the folders you specified on the Default Stores page during installation. Each virtual machine uses the following files:

- A virtual machine configuration (.xml) file in XML format that contains the virtual machine configuration information, including all settings for the virtual machine
- One or more virtual hard disk (.vhd or .vhdx) files to store the guest operating system, applications, and data for the virtual machine

A virtual machine may also use a saved-state (.vsv) file, if the machine has been placed into a saved state.

With each release of Windows Server, Hyper-V has been updated with new features and functionality. These updated features and functionality include:

- **Host resource protection:** Prevents a virtual machine from hogging all the resources on a Hyper-V host so that other virtual machines have sufficient resources to function.
- **Hyper-V Manager improvements:** Allows you to use alternate credentials when connecting to a Hyper-V host.
- **Nested virtualization:** Allows you to install and configure a Hyper-V role on a virtual machine running Windows Server 2016.
- **Rolling Hyper-V cluster upgrade:** Allows you to upgrade a Windows Server 2012 R2 cluster to Windows Server 2016 by adding Windows Server 2016 nodes on an existing cluster. You can then move the load to the Windows Server 2016 nodes, and retire the Windows Server 2012 R2 nodes.
- **Shielded virtual machines:** Secures a virtual machine by encrypting the virtual machine, which can only be accessed by the administrators of the virtual machine. This can also be used to prevent access from Hyper-V host administrators.
- **Start order priority:** Allows you to specify a specific startup order for virtual machines.
- **Storage Quality of Service (QoS):** Improves storage performance by allowing you to create and assign storage QoS policies on a Scale-Out File Server. This can be used to limit or reserve an amount of storage throughput.
- **Windows PowerShell Direct:** Allows you to run Windows PowerShell cmdlets on a virtual machine from the Hyper-V host.

Determining Hardware and Compatibility Requirements for Installing Hyper-V

Deploying Hyper-V is more complex than just installing the Hyper-V server role. As mentioned in Lesson 6, you need to determine the resources (processing, memory, and storage) required for each virtual machine running on the Hyper-V host, and you also need to plan for high availability (if high availability is a requirement).

CERTIFICATION READY
Determine hardware and compatibility requirements for installing Hyper-V
Objective 3.1

To run Hyper-V, you need the following:

- A 64-bit processor that incorporates second level address translation (SLAT) technology
- A minimum of 4 GB of memory (running more than one VM at a time requires more)
- Intel Virtualization Technology (Intel VT) or AMD Virtualization (AMD-V) enabled
- Hardware-enforced Data Execution Prevention (DEP) Enabled (Intel DX and AMD NX bit)

Modern processors such as processors developed by Intel and AMD have built-in capabilities that are used to simulate virtual machines. *Second level address translation (SLAT)*, also known as nested paging, reduces overhead needed to map virtual to physical addresses. Thus, you can run more virtual machines at the same time. Intel calls it, Extended Page Table (EPT), whereas AMD calls it Rapid Virtualization Indexing (RVI).

Data Execution Prevention (DEP) is a system-level memory protection feature that allows the system to mark one or more pages of memory as nonexecutable. With virtualization, it is used to segregate areas of memory for either storage of processor instructions or for storage of data. This feature (which may be labeled Data Execution Prevention, XD, Execute Disable, or NX) must be enabled in the BIOS Setup program.

The Intel VT and AMD-V are a series of extensions for hardware virtualization, which can be used to assign specific I/O devices to specific virtual machines and to support I/O devices such as network switches. Like DEP, Intel VT or AMD-V needs to be enabled in the BIOS Setup program.

In addition to the processor and motherboard that supports virtualization, you also need to ensure that you have sufficient hardware resources to run the virtual machines, including processor, memory, storage, and network.

Hyper-V hosts can support the following:

- Up to 512 logical processors and 2,048 virtual processors
- 24 TB of memory
- 1,024 virtual machines per server

Installing Hyper-V

Before you install Hyper-V, you ensure that the host running Windows Server 2016 is installed with all necessary drivers and updates. You can then install the Hyper-V server role by using Server Manager or the Windows PowerShell `Install-WindowsFeature` cmdlet.

CERTIFICATION READY
Install Hyper-V
Objective 3.1

To install Hyper-V using Server Manager on Windows Server 2016, you must have the Windows Server 2016 Standard or Datacenter edition. You will also need to have administrative permissions for the host.

INSTALL THE HYPER-V ROLE

GET READY. To install the Hyper-V Role, perform the following steps.

1. Open **Server Manager.**
2. In the Server Manager window, open the **Manage** menu and click **Add Roles and Features.**
3. When the Add Roles and Features Wizard opens, on the Before You Begin page, click **Next.**
4. On the Installation Type page, Role-based or feature-based installation is already selected. Click **Next.**
5. When the Select Destination Server page appears, select the server on which you want to install Hyper-V and click **Next.** The Select Server Roles page appears, as shown in Figure 7-1.

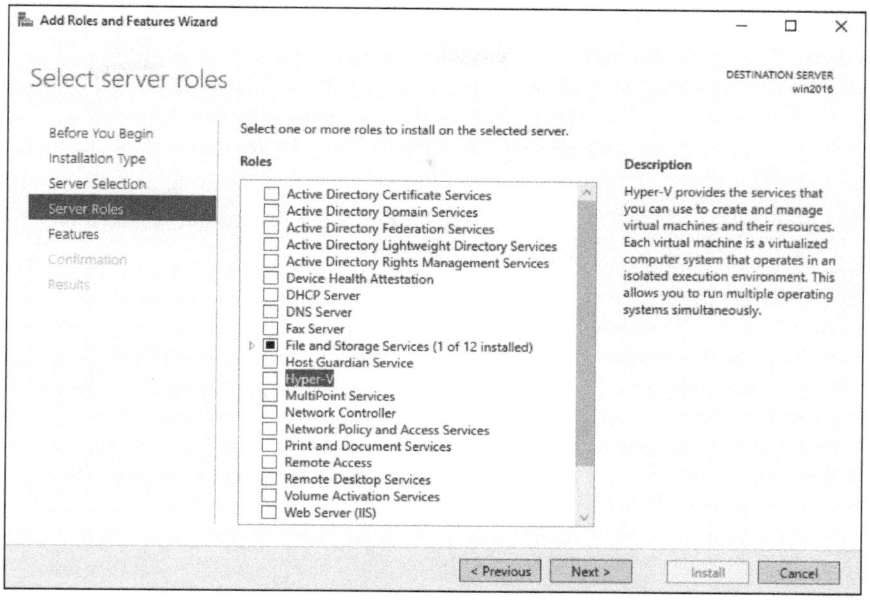

Figure 7-1

The Select Server Roles page of the Add Roles and Features Wizard

6. Select the **Hyper-V** role. When you are prompted to add features, click the **Add Features** button. Click **Next**.

7. When the Hyper-V page appears, click **Next**.

8. On the Create Virtual Switches page, select the check box for a network adapter and click **Next**.

9. When the Virtual Machine Migration page appears, click **Next**.

10. When the Default Stores page appears, specify alternatives to the default locations for virtual hard disk and virtual machine configuration files, if desired, and click **Next**.

11. On the Confirm Installation Selections page, select **Restart the destination server automatically if required** and then click **Yes**. Click **Install**. The host may restart several times as the system is rebooted.

To install Hyper-V on Server Core, use the following Windows PowerShell command:

```
Install-WindowsFeature -Name Hyper-V
-IncludeManagementTools -Restart
```

Windows will restart to complete the installation.

Installing Management Tools

Hyper-V is managed using the Hyper-V Manager or Windows PowerShell with the Hyper-V Module for Windows PowerShell. Typically, when you install Hyper-V on Windows Server 2016, the additional features that are installed include the Hyper-V GUI Management Tools and Hyper-V Module for Windows PowerShell.

CERTIFICATION READY
Install management tools
Objective 3.1

The Hyper-V Manager (as shown in Figure 7-2) is the administrative tool to create, change, and delete virtual machines and virtual switches, and it allows you to manage virtual storage. For computers running Windows Server 2016, you can open Server Manager and use Add

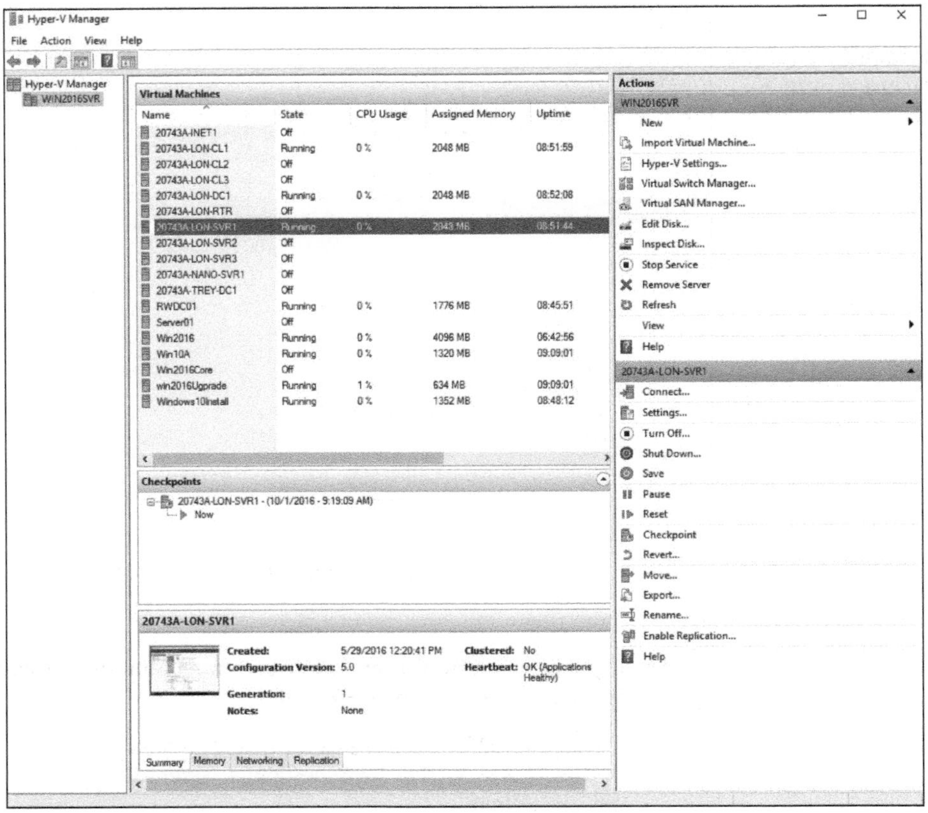

Figure 7-2

Managing VMs with Hyper-V
Manager

Roles and Features to install the Remote Administration Tools\Role Administration
Tools\Hyper-V Management Tools. For clients running Windows 10, you can install the
Hyper-V Management Tools by opening Programs and Features > Turn Windows features
on or off.

You will manage virtual machines by opening the Virtual Machine Connection program,
right-clicking the virtual machine in Hyper-V Manager, and choosing Connect. You can also
manage Hyper V using the Hyper-V Module for Windows PowerShell, which can also be
used with scripting.

INSTALL THE HYPER-V MANAGEMENT TOOLS ON A CLIENT RUNNING WINDOWS 10

GET READY. To install the Hyper-V management tools, perform the following steps.

1. Log on to a client running Windows 10 with administrator access, such as
   adatum\administrator with the password of **Pa$$w0rd.**
2. Right-click **Start** and choose **Programs and Features.**
3. When the Control Panel Programs and Features window opens, click the **Turn
   Windows features on or off** option.
4. When the Windows Features dialog box opens, expand the **Hyper-V** node and select
   the **Hyper-V Management Tools**, as shown in Figure 7-3. Click **OK.**

Figure 7-3

Installing the Hyper-V
Management Tools
in Windows 10

5. When the installation is complete, click **Close**.

To install the Hyper-V Management Tools using Windows PowerShell, use the
`Install-WindowsFeature` command:

```
Install-WindowsFeature -Name Hyper-V-Tools

-IncludeManagementTool
```

Performing Remote Management of Hyper-V Hosts

After you install the Hyper-V Management Tools, you can manage Hyper-V hosts
locally or remotely. Because the Hyper-V hosts are in a server room or data center, you
can manage your VMs remotely from your office desk or home through a virtual private
network (VPN) tunnel. In addition, you can manage multiple Hyper-V hosts using a
single instance of Hyper-V Manager.

CERTIFICATION READY
Perform remote management
of Hyper-V hosts
Objective 3.1

When you open Hyper-V Manager on a Hyper-V host, the local host will already be added to
the console. To manage other hosts or remote hosts, you just add the other hosts to Hyper-V
Manager.

→ **MANAGE REMOTE HYPER-V HOSTS**

GET READY. To manage remote Hyper-V hosts on a server running Windows Server 2016,
perform the following steps.

1. Log on to a computer running Windows Server 2016 with an administrator account,
   such as **adatum\administrator** with the password of **Pa$$w0rd**.
2. If Server Manager does not open, click **Start** and click **Server Manager**.
3. Open the **Tools** menu and click **Hyper-V**.
4. When Server Manager opens, right-click the **Hyper-V Manager** node and choose
   Connect to Server.
5. When the Select Computer dialog box opens (as shown in Figure 7-4), with
   Another computer option already selected, in the Another computer text box, type
   the name of the server, such as **LON-SVR1**, and click **OK**.

Figure 7-4

Adding another computer to Hyper-V Manager

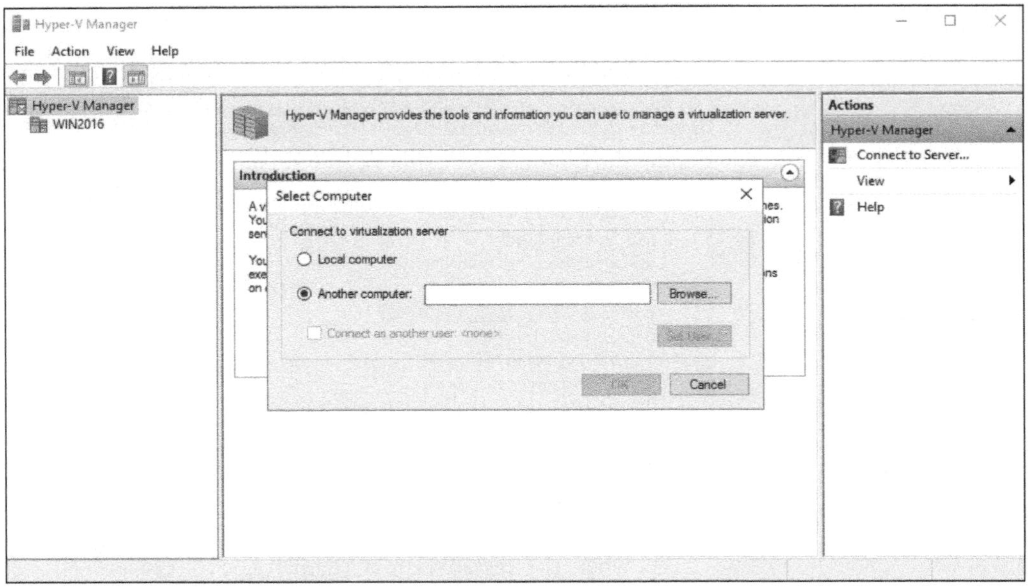

Upgrading from Existing Versions of Hyper-V

> To upgrade Windows Server 2012 R2 running Hyper-V, simply insert the Windows Server 2016 installation disc, access the disk, and double-click the setup program to start the upgrade. The upgrade process was discussed in Lesson 2. When you have Windows Server 2012 R2 running Windows Server 2012 or 2012 R2 virtual machines, you can mount the ISO file on each VM and then access the virtual disk to upgrade Windows.

CERTIFICATION READY
Upgrade from existing versions of Hyper-V
Objective 3.1

CERTIFICATION READY
Move and convert VMs from previous versions of Hyper-V to Windows Server 2016 Hyper-V
Objective 3.2

Before you perform any upgrade, you should make sure you have a current backup of the hosts and any VMs. If you have VMs running on a cluster, you should move the VMs to the other cluster nodes. If you do not have a cluster, and you cannot migrate the servers, you should shut down the servers before upgrading the host. You should also delete any checkpoints. After the upgrade is complete, be sure to apply the newest updates from Microsoft.

When you create a virtual machine, the configuration file will be a specific ***VM configuration version*** based on the host operating system. The various features and related features are listed in Table 7-1. When you move or import a virtual machine to a Hyper-V host running Windows Server 2016, or you upgrade a Hyper-V host from Windows Server 2012 R2 to Windows Server 2016, the virtual machine version is not updated to the newest version. If you are sure that you will not have to run the VMs on an older host operating system, you should upgrade the virtual machine version so that you can take advantage of the additional features.

Table 7-1

Virtual Machine Configuration Versions

HOST VERSION	VM CONFIGURATION VERSION	ADDED FEATURES
Windows 8.1 and Windows Server 2012 R2	Version 5	
Windows 10 build earlier than 10565	Version 6.2	Version 5 features plus Virtual Machine Grouping, PowerShell Direct, Production Checkpoints, Secure Boot for Linux, and the ability to hot add/remove static memory

Host Version	VM Configuration Version	Added Features
Windows 10 build 10565 or newer	Version 7	Virtual 6.2 features plus Virtual Trusted Platform Module
Windows Server 2016	Version 7.1	Virtual 7 features plus virtual machine multi queues

TAKE NOTE*

Once the configuration version has been updated, you will not be able to revert back to an earlier version without restoring from backup, or creating a virtual machine and pointing to the existing virtual disks.

→ UPGRADE THE VM VERSION

GET READY. To upgrade the VM version of a virtual machine running on a Windows Server 2016 Hyper-V, perform the following steps.

1. Log on to a computer running Windows Server 2016 with an administrator account, such as **adatum\administrator** with the password of **Pa$$w0rd**.
2. If Server Manager does not open, click **Start** and click **Server Manager**.
3. Open the **Tools** menu and click **Hyper-V**.
4. You can view the Configuration version by looking in the Configuration Version. Then, to upgrade a VM configuration version, right-click the VM and choose **Upgrade Configuration Version**, as shown in Figure 7-5.

Figure 7-5

Upgrading a VM configuration version

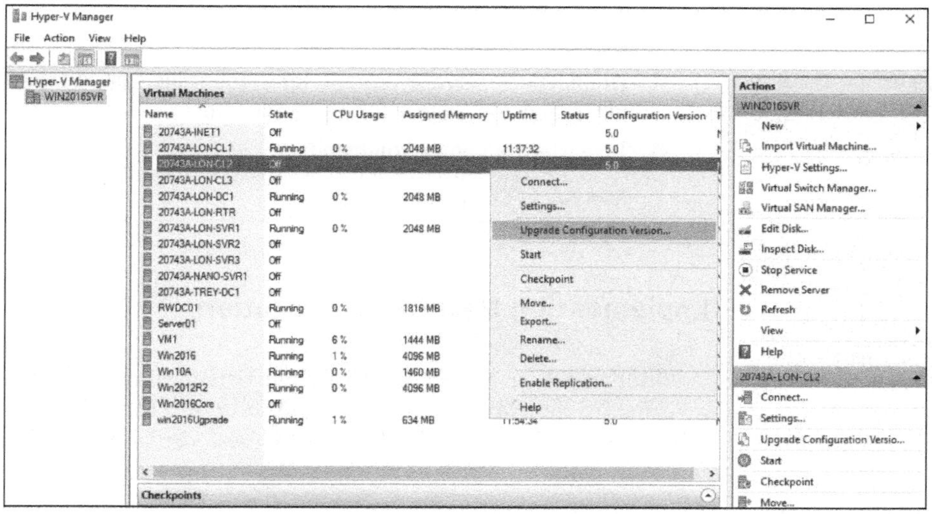

5. When the Upgrade Configuration Version dialog box opens, click the **Upgrade** button.

Configuring Virtual Machines Using Windows PowerShell Direct

Windows PowerShell can be used to create remote sessions to run Windows PowerShell cmdlets on a remote host. However, in Windows Server 2016, *PowerShell Direct* has been added, which allows you to connect to a virtual machine via the Hyper-V host, even if the VM does not have a network connection.

To use PowerShell Direct, you need the following:

- The host operating system must be Windows Server 2016 or Windows 10.
- The guest operating system must be Windows Server 2016 or Windows 10.
- You must run Windows PowerShell as an administrator.
- You must provide credentials to authenticate to the virtual machine.
- The virtual machine configuration version must be updated.
- The virtual machine must be running locally on the host.
- The virtual machine must be turned on and running with at least one configured user profile.

To enter a session on a virtual machine, use the following command:

```
Enter-PSSession -VMName VM1
```

To invoke a command on a virtual machine, use the following command:

```
Invoke-Command -VMName VM1 -ScriptBlock {Windows PowerShell commands}
```

⊖ MANAGE REMOTE HYPER-V HOSTS

GET READY. To manage remote Hyper-V hosts on a server running Windows Server 2016, perform the following steps.

1. Log on to a computer running Windows Server 2016 with an administrator account, such as **adatum\administrator** with the password of **Pa$$w0rd**.
2. On the taskbar, click the **Windows PowerShell** tile.
3. When the Administrator: Windows PowerShell window opens, enter the following command and then press **Enter**:

   Enter-PSSession -VMName "VM1"
4. When you receive a prompt for credentials, use **adatum\administrator** as the user name and **Pa$$w0rd** for the password.
5. Type the following command:

   Restart-Computer

Implementing Nested Virtualization

Windows Server 2016 supports nested virtualization, which allows a Hyper-V guest virtual machine to become a Hyper-V host and run a Hyper-V guest operating system. In other words, it allows you to run a guest virtual machine in a guest virtual machine.

To enable nested virtualization, you need the following:

- Hyper-V must be running Windows Server 2016 or Windows 10.
- The virtual memory must be 4 GB of memory or more.
- The virtual machine that is running Hyper-V must be the same build as the host.
- Disable Dynamic Memory of the virtual machine.
- Enable Virtualization Extensions of the vCPU.

To enable the Virtualization Extension of the vCPU, run the following Windows PowerShell command:

```
Set-VMProcessor -VMName "VMName"

-ExposeVirtualizationExtensions $true
```

The following features are disabled or will fail after you enable nested virtualization:

- Virtual-based security
- Device Guard
- Dynamic Memory
- Hot add Static Memory
- Checkpoints
- Live migration
- Save or Restore state

For guest virtual machines to communicate on the external network, you must enable MAC spoofing for the VM that is hosting Hyper-V. If you do not enable MAC spoofing, network packets from guest virtual machines are not recognized as legitimate and are blocked.

 ENABLE MAC SPOOFING

GET READY. To enable MAC spoofing for the virtual machine running Hyper-V, perform the following steps.

1. Log on to a computer running Windows Server 2016 with an administrator account, such as **adatum\administrator** with the password of **Pa$$w0rd**.
2. If Server Manager does not open, click **Start** and click **Server Manager**.
3. Open the **Tools** menu and click **Hyper-V**.
4. If the virtual machine is on, perform a shutdown of the virtual machine by right-clicking the virtual machine and choosing **Shutdown**. When you are prompted to determine whether you want to shut down the operating system, click the **Shut Down** button.
5. Right-click the virtual machine and choose **Settings**.
6. When the Settings dialog box opens, expand the **Network Adapter** node and select the **Advanced Features** node, as shown in Figure 7-6.

Figure 7-6

Configuring Network Adapter Advanced Features

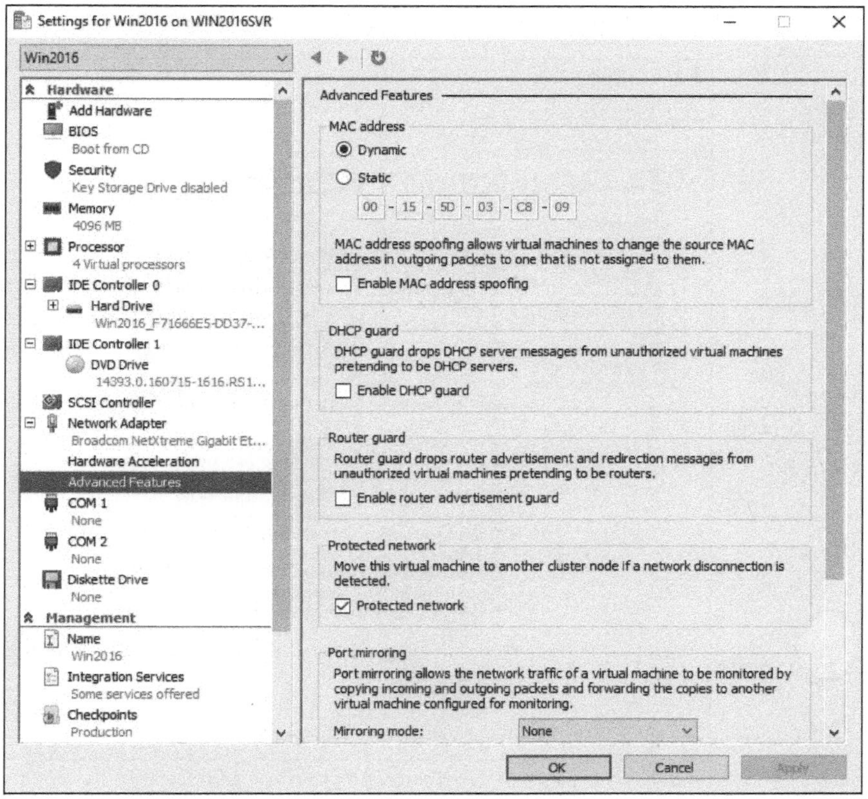

7. Select the **Enable MAC address spoofing** option and click **OK**.

8. Right-click the virtual machine and choose **Start**.

Delegating Virtual Machine Management

By default, Hyper-V allows the administrators group to create and manage virtual machines. You can grant administrative access by adding a user to the Administrators or the Hyper-V Administrators group. However, you can also allow a non-administrative user to create and control virtual machines by using the Authorization Manager console.

CERTIFICATION READY
Delegate virtual machine management
Objective 3.1

To grant access to a user to a virtual machine or machines, you use the Windows PowerShell `Grant-VMConnectAccess` cmdlet to grant Console Read or Console Read/Write access. To revoke access, use the Windows PowerShell `Revoke-VMConnectAccess` cmdlet.

For example, if you want to grant permissions to a user named User1 in the Adatum domain for connecting to a virtual machine named VM1, you could run the following cmdlet:

```
Grant-VMConnectAccess -VMName VM1 -UserName "Adatum\user1"
```

➡ ADD A USER TO THE HYPER-V ADMINISTRATORS GROUP

GET READY. To add a user to the Hyper-V Administrators group, perform the following steps.

1. Log on to a computer running Windows Server 2016 with an administrator account, such as **adatum\administrator** with the password of **Pa$$w0rd**.

2. If Server Manager does not open, click **Start** and click **Server Manager**.

3. Open the **Tools** menu and click **Computer Management**.

4. When the Computer Management console opens, expand the **Local Users and Groups** node and click **Groups**.

5. Double-click the **Hyper-V Administrators** group. The Hyper-V Administrators Properties dialog box opens, as shown in Figure 7-7.

Figure 7-7

Adding a user to Hyper-V Administrators Properties

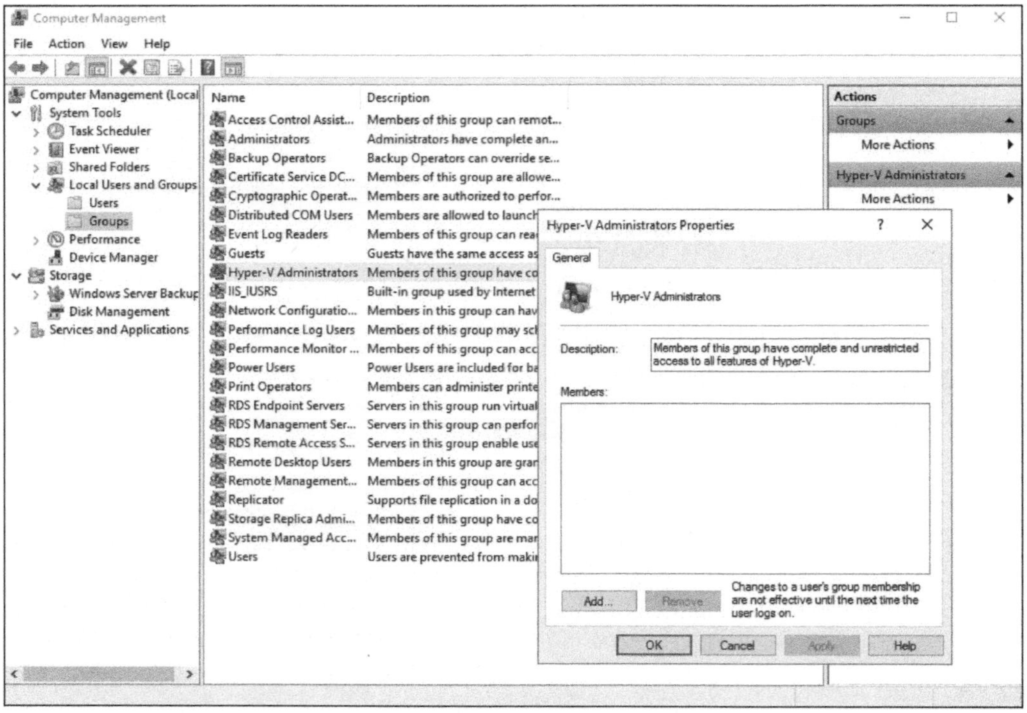

6. Click **Add**.

7. When the Select Users dialog box opens, type the name of the user that you want to add and click **OK**.

8. To close the Hyper-V Administrators Properties dialog box, click **OK**.

SKILL SUMMARY

IN THIS LESSON YOU LEARNED:

- By using virtual machine technology, you can run multiple operating systems concurrently on a single machine, which allows separation of services while keeping cost to a minimum. It can also be used to create Windows test systems in a safe, self-contained environment.

- Hyper-V is a hardware virtualization server role that enables you to create and manage virtual machines (VMs) using a virtual switch. By using hardware virtualization, you can subdivide the single physical computer to be subdivided into, and allocated to, multiple virtual machines.

- The physical machine that Hyper-V and the virtual machines run on is often referred to as the host.

- Hyper-V is managed using the Hyper-V Manager or Windows PowerShell with the Hyper-V Module for Windows PowerShell. Typically, when you install Hyper-V on Windows Server 2016, the additional features that are installed include the Hyper-V GUI Management Tools and Hyper-V Module for Windows PowerShell.

- Windows PowerShell can be used to create remote sessions to run Windows PowerShell cmdlets on a remote host. However, in Windows Server 2016, PowerShell Direct has been added, which allows you to connect to a virtual machine via the Hyper-V host, even if the VM does not have a network connection.

- Windows Server 2016 supports nested virtualization, which allows a Hyper-V guest virtual machine to become a Hyper-V host and run a Hyper-V guest operating system. In other words, it allows you to run a guest virtual machine in a guest virtual machine.

■ Knowledge Assessment

Multiple Choice

Select the correct answer for each of the following questions.

1. Regarding virtualizing servers, the Windows Server 2016 module responsible for abstracting the computer's hardware is called a _____.
   a. virtual machine (VM)
   b. hypervisor
   c. virtualization architecture
   d. host operating system

2. Server virtualization in Windows Server 2016 means each VM has its own _____.
   a. disk partition, but uses the physical hardware
   b. virtual hardware, but directly uses the physical memory
   c. virtual hardware configuration and operating system
   d. virtual hardware configuration, but uses the host operating system

3. Windows Server 2016 uses a virtualization architecture called Type I virtualization. Choose the interaction between the host operating system (OS), physical hardware, and guest OS.
    a. Guest OSs access hardware through the host OS.
    b. Guest OSs request processor time from the host OS.
    c. Both guest OSs and the host OS access hardware through the hypervisor.
    d. The host OS accesses hardware through the hypervisor and then allocates it to the guest OSs.

4. As far as Hyper-V is concerned, which of the following is the primary difference between the Standard and Datacenter editions of Windows Server 2016?
    a. The retail cost
    b. The number of VMs they support
    c. The number of OSs able to be installed as VMs
    d. The number of VMs able to run Windows Server 2016

5. A subset of Windows Server 2016 as a dedicated product for virtualization and provided free by Microsoft is called _____.
    a. Hyper-V Manager
    b. Hyper-V Server
    c. Hyper-V role
    d. hypervisor

6. If you want to install additional roles along with Hyper-V, which of the following solutions is recommended?
    a. Microsoft recommends that you install other roles on one of the VMs you create with Hyper-V.
    b. Microsoft recommends you install only roles related to Hyper-V.
    c. Microsoft recommends you install only roles on the parent partition.
    d. There are no recommendations for roles installed with Hyper-V.

7. Which operating systems can be installed on a VM?
    a. Windows Server 2012 R2 and newer
    b. Windows Server 2008 and newer
    c. Any Microsoft Windows edition
    d. Several Microsoft products as well as Red Hat and SuSE Linux

8. Which Windows PowerShell cmdlet must be executed to support Hyper-V nested virtualization?
    a. `Execute-VMProcessor`
    b. `Set-NestedVirtualization`
    c. `Enable-NestedVirtualization`
    d. `Set-VMProcessor`

9. Which of the following allows you to connect to a virtual machine via the Hyper-V host without a network connection via Windows PowerShell in Windows Server 2016?
    a. Remote VM
    b. PowerShell Find
    c. PowerShell Direct
    d. PowerShell Remote

10. Which Windows PowerShell cmdlet can be used to grant access to a virtual machine?
    a. `Grant-VMRights`
    b. `Grant-VMPermissions`
    c. `Grant-VMConnectAccess`
    d. `Grant-VMAccess`

Best Answer

Choose the letter that corresponds to the best answer. More than one answer choice may achieve the goal. Select the BEST answer.

1. Hyper-V in Windows Server 2016 is a Type I virtualization architecture. Which of the following is the fundamental difference between Hyper-V and older, Type II virtualization architectures?
   a. Hyper-V creates environments called partitions, each with its own operating system installed.
   b. Its hypervisor designates the first partition as the parent partition and all subsequent partitions as child partitions.
   c. Its hypervisor is an abstraction layer and interacts directly with computer hardware, rather than as a host OS application.
   d. Computer subsystems such as Plug and Play and power management are managed by Hyper-V's parent partition.

2. Windows Server 2016 includes Hyper-V in which of the following edition(s)?
   a. All editions
   b. The Datacenter edition, only
   c. The Standard and Datacenter editions
   d. The Essentials, Standard, and Datacenter editions

3. After installing the Hyper-V role, which of the following is the startup procedure for Windows Server 2016?
   a. The newly installed hypervisor starts first, and then loads the operating system as the primary or parent partition.
   b. The actual startup procedure is not altered.
   c. The newly installed hypervisor starts first, and then loads the operating system as a child partition.
   d. The newly installed hypervisor starts second, after the operating system loads as a partition.

4. Which of the following best describes Resource Monitoring in Windows Server 2016?
   a. Resource Monitoring is a PowerShell-based feature that enables you to document virtual machine usage.
   b. Resource Monitoring is a Server Manager feature that enables you to monitor virtual machine resources.
   c. Resource Monitoring is a PowerShell-based feature that enables you to redistribute virtual machine resources.
   d. Resource Monitoring is a Server Manager feature that enables you to document virtual machine communications.

Build a List

1. Specify the correct order of steps necessary to installing the Hyper-V role.

   _____ Choose Role-based or feature-based installation from the Select Installation Type page.

   _____ Select network adapter on the Create Virtual Switches page.

   _____ Select the server on which to add the Hyper-V role. Add applicable dependencies.

   _____ From Server Manager's Manage menu, choose Add Roles and Features.

   _____ Log on to Windows Server 2016 with administrative privileges.

   _____ Specify virtual hard disk and virtual machine configuration file locations.

■ Business Case Scenarios

Scenario 7-1: Isolating Server Applications

You manage two network accounting applications, neither of which is processor hungry. Both applications must be kept totally isolated from each other and from all other applications. Both applications will access a centralized database server. Which server configuration solution do you recommend?

Scenario 7-2: Training with Hyper-V

You are setting up a class so that you can train several junior administrators on Windows Server 2016 Hyper-V. You don't have dedicated Hyper-V hosts, but you do have plenty of resources on your current Hyper-V environment. Describe your proposed solution.

Configuring Virtual Machine (VM) Settings

70-740 EXAM OBJECTIVE

Objective 3.2 – Configure virtual machine (VM) settings. This objective may include but is not limited to the following: Add or remove memory in running a VM; configure Dynamic Memory; configure Non-Uniform Memory Access (NUMA) support; configure smart paging; configure Resource Metering; manage Integration Services; create and configure Generation 1 and 2 VMs and determine appropriate usage scenarios; implement enhanced session mode; create Linux and FreeBSD VMs; install and configure Linux Integration Services (LIS); install and configure FreeBSD Integration Services (BIS); implement Secure Boot for Windows and Linux environments; implement Discrete Device Assignment (DDA). *Move and convert VMs from previous versions of Hyper-V to Windows Server 2016 Hyper-V is covered in Lesson 7.*

Objective 5.5 – Manage VM Movement in Clustered Nodes. Import, export, and copy VMs. *Other Objective 5.5 topics are covered in Lesson 18.*

LESSON HEADING	EXAM OBJECTIVE
Configuring Virtual Machines	Implement enhanced session mode
– Creating Virtual Machines	Add or remove memory in running a VM
– Implementing Enhanced Session Mode	Configure Dynamic Memory
– Managing Virtual Memory, Including Startup Memory, Dynamic Memory, and Smart Paging	Configure smart paging
– Configuring Non-Uniform Memory Access (NUMA) Support	Configure Non-Uniform Memory Access (NUMA) support
– Managing Integration Services	Manage Integration Services
– Creating and Configuring Generation 1 and 2 VMs	Create and configure Generation 1 and 2 VMs and determine appropriate usage scenarios
– Importing, Exporting, and Copying VMs	Export and import VMs
	Import, export, and copy VMs
– Implementing Discrete Device Assignment (DDA)	Implement Discrete Device Assignment (DDA)
– Creating Linux and FreeBSD VMs	Create Linux and FreeBSD VMs
– Implementing Security Options for Windows and Linux Virtual Machines, Including Secure Boot	Install and configure Linux Integration Services (LIS)
	Install and configure FreeBSD Integration Services (BIS)
	Implement Secure Boot for Windows and Linux environments
Configuring Resource Metering	Configure Resource Metering

KEY TERMS

BitLocker Drive Encryption	**Host Guarding Service (HGS)**	**Non-Uniform Memory Access (NUMA)**
Discrete Device Assignment (DDA)	**Hyper-V Resource Metering**	**Secure Boot**
enhanced session mode	**maximum RAM**	**smart paging**
Generation 1	**memory buffer**	**startup RAM/Memory**
Generation 2	**memory weight**	**Trusted Platform Module (TPM)**
guarded host	**minimum RAM**	**virtual machine (VM)**

■ Configuring Virtual Machines

THE BOTTOM LINE

A *virtual machine (VM)* is a self-contained, isolated unit that can be easily moved from one physical computer to another, runs its own operating system, and includes its own virtual hardware configuration.

Within the Hyper-V Manager console, you can create virtual machines, import VMs (Action > Import Virtual Machine), and create virtual hard disks (Action > New > Virtual Hard Disk) to be used by VMs or by the host PC. You can also manage a VM's configuration by modifying the startup order of devices (for example, CD, IDE, network adapter, floppy), allocate memory, determine the number of virtual processors to use, and add hard drives/CD drives to an IDE/SCSI controller.

Creating Virtual Machines

After the Hyper-V host has been installed, you can begin creating virtual machines and configuring them. The easiest way to create a virtual machine is to open Hyper-V and use the New Virtual Machine Wizard. The wizard allows you to define the number of virtual processors, the amount of virtual memory, and how large the virtual disks will be.

After the virtual machine is created, you have to install an operating system, just as you would have to install on a physical machine. Some of the operating systems that Hyper-V supports are:

- Windows 10
- Windows 8.1
- Windows 8
- Windows 7 with SP1
- Windows 7
- Windows Vista with SP2
- Windows Server 2016
- Windows Server 2012 R2

- Windows Server 2012
- Windows Server 2008 R2 with SP1
- Windows Server 2008 with SP2
- Windows Small Business Server 2011
- CentOS and Red Hat Enterprise Linux
- Debian virtual machines on Hyper-V
- SUSE
- Oracle Linux
- Ubuntu
- FreeBSD

When you create a virtual machine, you must define the virtual machine virtual hardware, including:

- The name of the virtual machine
- The location where the virtual machine will be stored
- The VM generation
- How much memory the virtual machine will use
- The virtual switch the virtual machine is connected to
- A virtual hard disk used by the operating system
- The operating system installation options

Windows Server 2016 Hyper-V virtual machines support the following:

- For Generation 1, each VM can have up to 1 TB for memory. For Generation 2, each VM can have up to 12 TB.
- For Generation 1, each VM can have up to 64 virtual processors. For Generation 2, each VM can have up to 240 virtual processors.
- Each VM can have up to eight Hyper-V-specific network adapters and four legacy network adapters.
- Each VM can have up to 256 virtual SCSI disks and four virtual IDE drives.

CREATE A VIRTUAL MACHINE

GET READY. To create a virtual machine on Hyper-V, perform the following steps.

1. Log on to a computer running Windows Server 2016 with an administrator account, such as **adatum\administrator** with the password of **Pa$$w0rd**.
2. If Server Manager does not open, click **Start** and click **Server Manager**.
3. Open the **Tools** menu and click **Hyper-V**.
4. When Hyper-V Manager opens, right-click the host node and choose **New > Virtual Machine**.
5. When the New Virtual Machine Wizard opens, on the Before You Begin page, click **Next**.
6. On the Specify Name and Location page (as shown in Figure 8-1), in the Name text box, type the name of the virtual machine.

Figure 8-1

Creating a virtual machine

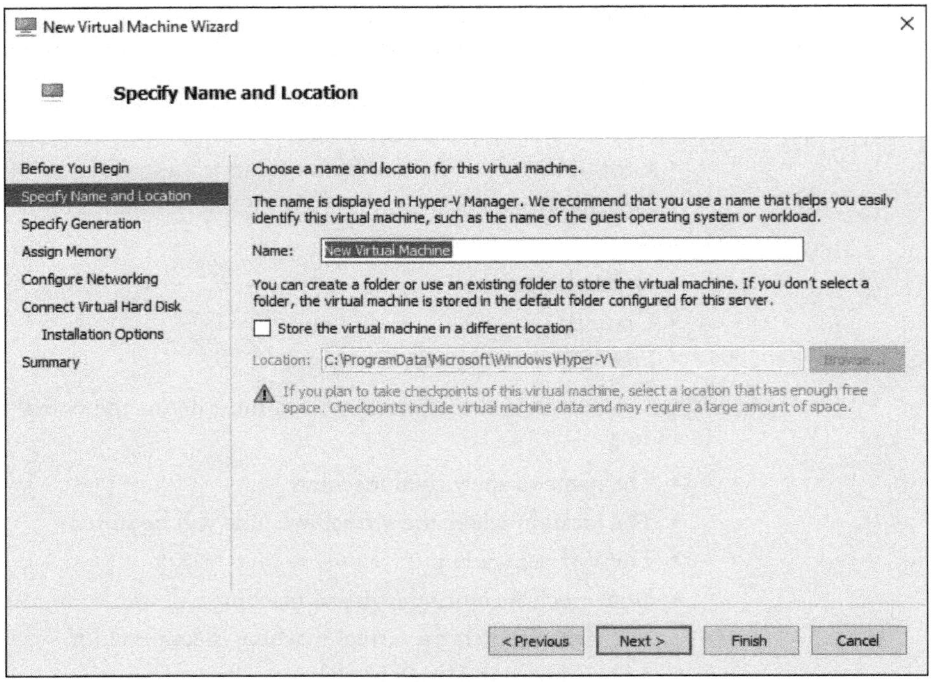

7. The default location to store the VM is the C:\ProgramData\Microsoft\Windows\Hyper-V\ folder. Click **Next**.

8. On the Specify Generation page, Generation 1 is already selected. Click **Next**.

9. On the Assign Memory page, the default startup memory is 1024. In the Startup memory box, type **2048**. Click **Next**.

10. Normally, you would select a virtual switch. However, because a virtual switch is not configured yet, on the Configure Networking page, click **Next**.

11. On the Connect Virtual Hard Disk page, change the size to **50** GB (as shown in Figure 8-2). Click **Next**.

Figure 8-2

Creating a virtual hard disk

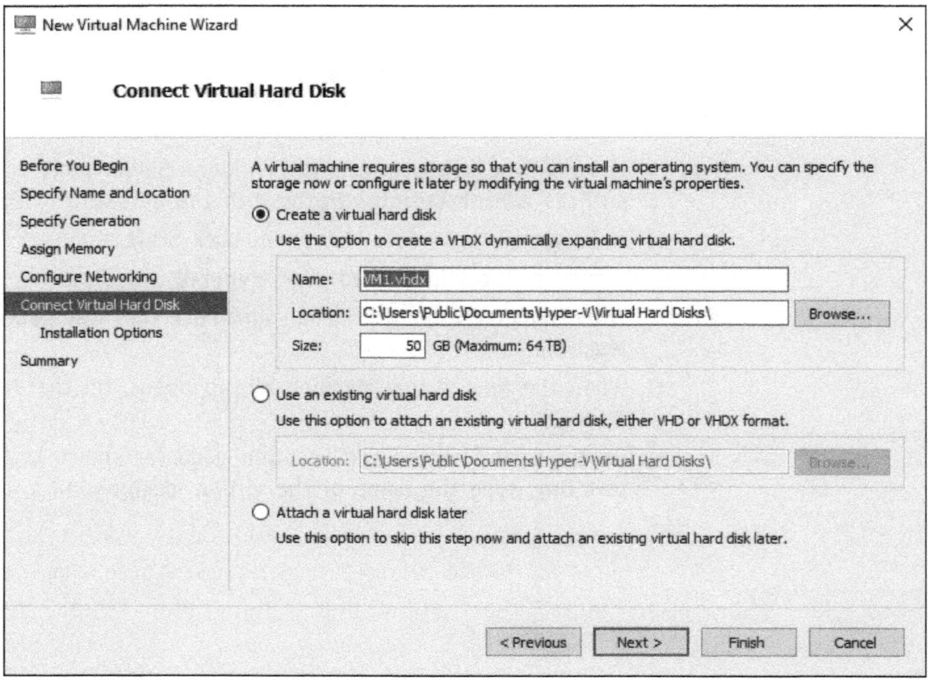

12. On the Installation Options page (as shown in Figure 8-3), select the **Install an operating system from a bootable CD/DVD-ROM** option.

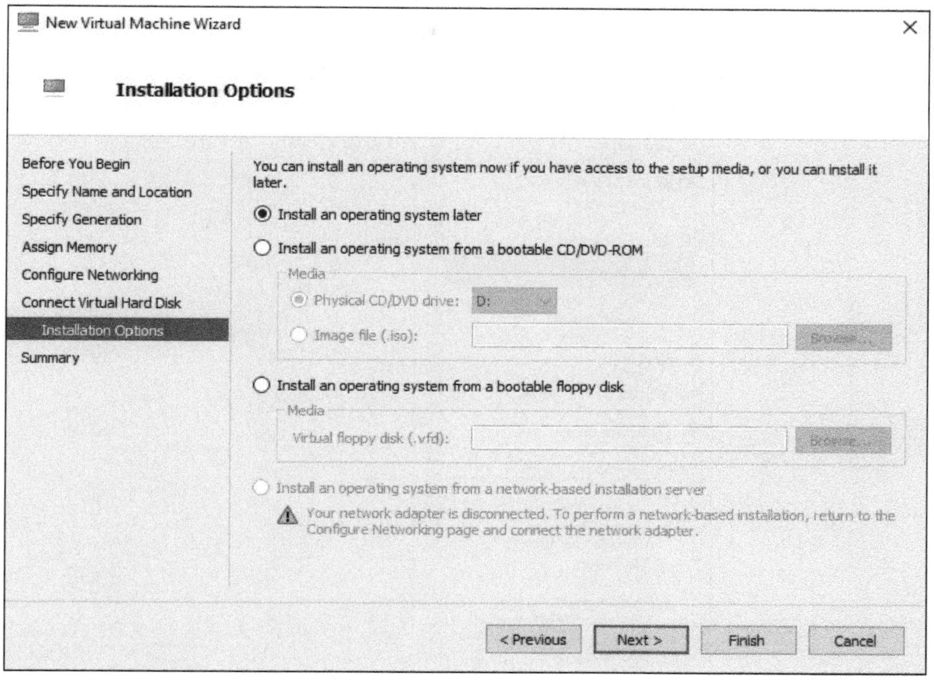

Figure 8-3

Specifying installation options

13. Select the **Image file (.iso)** option. Then click the **Browse** button. When the Open dialog box opens, browse to and double-click a Windows installation ISO file. Click **Next**.

14. On the Summary page, click **Finish**.

When you open the Settings dialog box for a virtual machine and select the DVD drive in the Hardware list, you see the interface shown in Figure 8-4. In the Media box, you can select one of the following options for the drive:

- **None:** Is the equivalent of a drive with no disk inserted
- **Image file:** Points to a disk image file with an .iso extension stored on one of the host computer's drives or on a shared network drive
- **Physical CD/DVD drive:** Links the virtual DVD drive to one of the physical DVD drives in the host computer

The ability to mount an image file to a virtual DVD drive is a particularly useful benefit for administrators who download operating system files as disk images. After you mount an installation disc, either physically or virtually, click Start in the Actions pane, which is the equivalent of turning on the virtual machine.

Starting a VM causes the thumbnail in the Hyper-V Manager to go live, displaying the contents of the computer's screen. To display the VM's activity at full size, click Connect in the Actions pane to open a new window for the virtual machine. You can then interact with the VM through that window as though you were sitting at a physical computer's console.

When the virtual machine boots from the disc you mounted, the operating system installation proceeds as though you were using a physical computer. During the installation process, you can work with the virtual hard disk drive just as you would a physical one,

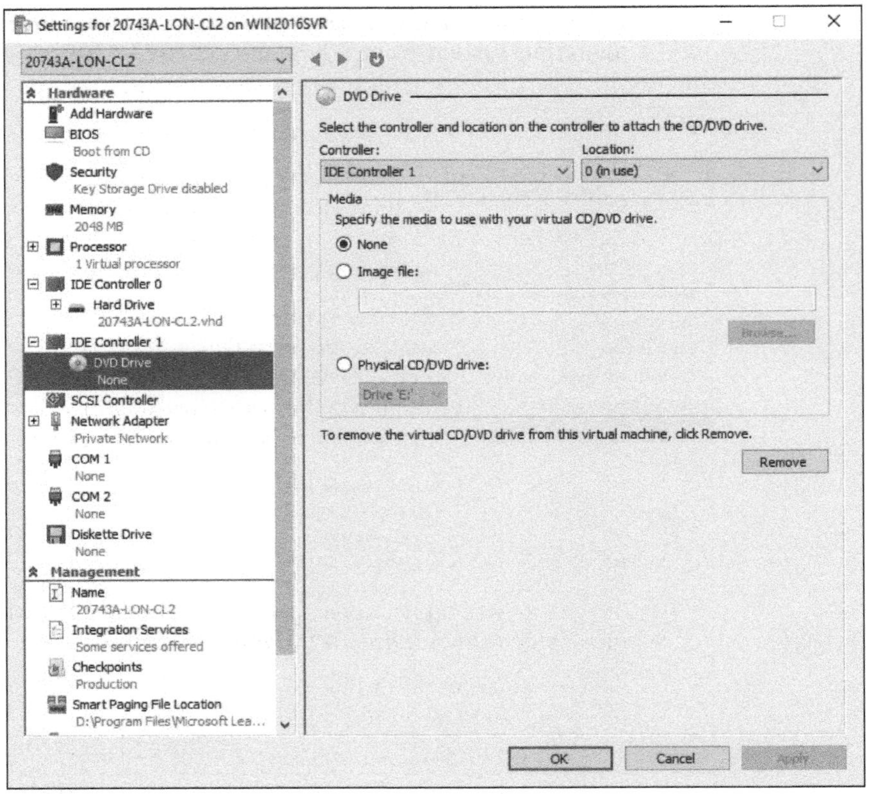

Figure 8-4

DVD drive settings for a virtual machine

creating partitions of various sizes and selecting one for the operating system. When the installation is complete, the virtual machine restarts, and you can then log on and use it as you would normally.

Implementing Enhanced Session Mode

> There are several ways to connect to virtual machines by using Virtual Machine Connection. You can open Hyper-V Manager and double-click the virtual machine in Hyper-V Manager, or right-click the virtual machine and choose Connect. You can also run VMConnect.exe and specify the virtual machine that you want to open.

CERTIFICATION READY
Implement enhanced session mode
Objective 3.2

By default, Virtual Machine Connection connects remotely over the VMBus by using TCP port 2179 using the Remote Desktop Protocol (RDP). If you want to modify the default port, you can open the registry and modify HKLM\SOFTWARE\Microsoft\Windows NT\CurrentVersion\Virtualization.

Virtual Machine Connection only supports a single connection. If a connection is already established, and a second user connects to the same virtual machine, the first user will be disconnected, and the second user will take over the session. Because the second user can view the first user's desktop, documents, and applications, this is considered a privacy and security issue.

Starting with Windows Server 2012 R2, Hyper-V supports enhanced session mode. By using *enhanced session mode*, you can connect to a running VM with the same features as Remote Desktop Services (RDS), even if the virtual machine does not have network connectivity or does not have the Remote Desktop feature enabled on the guest operating system. If the virtual machine is turned off, you can connect to it only by using simple mode. In addition, enhanced session mode allows you to redirect local drives, printers, USBs, and other devices to the virtual machine, and you can use a shared Clipboard, redirected folders, rich copy (similar to rich text that copies the text and the text formatting) and paste for copying files or graphics, and redirected sound from virtual machines.

You can configure enhanced session mode options at the following levels:

- **Server settings:** Affects all virtual machines that are running on the Hyper-V host. The default setting for the Allow enhanced session mode is set to Disabled on Hyper-V in Windows Server 2016, and is set to Enabled on Windows 10.

- **User settings:** Determines if the Virtual Machine Connection tool attempts to use enhanced session mode.

- **Guest operating system:** Is available only if you connect to virtual machines that are running Windows Server 2012 R2 or higher, or Windows 8.1 or higher and Remote Desktop Services is running on the virtual machine. The user account you will be using to sign in to the virtual machine must be a member of the Remote Desktop Users local group.

ENABLE ENHANCED SESSION MODE

GET READY. To enable enhanced session mode, perform the following steps.

1. Log on to a computer running Windows Server 2016 with an administrator account, such as **adatum\administrator** with the password of **Pa$$w0rd**.
2. If Server Manager does not open, click **Start** and click **Server Manager**.
3. Open the **Tools** menu and click **Hyper-V**.
4. Right-click the host and choose **Hyper-V Settings**.
5. When the Hyper-V Settings window opens, under the Server section, select the **Enhanced Session Mode Policy** node.
6. On the Enhanced Session Mode Policy page, select the **Allow enhanced session mode** check box, as shown in Figure 8-5.

Figure 8-5

Enabling enhanced session mode

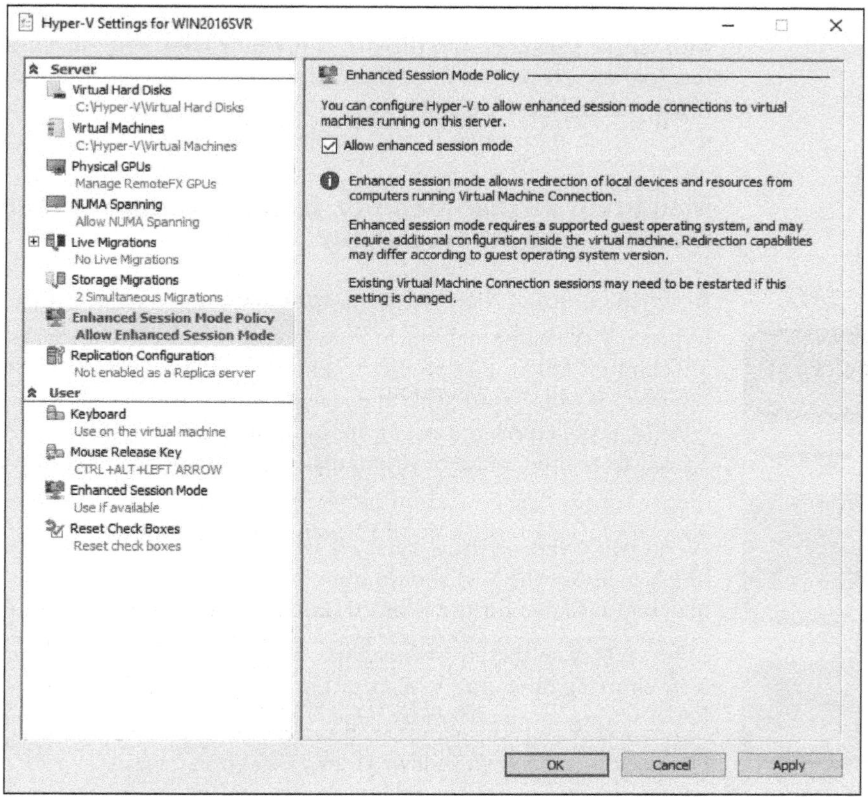

7. Under the User section, click **Enhanced Session Mode**. By default, the Use enhanced session mode option is already selected.

8. To close the Hyper-V Settings window, click **OK.**

9. In Hyper-V Manager, right-click a running VM and choose **Connect.**

10. When the Connect dialog box opens, you can specify the display configuration/resolution by moving the slider.

11. Click **Show Options** and click the **Local Resources** tab, as shown in Figure 8-6.

Figure 8-6

Specifying local resources

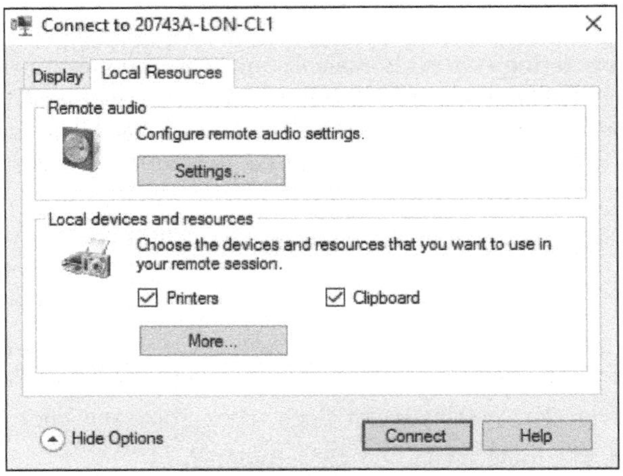

12. In the Local devices and resources section, click **More**, click **Drives**, and then click **OK.**

13. In the Connect to LON-CL1 window, click **Connect.**

At the user settings level, you configure enhanced session mode, which controls whether Virtual Machine Connection will attempt to use enhanced session mode when establishing connections with virtual machines. On the virtual machine level, you can control whether Guest services Integration Service is enabled (in other words, if the virtual machine offers enhanced session mode). In addition, the operating system in a virtual machine must support enhanced session mode, which means that it must be either Windows 8.1 or Windows Server 2012 R2.

Managing Virtual Memory, Including Startup Memory, Dynamic Memory, and Smart Paging

When you create a virtual machine, you define startup RAM, which is the amount of memory that a virtual machine will use when the computer boots and represents the minimum amount of physical memory the virtual machine will use. When specifying startup RAM, be sure that the startup RAM for all VMs does not exceed the physical RAM installed on the server. If you do exceed the physical RAM on the server, you need to remove some of the virtual machines or add memory to the host.

CERTIFICATION READY
Add or remove memory in running a VM
Objective 3.2

CERTIFICATION READY
Configure Dynamic Memory
Objective 3.2

CERTIFICATION READY
Configure smart paging
Objective 3.2

When you create a virtual machine with the New Virtual Machine Wizard, you specify how much memory the VM should use on the Assign Memory page. Obviously, the amount of memory available for use is based on the physical memory installed in the computer.

After you create the virtual machine, you can modify the amount of memory allocated to it by shutting down the VM, opening its Settings dialog box, and changing the Startup RAM setting on the Memory page. This enables you to experiment with various amounts of memory and dial in the optimum performance level for the system.

In the first versions of Hyper-V, shutting down the virtual machine was the only way to modify its memory allocation. In the Windows Server 2016 version, however, you can use a feature called Dynamic Memory to reallocate memory automatically to the VM from a shared memory pool as its demands change. If a virtualized server starts to experience larger amounts of client traffic, for example, Hyper-V can increase the memory allocated to the system, and then reduce it when the traffic subsides.

To use Dynamic Memory, you must enable it by selecting the Enable Dynamic Memory check box on the VM's Memory page of the Settings dialog box, and then configure the following settings:

- *Startup RAM/Memory* specifies the amount of memory that you want to allocate to the VM when it starts. When you are using Dynamic Memory, this value can be the minimum amount of memory needed to boot the system.

- *Minimum RAM* specifies the smallest amount of memory the VM can use at any time. Operating systems can conceivably require more memory to start up than they do to run, so this value can be smaller than the Startup RAM value.

- *Maximum RAM* specifies the largest amount of memory that the VM can use at any time. The value can range from a low equal to the Startup RAM value to a high of 1 TB.

- *Memory buffer* contains a percentage that Hyper-V uses to calculate how much memory to allocate to the VM, compared with its actual utilization, as measured by performance counters. For example, with the Memory buffer value set to 20%, a VM with applications and operating system that consume 1 GB of memory receives a dynamic allocation of 1.2 GB.

- *Memory weight* contains a relative value that specifies the priority of this VM, compared with the other VMs on the same computer. When the physical memory in the computer is insufficient to allocate the full buffered amount specified for each VM, the VMs with the highest memory weight settings receive priority.

Windows Server 2008 R2 Hyper-V introduced Dynamic Memory, but newer versions of Windows improved on the concept by adding the Minimum RAM setting. This enables Hyper-V to reduce the memory used by a virtual machine to a level lower than that needed to start the system, reclaiming that memory for other uses.

The problem with having minimum RAM values that are lower than the startup RAM values is that the supply of physical memory can become depleted with too many VMs running simultaneously at their minimum RAM values. When this occurs, a VM that has to restart might be unable to do so because not enough free memory is available to increase its memory allocation from its minimum RAM value to its startup RAM value.

⟶ CONFIGURE THE VIRTUAL MACHINE STATIC MEMORY

GET READY. To configure the virtual machine static memory, perform the following steps.

1. Log on to a computer running Windows Server 2016 with an administrator account, such as **adatum\administrator** with the password of **Pa$$w0rd.**
2. If Server Manager does not open, click **Start** and click **Server Manager.**
3. Open the **Tools** menu and click **Hyper-V.**
4. If the virtual machine is running, right-click the virtual machine and choose **Shut down.** When you are prompted to shut down the operating system, click the **Shut Down** button.

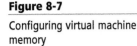 If the virtual memory has a virtual configuration of 6.2 or higher, you can increase or decrease the Startup RAM without turning off the computer.

5. Right-click the virtual machine and choose **Settings**.

6. Click the **Memory** node, as shown in Figure 8-7.

Figure 8-7

Configuring virtual machine memory

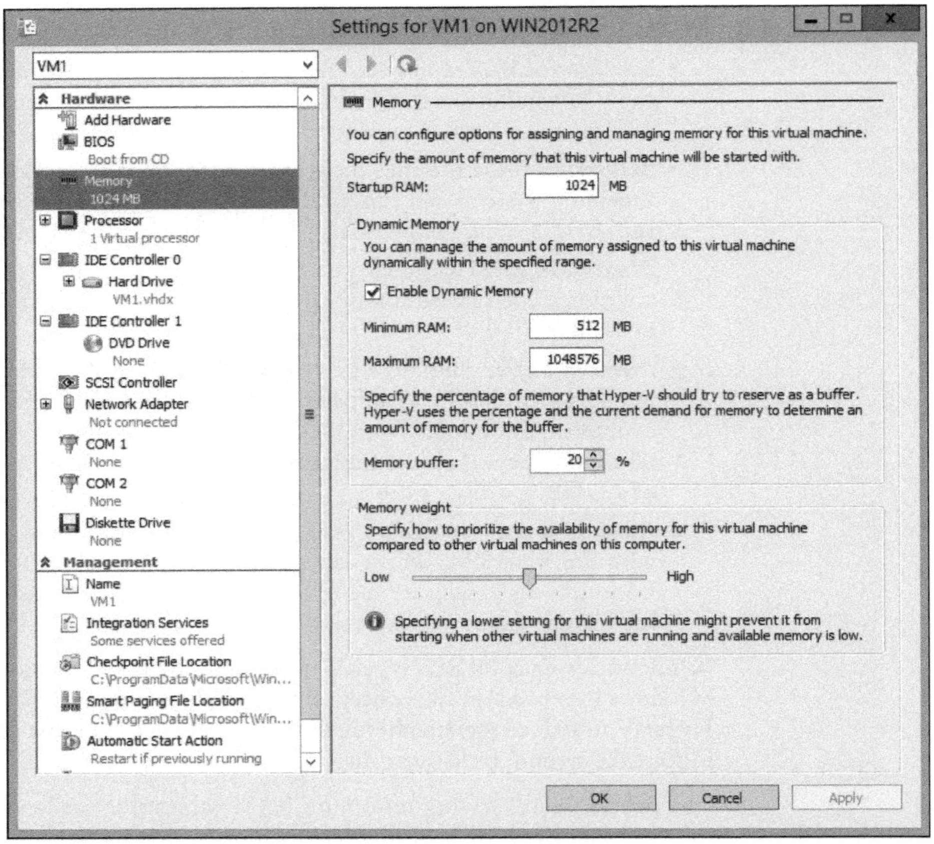

![Settings for VM1 on WIN2012R2 dialog showing Memory configuration with Startup RAM 1024 MB, Dynamic Memory enabled, Minimum RAM 512 MB, Maximum RAM 1048576 MB, Memory buffer 20%, and Memory weight slider]

7. Change the Startup RAM from 1024 MB to **2048** MB.

8. To enable Dynamic Memory, select the **Enable Dynamic Memory** check box. As shown in Figure 8-7, the Enable Dynamic Memory check box has already been selected because it was enabled when the VM was created. Then, specify the minimum and maximum memory for Dynamic Memory.

9. To specify the memory buffer, type the appropriate number.

10. To change the memory weight, slide the slider left or right as needed.

11. When done, click **OK**.

To address the possibility of running out of memory because the Hyper-V host does not have enough memory to run all of the virtual machines hosted on the Hyper-V host, Hyper-V includes a feature called *smart paging*. Smart paging is an advanced version of memory paging that allows a virtual machine to temporarily use hard disk space when there is a shortage of nonvolatile memory. With smart paging, when a VM has to restart and not enough memory is available to allocate its startup RAM value, the system uses hard disk space to make up the difference and begins paging memory contents to disk.

Disk-access rates are far slower than memory-access rates, of course, so smart paging incurs a severe performance penalty, but the paging occurs only for as long as it takes to restart the VM and return it to its minimum RAM allocation.

Hyper-V uses smart paging only in highly specific conditions, such as when a VM must be restarted, no free memory is available, and the memory needed cannot be freed up by other means.

➔ CONFIGURE THE SMART PAGING FILE LOCATION

GET READY. To configure the Smart Paging File Location, perform the following steps.

1. Log on to a computer running Windows Server 2016 with an administrator account, such as **adatum\administrator** with the password of **Pa$$w0rd**.
2. If Server Manager does not open, click **Start** and click **Server Manager**.
3. Open the **Tools** menu and click **Hyper-V**.
4. If the virtual machine is running, right-click the virtual machine and choose **Shut down**. When you are prompted to shut down the operating system, click the **Shut Down** button.
5. Right-click the virtual machine and choose **Settings**.
6. Under Management, click the **Smart Paging File Location** node.
7. In the Smart Paging File Location text box, specify the location of the smart paging file location.
8. To close the Settings dialog box, click **OK**.

Configuring Non-Uniform Memory Access (NUMA) Support

Non-Uniform Memory Access (NUMA) is a computer system architecture that is used with multiprocessor designs that organizes memory into regions; these regions are assigned access latencies, based on how these larger systems' processors and memory are interconnected. For large multiprocessor systems, NUMA divides memory and processors into groups called NUMA nodes. Processors can access local memory faster than remote memory. NUMA will schedule threads and allocate memory to increase performance by allocating storage and schedule threads to access data in the same NUMA node.

CERTIFICATION READY
Configure Non-Uniform
Memory Access (NUMA)
support
Objective 3.2

While spanning NUMA nodes can help you run more virtual machines at the same time by providing more memory than what is available on a single NUMA node, it can decrease overall performance. Aligning the nodes and sockets of a virtual machine to the hardware topology helps improve the performance of NUMA-aware workloads.

In Windows Server 2016, Hyper-V projects a virtualized NUMA topology to virtual machines, which is optimized to match the NUMA topology of the physical host. You can configure virtual NUMA topology at a virtual machine level. You can specify the maximum amount of memory, the maximum number of virtual processors, and the maximum number of virtual NUMA nodes. By default, these values are set to align with the physical NUMA topology. If you change the settings, you can restore the default virtual NUMA topology by clicking the Use Hardware Topology button.

⊘ **CONFIGURE NUMA**

GET READY. To configure NUMA, perform the following steps.

1. Log on to a computer running Windows Server 2016 with an administrator account, such as **adatum\administrator** with the password of **Pa$$w0rd**.

2. If Server Manager does not open, click **Start** and click **Server Manager**.

3. Open the **Tools** menu and click **Hyper-V**.

4. When Hyper-V opens, right-click the physical host and choose **Hyper-V Settings**.

5. When the Hyper-V Settings window opens, select the **NUMA Spanning** node.

6. On the NUMA Spanning page, the Allow virtual machine to span physical NUMA nodes option is already selected. To close the Hyper-V Settings window, click **OK**.

7. If the virtual machine is running, right-click the virtual machine and choose **Shut down**. When you are prompted to shut down the operating system, click the **Shut Down** button.

8. Right-click the virtual machine and choose **Settings**.

9. When the Settings window opens, expand the **Processor** node and click **NUMA**, as shown in Figure 8-8.

Figure 8-8

Configuring NUMA for a VM

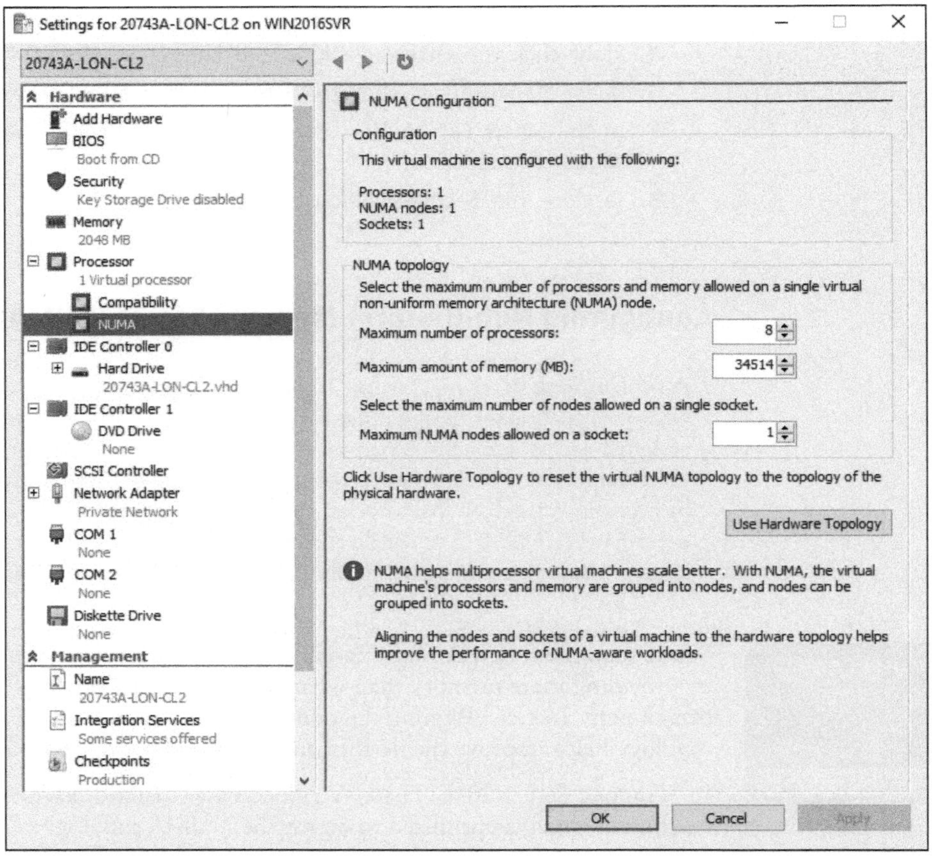

The top of the window shows the number of processors, NUMA nodes, and sockets being used by the virtual machines. In the NUMA topology section, you can specify the maximum number of processors, the maximum amount of memory, and the maximum number of nodes allowed on a single socket.

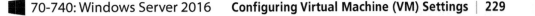

By default, the maximum number of processors, the maximum amount of memory, and the maximum number of nodes allowed on a single socket is set to align with the physical NUMA topology.

10. To restore the maximum number of processors, the maximum amount of memory, and the maximum number of nodes allowed on a single socket values to match the topology of the physical hardware, click the **Use Hardware Topology** button.

11. Close the Settings window by clicking **OK.**

Managing Integration Services

In some cases, the Hyper-V guest operating system does not function properly using the default drivers that are installed. For these operating systems, you can install guest integration services. Hyper-V Integration Services is a suite of utilities and drivers that are designed to enhance the performance of the virtual machine's guest operating systems. It also supports operating system shutdown, time synchronization, and backup support. Windows 8 and newer and Windows Server 2012 and newer already include the guest integration services.

When the operating system is not virtualization-aware, the virtual machine does not have the proper device drivers for some of the hardware that would allow the VM to run efficiently. In addition, it is unable to use features that are available only on virtual machines, such as time synchronization with the Hyper-V host, or releasing the mouse when the cursor reaches the edge of the virtual machine window. When the operating system includes Integration Services, Integration Services provide better interoperability with the Hyper-V environment and support for VMBus, synthetic devices, and other virtualization-specific features.

Hyper-V Integration Services that are available in virtual machines are:

- **Hyper-V Guest Shutdown Service:** Allows you to shut down a virtual machine without interacting directly with the operating system on the virtual machine via a Windows Management Instrumentation call
- **Hyper-V Time Synchronization Service:** Synchronizes the time on the virtual machine with the time on the Hyper-V host
- **Hyper-V Data Exchange Service:** Provides a method to set, delete, enumerate, and exchange specific registry key values between the virtual machine and the Hyper-V host
- **Hyper-V Heartbeat Service:** Verifies if an operating system that is running on a virtual machine is responding to requests
- **Hyper-V Volume Shadow Copy Requestor:** Allows the Hyper-V host to request the synchronization and backup of a running virtual machine
- **Hyper-V Remote Desktop Virtualization Service:** Enables the Remote Desktop Virtualization Host to communicate with and manage virtual machines that are part of a virtual desktop infrastructure (VDI) collection
- **Hyper-V Guest Service Interface:** Enables enhanced session mode communication with virtual machines, including device redirection, shared Clipboard, and drag-and-drop functionality between the Hyper-V host and virtual machines

→ INSTALL GUEST INTEGRATION SERVICES

GET READY. To install guest integration services, perform the following steps.

1. Log on to a computer running Windows Server 2016 with an administrator account, such as **adatum\administrator** with the password of **Pa$$w0rd**.
2. If Server Manager does not open, click **Start** and click **Server Manager**.
3. Open the **Tools** menu and click **Hyper-V**.
4. In the left pane, select a Hyper-V server.
5. In the Actions pane, start the virtual machine on which you want to install the guest integration services and click **Connect**. A Virtual Machine Connection window appears.
6. In the Virtual Machine Connection window, click **Action** and then click **Insert Integration Services Setup Disk**. Hyper-V mounts an image of the guest integration services disk to a virtual disk drive and displays an AutoPlay window.
7. Click **Install Hyper-V Integration Services**. A message box appears, prompting you to upgrade the existing installation.
8. Click **OK**. The system installs the package and prompts you to restart the computer.
9. Click **Yes** to restart the computer.

You can control which Integration Services are available to a virtual machine by opening the virtual machine settings and clicking the Integration Services node, as shown in Figure 8-9. By default, all Integration Services except Hyper-V Guest Service Interface are enabled for the virtual machines that you create in Hyper-V in Windows Server 2016.

Figure 8-9

Configuring a virtual machine's Integration Services

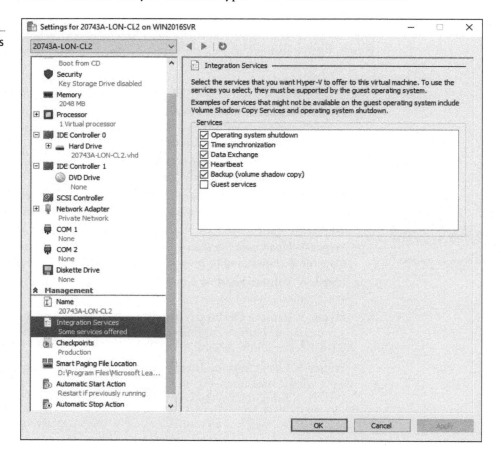

Creating and Configuring Generation 1 and 2 VMs

When you create a virtual machine, you specify if the virtual machine is a Generation 1 VM or a Generation 2 VM. Generation 1 uses the original Hyper-V BIOS-based architecture. Generation 2 is hypervisor aware, does not rely on synthetic or emulated hardware, which can give faster boot times, and does not perform as well. Unfortunately, the VM generation cannot be changed once the VM is created.

CERTIFICATION READY
Create and configure
Generation 1 and 2
VMs and determine
appropriate usage
scenarios
Objective 3.2

When you create virtual machines in Hyper-V, you have to choose one of the two virtual machine generations:

- *Generation 1*: Provides the same virtual hardware used in older versions of Hyper-V. Generation 1 VMs supports 32-bit and 64-bit guest operating systems. Generation 1 VMs can access a physical DVD drive.
- *Generation 2*: Provides new functionality on a virtual machine, including PXE boot by using a standard network adapter, boot from a SCSI virtual hard disk or DVD, Secure Boot, and UEFI firmware support. Generation 2 VMs only support 64-bit guest operating systems. Generation 2 VMs cannot access a physical DVD drive. Generation 2 virtual machines currently support only Windows Server 2012, Windows 8 (64-bit), and newer 64-bit Windows operating systems. However, only Windows Server 2012 R2 and newer Hyper-V hosts support Generation 2 VMs.

TAKE NOTE*

Once a virtual machine has been created, you cannot change its generation.

Because Windows Server 2012 or earlier Hyper-V hosts and Azure IaaS services do not support Generation 2 VMs, you should not choose Generation 2 if you are using Windows Server 2012 or Azure. Also if you have 32-bit VMs, you will need to use Generation 1 for those VMs. If you need better performance and better security, you should choose Generation 2.

Importing, Exporting, and Copying VMs

VMs are easy to create. By leveraging the exporting, importing, and copying functions of Hyper-V, you significantly reduce the time spent creating duplicate VMs.

CERTIFICATION READY
Export and import VMs
Objective 3.2

Exporting a VM is the process by which you take a partially or completely configured VM and create other VMs without having to perform the installation and configuration from scratch.

Importing and copying are related in that to do either, you must use the Import Virtual Machine Wizard:

CERTIFICATION READY
Import, export, and
copy VMs
Objective 5.5

- Importing is the process by which you take an existing set of VM files and re-create the exact same VM.
- Copying is the process of using an exported VM like a template to create as many additional VMs as you need.

In Windows Server 2016, there are three options available when you select the Import Virtual Machine Wizard:

- **Register the virtual machine in place (use the existing unique ID):** Used when you have manually placed the VM files where you want them, there is no other VM on the machine that has the same unique ID, and you just want Hyper-V to register the VM
- **Restore the virtual machine (use the existing unique ID):** Used when you have VM files on other media (external drive, file server, and so on), there is no other VM on the machine that has the same unique ID, and you want Hyper-V to organize the files and register the VM

• **Copy the virtual machine (create a new unique ID):** Used when you have an exported VM that you are using as a template and want to import many times

If you want to use an exported VM as a template to create multiple VMs, you should run sysprep on the VM prior to performing the export.

EXPORT A VM

GET READY. To export a VM, perform the following steps.

1. Log on to a computer running Windows Server 2016 with an administrator account, such as **adatum\administrator** with the password of **Pa$$w0rd**.
2. If Server Manager does not open, click **Start** and click **Server Manager.**
3. Open the **Tools** menu and click **Hyper-V.**
4. When Hyper-V Manager opens, right-click the VM and choose **Export.**
5. When the Export Virtual machine dialog box opens, in the Location dialog box, specify the path of where to save the exported virtual machine and then click the **Export** button.
6. In the Virtual Machines section of Hyper-V Manager, scroll to the right to view the status of the export, as shown in Figure 8-10.

Figure 8-10

Monitoring the export status of a VM

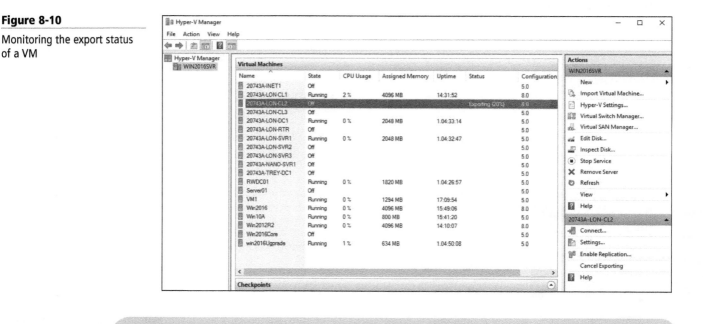

If your intention is to use your exported VM multiple times, it is important to name the VM something generic to avoid confusion later.

COPY OR IMPORT A VM

GET READY. To copy or import a VM, perform the following steps.

1. Log on to a computer running Windows Server 2016 with an administrator account, such as **adatum\administrator** with the password of **Pa$$w0rd**.
2. If Server Manager does not open, click **Start** and click **Server Manager.**

3. Open the **Tools** menu and click **Hyper-V.**

4. Right-click the Hyper-V host and choose **Import Virtual Machine.**

5. On the Before You Begin page, click **Next.**

6. On the Locate Folder page, specify the path of the folder or browse to it and select the folder of the exported VM, and then click **Next.**

7. On the Select Virtual Machine page, select the name of the VM to import and then click **Next.**

TAKE NOTE*

This should be the same name as the VM you are replacing.

8. On the Choose Import Type page (see Figure 8-11), select from the following choices:

   • **Register the virtual machine in-place (use the existing ID):** The import option that takes the existing VM and corresponding files and folder structure as it is and registers the VM with the host

   • **Restore the virtual machine (use the existing ID):** The import option that is similar to registering; however, it enables you to specify different paths for the files and folders

   • **Copy the virtual machine (create a new unique ID):** The copy option that will register the VM with a new name and location

   Click **Next.**

Figure 8-11

The Choose Import Type page

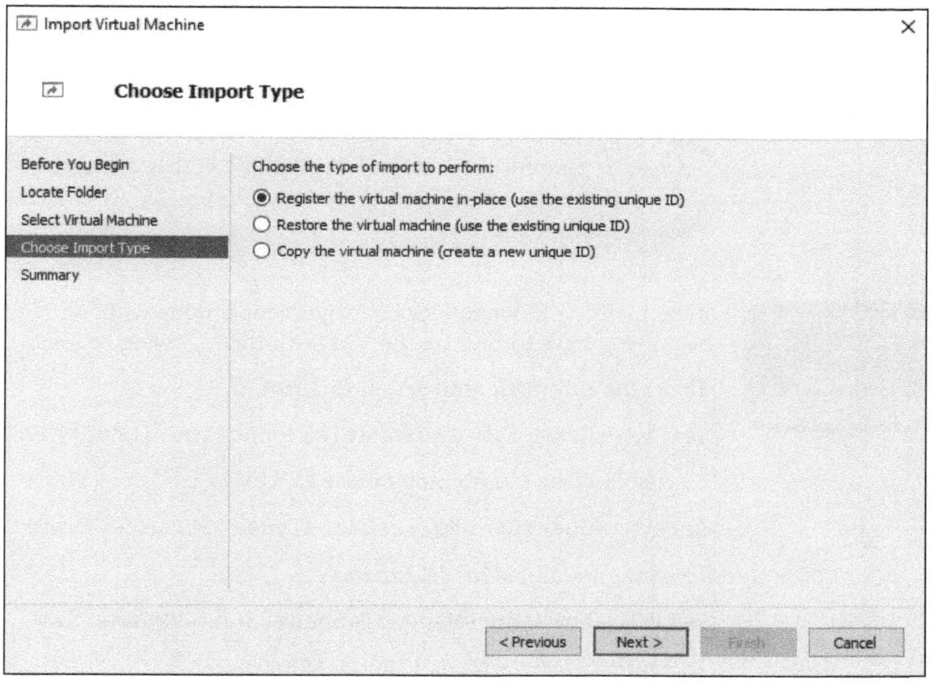

9. If you selected the Register option, you are presented with the Completing Import Wizard box. Verify that your selections are correct and then click **Finish.**

10. If you selected the Restore or Copy option, you are presented with the Choose Folders for Virtual Machine Files box. Select the **Store the virtual machine in a different location** check box.

    a. In the Virtual machine configuration folder box, specify the path of the folder or browse to it and select the folder where you want to place the current configuration.

b. In the Snapshot store box, specify the path of the folder or browse to it and select the folder where you want to place the current configuration.

c. In the Smart Paging Folder box, specify the path of the folder or browse to it and select the folder where you want to place the smart paging files.

Then, click **Next.**

11. On the Choose Folders to Store Virtual Hard Disks page, in the Location box, specify the path of the folder or browse to it and select the folder where you want to place the VM hard disk, and then click **Next.**

12. On the Completing Move Wizard, verify that your selections are correct and then click **Finish.**

TAKE NOTE*

When importing a VM multiple times, remember that the actual name of the VM will be the same as the exported VM in Hyper-V Manager. The VM name can be changed in Hyper-V Manager, but the file names should remain the same.

Prior to importing, copy the entire exported VM folder to the location where you want to store the new VM. This will avoid duplicate file naming conflicts.

Implementing Discrete Device Assignment (DDA)

Discrete Device Assignment (DDA) allows guest virtual machines to communicate directly with PCIe devices. It is used for VMs that need access to solid-state disk (SSD) drives or Graphical Processing Units (GPUs) that are connected directly to the PCIe bus that follows the Non-Volatile Memory Express (NVMe) standard. DDA allows faster access to these devices.

CERTIFICATION READY
Implement Discrete
Device Assignment (DDA)
Objective 3.2

Implementing Discrete Device Assignment is done with Windows PowerShell. Before you begin, you have to prepare the VM with the following actions:

To set the automatic stop action to TurnOff:

`Set-VM -Name $vm -AutomaticStopAction TurnOff`

To enable Write-Combining on the CPU:

`Set-VM -GuestControlledCacheTypes $true -VMName $vm`

To configure 32-bit MMIO space:

`Set-VM -LowMemoryMappedIoSpace 3Gb -VMName $vm`

To configure greater than 32-bit MMIO space:

`Set-VM -HighMemoryMappedIoSpace 33280Mb -VMName $vm`

The next thing you need to do is dismount the device as a display adapter from the host so that it will be available from DDA by using the following command:

`Dismount-VMHostAssignableDevice -force -LocationPath $locationPath`

You will then assign the device to the guest VM by using the following command:

`Add-VMAssignableDevice -LocationPath $locationPath -VMName $vm`

Creating Linux and FreeBSD VMs

> Most data centers will have a combination of Windows and Linux servers to provide all of the applications and services needed by an organization. Hyper-V provides a complete virtualization environment that also supports Linux and FreeBSD VMs, including CentOS, Red Hat Linux, Debian, Oracle Linux, SUSE, and Ubuntu.

CERTIFICATION READY
Create Linux and
FreeBSD VMs
Objective 3.2

Creating Linux and FreeBSD VMs is no different than creating a Windows VM. Simply right-click the Hyper-V host and choose New > Virtual Machine. Then specify the name of the virtual machine, specify the amount of memory, specify a virtual switch, and specify the operating system installation options. After the VM is created, you perform the Linux or FreeBSD installation from the installation ISO file.

CERTIFICATION READY
Install and configure
Linux Integration
Services (LIS)
Objective 3.2

Just as with Windows, for the best performance for Linux and FreeBSD systems, you need to install the appropriate Linux Integration Services (LIS) or FreeBSD Integration Services (BIS). Some recent distributions come with built-in support for LIS. In other situations, you will have to download the LIS or BIS and install the appropriate package within the Linux VM.

CERTIFICATION READY
Install and configure
FreeBSD Integration
Services (BIS)
Objective 3.2

In either case, you then need to activate LIS before you can use it. For example, for Ubuntu you will modify the /etc/initramfs-tools/modules file to add the following lines:

hv_vmbus

hv_storvsc

hv_blkvsc

hv_netvsc

After saving the changes, you need to reinitialize the modules and reboot the virtual machine:

```
sudo update-initramfs -u
sudo shutdown -r now
```

Implementing Security Options for Windows and Linux Virtual Machines, Including Secure Boot

> Windows Server 2016 includes multiple options that will help secure the virtual machines. These options include Secure Boot, encryption support, and shielding.

CERTIFICATION READY
Implement Secure Boot
for Windows and Linux
environments
Objective 3.2

Secure Boot is a Unified Extensible Firmware Interface (UEFI) that ensures that each component that is loaded during the boot process is digitally signed and validated. It allows the machine to boot using only software that is trusted by the PC manufacturer or the user and to help prevent malware.

When a computer boots, a boot loader is responsible for copying the operating system image into memory when the computer is started. If Secure Boot detects a boot loader that is not signed with the appropriate digital signature, it will block it.

To support Secure Boot for Windows and Linux virtual machines, the virtual machine must be Generation 2. You then open the virtual machine settings, select the Security node, and make sure the Enable Secure Boot option is selected. The Enable Secure Boot option is enabled by default.

BitLocker Drive Encryption is designed to protect against brute force attacks to gain access to your fixed drive or situations in which someone tries to install and access your fixed drive from another computer. It provides full disk encryption capabilities for fixed drives (including storage pools) and operating system drives. You can further enhance security by checking the integrity of boot files if a ***Trusted Platform Module (TPM)*** chip is available on your computer. The TPM is a dedicated cryptographic processor chip that the computer uses to store the BitLocker encryption keys.

By enabling the Enable Trusted Platform Module option, you use a virtualized Trusted Platform Module (TPM) chip available for the VM that will encrypt the virtual disk using BitLocker. By selecting the Encrypt State and VM migration traffic option to encrypt the virtual machine saved state and live migration traffic.

If you select the Enable Shielding option, you disable management features like console connection, PowerShell Direct, and some integration components. In addition, the Enable Secure Boot, Enable Trusted Platform Modules, and Encrypt State and virtual machine migration traffic options will be automatically selected and enforced.

The Hyper-V host that has a shielded virtual machine is known as a ***guarded host***, which runs the ***Host Guarding Service (HGS)*** server role. The HGS service will provide a transport key that will unlock and run a shielded VM. When you shield a virtual machine, the VM data and state is protected by using the virtual TPM, which will encrypt the VM disks. The vTPM device is encrypted with the transport key.

You can run the shielded virtual machine locally without setting up a Host Guarding Service. But if you migrate it to another host, you must update the Key Protector for the virtual machine to authorize the new host to run the virtual machine.

 ENABLE VM SECURITY OPTIONS

GET READY. To enable VM security options, perform the following steps.

1. Log on to a computer running Windows Server 2016 with an administrator account, such as **adatum\administrator** with the password of **Pa$$w0rd**.

2. If Server Manager does not open, click **Start** and click **Server Manager**.

3. Open the **Tools** menu and click **Hyper-V**.

4. If the virtual machine is running, right-click the virtual machine and choose **Shut down**. When you are prompted to shut down the operating system, click the **Shut Down** button.

5. Right-click a VM and choose **Settings**.

6. When the Settings dialog box opens, click the **Security** node.

7. On the Security page, as shown in Figure 8-12, Enable Secure Boot is already selected. To select the TPM, select the **Enable Trusted Platform Module** option. If you want to encrypt state and virtual machine migration traffic, select the **Encrypt state and virtual machine traffic** option.

Figure 8-12

Selecting security options

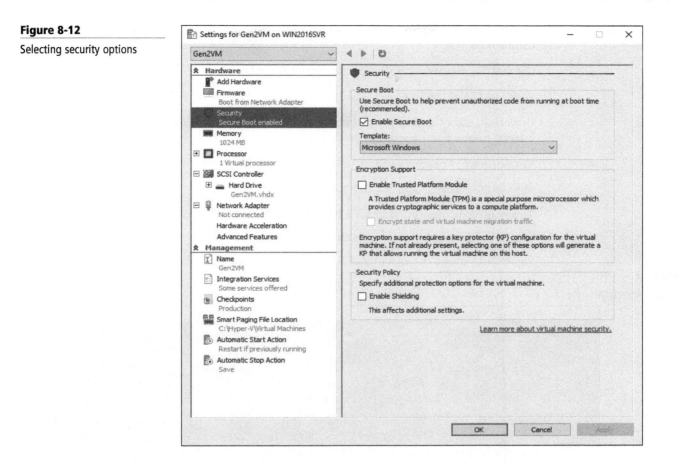

8. To shield the virtual machine, select the **Enable Shielding** option.
9. To close the Settings dialog box, click **OK**.

■ Configuring Resource Metering

THE BOTTOM LINE

Just as you need to monitor physical computers, you also need to monitor virtual machines (VMs). Everything you have learned in this lesson applies to VMs. To monitor a virtual machine running Windows, you can still use Server Manager, Computer Management, Event Viewer, Performance Monitor, and all of the other tools. Because a single host can have many virtual servers, you need to make sure that one virtual computer does not use all of the resources that would take away from the other machines.

CERTIFICATION READY
Configure Resource
Metering
Objective 3.2

Hyper-V Resource Metering is a tool that allows you to view the resource usage of a host and individual VMs. In Windows Server 2016, it is activated and viewed with Windows PowerShell. Hyper-V Resource Metering includes the following cmdlets:

- `Enable-VMResourceMetering` starts collecting data per virtual machine.
- `Disable-VMResourceMetering` disables resource metering per virtual machine.
- `Reset-VMResourceMetering` resets virtual machine resource-metering counters.
- `Measure-VM` displays resource-metering statistics for a specific virtual machine.

To enable Hyper-V resource metering on a Hyper-V host, execute the following PowerShell commands:

```
Get-VM -ComputerName <HostName> | Enable-
VMResourceMetering
```

By default, the collection interval for Hyper-V metering data is one hour. To change the interval to one minute, execute the following command:

```
Set-vmhost -computername <HostName>
-ResourceMeteringSaveInterval 00:01:00
```

To get all VMs metering data for a host, execute the following command:

```
Get-VM -ComputerName <HostName> | Measure-VM
```

Figure 8-13 shows the enabling of Resource Metering and the data collected.

Figure 8-13

Enabling Resource Metering

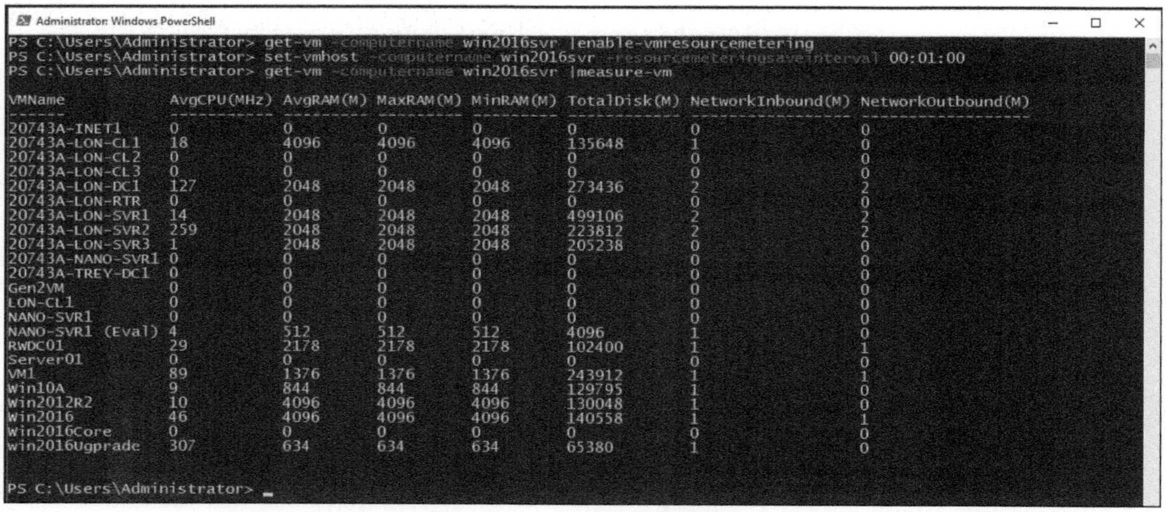

```
Administrator: Windows PowerShell
PS C:\Users\Administrator> get-vm -computername win2016svr |enable-vmresourcemetering
PS C:\Users\Administrator> set-vmhost -computername win2016svr -resourcemeteringsaveinterval 00:01:00
PS C:\Users\Administrator> get-vm -computername win2016svr |measure-vm

VMName             AvgCPU(MHz) AvgRAM(M) MaxRAM(M) MinRAM(M) TotalDisk(M) NetworkInbound(M) NetworkOutbound(M)
------             ----------- --------- --------- --------- ------------ ----------------- ------------------
20743A-INET1       0           0         0         0         0            0                 0
20743A-LON-CL1     18          4096      4096      4096      135648       1                 0
20743A-LON-CL2     0           0         0         0         0            0                 0
20743A-LON-CL3     0           0         0         0         0            0                 0
20743A-LON-DC1     127         2048      2048      2048      273436       2                 2
20743A-LON-RTR     0           0         0         0         0            0                 0
20743A-LON-SVR1    14          2048      2048      2048      499106       2                 2
20743A-LON-SVR2    259         2048      2048      2048      223812       2                 2
20743A-LON-SVR3    1           2048      2048      2048      205238       0                 0
20743A-NANO-SVR1   0           0         0         0         0            0                 0
20743A-TREY-DC1    0           0         0         0         0            0                 0
Gen2VM             0           0         0         0         0            0                 0
LON-CL1            0           0         0         0         0            0                 0
NANO-SVR1          0           0         0         0         0            0                 0
NANO-SVR1 (Eval)   4           512       512       512       4096         1                 0
RWDC01             29          2178      2178      2178      102400       1                 1
Server01           0           0         0         0         0            0                 0
VM1                89          1376      1376      1376      243912       1                 1
Win10A             9           844       844       844       129795       1                 0
Win2012R2          10          4096      4096      4096      130048       1                 0
Win2016            46          4096      4096      4096      140558       1                 1
Win2016Core        0           0         0         0         0            0                 0
win2016Ugprade     307         634       634       634       65380        1                 0

PS C:\Users\Administrator> _
```

To retrieve metering data for a particular VM, execute the following command:

```
Get-VM -ComputerName <HostName> -Name
"<VMName>" | Measure-VM
```

SKILL SUMMARY

IN THIS LESSON YOU LEARNED:

- A virtual machine (VM) is a self-contained, isolated unit that can be easily moved from one physical computer to another, runs its own operating system, and includes its own virtual hardware configuration.
- After the Hyper-V host has been installed, you can begin creating virtual machines and configuring them. The easiest way to create a virtual machine is to open Hyper-V and use the New Virtual Machine Wizard. The wizard allows you to define the number of virtual processors, the amount of virtual memory, and how large the virtual disks will be.

- There are several ways to connect to virtual machines by using Virtual Machine Connection. You can open Hyper-V Manager and double-click the virtual machine in Hyper-V Manager, or right-click the virtual machine and choose Connect. You can also run VMConnect.exe and specify the virtual machine that you want to open.

- Non-Uniform Memory Access (NUMA) is a computer system architecture that is used with multiprocessor designs; it divides memory into regions, which are assigned access latencies based on how these larger systems' processors and memory are interconnected. For large multiprocessor systems, NUMA divides memory and processors into groups called NUMA nodes.

- In some cases, the Hyper-V guest operating system does not function properly using the default drivers that are installed. For these operating systems, you can install guest integration services. Hyper-V integration services is a suite of utilities and drivers that are designed to enhance the performance of the virtual machine's guest operating systems. It also supports operating system shutdown, time synchronization, and backup support.

- VMs are easy to create. By leveraging the exporting, importing, and copying functions of Hyper-V, you significantly reduce the time spent creating duplicate VMs.

- Windows Server 2016 includes multiple options that will help secure the virtual machines. These options include Secure Boot, encryption support, and shielding.

■ Knowledge Assessment

Multiple Choice

Select the correct answer for each of the following questions.

1. Which two files are used for every VM?
   a. A saved-state file and a virtual machine configuration (.vmc) file in INF format
   b. A virtual machine configuration (.vmc) file in INF format and virtual hard disk (.vhd or .vhdx) files for the guest OS and data
   c. A saved-state file and virtual hard disk (.vhd or .vhdx) files for the guest OS, applications, and data
   d. A virtual machine configuration (.vmc) file in XML format and virtual hard disk (.vhd or .vhdx) files for the guest OS and data

2. When using the Create a Virtual Machine Wizard, how is the virtual hard disk created by default?
   a. You set the maximum size and it starts at that size.
   b. It starts at 40 GB and warns the administrator when nearly full.
   c. It starts small and dynamically expands up to the maximum size you specify.
   d. It starts small and continually expands to fill the available storage.

3. Which of the following options are available when selecting the Import Virtual Machine Wizard? (Choose two answers.)
   a. Copy the virtual machine
   b. Move the virtual machine's data by selecting where to move the items
   c. Register the virtual machine in place
   d. Move the virtual machine's data automatically

4. Which of the following statements best describes the primary purpose of the software package offered by Hyper-V called guest integration services?
   a. Guest integration services improves communications between the parent partition and child partitions.

    b. Guest integration services resolves compatibility issues of certain guest operating systems experiencing nonfunctioning features.

    c. Guest integration services improves data exchange between the parent partition and child partitions.

    d. Guest integration services improves time synchronization between the parent partition and child partitions.

5. In Hyper-V, which generation is needed to use Secure Boot or SCSI virtual hard disk?
    a. Generation 1
    b. Generation 2
    c. Generation 3
    d. Generations 1 and 2

6. Which of the following is used to connect to a virtual machine similar to Remote Desktop Services (RDS), even if the virtual machine does not have network connectivity or have the Remote Desktop featured enabled?
    a. Discrete Device Assignment
    b. Non-Uniform Memory Access
    c. Secure Boot
    d. Enhanced session mode

7. In Hyper-V, which of the following allows guest virtual machines to communicate directly with PCIe devices?
    a. Discrete Device Assignment
    b. Non-Uniform Memory Access
    c. Secure Boot
    d. Enhanced session mode

8. Which of the following features is used to ensure that each component loaded during the boot process is digitally signed and validated?
    a. Enhanced session mode
    b. Secure Boot
    c. Host Guarding Service
    d. BitLocker

9. In Hyper-V, which of the following is used to provide encryption keys when using Hyper-V to encrypt a VM and its disks?
    a. Host Guarding Service
    b. Memory buffer
    c. Non-Uniform Memory Access
    d. Secure Boot

10. Which Hyper-V tool is used to view the resource usage of a host and individual VMs?
    a. Host Guarding Service
    b. Resource Metering
    c. Non-Uniform Memory Access
    d. Discrete Device Assignment

11. Which of the following best describes Resource Monitoring in Windows Server 2016?
    a. Resource Monitoring is a PowerShell-based feature that enables you to document virtual machine usage.
    b. Resource Monitoring is a Server Manager feature that enables you to monitor virtual machine resources.
    c. Resource Monitoring is a PowerShell-based feature that enables you to redistribute virtual machine resources.
    d. Resource Monitoring is a Server Manager feature that enables you to document virtual machine communications.

Best Answer

Choose the letter that corresponds to the best answer. More than one answer choice may achieve the goal. Select the BEST answer.

1. When securing a virtual machine that is running on Hyper-V, which of the following options provides the best protection?
   a. Non-Uniform Memory Access
   b. BitLocker
   c. Secure Boot
   d. Shielding

Matching and Identification

1. Match the tool with the tasks it can perform:
   _____ a. Shutdown Services
   _____ b. Time Synchronization Service
   _____ c. Remote Desktop Virtualization Service
   _____ d. Data Exchange Service
   _____ e. Volume Shadow Copy Requestor
   1. Allows you to shut down a virtual machine using the Hyper-V console
   2. Used to set specific registry values between the virtual machine and Hyper-V host
   3. Allows to request the synchronization and backup of a running virtual machine
   4. Synchronizes time on the virtual machine with the Hyper-V host
   5. Enables the Remote Desktop Virtualization Host to communicate with and manage virtual machines

Build a List

1. Specify the correct order of steps necessary to exporting a VM in Windows Server 2016. Not all steps will be used.

   _____ Launch the Move Wizard.

   _____ Select Store as OVF file.

   _____ Specify the path of storage location.

   _____ Choose Export Type.

   _____ Select Export menu item.

   _____ Register the VM.

   _____ Select the Export button.

2. Specify the correct order of steps necessary to installing guest integration services.

   _____ Select a Hyper-V server.

   _____ Log on to the server with administrative privileges.

   _____ Click Install Hyper-V Integration Services.

   _____ From Server Manager's Tools menu, choose Hyper-V Manager.

   _____ In the Virtual Machine Connection window, click the Action menu and then choose Insert Integration Services Setup Disk.

   _____ In the Actions pane, start the virtual machine on which you want to install the guest integration services, and then click Connect.

Business Case Scenarios

Scenario 8-1: Exporting and Importing a VM

Management has decided to migrate all servers to Windows Server 2016 and all users to Windows 10. As the senior administrator for Contoso, you have been tasked with preparing a lab quickly so that the new features of both operating systems can be tested along with the current set of standard corporate applications and division-specific applications for three divisions. In a virtual environment, you need to create a simple Active Directory domain with DNS and DHCP, LOB application servers, and workstations to test each configuration. How many servers and workstations do you need and what do you do?

Scenario 8-2: Securing a VM

You administer a virtual machine running on Hyper-V that contains secret information, which needs to be protected at all costs. Describe how to ensure that the virtual machine is secure?

Configuring Hyper-V Storage

70-740 EXAM OBJECTIVE

Objective 3.3 – Configure Hyper-V storage. This objective may include but is not limited to identifying and resolving issues related to the following: Create VHDs and VHDX files using Hyper-V Manager; create shared VHDX files; configure differencing disks; modify virtual hard disks; configure pass-through disks; resize a virtual hard disk; manage checkpoints; implement production checkpoints; implement a virtual Fibre Channel adapter; configure storage Quality of Service (QoS).

LESSON HEADING	EXAM OBJECTIVE
Working with Virtual Disks	Create VHDs and VHDX files using Hyper-V Manager
– Creating VHDs and VHDX Files Using Hyper-V Manager	Configure differencing disks
	Configure pass-through disks
– Adding Virtual Disks to Virtual Machines	Modify virtual hard disks
	Resize a virtual hard disk
– Configuring Differencing Disks	Create shared VHDX files
– Configuring Pass-Through Disks	Configure storage Quality of Service (QoS)
– Editing Virtual Disks, Including Resizing and Converting Virtual Hard Disks	
– Creating Shared VHDX Files	
– Configuring Storage Quality of Service	
Managing Checkpoints	Manage checkpoints
	Implement production checkpoints
Understanding Shared Storage	Implement a virtual Fibre Channel adapter
– Planning and Implementing Fibre Channel SANs	
– Implementing a Virtual Fibre Channel Adapter	

■ Working with Virtual Disks

THE BOTTOM LINE

After you create a virtual machine (VM) in Windows Server 2016 Hyper-V, you emulate all the standard components that you typically find in a physical computer. Hyper-V uses a specialized *virtual hard disk (VHD)* format to package part of the space on a physical disk and make it appear to the VM as a physical hard disk drive.

After you create a new VM in Hyper-V by using the New Virtual Machine Wizard, the wizard creates a virtual storage subsystem. Generation 1 systems consists of two Integrated Drive Electronics (IDE) controllers and one Small Computer System Interface (SCSI) controller, as shown in Figure 9-1 while generation 2 machines have a SCSI Controller. The IDE controllers host the VM's system drive and its DVD drive. As with their physical equivalents, each IDE controller can host two devices, so you can create two additional virtual drives and add them to the system.

The SCSI controller, in the default VM configuration, is unpopulated, and you can create additional drives and add them to that controller to provide the VM with additional storage. You can also create additional SCSI controllers and add drives to them. By creating multiple drives and controllers, Hyper-V makes it possible to construct virtual storage subsystems that emulate almost any physical storage solution you might devise.

Creating VHDs and VHDX Files Using Hyper-V Manager

A virtual disk is a file that represents a physical disk drive to a guest operating system running on a virtual machine. The user can install a new operating system onto the virtual disk without repartitioning the physical disk or rebooting the host machine.

The New Virtual Hard Disk Wizard provides you with a simple way to create a virtual hard disk. With the wizard, you will have to specify the file format and the type of virtual disk.

The original file format used by Hyper-V is the *.vhd file format*. Unfortunately, the .vhd format is limited to 2 TB. The newer (and default format) is the *.vhdx file format*, which supports larger disks (up to 64 TB), larger block sizes, and protection from data corruption during power failures. However, .vhdx is not supported by operating systems before Windows 8.

Figure 9-1

The default VM drive controller configuration

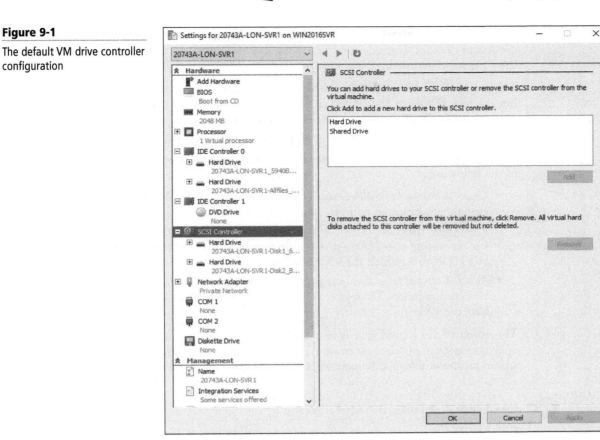

This wizard creates the following types of disks:

- Fixed virtual hard disk
- Dynamically expanding virtual hard disk
- Differencing virtual hard disk

Fixed-size virtual disks are virtual disks that you create with a specific size. For example, if you create a 100-GB, fixed-size virtual disk, the file that makes up the virtual disk will also be 100 GB. The advantage of using a fixed-size virtual disk is that because you are assigning all of the disk space up front, you will not overcommit because the disk space is already allocated. The disadvantage is that any disk space that you are not using is a wasted resource. Lastly, a fixed disk takes longer to move from one server to another.

Dynamic virtual disks start small and will grow as needed up to the specified size. The advantage of using dynamic virtual disks is that there is no wasted space. The disadvantage is that as a disk grows, you will need to manage and monitor storage utilization more carefully because the growing disk could fill up the storage space that could be holding other virtual disks, leaving no room for the dynamic disks to grow. In addition, because dynamic disks will grow over time, fragmentation of the virtual hard disk file will slightly affect the performance of the virtual disk. Lastly, some applications (such as Exchange Server) cannot use dynamic disks.

A ***differencing virtual disk*** is a virtual disk that is associated with another virtual hard disk in a parent-child relationship. In other words, you start with a parent disk and then create a differencing disk that points to the parent disk. As changes are made, the changes are written to the differencing disk, while the parent disk remains unchanged. The differencing virtual disk will expand dynamically as needed. When you use a differencing disk, you do not specify the size of the disk. Instead, the differencing disk will grow up to the size of the parent disk that it is associated with.

The graphical interface in Hyper-V Manager provides access to most of the VHD parameters, but the new Windows PowerShell cmdlets included in Windows Server 2012 and above provide the most granular control over the disk image format.

The New Virtual Machine Wizard includes a Connect Virtual Hard Disk page, with which you can add a single disk to your new VM. The options for this disk are limited and consist of the following:

- *Create a virtual hard disk* enables you to specify the name, location, and size of a new virtual hard disk, but you can create only a dynamically expanding disk by using the VHDX format.

- *Use an existing virtual hard disk* enables you to specify the location of an existing VHD or VHDX disk, which the VM presumably uses as its system disk.

- *Attach a virtual hard disk later* prevents the wizard from adding virtual disks to the VM configuration. Therefore, you need to manually add a disk later, before you start the VM.

The object of this wizard page is to create the disk on which you will install the VM's operating system, or select an existing disk on which an OS is already installed. The disk the wizard creates is always a dynamically expanding one connected to IDE Controller 0.

CREATE A VIRTUAL DISK

GET READY. To create a virtual disk in Hyper-V running on Windows Server 2016, perform the following steps.

1. Log on to a computer running Windows Server 2016 with an administrator account, such as **adatum\administrator** with the password of **Pa$$w0rd**.
2. If Server Manager does not open, click **Start** and click **Server Manager**.
3. Open the **Tools** menu and click **Hyper-V**.
4. If the virtual machine is running, right-click the virtual machine and choose **Shut down**. When you are prompted to shut down the operating system, click the **Shut Down** button.
5. Right-click a virtual machine and choose **Settings**.
6. When the Settings dialog box opens, click **IDE Controller 1**. As you can see, it already has one virtual disk that was created when the virtual machine was created.
7. On the IDE Controller page, select **Hard Drive** and click **Add**. The Hard Drive page opens, as shown in Figure 9-2.
8. With the Virtual hard disk option selected, click the **New** button.
9. When the New Virtual Hard Disk Wizard opens, on the Before You Begin page, click **Next**.
10. On the Choose Disk Format page, VHDX is already selected. Click **Next**.
11. On the Choose Disk Type page, select one of the following disk types and click **Next**:
    - Fixed size
    - Dynamically expanding
    - Differencing

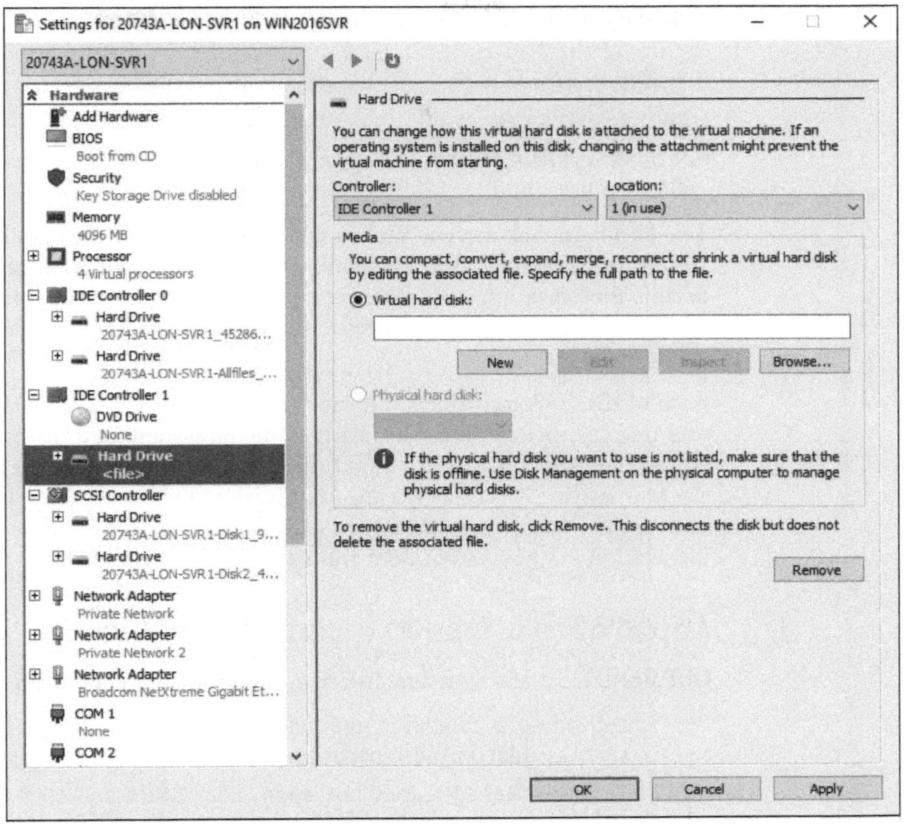

Figure 9-2

Creating a virtual disk

12. On the Specify Name and Location page, in the Name text box, specify a descriptive name for the disk. Click **Next**.

13. On the Create a New Blank Virtual Hard Disk page, specify the size of the disk, such as **10 GB**. Click **Next**.

14. On the Summary page, click **Finish**.

15. Click **OK** to close the Settings dialog box.

USING POWERSHELL

You can create new virtual hard disk files by using Windows PowerShell, with more control than is available through the graphical interface. To create a new disk image, you use the **New–VHD** cmdlet with the following basic syntax:

```
New-VHD –Path c:\filename.vhd|c:\filename.vhdx –Fixed|-Dynamic|-Differencing
–SizeBytes <size> [-BlockSizeBytes <block size>] [-LogicalSectorSizeBytes
512|4096] [-ParentPath <pathname>]
```

When using the cmdlet to create a disk image, the extension you specify for the file name determines the format (VHD or VHDX), and you can specify the block size and the logical sector size for the image, which you cannot do in the GUI. For example, the following command creates a 400-GB fixed VHDX image file with a logical sector size of 4 KB:

```
New-VHD –Path c:\diskfile.vhdx –Fixed –SizeBytes 400GB

-LogicalSectorSizeBytes 4096
```

Adding Virtual Disks to Virtual Machines

Creating virtual disk image files as a separate process enables you to exercise more control over their capabilities. After creating the VHD or VHDX files, you must add them to a VM for them to be useful.

To add a hard disk drive to a physical computer, you must connect it to a controller, and the same is true with a VM in Hyper-V. After you open the Settings dialog box for a VM in its default configuration, you see three controllers, labeled *IDE Controller 0, IDE Controller 1*, and *SCSI Controller*. These correspond to the controllers you might find in a typical physical server computer.

Each of the IDE controllers can support two devices, and the default VM configuration uses one channel on IDE Controller 0 for the system hard disk and one channel on IDE Controller 1 for the system's DVD drive. If you did not create a virtual disk as part of the new Virtual Machine Wizard (that is, if you chose the *Attach a virtual hard disk later* option), then you must add a hard disk image to IDE Controller 0 to use as a system drive. Generation 1 VMs cannot boot from the SCSI controller.

→ ADD A VIRTUAL DISK TO A VIRTUAL MACHINE

GET READY. To add a virtual disk to a virtual machine, perform the following steps.

1. Log on to a computer running Windows Server 2016 with an administrator account, such as **adatum\administrator** with the password of **Pa$$w0rd**.
2. If Server Manager does not open, click **Start** and click **Server Manager**.
3. Open the **Tools** menu and click **Hyper-V**.
4. If the virtual machine is running, right-click the virtual machine and choose **Shut down**. When you are prompted to shut down the operating system, click the **Shut Down** button.
5. Right-click a VM and choose **Settings**. The Settings dialog box for the VM opens.
6. Select **IDE Controller 0**.
7. In the IDE Controller box, select **Hard Drive** and click **Add**. The Hard Drive page appears.
8. In the Controller and Location drop-down lists, select the IDE controller and the channel you want to use for the hard disk.
9. With the **Virtual hard disk** option selected, click **Browse** and select the disk image file you want to add.
10. Click **OK** to close the Settings dialog box.

Although you cannot use a SCSI drive as the system disk in a Generation 1 VM, you can add virtual data disks to the SCSI controller. Unlike the IDE connectors, which support only two devices each, a SCSI connector in Hyper-V can support up to 64 drives. You can also add SCSI controllers to a VM, providing almost unlimited scalability for your virtual storage subsystem.

 In addition to these disk-editing functions provided by Hyper-V Manager, it is also possible to use the Disk Management snap-in to mount a VHD or VHDX file as a drive and access its contents, just as if it were a physical disk.

Configuring Differencing Disks

A differencing disk enables you to preserve an existing virtual disk image file in its original state, while mounting it in an OS and even modifying its contents. For example, when building a laboratory setup, you can create a baseline system by installing a clean copy of an OS on a new virtual disk and configuring the environment to your needs. Then, you can create a new child-differencing disk by using your baseline image as the parent. All subsequent changes you make to the system are written to the differencing disk, whereas the parent remains untouched. You can experiment on the test system, knowing that you can revert back to your baseline configuration by creating a new differencing disk.

CERTIFICATION READY
Configure differencing disks
Objective 3.3

You can create multiple differencing disks that point to the same parent image, enabling you to populate a lab network with as many VMs as you need, without having to repeatedly install the OS and while saving on disk space.

⊙ **CREATE A CLONED INSTALLATION WITH A DIFFERENCING DISK**

GET READY. To create a cloned version of a baseline installation with a differencing disk, perform the following steps.

1. **Install and configure the baseline VM:** Create a new VM with a new disk image file and install a guest OS on it. Configure the OS as needed and install any roles, features, applications, or services you need.

2. **Generalize the parent image:** Open an elevated command prompt on the baseline system and run the sysprep.exe utility. Sysprep configures the system to assign itself a new, unique security ID (SID) the next time the computer starts. This enables you to create multiple cloned systems from a single disk image.

3. **Create a parent disk image:** After you generalize the baseline installation, you no longer need the original VM. You can delete everything except the VHD or VHDX file containing the disk image. This file becomes your parent image. Open the properties sheet for the image file and set the read-only flag to ensure that the baseline does not change.

4. **Create a differencing disk:** By using the New Virtual Hard Disk Wizard or the New–VHD cmdlet for Windows PowerShell, create a new differencing disk, pointing to the baseline image you created and prepared previously as the parent image.

5. **Create a cloned VM:** Create a new VM and, on the Connect Virtual Hard Disk page, attach the differencing disk you created to it, by using the Use an existing virtual hard disk option.

You can then create additional cloned VMs, with differencing disks that use the same parent. Each one can function independently, and the parent disk will remain unchanged.

⊙ **CREATE A DIFFERENCING DISK**

GET READY. To create a differencing disk, perform the following steps.

1. Log on to a computer running Windows Server 2016 with an administrator account, such as **adatum\administrator** with the password of **Pa$$w0rd**.

2. If Server Manager does not open, click **Start** and click **Server Manager**.

3. Open the **Tools** menu and click **Hyper-V**.

4. If the virtual machine is running, right-click the virtual machine and choose **Shut down.** When you are prompted to shut down the operating system, click the **Shut Down** button.

5. Right-click a virtual machine and choose **Settings**.

6. Click the **SCSI controller** node.

7. On the SCSI Controller page, click **Hard Drive** and click **Add.**

8. When the Hard Drive Page opens, with the Virtual hard disk option selected, click the **New** button.

9. When the New Virtual Hard Disk Wizard opens, on the Before You Begin page, click **Next.**

10. On the Choose Disk Format page, VHDX is already selected. Click **Next.**

11. On the Choose Disk Type page, select the **Differencing** option.

12. On the Specify Name and Location page, in the Name text box, specify a descriptive name for the disk. Click **Next.**

13. On the Configure Disk page, in the Location text box, specify the path of the parent disk and click **Next.**

14. On the Create a New Blank Virtual Hard Disk page, specify the size of the disk, such as **10 GB.** Click **Next.**

15. On the Summary page, click **Finish.**

16. To close the Settings dialog box, click **OK.**

In the same way, if you create the differencing disk by using Windows PowerShell, you must run the New-VHD cmdlet with the -Differencing parameter and the -ParentPath parameter, specifying the location of the parent disk.

Configuring Pass-Through Disks

So far, this lesson has focused primarily on virtual hard disks, that is, areas of space on a physical disk drive allocated for use by VMs. However, it is also possible for VMs to access physical disks directly.

A *pass-through disk* is a type of virtual disk that points not to an area of space on a physical disk, but to a physical disk drive itself, installed on the host computer. After you add a hard drive to any of the controllers in a VM, you can select a physical hard disk, as opposed to a virtual one. You can perform this by opening the Disk Management console, right-clicking the disk, and choosing Offline.

+ MORE INFORMATION

For more information about managing disks with Disk Manager, refer to Lesson 3.

Before you can add a physical hard disk to a VM, you first need to connect the hard drive to the physical host computer and start the server. To use the disk as a pass-through disk, the VM must have exclusive access to the disk. Therefore, you then need to make sure that the disk is offline in Windows on the physical host computer.

You can attach a pass-through disk by performing the following steps:

1. Ensure that the physical hard disk is offline in Windows.

2. Use Hyper-V Manager to edit an existing virtual machine's properties.

3. Click an Integrated Drive Electronics (IDE) or SCSI controller, click Add, and then click Hard Drive.

4. In the Hard Drive dialog box, select Physical Hard Disk. In the drop-down list box, select the disk that you want to use as the pass-through disk.

⊘ **ATTACH A PASS-THROUGH DISK**

GET READY. To attach a pass-through disk, perform the following steps.

1. Log on to a computer running Windows Server 2016 with an administrator account, such as **adatum\administrator** with the password of **Pa$$w0rd.**

2. If Server Manager does not open, click **Start** and click **Server Manager.**

3. Open the **Tools** menu and click **Hyper-V.**

4. If the virtual machine is running, right-click the virtual machine and choose **Shut down.** When you are prompted to shut down the operating system, click the **Shut Down** button.

5. Right-click a virtual machine and choose **Settings.**

6. Click the **SCSI controller** node.

7. On the SCSI Controller page, click **Hard Drive** and click **Add.**

8. When the Hard Drive Page opens, select the Physical hard disk option, as shown in Figure 9-3.

Figure 9-3

Selecting a physical hard disk that can be used for pass-through drives

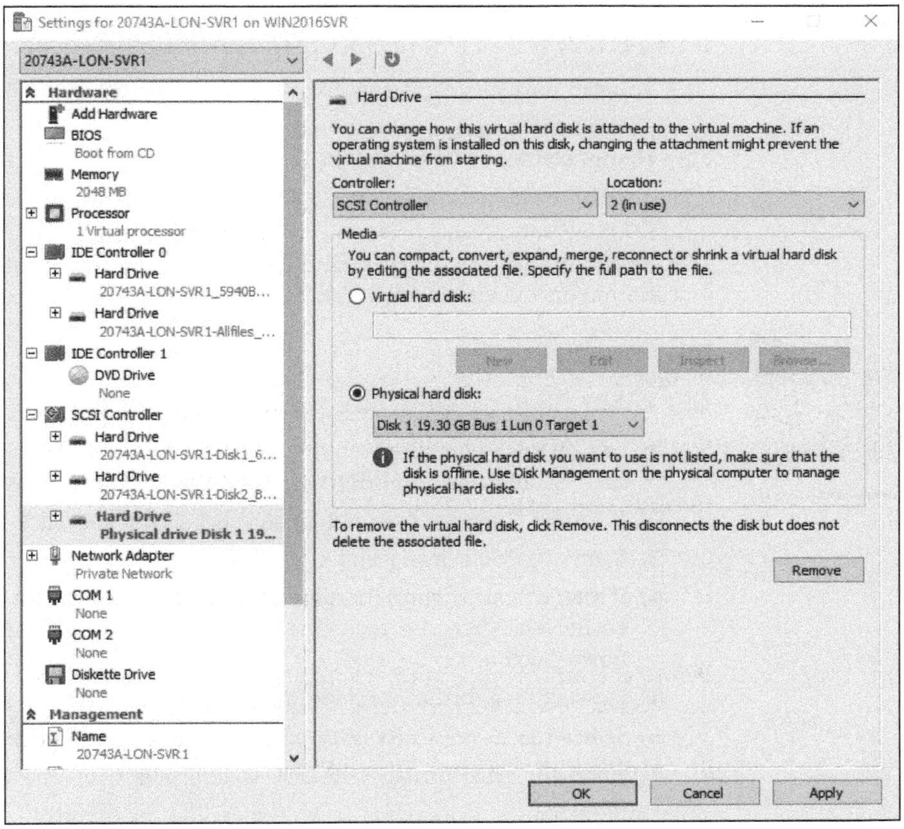

9. To close the Settings dialog box, click **OK.**

Editing Virtual Disks, Including Resizing and Converting Virtual Hard Disks

Just like physical disks in a computer, there will be times when you will need to edit a virtual disk. For example, if you start to run out of disk space, you might want to expand the disk. You can convert a virtual hard disk from .vhd format to .vhdx format or .vhdx to .vhd format, and you can convert from fixed-size to dynamically expanding or dynamically expanding to fixed-size.

After you create a virtual hard disk, whether you attach it to a VM or not, you can manage it by using the Edit Virtual Hard Disk Wizard in Hyper-V Manager. The options that appear on the wizard's Choose Action page depend on the current status of the image file you select. The actions that you can perform on the disks include:

- *Compact* reduces the size of a dynamically expanding or differencing disk by deleting empty space, while leaving the disk's capacity unchanged.
- *Convert* changes the type of format of a disk by copying the data to a new disk image file.
- *Expand* increases the capacity of the disk by adding empty storage space to the image file.
- *Shrink* reduces the capacity of the disk by deleting empty storage space from the file. The Shrink option does not appear unless there is free space in the file that the wizard can delete.
- *Merge* combines the data on a differencing disk with the parent disk to form a single composite image file. The Merge option only appears if you choose a differencing disk.

In Windows Server 2016, you can resize virtual hard disks that are used by a running virtual machine, only if the following prerequisites are met:

- You can only resize a virtual hard disk if the virtual hard disk is in .vhdx format.
- You can only resize a virtual hard disk if it is connected to a virtual SCSI controller. You cannot resize virtual hard disks that are connected to a virtual IDE controller.
- You can only resize a shared virtual hard disk if the virtual machine is running Windows Server 2016.
- You cannot shrink a virtual hard disk beyond the size of the current volumes that are hosted on the virtual hard disk.

⊙ EDIT A VIRTUAL DISK

GET READY. To edit a virtual disk, perform the following steps.

1. Log on to a computer running Windows Server 2016 with an administrator account, such as **adatum\administrator** with the password of **Pa$$w0rd**.
2. If Server Manager does not open, click **Start** and click **Server Manager**.
3. Open the **Tools** menu and click **Hyper-V**.
4. If the virtual machine is running, right-click the virtual machine and choose **Shut down**. When you are prompted to shut down the operating system, click the **Shut Down** button.
5. Right-click a virtual machine and choose **Settings**.
6. Select the desired disk that you want to edit and click the **Edit** button.
7. When the Edit Virtual Hard Disk Wizard opens, on the Before You Begin page, click **Next**.
8. On the Locate Disk page, click **Next**.
9. On the Choose Action page (as shown in Figure 9-4), select **Expand** and click **Next**.
10. On the Configure Disk page, specify the new size of the disks and click **Next**.
11. On the Summary page, click **Finish**.
12. To close the Settings dialog box, click **OK**.

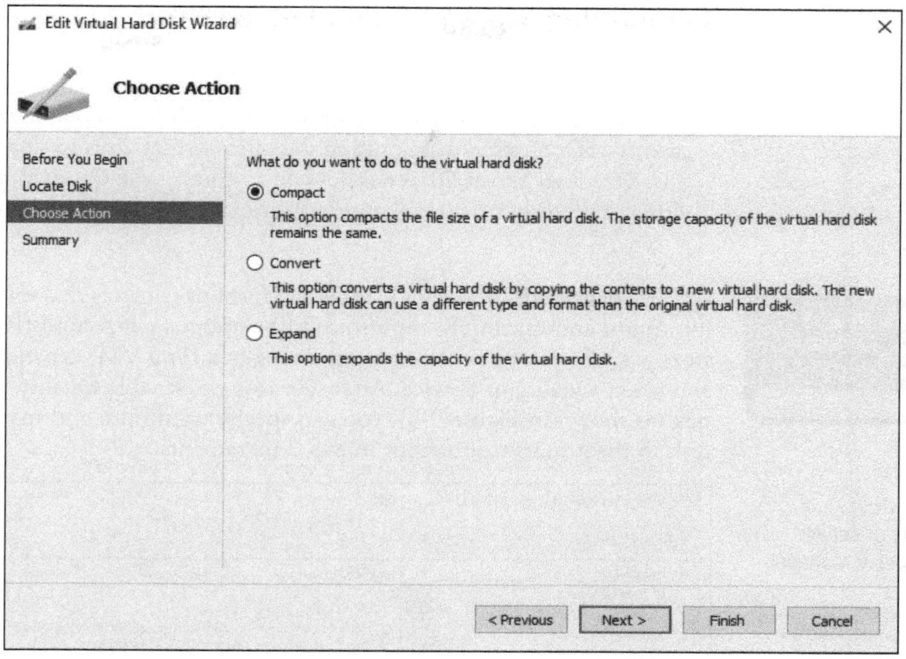

Figure 9-4

Modifying a virtual disk

| Edit Virtual Hard Disk Wizard | ✕ |

Choose Action

Before You Begin
Locate Disk
Choose Action
Summary

What do you want to do to the virtual hard disk?

⦿ Compact

This option compacts the file size of a virtual hard disk. The storage capacity of the virtual hard disk remains the same.

○ Convert

This option converts a virtual hard disk by copying the contents to a new virtual hard disk. The new virtual hard disk can use a different type and format than the original virtual hard disk.

○ Expand

This option expands the capacity of the virtual hard disk.

[< Previous] [Next >] [Finish] [Cancel]

USING POWERSHELL

You can execute some of the functions discussed in this section by using cmdlets included with Windows Server 2016 PowerShell, including the following:

- *Merge-VHD* merges a differencing disk into its parent disk.
- *Mount-VHD* mounts a virtual hard disk file into the local file system.
- *Dismount-VHD* dismounts a virtual hard disk file from the local file system.
- *Convert-VHD* converts the format, type, or block size of a virtual hard disk file.
- *ResizeVHD* expands or shrinks virtual hard disks.
- *OptimizeVHD* compacts dynamic or differencing disks.

After you expand a drive, you will need to open the Disk Management console or use Windows PowerShell to expand the drive in Windows. If you are Disk Management, you will open the Action menu and click Rescan Disks. Then, right-click the volume that needs to be expanded and choose Extend Volume to run the Extend Volume Wizard.

Creating Shared VHDX Files

Starting with Windows Server 2012 R2, you can share a virtual hard disk file between multiple virtual machines. This comes in handy when you are configuring a failover cluster that has two or more VMs that access the same disks.

CERTIFICATION READY
Create shared VHDX files
Objective 3.3

To use a Hyper-V shared virtual disk, you must use .vhdx files that are connected to a virtual SCSI controller. You cannot use .vhd files, or virtual disks that are connected to a virtual IDE controller. You can store the shared .vhdx file only on a failover cluster via a Cluster Shared Volume (CSV) or a Scale-Out File Server with SMB 3.0.

➕ MORE INFORMATION

For more information about Cluster Shared Volumes and Scale-Out File Servers, go to Lesson 15.

Configuring Storage Quality of Service

Because it is common for there to be more than one virtual hard disk hosted by a single physical hard disk, it is possible for one virtual disk to monopolize the input/output capacity of a physical disk, causing the other virtual disks to slow down. To help prevent this, Windows Server 2016 enables you to control the *Quality of Service (QoS)* for a given virtual hard disk, which will ensure high-quality performance for critical applications.

CERTIFICATION READY
Configure storage Quality of Service (QoS)
Objective 3.3

QoS management in Hyper-V takes the form of controls that enable you to specify the minimum and maximum input/output operations per second (IOPS) for a disk. To configure storage QoS, you open the Settings dialog box for a VM, expand a hard drive component, and select Quality of Service. After selecting the Enable Quality of Service management check box (as shown in Figure 9-5), you can specify minimum and maximum IOPS values for the disk to throttle its throughput in 8-KB increments.

Figure 9-5

Storage Quality of Service controls in Hyper-V Manager

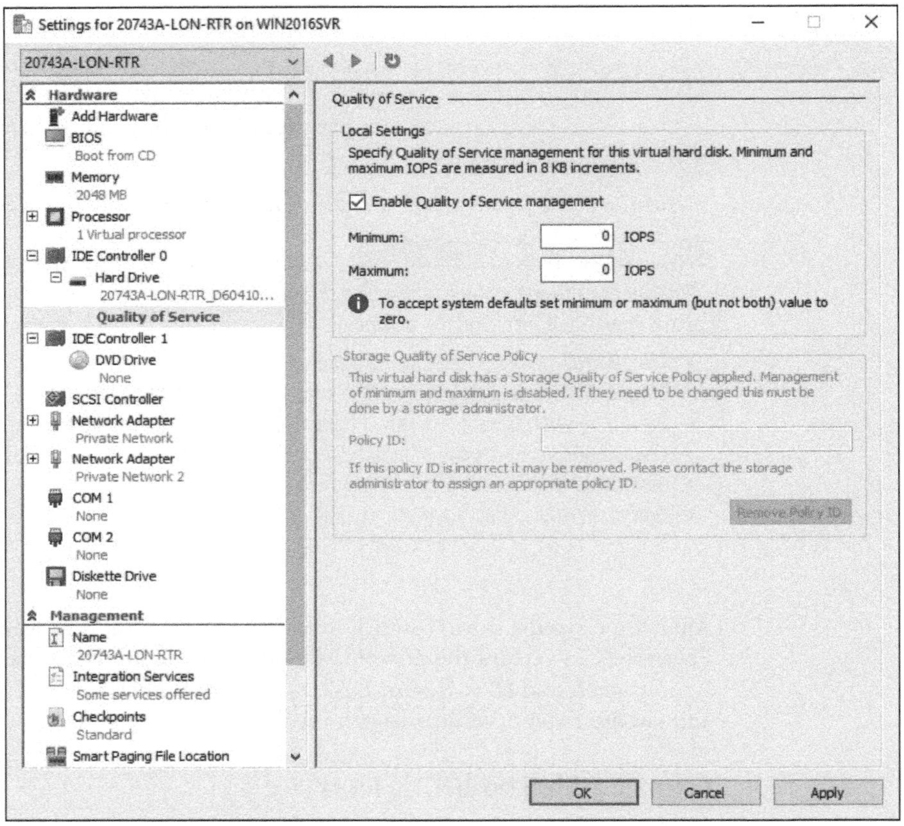

ENABLE QUALITY OF SERVICE

GET READY. To enable Quality of Service for a virtual disk, perform the following steps.

1. If Server Manager does not open, click **Start** and then click **Server Manager.**
2. Open the **Tools** menu and click **Hyper-V.**
3. Right-click a virtual machine and choose **Settings.**
4. When the Settings dialog box opens, navigate to and expand a virtual disk node and click **Quality of Service.**
5. Select the **Enable Quality of Service management** option.
6. In the Minimum and Maximum IOPS text boxes, specify the appropriate value.
7. To close the Settings dialog box, click **OK.**

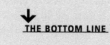

■ Managing Checkpoints

↓ **THE BOTTOM LINE**	In Hyper-V, a ***checkpoint*** is a snapshot, or captured image of the state, data, and hardware configuration of a VM at a particular moment in time. Windows Server 2016 has the ability to provide production checkpoints and standard checkpoints. Each virtual machine can have a maximum of 50 checkpoints.

CERTIFICATION READY
Manage checkpoints
Objective 3.3

CERTIFICATION READY
Implement production checkpoints
Objective 3.3

When you are testing an application and want to troubleshoot compatibility issues or test a new application update before rolling it out to production machines, you can use the Hyper-V snapshot feature (right-click the machine and choose Checkpoint, as shown in Figure 9-6). By taking a checkpoint, you can return to a known state on the VM (for example, the state before you installed the application). To revert to the previous state, right-click the checkpoint and choose Apply. When you no longer need the checkpoint, right-click the checkpoint and choose Delete Checkpoint.

Although checkpoints are a useful tool for you when implementing a test environment in Hyper-V, this tool is not recommended for heavy use in production environments. Apart from consuming disk space, the presence of snapshots can reduce the overall performance of a VM's disk subsystem.

A ***standard checkpoint*** is the traditional checkpoint that has been available since Windows Server 2008. When a checkpoint is created, any changes to the disk are stored in a .avhd file. When you delete a standard checkpoint, the data is merged with the previous checkpoint or

Figure 9-6

A checkpoint in Hyper-V Manager

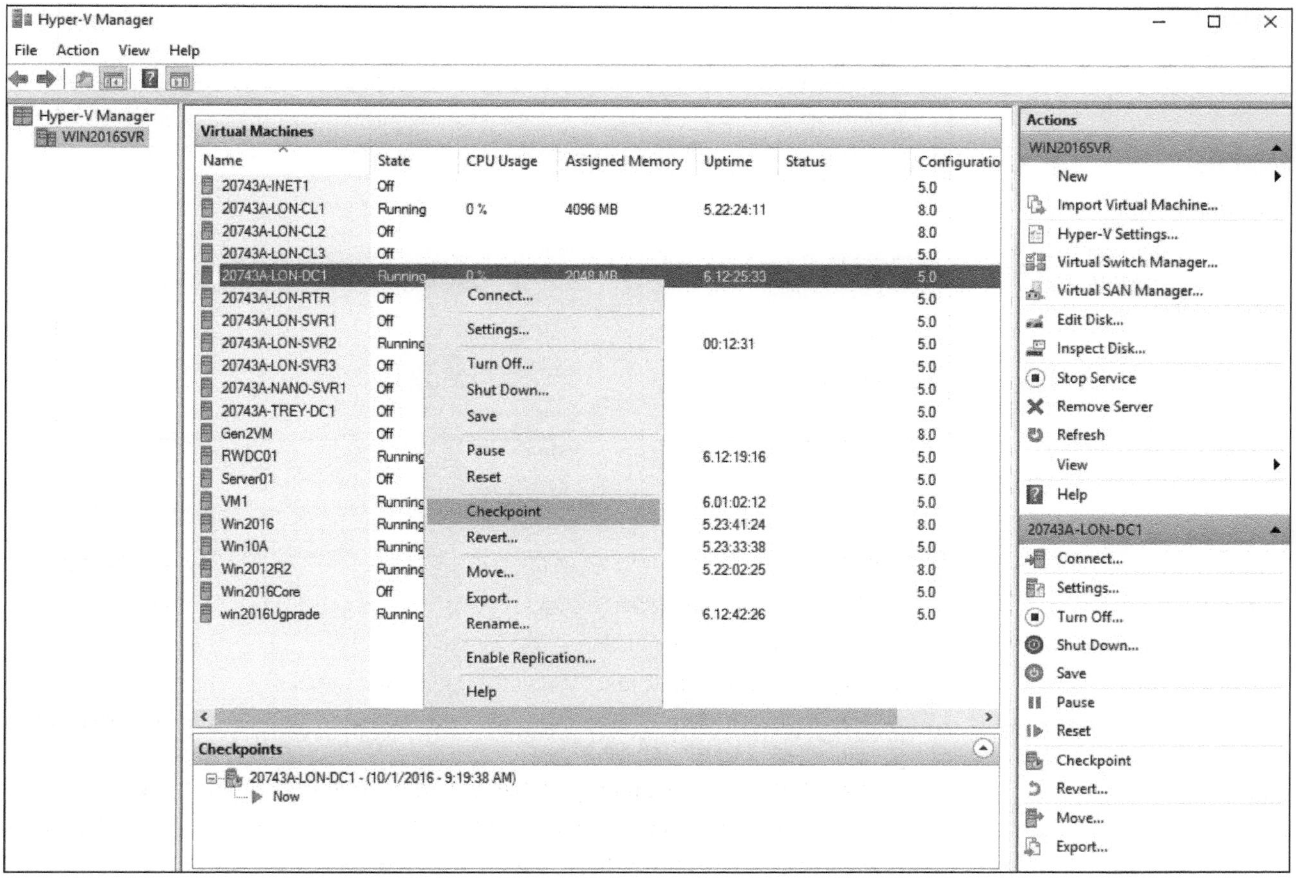

parent virtual hard disk. When you apply a checkpoint, you revert to the state of the system when the checkpoint was made. It is possible to create checkpoint trees that have different branches.

Volume Shadow Copy Service (VSS) is a Windows feature that enhances backup capability temporarily so that you can perform a backup of a system that is in a data or application-consistent state. It allows you to make a copy of files that are open or locked. VSS intercepts disk writes before they actually happen and writes them into a shadow copy buffer or snapshot. The backup software can then back up the volume that is consistent, or nonchanging. The snapshot, or shadow copy, is then deleted when the backup has completed, and the modified data is applied to the system.

Production checkpoints are introduced with Windows Server 2016, which uses VSS to free a file system, so that it can make a better backup that is closer to the state of the system when the checkpoint is created. Production checkpoints require a virtual machine to start from an offline state to restore the checkpoint. To configure the Checkpoint type, open the VM Settings.

CONFIGURE AND USE CHECKPOINTS

GET READY. To configure and use checkpoints, perform the following steps.

1. Log on to a computer running Windows Server 2016 with an administrator account, such as **adatum\administrator** with the password of **Pa$$w0rd**.
2. If Server Manager does not open, click **Start** and click **Server Manager**.
3. Open the **Tools** menu and click **Hyper-V**.
4. Right-click a VM and choose **Settings**.
5. When the Settings dialog box opens, under Management, click the **Checkpoints** node, as shown in Figure 9-7.

Figure 9-7

Managing Checkpoint settings

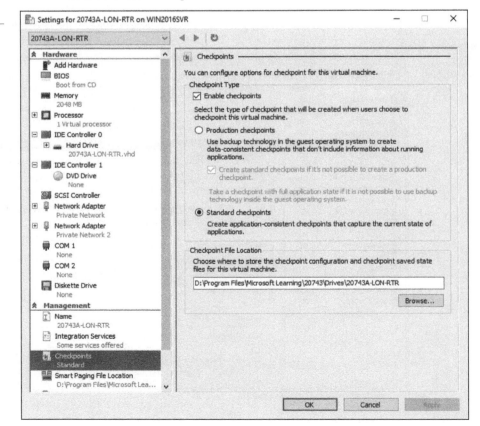

6. Ensure that the **Enabled checkpoints** option is enabled and that the Checkpoint Type is set to **Production Checkpoints**.

7. To close the Settings dialog box, click **OK**.

8. Right-click the VM and choose **Checkpoint**. The checkpoint is listed in the Checkpoints pane.

9. To delete the checkpoint, in the Checkpoints pane, right-click the checkpoint and choose **Delete Checkpoint**.

■ Understanding Shared Storage

↓ **THE BOTTOM LINE**

Many of the servers used in an organization require large amounts of disk space to provide the services and resources. For example, file servers need to store data files, and mail servers and database servers need to store large databases. Therefore, these servers typically need many hard drives connected directly to the machine, or the servers connect to shared storage. *Shared storage* devices have many hard drives to provide huge amounts of disk space.

There are two network storage solutions used in networking:

- *Network attached storage (NAS):* A NAS is a file-level data storage device that is connected to the server over a computer network to provide shared drives or folders usually using Server Message Block (SMB) or Network File System (NFS).

- *Storage area networks (SANs):* A SAN is a storage architecture that allows systems to attach to the storage in the SAN, and present the drives to the server just as if it was locally attached.

Accessing the shared files on a NAS is like accessing a shared folder on a server. To provide fault tolerance and better performance, most NAS devices use Redundant Array of Independent Disks (RAID). NAS devices can be managed with a web interface, and some enterprise NAS devices include a command-line interface accessible using Secure Shell (SSH).

If a server fails, the data is still stored in the SAN. You can then bring up another server, present the same storage to the server, and you have all your data intact. Typically, when you use clustering in a production environment and for a virtual environment such as Hyper-V, it is common and recommended to use a SAN. Of course, the robust SANs usually have a higher level of RAID such as RAID 10, spare drives, redundant power supplies, redundant network connections, and built-in monitoring tools.

Most SANs use the SCSI protocol for communication between servers and disk drive devices. By using the SCSI protocol, you can attach disks to a server using copper Ethernet cables or fiber-optic cables. The two standards used in SANs include:

- Fibre Channel
- iSCSI

Both of these technologies use a fabric, which is a network topology where devices are connected to each other through one or more high-efficient data paths. Besides allowing multiple servers to access the SAN, both of these technologies also allow the SAN to be in a different rack in the server room, in a separate room, or even in a separate building. Of course, when deciding on what is an acceptable performance, it always comes down to bandwidth and latency.

Fibre Channel is a gigabit-speed or higher network technology primarily used for a storage network. With Fibre Channel fabric, the network includes one or more Fibre Channel switches that enable the servers and storage devices to connect to each other through a virtual point-to-point connection. The switches route the packets in the fabric. Servers use a host bus adapter (HBA) to connect to the storage device.

Internet Small Computer System Interface (iSCSI) is a protocol that enables clients to send SCSI commands over a TCP/IP network using TCP port 3260. Different from Fibre Channel, you use standard Ethernet cabling and switches to connect servers to the SAN. Because you connect to the SAN over the network, you should use a minimum of two network adapters on the server, one for the SAN communications and one for standard network communications. Currently, the fastest network connection is Fibre Channel of Ethernet (FCoE), which is capable of 10 gigabits per second or more.

A *logical unit number (LUN)* is a logical reference to a portion of a storage subsystem. The LUN can be a disk, part of a disk, an entire disk array, or part of the disk array. So when configuring servers to attach to a SAN, you usually configure the SAN to assign a LUN to a specific server. In other words, the LUN allows the administrator to break the SAN storage into manageable pieces. If the LUN is not mapped to a specific server, the server cannot see or access the LUN.

Planning and Implementing Fibre Channel SANs

A Fibre Channel network can use various network media. Copper alternatives include video or miniature coaxial cable and, more commonly, shielded twisted pair (STP) with DB-9 or HSSDC (High-Speed Serial Data Connection) cable connectors. These are distinctly different from the standard unshielded twisted pair (UTP) cables and RJ-45 connectors used for an Ethernet network and require a specialized installation. Fiber-optic alternatives include 62.5 or 50 micrometer (or micron) multimode and 7 or 9 micrometer single mode, all using LC or SC connectors. These standard fiber-optic media options are familiar to any qualified fiber-optic contractor. Because Fibre Channel uses serial instead of parallel signaling, it can span much longer distances than a pure SCSI connection—up to 50 kilometers or more, in some cases.

TAKE NOTE*

When discussing Fibre Channel, you will often see *fibre* with the British spelling and *fiber* with the American English spelling. However, *fibre* is used to refer to the protocol that runs with Fibre Channel, whereas *fiber* (or *fiber optics*) refers to the media that Fibre Channel runs on.

Today, transmission speeds for Fibre Channel networks range from 1 Gbps to 10 Gbps for copper cables, and up to 16 Gbps for fiber optic. Maximum speeds depend on the type of cable the network uses, the lengths of the cable segments, and, in the case of fiber optic, the type of laser used to transmit the signals.

Fibre Channel networks can use any one of the following topologies:

- *Point-to-point (FC-P2P)* consists of two devices only, directly connected with a single cable.
- *Arbitrated loop (FC-AL)* consists of up to 127 devices, connected in a loop topology, similar to that of a token ring network. The loop can be physical, with each device connected to the next device, or virtual, with each device connected to a hub that implements the loop.
- *Switched fabric (FC-SW)* consists of up to 16,777,216 (2^{24}) devices, each of which is connected to a Fibre Channel switch. Unlike Ethernet switches, Fibre Channel switches provide redundant paths between the connected devices, forming a topology called a *mesh* or *fabric*. If a switch or a connection between switches fails, data can find an alternate path through the fabric to its destination.

Until recently, FC-AL was the most popular of the three topologies because few SANs require more than 127 connections and the arbitrated loop eliminates the need for expensive switches. The prices of Fibre Channel switches have dropped considerably over the last few years (perhaps due to competition from low-cost iSCSI components), and FC-SW has become the more popular Fibre Channel solution.

The Fibre Channel standards define five protocol layers:

- FC0 defines the physical elements of a Fibre Channel network, including cables, connectors, pinouts, and optical and electrical specifications.
- FC1 defines the data-link layer transmission protocol, including the 8b/10b encoding method used to generate Fibre Channel network signals.
- FC2 defines the basic transport mechanism of a Fibre Channel network, including the frame format and three service classes: a connection-oriented class, a connectionless class with acknowledgments, and a connectionless class without acknowledgments.
- FC3 defines a collection of common services often required by applications using Fibre Channel networks, including data striping, multicasting, and multiport hunt groups.
- FC4 defines the upper layer protocol mapping rules, which enable Fibre Channel networks to carry SCSI and other types of application layer traffic.

The most critical layer in the operation of a SAN is FC4, which enables the network to carry the SCSI traffic generated by the server and storage devices, replacing the lower layers native to the SCSI protocol. SANs typically use the Fibre Channel Protocol (FCP) to transmit SCSI traffic over the network. However, Fibre Channel networks can use a number of other protocols at the FC4 layer for storage area networking, as well as other applications.

A *World Wide Node Name (WWNN)* is used to uniquely identify a device in a SAN. Each device has its own unique WWNN, which is burned into hardware or assigned through software. A *World Wide Port Name (WWPN)* is a unique identifier for each Fibre Channel port presented to a SAN. Each port on a storage device has a unique and persistent WWPN. The WWNN and WWPN is expressed as 16 hexadecimal characters/8 bytes long. Three of the bytes are used for the vendor ID.

Implementing a Virtual Fibre Channel Adapter

Before Windows Server 2012, connecting a virtual client machine directly to Fibre Channel HBAs was difficult. Windows Server 2012 and higher support Virtual Fibre Channel for Hyper-V, which enables virtual client machines to connect directly to Fibre Channel HBAs. Virtual Fibre Channel in Hyper-V guest also supports many related features, such as a virtual SAN (vSAN), live migration, quick migration, MPIO, Import and Export, Save and Restore, Pause and Resume, and host-initiated backups.

CERTIFICATION READY
Implement a virtual Fibre
Channel adapter
Objective 3.3

In Windows Server 2016, you can have up to four virtual ports per virtual machine. Depending on your configuration, your hardware might restrict the number of virtual ports per HBA and the LUNs per port.

The virtual Fibre Channel feature has the following prerequisites:

- It requires a computer with one or more Fibre Channel HBAs or Fibre Channel over Ethernet (FCoE) converged network adapters.
- The HBAs and FCoE converged network adapters must use updated drivers that support virtual Fibre Channel. The HBA ports should be set up in a Fibre Channel topology that supports N_Port ID Virtualization (NPIV).
- It requires an NPIV-enabled storage area network (SAN).

- Virtual machines that are configured to use a virtual Fibre Channel adapter must use Windows Server 2008 or higher as the guest operating system. No other guest operating systems are currently supported for use with virtual Fibre Channel.
- You must ensure that NPIV is enabled on your host bus adapter.
- Virtual Fibre Channel LUNs cannot be used as boot media. Fibre Channel tape devices are not supported.

 ADD A VIRTUAL CHANNEL ADAPTER AND CONNECT TO A vSAN

GET READY. To add and connect a virtual channel adapter to a vSAN, perform the following steps.

1. In Server Manager, click **Tools** and then click **Hyper-V Manager**.
2. On the Hyper-V Manager screen, under Virtual Machines, click the name of the desired virtual machine.
3. In the Action pane, click **Settings**.
4. Under Add Hardware, notice a list of hardware options that you can add to your virtual machine. Click **Fibre Channel Adapter** and then click **Add**.
5. On the Settings page (see Figure 9-8), you must connect the virtual Fibre Channel adapter to a vSAN that you previously created. From the Virtual SAN drop-down list that shows *Not connected*, select the name of the required vSAN.

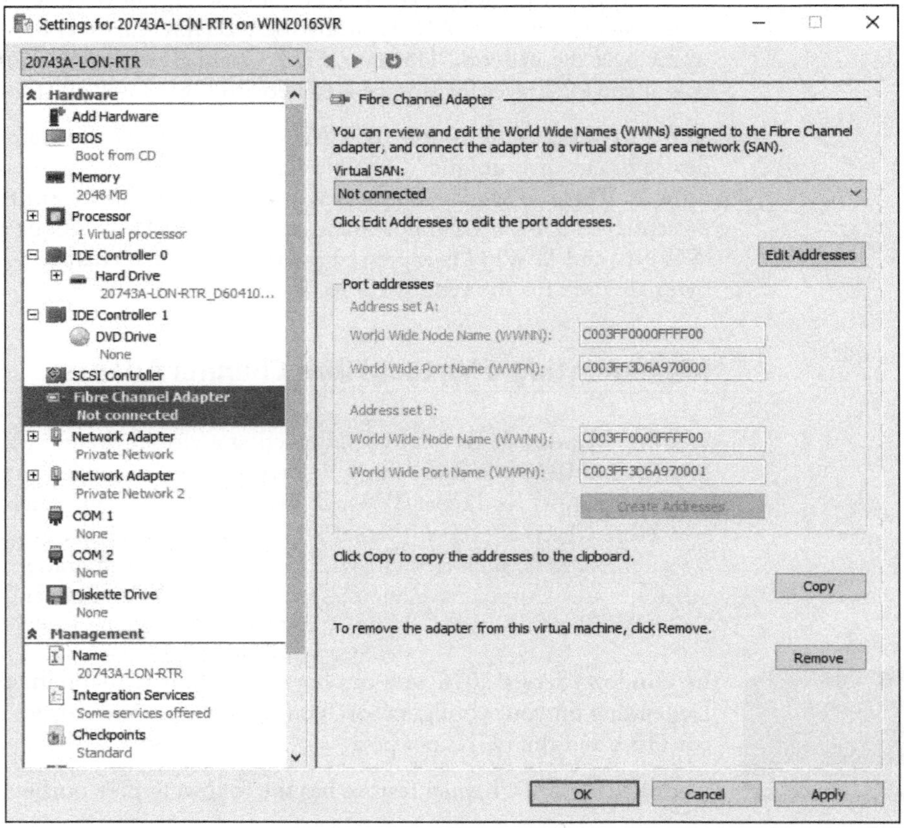

Figure 9-8

Connecting a Fibre Channel adapter to a virtual machine

![Settings dialog for 20743A-LON-RTR on WIN2016SVR showing the Fibre Channel Adapter configuration page with Virtual SAN set to "Not connected" and port addresses for Address set A and Address set B]

6. Configure your WWNNs (Set A and Set B) for your virtual Fibre Channel adapter. You can use the default automatically generated WWN or manually assign them. You need to configure both WWNN sets to ensure a successful live migration of your virtual machines.
7. Click **OK**.

SKILL SUMMARY

IN THIS LESSON YOU LEARNED:

- Hyper-V uses a specialized virtual hard disk (VHD) format to package part of the space on a physical disk and make it appear to the VM as a physical hard disk drive.

- A virtual disk is a file that represents a physical disk drive to a guest operating system running on a virtual machine. The user can install a new operating system onto the virtual disk without repartitioning the physical disk or rebooting the host machine.

- A differencing disk enables you to preserve an existing virtual disk image file in its original state, while mounting it in an OS and even modifying its contents.

- A pass-through disk is a type of virtual disk that points not to an area of space on a physical disk, but to a physical disk drive itself, installed on the host computer.

- In Hyper-V, a checkpoint is a snapshot, or captured image of the state, data, and hardware configuration of a VM at a particular moment in time. Windows Server 2016 has the ability to provide production checkpoints and standard checkpoints. Each virtual machine can have a maximum of 50 checkpoints.

- Windows Server 2012 and higher support Virtual Fibre Channel for Hyper-V, which enables virtual client machines to connect directly to Fibre Channel HBAs. Virtual Fibre Channel in Hyper-V guest also supports many related features, such as a virtual SAN (vSAN), live migration, quick migration, MPIO, Import and Export, Save and Restore, Pause and Resume, and host-initiated backups.

■ Knowledge Assessment

Multiple Choice

Select the correct answer for each of the following questions.

1. Which of the following statements about VHDX files is false?
   a. VHDX files can be as large as 64 TB.
   b. VHDX files can only be opened by computers running Windows Server 2012 and higher.
   c. VHDX files support larger block sizes than VHD files.
   d. VHDX files support 4-KB logical sectors.

2. Which of the following must be true about a pass-through disk?
   a. A pass-through disk must be offline in the guest OS that will access it.
   b. A pass-through disk must be offline in the parent partition of the Hyper-V server.
   c. A pass-through disk can only be connected to a SCSI controller.
   d. A pass-through disk must be added to a VM with the Disk Management snap-in.

3. The Merge function only appears in the Edit Virtual Hard Disk Wizard under which of the following conditions?
   a. When you select a VHDX file for editing
   b. When you select two or more disks for editing
   c. When you select a disk with free space available in it
   d. When you select a differencing disk for editing

4. Which of the following are valid reasons *not* to take snapshots of VMs? (Choose all that apply.)
   a. Snapshots can consume a large amount of disk space.
   b. Each snapshot requires a separate copy of the VM's memory allocation.
   c. Each snapshot can take several hours to create.
   d. The existence of snapshots slows down VM performance.

5. Which of the following is *not* required to add a Fibre Channel adapter to a Hyper-V VM?
   a. You must create a Fibre Channel virtual SAN.
   b. You must have a physical Fibre Channel adapter installed in the host computer.
   c. You must have a Fibre Channel adapter driver that supports virtual networking.
   d. You must have a SCSI cable connecting the Fibre Channel adapter to the storage devices.

6. Which Server Manager tool allows you to create a new virtual hard disk (VHD)?
   a. Hyper-V server
   b. Active Directory Domain Services (AD DS) manageability
   c. Hyper-V Manager
   d. File and storage services

7. When creating a new VHD, which Windows PowerShell feature is not offered by the graphical interface?
   a. You can specify the block size and the logical sector sizes.
   b. You can decide between VHD and VHDX disk types.
   c. You can choose among Fixed, Dynamic, or Differencing.
   d. You can specify the path.

8. Can you modify an existing VHD file?
   a. No, once created, a VHD file is fixed.
   b. Yes, but you can modify it only through Windows PowerShell.
   c. No, but you change it into a VHDX file.
   d. Yes, you can even modify it without mounting it to a VM.

9. Do VMs ever directly access a physical hard disk?
   a. No, VMs access only VHDs, areas of space on the physical hard disk.
   b. Yes, VMs access a physical hard disk by way of a "pass-through disk," a special virtual disk that directly accesses the physical disk if it is made exclusively available to the VM.
   c. No, VMs access physical hardware only through the hypervisor.
   d. Yes, VHDs correlate one to one with physical hard disks.

10. Creating a virtual SAN allows you to _____.
    a. eliminate the physical disks
    b. have VHDs communicate with physical hard disks
    c. make distant storage accessible to VMs
    d. reduce the load on the virtual machine

11. Which checkpoint uses Volume Shadow Copy Service, which can be used for a more efficient backup? (Choose all that apply.)
    a. Enhanced checkpoint
    b. Standard checkpoint
    c. Shadow checkpoints
    d. Production checkpoints

Best Answer

Choose the letter that corresponds to the best answer. More than one answer choice may achieve the goal. Select the BEST answer.

1. Deciding between two virtual disk formats (VHD and VHDX), you need one to accommodate image sizes up to 2 TB (terabytes) and be compatible with both Windows Server 2016's Hyper-V and Microsoft's older product, Virtual PC. Which format do you choose and why?
   a. VHD, because it supports up to 2-TB image files
   b. VHDX, because it supports file sizes far beyond 2 TB—up to 64 TB
   c. VHD, because it supports both new and old hypervisor products
   d. VHDX, because it supports larger block sizes for tuning storage performance

2. You need to connect a virtual hard disk with a virtual machine (VM). Which disk format do you choose and why?
   a. VHDX, because it's the only one available when creating a new disk
   b. VHD or VHDX if using an existing virtual hard disk
   c. VHD with an existing hard disk and a Type II hypervisor product
   d. Either one is possible and applicable.

3. You intend to create a new virtual hard disk, specifying a 700-GB VHDX image file with a logical sector size of 4 KB. How do you proceed?
   a. With Server Manager, using Hyper-V Manager's New Disk feature
   b. With the utilities included in Hyper-V's guest integration services
   c. Those exact specifications are not possible in Hyper-V Manager.
   d. With PowerShell, using the New-VHD cmdlet with appropriate parameters

4. Is it possible for a VM to access a hard disk directly?
   a. No. VMs access virtual hard disks, areas of space on the physical hard disk.
   b. Yes. VMs can have "pass-through disks," a special virtual disk that directly accesses the physical disk if made exclusively available to the VM.
   c. No. VMs can never access physical hardware, but only through the hypervisor.
   d. Yes. VMs use virtual hard disks, which are essentially the physical hard disks.

5. Which of the following is a key benefit of using differencing disks?
   a. They enable you to use baseline images.
   b. They enable you to keep a fixed image in its original state.
   c. They allow you to experiment without repercussions.
   d. They let you create parent and child-differencing disks.

Build a List

1. Specify the correct order of steps necessary to creating a new virtual hard disk.

   ____ Select to either create a blank virtual hard disk or to copy contents from an existing virtual or physical hard disk.

   ____ From Server Manager's Tools menu, select Hyper-V Manager, and then select a Hyper-V server.

   ____ From the Action menu, select New > Hard Disk.

   ____ Select one of the available hard disk types (fixed size, dynamically expanding, and differencing).

   ____ Choose the disk format, either VHD or VHDX.

   ____ Specify the Name and Location of the disk.

2. Specify the correct order of steps necessary to modifying a virtual disk.

___ Select one of the following edit options: Compact, Convert, Expand, Shrink, or Merge.

___ From Server Manager's Tools menu, select Hyper-V Manager and then select a Hyper-V server.

___ Browse to the name of the VHD or VHDX file to open.

___ In the Actions pane, select Edit Disk to bring up the Edit Virtual Hard Disk Wizard.

■ Business Case Scenarios

Scenario 9-1: Creating Differencing Disks

To conduct multiple tests, you need several VMs with the same baseline installation. You decide to employ differencing disks to create your VMs. Describe the necessary steps.

Scenario 9-2: Modifying Virtual Disks

You manage a virtual machine with a virtual disk that is almost full. Describe how to expand the VHD file.

Configuring Hyper-V Networking

70-740 EXAM OBJECTIVE

Objective 3.4 – Configure Hyper-V networking. This objective may include but is not limited to the following: Add and remove virtual network interface cards (vNICs); configure Hyper-V virtual switches; optimize network performance; configure MAC addresses; configure network isolation; configure synthetic and legacy virtual network adapters; configure NIC teaming in VMs; configure virtual machine queue (VMQ); enable Remote Direct Memory Access (RDMA) on network adapters bound to a Hyper-V virtual switch using Switch Embedded Teaming (SET); configure bandwidth management.

Lesson Heading	Exam Objective
Configuring Hyper-V Networking	Add and remove virtual network interface cards (vNICs)
– Adding and Removing Virtual Network Interface Cards (vNICs)	Configure synthetic and legacy virtual network adapters
– Configuring Hyper-V Virtual Switches	Configure Hyper-V virtual switches
– Optimizing Network Performance	Optimize network performance
– Configuring MAC Addresses	Configure virtual machine queue (VMQ)
– Configuring Network Isolation	Configure bandwidth management
– Configuring NIC Teamings in VMs	Configure MAC addresses
– Enabling Remote Direct Memory Access (RDMA) with Switch Embedded Teaming (SET)	Configure network isolation
	Configure NIC teaming in VMs
	Enable Remote Direct Memory Access (RDMA) on network adapters bound to a Hyper-V virtual switch using Switch Embedded Teaming (SET)

KEY TERMS

emulated network adapters

external virtual switch

internal virtual switch

IPsec task off-loading

legacy network adapters

local area network (LAN)

MAC spoofing

Media Access Control (MAC) address

NIC teaming

private virtual switch

single-root I/O virtualization (SR-IOV)

standard network adapters

Switch Embedded Teaming (SET)

synthetic network adapters

virtual LANs (VLANs)

virtual machine queue (VMQ)

■ Configuring Hyper-V Networking

↓
THE BOTTOM LINE

Hyper-V virtualization provides virtual networks for the virtual machines to communicate with other virtual machines and it allows the virtual machines to communicate with the physical network infrastructure. Just like a physical network, the virtual devices connect to virtual switches, which can provide security, isolation, and service levels.

CERTIFICATION READY
Add and remove virtual network interface cards (vNICs)
Objective 3.4

The Hyper-V virtual switch is a software-based layer-2 network system that can be managed with Hyper-V Manager. Each virtual machine will have a virtual network interface that you would connect to the virtual switch.

Adding and Removing Virtual Network Interface Cards (vNICs)

CERTIFICATION READY
Configure synthetic and legacy virtual network adapters
Objective 3.4

Each virtual machine can support a total of 12 virtual network adapters (8 Hyper-V synthetic adapters and 4 legacy network adapters). To add or remove network adapters to Generation 1 systems, or virtual machines running earlier than Windows 10 and Windows Server 2016, you must turn off the computer.

After you build a network out of physical computers, you install a network interface adapter in each one and connect it to a hardware switch. The same principle is true in a Hyper-V environment, except that you use virtual components rather than physical ones. Each virtual machine you create has at least one virtual network adapter, and you can connect that adapter to a virtual switch. This enables you to connect the virtual machines on your Hyper-V server in various network configurations that either include or exclude the systems on your physical network.

It is recommended that you use Hyper-V *standard network adapters* (previously called *synthetic network adapters*) because they communicate over the VMBus, which allows it to be faster than legacy network adapters. Hyper-V standard network adapters are available for both Generation 1 and Generation 2 virtual machines. It requires a driver that is included in Hyper-V Integration Services.

Legacy network adapters (previously known as *emulated network adapters*) are only available in Generation 1 virtual machines. Legacy adapters communicate by making calls to the hypervisor. They emulate an Intel 21140-based PCI Fast Ethernet Adapter and can be used to boot to a network so you can install an operating system from a service such as Windows Deployment Services.

→ ADD A VIRTUAL NETWORK INTERFACE CARD

GET READY. To add a virtual network interface card to a virtual machine, perform the following steps.

1. Log on to a computer running Windows Server 2016 with an administrator account, such as **adatum\administrator** with the password of **Pa$$w0rd**.
2. If Server Manager does not open, click **Start** and then click **Server Manager**.
3. Open the **Tools** menu and click **Hyper-V**.
4. If the virtual machine is a generation 1, right-click the virtual machine and choose **Shut down**. When you are prompted to shut down the operating system, click the **Shut Down** button.
5. Right-click a virtual machine and choose **Settings**.
6. When the Settings dialog box opens, Add Hardware is already selected. On the Add Hardware page, select **Network Adapter** and click **Add**.

Figure 10-1

Adding a virtual network
adapter

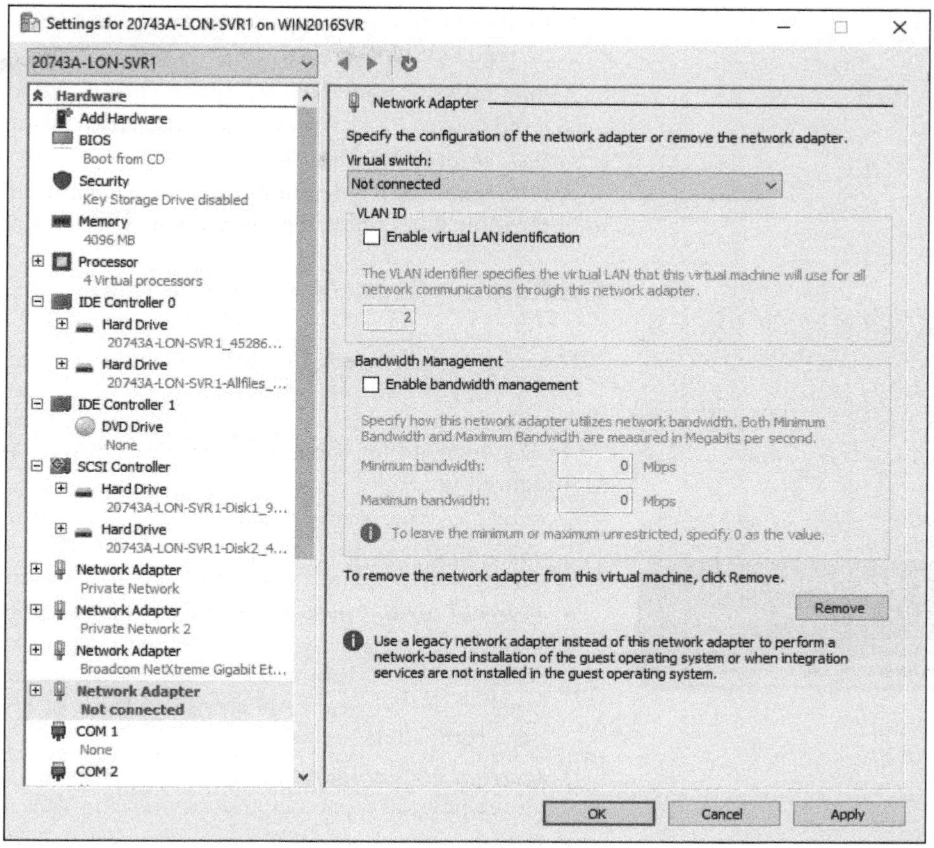

7. On the Network Adapter page (as shown in Figure 10-1), for the Virtual switch, select a virtual switch.

8. If your network is using virtual LANs (VLANs), you select the **Enable virtual LAN identification** check box. You would then specify the VLAN identifier.

9. To control bandwidth, select the **Enable bandwidth management** check box. Then in the Minimum bandwidth and Maximum bandwidth text boxes, specify the desired bandwidth in Mbps.

10. To create the virtual adapter and close the Settings dialog box, click **OK**.

To remove a virtual adapter, you just have to open the VM Settings dialog box, click the network adapter, and click the Remove button. You will then click the Apply or OK button.

If you are using standard network adapters, you can use the Advanced Features page to provide additional options supporting network adapter capabilities, as follows:

- **Static MAC address:** By default, virtual network adapters receive a dynamically assigned MAC address from the Hyper-V server. However, you can also create a static MAC address, by using this option. The only requirement is that no other adapter, virtual or physical, on the same network uses the same address.

- **Enable MAC address spoofing:** After enabled, the port in the virtual switch to which the virtual network adapter is connected can send and receive packets that contain any MAC address. The virtual switch port can also learn of new MAC addresses and add them in its forwarding table.

- **Enable DHCP guard:** This option prevents the adapter from processing messages sent by rogue DHCP servers.
- **Port mirroring mode:** This option enables the adapter to forward all the packets it receives over the network to another virtual adapter for analysis by using an application such as Network Monitor.
- **NIC teaming:** This option enables the adapter to add its bandwidth to other adapters in the same guest operating system in a NIC teaming arrangement.

Configuring Hyper-V Virtual Switches

To set up a test network that includes multiple systems, you need to configure a virtual switch using the Virtual Switch Manager, which can be opened from Hyper-V Manager. The virtual switch enables your VMs to communicate with each other and access your physical network for Internet access. The Hyper-V virtual switch supports unlimited virtualized ports.

Hyper-V includes three types of virtual switches:

- **External virtual switch:** Creates a virtual switch that binds to the physical network adapter. This enables your VMs to access your physical network. Starting with Windows Server 2016, you can map an external network to a wireless network adapter if you have installed the Wireless LAN service on the host Hyper-V server and if the Hyper-V server has a compatible network adapter.
- **Internal virtual switch:** Creates a virtual switch that is used only by the VMs that run on the physical computer and between the VMs and the physical computer.
- **Private virtual switch:** Creates a virtual switch that can only be used by the VMs running on the computer.

To create a virtual switch, under the Actions pane, click Virtual Switch Manager. From the Virtual Switch Manager box, select the type of switch to use and then click Create Virtual Switch. If you select the external switch type, you need to specify the physical network adapter (on the host) to connect the switch to.

 CREATE A VIRTUAL SWITCH

GET READY. To create a virtual switch in Hyper-V running on Windows Server 2016, perform the following steps.

1. Log on to a computer running Windows Server 2016 with an administrator account, such as **adatum\administrator** with the password of **Pa$$w0rd**.
2. If Server Manager does not open, click **Start** and click **Server Manager**.
3. Open the **Tools** menu and click **Hyper-V**.
4. Under Actions, click **Virtual Switch Manager**. The Virtual Switch Manager dialog box opens, as shown in Figure 10-2.
5. Select the type of switch that you want to create and click the **Create Virtual Switch** button.
6. On the New Virtual Switch page (as shown in Figure 10-3), in the Name text box, type a descriptive name for the switch.
7. Click **OK** to close the Virtual Switch Manager. When you are prompted to apply networking changes, click **Yes**.

Figure 10-2

Selecting the type of virtual switch

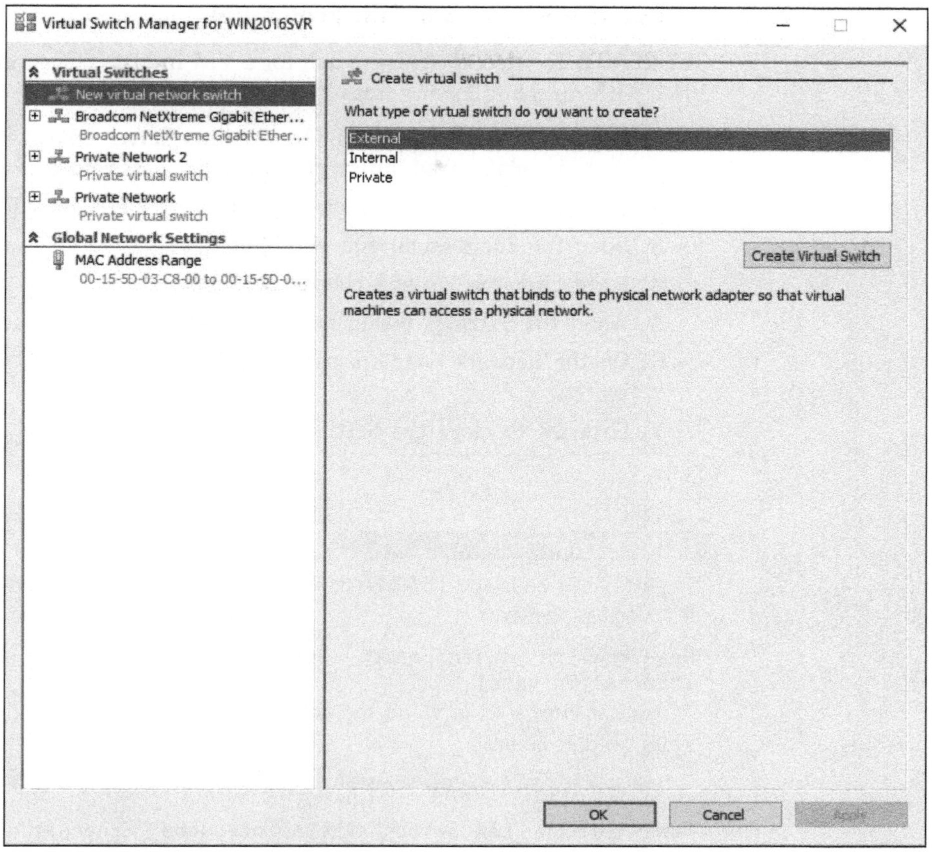

Figure 10-3

Configuring a virtual switch

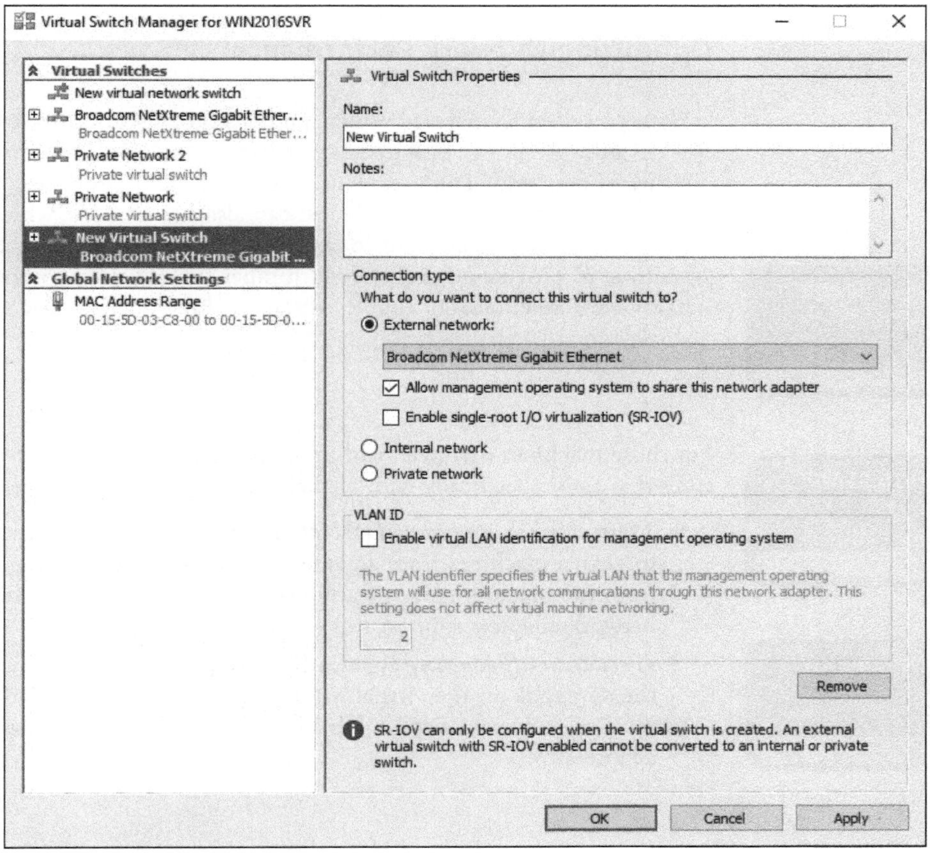

→ **SELECT A VIRTUAL SWITCH FOR A VM**

GET READY. To select a virtual switch for a VM in Hyper-V running on Windows Server 2016, perform the following steps.

1. Log on to a computer running Windows Server 2016 with an administrator account, such as **adatum\administrator** with the password of **Pa$$w0rd.**
2. If Server Manager is not open, click **Start** and then click **Server Manager.**
3. Open the **Tools** menu and click **Hyper-V.**
4. Right-click the VM and choose **Settings.**
5. When the Settings dialog box opens, click a network adapter.
6. On the Network Adapters page, for the Virtual switch, select the new virtual switch.
7. Click **OK** to close the Settings dialog box.

USING POWERSHELL

To create a new virtual switch with Windows PowerShell, you use the **New-VMSwitch** cmdlet with the following basic syntax:

```
New-VMSwitch <switch name> -NetAdapterName <adapter name> [-SwitchType
Internal|Private]
```

To create an External virtual switch, specify NetAdapterName parameter, which implicitly set the type of the virtual switch to External.

For example, to create an external switch called *LAN Switch*, you use the following command:

```
New-VMSwitch "LAN Switch" -NetAdapterName "Ethernet"
```

Optimizing Network Performance

First, you need to make sure that the physical network infrastructure is using at least 1 GB or faster links. As stated earlier in this book, it is recommended that you use the standard network adapters because they are faster than the legacy network adapters, and can reduce CPU overhead. You can also use VLANs, which help isolate networks, use bandwidth management to control the amount of traffic at one time, and use NIC teaming to provide larger bandwidth pipes. In addition, you can access network adapter hardware acceleration to enable virtual machine queue, IPsec task off-loading, and single-root I/O virtualization.

CERTIFICATION READY
Optimize network performance
Objective 3.4

CERTIFICATION READY
Configure virtual machine queue (VMQ)
Objective 3.4

CERTIFICATION READY
Configure bandwidth management
Objective 3.4

For those machines that need additional performance, some network adapters support features that assist specifically with virtualization and iSCSI storage, including:

- *Virtual machine queue (VMQ)* uses hardware packet filtering to deliver data directly to virtual machines from an external network, reducing the overhead of routing packets from the management operating system to the virtual machine. Only Hyper-V-specific network adapters support this feature.
- *IPsec task off-loading* enables IPsec task off-loading at the machine level, reducing the demands on the virtual machine's CPU by using a dedicated processor on the physical network adaptor. This feature is only supported on Hyper-V-specific network adapters.

- *Single-root I/O virtualization (SR-IOV)* allows a device, such as a network adapter, to distribute access to its resources among PCI Express hardware functions. You can configure a maximum number of off-loaded security associations from 1 to 4,096. This feature is supported only on Hyper-V standard network adapters.

 **OPTIMIZE NETWORK PERFORMANCE**

GET READY. To optimize network performance for Hyper-V virtual machines running on Windows Server 2016, perform the following steps.

1. Log on to a computer running Windows Server 2016 with an administrator account, such as **adatum\administrator** with the password of **Pa$$w0rd.**
2. If Server Manager is not open, click **Start** and click **Server Manager.**
3. Open the **Tools** menu and click **Hyper-V.**
4. Right-click the VM and choose **Settings.**
5. When the Settings dialog box opens, expand a network adapter node and click **Hardware Acceleration**, as shown in Figure 10-4.

Figure 10-4

Configuring Hardware Acceleration

Settings for 20743A-LON-SVR3 on WIN2016SVR

Hardware Acceleration

Specify networking tasks that can be offloaded to a physical network adapter.

Virtual machine queue

Virtual machine queue (VMQ) requires a physical network adapter that supports this feature.

☑ Enable virtual machine queue

IPsec task offloading

Support from a physical network adapter and the guest operating system is required to offload IPsec tasks.

When sufficient hardware resources are not available, the security associations are not offloaded and are handled in software by the guest operating system.

☑ Enable IPsec task offloading

Select the maximum number of offloaded security associations from a range of 1 to 4096.

Maximum number: [512] Offloaded SA

Single-root I/O virtualization

Single-root I/O virtualization (SR-IOV) requires specific hardware. It also might require drivers to be installed in the guest operating system.

When sufficient hardware resources are not available, network connectivity is provided through the virtual switch.

☐ Enable SR-IOV

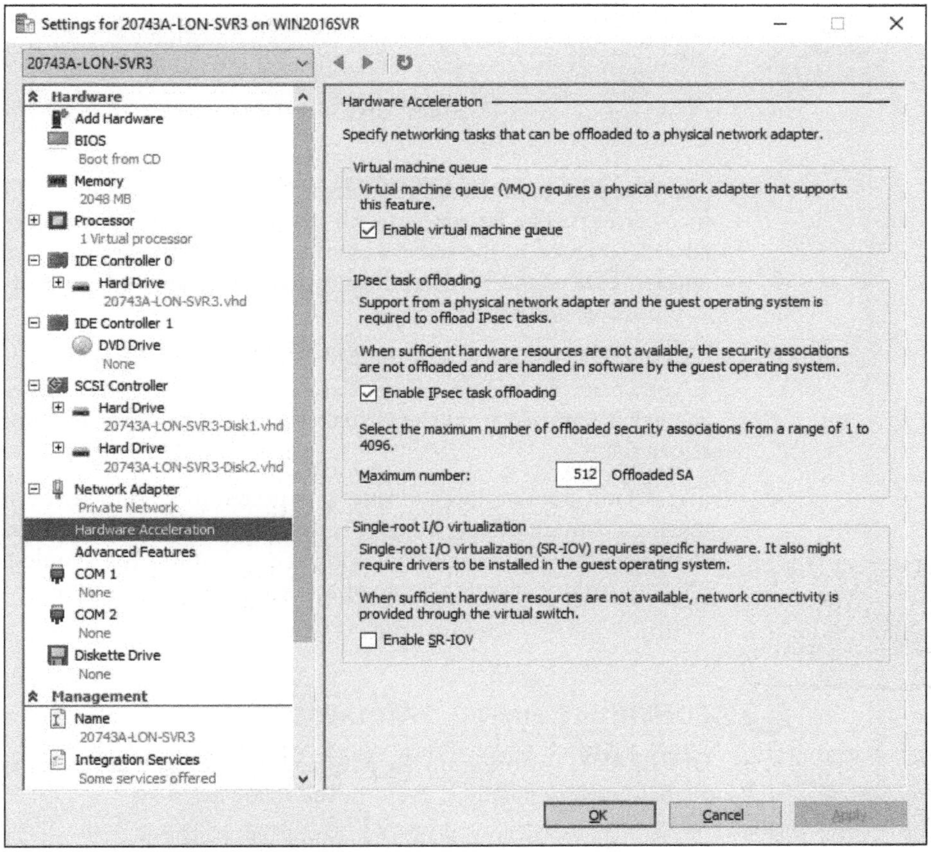

6. By default, Enable Virtual queue and Enable IPsec task off-loading is enabled. The default maximum number of IPsec tasks is 512. You can change the number of IPsec tasks by specifying a number from 1 to 4,096.
7. To enable single-root I/O virtualization, select the **enable SR-IOV** option.
8. To close the Settings dialog box, click **OK.**

Configuring MAC Addresses

Every network interface adapter has a ***Media Access Control (MAC) address*** (sometimes called a *hardware address*) that uniquely identifies the device on the network. On physical network adapters, the MAC is assigned by the manufacturer and permanently entered in the adapter's firmware. The MAC address is a 6-byte hexadecimal value—the first 3 bytes are an organizationally unique identifier (OUI) that specifies the manufacturer, and the last 3 bytes identify the adapter itself.

CERTIFICATION READY
Configure MAC addresses
Objective 3.4

The MAC address is essential to the operation of a LAN, so the virtual network adapters on a Hyper-V server require them. The server has at least one real MAC address, provided in its physical network adaptor, but Hyper-V cannot use that one address for all the virtual adapters connecting virtual machines to the network.

To provide MAC addresses for the virtual adapters, Hyper-V creates a pool of addresses and assigns addresses from this pool to virtual machines as you create them. To view or modify the MAC address pool for the Hyper-V server, you open the Virtual Switch Manager and select MAC Address Range under Global Network Settings.

TAKE NOTE*

Virtual network adapters in Hyper-V receive dynamically assigned MAC addresses by default, but you can choose to configure individual adapters with static MAC addresses as well, as described later in this lesson.

The first 3 bytes of the MAC address range are always 00-15-5D, which is an OUI registered by Microsoft. The fourth and fifth bytes of the MAC address are the last 2 bytes of the IP address assigned to the server's physical network adapter, converted to hexadecimals. The sixth and last byte of the MAC address contains the range of values from 00 to FF, which provides 256 possible addresses.

The Hyper-V server assigns the MAC addresses to the network adapters in virtual machines as you create the adapters. The adapters retain their MAC addresses permanently, or until the adapter is removed from the virtual machine. The server reclaims any unused addresses and reuses them.

The default pool of 256 addresses is expected to be sufficient for most Hyper-V virtual machine configurations, but if it is not, you can modify the Minimum and Maximum values to enlarge the pool. To prevent address duplication, you should change the second-to-last byte only, by making it into a range of addresses like the last byte.

 CONFIGURE THE MAC ADDRESS RANGE

GET READY. To configure the MAC address range that can be assigned dynamically to virtual network adapters, perform the following steps.

1. Log on to a computer running Windows Server 2016 with an administrator account, such as **adatum\administrator** with the password of **Pa$$w0rd**.
2. If Server Manager does not open, click **Start** and then click **Server Manager**.
3. Open the **Tools** menu and click **Hyper-V**.
4. Under Actions, click **Virtual Switch Manager**.
5. When the Virtual Switch Manager dialog box opens, under Global Network Settings, select **MAC Address Range**, as shown in Figure 10-5.

Figure 10-5

The MAC address range in the Virtual Switch Manager

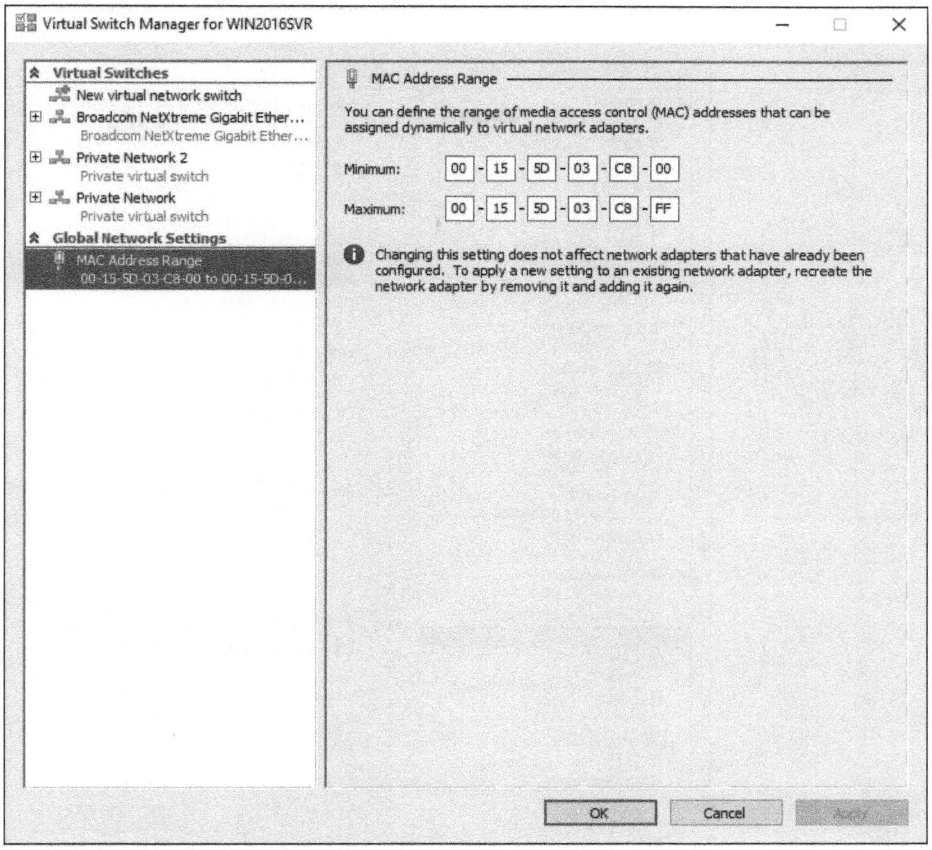

6. Specify the Minimum and Maximum MAC addresses.
7. To close the Virtual Switch Manager dialog box, click **OK**.

MAC spoofing is a technique that changes the MAC address of a network interface on a network device. Windows Network Load Balancing (NLB) is a form of clustering that allows multiple nodes to provide a server or application. Before you can use NLB, you need to enable spoofing of MAC addresses.

→ **CHANGE THE MAC ADDRESS OF A VIRTUAL NETWORK ADAPTER**

GET READY. To change the MAC address of a virtual network adapter, perform the following steps.

1. Log on to a computer running Windows Server 2016 with an administrator account, such as **adatum\administrator** with the password of **Pa$$w0rd**.
2. If Server Manager is not open, click **Start** and click **Server Manager**.
3. Open the **Tools** menu and click **Hyper-V**.
4. Right-click the VM and choose **Settings**.
5. If the virtual machine is running, right-click the virtual machine and choose **Shut down**. When you are prompted to shut down the operating system, click the **Shut Down** button.

Figure 10-6

The network adapters advanced features

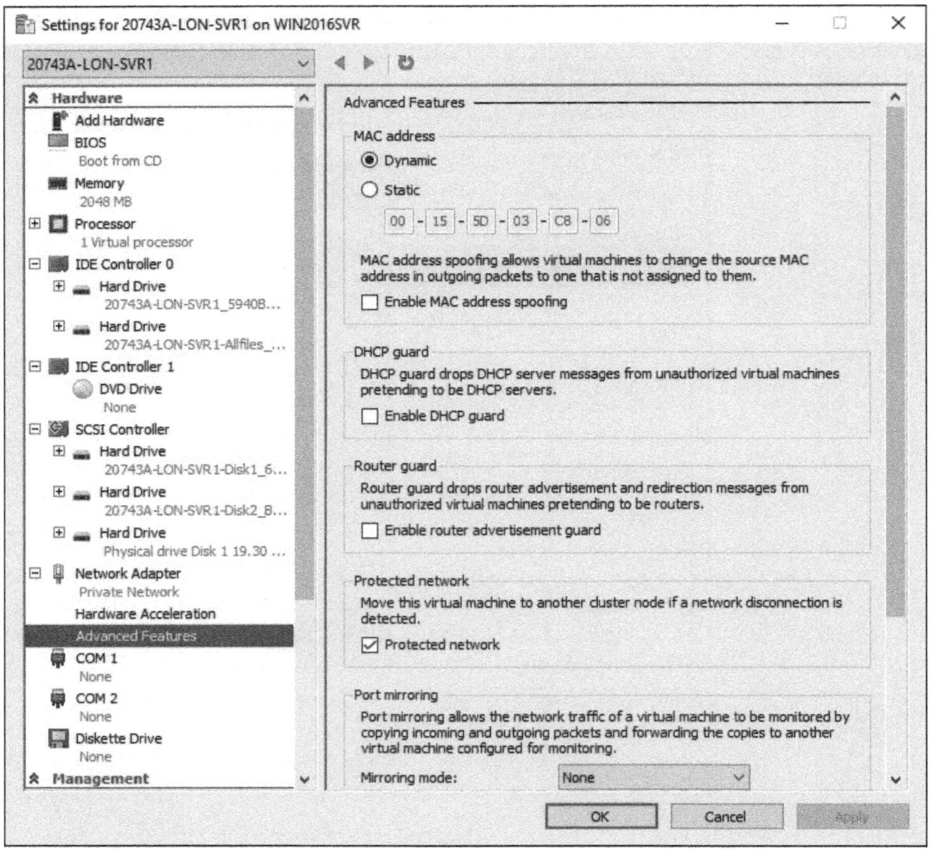

6. When the Settings dialog box opens, expand a network adapter node and click **Advanced Features**, as shown in Figure 10-6.

7. To specify a static MAC address, select the **Static** option. Then, specify the MAC address.

8. If you need to enable MAC address spoofing, select the **Enable MAC Address spoofing** option.

9. To close the Settings dialog box, click **OK**.

Configuring Network Isolation

If you isolate systems by performing network isolation, you limit what systems can talk with other systems. You can perform isolation by using internal or private switches, or by using VLANs.

CERTIFICATION READY
Configure network isolation
Objective 3.4

For testing and evaluation purposes, or for classroom situations, you might create isolated network environments. By creating internal or private virtual switches, you can create a network that exists only within the Hyper-V space, with or without the parent partition included.

An isolated network such as this suffers from the weaknesses of its strengths. If you install the guest operating systems by using Windows Deployment Services or configure the virtual machines by using DHCP, you must install and configure these services on your private network.

The guest operating systems also do not have access to the Internet, which prevents them from downloading operating system updates. Again, you must deploy appropriate substitutes on the private network.

To provide your systems with updates, install two network adapters on each of your virtual machines, by connecting one to a private switch and one to an external switch. This procedure enables the virtual machines to access the Internet and the private network.

A *local area network (LAN)* is a network of hosts covering a small physical area, like an office, a floor in a building, or a small group of buildings. LANs are used to connect multiple hosts. These LANs are then connected to other LANs using a router, which (as discussed) is a layer-3 device.

One of the challenges associated with LANs as they grow larger is that each device on the LAN broadcasts traffic onto the LAN. Although these broadcasts will not cross a router, if there are enough hosts, the aggregate broadcast traffic can saturate a network. One solution is to deploy more routers as a way to divide the network into more manageable segments. However, routers add latency to network traffic, and they require a routing protocol (discussed in the next section) for traffic to find its way from one part of the network to another.

Accordingly, *virtual LANs (VLANs)* were developed as an alternate solution to deploying multiple routers. VLANs are logical network segments used to create separate broadcast domains, but they still allow the devices on the VLAN to communicate at layer 2 without requiring a router. VLANs are created by switches, and traffic between VLANs is switched not routed, which creates a much faster network connection because there is no need for involvement of a routing protocol. Even though the hosts are logically separated, the traffic between these hosts is switched directly as if the hosts were on the same LAN segment.

VLANs provide a number of benefits over routed networks, including the following:

- Higher performance on medium or large LANs due to reduced broadcast traffic
- Better organization of devices on the network for easier management
- Additional security because devices can be put on their own VLAN

VLANs can be used to isolate a network. This is particularly helpful if you have virtual machines on different Hyper-V servers that you want to add to the isolated network. By connecting the network adapters to an external switch and configuring them with the same VLAN identifier, you can create a network within a network, which isolates the VLAN from other computers. You can, for example, deploy a DHCP server on your VLAN without it interfering with the other DHCP servers in your production environment.

> ✚ **MORE INFORMATION**
>
> To see how to define VLANs for a virtual network interface card, go to the "Adding and Removing Virtual Network Interface Cards (vNICs)" section of this lesson. To see how to define internal and private switches, go to the "Configuring Hyper-V Virtual Switches" section of this lesson.

Configuring NIC Teamings in VMs

> *NIC teaming*, also called bonding, balancing, and aggregation, is a Windows feature that enables administrators to join multiple network adapters into a single entity, for performance enhancement or fault-tolerance purposes. Hyper-V virtual machines can also take advantage of NIC teaming, but they are limited to teams of only two, as opposed to the host operating system, which can have teams of up to 64 NICs.

CERTIFICATION READY
Configure NIC teaming
in VMs
Objective 3.4

To use NIC teaming in Hyper-V, you must complete three basic tasks, as follows:

1. Create the NIC team in the Windows Server 2016 host operating system.
2. In Hyper-V Manager, create an external virtual switch using the NIC team.
3. Configure the network adapter in a virtual machine to connect to the virtual switch representing the NIC team.

NIC teaming in Windows Server 2016 supports two modes:

- **Switch Independent Mode:** All of the network adapters are connected to different switches, providing alternative routes through the network. Static teaming and LACP are switch dependent modes.
- **Switch Dependent Mode:** All of the network adapters are connected to the same switch, providing a single interface with their combined bandwidth.

In Switch Independent Mode, you can choose between two configurations. The active/active configuration leaves all of the network adapters functional, providing increased throughput. If one adapter fails, all of the traffic is shunted to the remaining adapters. In the active/standby configuration, one adapter is left offline, to function as a failover in the event the active adapter fails. In active/active mode, an adapter failure causes a performance reduction; in active/standby mode, the performance remains the same before and after an adapter failure.

In Switch Dependent Mode, you can choose static teaming, a generic mode that balances the traffic between the adapters in the team, or you can opt to use the Link Aggregation Control Protocol (LACP) defined in IEEE 802.3ax, assuming that your equipment supports it. When you select the *Static Teaming* teaming mode, you manually configure both the switch and the host to identify which links form the team.

There is one significant limitation to NIC teaming. If your traffic consists of large TCP sequences, such as a Hyper-V live migration, the system will shun using multiple adapters for those sequences, to minimize the number of lost and out-of-order TCP segments. You will therefore not realize any performance increase for large file transfers using TCP.

You can create and manage NIC teams using Server Manager or Windows PowerShell. To create a NIC team using Server Manager, use the following procedure.

 CREATE A NETWORK TEAM ON WINDOWS SERVER 2016

GET READY. To create a network team on Windows Server 2016, perform the following steps.

1. Log on to a computer running Windows Server 2016 with an administrator account, such as **adatum\administrator** with the password of **Pa$$w0rd**.
2. If Server Manager is not open, click **Start** and click **Server Manager**.
3. Click **All Servers** and then click the server that you want to create the team on. Then, right-click the server and choose **Configure NIC Teaming**.
4. When the NIC Teaming window opens, in the Teams section, click **TASKS > New Team**.
5. When the NIC Teaming dialog box opens (as shown in Figure 10-7), in the Team name text box, type **Team1**.
6. Select two adapters.
7. To show the Additional properties, click the **Additional properties** option. The Additional options allow you to specify the teaming mode, load balancing mode, and standby adapter.

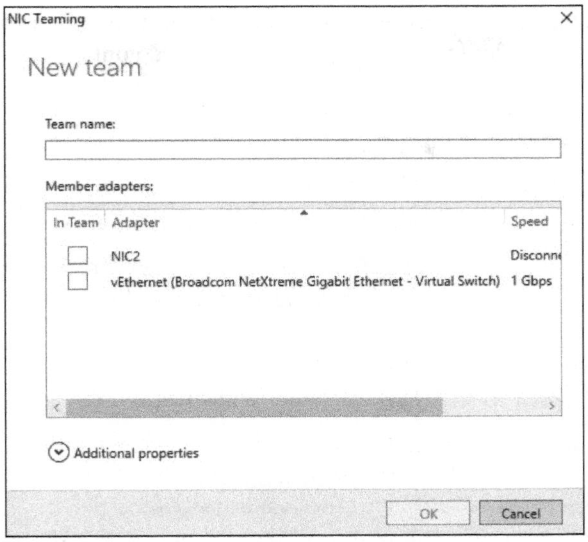

Figure 10-7

The NIC Teaming dialog box

8. To define a VLAN, click the **Primary team interface** link. If you need to specify a VLAN, click the Specify VLAN option, and type in the VLAN ID. Click **OK.**
9. To close the NIC Teaming dialog box, click **OK.**

Once you have created the NIC team, you can open the Virtual Switch Manager and create a new virtual switch by selecting the External network option and choosing Microsoft Network Adapter Multiplexor Driver from the drop-down list, as shown in Figure 10-8.

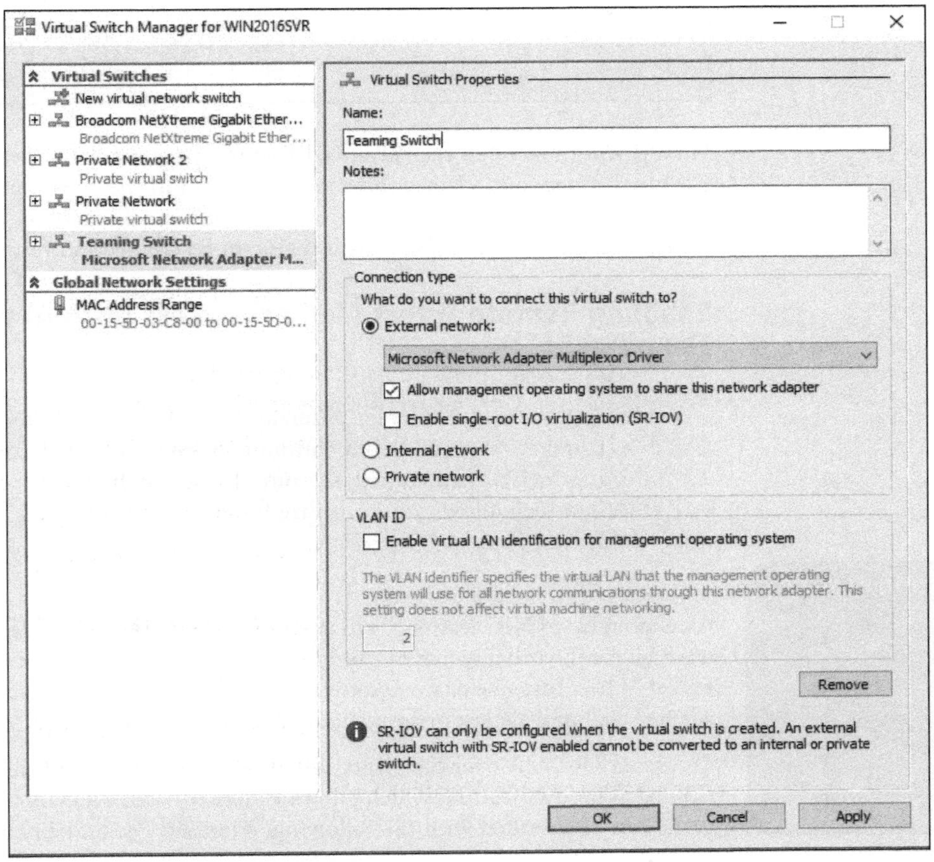

Figure 10-8

The Virtual Switch Properties settings for a NIC team switch

To configure a virtual machine to use a NIC team, you must use the Settings dialog box to modify the properties for a virtual network adapter, configuring it to use the team switch you created in the previous section, as shown in Figure 10-9.

Figure 10-9

The Network Adapter settings for a NIC team adapter

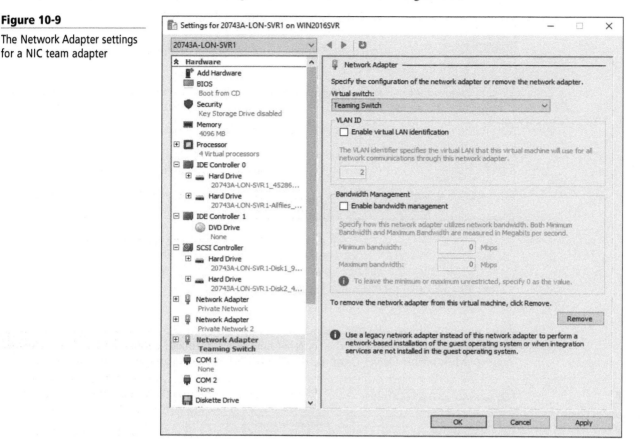

Finally, you must open the Advanced Features page for the network adapter and select the Enable this network adapter to be part of a team in the guest operating system check box. At this point, the NIC team is operational for the virtual machine. You can unplug one of the network cables, and the system will maintain its connection to the network.

Enabling Remote Direct Memory Access (RDMA) with Switch Embedded Teaming (SET)

A converged network allows for different types of communication within a single network, such as storage, video, and data communication. You can form a converged network by combining Switch Embedded Teaming (SET) with Remote Direct Memory Access (RDMA), which allows you to utilize fewer network adapters in your servers. RDMA was defined in Lesson 3.

CERTIFICATION READY
Enable Remote Direct Memory Access (RDMA) on network adapters bound to a Hyper-V virtual switch using Switch Embedded Teaming (SET)
Objective 3.4

An alternative to NIC teaming is to use SET. *Switch Embedded Teaming (SET)* allows you to use a Hyper-V virtual switch to team up to eight physical Ethernet adapters located on the same Hyper-V host into one or more software-based virtual network adapters. The virtual network adapters will provide fast performance and fault tolerance in the event of a network adapter failure.

To use any RDMA over converged Ethernet, you must install the Data Center Bridging (DCB) Windows feature, which allows Ethernet-based RDMA technologies to work better. DCB can be installed with the following Windows PowerShell command:

```
Install-WindowsFeature Data-Center-Bridging
```

To create a SET team, you have to create the Hyper-V Virtual Switch with the New-VMSwitch Windows PowerShell command, by including the `EnableEmbeddedTeaming` parameter in your command syntax. For example, to create a new virtual switch called Team2Switch, you would use the following command:

```
New-VMSwitch -Name Team2Switch -NetAdapterName "NIC 1","NIC 2"
-EnableEmbeddedTeaming $true
```

If you want to create a SET-capable switch with a single team member so that you can add a team member at a later time, you must use the `EnableEmbeddedTeaming` parameter.

```
New-VMSwitch -Name TeamedvSwitch -NetAdapterName "NIC 1"
-EnableEmbeddedTeaming $true
```

To add host vNICs and make them RDMA capable, use the following commands:

```
Add-VMNetworkAdapter -SwitchName SETswitch -Name SMB_1 -managementOS
```

```
Add-VMNetworkAdapter -SwitchName SETswitch -Name SMB_2 -managementOS
```

```
Enable-NetAdapterRDMA "vEthernet (SMB_1)","vEthernet (SMB_2)"
```

SKILL SUMMARY

IN THIS LESSON YOU LEARNED:

- Hyper-V virtualization provides virtual networks for the virtual machines to communicate with other virtual machines and it allows the virtual machines to communicate with the physical network infrastructure. Just like a physical network, the virtual devices connect to virtual switches, which can provide security, isolation, and service levels.

- To set up a test network that includes multiple systems, you need to configure a virtual switch using the Virtual Switch Manager, which can be opened from Hyper-V Manager. The virtual switch enables your VMs to communicate with each other and to access your physical network for Internet access.

- First, you need to make sure that the physical network infrastructure is using at least 1 GB or faster links. As stated earlier in this book, it is recommended that you use the standard network adapter because it is faster than the legacy network adapters, and can reduce CPU overhead. You can also use VLANS, which will help isolate networks, use bandwidth management to control the amount of traffic at one time, and use NIC teaming to provide larger bandwidth pipes. In addition, you can access network adapter hardware acceleration to enable virtual machine queue, IPsec task off-loading, and single-root I/O virtualization.

- Every network interface adapter has a Media Access Control (MAC) address (sometimes called a hardware address) that uniquely identifies the device on the network. On physical network adapters, the MAC address is assigned by the manufacturer and permanently entered in the adapter's firmware. The MAC address is a 6-byte hexadecimal value—the first 3 bytes are an organizationally unique identifier (OUI) that specifies the manufacturer, and the last 3 bytes identify the adapter itself.

- NIC teaming, also called bonding, balancing, and aggregation, is a Windows feature that enables administrators to join multiple network adapters into a single entity, for performance enhancement or fault-tolerance purposes. Hyper-V virtual machines can also take advantage of NIC teaming, but they are limited to teams of only two, as opposed to the host operating system, which can have teams of up to 64 NICs.

■ Knowledge Assessment

Multiple Choice

Select the correct answer for each of the following questions.

1. Which of the following are valid reasons for using an legacy network adapter rather than a synthetic one? (Choose all that apply.)
   a. You want to install the guest OS using a Windows Deployment Services server.
   b. There is no Guest Integration Services package available for the guest OS you plan to use.
   c. The manufacturer of your physical network adapter has not yet provided a synthetic network adapter driver.
   d. The emulated network adapter provides better performance.

2. Which of the following statements is *not* true about synthetic network adapters?
   a. Synthetic adapters communicate with the parent partition using the VMBus.
   b. Synthetic adapters require the Guest Integration Services package to be installed on the guest OS.
   c. Synthetic adapters provide faster performance than legacy adapters.
   d. Synthetic adapters can start the child VM using a PXE network boot.

3. Which of the following is the maximum number of ports supported by a Hyper-V virtual switch?
   a. 8
   b. 256
   c. 4,096
   d. Unlimited

4. Which of the following virtual switch types does *not* enable guest OSs to communicate with the parent partition?
   a. External
   b. Internal
   c. Private
   d. Isolated

5. How many dynamically assigned MAC addresses can be provided by a Hyper-V server by default?
   a. 8
   b. 256
   c. 4,096
   d. Unlimited

6. Virtual switches can be created after which of the following roles is installed?
   a. Hyper-V
   b. Application Server
   c. Remote Access
   d. Network Policy and Access Services

7. Creating the default virtual switch places it between _____ and _____.
   a. the physical switch; the network adapter in the host operating system
   b. the virtual adapter; the network adapter in the host operating system
   c. the network adapter; the virtual adapter in the host operating system
   d. the physical switch; the next upstream physical switch

8. Which of the following statements best describes how to create a virtual switch for the purpose of isolating virtual machines (VMs) from the external network and the host operating system?
   a. You must create an external virtual switch.
   b. You must create an internal virtual switch.

    c. You must create a private virtual switch.

    d. You cannot isolate VMs from the external network.

9. Which is faster, a standard network adapter or an legacy network adapters adapter?

    a. Standard, because it does not correspond to a real-world device

    b. Legacy, because it is legacy and more compatible

    c. Standard, because it uses the VMBus

    d. Legacy, because it uses the VMBus

10. Which of the following methods can be used to team up physical Ethernet adapters so that the hosts can have better performance and fault tolerance? (Choose two answers.)

    a. NIC teaming

    b. Virtual machine queue

    c. Remote Direct Memory Access

    d. Switch Embedded Teaming

Best Answer

Choose the letter that corresponds to the best answer. More than one answer choice may achieve the goal. Select the BEST answer.

1. Which of the following network interface configurations are recommended by Microsoft in a Hyper-V server?

    a. Two physical adapters providing multiple virtual adapters

    b. One physical adapter per Hyper-V server, providing for several network and SAN connections

    c. One physical adapter per partition, providing for multiple network connections per partition

    d. At least two physical network adapters: one adapter servicing the parent partition and the other to the child partitions

2. Which of the following best describes the key benefit for creating a virtual switch?

    a. Virtual switches enable virtual machines (VMs) to participate on the networks to which the physical adapters are connected.

    b. Virtual switches require no physical space in the rack.

    c. Virtual switches enable the Hyper-V server to participate on the networks to which the physical adapters are connected.

    d. Virtual switches have unlimited ports, freeing network administrators from connecting physical switches by uplinks or crossover circuits.

3. Which of the following best describes the MAC address range in the Virtual Switch Manager?

    a. The MAC of the Hyper-V server is associated with the physical adapter's MAC address.

    b. The first 3 bytes are fixed. The fourth and fifth bytes associate to the adapter's IP address. The sixth byte provides 256 options.

    c. The first 1 byte is fixed. The next 3 bytes associate to the adapter's IP address. The last 2 bytes provide 256 options.

    d. The first 3 bytes are fixed. The fourth byte associates to the adapter's IP address. The fifth and sixth byte provides 256 options.

4. In which of the following locations can you make configuration changes to optimize network performance?

    a. In Server Manager, Advanced Network Features

    b. In the Settings dialog box of any VM

    c. In the Hardware Acceleration page under VM settings

    d. In any virtual network adapter, Advanced settings

5. Which network communication occurs after creating a *private* virtual switch?
   a. The VM on the parent partition can communicate with the physical network.
   b. VMs on both the parent and child partitions can communicate with each other.
   c. VMs on the child partitions can communicate with each other only.
   d. VMs on child partitions and parent partitions cannot communicate with each other.

Build a List

1. Specify the correct order of steps necessary to creating a virtual switch.

   _____ If applicable, configure the virtualization or management options.

   _____ Click Create Virtual Switch after selecting a switch type option (External, Internal, or Private).

   _____ In the Server Manager Tools menu, select Hyper-V Manager, and then select a Hyper-V server.

   _____ From the Actions pane, select Virtual Switch Manager.

2. Specify the correct order of steps necessary to creating a virtual network adapter.

   _____ In the Server Manager Tools menu, select Hyper-V Manager, and then select a Hyper-V server.

   _____ If applicable, select the Enable virtual LAN identification check box.

   _____ In the Add Hardware list, select Network Adapter and click Add.

   _____ In the Virtual Machines list, select a virtual machine and, in the Actions pane, click Settings.

   _____ In the Virtual Switch drop-down list, select the switch to which you want to connect the network adapter.

■ Business Case Scenarios

Scenario 10-1: Creating a New Virtual Switch

You need all VMs networked to each other as well as to the host operating system. Only the host operating system will be connected to the external network. Describe your proposed solution.

Scenario 10-2: Isolating Test Systems

Your virtual machines are running on a Hyper-V host. You need to duplicate an accounting system and place it in an isolated test network. You must make sure that users cannot access these systems through the production network and you must make sure that they do not interfere with the systems that make up production accounting systems. Describe your proposed solution.

Installing and Configuring the Windows Nano Server

70-740 EXAM OBJECTIVE

Objective 1.2 – Install and configure Nano Server. This objective may include but is not limited to the following: Determine appropriate usage scenarios and requirements for Nano Server; install Nano Server; implement roles and features on Nano Server; manage and configure Nano Server; manage Nano Server remotely using Windows PowerShell.

Objective 1.3 - Create, manage, and maintain images for deployment. This objective may include but is not limited to the following: Manage and maintain Nano Server images using Windows PowerShell. *Other Objective 1.3 topics are covered in Lesson 6 and Lesson 3.*

Lesson Heading	Exam Objective
Installing and Configuring Windows Nano Server	Determine appropriate usage scenarios and requirements for Nano Server
– Determining Appropriate Usage Scenarios and Requirements for Nano Server	Install Nano Server
	Manage and configure Nano Server
– Installing Nano Server	Manage Nano Server remotely using Windows PowerShell
– Managing and Configuring Nano Server	Manage and maintain Nano Server images using Windows PowerShell
– Implementing Roles and Features on Nano Server	Implement roles and features on Nano Server

KEY TERMS

Nano Recovery Tool   **Nano Server**

283

■ Installing and Configuring Windows Nano Server

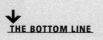
THE BOTTOM LINE

Nano Server is a new installation option for Windows Server 2016. Although it has a small hardware footprint for Server Core, it has no local sign-in capability. It supports only 64-bit applications, tools, and agents.

Different from installing Windows Server Core, you must create a virtual hard disk. You can then use the virtual hard drive on a virtual machine to support a virtualized Nano Server in Hyper-V, or you can configure the Nano Server to start from a .vhd file.

Determining Appropriate Usage Scenarios and Requirements for Nano Server

There are many scenarios where you could take advantage of the Nano Server. For example, if you require higher security, or require a smaller hardware footprint, you should check to see if the Nano Server can run your services and applications.

CERTIFICATION READY
Determine appropriate usage scenarios and requirements for Nano Server.
Objective 1.2

Some of the scenarios used by Nano Servers include:

- A Hyper-V host computer
- A storage host for a Scale-Out File Server
- A DNS server
- A web server running Internet Information Services (IIS)
- A host computer that runs a container

To install the Nano Server, you need a server running Windows Server 2016 and 800 MB of free disk space. Of course, you might need additional disk space to store data and additional processor and memory for the load that the Nano Server is running.

Installing Nano Server

As mentioned before, Nano Server cannot be installed directly from the installation media during setup. Instead, you must access the Windows Server 2016 installation media NanoServer folder to generate a Nano Server image.

CERTIFICATION READY
Install Nano Server
Objective 1.2

Nano Server is installed using one of three methods:

- Deploying a VHD image that will be hosted as a virtual machine on a Hyper-V host
- Deploying a VHD as a bootable drive on a physical computer
- Deploying a Nano Server WIM file on a physical computer

To create the Nano Server image, use the Windows PowerShell cmdlet New-NanoServerImage. The options available include the following:

- **Edition:** Lists the Windows Server 2016 edition of the Nano Server. Options are Standard or Datacenter.
- **Deployment type:** Lists the type of deployment. Use *Host* for WIM or bootable VHD and *Guest* for VHDs hosted in Hyper-V.
- **Media path:** Lists the path to the root of the Windows Server 2016 installation media.
- **Base path:** Optionally copies the server binary files to this folder, if you are creating a WIM file.
- **Target path:** Identifies the path and file name, including extension, of the Nano Server image. Options include .vhd, .vhdx, and .wim.

- **Computer name:** Identifies the name of the target Nano Server computer.
- **Computer:** Installs the Hyper-V role.
- **Clustering:** Installs failover clustering.
- **Containers:** Installs host support for Windows Containers.
- **GuestDrivers:** Installs Hyper-V guest drivers for hosting Nano Server as a virtual machine.
- **OEMDrivers:** Installs the same basic drivers for a variety of network adapters and storage controllers that are included in the Server Core installation of Windows Server 2016.
- **Storage:** Installs the File Server role and other storage components.
- **Defender:** Installs Windows Defender anti-malware, including a default signature file.
- **Packages:** Installs certain roles and features. Depending on the packages that are installed, you might need additional package switches.
  - To install Internet Information Server (IIS), use `-Packages Microsoft-NanoServer-IIS-Package`.
  - To install the System Center Virtual Machine Manager agent, use `-Packages Microsoft-Windows-Server-SCVMM-Package`.
  - To install the Network Performance Diagnostics Service (NPDS), use `-Packages Microsoft-NanoServer-NPDS-Package`.
  - To install Data Center Bridging, use `-Packages Microsoft-NanoServer-DCB-Package`.
  - To install the DNS Server role, use `-Packages Microsoft-NanoServer-DNS-Package`.
  - To install Desired State Configuration (DSC), use `-Packages Microsoft-NanoServer-DSC-Package`.
  - To install Secure Startup, use `-Packages Microsoft-NanoServer-SecureStartup-Package`.
  - To install Shielded Virtual Machine, use `-Packages Microsoft-NanoServer-ShieldedVM-Package`.

The steps to create an image include the following:

1. Copy the NanoServerImageGenerator folder from the NanoServer folder on the Windows Server 2016 installation media to a folder on your local machine.
2. Start Windows PowerShell as an administrator and change the directory to the NanoServerImageGenerator folder on your local drive.
3. Import the NanoServerImageGenerator module by using the following Windows PowerShell `Import-Module` cmdlet:

   ```
   Import-Module .\NanoServerImageGenerator -Verbose
   ```
4. Create the VHD or WIM by using the `New-NanoServerImage` cmdlet with the following syntax:

   ```
   New-NanoServerImage -Edition <edition>
   -DeploymentType <deployment type> -MediaPath <media path>
   -BasePath <base path> -TargetPath <target path> -ComputerName
   <computer name>
   -Packages <packages> -<other package switches>
   ```

DEPLOYING A VHD IMAGE AS A VIRTUAL MACHINE

To create a Nano Server called NANO-SVR1 that will be stored in the nano-svr1.vhdx file, with IIS installed, use the following command:

```
new-NanoServerImage -DeploymentType Guest -Edition Standard -mediapath
C:\ -Basepath c:\nano -targetpath c:\nano\nano-svr1.vhdx -computername
NANO-SVR1

-storage -package Microsoft-NanoServer-IIS-Package
```

When you are prompted to type in a password, type Pa$$w0rd. It will then take a few minutes to generate the nano-svr1.vhdx file.

Once the .vhd or .vhdx file is created, you need to deploy the Nano Server to Hyper-V, by using the following steps:

1. Open Hyper-V Manager.
2. Create a new virtual machine with the new virtual disk file.
3. Boot the virtual machine.
4. Use Hyper-V to connect to the virtual machine.
5. Log on to the Nano Server Recovery Console using the administrator account and password.
6. Obtain the IP address for the virtual machine and connect to the Nano Server by using the remote management tools to manage the server.

CREATE A VIRTUAL MACHINE

GET READY. To create a virtual machine on Hyper-V to run a Nano Server, perform the following steps.

1. Log on to a computer running Windows Server 2016 with an administrator account, such as **adatum\administrator** with the password of **Pa$$w0rd.**
2. If Server Manager does not open, click **Start** and click **Server Manager.**
3. Open the **Tools** menu and click **Hyper-V.**
4. When Hyper-V Manager opens, right-click the host node and choose **New > Virtual Machine.**
5. When the New Virtual Machine Wizard opens, on the Before You Begin page, click **Next.**
6. On the Specify Name and Location page, in the Name text box, type **NANO-SVR1.** Click **Next.**
7. On the Specify Generation page, select **Generation 2** and click **Next.**
8. On the Assign Memory page, select the **Use Dynamic Memory for this virtual machine** option and click **Next.**
9. On the Configure Networking page, for the Connection option, select a switch, such as **Private Network.** Click **Next.**
10. On the Connect Virtual Hard Disk page, select the **Use an existing virtual hard disk** option.
11. Click the **Browse** button.
12. When the Open dialog box opens, navigate to and click the **C:\nano\nano-svr1 .vhdx** file. Click **Open.**
13. Back on the Connect Virtual Hard Disk page, click **Next.**
14. On the Summary page, click **Finish.**
15. Right-click the NANO-SVR1 and choose **Start.**
16. Right-click the NANO-SVR1 and choose **Connect.**
17. On the logon screen, as shown in Figure 11-1, type **administrator.** Then, press the **Tab** key. Then, in the Password box, type **Pa$$w0rd.**

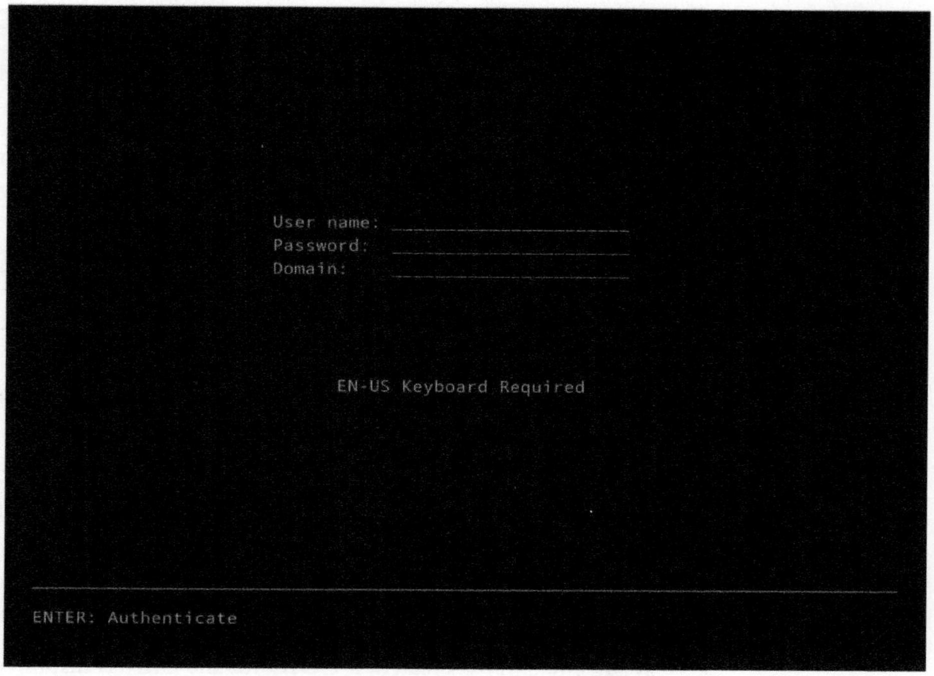

Figure 11-1

Logging on to a Nano Server

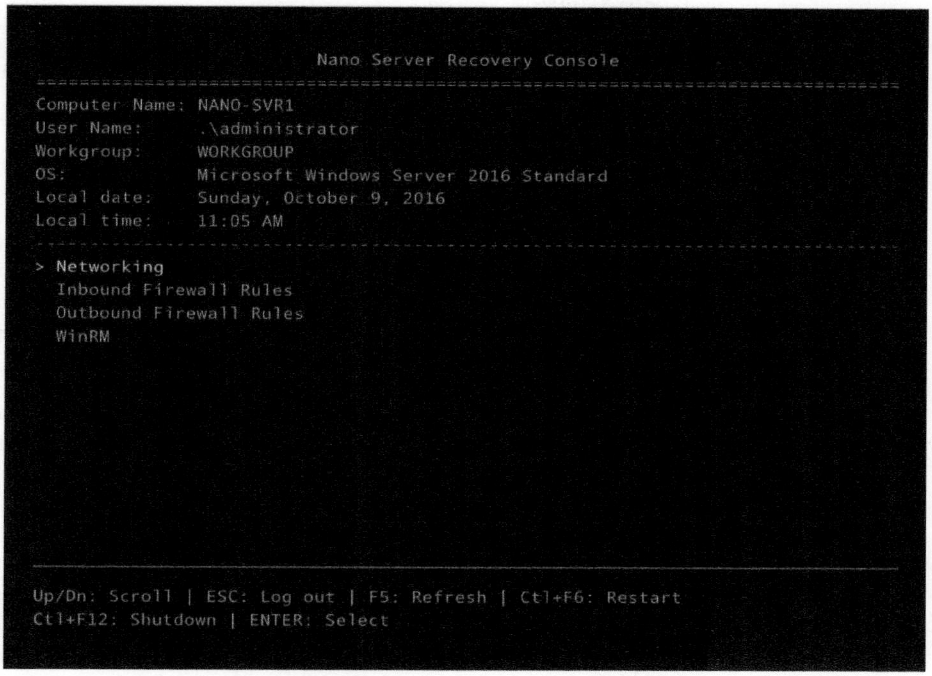

Figure 11-2

Accessing the Nano Server Recovery Console

18. When the Nano Server Recovery Console opens (as shown in Figure 11-2), Networking is already selected. Press **Enter.**

19. With the Ethernet adapter and MAC address already selected, press **Enter.**

20. Record the IP address and press **Esc** twice.

DEPLOYING THE NANO SERVER VHD ON A PHYSICAL COMPUTER

To create a Nano Server called NANO-SVR1 that will be stored in the nano-svr1.vhdx file, with IIS installed, use the following command:

```
new-NanoServerImage -DeploymentType Host -Edition Standard -mediapath
C:\ -Basepath c:\nano -targetpath c:\nano\nano-svr2.vhdx -computername
NANO-SVR2

-storage -package Microsoft-NanoServer-IIS-Package

-OEMDrivers
```

The main difference when running this command is that you set the DeploymentType to Host, and you must include the -OEMDrivers so that the most common hardware drivers are installed.

After the image is booted, mount the VHD file to the local computer and then use the bcd-boot command to add a boot entry to the Windows Boot Manager boot menu, by opening a command prompt and executing the commands:

1. To create a boot entry called "Nano Server," execute the following command:

   ```
   bcdedit /copy {current} /d "Nano Server"
   ```

   When the entry is created, a GUID for the entry is displayed, such as {0141898c-3e9e-11e3-8aa8-9b1588913cd5}. You need the GUID for the remaining commands.

2. Then, execute the following commands:

   ```
   bcdedit /set {GUID} device vhd=[c:]\Nano\nano-svr2.vhdx

   bcdedit /set {GUID} osdevice vhd=[c:] \Nano\nano-svr2.vhdx

   bcdedit /set {GUID} path \windows\system32\boot\winload.exe
   ```

DEPLOYING A NANO SERVER WIM FILE

To create a Nano Server WIM, use the following command:

```
new-NanoServerImage -DeploymentType Host -Edition Standard -mediapath
C:\ -Basepath c:\nano -targetpath c:\nano\nano-svr3.wim -computername
NANO-SVR3

-storage -package Microsoft-NanoServer-IIS-Package
```

Once the WIM file is created, you can deploy it by using WinPE:

1. Ensure the .wim file is accessible from WinPE.
2. Boot into WinPE on the local server.
3. Use diskpart.exe to prepare the local hard drive.
4. Apply the Nano Server image by using dism.exe.
5. Add the WIM file to the boot menu using the bcdboot.exe.
6. Remove the WinPE media if applicable, and reboot the system by using the following command:

   ```
   Wpeutil.exe reboot
   ```

To prepare the local hard drive with Diskpart, execute the following at a command prompt:

```
Diskpart.exe

Select disk 0
```

```
Clean

Convert GPT

Create partition efi size=100

Format quick FS=FAT32 label="System"

Assign letter="s"

Create partition msr size=128

Create partition primary

Format quick FS=NTFS label="NanoServer"

Assign letter="n"

List volume

Exit
```

To apply the Nano Server image using the dism.exe command, execute the following command at a command prompt:

```
Dism.exe /apply-image /imagefile:.\Nano\NANO-SVR3.wim /index:1 /
applydir:n:\
```

Then, to add to the boot menu, execute the following command:

```
Bcdboot.exe n:\Windows /s s:
```

Managing and Configuring Nano Server

After you install and place the Nano Server, you need to configure the Nano Server, including configuring networking and firewall, adding the server to the domain, and adding roles and features. You can then manage the server using Server Manager, Windows PowerShell, and other management tools.

CERTIFICATION READY
Manage and configure
Nano Server.
Objective 1.2

Before you make significant changes to a Nano Server running as a virtual machine, , you should back up the VM and consider creating a checkpoint of the VM. The disadvantage of the Nano Server is that you can only perform a small set of tasks on the running Nano Server. All other tasks will have to be done remotely.

USING THE NANO RECOVERY TOOL

The main local tool to configure the Nano Server tool is the ***Nano Recovery Tool***. It has all of the tools that will help you establish connectivity to your remote management tools. The front page shows the following:

- Computer name
- User name
- Workgroup or domain name
- The operating system
- Local date and time

You can also configure the following:

- Networking
- Inbound and outbound firewall rules
- WinRM

From the Networking page, perform the following:

- View the MAC address.
- Enable or disable DHCP.
- Configure an IPv4 address and subnet mask.
- Configure an IPv6 address.

When you access the inbound firewall rules or the outbound firewall rules, you can view the various firewall rules. When you select a firewall rule, you can use the F4 key to enable or disable a rule.

The Windows Remote Management (WinRM) protocol allows you to remotely connect to a computer and execute commands remotely using Windows PowerShell or Windows Remote Shell, as discussed in Lesson 2.

To enable Windows Remote Management, select WinRM, and then on the Windows Remote Management page, press Enter twice to confirm.

MANAGING NANO SERVER REMOTELY USING WINDOWS POWERSHELL

As discussed in Lesson 2, to connect to a remote computer you need to enable WinRS on the remote server. To enable WinRS, use the Nano Server Recovery Console, as shown earlier in this lesson. You can then be on another server or a client that has Windows PowerShell to use the `Enter-pssession` cmdlet to connect to the Nano Server computer and execute the appropriate Windows PowerShell commands.

To manage Nano Server with Windows PowerShell remoting, you need to add the IP address of the Nano Server to your management computer's list of trusted hosts. To add the Nano Server to the list of trusted hosts, run this command at an elevated Windows PowerShell prompt:

```
Set-Item WSMan:\localhost\Client\TrustedHosts "<IP address of Nano Server>"
```

MANAGING NANO SERVER REMOTELY USING ADMINISTRATIVE TOOLS

In Lesson 2, you learned how to redirect an administrative tool based on the Microsoft Management Console (MMC): Open an administrative tool on a remote computer, click and then right-click the snap-in, then choose Connect to another computer.

ADDING NANO SERVER TO DOMAIN

To add a computer to a domain, on a domain controller, use the djoin.exe command to provision the computer and generate an odjblob file and then use use the `Set-Item WSMAN:` command to add the Nano Server to a trusted host list. Next, open a remote PowerShell session on the Nano Server to configure the firewall, to copy the odjblob file, and to apply the file to the Nano Server.

 ADD A NANO SERVER TO A DOMAIN

GET READY. To add a Nano Server to a domain, perform the following steps.

1. Log on to your domain controller, such as **LON-DC1**, as **adatum\administrator** with the password of **Pa$$w0rd**.
2. Right-click **Start** and choose **Windows PowerShell (Admin)**.
3. At the command prompt, type the following cmdlet and then press **Enter**:

   ```
   djoin.exe /provision /domain adatum /machine nano-svr1 /savefile
   .\odjblob
   ```

4. At the command prompt, type the following cmdlet and then press **Enter**. Your IP address will be different.

   Set-Item WSMan:\localhost\Client\TrustedHosts "172.16.0.X"

   where *X* is the IP address of the server. Type **Y**, and when prompted, press **Enter**.

5. At the command prompt, type the following cmdlet and then press **Enter**. Your IP address will be different.

   $ip = "172.16.0.X"

6. At the command prompt, type the following cmdlet and then press **Enter**:

   Enter-PSSession -ComputerName $ip -Credential $ip\Administrator

7. In the Windows PowerShell credential request dialog box, in the Password box, type **Pa$$wOrd** and then click **OK**.

8. At the command prompt, type the following cmdlet and then press **Enter**:

   netsh advfirewall firewall set rule group="File and Printer Sharing" new enable=yes

9. At the command prompt, type the following cmdlet and then press **Enter**:

   Exit-PSSession

10. At the command prompt, type the following command and then press **Enter**. Your IP address will be different.

    net use z: \\172.16.0.X\c$

11. At the command prompt, type **Z:** and then press **Enter**.

12. At the command prompt, type the following command and then press **Enter**:

    copy c:\odjblob

13. At the command prompt, type the following cmdlet and then press **Enter**:

    Enter-PSSession -ComputerName $ip -Credential $ip\Administrator

14. In the Windows PowerShell credential request dialog box, in the Password box, type **Pa$$wOrd** and then click **OK**.

15. At the command prompt, type **cd** and then press **Enter**.

16. At the command prompt, type the following cmdlet and then press **Enter**:

    djoin /requestodj /loadfile c:\odjblob /windowspath c:\windows /localos

17. To reboot the computer, at the command prompt, type the following cmdlet and then press **Enter**:

    shutdown /r /t 5

Implementing Roles and Features on Nano Server

If you already used the `Set-Item WSMan:\localhost\Client\TrustedHosts` command on a remote computer, you can use the remote computer to get and add Windows server roles and features.

CERTIFICATION READY
Implement roles and
features on Nano Server.
Objective 1.2

To view a list of current Window Server roles and features, you can execute the following Windows PowerShell command from a remote computer:

`Get-WindowsFeature -comp nano-svr1`

When you run the `get-windowsfeature` command, it looks similar to Figure 11-3.

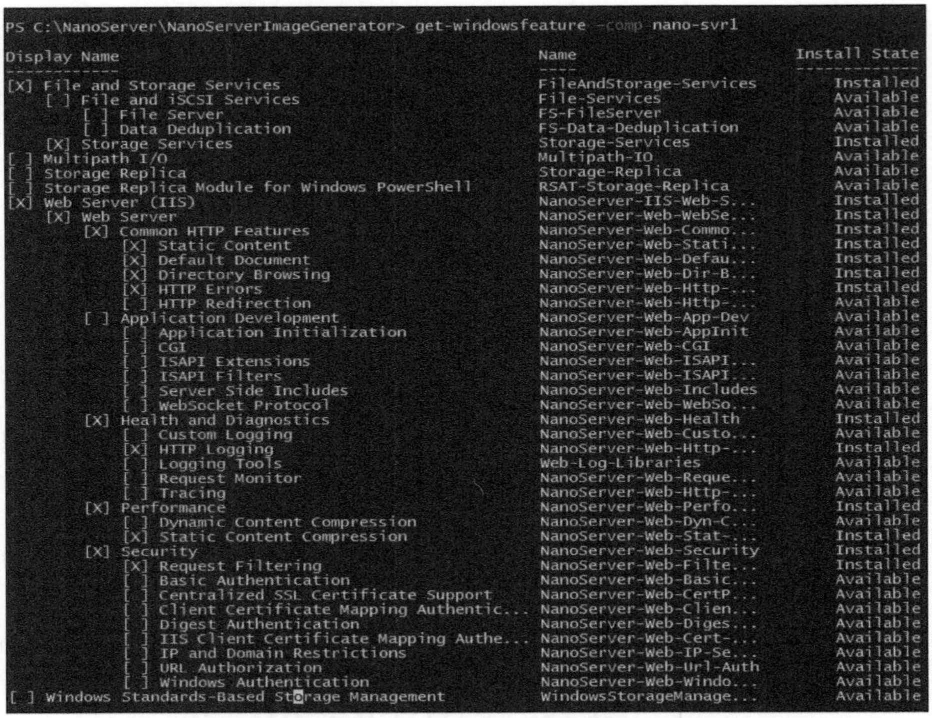

Figure 11-3

Using the get-windows
feature cmdlet

```
PS C:\NanoServer\NanoServerImageGenerator> get-windowsfeature -comp nano-svr1

Display Name                                        Name                        Install State
------------                                        ----                        -------------
[X] File and Storage Services                       FileAndStorage-Services     Installed
    [ ] File and iSCSI Services                     File-Services               Available
        [ ] File Server                             FS-FileServer               Available
        [ ] Data Deduplication                      FS-Data-Deduplication       Available
    [X] Storage Services                            Storage-Services            Installed
[ ] Multipath I/O                                   Multipath-IO                Available
[ ] Storage Replica                                 Storage-Replica             Available
[ ] Storage Replica Module for Windows PowerShell   RSAT-Storage-Replica        Available
[X] Web Server (IIS)                                NanoServer-IIS-Web-S...     Installed
    [X] Web Server                                  NanoServer-Web-WebSe...     Installed
        [X] Common HTTP Features                    NanoServer-Web-Commo...     Installed
            [X] Static Content                      NanoServer-Web-Stati...     Installed
            [X] Default Document                    NanoServer-Web-Defau...     Installed
            [X] Directory Browsing                  NanoServer-Web-Dir-B...     Installed
            [X] HTTP Errors                         NanoServer-Web-Http-...     Installed
            [ ] HTTP Redirection                    NanoServer-Web-Http-...     Available
        [ ] Application Development                 NanoServer-Web-App-Dev      Available
            [ ] Application Initialization          NanoServer-Web-AppInit      Available
            [ ] CGI                                 NanoServer-Web-CGI          Available
            [ ] ISAPI Extensions                    NanoServer-Web-ISAPI...     Available
            [ ] ISAPI Filters                       NanoServer-Web-ISAPI...     Available
            [ ] Server Side Includes                NanoServer-Web-Includes     Available
            [ ] WebSocket Protocol                  NanoServer-Web-WebSo...     Available
        [X] Health and Diagnostics                  NanoServer-Web-Health       Installed
            [ ] Custom Logging                      NanoServer-Web-Custo...     Available
            [X] HTTP Logging                        NanoServer-Web-Http-...     Installed
            [ ] Logging Tools                       Web-Log-Libraries           Available
            [ ] Request Monitor                     NanoServer-Web-Reque...     Available
            [ ] Tracing                             NanoServer-Web-Http-...     Available
        [X] Performance                             NanoServer-Web-Perfo...     Installed
            [ ] Dynamic Content Compression         NanoServer-Web-Dyn-C...     Available
            [X] Static Content Compression          NanoServer-Web-Stat-...     Installed
        [X] Security                                NanoServer-Web-Security     Installed
            [X] Request Filtering                   NanoServer-Web-Filte...     Installed
            [ ] Basic Authentication                NanoServer-Web-Basic...     Available
            [ ] Centralized SSL Certificate Support NanoServer-Web-CertP...     Available
            [ ] Client Certificate Mapping Authentic... NanoServer-Web-Clien... Available
            [ ] Digest Authentication               NanoServer-Web-Diges...     Available
            [ ] IIS Client Certificate Mapping Authe... NanoServer-Web-Cert-... Available
            [ ] IP and Domain Restrictions          NanoServer-Web-IP-Se...     Available
            [ ] URL Authorization                   NanoServer-Web-Url-Auth     Available
            [ ] Windows Authentication              NanoServer-Web-Windo...     Available
[ ] Windows Standards-Based Storage Management      WindowsStorageManage...     Available
```

To install a Windows feature that is included with the Nano Server, use the Windows PowerShell install-windowsfeature cmdlet. For example, to install the File Server server role (FS-FileServer), execute the following command:

```
Install-WindowsFeature FS-FileServer -comp nano-svr1
```

To install a Windows feature from a package that is not included with the Nano image after you have created the Nano Server image, you need to shut down the Nano Server and mount the disk image of the Nano Server on the Hyper-V server with the Windows PowerShell Mount-DiskImage cmdlet. For example, if the Nano Server image was c:\Images\nanoserver .vhd, execute the following command:

```
Mount-DiskImage -ImagePath 'C:\Images\nanoserver.vhd'
```

The image will be mounted as a drive letter.

To install a package that is not already included with the Nano Server, use the Add-WindowsPackage cmdlet. If the image was mounted to the E drive, to install the DNS Server package, execute the following command:

```
Add-WindowsPackage -Path E:\ -PackagePath C:\NanoServer\Packages\
Microsoft-NanoServer-DNS-Package.cab
```

When you are done, dismount the disk image using the Dismount-DiskImage cmdlet. For the example, to dismount the C:\Images\nanoserver.vhd image, use the following command:

```
Dismount-DiskImage -ImagePath 'C:\Images\nanoserver.vhd'
```

UPDATING A NANO SERVER

To install the updates, visit the Microsoft Update Catalog to download cumulative updates for Windows Server 2016. After you download the .msu files and save them to a local directory such as C:\ServicingPackages, expand the .cab files from the .msu files into separate directories and then copy the .cabs into a single folder.

```
mkdir C:\ServicingPackages_expanded
```

```
mkdir C:\ServicingPackages_expanded\KB3176936
```

```
mkdir C:\ServicingPackages_expanded\KB3192366
```

```
Expand C:\ServicingPackages\KB3176936.msu -F:* C:\
ServicingPackages_expanded\KB3176936
```

```
Expand C:\ServicingPackages\KB3192366.msu -F:* C:\
ServicingPackages_expanded\KB3192366
```

```
mkdir C:\ServicingPackages_cabs
```

```
copy C:\ServicingPackages_expanded\KB3176936\Windows10.0-
KB3176936-x64.cab C:\ServicingPackages_cabs
```

```
copy C:\ServicingPackages_expanded\KB3192366\Windows10.0-
KB3192366-x64.cab C:\ServicingPackages_cabs
```

When you build the image, you can use:

```
New-NanoServerImage -ServicingPackagePath 'C:\ServicingPackages_
cabs\Windows10.0-KB3176936-x64.cab', 'C:\ServicingPackages_cabs\
Windows10.0-KB3192366-x64.cab' -<other parameters>
```

To apply the cumulative update on a running Nano Server, use the `Edit-NanoServerImage` cmdlet. For example, you might perform the following:

```
Edit-NanoServerImage -ServicingPackagePath 'C:\ServicingPackages_
cabs\Windows10.0-KB3176936-x64.cab', 'C:\ServicingPackages_cabs\
Windows10.0-KB3192366-x64.cab' -TargetPath .\NanoServer.vhdx
```

SKILL SUMMARY

IN THIS LESSON YOU LEARNED:

- Nano Server is a new installation option for Windows Server 2016. Although it has a small hardware footprint for Server Core, it has no local sign-in capability. It supports only 64-bit applications, tools, and agents.

- To install the Nano Server, you need a server running Windows Server 2016 and 800 MB of free disk space. Of course, you might need additional disk space to store data and additional processor and memory for the load that the Nano Server is running.

- The Nano Server cannot be installed directly from the installation media during setup. Instead, you access the Windows Server 2016 installation media NanoServer folder to generate a Nano Server image.

- After you install and place the Nano Server, you need to configure the Nano Server, including configuring networking and firewall, adding the server to the domain, and adding roles and features. You can then manage the server using Server Manager, Windows PowerShell, and other management tools.

- The main local tool to configure the Nano Server tool is the Nano Recovery Tool. It has all of the tools that will help you establish connectivity to your remote management tools.

■ Knowledge Assessment

Multiple Choice

Select the correct answer for each of the following questions.

1. Which type of server has a smaller hardware footprint than Server Core and has no local sign-in capability?
   a. Server with Desktop Experience
   b. Nano Server
   c. Reduced Footprint Server
   d. Compressed Server

2. Which of the following is the minimum amount of disk space for a Nano Server?
   a. 400 MB
   b. 800 MB
   c. 1 GB
   d. 1.4 GB

3. Which of the following are methods used to install Nano Server? (Choose three answers.)
   a. Deploy a VHD as a bootable drive on a physical computer.
   b. Deploy a WIM file in Hyper-V.
   c. Deploy a Nano Server WIM file on a physical computer.
   d. Deploy a VHD image that will be hosted as a virtual machine on a Hyper-V host.

4. Which Windows PowerShell cmdlet is used to create a Nano Server?
   a. `Set-NanoServerImage`
   b. `New-NanoServer`
   c. `New-NanoServerImage`
   d. `Create-NanoServer`

5. Which Nano Server tool is used to configure networking, firewall rules, and WinRM?
   a. Nano Recovery Tool
   b. Nano Setup Tool
   c. Nano Configuration Tool
   d. Nano Remote Configuration Tool

6. Which Windows PowerShell cmdlet is used to add a Windows package to a Nano Server that is not included with the Nano Server?
   a. `Install-WindowsFeature`
   b. `Update-WindowsFeature`
   c. `Add-WindowsPackage`
   d. `Add-Features`

Best Answer

Choose the letter that corresponds to the best answer. More than one answer choice may achieve the goal. Select the BEST answer.

1. Which type of server should be used to create a secure virtual machine that has the smallest security footprint?
   a. Core Server
   b. Nano Server
   c. Server with Desktop Experience
   d. Reduced Server

Build a List

1. Specify the correct order of the steps necessary for adding a Nano Server to a domain.

   _____ On a domain controller, use the `Set-Item WSMan` cmdlet that will add the computer to the trusted host list.

   _____ Connect to the Nano Server with the `Enter-PSSession` cmdlet.

   _____ Reboot the Nano Server.

   _____ Configure the Windows Firewall on the Nano Server.

   _____ On a domain controller, run the djoin.exe cmdlet.

   _____ Copy the odjblob file to the NanoServer and use the djoing command.

■ Business Case Scenarios

Scenario 11-1: Adding Features on a Nano Server

You are ready to create the Nano Server. You need to deploy the DNS server role on one server and the web services on two other Nano Servers. On all Nano Servers, you need to make sure Defender and Desired State Package (DSC) package is installed. Describe your recommended course of action.

12 LESSON

Deploying and Managing Windows Containers

70-740 EXAM OBJECTIVE

Objective 4.1 – Deploy Windows containers. This objective may include but is not limited to the following: Determine installation requirements and appropriate scenarios for Windows containers; install and configure Windows Server container host in physical or virtualized environments; install and configure Windows Server container host to Windows Server Core or Nano Server in a physical or virtualized environment; install Docker on Windows Server and Nano Server; configure Docker daemon start-up options; configure Windows PowerShell for use with containers; install a base operating system; tag an image; uninstall an operating system image; create Windows Server containers; create Hyper-V containers.

Objective 4.2 – Manage Windows containers. This objective may include but is not limited to the following: Manage Windows containers using PowerShell; manage container networking; manage container data volumes; manage Resource Control; create new container images using Dockerfile; manage container images using DockerHub repository for public and private scenarios; manage container images using Microsoft Azure.

LESSON HEADING	EXAM OBJECTIVE
Deploying Windows Containers	Determine installation requirements and appropriate scenarios for Windows containers
– Determining Appropriate Scenarios for Windows Containers	
– Determining Windows Container Installation Requirements	Install and configure Windows Server container host in physical or virtualized environments
	Install and configure Windows Server container host to Windows Server Core or Nano Server in a physical or virtualized environment
– Installing and Configuring Windows Server Container Host	Configure Windows PowerShell for use with containers
– Installing and Configuring Docker	Install Docker on Windows Server and Nano Server
	Configure Docker daemon start-up options
Managing Windows Containers	Install a base operating system
– Managing Base Container Images	Tag an image
– Managing Containers with Docker	Uninstall an operating system image
– Managing Windows Containers using Windows PowerShell	Manage Windows containers using PowerShell
	Create Windows Server containers
– Managing Container Networking	Create Hyper-V containers
– Managing Container Data Volumes	Manage Windows containers using the Docker daemon
– Managing Resource Control	Manage container networking

LESSON HEADING	EXAM OBJECTIVE
– Creating New Container Images Using Dockerfile	Manage container data volumes
	Manage Resource Control
– Managing Container Images Using DockerHub Repository	Create new container images using Dockerfile
	Manage container images using DockerHub repository for public and private scenarios
– Managing Container Images Using Microsoft Azure	Manage container images using Microsoft Azure

KEY TERMS

container host	Docker	Microsoft Azure
ContainerImage	Docker Build	NanoServerPackage
container image	Docker container	NuGet
container OS image	Dockerfile	OneGet
container repository	DockerHub	PackageManagement
containers	DockerMsftProvider	sandbox
data volumes	Hyper-V containers	Windows Server containers

■ Deploying Windows Containers

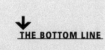

THE BOTTOM LINE

Windows Server 2016 introduced ***containers***, which are lightweight virtual machines that can provide an isolated environment for applications, similar to a virtual machine running on a Hyper-V host. The containers provide a separate operating environment for installed applications that does not affect the rest of the operating system and the operating system does not affect the container. A container is typically used to run a single application.

CERTIFICATION READY
Determine installation requirements and appropriate scenarios for Windows containers
Objective 4.1

Containers are also referred to as container-based OS virtualization. Windows as shown in Figure 12-1. The container has a virtual namespace with access to files, network ports, and its own list of running processes, which provide the security and reliability of the apps that run within the containers. Because the container is based on another instance, containers can be created quickly.

The container host uses namespace isolation to run one or more Windows containers. When the ***container image*** is created, it is derived from the container OS Image (base image, additional binary/libraries, middleware) and applications/data, is stored in a repository, and can

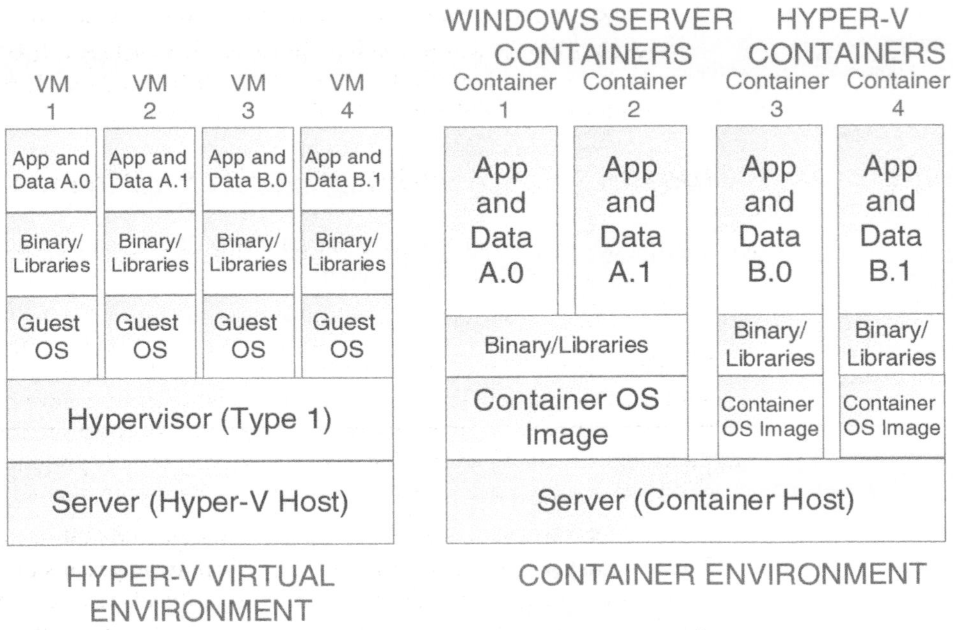

Figure 12-1

Comparing Hyper-V virtual
machines and containers

be interconnected with other containers to create a larger application. Windows Server 2016
supports two different types of containers, or run times:

- *Windows Server containers*: Shares the OS kernel with the container host and with all
  other containers that run on the host. Because it shares the OS kernel with the base container, it does not provide complete isolation of the containers. However, it does provide
  a faster startup.

- *Hyper-V containers*: Provides a more isolated environment than Windows Server containers as they do not share container OS images with other Hyper-V containers. Each
  Hyper-V container has its own OS.

The containers use the following terms:

- The *container host* is a physical or virtual computer that is configured with the
  Windows container feature.

- The *container OS image* provides the OS environment.

- The *sandbox* provides a layer that consists of all changes made to the container,
  including file system and registry modifications and software installations. You can keep
  or discard these changes as needed.

- The *container repository* is the place that the container image and its dependencies
  (such as libraries) are stored. By using a container repository, you can reuse the image
  multiple times on a container host.

When you create a container image, you discard the changes to make sure that the container
stays pristine or you can save the changes. You can also use the create container that inherits
the container changes or converts the changes into a new container image.

PackageManagement (also referred to as *OneGet*) is used to discover and install software
packages over the Internet. PackageManagement is accessed from the https://www
.powershellgallery.com. It is a manager of existing package managers/package providers
that can be accessed with Windows PowerShell. Some package manager providers include:

- *ContainerImage*: Helps you discover, download, and install Windows Container
  OS images.

- *NanoServerPackage*: Helps you discover, install, and download Nano Server Packages.

- *DockerMsftProvider:* Allows you to discover, install, and update Docker images.
- *NuGet:* Allows you to produce and consume packages. It is used for the Microsoft development platform, including .NET. It is also a searchable repository for scripts and modules around the PowerShell scripting language.

Determining Appropriate Scenarios for Windows Containers

Windows Server and Hyper-V containers have several practical applications for enterprise environments.

Windows Server containers are preferred when the OS trusts the apps that it hosts, and all the apps trust each other. This is particularly useful when you have multiple container apps and the apps compose a shared service of a larger app. In these situations, the apps deployed in the container should be stateless, which is an application program that does not record data generated in one session, such as user settings and events that occur.

Windows Server containers can be used to package and deliver distributed apps quickly. The benefits can be seen if you need to perform deployments on a regular basis, or for containers that change often. Containers can be easily adapted to deploy a test environment that matches your production environment and you can deploy this container in Microsoft Azure without changing it.

Hyper-V containers each have their own copy of the Windows OS kernel, and have memory assigned directly to them. As a result, the Hyper-V containers provide better isolation, which can allow untrusted apps to run on the same host. In these situations, each Hyper-V container would be assigned to a different tenant. If malware or malicious attacks compromised one container host, or VM, the other VMs that belong to other customers would be unaffected.

Determining Windows Container Installation Requirements

Just as you plan a virtual machine deployment, you need to plan for Windows containers. After you determine your needs and determine the appropriate scenario, you need to understand the container host and container requirements.

The Windows container role is only available on:

- Windows Server 2016 and higher, Full and Server Core
- Nano Server
- Windows 10 (build 14352 and newer)

If you want to use Hyper-V containers, you need to install the Hyper-V role. Windows Server container hosts must have the Windows OS installed to C:\, which does not apply if only Hyper-V containers will deploy.

If you deploy a Windows container host on a Hyper-V VM that is hosting Hyper-V containers, you need to enable nested virtualization. Nested virtualization has the following requirements:

- At least 4 gigabytes (GB) of memory available for the virtualized Hyper-V host
- On the host system, you need:
  - Windows Server 2016 and newer
  - Windows 10 (build 10565 and newer)

- On the container host VM, you need:
  - Windows Server 2016 (Full or Server Core)
  - Nano Server
- A processor with Intel VT-x
- The container host VM requires at least two virtual processors

Microsoft restricts which image you can use with each container type, as outlined in Table 12-1.

Table 12-1

Containers That Run on Host Operating Systems

HOST OS	WINDOWS SERVER CONTAINER	HYPER-V CONTAINER
Windows Server with Desktop Experience	Server Core image or Nano Server	Server Core image or Nano Server
Windows Server Core	Server Core image or Nano Server	Server Core image or Nano Server
Windows Server Nano	Nano Server	Server Core image or Nano Server
Windows 10	Not Available	Server Core image or Nano Server

Installing and Configuring Windows Server Container Host

Before you can use containers in Windows Server 2016, you need to deploy a container host, which can be a physical host computer or a VM. You can use Windows Server 2016 with or without Desktop Experience or Nano Server.

CERTIFICATION READY

Install and configure Windows Server container host in physical or virtualized environments

Objective 4.1

CERTIFICATION READY

Install and configure Windows Server container host to Windows Server Core or Nano Server in a physical or virtualized environment

Objective 4.1

CERTIFICATION READY

Configure Windows PowerShell for use with containers

Objective 4.1

If you choose to deploy Windows Server containers on a Nano server, you need to prepare a Nano Server virtual hard disk with the container and Hyper-V capabilities by using the `–Computer` and `–Containers` switches:

`New-NanoServerImage -MediaPath $WindowsMedia`

`-BasePath c:\nano -TargetPath C:\nano\NanoContainer.vhdx -GuestDrivers`

`-ReverseForwarders -Compute -Containers`

If you want to deploy Windows Server host for containers, you perform the following high-level steps:

1. Install the container feature using Server Manager or by using the following Windows PowerShell command:

   `Install-WindowsFeature Containers`

2. Create a virtual switch in Hyper-V Manager, or using the Windows PowerShell New-VMSwitch cmdlet.

3. If you want to use a virtual switch configured with Network Address Translation (NAT), you must configure the NAT settings with the following Windows PowerShell command: `New-NetNat -Name ContainerNat`

   `-InternalIPInterfaceAddressPrefix "172.16.0.0/12"`

4. Configure media access control (MAC) address spoofing. For example, you can type the following Windows PowerShell command and then press Enter:

```
Get-VMNetworkAdapter -VMName Container Host VM | Set-
VMNetworkAdapter -MacAddressSpoofing On
```

To view the available package providers, you use the Windows PowerShell `Find-PackageProvider` cmdlet, as shown in Figure 12-2. To display the registered PowerShell galleries, you use the `Get-PSRepository` cmdlet.

Figure 12-2

Displaying available package providers

```
PS C:\Users\Administrator> Find-PackageProvider

Name                Version     Source      Summary
----                -------     ------      -------
GistProvider        0.6         PSGallery   Gist-as-a-Package - PackageManagement PowerShell Provider t
TSDProvider         0.2         PSGallery   PowerShell PackageManager provider to search & install TypeS
MyAlbum             0.1.2       PSGallery   MyAlbum provider discovers the photos in your remote file re
ContainerImage      0.6.4.0     PSGallery   This is a PackageManagement provider module which helps in d
DockerMsftProvider  1.0.0.1     PSGallery   PowerShell module with commands for discovering, installing,
NanoServerPackage   1.0.1.0     PSGallery   A PackageManagement provider to  Discover, Save and Install
PowerShellGet       1.1.1.0     PSGallery   PowerShell module with commands for discovering, installing,
GitHubProvider      0.5         PSGallery   GitHub-as-a-Package - PackageManagement PowerShell Provider
ChocolateyGet       1.0.0.1     PSGallery   An PowerShell OneGet provider that discovers packages from h
OfficeProvider      1.0.0.1     PSGallery   OfficeProvider allows users to install Microsoft Office365 P
GitLabProvider      1.3.4       PSGallery   GitLab PackageManagement provider
WSAProvider         1.0.0.4     PSGallery   Provider to Discover, Install and inventory windows server a
0install            2.12.0      PSGallery   Zero Install is a decentralized cross-platform software-inst

PS C:\Users\Administrator> Get-PSRepository

Name        InstallationPolicy     SourceLocation
----        ------------------     --------------
PSGallery   Untrusted              https://www.powershellgallery.com/api/v2/
```

To deploy Windows Server containers, use the following high-level steps:

1. Install the required Windows PowerShell module with the following command:

```
Install-PackageProvider ContainerImage -Force
```

2. List the available images by name, version number, and description, using the `Find-ContainerImage` command.

3. Install the named image with the following command:

```
Install-ContainerImage -Name ImageName -Version Number
```

To run Hyper-V containers, you need to install the Hyper-V role and the container feature. If the host machine is a virtual machine, you need to enable nested virtualization before installing Hyper-V.

Because the Windows Server containers and host share a single kernel, the container's base image must match the host. If the versions are different, the container might start, but functionality might be degraded. Therefore, Windows Server containers are blocked from starting when the build number is different. For example, the Windows Server 2016 RTM version is 10.0.14393.0 (Major.Minor.Build.Revision). The Windows Server 2016 Technical Preview was 10.0.14393.0.

Since the final release of Windows Server 2016, Microsoft has decided to shift more into using Docker to create and manage containers. Containers created with Windows and containers created with Docker are not compatible.

Installing and Configuring Docker

Docker is a collection of open source tools, solutions, and cloud-based services that are used for creating and managing containers. A *Docker container* is a software wrapped in a complete file system that includes everything it needs to run. Each Docker container runs as an isolated process in the user space on the host OS.

CERTIFICATION READY
Install Docker on
Windows Server and
Nano Server
Objective 4.1

CERTIFICATION READY
Configure Docker
daemon start-up options
Objective 4.1

The Open Container Initiative is an open industry standard with Microsoft as one of the founding members, so that developers can create, manage, and deploy both Windows Server and Linux containers by using the similar Docker tool sets. The tool set can be used to manage Windows Server containers and Hyper-V containers. On Windows Server 2016, you can install the Docker daemon for Windows Server hosts, which can be used with Docker containers, tools, and workflows in production Windows environments. At the time of this writing, Windows containers run on Windows Server 2016 or Windows 10 and they cannot be used to run Linux containers. However, the Docker tools used to create Windows containers are similar to the Docker tools used on Linux machines to create Linux containers.

INSTALLING AND CONFIGURING DOCKER ON WINDOWS SERVER 2016 WITH DESKTOP EXPERIENCE

Windows Server 2016 does not include the Docker Engine; you need to install and configure it separately. Before you install Docker, you need to install the Windows container feature. You then need to install the KB3176936 cumulative patch or the latest Windows Server 2016 cumulative patch. You will also need an Internet connection so that you can download the appropriate files.

 INSTALL DOCKER ON WINDOWS SERVER 2016

GET READY. To install Docker on Windows Server 2016 and enable the container feature, perform the following steps.

1. Log on to LON-SVR1 as **adatum\administrator** with the password of **Pa$$WOrd**.
2. Click **Start**. When the Start menu appears, type **PowerShell**. From the results, right-click **Windows PowerShell**, and choose **Run as Administrator**. The Administrator: Windows PowerShell window opens.
3. To install the OneGet PowerShell module, execute the following Windows PowerShell command:

   `Install-Module -Name DockerMsftProvider`

   `-Repository psgallery –Force`

   If you are prompted to install NuGet, type **Y**.
4. To use OneGet to install the latest version of Docker, execute the following Windows PowerShell command:

   `Install-Package -Name docker -ProviderName DockerMsftProvider`

   If a message appears stating that the package source is not trusted and prompting you to determine whether you want to install software from DockerDefault, type **Y**.
5. To restart the computer, execute the following Windows PowerShell command:

   `Restart-Computer -Force`

The Docker service will already be added to the Services console and will already be set to Automatic. Therefore, after the reboot, the Docker service will automatically restart.

INSTALLING AND CONFIGURING DOCKER ON NANO SERVER

Similar to Windows Server 2016, Docker is not included with Nano Server. Therefore, you need to download the software via the Windows PowerShell command prompt.

INSTALL DOCKER ON NANO SERVER

GET READY. To install Docker on Nano Server, perform the following steps.

1. Log on to LON-SVR1 as **adatum\administrator** with the password of **Pa$$W0rd**.
2. Click **Start**. When the Start menu appears, type **PowerShell** and press **Enter**.
3. Because the Nano Server does not have interactive logon capabilities, you need to add the Nano Server to the trusted hosts of the remote system, using the following Windows PowerShell command:

   ```
   Set-Item WSMan:\localhost\Client\TrustedHosts <IP_ADDRESS_OF_
   NANOSERVER> -Force
   ```

4. To create a remote PowerShell session, execute the following Windows PowerShell command:

   ```
   Enter-PSSession –ComputerName <IP_ADDRESS_OF_NANOSERVER>
   -Credential ~\Administrator
   ```

5. To use the Nano Server, you need to install critical updates. This can be performed with the following Windows PowerShell commands:

   ```
   $sess = New-CimInstance -Namespace root/Microsoft/Windows/
   WindowsUpdate -ClassName MSFT_WUOperationsSession

   Invoke-CimMethod -InputObject $sess -MethodName
   ApplyApplicableUpdates
   ```

6. Reboot the Nano Server by using the following Windows PowerShell command:

   ```
   Restart-Computer
   ```

7. Then, to create a remote PowerShell session, execute the following Windows PowerShell command:

   ```
   Enter-PSSession –ComputerName <IP_ADDRESS_OF_NANOSERVER>
   -Credential ~\Administrator
   ```

8. To install the OneGet PowerShell module, use the following Windows PowerShell command:

   ```
   Install-Module -Name DockerMsftProvider

   -Repository PSGallery –Force
   ```

9. To use OneGet to install the latest version of Docker, use the following command:

   ```
   Install-Package -Name docker -ProviderName DockerMsftProvider
   ```

10. Reboot the Nano Server by using the following Windows PowerShell command:

    ```
    Restart-Computer
    ```

Because you cannot manage Docker on Nano Server directly, you must prepare the container host by performing the following steps:

1. Create a firewall rule on the container host for the Docker connection (port 2375 for an unsecure connection, or port 2376 for a secure connection) using the following command:

   ```
   netsh advfirewall firewall add rule name="Docker daemon " dir=in
   action=allow protocol=TCP localport=2375
   ```

2. Configure the Docker Engine to accept incoming connections over TCP by first creating a daemon.json file at c:\ProgramData\docker\config\daemon.json on the Nano Server host using the following Windows PowerShell command:

```
new-item -Type File c:\ProgramData\docker\config\daemon.json
```

Then, run the following Windows PowerShell command to add connection configuration to the daemon.json file:

```
Add-Content 'c:\programdata\docker\config\daemon.json' '{ "hosts":
["tcp://0.0.0.0:2375", "npipe://"] }'
```

Use port 2376 if you are using secure connection.

3. Restart the Docker service by running the following Windows PowerShell command:

```
Restart-Service docker
```

If you plan to use Hyper-V containers, you need to install the Hyper-V role on a Nano Server container host with the following two commands:

```
Install-NanoServerPackage Microsoft-NanoServer-Compute-Package
```

```
Restart-Computer
```

To manage Docker remotely, you must install the Docker client on a remote system, such as your client workstation. To download and install the Docker client, follow these steps:

To download the Docker client, execute the following Windows PowerShell command:

```
Invoke-WebRequest "https://download.docker.com/components/engine/
windows-server/cs-1.12/docker.zip" -OutFile "$env:TEMP\docker.zip"
-UseBasicParsing
```

To extract the compressed package, use the following Windows PowerShell command:

```
Expand-Archive -Path "$env:TEMP\docker.zip"
```

```
-DestinationPath $env:ProgramFiles
```

To add the Docker directory to the system path, run the following two Windows PowerShell commands:

```
$env:path += ";c:\program files\docker"
```

```
[Environment]::SetEnvironmentVariable("Path", $env:Path + ";C:\Program
Files\Docker", [EnvironmentVariableTarget]::Machine)
```

Once completed, you can access the remote Docker host with the docker -H parameter:

```
docker -H tcp://<IPADDRESS>:2375 run -it microsoft/nanoserver cmd
```

To create an environmental variable DOCKER_HOST, which removes the -H parameter requirement, execute the following Windows PowerShell command:

```
$env:DOCKER_HOST = "tcp://<ipaddress of server>:2375"
```

With this variable set, the command is reduced to the following:

```
docker run -it microsoft/nanoserver cmd
```

■ Managing Windows Containers

↓
THE BOTTOM LINE

As an administrator, you must know how to manage the containers on a server. This is mostly done with the **docker** command.

In addition to creating containers, you can use the docker command to you can create and delete container images, delete containers, start and stop containers, and configure container networks. The **docker** command is one of those programs that features hundreds of available options. To see those options, search online for "docker commands."

Managing Base Container Images

As you might recall from earlier in the lesson, containers are built on a base image. Therefore, you need to install base images for Windows Server Core and/or Nano Server before using containers.

CERTIFICATION READY
Install a base operating system
Objective 4.1

To install the Nano Server base image, execute the following Windows PowerShell command:

```
docker pull microsoft/nanoserver
```

To install the Windows Server Core base image, execute the following Windows PowerShell command:

```
docker pull microsoft/windowsservercore
```

CERTIFICATION READY
Tag an image
Objective 4.1

To display the operating system container images, execute the following Windows PowerShell command:

```
docker images
```

CERTIFICATION READY
Uninstall an operating system image
Objective 4.1

To delete or uninstall a container image, use the following Windows PowerShell command:

```
docker rmi <image_ID>
```

If the image is in use, you can add the −f parameter to force the removal, as shown in Figure 12-3:

```
docker rmi −f <image_ID>
```

Figure 12-3

Removing a container image

To delete all images, use the following Windows PowerShell command:

```
docker rmi $(docker images -q)
```

You can tag an image with the `docker tag <image> <tag>` command, which can be used to help identify an image. A tag may contain lowercase characters, digits, and separators. A separator is defined as a period, one or two underscores, or one or more dashes. A name component may not start or end with a separator. Therefore, to give an image the tag of *Serverstandardbuild-1-2-2017*, you would type the following:

```
docker tag Microsoft/windowsservercore serverstandardbuild-1-2-2017
```

Managing Containers with Docker

The `docker` command allows you to manage your Docker containers, including listing your images and Docker containers, starting and quitting a Docker container, and removing Docker containers.

CERTIFICATION READY
Create Windows Server containers
Objective 4.1

CERTIFICATION READY
Create Hyper-V containers
Objective 4.1

CERTIFICATION READY
Manage Windows containers using the Docker daemon
Objective 4.1

The `docker` command can also be used to view your images saved in the repository and view your running containers:

- **docker images:** Lists the installed images on your container host. You use container images as a base for your containers.
- **docker ps:** Lists the running containers.
- **docker ps -a:** Lists all containers.

To create a container, you use the `docker run` command. For example, to copy the container `Microsoft/windowsservercore` and to open an interactive session with the container, use the following command:

```
docker run --name IIS -it Microsoft/windowsservercore
```

To start a Hyper-V container, you just have to add the `--isolation=hyperv` option. For example, to create the IIS container as a Hyper-V container, use the following command:

```
docker run --name IIS -it -hyper-v Microsoft/windowsservercore
```

To stop the running container, you just have to type `exit`. To commit the changes and create a new container, open another Windows PowerShell window and use the `docker commit` command. For example, to save the changes while creating a new IIS container, run the following command:

```
docker commit iis
```

To start a container, use the `docker start` command. For example, to start a container based on container ID, execute the following command:

```
docker start 64c20e22f795
```

To stop a container, use the `docker stop` command. For example, to stop a container based on container ID, execute the following command:

```
docker stop 64c20e22f795
```

Similarly, you can use the `docker restart` command to restart a container.

To access a running container, you can use the `exec` option and `cmd` option. For example, to access the eefba14d9760 container, use the following command:

```
docker exec -it eefba14d9760 cmd
```

To move a container, use the `docker rm` command. For example, you can use the following commands to remove a container based on the container ID and name:

```
docker -rm 64c20e22f795
```

```
docker -rm IIS4
```

To stop and remove all containers, use the following two commands:

```
docker stop $(docker ps -a -q)
docker rm $(docker ps -a -q)
```

Managing Windows Containers using Windows PowerShell

You can also use Windows PowerShell to manage your Docker images, containers and networks. However, before you can do this, you will need to download and install the docker-powershell module.

To register and install the module, you will need to perform the following commands using Windows PowerShell:

```
Register-PSRepository -Name DockerPS-Dev -SourceLocation https://
ci.appveyor.com/nuget/docker-powershell-dev
```

```
Install-Module Docker -Repository DockerPS-Dev -Scope CurrentUser
```

Then to show the docker commands, you can then execute the following Windows PowerShell command:

```
Get-Command -Module Docker -CommandType Cmdlet
```

For example, to list your container images, you can perform the following Windows PowerShell command:

```
Get-ContainerImage
```

To run the nanoserver container, you can use the Run-ContainerImage cmdlet:

```
Run-ContainerImage microsoft/nanoserver:latest powershell -In -T
```

To create new container from the container image named Image01 from the publisher Adatum, use the following Windows PowerShell command:

```
New-Container -ContainerImageName "Image01" -ContainerImagePublisher
"Adatum" -ContainerImageVersion 1.1.0.0
```

To start the Container01, you would use the following Windows Powershell command:

```
Start-Container -Name "Container01"
```

To stop the running Container01, you would use the following Windows Powershell command:

```
Stop-Container -Name "Container01"
```

To remove a container called Container01, use the following WindowsPowerShell command:

```
Remove-Container -Name "Container01"
```

Managing Container Networking

Similar to a virtual machine, each container has a virtual network adapter, which is connected to a virtual switch. To enforce isolation between containers on the same host, a network compartment is created for each Windows Server and Hyper-V container into which the network adapter for the container is installed.

Windows containers support four different networking drives or modes:

- **Network Address Translation:** Each container receives an IP address from an internal, private IP prefix. The container host performs port forwarding/mapping from the public address to the private address and vice versa.
- **Transparent:** Each container endpoint is directly connected to the physical network. Addresses can be assigned statically or dynamically using an external DHCP server.
- **L2 Bridge:** Each container endpoint is in the same IP subnet as the container host. The IP addresses must be assigned statically from the same prefix as the container host. All containers have the same MAC address, due to Layer-2 address translation.
- **L2 Tunnel:** This mode is used with private and public cloud deployments, specifically with Microsoft Cloud Stack.

To view the current network connection for the container host, execute the following Windows PowerShell command:

```
Get-ContainerNetwork
```

By default, the Windows Docker Engine creates a default NAT network with an IP prefix of 17.16.0.0/12. If you want to change the NAT network, you first have to remove the current container by executing the following Windows PowerShell command:

```
Get-ContainerNetwork | Remove-ContainerNetwork
```

To create a user-defined NAT network, you use the docker network create command. For example, to define the 192.168.1.0/24 prefix, use the following command:

```
docker network create -d nat --subnet=192.168.1.0/24
--gateway=192.168.1.1 MyNatNetwork
```

You then have to change the options in the C:\ProgramData\Docker\config\daemon.json configuration file, which might need be to be created if it does not exist.

To create a port mapping between a host and container endpoint, you need to specify the port translation when you execute the docker run command with the –p option. For example, to create a static mapping between port TCP:80 of the container host and TCP:80 of the container, execute the following command:

```
docker run -it -p 80:80 <image> <cmd>
```

If you want to create a static mapping between port 8080 of the container host and port 80 of the container, use the following command:

```
docker run -it -p 8080:80 windowsservercore cmd
```

To use the Transparent networking mode, create a container network with the driver name "transparent" with the following command:

```
docker network create -d transparent MyTransparentNetwork
```

If you want to use DHCP on a virtualized container host, you must enable MACAddressSpoofing on the virtual machine's network adapter. If you don't, Hyper-V host will block network traffic from the containers in the VM with multiple MAC addresses. To enable MACAddressSpoofing, use the following Windows PowerShell command:

```
Get-VMNetworkAdapter -VMName ContainerHostVM | Set-VMNetworkAdapter
-MacAddressSpoofing On
```

To use the L2 Bridge Networking mode, create a container network with the driver name "l2bridge" with the following command:

```
docker network create -d l2bridge --subnet=192.168.1.0/24
--gateway=192.168.1.1 MyBridgeNetwork
```

Managing Container Data Volumes

Containers are meant to run specific applications. However, when using containers, it is better not to use the storage on the container and use **data volumes** to keep data on the container host. Data volumes are stored in C:\programdata\docker\volumes.

CERTIFICATION READY
Manage container data volumes
Objective 4.2

To create a data volume, use the following command:

```
docker volume create --name volume01
```

To view all volumes, use the following command:

```
docker volume ls
```

To attach a volume to a container type and assign it to the c:\volume01 folder, use the following command:

```
docker run --name test01 -it -v c:\programdata\docker\volumes\
volume01:c:\volume01 microsoft/windowsservercore cmd
```

The mounted folder will show as a <SYMLINKD> link, as shown in Figure 12-4.

Figure 12-4

Showing an attached container data volume

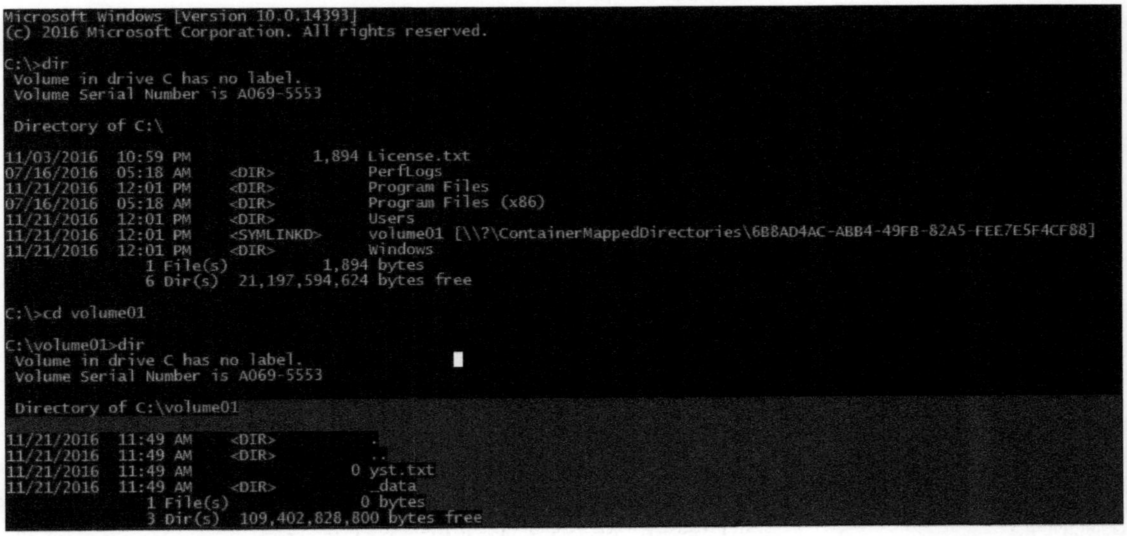

Managing Resource Control

Similar to running a VM in a virtual environment, you also need to monitor the performance of containers and the host that they are running on.

CERTIFICATION READY
Manage Resource Control
Objective 4.2

To view the running containers, you can use the `docker ps` command. You can then view the top processes running on a specific container by using the `docker top <container_id>` command.

When you use the `docker run` command to create containers, you can specify memory and processor settings that will give better control of processor and memory utilization. Some of the options include:

- **--memory="":** Memory limit (format: <number>[<unit>]). Number is a positive integer. Unit can be one of b, k, m, or g. Minimum is 4M.
- **--memory-swap="":** Total memory limit (memory + swap, format: <number>[<unit>]). Number is a positive integer. Unit can be one of b, k, m, or g.
- **--memory-reservation="":** Memory soft limit (format: <number>[<unit>]). Number is a positive integer. Unit can be one of b, k, m, or g.
- **--cpu-shares=0:** CPU shares (relative weight).
- **--cpu-period=0:** Limit the CPU CFS (Completely Fair Scheduler) period.
- **--cpuset-cpus="":** CPUs in which to allow execution (0-3, 0,1).
- **--cpuset-mems="":** Memory nodes (MEMs) in which to allow execution (0-3, 0,1). Only effective on NUMA systems.

For example, if you want to limit the memory of the container to 1,024 MB, execute the following command:

```
docker run –name web –it –memory "1024M" Microsoft/windowsservercore
```

To allow only one virtual processor for the container, use the following command:

```
docker run –name web –it –memory –cpuset-cpus "0" Microsoft/windowsservercore
```

Of course, you can combine these two options by executing the following:

```
docker run –name web –it –memory "1024M" –cpuset-cpus "0" Microsoft/windowsservercore
```

Creating New Container Images Using Dockerfile

Dockerfile is a text document that contains all the commands a user could call to assemble an image, including using an existing image as a base. Dockerfile can then be used to automate the creation of container images, which can be performed in rapid and precise re-creation of container images.

CERTIFICATION READY
Create new container images using Dockerfile
Objective 4.2

The main components to automate the creation of container images is the Dockerfile and the Docker Build. The **Docker Build** command consumes a Dockerfile and then triggers the image creation process.

A simple Dockerfile might look like the following:

```
# Indicates that the windowsservercore image will be used as the base
image

FROM windowsservercore

# Metadata indicating an image maintainer.

MAINTAINER administrator@adatum.com

# Uses dism.exe to install the IIS role.

RUN dism.exe /online /enable-feature /all /featurename:iis-webserver /
NoRestart

# Creates an html file and adds content to this file.
```

```
RUN echo "Hello World - Dockerfile" > c:\inetpub\wwwroot\index.html
# Sets a command or process that runs each time a container is run
from the new image.
CMD [ "cmd" ]
```

As you can see from the comments (which start with #), it uses the WindowsServerCore as the base image. It then uses DISM to install IIS on the server and to add content to the c:\inetpub\wwwroot\index.html file. When the container is executed, a command process is executed.

After you create a Dockerfile and save it to disk in the DockerFiles folder, you can use Docker Build to create the new image using the docker build command. For example, the following command creates an image named IIS:

```
docker build c:\dockerfiles -t iis
```

If you

Managing Container Images Using DockerHub Repository

> *DockerHub* is a cloud-based public registry service that is used for building and shipping applications and containers. It allows for centralized resources for container image discovery, distribution, change management, and workflow automation.

CERTIFICATION READY
Manage container
images using DockerHub
repository for public and
private scenarios
Objective 4.2

DockerHub repositories allow you to build and save your container images on the cloud, so that you can access them from anywhere that has an Internet connection. You can then share the images with coworkers, customers, or anyone else who requires access to them. You can also use DockerHub for automated builds and it can be integrated with GitHub or Bitbucket, which is often used to store source code.

To use DockerHub, you need to create a Docker ID at https://hub.docker.com. The Docker ID and related password will be used to access the DockerHub from the command-line interface (CLI) by using the following command:

```
docker login
```

To logout of docker, you would just use the following command:

```
docker logout
```

You can search the DockerHub repository and images by using the Search feature on the DockerHub website, or you can use the docker search command from the CLI. The search results can be filtered by searching an image name, user name, or description.

Image search results are based on criteria such as image name, user name, or description. Using the search criteria *IIS* will returns from all the repositories and images that contain IIS in the image name, user names, or description:

```
docker search IIS
```

After you locate the image you want, you can download it with the docker pull command from the CLI. For example, if the image was actually called IIS, you could use the following command to pull the image:

```
docker pull iis
```

If you want to share an image with others, you use the docker push command:

```
docker push Docker ID/Image Name
```

Managing Container Images Using Microsoft Azure

> In some situations, you might have a need to deploy container images to the cloud, such as Microsoft Azure. Because containers are extremely lightweight when compared with virtual machine images, you can easily transfer and run multiple containers on a single host.

CERTIFICATION READY
Manage container images using Microsoft Azure
Objective 4.2

Microsoft Azure is a cloud-computing platform used for building, deploying, and managing applications and services through a global network of Microsoft-managed data centers. Although Microsoft Azure has its own web-based tools, you can also use System Center 2016 Virtual Machine Manager (VMM) and App Controller.

Microsoft Azure includes the following features:

- Websites with support for ASP.NET, PHP, Node.js, or Python that can be deployed using FTP, Git, Mercurial, or Team Foundation Server
- Virtual machines that run both Windows Server and Linux virtual machines
- Cloud services, including the Microsoft Platform as a Service (PaaS) environment that is used to create scalable applications and services
- Data management using SQL Database (formerly known as SQL Azure Database) that can integrate with Active Directory, Microsoft System Center, and Hadoop
- Media services that use PaaS to provide encoding, content protection, streaming, and/ or analytics

With Azure, you can deploy Docker using one of the following methods:

- A Docker Machine Azure driver to deploy Docker hosts within Azure
- An Azure Docker VM extension for template deployments
- An Azure container service cluster

Azure Docker fully supports Windows containers that are deployed to Windows virtual machines running on Microsoft Azure. For these situations, you can use the Docker Machine Azure driver to deploy Docker hosts on Azure.

Of course, similar to DockerHub, you need to have an Azure account. Then, you can create Docker host VMs on Azure by using the `docker-machine create` command with the `-d azure` Azure driver option. For example, to create a VM named DockerVM that is accessible from port 80 and can be accessed via Secure Shell (SSH), you use the following command:

```
docker-machine create -d azure \

--azure-ssh-user ops \

--azure-subscription-id Azure_Subscription_ID \

--azure-open-port 80 \

machine
```

For a template-based deployment, you can use the Docker VM extension for Azure VMs, which allows you to integrate with Azure Resource Manager template deployments. The Azure Docker VM extension installs and configures the Docker daemon, the Docker client, and Docker Compose in your Linux VM. You can also use Docker Compose to define and deploy container apps and you can use the Azure Resource Manager template to deploy a solution throughout the development life cycle.

Lastly, the Azure Container Service provides the rapid deployment of open source container clustering through Docker Swarm cluster, which can be accessed via Azure Resource Manager templates or the Azure portal. Docker Swarm clusters are ideal for production-ready, scalable deployments that take advantage of the additional scheduling and management tools that Docker Swarm provides. Docker Swarm provides container workloads across a pooled set of Docker hosts, which allows you to manage a collection of VMs as a set.

SKILL SUMMARY

IN THIS LESSON YOU LEARNED:

- Windows Server 2016 introduced containers, which are lightweight virtual machines that can provide an isolated environment for applications, similar to a virtual machine running on a Hyper-V host. The containers provide a complete operating environment for installed applications that does not affect the rest of the operating system and the operating system does not affect the container. A container is usually used to run a single application.

- PackageManagement (also referred to as OneGet) is used to discover and install software packages over the Internet. Package Management is accessed from https://www .powershellgallery.com.

- Docker is a collection of open source tools, solutions, and cloud-based services that are used for creating and managing containers. A Docker container is a software wrapped in a complete file system that includes everything it needs to run. Each Docker container runs as an isolated process in the user space on the host OS.

- The docker command allows you to manage your Docker containers, including listing your images and Docker containers, starting and quitting a Docker container, and removing Docker containers.

- The Dockerfile is a text document that contains all the commands a user could call to assemble an image, including using an existing image as a base. The Dockerfile can then be used to automate the creation of container images, which can be performed in rapid and precise re-creation of container images.

- DockerHub is a cloud-based public registry service that is used for building and shipping applications and containers. It allows for centralized resources for container image discovery, distribution, change management, and workflow automation.

■ Knowledge Assessment

Multiple Choice

Select the correct answer for each of the following questions.

1. Which of the following is a lightweight virtual machine that can provide an isolated environment for applications?
   a. Containers
   b. ESXi node
   c. VDI node
   d. Virtual namespace

2. Microsoft PackageManagement is also known as which of the following?
   a. Sandbox
   b. DockerMsftProvider
   c. NuGet
   d. OneGet

3. Which type of container is used for a more isolated environment?
   a. Windows Server containers
   b. Hyper-V containers
   c. Container repository
   d. OneGet container

4. Which Windows roles or features are required to use Windows or Hyper-V containers? (Choose all that apply.)
   a. Container
   b. Docker
   c. Hyper-V
   d. OneGet

5. Which types of base images can be used with containers? (Choose all that apply.)
   a. WindowsDocker
   b. WindowsServerwithDesktop
   c. WindowsserverCore
   d. Nanoserver

6. Which command is used to create a Docker container?
   a. `docker start`
   b. `docker new`
   c. `docker run`
   d. `docker tag`

7. Which of the following is used as a mount point in Docker containers?
   a. PackageManagement
   b. Sandbox
   c. Container repository
   d. Data volumes

8. Which of the following is an industry standard for containers?
   a. Docker container
   b. Hyper-V container
   c. Windows container
   d. Resource container

9. Which command is used to view running containers?
   a. `ps -a`
   b. `docker ps -a`
   c. `docker ps`
   d. `docker image`

10. Which command is used to upload a container to the DockerHub?
    a. `docker ssh`
    b. `docker azure`
    c. `docker pull`
    d. `docker push`

Best Answer

Choose the letter that corresponds to the best answer. More than one answer choice may achieve the goal. Select the BEST answer.

1. Which type of container provides the best security for an application?
   a. Windows Server containers
   b. Hyper-V containers
   c. Container repository
   d. OneGet container

Matching and Identification

1. Match the term with its definition:

   ___ **a.** container host

   ___ **b.** container OS image

   ___ **c.** container repository

   ___ **d.** DockerMsftProvider

   ___ **e.** scanstate

   1. Used to discover, download, and install Windows container OS images

   2. A physical or virtual computer that is configured with the Windows container feature

   3. The place that a container image and its dependencies are stored

   4. The repository that allows you to discover, install, and update Docker images

   5. Used as a base operating system for the container

Build a List

1. Specify the correct order of steps necessary to installing Docker on Windows Server 2016.

   _____ Install the OneGet PowerShell module.

   _____ Install the container feature.

   _____ Install the docker package from the DockerMsftProvider.

   _____ Reboot the computer.

Business Case Scenarios

Scenario 12-1: Deploying a Website

Describe how to deploy a website and make it as secure as possible while reducing its resources used.

Scenario 12-2: Running Multiple Containers

You are an administrator of a Hyper-V server that is running 15 containers. You have noticed that one container is using much more memory and processing than the other containers, which is affecting the performance of the other containers. Describe how to ensure that the container does not use too many resources.

13 LESSON

Implementing Failover Clustering

70-740 EXAM OBJECTIVE

Objective 5.2 – Implement failover clustering. This objective may include but is not limited to the following: Implement Workgroup, Single, and Multi-Domain clusters; configure quorum; configure cluster networking; restore single node or cluster configuration; configure cluster storage; implement Cluster-Aware Updating; implement Cluster Operating System Rolling Upgrade; configure and optimize clustered shared volumes (CSVs); configure clusters without network names; implement a Clustered Storage Spaces solution using Shared SAS storage enclosures; implement Storage Replica*; implement Cloud Witness.

The following objectives are covered in Lesson 14: Implement Scale-Out File Server (SoFS); determine different scenarios for the use of SoFS versus clustered File Server; determine usage scenarios for implementing guest clustering; implement VM resiliency; implement shared VHDX as a storage solution for guest clusters.

Implement Storage Replica is covered in Lesson 4.

LESSON HEADING	EXAM OBJECTIVE
Understanding Fault Tolerance	
Implementing Failover Clustering	Implement Workgroup, Single, and Multi-Domain clusters
– Implementing Workgroup, Single, and Multi-Domain Clusters	Configure cluster networking
– Understanding Failover Clustering Requirements	Configure cluster storage
– Configuring Cluster Networking	Configure and optimize clustered shared volumes (CSVs)
– Installing and Creating a Failover Cluster	
– Configuring Cluster Storage	Configure quorum
– Configuring and Optimizing Cluster Shared Volumes	Implement Cloud Witness
	Implement Cluster-Aware Updating
– Configuring Quorum	Implement Cluster Operating System Rolling Upgrade
– Implementing Cluster-Aware Updating	
– Implementing Cluster Operating System Rolling Upgrade	Configure clusters without network names
– Configuring Clusters Without Network Names	Implement a Clustered Storage Spaces solution using Shared SAS storage enclosures
– Implementing a Clustered Storage Spaces Solution	
– Restoring Single Node or Cluster Configuration	Restore single node or cluster configuration

KEY TERMS

Active Directory–detached cluster	cluster virtual server	Nodes
active-passive cluster	dependent resource	nonauthoritative restore
authoritative restore	failover cluster	Private network
Azure Cloud Witness	heartbeats	Public-and-private network
cluster	Microsoft Failover Cluster Virtual Adapter	Public network
Cluster-Aware Updating (CAU)	multi-domain clusters	quorum
clustered services	No Majority (no witness)	single-domain clusters
cluster resource	Node Majority	Storage Spaces
Cluster Shared Volume (CSV)	Node Majority with Witness (disk or file share)	workgroup and domain clusters
cluster storage		workgroup clusters

■ Understanding Fault Tolerance

THE BOTTOM LINE

When a server goes down, it most likely adversely impacts revenue and productivity. If your network contains an external website or database that controls your sales, ordering, inventory, or production, server downtime can be detrimental to these business needs. If it is an internal server, it might not allow your users to perform their jobs.

As a server administrator, you need to minimize downtime by identifying potential failures and taking steps to avoid those failures and to reduce their effects. High availability is a combination of technology, protocols, and redundant hardware that ensures a higher degree of operational continuity during a given measurement period, while reducing the chances of disaster and failure. Generally, the term *downtime* is used to refer to periods when a system is unavailable. Availability is usually expressed as a percentage of uptime in a given year, as shown in Table 13-1.

Table 13-1

Availability Guidelines

AVAILABILITY %	DOWNTIME PER YEAR	DOWNTIME PER MONTH
99%	3.65 days	7.20 hours
99.9% ("three nines")	8.76 hours	43.8 minutes
99.99% ("four nines")	52.6 minutes	4.32 minutes
99.999% ("five nines")	5.26 minutes	25.9 seconds
99.9999% ("six nines")	31.5 seconds	2.59 seconds

When designing servers and the services they provide, they are often assigned service-level agreements (SLA), which state the level of availability those servers or services must maintain. Of course, to have a server design that can support five or six nines is much more expensive than supporting an availability of 99%.

If there is miscommunication about service-level expectations between the customer and the IT department, poor business decisions, unsuitable investment levels, and customer dissatisfaction are likely to occur. Therefore, you need to express availability requirements clearly so that there are no misunderstandings about the implications.

To make a server more fault tolerant, you should first look at which components are the most likely to fail and implement technology to make a system less likely to fail. Some of the components that are made redundant within a system are usually the following:

- **Disks:** Use some form of RAID and hot spares.
- **Power supplies:** Use redundant power supplies.
- **Network cards:** Use redundant network cards.

Although you can make these components fault tolerant, the entire server still won't be fault tolerant. Instead, you can use a cluster to provide server redundancy.

A *cluster* is a group of linked computers that work together as one computer. Based on the technology used, clusters can provide fault tolerance (often referred to as *availability*), load balancing, or both. If the system fails, including the processor, memory, or motherboard, a cluster that provides fault tolerance can still service requests.

The two most popular forms of clusters are failover clusters and load-balancing clusters. Common uses of clusters include:

- A load-balancing cluster for the front end that provides the web interface to the back-end servers
- A failover cluster for back-end servers, such as a database (such as SQL Server) or mail server (such as Exchange Server)

■ Implementing Failover Clustering

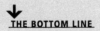
THE BOTTOM LINE

A *failover cluster* is a set of servers that work together to increase the availability of services and applications. The clustered servers (called *nodes*) are connected through a network connection (physical or virtual) and by software. If one of the nodes fails, another node may take over to provide services (a process known as *failover*). However, the failover may not be immediate and manual failover may be required, or desired. Failover clusters can be used for a wide range of network services, including database applications such as Exchange Server or SQL Server, file servers, or network services such as Dynamic Host Configuration Protocol (DHCP) services.

The most common failover cluster is the *active-passive cluster*. In an active-passive cluster, both servers are configured to work as one, but only one at a time. The active node provides the network services, whereas the passive node waits for something to happen to the active node where it cannot provide network services. If the active node goes down, the passive node becomes the active node and resumes providing the network services. When the failed node is restored, it becomes the passive node.

Active-passive clusters provide high availability, but do not provide scalability. The only exception to the scalability is if you implement file servers on Cluster Shared Volumes (CSVs), which are discussed later in this lesson. If you need higher performance, you can typically reduce the load or use more powerful hardware for the individual nodes.

Another type of failover cluster is the active-active cluster that is designed to provide fault tolerance and load balancing. Network services are split into two groups. One cluster node runs one set of network services while the other cluster node runs the other set of network services.

Both nodes are active. If one of the nodes fails, the remaining node takes over providing all the network services.

Failover clustering is best suited for stateful applications that are derived from a single set of data. For example, a database is stored in a single location and there can be only one database instance running.

To create a failover using Windows Server 2016, you need a minimum of two servers (physical or virtual) that meet the minimum requirements of Windows Server 2016 and that have identical hardware components. In addition, the servers must run the same Windows Server 2016 Standard or Windows Server 2016 Datacenter (including the same hardware version), and the servers should have the same software updates and service packs. While earlier versions of Windows servers required the nodes to be part of the same domain, starting with Windows Server 2016, you can use a single-domain cluster, a multiple domain cluster, or a workgroup cluster.

When you create the cluster, you assign network resources to the cluster, which can be enabled or disabled when the node is active or inactive. Every cluster has a ***cluster virtual server*** assigned, which includes the network name, and an IP address assigned to it.

Clustered services are services or applications that are made highly available by installing them on a failover cluster. Clustered services are active on one node, but can be moved to another node.

A ***cluster resource*** is the most basic and smallest configurable unit that may provide a service to clients, or is an important component that makes up the cluster. It can be a network application server or hardware device, such as a storage device, that is defined and managed by the cluster server. At any time, a resource can run only on a single node in a cluster, and is online on a node when it provides its service to that specific node.

So if you have an active-passive cluster, the active node will have the cluster virtual server with a virtual IP address and cluster resources (resources that you are providing and making fault tolerant with the cluster). When the active cluster goes offline, the passive cluster becomes the active node and the resources switch over to the new active node.

A ***dependent resource*** is a resource that depends on or is required by another resource to operate. For example, because a network name must be associated with an IP address, a network name is considered a dependent resource.

To perform graceful failover from one node to another node, the dependent resources are taken offline before the resources upon which they depend are taken offline. When the resources are brought online, the resources that are required for the other services to function are brought online first. A resource can specify one or more resources on which it is dependent. Resource dependencies also determine bindings. For example, clients are bound to the particular IP address on which a network name resource depends.

A failover cluster consists of the following components:

- **Nodes:** Servers that make up the cluster and that run the Cluster service. They host the resources and applications associated with the cluster. In Windows Server 2016, a failover cluster can have 64 physical nodes and can run 8,000 virtual machines on each cluster.
- **Network:** A common network that connects the cluster nodes. Three types of networks can be used in a cluster: public, private, and public-and-private.
- ***Cluster storage***: A storage system that is shared between cluster nodes and usually connects using Fibre Channel or iSCSI.
- **Clients:** Computers (or users) that use the Cluster service.
- **Cluster service:** The service that runs on Windows servers that manages and coordinates cluster resources to provide high availability.

CERTIFICATION READY
Implement Workgroup,
Single, and Multi-Domain
clusters
Objective 5.2

Implementing Workgroup, Single, and Multi-Domain Clusters

To create a cluster in Windows Server 2016, you first install the Failover Clustering feature. You then validate your hardware configuration and then create a cluster using the Failover Cluster Manager.

TAKE NOTE *

If you have previously installed and have Network Load Balancing (NLB) running, you should remove this feature. In addition, you should also remove any secondary addresses where the same address is used by the same server.

Windows Server 2016 introduces several types of clusters, which you use depending on your domain-membership scenario. They include:

- *Single-domain clusters*: Cluster nodes are members of the same domain.
- *Workgroup clusters*: Cluster nodes are not joined to the domain.
- *Multi-domain clusters*: Cluster nodes are members of the different domains.
- *Workgroup and domain clusters*: Cluster nodes consist of a mix of domain servers and members that are not joined to the domain.

If your servers are not part of an Active Directory domain, you cannot use Kerberos authentication when accessing cluster resources. Instead, you must use NTLM authentication. Thus, if you require Kerberos authentication, you need to select single-domain or multi-domain clusters.

Understanding Failover Clustering Requirements

To use a failover cluster, you should determine the resources and services that need to be provided by the cluster and that are critical to your organization. Therefore, you need to select the proper hardware to provide a reliable environment.

When creating a cluster, you should think "identical systems are best." Therefore, you should consider the following when selecting systems:

- Each node should have the same or similar hardware on each failover cluster node, including network adapters, SAS or Fibre Channel storage connections, motherboard, processor family, and BIOS (including BIOS version). Network adapters and storage connection adapters should have the same firmware and same firmware version.

- All hardware that you select for a failover cluster should meet the Certified for Windows Server 2016 logo requirements. When hardware is certified, the hardware has been independently tested to ensure that the hardware provides reliability, availability, stability, security, and platform compatibility. In addition, Microsoft provides official support for those items within a cluster.

- If you use iSCSI storage connections, each clustered server should have one or more network adapters or host bus adapters dedicated to the cluster storage. Of course, the adapters should be identical between nodes and it is recommended to use 1-Gbps Ethernet connections or higher.

- Each network adapter in each node should be identical and should be configured identically, including the same IP protocol version, speed, duplex, and flow control capabilities.

- When planning the network connections, you should always plan for redundant paths, including using network adapter teaming that connects to different switches.
- Each cluster node must run the same edition of Windows Server 2016.
- Each cluster node must have the same service packs and updates.
- Each node within the cluster should have the same Windows Server 2016 roles and features.
- It is recommended that you do not install the Active Directory Domain Services (AD DS) role on any of the nodes. Remember that multiple domain controllers provide fault tolerance without having a cluster.

Configuring Cluster Networking

Failover clustering uses only IP-based protocols and is, therefore, suited only to IP-based applications. Failover clustering now supports both IPv4 and IPv6.

CERTIFICATION READY
Configure cluster networking
Objective 5.2

When you connect the cluster to the network, you should consider using the following networks:

- *Private network*: Used by cluster nodes to communicate with each other
- *Public network*: Used by the clients to access the cluster and its shared resources
- *Public-and-private network*: Used to communicate with external storage systems

A failover cluster has full connectivity and communication with the other nodes in the cluster using a private network. In addition, the cluster is aware when a node is added or removed from the cluster. Cluster nodes are kept aware of the status of the other nodes and services through the use of *heartbeats*. Heartbeats transmit and receive using UDP port 3343 unicast (legacy clusters used UDP broadcast).

Each node of the cluster has a computer name and IP address. In addition, the cluster has a cluster name and cluster IP address. When users connect to the cluster, the users connect using the cluster name and cluster IP address. Therefore, no matter which node is active, users connect to the active node.

Because clusters usually need to access shared storage, the cluster should have a public-and-private network to communicate with the shared storage. If the cluster communicates to shared storage using Fibre Channel, the Fibre Channel connects using a dedicated network known as a *fabric*. If the cluster connects to shared storage using iSCSI, you can use the public network or use a dedicated public-and-private network to handle iSCSI traffic. Sharing a public network can cause contention and latency issues for the users and the shared resources. However, you can use the public network for a test network.

The Windows Server 2016 Failover Cluster uses a virtual network adapter called *Microsoft Failover Cluster Virtual Adapter* to communicate between nodes in the cluster. It is assigned an APIPA address (169.254.0.0/16) and an fe80::/10 prefix. The Microsoft Failover Cluster Virtual Adapter is used as an alternative network if the private network or connection fails.

After the cluster is created, you can right-click a cluster network and choose Properties. When the Cluster Network Properties dialog box opens, you can define whether cluster network traffic will communicate over the cluster network, as shown in Figure 13-1. You can also specify whether clients can connect through the network.

Figure 13-1

Configuring cluster network
properties

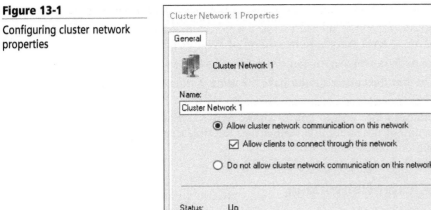

Installing and Creating a Failover Cluster

Initially installing a failover cluster is a three-step process:

1. Install the Failover Clustering feature.
2. Validate the cluster configuration.
3. Create the cluster.

You must first install the Failover Clustering feature, which installs the Failover Cluster
Manager. You can then use the Failover Cluster Manager to validate the cluster configuration
and create the cluster. When you validate the cluster configuration of servers and components
that will make up the cluster, you are validating whether everything is compatible within
the cluster and that you have the minimum resources to make a cluster. The four main tests
include inventory, network, storage, and system configuration.

 INSTALL THE FAILOVER CLUSTERING FEATURE

GET READY. To install the Failover Clustering feature, perform the following steps.

1. On the taskbar, click the **Server Manager** button to open Server Manager.
2. At the top of Server Manager, click **Manage** and click **Add Roles and Features**.
   The Add Roles and Feature Wizard opens.
3. On the Before You Begin page, click **Next**.
4. Select **Role-based or feature-based installation** and then click **Next**.
5. On the Select Destination Server page, click **Next**.
6. On the Select Server Roles page, click **Next**.

7. On the Select Features page, click **Failover Clustering** and click **Next**.

8. When you are prompted to add features required for Failover Clustering, click **Add Features**.

9. Back on the Select Features page, click **Next**.

10. On the Confirm Installation Selections page, click **Install**.

11. When the installation is complete, click **Close**.

VALIDATE CLUSTER CONFIGURATION

GET READY. To validate the cluster configuration, perform the following steps.

1. Open Server Manager.

2. Click **Tools > Failover Cluster Manager**. The Failover Cluster Manager opens, as shown in Figure 13-2.

Figure 13-2

Opening the Failover Cluster Manager

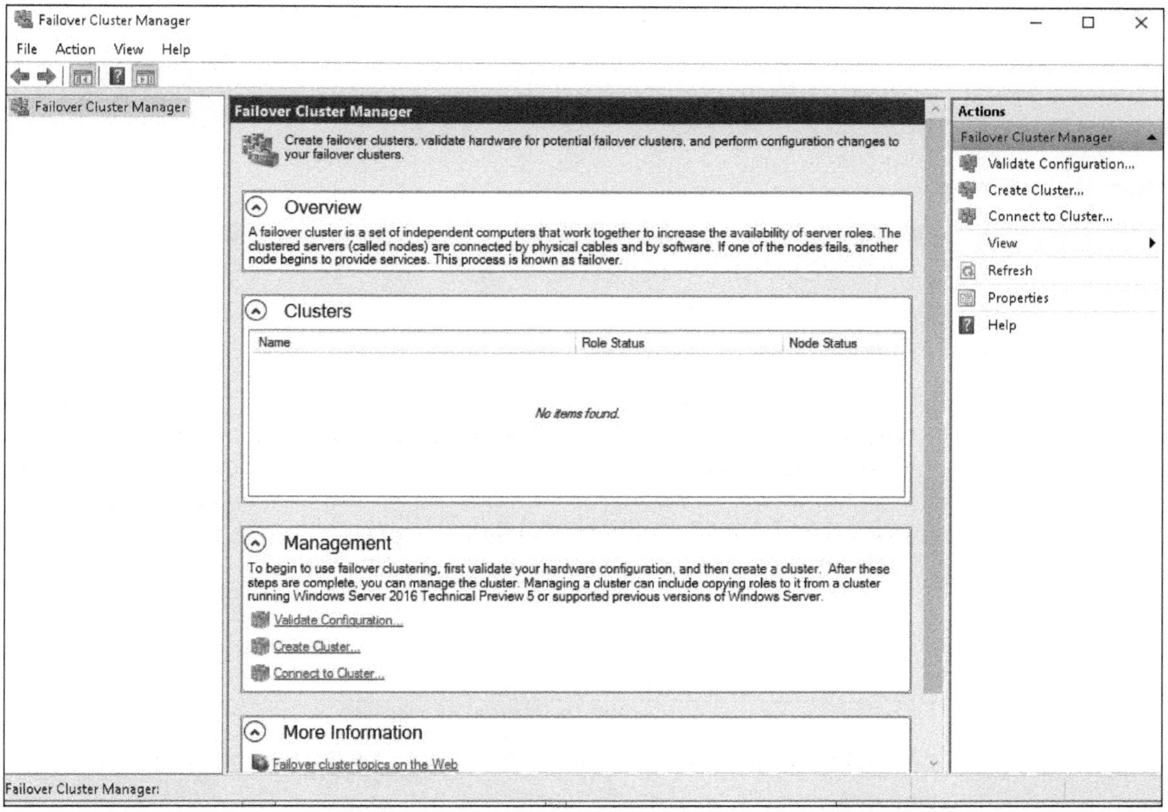

3. In the Actions pane, click **Validate Configuration**. The Validate a Configuration Wizard starts.

4. On the Before You Begin page, click **Next**.

5. In the Enter name text box, type the name of the first server in the cluster, such as **LON-SVR1**, and then click **Add**. Repeat for other servers that will be used within the cluster, such as **LON-SVR2**. After the computers have been added, click **Next**.

6. With the Run all tests (recommended) option selected, click **Next**.

7. On the Confirmation page, click **Next**.

8. When the testing is done, the Summary page appears. Click **View Reports**. The Failover Cluster Validation Report opens, as shown in Figure 13-3.

Figure 13-3

Viewing the Failover Cluster Validation Report

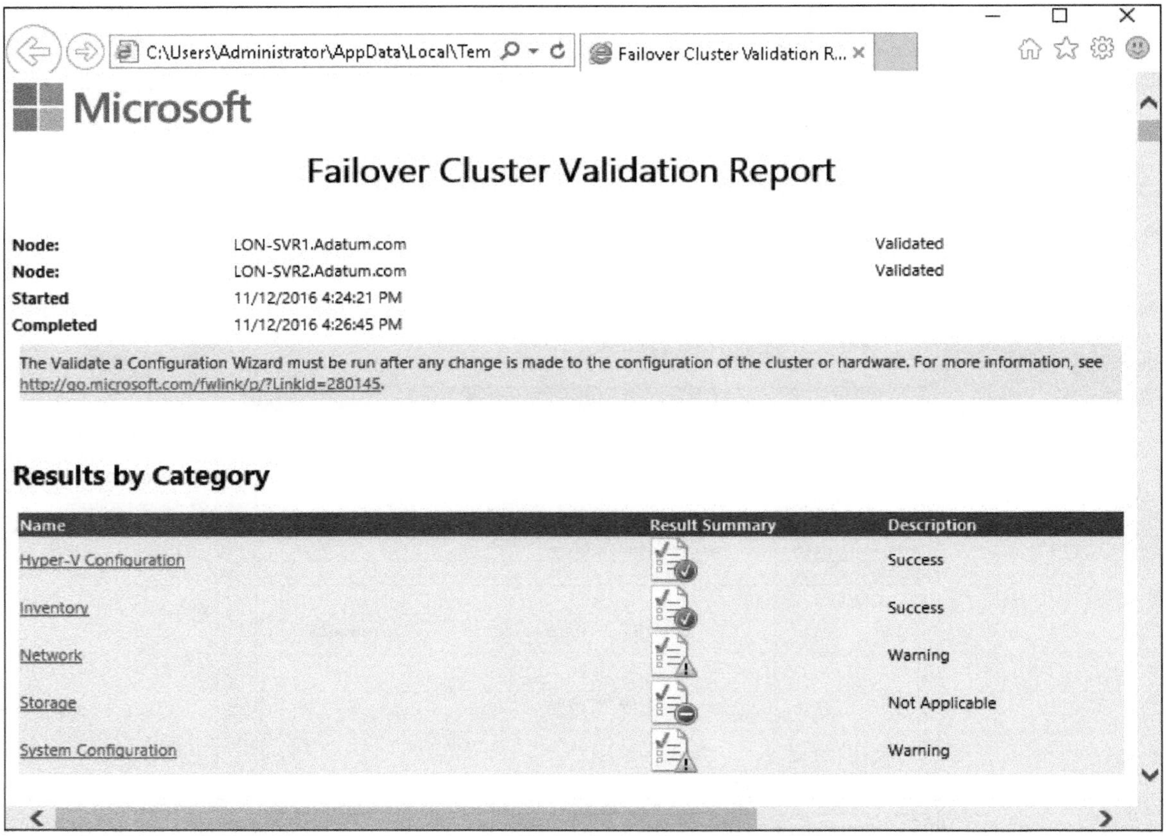

9. Close the report.

10. After the cluster has been validated, the Create Cluster Wizard opens. For now, you can close the wizard.

CREATE A CLUSTER

GET READY. To create a cluster, perform the following steps.

1. With the Failover Cluster Manager already open, in the Actions pane, click **Create Cluster**. The Create Cluster Wizard opens.

2. On the Before You Begin page, click **Next**.

3. On the Select Servers page, type the name of the first server of the cluster and click **Add**. Repeat for the other nodes of the cluster. When done, click **Next**.

4. On the Access Point for Administering the Cluster page (see Figure 13-4), type the name of the cluster, such as **Cluster01**, in the Cluster Name text box. In the *Click here to type an address* text box, type the address that will be assigned to the entire cluster (such as **172.16.0.22**) and click **Next**.

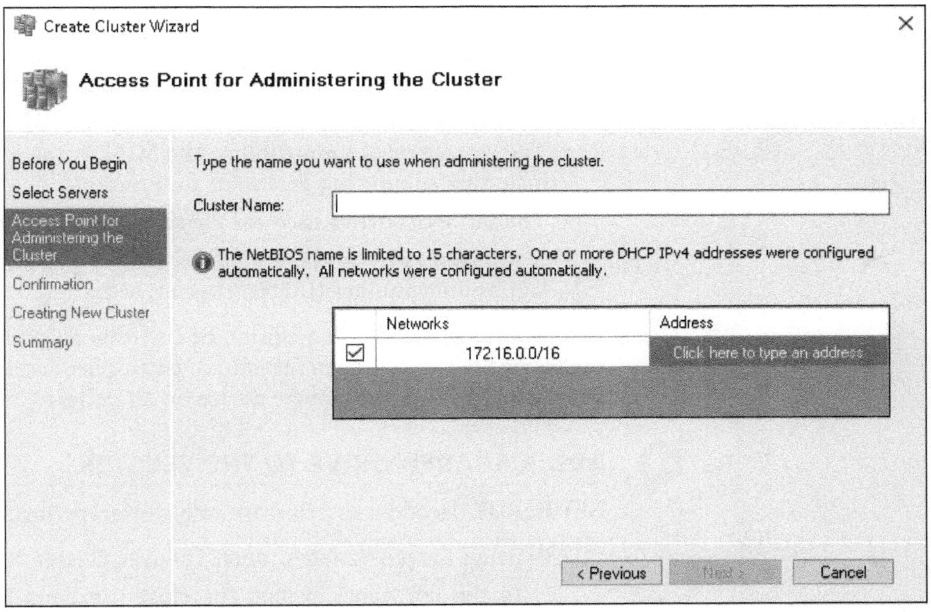

Figure 13-4

Specifying the name and IP address of the cluster

5. When the Confirmation page appears, click **Next**.
6. When the cluster is created, click **Finish**.

Configuring Cluster Storage

Most failover clusters use shared storage to provide consistent data to all cluster nodes. Shared storage is accessed over a network so that it can support multiple systems simultaneously.

CERTIFICATION READY
Configure cluster storage
Objective 5.2

There are four shared-storage options for a failover cluster:

- **Shared serial attached SCSI (SAS):** A low-cost option that requires the cluster nodes to be physically close to the drives. Typically, the SAS has a limited number of connections for cluster nodes.
- **Internet SCSI (iSCSI):** A type of storage area network (SAN) that transmits SCSI commands over an IP network. iSCSI drives can be connected to a Windows server using the iSCSI initiator, which is included with Windows Server 2016.
- **Fibre Channel:** A form of SAN technology that is based on fiber optics. It typically offers better performance than iSCSI SANs but is more expensive because it requires specialized equipment.
- **Fibre Channel over Ethernet (FCoE):** A form of SAN technology that uses the Fibre Channel protocol using 10-Gigabit Ethernet networks or higher on a converged network.

+ MORE INFORMATION

For more information on iSCSI technology, refer to Lesson 4.

To use a shared disk, you must use the following guidelines:

- For the disk type, use basic disks, not dynamic disks.
- For the file system type, format the disk as New Technology File System (NTFS).
- For the partition style of the disk, you can use either Master Boot Record (MBR) or globally unique identifier (GUID) partition table (GPT).
- The storage device must follow the SCSI Primary Commands-3 (SPC-3) standard, including supporting Persistent Reservations.
- The miniport driver used for the storage must work with the Storport storage driver.
- A storage device can be assigned to only one cluster. This is usually accomplished with logical unit number (LUN) masking or zoning.

Before you add storage to a cluster, be sure that all nodes can see the storage device and that the storage device has been initialized, partitioned, and formatted and that the same drive letter is assigned to the storage device on all nodes.

 ADD A SHARED DRIVE TO THE CLUSTER

GET READY. To add a shared drive to a cluster, perform the following steps.

1. Using Server Manager, open Failover Cluster Manager.
2. In the left pane, expand the cluster, expand **Storage**, and click **Disks**. The available shared disks are displayed.
3. Right-click **Disks** and click **Add Disk**.
4. When the Add Disks to a Cluster dialog box opens, select the disks that you want to include (see Figure 13-5), and click **OK**. The disks appear as shown in Figure 13-6.

Figure 13-5

Adding a disk to a cluster

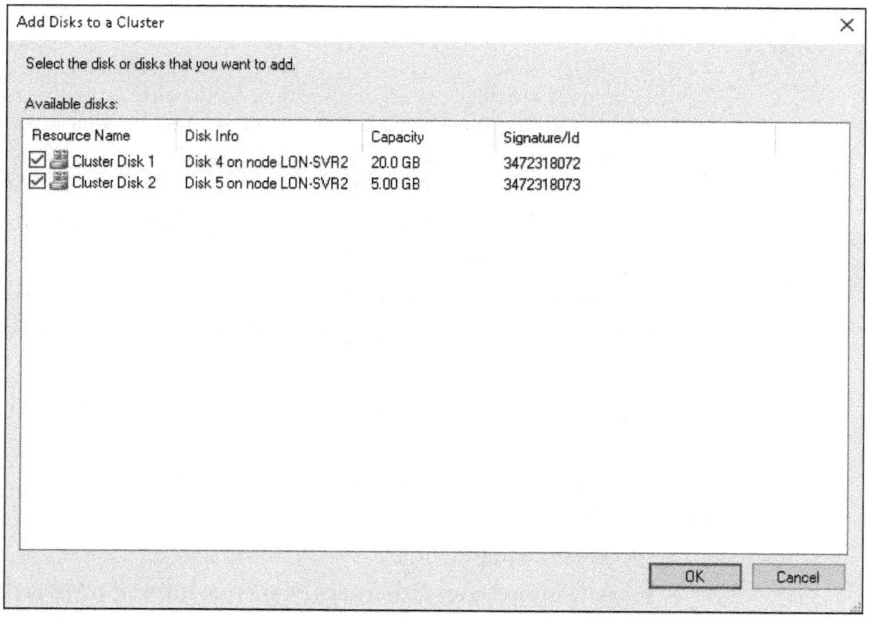

Add Disks to a Cluster ✕

Select the disk or disks that you want to add.

Available disks:

Resource Name	Disk Info	Capacity	Signature/Id
☑ 🖳 Cluster Disk 1	Disk 4 on node LON-SVR2	20.0 GB	3472318072
☑ 🖳 Cluster Disk 2	Disk 5 on node LON-SVR2	5.00 GB	3472318073

OK   Cancel

Figure 13-6
Displaying a cluster's shared disk

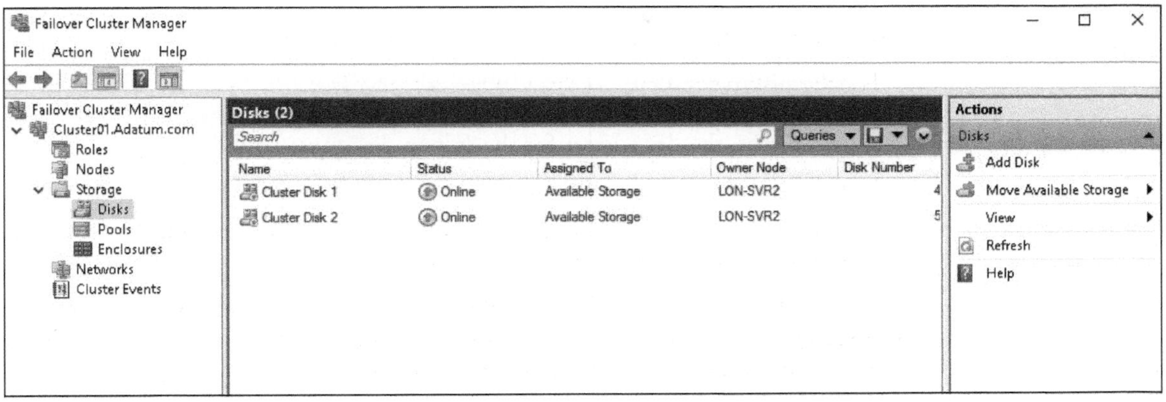

Configuring and Optimizing Cluster Shared Volumes

Traditionally, a single node controls a LUN on the shared storage. However, starting with Windows Server 2008 R2, Windows can use a ***Cluster Shared Volume (CSV)***, which allows multiple nodes to share a single LUN concurrently. Instead of taking control of the entire LUN, a node takes control of an individual file. With CSV, a clustered role can fail over quickly from one node to another node without requiring a change in drive ownership, or dismounting and remounting a volume. After a disk has been added to a CSV, the volumes appear as Cluster Shared Volume File System (CSVFS).

CERTIFICATION READY
Configure and optimize clustered shared volumes (CSVs)
Objective 5.2

Because volumes appear as CSVFS, applications can quickly see that the volume is a CSV; it then knows how to handle the volume. To make the volumes available to all cluster nodes, the volumes use a single file namespace, with the same name and path on any node in a cluster.

CSV in Windows Server 2012 and later has the following improvements:

- Multi-subnet support for CSVs so that you can achieve faster throughput when integrated with Server Message Block (SMB) Multichannel and allows the network adapters to support Remote Direct Memory Access (RDMA).
- Support for BitLocker volume encryption. Each node performs decryption by using the computer account for the cluster itself.
- Support for SMB 3.0 storage.
- Support for integration with Storage Spaces, which virtualizes storage on clusters of inexpensive disks.
- Support for Windows Server 2012 and later to scan and repair CSV volumes with zero offline time.

Windows Server 2016 can be provided with NTFS or Resilient File System (ReFS). CSV applications include:

- Clustered virtual hard disk (VHD) files for clustered Hyper-V virtual machines.
- Scale-Out File Server file shares to be used with the Scale-Out File Server clustered role. Scale-Out File Server clusters are explained in Lesson 14.

To use CSV:

- The disk or storage space must be a basic disk.
- If you want to use storage space for a CSV, Windows Server 2012 supports simple space or a mirror space, while Windows Server 2012 R2 and Windows Server 2016 can also be configured as a parity space. Storage spaces was discussed in lesson 4, Implementing Server Storage.
- On all nodes, the drive letter for the system disk must be the same.
- The NTLM protocol must be enabled on all nodes. This is enabled by default.

A CSV cannot be used as a quorum witness disk. In addition, in Windows Server 2016, CSV does not support enabling compression on CSV.

To add storage to the CSV, you must make the LUN available as shared storage to the cluster, and the shared disk must be added to the cluster. When you add a disk to the CSV, the LUN's drive letter or mount point is removed. It should also be noted that you cannot add shared storage to the CSV if it is in use.

➔ ADD A VOLUME TO A CSV

GET READY. To add a volume to a CSV, perform the following steps.

1. Open Failover Cluster Manager.
2. When the Failover Cluster Manager opens, expand the **Storage** node and click the **Disks** node.
3. Right-click the volume that you want to convert to a Cluster Shared Volume and click **Add to Cluster Shared Volumes**. To convert a volume from Cluster Shared Volumes, right-click the CSV, choose **Remove from Cluster Shared Volumes**, and then click **Yes** when prompted.

Windows Server 2016 has added new CSV functionality, including the following:

- Optimized CSV placement policies
- Increased CSV resiliency
- CSV diagnosibility
- CSV cache allocation
- CSV interoperability

With Windows Server 2012, one node is the coordinator node or owner for CSV. The coordinator node owns the physical disk resources associated with a LUN, including all I/O operations. With Windows Server 2016, the CSV ownership is automatically distributed and rebalanced across the failover cluster nodes based on the number of CSVs that each node owns. Ownership is automatically rebalanced when a CSV fails over, a node rejoins the cluster, a new node is added to the cluster, a cluster node is restarted, or failover is started after being shut down.

With Windows Server 2016, there are multiple Server service instances per failover cluster node. The default instance handles incoming traffic from Server Message Block (SMB) clients that access regular file shares. Another CSV instance handles only internode CSV traffic.

Problems with the Server service will impact the CSV coordinator node to accept I/O requests from other nodes and to perform the orchestration of metadata updates. In Windows Server 2016, if the Server service becomes unhealthy on a node, CSV ownership automatically transitions to another node.

In Windows Server 2016, you can view the state of a CSV on a per-node basis, including where I/O is connected directly or redirected, or whether the CSV is unavailable. If the CSV is in I/O redirected mode, you can view the reason. To view the state information and the redirection reason, use the Windows PowerShell cmdlet `Get-ClusterSharedVolumeState`.

In Windows Server 2016, you can now allocate up to 80% of the total physical memory. Increasing the CSV Cache limit is more beneficial for Scale-Out File Server scenarios. To control the CSV Cache, use the following Windows PowerShell cmdlets:

- `CsvEnableBlockCache`: Allows you to enable CSV Cache on an individual disk. The default setting is 0 for disabled; setting to a value of 1 enables CSV Block Cache on that disk.
- `SharedVolumeBlockCacheSizeInMB`: Defines how much memory (in megabytes) you want to reserve for the CSV Cache on each node in the cluster. Configuring a value of 0 disables CSV Block Cache.

In Windows Server 2016, CSV functionality has been enhanced to include support for the following features:

- Resilient File System (ReFS)
- Deduplication
- Parity storage spaces
- Tiered storage spaces
- Storage Spaces write-back caching

Configuring Quorum

> A *quorum* is used with a failover cluster to determine the number of failures that the cluster can sustain. If a quorum (the majority of the votes) is not reached, the cluster will stop running. Each voting element, except the file sharing witness, contains a copy of the cluster configuration, and the Cluster service works to keep all copies synchronized at all times.

CERTIFICATION READY
Configure quorum
Objective 5.2

For example, if a cluster has five nodes, it needs three nodes running to have a majority. Therefore, two nodes can fail and the cluster will still continue to function. If there is an even number of nodes, the cluster needs to have a witness assigned to the cluster to break the tie. The witness can be either a disk or a file share.

A cluster protects only against hardware failure, such as a server with a faulty power supply, motherboard, or processor. A quorum will not protect if a remaining cluster node does not have the resources to run properly, such as sufficient disk space, processing power, random access memory (RAM), or network bandwidth.

CONFIGURING A WITNESS DRIVE

For a simple failover cluster that has only two nodes, you want to configure a quorum drive. Therefore, you need to add a shared drive that is seen by all nodes.

When you configure the quorum, there are three possible quorum configurations:

- *Node Majority (no witness)*: Recommended for clusters with an odd number of nodes. It can sustain failures of half the nodes (rounding up) minus one.
- *Node Majority with Witness (disk or file share)*: Recommended for clusters with an even number of nodes. It can sustain failures of half the nodes (rounding up) if the witness remains online.
- *No Majority (disk witness only)*: Not recommended because the disk would be a single point of failure. This configuration allows the cluster to function as long as one node is available and the disks are online.

If you use a witness disk, the disk must be at least 512 MB. It must be dedicated for cluster use and not assigned to a clustered role. It cannot be a volume that is a CSV. The cluster database is stored in the disk witness, whereas it is not stored in the file share witness.

With Windows Server 2016, to reduce the risk that a cluster will go down because of the witness failure, by default the cluster determines quorum management options, including the quorum witness. Therefore, if you have an odd number of votes, the quorum witness does not have a vote; if you have an even number of votes, the quorum witness has a vote. In addition, if the witness resource is offline or has failed, the cluster sets the witness vote to "0". You can view the assigned quorum vote and the current quorum vote for each cluster node in the Failover Cluster Manager user interface (UI) by clicking the Nodes node.

To view the quorum witness vote, use the following Windows PowerShell command:

```
(Get-Cluster).WitnessDynamicWeight
```

A value of "0" indicates that the witness does not have a vote. A value of "1" indicates that the witness has a vote.

CONFIGURE THE CLUSTER QUORUM SETTINGS USING TYPICAL SETTINGS

GET READY. To configure the Cluster Quorum settings using typical settings, perform the following steps.

1. Open Server Manager and then open Failover Cluster Manager.
2. In the left pane, right-click the cluster, choose **More Actions**, and then choose **Configure Cluster Quorum Settings.**
3. When the Configure Cluster Quorum Wizard starts, click **Next.**
4. On the Select Quorum Configuration Option page, verify that **Use default quorum configuration** is already selected (see Figure 13-7). Click **Next.**

Figure 13-7

Selecting the quorum configuration

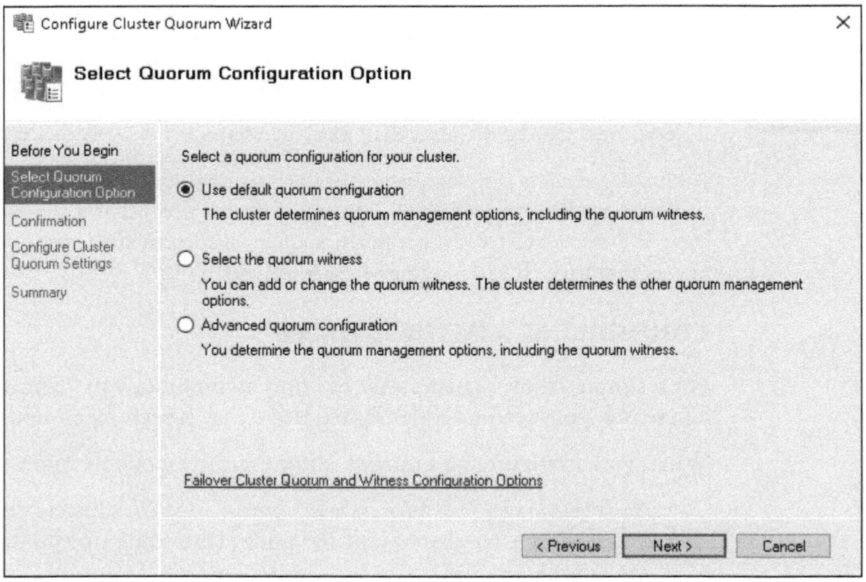

5. On the Confirmation page, with a Disk Witness being displayed, click **Next.**
6. On the Summary page, click **Finish.** The quorum disk will be labeled as *Disk Witness in Quorum.*

ADD OR CHANGE THE QUORUM WITNESS

GET READY. To add or change the quorum witness, perform the following steps.

1. Open Server Manager and then open Failover Cluster Manager.
2. In the left pane, right-click the cluster, choose **More Actions**, and then click **Configure Cluster Quorum Settings.**
3. When the Configure Cluster Quorum Wizard starts, click **Next.**
4. On the Select Quorum Configuration Option page, click **Select the quorum witness** and click **Next.**
5. On the Select Quorum Witness page (see Figure 13-8), click **Configure a disk witness** and click **Next.**

Figure 13-8

Selecting the quorum witness

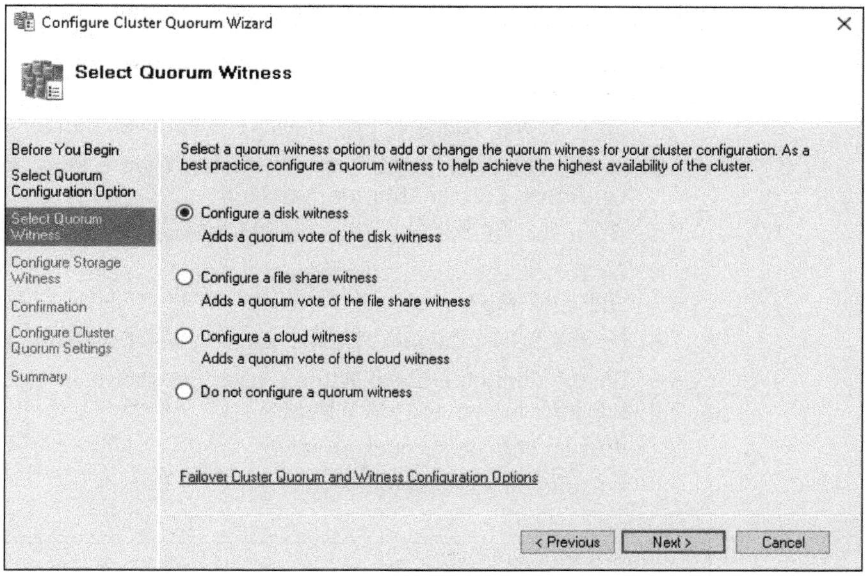

> **Configure Cluster Quorum Wizard**   ✕
>
> **Select Quorum Witness**
>
> Before You Begin
> Select Quorum Configuration Option
> **Select Quorum Witness**
> Configure Storage Witness
> Confirmation
> Configure Cluster Quorum Settings
> Summary
>
> Select a quorum witness option to add or change the quorum witness for your cluster configuration. As a best practice, configure a quorum witness to help achieve the highest availability of the cluster.
>
> ⦿ Configure a disk witness
>   Adds a quorum vote of the disk witness
>
> ◯ Configure a file share witness
>   Adds a quorum vote of the file share witness
>
> ◯ Configure a cloud witness
>   Adds a quorum vote of the cloud witness
>
> ◯ Do not configure a quorum witness
>
> Failover Cluster Quorum and Witness Configuration Options
>
> < Previous   Next >   Cancel

6. On the Configure Storage Witness page (see Figure 13-9), click the drive to be used as a storage witness and click **Next.**

Figure 13-9

Selecting the storage witness

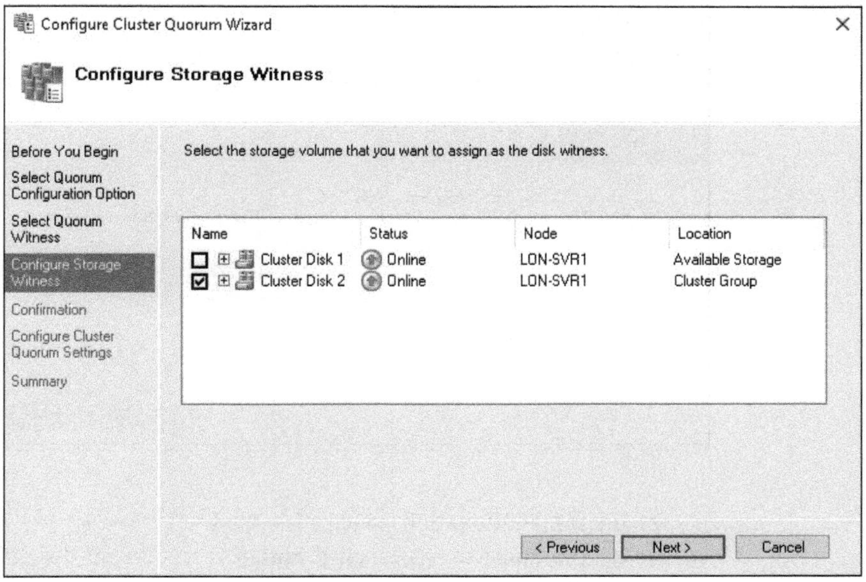

> **Configure Cluster Quorum Wizard**   ✕
>
> **Configure Storage Witness**
>
> Before You Begin
> Select Quorum Configuration Option
> Select Quorum Witness
> Configure Storage Witness
> Confirmation
> Configure Cluster Quorum Settings
> Summary
>
> Select the storage volume that you want to assign as the disk witness.
>
> | Name | Status | Node | Location |
> | --- | --- | --- | --- |
> | ☐ ⊞ Cluster Disk 1 | ● Online | LON-SVR1 | Available Storage |
> | ☑ ⊞ Cluster Disk 2 | ● Online | LON-SVR1 | Cluster Group |
>
> < Previous   Next >   Cancel

7. On the Confirmation page, click **Next.**
8. On the Summary page, click **Finish.**

CONFIGURING CLOUD WITNESS

Besides file share witness and disk witness, Windows Server 2016 supports *Azure Cloud Witness*, which is an ideal option when you run an Internet-connected stretch cluster that stretches over multiple geographical locations. Similar to a file share witness, the Azure Cloud Witness does not store a copy of the cluster database.

CERTIFICATION READY
Implement Cloud Witness
Objective 5.2

You should also consider the capacity of the nodes in your cluster and their ability to support the services and applications that might fail over to that node. For example, a cluster that has four nodes and a disk witness still has quorum after two nodes fail. However, if you have several applications or services deployed on the cluster, each remaining cluster node might not have the capacity to provide services.

⊕ ADD OR CHANGE THE CLOUD WITNESS

GET READY. To add or change the cloud witness, perform the following steps.

1. Open **Server Manager** and then open **Failover Cluster Manager**.
2. In the left pane, right-click the cluster, choose **More Actions**, and then click **Configure Cluster Quorum Settings**.
3. When the Configure Cluster Quorum Wizard starts, click **Next**.
4. On the Select Quorum Configuration Option page, click **Select the quorum witness** and click **Next**.
5. On the Select Quorum Witness page, select **Configure a cloud witness**.
6. On the Configure Cloud Witness page (as shown in Figure 13-10), enter the following information and click **Next**:
   - Azure storage account name
   - Azure storage account key

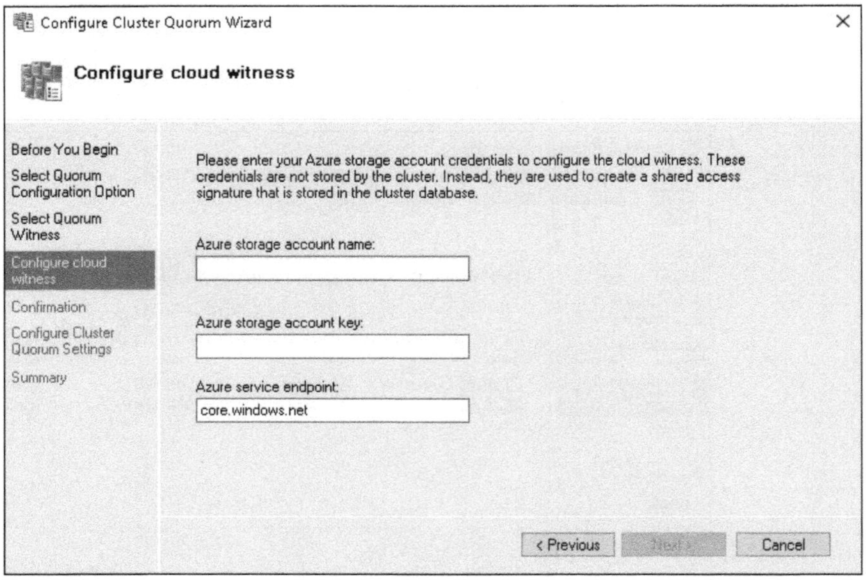

Figure 13-10

Configuring a cloud witness

7. On the Confirmation page, click **Next**.
8. On the Summary page, click **Finish**.

Implementing Cluster-Aware Updating

Applying Windows updates to nodes in a cluster always needs more attention and planning because having one update on one node and not on the other node can cause problems or corruption of data. If you don't want downtime, you must move resources manually from the node that you are updating, perform the updates on the first node, and then change the resources to another node and perform the updates on the next node. Starting with Windows Server 2012, *Cluster-Aware Updating (CAU)* lets administrators update cluster nodes automatically, with little or no downtime, particularly if you use Hyper-V with live migration.

CERTIFICATION READY
Implement Cluster-Aware
Updating
Objective 5.2

You can use CAU in one of the following two modes:

- Remote-updating mode
- Self-updating mode

With remote-updating mode, you install the failover clustering administrative tools on a CAU orchestrator (a remote computer running Windows 10 or Windows Server 2016 that is not a member of the cluster). The CAU is included in the Remote Server Administration Tool (RSAT). The administrator triggers the update process on the orchestrator computer. Remote-updating mode is useful for monitoring real-time progress during the Updating Run, and for clusters that run on Server Core installations of Windows Server 2016.

With self-updating mode, the CAU (installed on a node on the cluster) updates the cluster at scheduled times by using a default or custom Updating Run profile. During the Updating Run, the CAU orchestrator process starts on the node that currently owns the CAU clustered role, and the process sequentially performs updates on each cluster node. You can use self-updating mode, which allows the CAU to update the failover cluster by using a fully automated, end-to-end updating process, or you can trigger the updates manually. When using self-updating mode, you can check the progress of updates by connecting to the cluster and running the `Get-CauRun` Windows PowerShell cmdlet.

 UPDATE THE SERVER USING CLUSTER-AWARE UPDATING

GET READY. To update the server using Cluster-Aware Updating, perform the following steps.

1. Using Server Manager, open Failover Cluster Manager.
2. Click the cluster and click **Cluster-Aware Updating**. If you are prompted for credentials, log on as **adatum\administrator** with the password of **Pa$$w0rd**. The cluster and nodes are displayed.
3. Click the **Connect to a failover cluster** option and select your cluster. Click **Connect**. The cluster nodes appear, as shown in Figure 13-11.

Figure 13-11

Connecting to a cluster

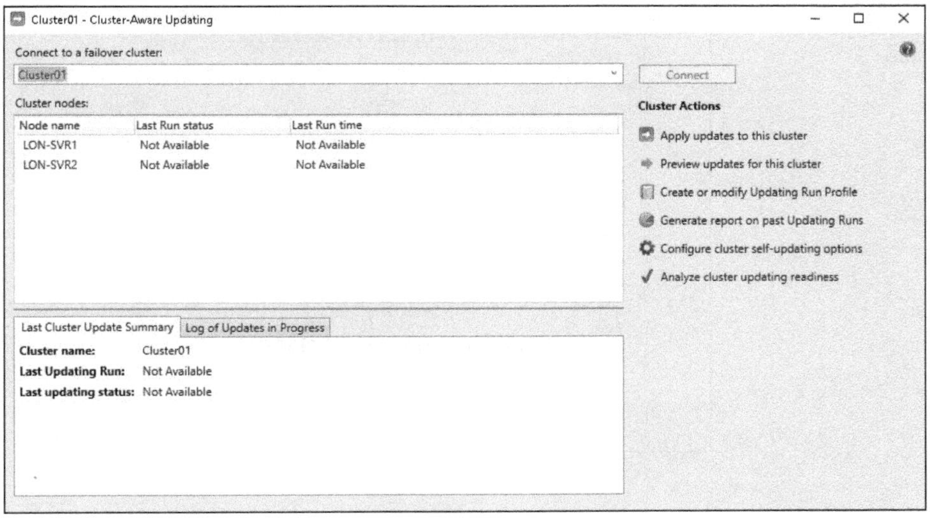

| Cluster01 - Cluster-Aware Updating | | | □ × |

Connect to a failover cluster:

| Cluster01 | ∨ | Connect |

Cluster nodes:

Node name	Last Run status	Last Run time
LON-SVR1	Not Available	Not Available
LON-SVR2	Not Available	Not Available

Cluster Actions

- Apply updates to this cluster
- Preview updates for this cluster
- Create or modify Updating Run Profile
- Generate report on past Updating Runs
- Configure cluster self-updating options
- Analyze cluster updating readiness

| Last Cluster Update Summary | Log of Updates in Progress |

Cluster name: Cluster01
Last Updating Run: Not Available
Last updating status: Not Available

4. To install the cluster-aware role on the cluster, click **Configure cluster self-updating options.**

5. When the Configure Self-Updating Options Wizard starts, click **Next.**

6. Click the **Add the CAU clustered role, with self-updating mode enabled, to this cluster** and click **Next.**

7. On the Specify Self-Updating Schedule page (see Figure 13-12), specify how often it should do self-updating and when it should occur. Click **Next.**

Figure 13-12

Scheduling self-updating

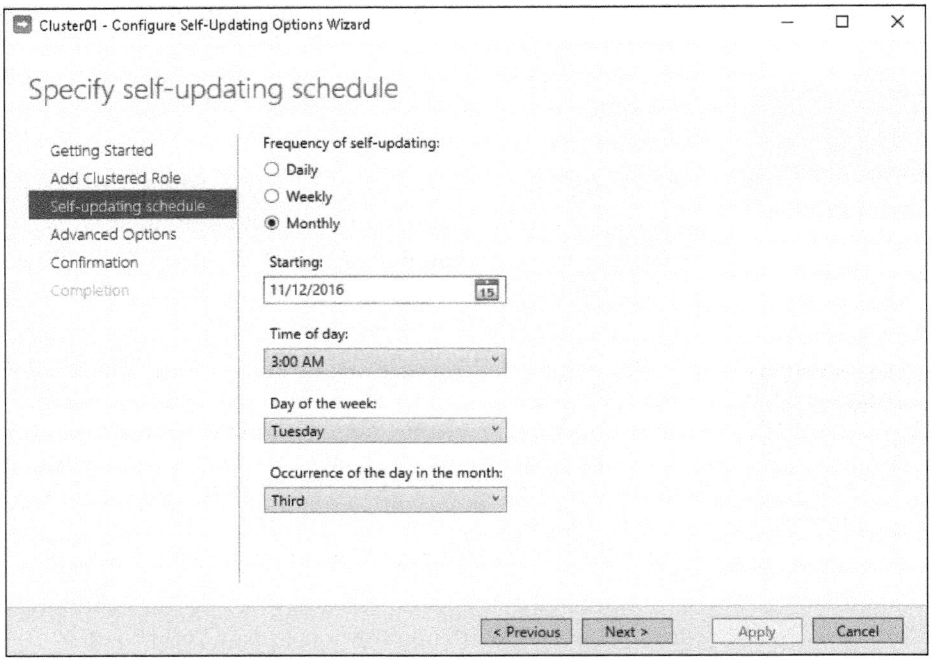

8. On the Advanced Options page (see Figure 13-13), you can modify the options that define how self-updating runs. Click **Next.**

Figure 13-13

Modifying advanced options

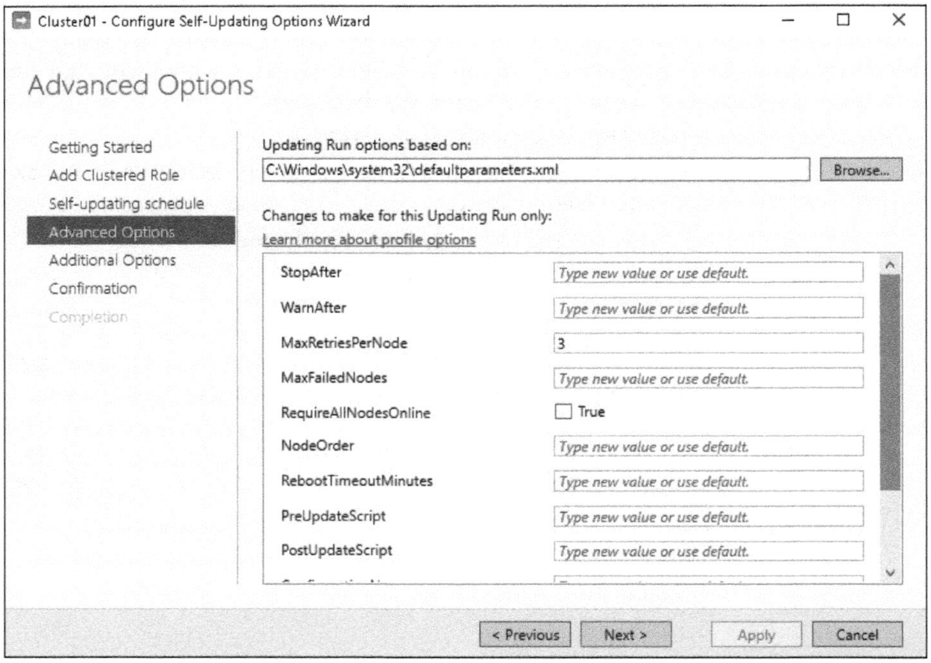

9. If you want recommended updates, click **Give me recommended updates the same way that I receive important updates** option and click **Next**.

10. On the Confirmation page, click **Apply**.

11. On the Completion page, click **Close**.

12. To manually apply updates, click **Apply updates to this cluster**.

13. When the Cluster-Aware Updating Wizard starts, click **Next**.

14. On the Confirmation page, click **Update**.

15. When the scheduling of the immediate updating is successful, click **Close**.

Implementing Cluster Operating System Rolling Upgrade

> When you have a cluster running on Windows Server 2016 and you want to upgrade Windows Server 2012 or Windows Server 2012 R2 to Windows Server 2016, you need to plan your upgrade. Otherwise, your server might be down longer than you'd like.

CERTIFICATION READY
Implement Cluster
Operating System Rolling
Upgrade
Objective 5.2

To replace cluster nodes or upgrade to a newer version of Windows, you need to migrate cluster roles or services from one cluster to another. You can migrate clusters running Windows Server 2016. You can migrate these roles and configuration in one of two ways:

- Migrate from an existing cluster to a new cluster that is running Windows Server 2016
- Perform an in-place migration on a two-node cluster

When you migrate from an existing cluster to a new cluster, you create a new cluster consisting of two cluster nodes running Windows Server 2016. You then migrate from the existing cluster to the new cluster.

To perform an in-place migration on a two-node cluster, you actually perform a migration when you don't have extra computers to form a new cluster. Instead of migrating to a new cluster, you basically upgrade to Windows Server 2016. To accomplish this, perform the following:

1. Remove resources from one node and evict that node from a cluster.
2. Perform a clean installation of Windows Server 2016 on the evicted server.
3. Create a one-node failover cluster.
4. Migrate the clustered services and applications from the old cluster node to the new one-node failover cluster.
5. Remove the old node from the cluster.
6. Install Windows Server 2016 on the second cluster node and configure the Failover Clustering features.

To perform the actual migration, use the Cluster Migration Wizard. Because the Cluster Migration Wizard does not copy data from one storage location to another, you must copy or move data or folders (including shared folder settings) during a migration. Although you can migrate physical disk resource settings to and from disks that use mount points, you cannot migrate mount-point information that does not use drive letters and is mounted in a folder on another hard disk drive.

⊕ RUN THE MIGRATE A CLUSTER WIZARD

GET READY. To run the Migrate a Cluster Wizard , perform the following steps.

1. On a node of the new cluster, use Server Manager to open the Failover Cluster Wizard.
2. Right-click the cluster, click **More Actions**, and click **Copy Cluster Roles.**
3. When the Migrate a Cluster Wizard opens, click **Next.**
4. On the Specify Old Cluster page, in the Cluster or cluster node to migrate from text box, type the name of the cluster or a name of one of the cluster nodes. Click **Next.**
5. On the Select Services and Applications page, select the resources that you want to migrate and click **Next.**
6. On the Customize Virtual Machine Networks page, select the virtual network switch and click **Next.**
7. On the Confirmation page, click **Next.**
8. When the wizard is complete, click **Finish.**

At this point, the target cluster is ready to take over. So, during a scheduled maintenance window, you need to shut down all servers on the old cluster, configure the storage, and start the servers on the Windows Server 2016 cluster.

Configuring Clusters Without Network Names

Windows Server 2012 R2 introduced the *Active Directory–detached cluster*, which allows you to deploy a failover cluster without any dependencies in Active Directory Domain Services (AD DS) for network names. When you create an Active Directory–detached cluster, you register the cluster network names with the network names of the clustered roles to your DNS servers without creating computer objects in AD DS.

Active Directory–detached clusters simplify the process of deploying, managing, and maintaining your failover cluster. Because the hosts of an Active Directory–detached cluster are joined to an Active Directory domain, Kerberos authentication is used when performing internode cluster communications, However, when accessing the cluster network name—which does not have an Active Directory account—NT LAN Manager (NTLM) authentication is used when communicating with the cluster as a whole.

If the cluster applications require Kerberos authentication, it is not recommended to use Active Directory–detached clusters. Therefore, you should consider the following:

- Because the Server Message Block (SMB) traffic recommends using Kerberos, you should not use Active Directory–detached clusters.
- If you require live migration, which requires Kerberos authentication, you should not use Active Directory–detached clusters for Hyper-V.
- Because Message Queuing stores properties in AD DS, you cannot use Active Directory–detached clusters.
- If you have an Active Directory–detached cluster with a SQL server, you should use SQL Server authentication.
- BitLocker Drive Encryption is not supported with Active Directory–detached clusters.
- Cluster-Aware Updating (CAU) in self-updating mode is not supported with Active Directory–detached clusters. However, CAU is supported in remote-updating mode.

- If you deploy a highly available file server by using this deployment method, you cannot use Server Manager to manage the file server. Instead, you must use Windows PowerShell or Failover Cluster Manager.
- After you create the cluster, you cannot change the cluster to an Active Directory–detached cluster or an Active Directory–attached cluster.

Before you create the failover cluster, you must ensure that all servers that you want to add as cluster nodes meet the following prerequisites:

- All servers must be running Windows Server 2016.
- All servers must be joined to the same Active Directory domain.
- All servers must have the Failover Clustering feature installed.
- All servers must use supported hardware and the collection of servers must pass all cluster validation tests.

To deploy an Active Directory–detached cluster, you must create the failover cluster with the Windows PowerShell `New-Cluster` cmdlet with the `-AdministrativeAccessPoint` parameter set to a value of `Dns`.

For example, to create a failover cluster called Cluster1 using the two nodes (Node1 and Node2) and using an administrative access point of type DNS (Active Directory–detached), use the following command:

```
New-Cluster Cluster1 -Node Node1,Node2 -StaticAddress 192.168.1.16
-NoStorage -AdministrativeAccessPoint Dns
```

To verify the type of administrative access point for a failover cluster, use the following Windows PowerShell command:

```
(Get-Cluster).AdministrativeAccessPoint
```

Implementing a Clustered Storage Spaces Solution

You can group local disks—USB, Serial ATA (SATA), or serial-attached SCSI (SAS)—into storage pools and then create virtual disks called *Storage Spaces* from the available capacity in the storage pools. Storage Spaces can also provide resiliency (such as using mirroring or parity) and scalability. You can deploy clustered storage spaces by using Storage Spaces and Failover Clustering to provide solutions that are resilient, highly available, and cost efficient.

CERTIFICATION READY
Implement a Clustered Storage Spaces Solution using Shared SAS storage enclosures
Objective 5.2

Although you cannot use a storage space to host the Windows system drive, you can use clustered storage spaces to help protect against the following:

- Physical disk failures
- Data access failures
- Data corruptions and volume unavailability
- Server node failures

By using CSVs, you can combine the storage access into a single namespace, which all cluster nodes can access at the same time, and you can easily take a server offline for maintenance.

To deploy clustered storage spaces, you need a small collection of servers and a set of Shared serial-attached SCSI enclosures, which must be connected to all servers with redundant paths. All physical disks used to create a clustered pool must pass the failover cluster validation tests. Clustered storage spaces must use fixed provisioning. Simple, mirror, and parity storage spaces are supported. Storage spaces formatted with NTFS and ReFS can be added to the CSV.

⊕ **CONFIGURE A CLUSTERED STORAGE SPACE**

GET READY. To configure a clustered storage space, perform the following steps.

1. Using Server Manager, click **Manage > Add Roles and Features.**
2. On the Before You Begin page, click **Next.**
3. On the Select Installation Type page, click **Next.**
4. On the Select Destination Server page, click the server to which you want to install and then click **Next.**
5. On the Select Server Roles page, click the **File Server** role and then click **Next.**
6. On the Select Features page, click **Next.**
7. On the Confirm Installations Selections page, click **Install.**
8. When the installation is complete, click **Close.**
9. Using Server Manager, click **Tools > Failover Cluster Manager.**
10. In the left pane, expand the cluster node, expand the **Storage** node, and then click the **Pools** node (see Figure 13-14).

Figure 13-14

The Pools node

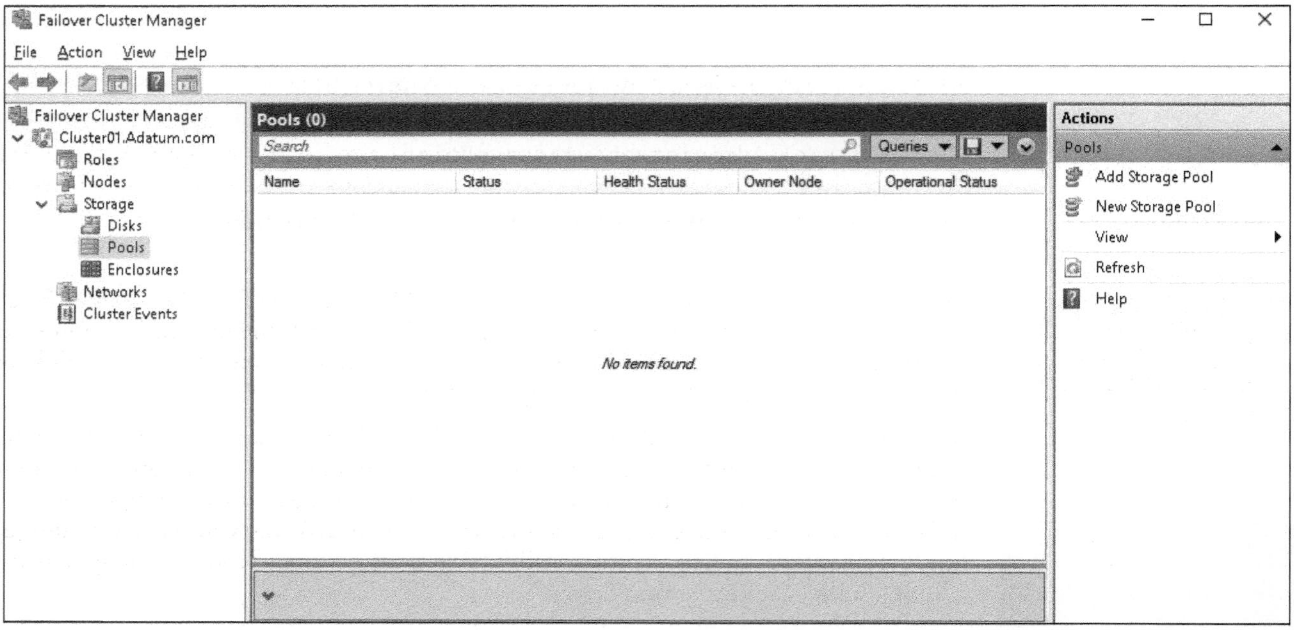

11. Right-click **Pools** and choose **New Storage Pool.**
12. On the Before You Begin page, click **Next.**
13. On the Storage Pool Name page, in the Name text box, type the name of the storage pool. Then, select the storage subsystem that is available to the cluster and click **Next.**
14. Select a minimum of three physical disks and then click **Next.**
15. On the Confirmation page, click **Create.**
16. Once the storage pool is created, click **Close.**
17. Right-click the storage pool and choose **New Virtual Disk.**

18. On the Before You Begin page, click **Next**.

19. On the Storage Pool page, select the server and storage pool for the virtual disk and then click **Next**.

20. On the Virtual Disk Name page, in the Name text box and the Description text box, provide a name and description for the virtual disk, respectively, and then click **Next**.

21. On the Storage Layout page, specify the desired Storage Layout (**Simple**, **Mirror**, or parity). Click **Next**.

22. On the Size page, specify the size of the virtual disk and then click **Next**.

23. On the Confirmation page, click **Create**.

24. Once the virtual disk is created, the Create a volume when this wizard closes option is already selected. Click **Close**.

25. On Before You Begin page, click **Next**.

26. On the Server and Disk page, verify the correct selection of the disk and server that must be provisioned and then click **Next**.

27. On the Size page, specify the size of the volume and then click **Next**.

28. On the Drive Letter or Folder page, select the desired drive letter and then click **Next**.

29. On the File System Settings page, select the file system settings and then click **Next**.

30. On the Confirmation page, click **Create**. The new volume will be created on the virtual disk and will be added to the failover cluster.

Restoring Single Node or Cluster Configuration

Because configuring a cluster is time consuming and sometimes complex, it is important that you back up the cluster configuration. You can back up the cluster configuration and restore using Windows Server Backup or a non-Microsoft Backup tool.

Before you put a cluster into production, you should test failover to make sure it is functioning properly. In addition, be sure that each node runs with the necessary resources. Lastly, you should test the backup and recovery process so that if a disaster occurs, you will know the steps to bring the cluster back in a timely manner.

Assuming that you have installed the Windows Server Backup feature, before you can perform a backup, the cluster needs to be running and you must have a quorum. The Cluster service keeps track of the cluster configuration. When a change is made, it replicates the configuration to all cluster nodes. If the cluster has a witness disk, the Cluster service also replicates the configuration to the witness disk. Therefore, be sure to back up the system state, Cluster folders, and the witness disk.

You still have to back up the individual applications running on the server and the associated data, such as SQL databases, Exchange databases, or shared files. To back up application data, you can install backup software on the cluster node that owns the disk resource, or you can run the backup against the clustered resource over the network. If you use CSV volumes, you can run backup from any node that is attached to the CSV volume.

To restore the cluster, you can perform one of two types of restores:

- *Nonauthoritative restore*: A type of restore that restores the information that was performed when originally backed up but is overwritten by current information stored on other cluster nodes

- *Authoritative restore*: A type of restore that restores the information that was performed when originally backed up but is marked as the current and authoritative configuration, which will then overwrite the configuration on the other nodes

If you have a single cluster node that has failed, you can perform the nonauthoritative restore. After fixing or replacing the failed node, perform a nonauthoritative restore, including the system state. When you restart the node, the restored node joins the cluster and automatically receives the latest cluster configuration from the other nodes or the witness disk.

Alternatively, you can remove a node and add a new node to the cluster. The new node automatically receives the cluster information.

If an administrator accidently removed clustered resources or modified other cluster settings and you need to restore the cluster back to a specific point in time before the changes were made, you will perform an authoritative restore. To perform an authoritative restore, you need to stop the cluster restores on all nodes. You then perform a system state recovery on a single node. After the restore, restart the cluster service, so that the cluster service will mark the current configuration as the most recent configuration. As you bring the remaining cluster nodes online and start the cluster service, the other nodes will receive the restored configuration.

With Windows Server 2016, if you manually force quorum to start the cluster (such as when you start the Cluster service with the /fq switch), the partition that you started with force quorum is considered authoritative. However, when the partition nodes are brought back online, the partitioned nodes automatically restart the Cluster service and the partitions are joined back to the cluster.

In Windows Server 2012 R2, when a node fails, you can now specify which node is removed for a quorum vote (by specifying the LowerQuorumPriorityNode ID property).

To set the property, run the following Windows PowerShell command (whereby node 1 is considered less critical):

```
(Get-Cluster).LowerQuorumPriorityNodeID = 1
```

SKILL SUMMARY

IN THIS LESSON YOU LEARNED:

- A failover cluster is a set of servers that works together to increase the availability of services and applications. The clustered servers (called nodes) are connected through a network connection (physical or virtual) and by software. If one node fails, another node begins to provide services (a process known as failover).

- Most failover clusters use shared storage to provide consistent data to all cluster nodes. Shared storage is accessed over a network so that it can support multiple systems simultaneously.

- Traditionally, a single node controls a LUN on the shared storage. However, starting with Windows Server 2008 R2, Windows can use a Cluster Shared Volume (CSV), which allows multiple nodes to share a single LUN concurrently. Instead of taking control of the entire LUN, a node takes control of an individual file.

- A quorum is used with a failover cluster to determine the number of failures that the cluster can sustain. If a quorum (the majority of the votes) is not reached, the cluster will stop running. Each voting element, except the file share witness contains a copy of the cluster configuration, and the Cluster service works to keep all copies synchronized at all times.

- Cluster-Aware Updating (CAU) lets administrators update cluster nodes automatically, with little or no downtime, particularly if you use Hyper-V with live migration.

- You can group local disks—USB, Serial ATA (SATA), or serial-attached SCSI (SAS)—into storage pools and then create virtual disks called Storage Spaces from the available capacity in the storage pools. Storage Spaces can also provide resiliency (such as using mirroring or parity) and scalability. You can deploy clustered storage spaces by using Storage Spaces and Failover Clustering to provide solutions that are resilient, highly available, and cost efficient.

Multiple Choice

Select the correct answer for each of the following questions.

1. Which type of clustering is used for back-end databases?
   a. Network Load Balancing (NLB)cluster
   b. Failover cluster
   c. Aggregated cluster
   d. Power cluster

2. Which of the following is the maximum number of nodes there can be on a single cluster?
   a. 2
   b. 8
   c. 32
   d. 64

3. Which of the following can be used by networks in a Windows failover cluster? (Choose all that apply.)
   a. Public-and-private
   b. Private
   c. Public
   d. Central

4. Which of the following ports are used by heartbeats?
   a. 80
   b. 2232
   c. 3343
   d. 3389

5. Which of the following are SAN technologies that are used for centralized storage when configuring failover clusters? (Choose all that apply.)
   a. SAS
   b. Fibre Channel
   c. Serial ATA
   d. iSCSI

6. Which type of storage allows multiple nodes to access the storage at the same time?
   a. Cluster Shared Volume (CSV)
   b. FAT Volume
   c. LAN Volume
   d. WAN Volume

7. Which of the following is used to provide quorum when there are only two nodes in a cluster? (Choose all that apply.)
   a. Heartbeats
   b. Witness disk
   c. CSV disk
   d. Shared folder

8. Which of the following allows a cluster node to be automatically patched with little or no downtime?
   a. Cluster-Aware Updating
   b. Cluster Auto Update
   c. Cluster Free Update
   d. Orchestrated Updates

9. Which type of quorum should be used when there are three nodes in a failover cluster?
   a. Node Majority
   b. Node and Disk Majority
   c. Node and File Share Majority
   d. No Majority

10. Which Windows PowerShell cmdlet should be used to check the progress of updates when using CAU?
    a. `InspectCAU`
    b. `Show-CAU`
    c. `Run-CAU`
    d. `Get-CAURUN`

11. Which of the following allows a failover cluster to be deployed without creating an Active Directory computer account for the cluster network name?
    a. `-Administrative AccessPoint`
    b. A Kerberos-free cluster
    c. A virtual failover cluster
    d. An Active Directory–detached cluster

Best Answer

Choose the letter that corresponds to the best answer. More than one answer choice may achieve the goal. Select the BEST answer.

1. An Active Directory domain called *contoso.com* has two servers called *Server1* and *Server2*, both of which are running Windows Server 2016. Server1 and Server2 make up the failover cluster called *Cluster1*. A third node is added. Which of the following must be configured so that the cluster will stop if two of the nodes fail?
   a. Failover settings
   b. Host priority
   c. Cluster Quorum settings
   d. Quick migration

2. When creating a failover cluster that connects to an iSCSI SAN, which of the following is the minimum number of network adapters recommended for each node?
   a. 1
   b. 2
   c. 3
   d. 4

3. As an administrator for the Contoso Corporation, you manage a two-node failover cluster with a witness disk. One of the servers failed and the entire server has been replaced. To add the replacement server to the cluster, which of the following actions should be taken?
   a. You should perform an authoritative restore.
   b. You should perform a nonauthoritative restore.
   c. You should create an image from the remaining server and restore to the new server.
   d. You should install Windows and the cluster, and copy the cluster folder from the witness disk to the new server.

4. For a failover cluster, which type of network should be used to communicate with an iSCSI device?
   a. Private
   b. Public

    c. Public-and-private

    d. Internal

Matching and Identification

1. Match the appropriate term with its description.

    ____ **a.** `Failover cluster`

    ____ **b.** `Node`

    ____ **c.** `Quorum`

    ____ **d.** `Cluster Shared Volume (CSV)`

    ____ **e.** `Cluster-Aware Updating (CAU)`

    ____ **f.** `Heartbeat`

    1. Used by nodes to keep aware of the status of other nodes

    2. Computers that make up a cluster

    3. A set of independent computers to provide high availability for a service

    4. Updates cluster nodes automatically

    5. A volume that allows multiple nodes to share a single LUN

    6. Determines the number of failures that a cluster can sustain at the same time

Build List

1. Specify the correct order of the three basic steps necessary to installing and creating a failover cluster. Not all steps will be used.

    _____ Create the cluster.

    _____ Validate the cluster configuration.

    _____ Define the heartbeats parameters.

    _____ Install the Failover Clustering feature.

    _____ Install the Microsoft Failover Cluster Virtual Adapter.

2. Specify the correct order of steps necessary to upgrading a cluster to Windows Server 2016.

    _____ Create a one-node failover cluster.

    _____ Evict the node from a cluster.

    _____ Remove the last node from the cluster and install Windows Server 2016.

    _____ Perform a clean installation of Windows Server 2016 on the evicted server.

    _____ Add a second node to the new cluster.

    _____ Remove resources from one node.

    _____ Migrate the clustered services and applications from the old cluster node to the new failover cluster.

■ Business Case Scenarios

Scenario 13-1: Configuring a Redundant Server

As an administrator at the Contoso Corporation, you manage a server that acts as a file server for clients. Describe how to ensure that the server is up at all times.

Scenario 13-2: Upgrading a Cluster to Windows Server 2016

As an administrator at the Contoso Corporation, you manage a cluster used as a file server that is running Windows Server 2012 R2. You do not have any other free servers. Describe how to upgrade the cluster to Windows Server 2016.

Managing Failover Clustering

70-740 EXAM OBJECTIVE

Objective 5.4 – Manage failover clustering. This objective may include but is not limited to the following: Configure role-specific settings, including continuously available shares; configure VM monitoring; configure failover and preference settings; implement stretch and site-aware failover clusters; enable and configure node fairness.

Objective 5.2 – Implement failover clustering. This objective may include but is not limited to the following: Implement Scale-Out File Server (SoFS); determine different scenarios for the use of SoFS versus clustered File Server; determine usage scenarios for implementing guest clustering; implement VM resiliency; implement shared VHDX as a storage solution for guest clusters. *Other Objective 5.2 topics are covered in Lesson 14.*

Objective 5.5 – Managing VM movement in clustered nodes. This objective may include but is not limited to: Configure drain on shutdown. *Other Objective 5.5 topics are covered in Lesson 8 and Lesson 15.*

LESSON HEADING	EXAM OBJECTIVE
Managing Failover Clustering Roles	Configure role-specific settings, including continuously available shares
– Configuring Roles	
– Implementing the Clustered File Server	Implement Scale-Out File Server (SoFS)
– Implementing the Scale-Out File Server	Determine different scenarios for the use of SoFS versus clustered File Server
– Determining Scenarios for Scale-Out File Servers and Clustered File Servers	
– Implementing VM Resiliency	Implement VM resiliency
– Implementing Shared VHDX as a Storage Solution for Guest Clusters	Implement shared VHDX as a storage solution for guest clusters
Managing Failover Clustering	Configure drain on shutdown
– Performing Maintenance Tasks, Including Configuring Drain Settings on Shutdown	Enable and configure node fairness
– Configuring Failover and Preference Settings	Configure VM monitoring
– Enabling and Configuring Node Fairness	
– Configuring VM Monitoring	

(continued)

LESSON HEADING	EXAM OBJECTIVE
Implementing Stretch and Site-Aware Failover Clusters	Configure failover and preference settings
	Implement stretch and site-aware failover clusters
– Configuring Multi-Site Storage and Network Settings	
– Configuring Quorum and Failover Settings	
– Implementing Stretch Clusters	
Determining Usage Scenarios for Implementing Guest Clustering Solution Using Shared SAS Storage Enclosures	Determine usage scenarios for implementing guest clustering

KEY TERMS

asynchronous replication

cluster-aware clustered role

drain

general Use File Server

generic application

generic clustered role

generic script

generic service

highly available virtual machines

multi-site failover cluster

Node Fairness

preferred node

Scale-Out File Server

Shared serial-attached SCSI (SAS)

synchronous replication

transaction

Virtual Machine Monitoring

■ Managing Failover Clustering Roles

THE BOTTOM LINE

Failover clusters provide high availability and scalability to many server applications, such as Microsoft Exchange, Microsoft SQL, and Hyper-V. You can use the High Availability Wizard to configure a *clustered role* (formerly called a *clustered service* or *application*), which is a service or application that you make highly available.

Similar to storage, if a server has a problem, a clustered role can fail over to another server. Clustered roles are divided into the following two types:

- Cluster-aware
- Generic

A *cluster-aware clustered role* is designed to work with Windows Server 2016 failover clusters. Examples include the File Server clustered role and the Virtual Machine clustered role.

A *generic clustered role* provides high availability for a service, application, or script that is not originally designed to run in a cluster. As a result, the cluster cannot detect the state of the generic application, script, or service as it can with a cluster-aware role. Generic cluster roles include the following:

- *Generic application:* The cluster software starts the generic application, and then periodically queries the operating system to see whether the application still runs.

- *Generic script*: You create a script that runs in Windows Script Host, which monitors and controls an application. The state of the application is determined by the script.
- *Generic service*: The cluster software starts the service. Similar to generic applications, the cluster service periodically queries the Service Controller to determine whether the service is still running.

Depending on the cluster role or application that you try to run, one or more server roles or applications on each node might be required. In addition, some applications, such as mail and database applications, might require additional configuration to work properly in a clustered environment. Microsoft provides thorough documentation to configure Microsoft Exchange or Microsoft SQL to run on a failover cluster on the technet.microsoft.com website.

Configuring Roles

> To add a clustered role, you right-click the Roles node and choose Configure Role, which starts the High Availability Wizard.

In the High Availability Wizard, you can choose from the following services and applications (see Figure 14-1):

- **DFS Namespace Server:** Provides a virtual view of shared folders in an organization, which allows users to access shared folders that are distributed among multiple folders.
- **DHCP Server:** Automatically provides TCP/IP hosts with valid IP addresses.
- **Distributed Transaction Coordinator (DTC):** Supports distributed applications that perform transactions. A *transaction* is a set of related tasks, such as updates to databases that either succeed or fail as a unit.
- **File Server:** Provides a central location on your network where you can store and share files with users.
- **Generic Application:** Allows you to run an application that is not specifically designed to run on a cluster.
- **Generic Script:** Allows you to run scripts that are used to start and monitor applications.
- **Generic Service:** Allows you to run services that are not specifically designed to run on a cluster.
- **Hyper-V Replica Broker:** Redirects all VM-specific events to the appropriate node in the replica cluster.
- **iSCSI Target Server:** Allows you to provide iSCSI storage devices to iSCSI clients known as *iSCSI initiators*.
- **Internet Storage Name Service (iSNS) Server:** Provides a directory of iSCSI targets.
- **Message Queuing:** Enables distributed applications that are running at different times to communicate across heterogeneous networks and with computers that might be offline.
- **Other Server:** Provides a client access point and storage. After completing the Failover cluster wizard, you would then add an application.
- **Virtual Machine:** Runs on a physical computer as a virtualized computer system. Multiple virtual machines (VM) can run on one computer.
- **WINS Server:** Enables users to access resources by a NetBIOS name instead of requiring them to use IP addresses that are difficult to recognize and remember.

Figure 14-1

Selecting a role to install on a cluster

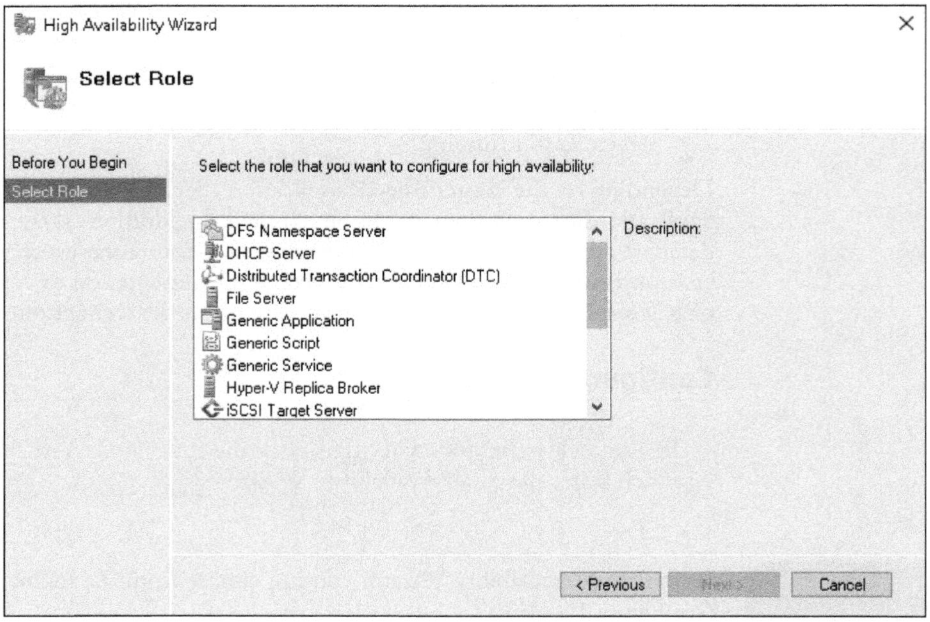

High Availability Wizard   ×

Select Role

Before You Begin

Select Role

Select the role that you want to configure for high availability:

DFS Namespace Server   Description:
DHCP Server
Distributed Transaction Coordinator (DTC)
File Server
Generic Application
Generic Script
Generic Service
Hyper-V Replica Broker
iSCSI Target Server

‹ Previous   Next ›   Cancel

Clusters can be used for a wide range of applications to provide high availability. However, popular uses of clustering include file services and VMs.

When you deploy highly available file services and VMs, you use a shared disk to store data files or VM files. Therefore, you need to choose a shared disk that is highly available and has high performance.

Implementing the Clustered File Server

File servers in a cluster can be configured for general use—*General Use File Server*—which is almost the same as it was in Windows Server 2008 R2. It provides a central location for users to share files or for server applications that open and close files frequently. It also supports SMB, Network File System (NFS), Data Deduplication, File Server Resource Manager, DFS Replication, and other File Services role services. SMB 3.0 is supported by Windows Server 2012 and higher.

Before you install and configure the File Server role, be sure that you install the appropriate file server roles for Windows Server 2016, such as File Server or Server for NFS. Then, when you deploy the General Use File Server role, you will first add the File Server role, and then create the file shares.

 DEPLOY THE GENERAL USE FILE SERVER ROLE

GET READY. To deploy the General Use File Server role, perform the following steps.

1. Open Server Manager and click **Tools > Failover Cluster Manager**. The Failover Cluster Manager opens.
2. Right-click **Roles** and choose **Configure Roles**. Alternatively, you can click the cluster and under Actions, click **Configure Role.**
3. When the High Availability Wizard opens, on the Before You Begin page, click **Next**.
4. On the Select Role page, click **File Server** and then click **Next**.
5. On the File Server Type page (see Figure 14-2), click **File Server for general use** and then click **Next**.

Figure 14-2

Selecting the file server type

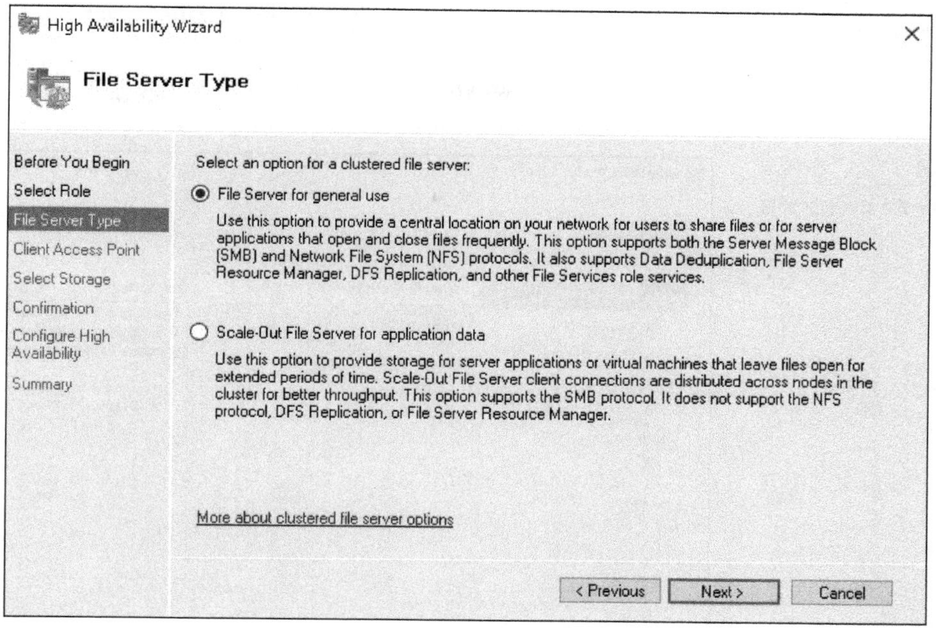

High Availability Wizard   ✕

File Server Type

Before You Begin
Select Role
File Server Type
Client Access Point
Select Storage
Confirmation
Configure High Availability
Summary

Select an option for a clustered file server:

◉ File Server for general use

Use this option to provide a central location on your network for users to share files or for server applications that open and close files frequently. This option supports both the Server Message Block (SMB) and Network File System (NFS) protocols. It also supports Data Deduplication, File Server Resource Manager, DFS Replication, and other File Services role services.

○ Scale-Out File Server for application data

Use this option to provide storage for server applications or virtual machines that leave files open for extended periods of time. Scale-Out File Server client connections are distributed across nodes in the cluster for better throughput. This option supports the SMB protocol. It does not support the NFS protocol, DFS Replication, or File Server Resource Manager.

More about clustered file server options

< Previous   Next >   Cancel

6. On the Client Access Point page (see Figure 14-3), in the Name text box, type a NetBIOS name that the clients will access for the clustered role. Next, in the Address column, type an IP address.

Figure 14-3

Specifying the file server name and IP address

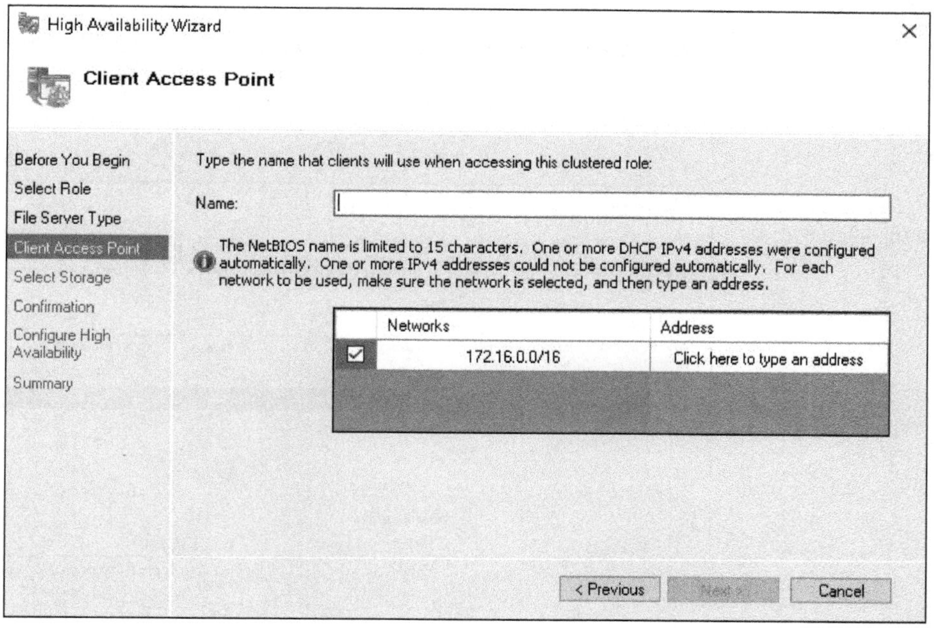

High Availability Wizard   ✕

Client Access Point

Before You Begin
Select Role
File Server Type
Client Access Point
Select Storage
Confirmation
Configure High Availability
Summary

Type the name that clients will use when accessing this clustered role:

Name: |

ℹ The NetBIOS name is limited to 15 characters. One or more DHCP IPv4 addresses were configured automatically. One or more IPv4 addresses could not be configured automatically. For each network to be used, make sure the network is selected, and then type an address.

	Networks	Address
☑	172.16.0.0/16	Click here to type an address

< Previous   Next >   Cancel

7. On the Select Storage page, enter a storage location for the data and click **Next**. The disk cannot be assigned as a Cluster Shared Volume (CSV).

8. On the Confirmation page, click **Next**.

9. On the Summary page, click **Finish**.

10. To create a file share, right-click the **File Server Role** and choose **Add File Share**.

11. When the New Share Wizard opens (see Figure 14-4), select the appropriate file share profile. Click **SMB Share – Quick** and click **Next**.

Figure 14-4

Selecting the file share profile

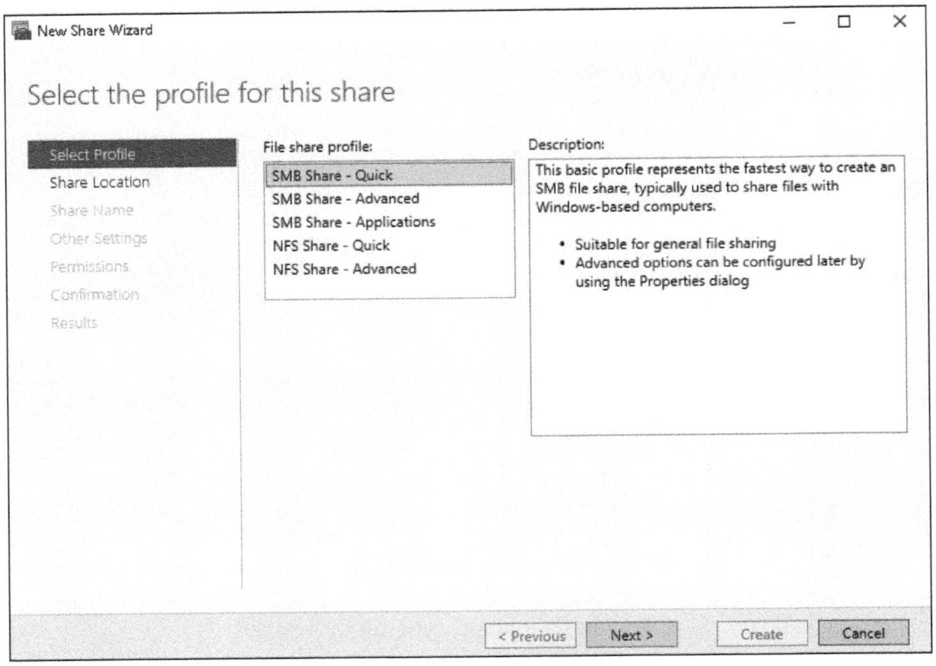

12. On the Share Location page, be sure that the **File Server** cluster role is selected. Then, with **Type a custom path** selected (see Figure 14-5), type a path (such as **E:\Data**) in the text box. Click **Next**.

Figure 14-5

Selecting the share location

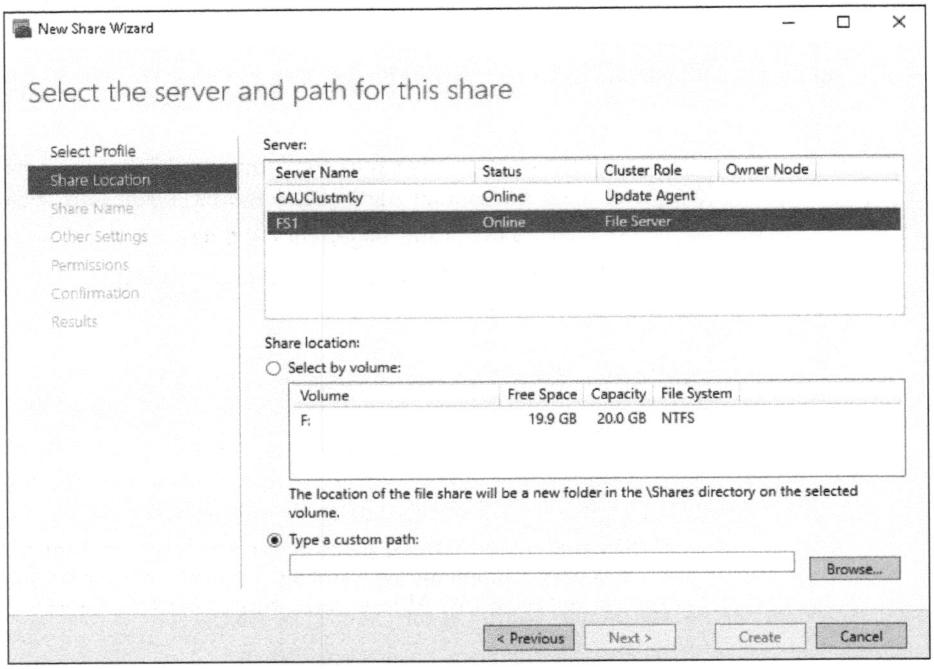

13. On the Share Name page, in the Share name box, type a name and click **Next**.
14. On the Other Settings page (see Figure 14-6), select or deselect the desired options and click **Next**.

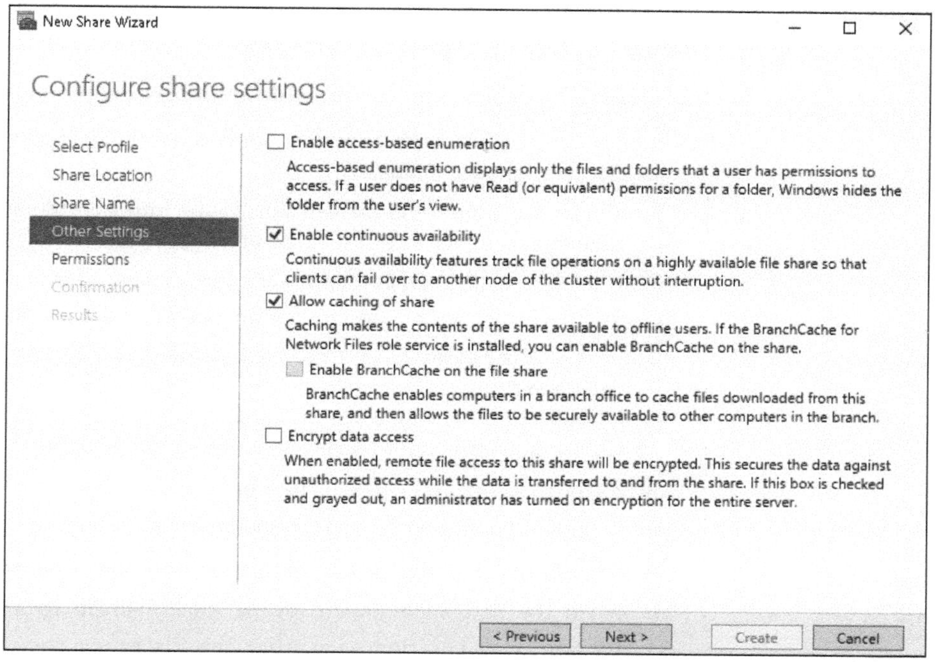

Figure 14-6

Selecting other settings

15. On the Permissions page, configure the NTFS and Share permissions as necessary by clicking **Customize permissions**. When done, click **Next**.
16. On the Confirmation page, click **Create**.
17. When the installation is complete, click **Close**.

TAKE NOTE*

The Enable continuous availability and Encrypt data access options are selected by default. The Enable continuous availability option takes advantage of SMB v3 functionality (Transparent Failover), whereas the Encrypt data access option enables encrypting the SMB connections.

Implementing the Scale-Out File Server

The type of file server that you can use with a cluster is the Scale-Out File Server (introduced in Windows Server 2012), which is intended for application data, such as Hyper-V VM files, file shares that require reliability, manageability, and high performance. Different from a General Use File Server cluster, the *Scale-Out File Server* cluster is an active-active failover cluster where all files shares are online on all nodes simultaneously. Although the Scale-Out File Server supports SMB, it does not support NFS, Data Deduplication, DFS Replication, or File Server Resource Manager.

CERTIFICATION READY
Implement Scale-Out File
Server (SoFS)
Objective 5.2

To support multiple nodes to access the same volume at the same time, the Scale-Out File Server uses a CSV. It also uses a CSV cache, which is a read cache that significantly improve performance in certain scenarios, such as when creating a Virtual Desktop Infrastructure.

DEPLOY A SCALE-OUT FILE SERVER

GET READY. To deploy a Scale-Out File Server, perform the following steps.

1. Open Server Manager and click **Tools > Failover Cluster Manager.** The Failover Cluster Manager opens.
2. Right-click **Roles** and choose **Configure Roles.** Alternatively, you can click the cluster and under Actions, click **Configure Role.**
3. When the High Availability Wizard opens, click **Next.**
4. On the Select Role page, click **File Server** and click **Next.**
5. On the File Server Type page, click **Scale-Out File Server for application data** and click **Next.**
6. On the Client Access Point page, type the name that clients will use to access the file server. Click **Next.**
7. On the Confirmation page, click **Next.**
8. On the Summary page, click **Finish.**
9. Click **Roles.** Right-click the file server role and choose **Add File Share.**
10. When the New Share Wizard opens, click **SMB Share – Quick** and then click **Next.**
11. On the Share Location page, click the file server name and click **Select by volume.** Click **Next.**
12. On the Share Name page, type the name of the share and click **Next.**
13. On the Other Settings page, verify that **Enable continuous availability** is selected and then click **Next.**
14. On the Permissions page, configure the NTFS and Share permissions as necessary by clicking **Customize permissions.** When done, click **Next.**
15. When the installation is complete, click **Close.**

Determining Scenarios for Scale-Out File Servers and Clustered File Servers

Clustered file servers and Scale-Out File Servers give you fault tolerance. The Scale-Out File Server is an active-active failover cluster where all of the file shares are online on all nodes simultaneously. However, it does not support NFS, Data Deduplication, DFS Replication, or File Server Resource Manager. On the other hand, clustered file server/General Use File Server is usually an active-passive failover cluster. However, clustered file servers do support NFS, Data Deduplication, DFS Replication, and File Server Resource Manager.

CERTIFICATION READY
Determine different
scenarios for the use of
SoFS versus clustered
File Server
Objective 5.2

As discussed in the previous two sections, Scale-Out File Servers use a CSV, while the clustered file server uses a standard clustered shared drive. Scale-Out File Servers provide solid performance with a few big files (such as larger databases and virtual machines), with little metadata activity. However, Scale-Out File Servers do not perform as well with many small files or with lots of metadata activity.

Implementing VM Resiliency

One popular use of failover clusters is to have Hyper-V provide highly available virtual machines. A failover cluster that is made up of two or more virtual machines is typically referred to as a guest cluster, which is used to provide highly available virtual machines. *Highly available virtual machines* can be migrated to another physical host in a failover cluster to provide continuing service when the current host goes down or needs maintenance. Different from the other types of clusters, the Hyper-V nodes must be composed of physical hosts. You cannot run Hyper-V on a VM. In addition, to avoid losing network connectivity, you must create the same virtual networks on all physical hosts that participate in the cluster.

CERTIFICATION READY
Implement VM resiliency
Objective 5.2

To make a VM highly available, all the VM storage locations must be on shared storage that all nodes can access. In addition, the storage needs to be configured as a CSV.

In addition to the network and storage requirements, to deploy Hyper-V on a failover cluster, you must meet the following hardware requirements:

- Physical hosts should have similar hardware.
- Physical hosts require an x64-based processor with hardware-assisted virtualization and hardware-enforced Data Execution Prevention (DEP).
- The processors should be the same architecture and version.
- To provide network redundancy, you can connect cluster nodes to multiple networks and/or use teamed network adapters, redundant switches, and redundant routers.
- To provide interhost communications, you need one network adapter for each host to form the private network.
- If you use a serial attached SCSI (SAS) or Fibre Channel, the mass-storage device controllers in all physical hosts should be identical and should use the same firmware version.
- If you use iSCSI, each physical host should have one or more network adapters that are dedicated to the cluster storage.
- The network adapters that you use to connect to the iSCSI storage target should be identical, and you should use a gigabit Ethernet or faster network adapter.
- When creating shared storage, use basic disks, not dynamic disks.
- Format the disks with the NTFS file system.
- Use either Master Boot Record (MBR) or GUID partition table (GPT).
- If you use a storage area network (SAN), the miniport driver that the storage uses must work with the Microsoft Storport storage driver.
- If you use a SAN, consider using multi-path I/O software.
- To protect against host failure, it is recommended that you place virtual machines that are part of the same guest cluster on different physical hosts.

To deploy Hyper-V on a failover cluster, you must meet the following software requirements:

- All physical hosts must run the Windows Server 2016 Standard edition or Windows Server 2016 Datacenter edition. In addition, you should have the same edition. However, different editions are supported during a rolling upgrade.
- All physical hosts must be either Full installations or Server Core installations.
- All physical hosts should have the same Windows updates and service packs.
- Network settings, such as speed, duplex mode, flow control, and media type settings, are the same.

- Make sure that the private network uses a unique subnet.
- Use DNS Dynamic update protocol.
- All servers must be in the same Active Directory Domain Services (AD DS) domain.
- When you first create a cluster or add servers to a cluster, you must be logged on to the domain with an administrator's account on all the cluster's servers. If the account is not a domain administrator, the account must have the Create Computer Objects permission in the domain.

To deploy a highly available VM, you will perform the following steps:

1. Connect both host computers to the network and storage.
2. Install and configure the required versions of Windows Server 2016.
3. Configure the network settings and join the computers to the AD DS domain.
4. Configure the connection to the shared storage and partition and format the disks with Disk Manager.
5. Install the Hyper-V role.
6. Create the necessary virtual switches.
7. Install the failover clustering features on the host servers.
8. Validate the cluster configuration using the Validate This Cluster Wizard.
9. Create the cluster.
10. Enable Clustered Shared storage for the cluster.
11. Create a VM on one of the cluster nodes. Be sure that the virtual hard disk and VM configuration files are stored on the shared CSV volume.
12. Using the High Availability Wizard, select the Virtual Machine role and select the appropriate VMs from the available list (see Figure 14-7) that you want to make highly available.
13. Install the guest operating system on the VM.
14. Test VM failover.

Figure 14-7

Selecting a VM for high availability

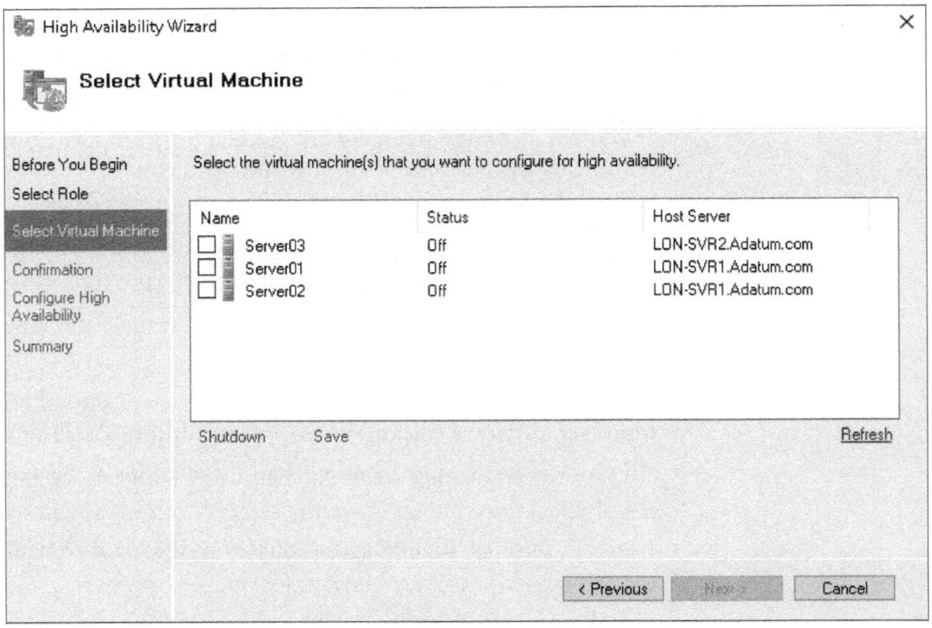

Another way to make a VM highly available is to store the VM files on a highly available SMB 3.0 file share, instead of using host or guest clustering. To accomplish this, you need the following:

- One or more computers that are running Windows Server 2016 with the Hyper-V role installed.
- One or more computers that are running Windows Server 2016 with the File and Storage Services role installed.
- The servers must be part of the same Active Directory domain.

After you have the servers in place, you create a Scale-Out File Server cluster and deploy the new SMB file share for applications. When the file shares are ready, you can deploy new servers or migrate existing VMs to the SMB file share.

Implementing Shared VHDX as a Storage Solution for Guest Clusters

Starting with Windows 2012 R2, Hyper-V can use shared VHDX files that allow you to create a virtual hard disk file and share it among multiple virtual machines, just like it was a Shared serial-attached SCSI disk. Although it does not eliminate the need for physical shared storage, it does hide the underlying storage architecture. It can also be useful in cloud-based cluster nodes.

CERTIFICATION READY
Implement shared VHDX as a storage solution for guest clusters
Objective 5.2

With Hyper-V, you can share a virtual hard disk (.vhdx), which can then provide the shared storage that is necessary for a Hyper-V guest failover cluster. The guest cluster can span multiple host clusters. Because a CSV cannot span clusters, you must use SMB 3.0 shares to store the shared VHDX files.

Using a shared virtual hard disk is ideal for:

- SQL Server database files
- File server services running within a virtual machine
- Database files that reside on shared disks

You will need at least two shared VHDX files:

- A 1-GB VHDX file to use as the quorum or witness disk
- One or more data VHDX files to store the clustered data

You should then create virtual machines, install and configure the operating systems, and configure the IP address of at least two networks (the management or client access IP address and a cluster private network IP address). Next, you need to add the VHDX files to the virtual SCSI controllers of each of the guest cluster virtual machines.

If the shared storage is a CSV disk, navigate to: C:\ClusterStorage\VolumeX, where *C:* represents the system drive, and *X* represents the volume number. If the shared storage is an SMB file share, navigate to: \\ServerName\ShareName, where *ServerName* represents the client access point for the Scale-Out File Server and *ShareName* represents the name of the SMB file share.

CREATE A SHARED VHDX DRIVE

GET READY. To create a shared VHDX drive, perform the following steps.

1. Open Server Manager and click **Tools > Hyper-V Manager**. The Hyper-V Manager opens.
2. Right-click the desired virtual machine that is turned off and choose **Settings**.
3. In the Settings dialog box, select **SCSI Controller**. Then, from the SCSI Controller page, click **Shared Drive** and then click **Add**.

4. On the Shared Drive page, click the **New** button.

5. When the New Virtual Hard Disk Wizard opens, on the Before You Begin page, click **Next**.

6. On the Choose Disk Format page, VHD Set is already selected. Click **Next**.

7. On the Choose Disk Type page, click **Next**.

8. On the Specify Name and Location Page, specify a descriptive name and then specify the location of the virtual hard disk page. Notice that the shared file has a .vhds extension. Click **Next**.

9. On the Configure Disk page, specify the size of the virtual hard disk in GB and click **Next**.

10. On the Summary page, click **Finish**.

11. Back on the Settings dialog box, click **OK**.

■ Managing Failover Clustering

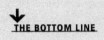

THE BOTTOM LINE

After you have installed and configured the cluster and cluster nodes and installed the cluster roles, you need to know how to manage the failover cluster. For example, you might need to know how to switch roles from one node to another and how to monitor the cluster.

The Failover Cluster Manager is used to manage and monitor the cluster and its nodes. Most common options can be accessed from the Cluster page, as shown in Figure 14-8.

Figure 14-8

Managing the failover cluster

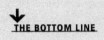

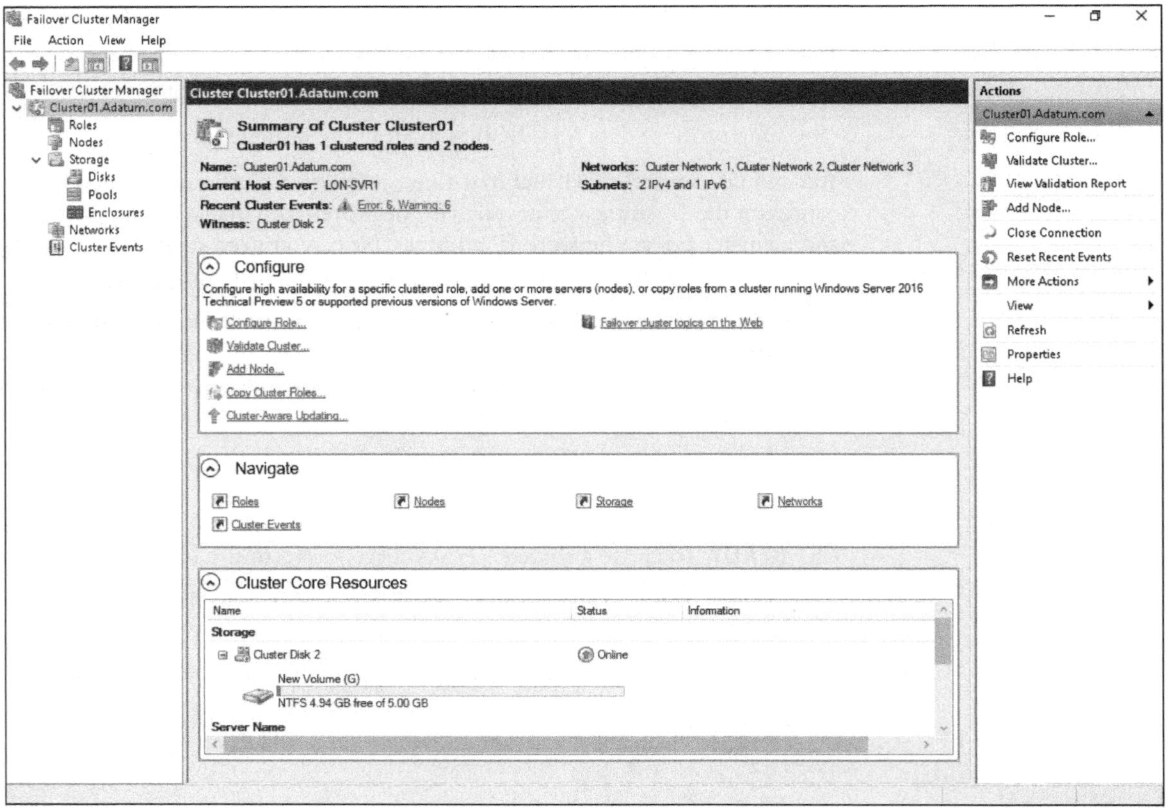

When a failover occurs (intentionally triggered by an administrator or an unplanned event such as a hardware failure), the failover attempt will consist of the following steps:

1. The Cluster service takes all the resources in the instance offline, in an order that is determined by the instance's dependency hierarchy. To perform a graceful shutdown of the resources, dependent resources are taken offline first, and then the supporting resources are taken offline.

2. The Cluster service transfers the instance to the node that is listed next on the instance's list of preferred owners.

3. If the instance is moved successfully, the Cluster service attempts to bring the resources online. The components that provide services for other components are started first, and then the dependent resources are brought online.

Failover is complete when all the resources are online on the new node. Depending on how you have the cluster configured, when the offline node becomes active again, the Cluster service can fail back the instance to the original offline node, or continue with the current node.

Performing Maintenance Tasks, Including Configuring Drain Settings on Shutdown

> The Failover Cluster console allows you to manage your cluster, including failing over a role from one node to another, removing nodes, deleting clusters, and so on.

CERTIFICATION READY
Configure drain on shutdown
Objective 5.5

Most of the maintenance tasks performed on a cluster are done using the failover cluster, including the following:

- To **drain** the roles (change roles to other nodes gracefully before a node is shut down), you right-click a node and choose Pause > Drain Roles.
- To resume a node, you right-click the node and choose Resume > Fail Roles Back *or* Do Not Fail Roles Back.
- To stop the Cluster service, right-click the node and choose More Actions > Stop Cluster Service.
- To take offline a shared storage device that is used by a cluster, right-click the disk and choose Take Offline. When you are prompted to confirm whether you are sure, click Yes.
- To bring a shared storage device back online, right-click the drive and choose Bring Online.
- To manually change a shared disk or role, right-click the shared disk or role and choose Move > Best Possible Node (or choose Select Node). When you choose Select Node, you are prompted for the node to change the disk or resource to.
- To add a new node to the cluster, right-click Node and choose Add Node to run the Add Node Wizard.
- To permanently remove a node from the cluster, right-click the server that you want to remove and choose More Actions > Evict.
- To delete a cluster, right-click the cluster and choose More Actions > Destroy Cluster.

USING WINDOWS POWERSHELL

You can configure and manage failover clusters using PowerShell. Some of the cmdlets include the following:

- `Add-ClusterCheckpoint`: Adds a cryptographic or registry checkpoint for a resource
- `Add-ClusterDisk`: Makes a new disk available for use in a failover cluster
- `Add-ClusterFileServerRole`: Creates a clustered file server resource group that includes one or more disks, on which shared folders can be created for users

- `Add-ClusterGenericApplicationRole`: Configures high availability for an application that was not originally designed to run in a failover cluster
- `Add-ClusterGenericScriptRole`: Configures an application controlled by a script that runs in Windows Script Host, within a failover cluster
- `Add-ClusterGenericServiceRole`: Configures high availability for a service that was not originally designed to run in a failover cluster
- `Add-ClusterGroup`: Adds an empty resource group to the failover cluster configuration, in preparation for adding clustered resources to the group
- `Add-ClusteriSCSITargetServerRole`: Creates a highly available iSCSI Target Server
- `Add-ClusterNode`: Adds a node, or server, to a failover cluster
- `Add-ClusterPrintServerRole`: Creates a clustered print server, a resource group that includes a printer, and a disk for storing print job information and printer drivers
- `Add-ClusterResource`: Adds a resource to a clustered role, or resource group, in a failover cluster
- `Add-ClusterResourceDependency`: Adds a resource to the list of resources on which a particular resource depends, using AND as the connector, within a failover cluster
- `Add-ClusterResourceType`: Adds a resource type to a failover cluster and specifies information such as the dynamic-link library (DLL) to be used with that resource type
- `Add-ClusterScaleOutFileServerRole`: Creates a clustered file server for scale-out application data
- `Add-ClusterServerRole`: Creates a highly available basic server
- `Add-ClusterSharedVolume`: Makes a volume available in CSVs in a failover cluster
- `Add-ClusterVirtualMachineRole`: Creates a clustered virtual machine, that is, a virtual machine that can be failed over if necessary to a different server in the failover cluster
- `Add-ClusterVMMonitoredItem`: Configures monitoring for a service or Event Tracing for Windows (ETW) event in a virtual machine
- `Block-ClusterAccess`: Prevents the specified user or users from accessing a failover cluster
- `Clear-ClusterDiskReservation`: Clears the persistent reservation on a disk in a failover cluster
- `Clear-ClusterNode`: Clears the cluster configuration from a node that was evicted from a failover cluster
- `Get-Cluster`: Gets information about one or more failover clusters in a given domain
- `Get-ClusterAccess`: Gets information about permissions that control access to a failover cluster
- `Get-ClusterAvailableDisk`: Gets information about the disks that can support failover clustering and are visible to all nodes, but are not yet part of the set of clustered disks
- `Get-ClusterCheckpoint`: Retrieves a cryptographic or registry checkpoint for a resource in a failover cluster
- `Get-ClusterGroup`: Gets information about one or more clustered roles, or resource groups, in a failover cluster
- `Get-ClusterLog`: Creates a log file for all nodes, or a specific node, in a failover cluster
- `Get-ClusterNetwork`: Gets information about one or more networks in a failover cluster
- `Get-ClusterNetworkInterface`: Gets information about one or more network adapters in a failover cluster
- `Get-ClusterNode`: Gets information about one or more nodes, or servers, in a failover cluster

- `Get-ClusterOwnerNode`: Gets information about which nodes can own a resource in a failover cluster or information about the order of preference among owner nodes for a clustered role
- `Get-ClusterParameter`: Gets detailed information about an object in a failover cluster, such as a cluster resource
- `Get-ClusterQuorum`: Gets information about the quorum configuration of a failover cluster
- `Get-ClusterResource`: Gets information about one or more resources in a failover cluster
- `Get-ClusterResourceDependency`: Gets information about the dependencies that have been configured between clustered resources in a failover cluster
- `Get-ClusterResourceDependencyReport`: Generates a report that lists the dependencies between resources in a failover cluster
- `Get-ClusterResourceType`: Gets information about one or more resource types in a failover cluster
- `Get-ClusterSharedVolume`: Gets information about CSVs in a failover cluster
- `Get-ClusterVMMonitoredItem`: Retrieves the list of services and events currently being monitored in the virtual machine
- `Grant-ClusterAccess`: Grants access to a failover cluster, either full access or read-only access
- `Move-ClusterGroup`: Moves a clustered role, or a resource group, from one node to another in a failover cluster
- `Move-ClusterResource`: Moves a clustered resource from one clustered role to another within a failover cluster
- `Move-ClusterSharedVolume`: Moves a CSV to ownership by a different node in a failover cluster
- `Move-ClusterVirtualMachineRole`: Moves the ownership of a clustered virtual machine to a different node
- `New-Cluster`: Creates a new failover cluster
- `Remove-Cluster`: Destroys an existing failover cluster
- `Remove-ClusterAccess`: Removes a user from the access list on the cluster
- `Remove-ClusterCheckpoint`: Removes a cryptographic or registry checkpoint for a resource in a failover cluster
- `Remove-ClusterGroup`: Removes a clustered role, also called a *resource group*, from a failover cluster
- `Remove-ClusterNode`: Removes a node from a failover cluster
- `Remove-ClusterResource`: Removes a clustered resource from the failover cluster
- `Remove-ClusterResourceDependency`: Removes a dependency between two resources in a clustered role within a failover cluster
- `Remove-ClusterResourceType`: Removes a resource type from a failover cluster
- `Remove-ClusterSharedVolume`: Removes a volume from the CSVs in a failover cluster and places it in Available Storage in the cluster
- `Remove-ClusterVMMonitoredItem`: Removes monitoring of a service or custom event that is currently being monitored
- `Repair-ClusterSharedVolume`: Runs repair tools on a CSV locally on a cluster node
- `Reset-ClusterVMMonitoredState`: Resets the Application Critical state of a virtual machine, so that the virtual machine is no longer marked as being in a critical state in the cluster

- `Resume-ClusterNode`: Resumes activity on a failover cluster node after it has suspended it, or paused
- `Resume-ClusterResource`: Turns off maintenance for a disk resource or CSV within a failover cluster
- `Set-ClusterLog`: Sets the size and level of detail for the cluster log
- `Set-ClusterOwnerNode`: Specifies which nodes can own a resource in a failover cluster or specifies the order of preference among owner nodes for a clustered role, or a resource group
- `Set-ClusterParameter`: Controls specific properties of an object in a failover cluster, such as a resource, a group, or a network
- `Set-ClusterQuorum`: Configures quorum options for a failover cluster
- `Set-ClusterResourceDependency`: Specifies the resources that a particular resource depends on within a failover cluster
- `Start-Cluster`: Starts the Cluster service on all nodes of the cluster on which it is not yet started
- `Start-ClusterGroup`: Brings one or more clustered services and applications, also known as *resource groups*, online on a failover cluster
- `Start-ClusterNode`: Starts the Cluster service on a node in a failover cluster
- `Start-ClusterResource`: Brings a resource online in a failover cluster
- `Stop-Cluster`: Stops the Cluster service on all nodes in a failover cluster, which stops all services and applications configured in the cluster
- `Stop-ClusterGroup`: Takes one or more clustered services and applications, also known as *resource groups*, offline on a failover cluster
- `Stop-ClusterNode`: Stops the Cluster service on a node in a failover cluster
- `Stop-ClusterResource`: Takes a resource offline in a failover cluster
- `Suspend-ClusterNode`: Suspends activity on a failover cluster node, that is, pauses the node
- `Suspend-ClusterResource`: Turns on maintenance for a disk resource or CSV so that you can run a disk maintenance tool without triggering failover
- `Test-Cluster`: Runs validation tests for failover cluster hardware and settings
- `Test-ClusterResourceFailure`: Simulates a failure of a cluster resource
- `Update-ClusterIPResource`: Renews or releases the DHCP lease for an IP address resource in a failover cluster
- `Update-ClusterNetworkNameResource`: Registers existing Network Name resources with a DNS server in a way that does not interrupt cluster availability

Configuring Failover and Preferences Settings

Usually in a cluster, one node is the same as another. However, you do have some control on which server is the preferred node and if a server fails back when the server is brought back online.

You have multiple nodes in a cluster. To specify that one node is the ***preferred node***, you can right-click a role and choose Properties. Then, in the Properties dialog box, select the General tab (see Figure 14-9). You can then click the server that you prefer and click the Up button to place it first in the list.

The default value for the maximum number of failures is n-1, where *n* is the number of nodes. Although you can change this value, it is recommended that you keep the value relatively low or the application or service will keep bouncing between nodes.

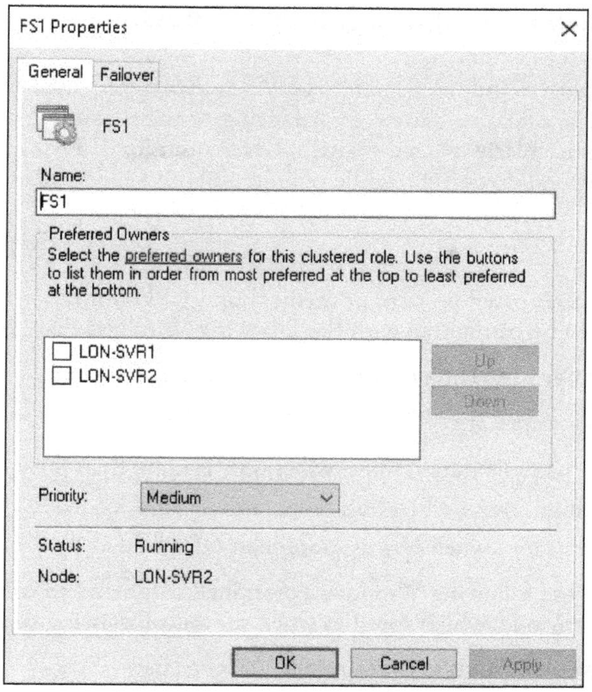

Figure 14-9

Specifying the preferred owner

FS1 Properties   ×

General | Failover

FS1

Name:
FS1

Preferred Owners

Select the preferred owners for this clustered role. Use the buttons to list them in order from most preferred at the top to least preferred at the bottom.

☐ LON-SVR1
☐ LON-SVR2

Up
Down

Priority: Medium

Status: Running
Node: LON-SVR2

OK   Cancel   Apply

If a cluster has multiple roles, you can specify the priority for each role. Roles with higher priorities are started before roles with lower priorities. If you don't want a role to start, you select *No Auto Start*.

When you click the Failover tab (see Figure 14-10), you can specify the number of times the Cluster service will attempt to restart or fail over. In the Failback option, you can specify not to fail back to the preferred owner after the preferred owner is brought back online and when the failback will occur.

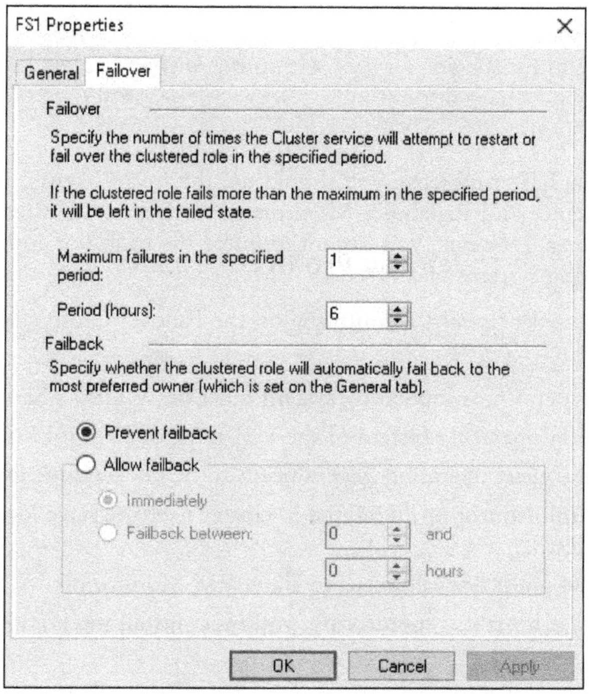

Figure 14-10

Specifying Failover and Failback options

FS1 Properties   ×

General | Failover

Failover

Specify the number of times the Cluster service will attempt to restart or fail over the clustered role in the specified period.

If the clustered role fails more than the maximum in the specified period, it will be left in the failed state.

Maximum failures in the specified period: 1

Period (hours):   6

Failback

Specify whether the clustered role will automatically fail back to the most preferred owner (which is set on the General tab).

◉ Prevent failback
○ Allow failback
    ○ Immediately
    ○ Failback between: 0   and
                            0   hours

OK   Cancel   Apply

Enabling and Configuring Node Fairness

> Starting with Windows Server 2016, *Node Fairness* is used to optimize the utilization of nodes in a failover cluster, by balancing or redistributing VMs running on a failover cluster, particularly when a node gets overcommitted. VMs are live migrated to idle nodes with no downtime, while maintaining possible owners and anti-affinity rules.

CERTIFICATION READY
Enable and configure
node fairness
Objective 5.4

Node Fairness is based on current memory and CPU utilization. The aggressiveness of balancing can be configured with the following Windows PowerShell command:

```
(Get-Cluster).AutoBalancerLevel = <value>
```

The available values are:

- **1:** Low (default value), move when host is more than 80% loaded
- **2:** Medium, move when host is more than 70% loaded
- **3:** High, move when host is more than 60% loaded

You can use the following Windows PowerShell command to configure the AutoBalancerMode, which specifies when the AutoBalancing will occur:

```
(Get-Cluster).AutoBalancerMode = <value>
```

The available values are:

- **0:** Disabled
- **1:** Balance on node join only
- **2:** Default value, balance on node join and every 30 minutes

To view the settings for your cluster, you can use the following Windows PowerShell command:

```
Get-Cluster | fl AutoBalancer*
```

Configuring VM Monitoring

> With Windows Server 2016, you can use *Virtual Machine Monitoring*, which is used to monitor specific services within the VM and reacts if there is a problem with a service.

CERTIFICATION READY
Configure VM monitoring
Objective 5.4

Any time you have problems, you should use the Event Viewer, Failover Cluster Manager, and Performance and Reliability Monitors to verify that a cluster runs and how well the cluster is doing. However, you cannot monitor the health of applications running inside the guest operating systems of a Hyper-V VM.

Before you can set up VM Monitoring on the Failover Cluster Manager, you must have the following:

- The Hyper-V host operating system must be Windows Server 2016.
- The guest operating system of the VM must be Windows Server 2012 or higher.
- The VM guest operating system needs to be on the same domain as the Hyper-V host.
- The administrator of the Hyper-V cluster needs to have local administrator rights on the VM guest.
- The VM guest firewall needs to allow VM Monitoring.
- To enable heartbeat monitoring, you must install integration services on the VM.

To enable VM Monitoring, right-click the VM in the Failover Cluster Manager and choose More Actions > Choose Configure Monitoring. In the Select Services dialog box, select the services that you want to monitor and click OK. You can also enable VM Monitoring with the following Windows PowerShell command:

```
Add-ClusterVMMonitoredItem -VirtualMachine "VM_Name" -Service
Name_of_Service
```

When the service is determined to be unhealthy, the Event ID 1250 is shown in the System logs. VM Monitoring will then restart the VM gracefully on the host that it's currently running on. If the VM fails again, VM Monitoring will move the VM to another node and start the VM. Virtual Machine Monitoring gives you a finer granularity of the kind of monitoring you want to have for your VMs. It also brings the added benefit of additional health checking and availability. Without Virtual Machine Monitoring, if a particular service has a problem, you will have to recognize the problem and then manually restart the service or move the VM to another host.

◼ Implementing Stretch and Site-Aware Failover Clusters

↓
THE BOTTOM LINE

Many companies have only one office, which is used to define a single site. If the site goes down, such as from a fire or flooding, the company would be at a standstill until a minimum number of servers were brought up and the data was restored from backups that were stored off-site. For larger companies, this type of solution is unacceptable. Therefore, assuming that the company has the money and resources, a backup site needs to be established so that it can be brought online and allow the company to function while the primary site is fixed and brought back online.

At the beginning of this lesson, using Hyper-V Replicas were used to make a backup copy of servers. The replicas can be used to replicate to a second site. However, the Hyper-V Replica is a cold server that must be brought online when the primary site is unavailable.

Another solution is to create a ***multi-site failover cluster***. A multi-site failover cluster has the following advantages, as compared with a replica VM:

- When a failure occurs, a multi-site cluster automatically fails over the clustered service or application to another.
- Because a site fails over automatically, a multi-site cluster has less administrative overhead than a cold standby server, which needs to be turned on and configured.

A multi-site failover cluster is similar to a standard failover cluster; however, you must take into account that the two sites are usually connected with a significantly slower WAN link as compared with links found in local area networks (LANs).

Configuring Multi-Site Storage and Network Settings

Because of the slower WAN link, there is no shared storage that cluster nodes on the two sites can use. Therefore, you need to use two separate storage systems, one at each site, and have some method to replicate the data between the two sites.

Because Microsoft Windows does not include a built-in mechanism for data replication, you need to use one of the following three methods:

- Block-level, hardware-based replication
- Software-based file replication
- Application-based replication

Some SANs have the capability to replicate data between SAN units. If not, you need to purchase another hardware system or software-based replication system to perform the replication. You should also check whether the shared application or service that you are running on the cluster has built-in replication. For example, both Microsoft Exchange and Microsoft SQL Server have replication built in to the software. Exchange Server has continuous replication, and SQL Server has several types of replication, including log shipping. In some situations, if the data that you replicate are small files that are typically closed, you can use Distributed File System (DFS) Replication.

When you configure multi-site replication, the replication is either synchronous or asynchronous. With **synchronous replication**, data is written to the remote site and then waits for a receive message stating that the data has been written to the remote site properly. If the message is not received, the data will be sent again. Although the synchronous replication keeps both sites the same, any slowness or delays over a WAN link slow the cluster application or service because the application or service waits for the data to be written to the remote site. Therefore, to use synchronous replication, you need high bandwidth between the two sites and low latency.

With **asynchronous replication**, the data is written to the primary storage device and then is written separately to the remote storage device, typically on its own schedule. However, most of these systems are written only after a short delay. The advantage of asynchronous replication is that it keeps the performance high for the clustered application or service.

Lastly, your network needs basic network services functioning when a site goes down, which includes Active Directory Domain Services (AD DS) and Domain Name System (DNS). Therefore, you need multiple domain controllers through your organization, including at least one at the secondary site. In addition, you should have multiple DNS servers, including at least one at the secondary site. Of course, for clients to use DNS at the secondary site, make sure that the secondary DNS server for the clients points to the DNS server at the secondary site.

Configuring Quorum and Failover Settings

Any time you deal with WAN links, you have to take into account that those links will have slower bandwidth and higher latency. Because failover is triggered by missing heartbeats, you might need to tweak the quorum and failover settings so that the failover will work more efficiently if it is a multi-site cluster.

CERTIFICATION READY
Configure failover and preference settings
Objective 5.4

By default, the heartbeat occurs once every second (1,000 milliseconds). If a node misses five consecutive heartbeats, another node will initiate failover.

For a cluster to operate properly over multiple sites, you should have at least one low-latency and reliable network connection between sites to carry the cluster heartbeats. If not, you will need to use the Failover settings (right-click the role, choose Properties, and then click the Failover tab) to specify the maximum failures in a specified period, so that a cluster does not fail over prematurely or unnecessarily.

Remember that you need enough nodes and votes to reach quorum, even if a site is down. Because the sites are geographically dispersed, you cannot use quorum configuration that requires a witness disk. If there are an odd number of nodes, use the Node Majority quorum. If there are an even number of nodes, which is typical in a geographically dispersed cluster, you can use the Node Majority with File Share Majority quorum.

If you use the Node Majority with File Share Majority quorum, you need to place the file share witness at a third site. In a multi-site cluster, a single server can host the file share witness. However, you must create a separate file share for each cluster.

With Windows Server 2016, you can adjust cluster quorum settings, including specifying which nodes can vote and which nodes cannot vote when determining quorum (see Figure 14-11). This might help you implement solutions across multiple sites and tweak settings after a major failure has occurred.

Figure 14-11

Selecting which nodes can vote

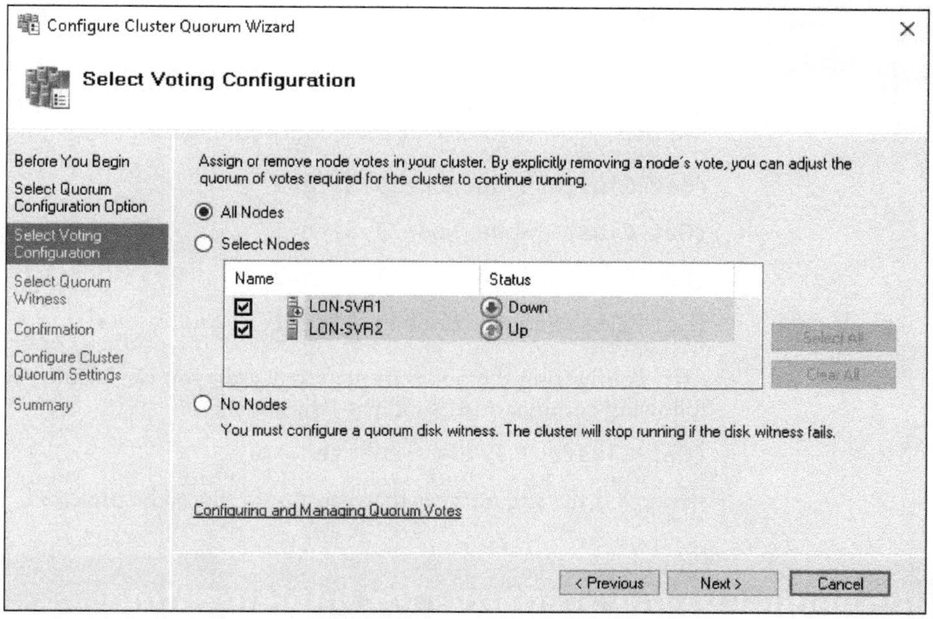

When you set up the multi-site failover cluster, it is not much different from normal local failover clusters. The high-level steps that you should perform when configuring a multi-site failover cluster are the following:

1. Ensure that you have enough cluster nodes at each site and that each node has similar hardware configuration and the same version of operating system and service packs.

2. Ensure that sites have stable connections, with sufficient bandwidth and low network latency. Latency validates when you run the Validate a Configuration Wizard in Failover Cluster Manager.

3. Ensure that you have a reliable storage replication mechanism between sites.

4. Make sure you have the basic network services available on each site, including AD DS, DNS, and DHCP.

5. Run the Validate a Configuration Wizard on all nodes and fix any problems that it might indicate.

6. Create a cluster.

7. Configure the cluster quorum mode.

8. Configure failover/failback settings.

9. Create the clustered role.

10. Test failover and failback.

Implementing Stretch Clusters

> When you implement a stretch cluster, Microsoft recommends using an Azure Cloud Witness. However, when you use an Azure Cloud Witness or a file share witness, you use the dynamic witness mode, which is the default mode in Windows Server 2016. Dynamic quorum and witness is used to avoid cluster shutdown when you lose an entire site, which might mean that you lose half or more of the cluster nodes at the same time.

To help you differentiate sites for cluster nodes, you can run the following commands to configure the nodes as site-aware:

```
(Get-ClusterNode Node1).Site=X
```

where *X* is the site number. For example, if you have four cluster nodes distributed between two sites, you would execute these four commands:

```
(Get-ClusterNode Node1).Site=1

(Get-ClusterNode Node2).Site=1

(Get-ClusterNode Node3).Site=2

(Get-ClusterNode Node4).Site=2
```

After configuring the nodes in preferred sites, you can identify a preferred site by running the following command in Windows PowerShell:

```
(Get-Cluster).PreferredSite = X
```

where *X* is the site number that you would like to be preferred.

■ Determining Usage Scenarios for Implementing Guest Clustering Solution Using Shared SAS Storage Enclosures

THE BOTTOM LINE

Guest clustering requires centralized storage. Larger organizations will have a SAN, which can be connected to your Hyper-V hosts via Fibre or iSCSI. However, smaller organizations might have a need for redundant systems, but cannot afford a SAN. In these situations, the small organization can look at shared SAS storage enclosures.

Shared serial-attached SCSI (SAS) is an option for smaller companies that give the benefits of storage area networks without the cost associated with iSCSI or Fibre Channel. You can then connect two or more servers with SAS cables to the SAS storage enclosure. The disadvantage of using SAS is you are limited in distance and most servers might need a SAS adapter if SAS is not available on the system motherboard.

SKILL SUMMARY

IN THIS LESSON YOU LEARNED:

- Failover clusters provide high availability and scalability to many server applications, such as Microsoft Exchange, Microsoft SQL, and Hyper-V. You can use the High Availability Wizard to configure a clustered role (formerly called a clustered service or application), which is a service or application that you make highly available.

- Scale-Out File Server cluster is an active-active failover cluster where all files shares are online on all nodes simultaneously. Although the Scale-Out File Server supports SMB, it does not support NFS, Data Deduplication, DFS Replication, or File Server Resource Manager.

- One popular use of failover clusters is to have Hyper-V provide highly available virtual machines. A failover cluster that is made up of two or more virtual machines is typically referred to as a guest cluster, which is used to provide highly available virtual machines. Highly available virtual machines can be migrated to another physical host in a failover cluster to provide continuing service when the current host goes down or needs maintenance.

- The Failover Cluster Manager is used to manage and monitor the cluster and its nodes. Most common options can be accessed from the cluster page.

- Usually in a cluster, one node is the same as another. However, you do have some control on which server is the preferred node and if a server fails back when the server is brought back online.

■ Knowledge Assessment

Multiple Choice

Select the correct answer for each of the following questions.

1. Which of the following should be configured to make a service or application highly available?
   a. Role
   b. Resource
   c. Device
   d. Storage

2. Which type of role is designed to work with Windows Server 2016 failover clusters?
   a. Generic clustered role
   b. Available role
   c. Cluster-aware clustered role
   d. Clustered update role

3. Which type of file server resembles the file server used in Windows Server 2008 R2?
   a. General Use File Server
   b. Scale-Out File Server
   c. Highly Available CSV
   d. Direct Access File Server

4. Which type of volume should be used for highly available virtual machines?
   a. SAS
   b. GPT
   c. DEP
   d. CSV

5. Which of the following should be configured to make one node be an active node while it is available?
   a. Failback partner
   b. Prioritized member
   c. Preferred owner
   d. Primary Active node

6. Which Windows PowerShell cmdlet is used to enable VM Monitoring?
   a. `Set-ClusterVMMonitoredItem`
   b. `Get-ClusterVMMonitoredItem`
   c. `Configure-ClusterVMMonitoredItem`
   d. `Add-ClusterVMMonitoredItem`

7. Which type of application or service should be configured on a cluster for an application or service that was not made for a cluster?
   a. Generic clustered role
   b. Available role
   c. Cluster-aware clustered role
   d. Clustered update role

8. Which of the following is supported by a Scale-Out File Server? (Choose all that apply.)
   a. NFS
   b. Data Deduplication
   c. SMB
   d. DFS Replication

9. As an administrator for the Contoso Corporation, you manage a two-node failover cluster with a witness disk. You need to take one of the servers down for maintenance. Which of the following should be performed?
   a. You should stop the Cluster service.
   b. You should unplug the network connections of the server before shutting down.
   c. You should drain the roles for the server that needs to be shut down.
   d. You should add a new node and then remove the node that needs to be taken down for maintenance.

Best Answer

Choose the letter that corresponds to the best answer. More than one answer choice may achieve the goal. Select the BEST answer.

1. The contoso.com site uses two servers called *Server1* and *Server2* that run Windows Server 2016 and have the Failover Clustering feature installed. As an administrator, you decide to add two more nodes to the cluster. You manage a folder for which you wants all the servers to provide services. Which of the following should be configured?
   a. File Server for general use
   b. Scale-Out File Server
   c. Preferred Server
   d. Handling priority

2. The contoso.com site uses two servers called *Server1* and *Server2* that run Windows Server 2016 and have the Failover Clustering feature installed. As an administrator, you have configured the application named *APP1* on the cluster. You need to make sure that Server2 handles all requests for App1. Which of the following should be configured?
   a. Preferred owner
   b. Possible owner
   c. Host priority
   d. Handling priority

3. The contoso.com site uses two servers called *Server1* and *Server2* that run Windows Server 2016 and have the Failover Clustering feature installed. As an administrator, you want to make a highly available file server that supports DFS. Which of the following should be configured?
   a. File Server for general use
   b. Scale-Out File Server
   c. Preferred Server
   d. Handling priority

4. The contoso.com site uses two servers called *Server1* and *Server2* that run Windows Server 2016 and have the Failover Clustering feature installed. As an administrator, you want to install a cluster that provides high availability for DHCP and a shared folder. You want to make sure that if two heartbeats are missed, the DHCP service is switched to another node on the cluster. Which of the following should be configured?
   a. Preferred owner
   b. Failover settings
   c. Host priority
   d. Handling priority

5. The contoso.com site uses two servers called *Server1* and *Server2* that run Windows Server 2016 and have the Failover Clustering feature installed. As an administrator, you configure the server to run a highly available virtual machine that is the DHCP server. Which of the following should be configured to monitor the DHCP service?
   a. Enable event forwarding
   b. Enable VM Monitoring
   c. Enable service monitoring
   d. Enable event subscriptions

Matching and Identification

1. Identify which of the following can be made highly available using the High Availability Wizard?

   _____ a. DFS Namespace Server

   _____ b. iSCSI client

   _____ c. Print services

   _____ d. DHCP Server

   _____ e. Message Queuing

   _____ f. Name resolver

   _____ g. WINS Server

   _____ h. Virtual machine

Build a List

1. Specify the correct order of steps necessary to creating a General Use File Server.

_____ Select File Server.

_____ Install the Failover Cluster feature.

_____ Create the cluster.

_____ Select File Server for general use.

_____ Start the High Availability Wizard.

_____ Select the storage to be used.

_____ Specify a name and IP address for the clients to access.

_____ Define a share by selecting a file share profile.

2. Specify the correct order of steps necessary to creating a Scale-Out File Server.

_____ Select File Server for general use.

_____ Install the Failover Cluster feature.

_____ Create the cluster.

_____ Enable continuous availability.

_____ Define a share by selecting a file share profile.

_____ Start the High Availability Wizard.

_____ Select File Server.

3. Specify the correct order of steps necessary to deploying a highly available virtual machine.

_____ Create the cluster.

_____ Install Windows Server 2016.

_____ Validate the cluster.

_____ Connect both computers to network and storage.

_____ Test the virtual machine failover.

_____ Install Hyper-V.

_____ Install the Failover Clustering feature.

_____ Prepare the disk to be used as a shared volume.

_____ Create a virtual machine.

_____ Use the High Availability Wizard to make the VM highly available.

_____ Create the necessary virtual switches.

_____ Enable the Clustered Shared storage.

■ Business Case Scenarios

Scenario 14-1: Deploying a Clustered File Server

As an administrator for the Contoso Corporation, you manage client software that receives its configuration from a shared folder. Therefore, you need to make sure that this shared folder is highly available. Because it is used by hundreds of users, many at the same time, you want to make sure that performance is high. Describe your recommended solution.

Scenario 14-2: Deploying a High Availability Virtual Machine

As an administrator for the Contoso Corporation, you manage an enterprise database application that has to be highly available. The application currently runs on a VM. Describe how to make the VM highly available.

15 LESSON

Implementing High Availability and Disaster Recovery Options in Hyper-V

70-740 EXAM OBJECTIVE

Objective 5.1 – Implement high availability and disaster recovery options in Hyper-V. This objective may include but is not limited to the following: Implement Hyper-V Replica; implement Live Migration; implement Shared Nothing Live Migration; configure CredSSP or Kerberos authentication protocol for Live Migration; implement Storage Migration.

Objective 5.5 – Manage VM movement in clustered nodes. This objective may include but is not limited to the following: Perform a Live Migration; perform a Quick Migration; perform a Storage Migration; configure VM Network Health Protection.

LESSON HEADING	EXAM OBJECTIVE
Implementing Virtual Machine Movement	Implement Live Migration
• Implementing Live Migration	Implement Shared Nothing Live Migration
• Implementing Quick Migration	Perform a Live Migration
• Implementing Storage Migration	Configure CredSSP or Kerberos authentication protocol for Live Migration
	Perform a Quick Migration
	Implement Storage Migration
	Perform a Storage Migration
Implementing Hyper-V Replica	Implement Hyper-V Replica
Configuring VM Network Health Protection	Configure VM Network Health Protection

KEY TERMS

Credential Security Support Provider (CredSSP)

Hyper-V Replica

Hyper-V Replica Broker server role

Kerberos

Live Migration (LM)

Network Health Protection

Quick Migration

shared nothing migration

Storage Migration

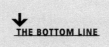

■ Implementing Virtual Machine Movement

THE BOTTOM LINE

Because of the ease with which virtual machines (VMs) can be created and the speed with which the services they provide grow, VM management can quickly become a problem. When this happens, you need a way to move the VM and its storage quickly and with as little inconvenience to your users as possible.

As a server administrator, VMs are one of the best tools to use for providing functionality on demand. With relative speed and ease, you can deliver additional applications as soon as they are needed rather than waiting for the purchase of new hardware.

However, there comes a time when that new application grows from being hardly used to being a mission-critical application that everyone in your organization relies on daily or even hourly. When that happens, inevitably, the server with which you started is no longer powerful enough to handle the load.

In these growth scenarios—when a more powerful server or more storage space is required—because the application started as a VM, it can be moved to that more powerful server or larger disk with relative ease and no server downtime. The challenge, however, is to move the existing VM from one physical computer to another *and* not impact your users.

In prior versions, moving VMs required either a cluster or powering the VM down and moving the files manually. Starting with Windows Server 2012, live VM movement is no longer limited to a cluster. You can now move an entire VM and its storage to another physical machine with ease while it is online and being used. Three processes are used to move an entire VM or its parts while it runs:

- *Live Migration (LM):* The process of moving an entire VM or parts of a VM to another physical server without a cluster
- *Quick Migration:* The process of moving an entire VM or parts of a VM to another physical server using a cluster
- *Storage Migration:* The process of moving the storage of a VM from one physical server to another without a cluster

Implementing Live Migration

LM is the process of moving a VM or its storage from one physical server to another without turning off the VM and without any perceived or actual downtime. In prior versions, the process of performing LM required the VM to be hosted within a clustered environment. In Windows Server 2012 or later, although that is still possible, it is no longer a requirement.

CERTIFICATION READY
Implement Live
Migration
Objective 5.1

CERTIFICATION READY
Implement Shared
Nothing Live Migration
Objective 5.1

CERTIFICATION READY
Perform a Live Migration
Objective 5.5

LM allows you to move the entire VM or its storage from one physical host to another without interrupting your users. This process is sometimes referred to as a ***shared nothing migration*** because the storage is mirrored over the network to the destination server while the VM continues to run and provide network services.

LM requires four steps to properly move a running VM. To perform an LM, your systems must perform the following steps:

1. Configure LM prerequisites.
2. Configure LM security (constrained delegation, if needed).
3. Configure the source and destination computers for LM.
4. Move a running VM or VM storage.

CONFIGURING LIVE MIGRATION, INCLUDING AUTHENTICATION

To support LM, you need two or more Windows Server 2016 servers with the Hyper-V role enabled, and they must meet the following requirements:

- They must use processors from the same manufacturer (for example, all Intel or all AMD).
- All hosts must support hardware virtualization.
- They must belong to the same Active Directory domain or two domains that trust one another; LM does not work with servers that are in a workgroup.
- The VMs must be configured to use VHD, VHDX, or virtual Fibre Channel disks.
- It is recommended they use a private network dedicated to LM traffic.
- Membership in one of the following groups on both the source and destination machines or in Active Directory for both domains (if using trusted domains) is required:
  - Administrators
  - Domain Admins
  - Hyper-V Administrators

In addition, you need to ensure that you have Hyper-V remote management tools installed and configured that can remotely manage both Hyper-V hosts.

Finally, you need to consider how you will perform the actual migration and from where you can or need to sign in to perform it. Will you perform the LM via a Keyboard, Video, and Monitor switch (KVM), through an attached monitor session, using Remote Desktop, using remote management tools, or through a Windows PowerShell session?

The answer to this consideration determines whether you will utilize *Credential Security Support Provider (CredSSP)* protocol, which enables you to securely delegate a user's credentials from a client to a target server, or whether you will use Kerberos to authenticate LM traffic. If you are not using remote management tools to perform a LM, you must sign on to the source server and use CredSSP to authenticate the LM. If you are using remote management tools, you need to configure constrained delegation and select Kerberos as the authentication protocol. *Kerberos* is a network authentication protocol that is designed to provide strong authentication for client/server applications by using secret-key cryptography and is used by Active Directory domains.

 ### CONFIGURE CONSTRAINED DELEGATION

GET READY. To configure constrained delegation, perform the following steps.

1. On LON-DC1, right-click **Start** and choose **Windows PowerShell (Admin)**.
2. In the Administrator: Windows PowerShell window, execute the following commands:

   ```
   setspn -S "Microsoft Virtual System Migration Services/LON-SVR1"
   LON-SVR1

   setspn -S "Microsoft Virtual System Migration Services/LON-SVR1.
   Adatum.com" LON-SVR1

   setspn -S "Microsoft Virtual System Migration Services/LON-SVR2"
   LON-SVR2

   setspn -S "Microsoft Virtual System Migration Services/LON-SVR2.
   Adatum.com" LON-SVR2
   ```

3. Close the Windows Administrator: Windows PowerShell window.
4. Using Server Manager, open the Active Directory Users and Computers snap-in.
5. In the navigation pane, expand the domain name and select the **Computers** folder.

6. In the Computers folder, identify the two (or more) servers you will use in this process: **LON-SVR1** and **LON-SVR2**.

7. Right-click the account of **LON-SVR1** (the server you are moving from) and choose **Properties**.

8. In the Properties dialog box, click the **Delegation** tab.

9. On the Delegation tab, select **Trust this computer for delegation to specified services only** and then select **Use Kerberos only**.

10. Click **Add**.

11. In the Add Services dialog box, click **Users or Computers**. The Select Users or Computers dialog box opens.

12. Type the name **LON-SVR2** (the server you are moving to).

13. Click **Check Names** to verify that you typed the name correctly and then click **OK**.

14. Back in the Add Services dialog box, the list of available services is displayed. Select both of the following and then click **OK**.

   • To move VM storage, select **CIFS**. This is required for moving the VM storage either with or without the VM.

   • To move VMs, select **Microsoft Virtual System Migration Service**.

15. Back in the Properties dialog box, on the Delegation tab, verify your selections and then click **OK** (see Figure 15-1).

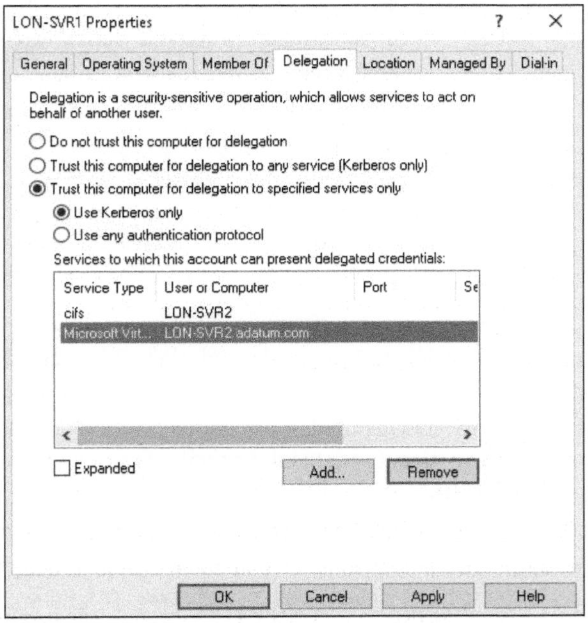

Figure 15-1

Verifying Delegation settings

16. For the next part of the process, repeat Steps 5 through 15, substituting the appropriate server name(s) where needed.

CONFIGURE THE SOURCE AND DESTINATION COMPUTERS FOR LM

GET READY. To prepare both the source and destination computers for an LM, perform the following steps.

1. On LON-SVR1, using Server Manager, click **Tools** and then click **Hyper-V Manager**.

2. In the navigation pane, click **LON-SVR1**.

3. In the Action pane, select **Hyper-V Settings**.

4. In the Hyper-V Settings dialog box, click **Live Migrations**.

5. In the Live Migrations pane, select **Enable incoming and outgoing live migrations** (see Figure 15-2).

Figure 15-2

Enabling the Live Migrations pane

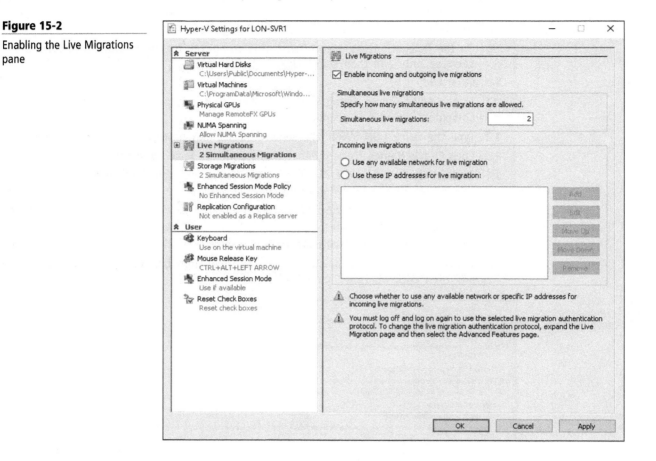

6. Expand the **Live Migrations** node and click **Advanced Features**.

7. In the Authentication protocol section, select **Use Kerberos** if you are using the Hyper-V remote management tools and have configured constrained delegation; otherwise, leave **Use Credential Security Support Provider (CredSSP)** selected.

8. Click the **Live Migrations** node again. In Simultaneous live migrations, specify a different number if you don't want to use the default of 2.

9. In Incoming live migrations, if you have configured dedicated network connections to accept LM traffic, select **Add** to type the IP address information. If you have not configured a dedicated network for LM, select **Use any available network for live migration** and then click **OK**.

USING WINDOWS POWERSHELL

You can configure and manage LM using the following cmdlets:

- PS C:\> Enable-VMMigration
- PS C:\> Set-VMMigrationNetwork [IP Address]
- PS C:\> Set-VMHost -VirtualMachineMigrationAuthenticationType Kerberos

MOVING VMs USING LIVE MIGRATION

The machines are now ready for the LM. In the sixth step of the following exercise, you are presented with three options for moving virtual machines. These options allow you the flexibility to either move the entire VM to one location or allow you to selectively move the various pieces to different locations.

TAKE NOTE*　As a best practice, keep in mind that unless there is some overwhelming technical need to do otherwise, it is best to keep virtual machines and disks together.

As shown in Figure 15-3, the two options for moving VMs are:

- **Move the virtual machine:** This is simplest because it moves all of the files of the VM to one location at one time.
- **Move the virtual machine's storage:** This provides the most options on where you can store the various components. Options include:
  - Move all of the virtual machine's data to a single location
  - Move the virtual machine's data to different locations
  - Move only the virtual machine's virtual hard disks

A storage live migration can move a virtual machine's storage while the VM is running.

Figure 15-3

Choose Move Type window

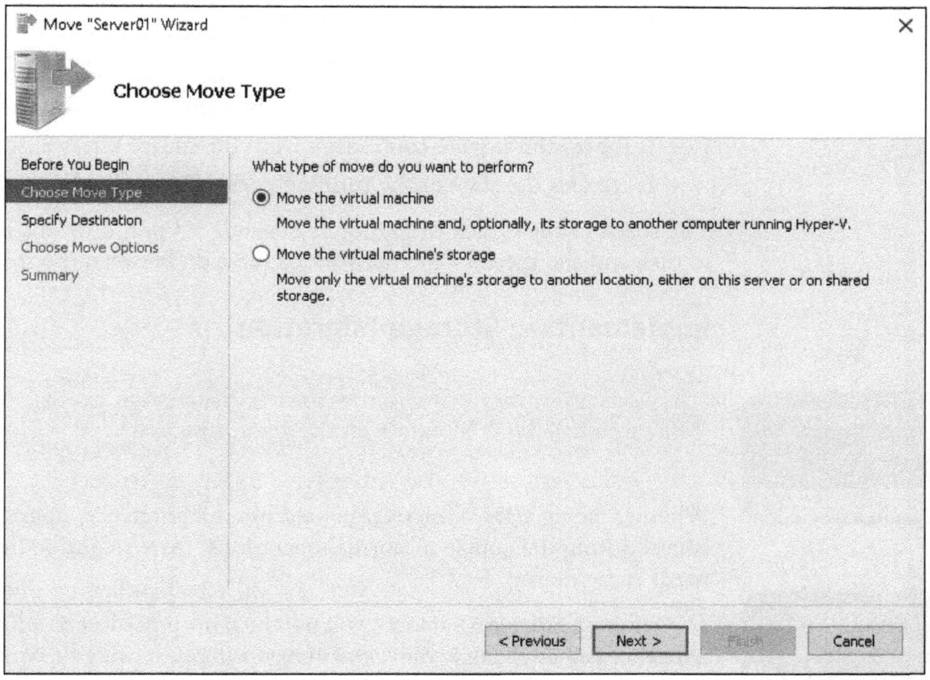

MOVE A RUNNING VM TO ANOTHER HYPER-V HOST

GET READY. To move a running VM to a single location, perform the following steps.

1. On LON-SVR1, open Hyper-V Manager.
2. In the Virtual Machines section of Hyper-V Manager, right-click the VM and choose **Move** to launch the Move Wizard.
3. On the Before You Begin page, click **Next**.
4. On the Choose Move Type page, select **Move the virtual machine**. Click **Next**.
5. On the Specify Destination page, browse to or type the name of the destination computer (such as **LON-SVR2**) and then click **Next**.

6. On the Choose Move Options page, select **Move all of the virtual machine's data to a single location**; this is the default and moves everything. Click **Next**.

7. On the Choose a new location for virtual machine page, in the New location Folder text box, type the path of the folder on the destination computer or browse to it and select the folder where you want to place the VM. Click **Next**.

8. On the Completing Move Wizard page, verify that your selections are correct and then click **Finish**.

Implementing Quick Migration

Windows Server 2016 includes a way to move a running VM that is hosted in a cluster called a Quick Migration.

Quick Migration is another process of moving a running VM from one physical host to another. However, Quick Migration occurs only within the confines of a cluster.

Quick Migration allows you to:

- Consolidate physical servers.
- Maintain availability of a production VM during host maintenance.
- Quickly restore services after service outages.

The process by which Quick Migration works is as follows:

- Quick Migration saves the state of the running guest VM to disk or shared storage.
- It moves the storage connection from the source physical server to the destination server.
- It restores the state of the running guest VM to the destination server.

The speed of the Quick Migration is dependent upon how much memory needs to be written to disk and the speed of the network connection between the source and destination servers.

Implementing Storage Migration

As VMs grow, they can outgrow their initial storage. Storage Migration is yet another way to move live VM data without disrupting users.

Whether facing a server or storage hardware maintenance, upgrades, or other performance issues, during the course of normal operations, there might be times when the VM storage needs to be moved.

To perform a Storage Migration, you use the same procedure as a Live Migration. The only difference is that you only move the storage without moving the virtual machine to a different host.

 MOVE THE VM's DATA TO A SINGLE LOCATION

GET READY. To move a running VM's data to a single location, perform the following steps.

1. Open Hyper-V Manager and in the navigation pane, select the name of the source server.

2. In the Virtual Machines section of Hyper-V Manager, right-click the VM and choose **Move** to launch the Move Wizard.

3. On the Before You Begin page, click **Next**.

4. On the Choose Move Type page, select **Move the virtual machine's storage** and then click **Next**.

5. On the Choose Options for Moving Storage page, select **Move the virtual machine's data to a single location**. This is the default and moves everything. Click **Next**.

6. On the Choose a New Location for Virtual Machine page, under the New location section Folder text box, type the path of the folder on the destination computer or browse to it and select the folder where you want to place the VM storage. Click **Next**.

7. On the Completing Move Wizard page, verify that your selections are correct and then click **Finish**.

 MOVE A RUNNING VM's DATA BY SELECTING WHERE TO MOVE THE ITEMS

GET READY. To move a running VM's data by selecting where to move the items, perform the following steps.

1. Open Hyper-V Manager and in the navigation pane, select the name of the source server.

2. In the Virtual Machines section of Hyper-V Manager, right-click the virtual machine and choose **Move** to launch the Move Wizard.

3. On the Before You Begin page, click **Next**.

4. On the Choose Move Type page, select **Move the virtual machine's storage**. Click **Next**.

5. On the Choose Move Options page, select the **Move the virtual machine's data to different locations** option. Click **Next**.

6. On the Specify Destination page, browse to or type the name of the destination computer and then click **Next**.

7. On the Select Items to Move page, as shown in Figure 15-4, select the items that you want to move and click **Next**.

Figure 15-4

Selecting items to move

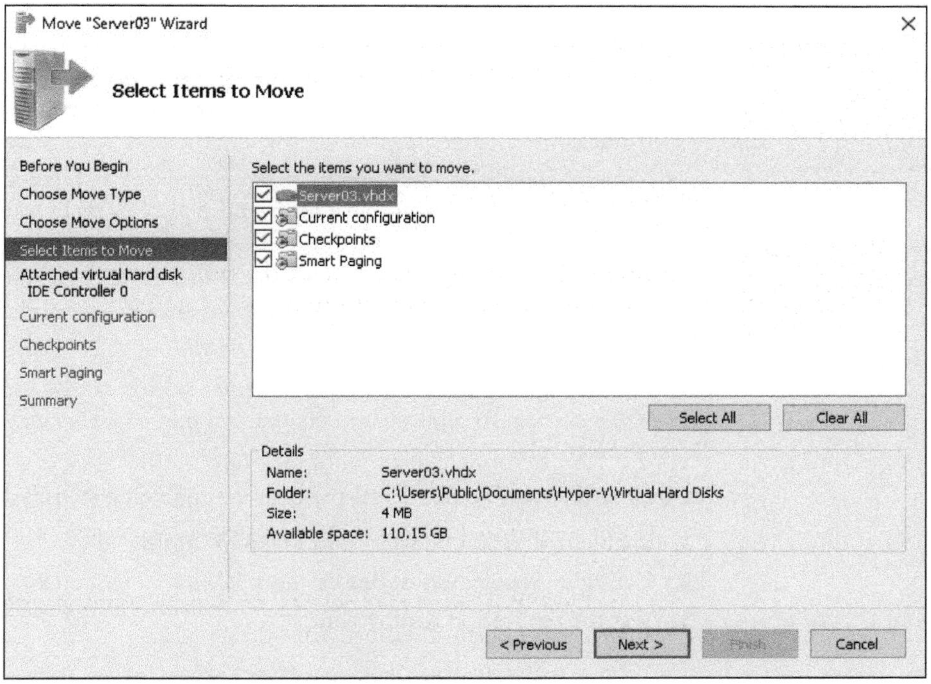

```
Move "Server03" Wizard                                                          ×

          Select Items to Move

Before You Begin            Select the items you want to move.
Choose Move Type            ☑ 📀 Server03.vhdx
Choose Move Options         ☑ 📄 Current configuration
Select Items to Move        ☑ 📄 Checkpoints
Attached virtual hard disk  ☑ 📄 Smart Paging
   IDE Controller 0
Current configuration
Checkpoints
Smart Paging
Summary
                                                        Select All      Clear All

                            Details
                            Name:            Server03.vhdx
                            Folder:          C:\Users\Public\Documents\Hyper-V\Virtual Hard Disks
                            Size:            4 MB
                            Available space: 110.15 GB


                                      < Previous    Next >     Finish     Cancel
```

8. On the Choose Move Options page, select **Move the virtual machine's data by selecting where to move the items** and then click **Next**.

9. On the Choose a New Location for Attached Virtual Hard Disk page, click **Browse**. In the Select Folder dialog box, navigate to and click the desired drive and folder in which you want to store the new components, and then click the **Select Folder** button. Then click **Next**.

10. On the Summary page, click **Finish**.

■ Implementing Hyper-V Replica

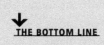
THE BOTTOM LINE

The reason that you perform backups is to be ready when you need to perform data recovery. Using clustering, you can provide fault tolerance for servers. However, when disasters occur that cause the cluster to fail or the virtual machine (VM) or data that you have on the central storage device becomes corrupted, it takes time to perform any repairs and restore from backup. To help overcome this problem, Hyper-V Replica was created.

CERTIFICATION READY
Implement Hyper-V Replica
Objective 5.1

Hyper-V Replica (offline copy) allows you to replicate a Hyper-V VM from one Hyper-V host at a primary site to another Hyper-V host at the replica site. The Hyper-V Replica is used as a spare server, which is stored on another central storage device at another site. It would also be a cold server, since the server is off until you need it and will need to be powered on and some configuration may be needed depending on where the replica resides when it is turned on and how it is to be used.

To keep the replica updated, Hyper-V Replica tracks the write operations on the primary VM and then replicates the changes to the replica over a wide area network (WAN) link. If the primary site goes down, you can then bring up the replica server in minutes. In addition, Hyper-V Replica enables you to restore virtualized workloads to a point in time depending on the Recovery History selections for the VM.

Hyper-V Replica consists of the following components:

- **Replication engine:** The component that manages the replication configuration details and manages initial replication, delta replication, failover, and test-failover operations.
- **Change tracking:** The component that tracks changes on the primary copy of the VM. It tracks the changes regardless of where the VM .vhdx files reside.
- **Network module:** The component that provides a secure and efficient way to transfer VM replicas between primary hosts and replica hosts by using compression and encryption (using HTTPS and certificate-based authentication).
- *Hyper-V Replica Broker server role:* A new server role (introduced in Windows Server 2012) that redirects all VM-specific events to the appropriate node in the replica cluster. It is configured as part of the failover cluster.

Hyper-V Replica is part of the Hyper-V server role. It can be used on servers that are not part of the cluster. To replicate servers that are part of a cluster, you use the Hyper-V Replica Broker server role.

To deploy Hyper-V Replica, you perform the following steps:javascript:;

1. Enable replication between two Hyper-V hosts.
2. Configure replication of one or more VMs.
3. Test the replication deployment.

To enable Hyper-V Replica, you configure the Hyper-V server settings, including selecting the authentication and port options and configuring authorization options. In addition, you must configure the location for replica files.

To use encryption for the replication, you need to use certificate-based authentication (HTTPS). You then need to use an existing X.509v3 certificate or create a self-signed certificate. In either case, the certificate needs to meet the following criteria:

- The certificate must not be expired or revoked.
- The certificate must include both client and server authentication extensions for enhanced key usage (EKU) and an associated private key.
- The certificate must terminate at a valid root certificate in the Trusted Root Certification Authorities store on the replica server.
- If the VM is hosted by a stand-alone server, the subject common name (CN) contains the fully qualified domain name (FQDN) of the host. If the VM is hosted by a failover cluster, the subject common name (CN) should contain the FQDN of the Hyper-V Replica Broker.

⊖ ENABLE HYPER-V REPLICATION

GET READY. To enable Hyper-V replication, perform the following steps on both Hyper-V hosts.

1. Using Server Manager, open Hyper-V Manager. The Hyper-V Manager console opens.
2. Right-click the **Hyper-V** host and choose **Hyper-V Settings**.
3. In the Hyper-V Settings dialog box, click **Replication Configuration**.
4. In the Replication Configuration section, click to enable the **Enable this computer as a Replica server** option (see Figure 15-5).
5. To enable Kerberos authentication, click to select **Use Kerberos (HTTP)**.

Figure 15-5

Configuring host replication

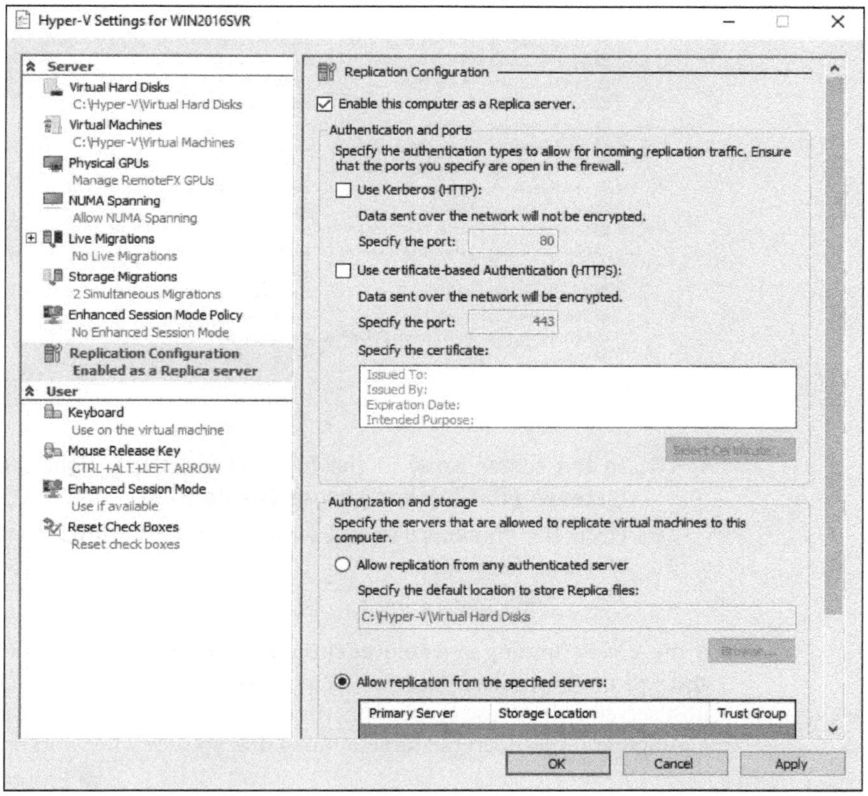

6. To use certificate-based authentication, click to select **Use certificate-based authentication (HTTPS)**.

7. In the Authorization and storage section, click to select **Allow replication from any authenticated server** and then click **Browse**.

8. Click **Computer**, double-click **Local Disk (E)**, and then click **New folder**. In the Name text box, type **VMReplica** and then press **Enter**.

9. Select the **E:\VMReplica** folder and then click **Select Folder**.

10. Click **OK** to close the Hyper-V Settings dialog box.

11. When inbound traffic needs to be allowed in the firewall, click **OK**.

12. Open Control Panel, click **System and Security**, and then click **Windows Firewall**.

13. Click **Advanced settings**.

14. In the Windows Firewall with Advanced Security console, click **Inbound Rules**, as shown in Figure 15-6.

Figure 15-6

Configuring inbound rules

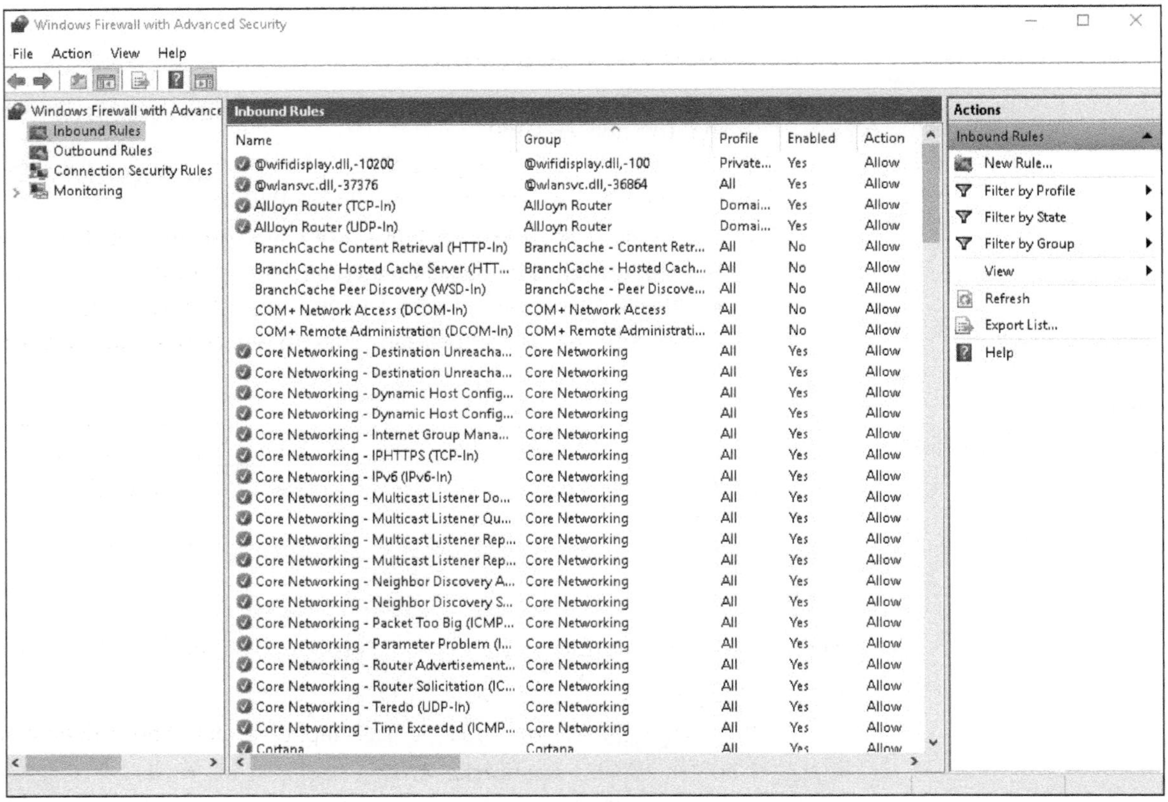

15. In the center pane, in the Inbound Rules list, right-click **Hyper-V Replica HTTP Listener (TCP-In)** and choose **Enable Rule**.

16. Close the Windows Firewall with Advanced Security console, and then close Windows Firewall.

If the VM is running in a failover cluster, the replication options in Hyper-V will be grayed out and will not be available. Instead, you have to open the Failover Cluster Manager, right-click the host server, and choose Hyper-V Settings. In the Hyper-V Settings dialog box, click Replication Configuration to open the same options that you see when you open the Hyper-V Settings.

INSTALL AND CONFIGURE THE HYPER-V REPLICA BROKER

GET READY. To install and configure the Hyper-V Replica Broker, perform the following steps.

1. Using Server Manager, open Failover Cluster Manager.
2. Right-click **Roles** and choose **Configure Role**.
3. In the High Availability Wizard, click **Next**.
4. On the Select Role dialog page, click **Hyper-V Replica Broker** and click **Next**.
5. On the Client Access Point page, specify the name and IP address of the client access point and click **Next**.
6. On the Confirmation page, click **Next**.
7. On the Summary page, click **Finish**.
8. With Failover Cluster Manager, click **Roles**, right-click **Hyper-V Replica Broker**, and choose **Replication Settings**.
9. In the Replication Configuration section, click to enable **Enable this computer as a Replica server**.
10. To enable Kerberos authentication, click to select **Use Kerberos (HTTP)**.
11. To use certificate-based authentication, click to select **Use certificate-based authentication (HTTPS)**.
12. In the Authorization and storage section, click to select **Allow replication from any authenticated server** and then click **Browse**.
13. Click **Computer**, double-click **Local Disk (E)**, and then click **New folder**. In the Name text box, type **VMReplica** and then press **Enter**.
14. Select the **E:\VMReplica** folder and then click **Select Folder**.
15. Click **OK** to close the Hyper-V Replica Broker Configuration dialog box.

After you enable replication on the host, you need to configure the VMs to replicate. During this configuration, you must specify the replica server name, options for the connection, and the virtual hard disks that you want to replicate. Lastly, you can configure the recovery history and the initial replication method.

 CONFIGURE REPLICATION FOR A VM

GET READY. To configure replication for a VM, perform the following steps.

1. Using Server Manager, open Hyper-V Manager.
2. Right-click the VM that you want to replicate and choose **Enable Replication**.
3. When the Enable Replication Wizard begins, click **Next**.
4. On the Specify Replica Server page, in the Replica server text box, type the name of the replica server that you want to copy to. Click **Next**.
5. On the Specify Connection Parameters page (see Figure 15-7), click **Next**.
6. On the Choose Replication VHDs page, the virtual hard disks are already selected. Click **Next**.
7. On the Configure Recovery History page, the Only the latest recovery point option is already selected. Click **Next**.
8. On the Choose Initial Replication Method page (see Figure 15-8), the Send initial copy over the network option and the Start replication immediately option are already selected. Click **Next**.
9. On the Summary page, click **Finish**.

Figure 15-7

Configuring the connection parameters

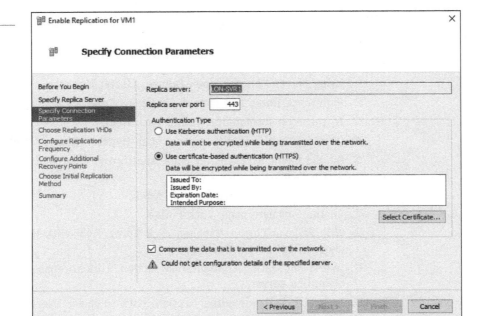

Figure 15-8

Configuring initial replication methods

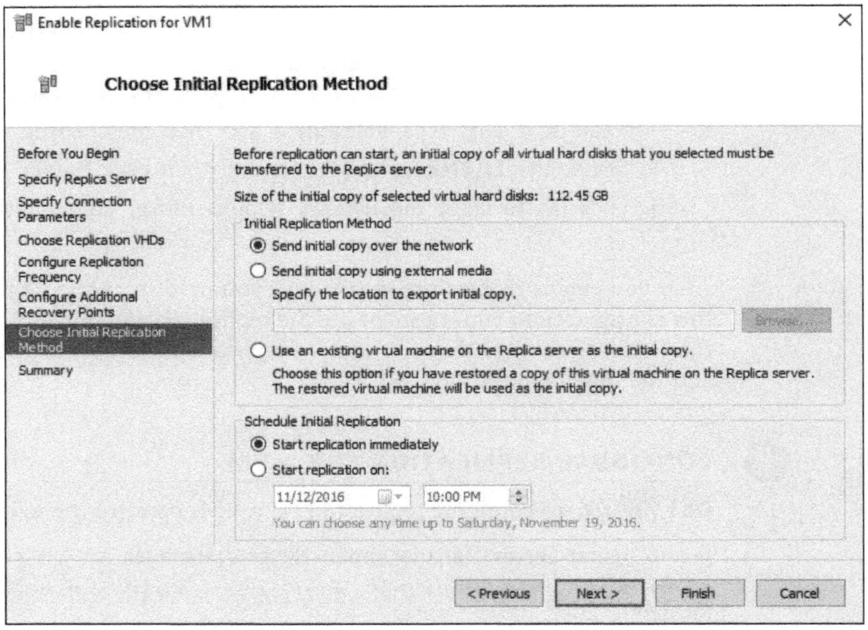

10. If an Enable Replication message appears notifying you that Replication enabled successfully but the network adapters for the Replica VM are not connected to any network, click **Settings**.

11. In the Settings dialog box, select the virtual switch that you want to use and click **OK**. After a period of time, the server will be replicated to the second Hyper-V host.

After you start the replication, you can check on the status of the replication by right-clicking the VM and choosing Replication > View Replication Health. Figure 15-9 shows the replication health of a VM.

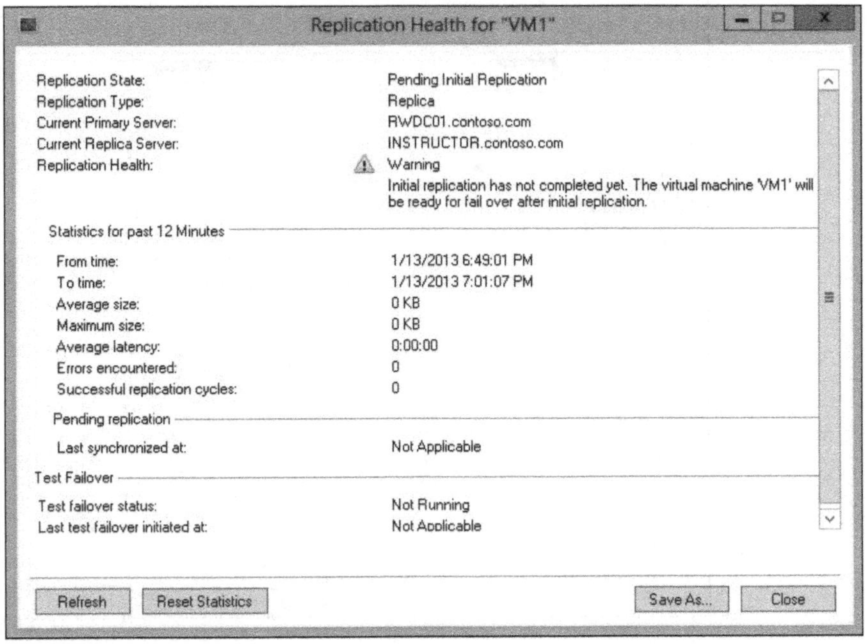

Figure 15-9

Viewing replication health

Replication Health for "VM1"

Replication State:	Pending Initial Replication
Replication Type:	Replica
Current Primary Server:	RWDC01.contoso.com
Current Replica Server:	INSTRUCTOR.contoso.com
Replication Health:	⚠ Warning
	Initial replication has not completed yet. The virtual machine 'VM1' will be ready for fail over after initial replication.

Statistics for past 12 Minutes

From time:	1/13/2013 6:49:01 PM
To time:	1/13/2013 7:01:07 PM
Average size:	0 KB
Maximum size:	0 KB
Average latency:	0:00:00
Errors encountered:	0
Successful replication cycles:	0

Pending replication

Last synchronized at:	Not Applicable

Test Failover

Test failover status:	Not Running
Last test failover initiated at:	Not Applicable

Refresh   Reset Statistics   Save As...   Close

■ Configuring VM Network Health Protection

THE BOTTOM LINE

A network outage can have serious repercussions to a virtual infrastructure. For a larger virtual infrastructure, you should always use network teaming to provide network redundancy to help protect against faulty cabling, or switches. *Network Health Protection* was introduced with Windows Server 2012 R2. It provides network high availability with Hyper-V, which automatically migrates from one failover cluster node to another failover cluster node if network connectivity on a specific network adapter becomes disconnected.

CERTIFICATION READY
Configure VM Network
Health Protection
Objective 5.5

When Network Health Protection is enabled, it checks every 60 seconds to see if a network connection is available or not. Once it discovers a disconnect, the resource checks the other nodes to see if the resources needed to run the VM are available. If the resources are available, the cluster resource initiates a Live Migration to move to another failover cluster node. In many cases, a network failure requires the VM to wait in a queued state for movement to another failover cluster node.

 CONFIGURE THE PROTECTED NETWORK SETTING

GET READY. To configure the protected network setting, perform the following steps.

1. Using Server Manager, open Hyper-V Manager.
2. In Hyper-V Manager, right-click a VM and choose **Settings**.
3. In the Settings dialog box, click the **Network Adapter**.
4. Expand the **Network Adapter** and click **Advanced Features**.

Figure 15-10

Configure protected network
setting

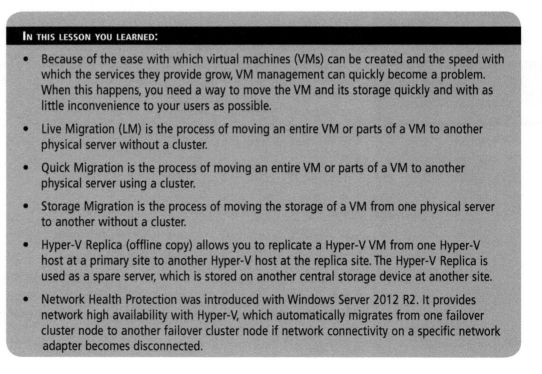

5. By default, **Protected network** is already selected, as shown in Figure 15-10.
6. To close the Settings dialog box, click **OK**.

SKILL SUMMARY

IN THIS LESSON YOU LEARNED:

- Because of the ease with which virtual machines (VMs) can be created and the speed with which the services they provide grow, VM management can quickly become a problem. When this happens, you need a way to move the VM and its storage quickly and with as little inconvenience to your users as possible.

- Live Migration (LM) is the process of moving an entire VM or parts of a VM to another physical server without a cluster.

- Quick Migration is the process of moving an entire VM or parts of a VM to another physical server using a cluster.

- Storage Migration is the process of moving the storage of a VM from one physical server to another without a cluster.

- Hyper-V Replica (offline copy) allows you to replicate a Hyper-V VM from one Hyper-V host at a primary site to another Hyper-V host at the replica site. The Hyper-V Replica is used as a spare server, which is stored on another central storage device at another site.

- Network Health Protection was introduced with Windows Server 2012 R2. It provides network high availability with Hyper-V, which automatically migrates from one failover cluster node to another failover cluster node if network connectivity on a specific network adapter becomes disconnected.

Knowledge Assessment

Multiple Choice

Select the correct answer for each of the following questions.

1. Which of the following allows the placement of an offline copy of a VM that is regularly updated?
   a. Data deduplication
   b. DFS replication
   c. Cluster replication
   d. Hyper-V Replica

2. Which component of the Hyper-V Replica performs the replication of VMs?
   a. Replication engine
   b. Change Tracking
   c. Network module
   d. Change Manager

3. How is data replicated when replicating to a Hyper-V Replica?
   a. HTTP
   b. Telnet
   c. FTP
   d. TFTP

4. Which program is normally used to enable Hyper-V replication?
   a. Hyper-V Manager
   b. Hyper-V Replica
   c. Failover Cluster Manager
   d. Hyper-V Replica Broker

5. When a VM is replicated as a Hyper-V Replica, the replicated VM is considered to be which of the following?
   a. Cold server
   b. Warm server
   c. Hot server
   d. Dynamic server

6. Which of the following provides encryption for Hyper-V replication over the network?
   a. HTTPS
   b. SSH
   c. SFTP
   d. TFTP

7. If a secondary site is available to be used as a backup site, which basic network services are necessary? (Choose all that apply.)
   a. SMTP
   b. SQL Server
   c. AD DS
   d. DNS

8. Which of the following advanced options are available when selecting where to move items during an LM?
   a. Copy the virtual machine.
   b. Move the virtual machine's data by selecting where to move the items.
   c. Register the virtual machine in place.
   d. Move the virtual machine's data automatically.

9. When using remote management tools to perform LM, which of the following needs to be configured?
   a. CredSSP
   b. Kerberos
   c. OVF
   d. Constrained delegation

10. Which of the following is the name of the process for moving an entire VM or parts of a VM to another physical server without a cluster?
    a. Quick Migration
    b. Storage Migration
    c. Constrained delegation
    d. Live Migration

11. Which of the following is the name of the process for moving an entire VM or parts of a VM to another physical server using a cluster?
    a. Quick Migration
    b. Storage Migration
    c. Constrained delegation
    d. Live Migration

12. Two servers, Server1 and Server2 are running Windows Server 2016 and the Hyper-V server role. VMs need to be replicated between Server1 and Server2, encryption with SSL needs to be used, and a digital certificate for SSL is needed. Which of the following intended purposes of the certificate are needed? (Choose two answers.)
    a. Client authentication
    b. Server authentication
    c. IP security
    d. KDC authentication

13. Three physical hosts, called Server1, Server2, and Server3, are all running Windows Server 2016. Server1 and Server2 make up the failover cluster Cluster1. Cluster1 has the Hyper-V Replica Broker server role installed and is hosting several VMs. Which of the following tools are needed to configure the VMs to replicate to Server3? (Choose two answers.)
    a. Hyper-V Manager console connected to Server3
    b. Hyper-V Manager console connected to Cluster1
    c. Failover Cluster Manager console connected to Cluster1
    d. Failover Cluster Manager console connected to Server3

Best Answer

1. Which of the following is used to enable Hyper-V Replica if a failover cluster is installed on a server where Hyper-V is installed?
   a. Hyper-V Manager
   b. Hyper-V Replica
   c. Failover Cluster Manager
   d. Hyper-V Replica Broker

2. Two servers, Server1 and Server2, are running Windows Server 2016. Both servers have the Hyper-V server role installed. Server1 is in the primary site and Server2 is in the secondary site, which are connected over a slow WAN link. Server1 is running a VM.

If Server1 fails, how can you start a copy of the VM on Server2, while keeping the cost low?

a. Install MPIO on Server1 and modify the storage locations of the VM.

b. Install MPIO on Server2 and modify the storage locations of the VM.

c. On Server1, modify the Replication Configuration settings and enable the replication of VM.

d. On Server2, modify the Replication Configuration settings and enable the replication of the VM.

Matching and Identification

1. Identify the components of Hyper-V Replica.

   _____ **a.** Hyper-V Replica Broker Server Role

   _____ **b.** Network module

   _____ **c.** Change tracking

   _____ **d.** Address module

   _____ **e.** Replication engine

   _____ **f.** Replication Authentication Module

   _____ **g.** Replication plug-in

Build a List

1. Specify the correct order of the steps necessary to deploying Hyper-V Replica. Not all steps will be used.

   _____ Enable replication between two Hyper-V hosts.

   _____ Configure replication of one or more VMs.

   _____ Schedule when the system will be replicated each day.

   _____ Test the replication deployment.

   _____ Enable the Replication Service using the Services console.

2. Specify the correct order of the steps necessary to enabling Hyper-V replication between Server1 and Server2. Not all steps will be used.

   _____ Drag the VM to the Allow side.

   _____ Click Replication Configuration.

   _____ Open the firewall for replication.

   _____ Enable the Replica Service.

   _____ Enable the Enable this computer as a replica server option.

   _____ Install IPsec.

   _____ Using Hyper-V Manager, right-click the host and choose Hyper-V Settings.

   _____ Specify the location to store the replicas.

■ Business Case Scenarios

Scenario 15-1: Replicating a VM to a Secondary Site

You are an administrator managing multiple sites within your corporation. At the main office, you manage most of the servers for your company. The secondary site is a data recovery site in the event there might be a major problem at the primary site. The primary servers are VMs on Server01 that need to run all the time. Describe how to create a backup copy of Server01 at the secondary site?

Scenario 15-2: Performing Live Migration

Server01 is in need of maintenance. You use Live Migration to move a VM from Server01 to Server02. When the maintenance is complete, you try to move the VM back to Server01 from the Hyper-V Manager on Server01 and encounter the following error: Virtual machine migration operation failed at migration Source. Failed to establish a connection with host Server01: No credentials are available in the security package (0x8009030E). Why does this occur?

Implementing Storage Spaces Direct

70-740 EXAM OBJECTIVE

Objective 5.3 – Implement Storage Spaces Direct. This objective may include but is not limited to the following: Determine scenario requirements for implementing Storage Spaces Direct; enable Storage Spaces Direct using Windows PowerShell; implement a disaggregated Storage Spaces Direct scenario in a cluster; implement a hyper-converged Storage Spaces Direct scenario in a cluster.

LESSON HEADING	EXAM OBJECTIVE
Implementing Storage Spaces Direct	Determine scenario requirements for implementing Storage Spaces Direct
– Determining Scenario Requirements for Implementing Storage Spaces Direct	Enable Storage Spaces Direct using Windows PowerShell
– Enabling Storage Spaces Direct Using Windows PowerShell	Implement a hyper-converged Storage Spaces Direct scenario in a cluster
– Implementing a Hyper-Converged Storage Spaces Direct Scenario in a Cluster	Implement a disaggregated Storage Spaces Direct scenario in a cluster
– Implementing a Disaggregated Storage Spaces Direct Scenario in a Cluster	

KEY TERMS

disaggregated deployment scenario

hyper-converged deployment scenario

Storage Spaces Direct

■ Implementing Storage Spaces Direct

THE BOTTOM LINE

In Lesson 4, Storage Spaces was discussed, showing how to combine multiple disks into a single logical volume that can be mirrored to protect against one or more drive failures. *Storage Spaces Direct* goes one step further by using industry-standard servers with local-attached drives to create highly available, highly scalable, software-defined storage at a fraction of the cost of a traditional SAN or NAS array. It can use the internal disks as nodes in a cluster, or by directly attaching to nodes in a cluster via an enclosure, which can be aggregated to form a virtual disk.

The advantage of using Storage Spaces is to use inexpensive storage with or without external storage and to use different types of storage in the same pool, such as SATA, SAS, USB, or SCSI. If necessary, you can add additional drives or servers to grow a pool, and you can designate drives as hot spares.

You cannot use Storage Spaces for the boot or system volume. You cannot use VHDs and pass-through disks in a virtual machine. In addition, you cannot use Fibre Channel or iSCSI.

The Storage Spaces Direct feature consists of the following components (as shown in Figure 16-1):

- **Network:** The network interface card must be capable of Remote Direct Memory Access (RDMA) or two network interface cards must be present to ensure performance and minimize latency.
- **Servers:** Each server or storage node has local internal disks or an enclosure with multiple disks that connects externally. Similar to multiple disks used in Storage Spaces, Storage Spaces Direct requires at least two servers, and a maximum of 16 servers. Additional servers will be needed based on the resilience chosen. Intranode communications is provided by SMB via a Software Storage Bus, which combines storage of each node so they are visible to the Storage Spaces layer.
- **Storage pools:** The storage pool uses local storage from all servers.

Figure 16-1

Storage Spaces Direct, hyper-converged and disaggregated

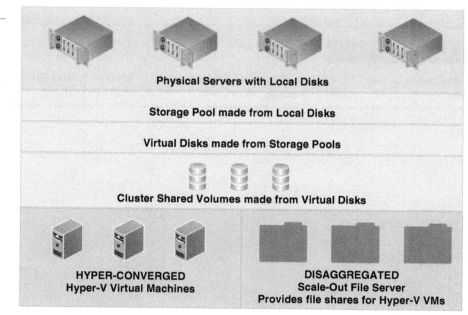

- **Storage spaces:** Virtual disks are created from the storage pool. Based on the resiliency chosen, you can provide fault tolerance for disk and server failure because the data is stored on disks on different servers.
- **CSVs:** CSVs consolidate all volumes into a single namespace, which is accessible through the file system on any cluster node.
- **Scale-Out File Server:** Scale-Out File Server provides access to the storage system by using SMB 3.0. The Scale-Out File Server is only needed for the disaggregated configuration.

Determining Scenario Requirements for Implementing Storage Spaces Direct

Storage Spaces Direct can be used to store Hyper-V virtual machine (VM) files or for second storage for Hyper-V Replica virtual machine files. Microsoft recognizes two deployment scenarios, including disaggregated deployment and hyper-converted deployment. You can also use Storage Spaces Direct with Azure virtual machines.

Storage Spaces Direct in the current implementation requires a minimum of 2 servers, and it supports up to 12 servers. You can add up to 240 disks to a storage pool.

In the ***hyper-converged deployment scenario***, the Hyper-V and Storage Spaces Direct components are on the same cluster. The virtual machine's files are stored on a Cluster Shared Volume. You can scale Hyper-V computer clusters and storage together, without configuring file access and permissions. Once Storage Spaces Direct is configured and the CSV volumes are available, you configure and provision Hyper-V as a failover cluster.

In the ***disaggregated deployment scenario***, one cluster is for Hyper-V and the other is used as a Scale-Out File Server. This solution gives extra processing power for the virtualization systems, while providing extra storage capacity. Because you are using a Scale-Out File Server, the file share is accessed over the network using the Server Message Block (SMB) 3.0 protocol.

Other uses for Storage Spaces Direct are storage of Hyper-V Replica files or backup or archival of virtual machine files. In addition, Microsoft supports Storage Spaces Direct for SQL Server 2012 or later to store both system and user database files. However, Microsoft does not support using Storage Spaces Direct for Microsoft Exchange.

If you have a multi-tenant scenario where you need to isolate clients from others, you can delegate on a per–storage pool basis. In these situations, you can control and isolate access by using Access Control Lists (ACLs), which can be fully integrated with Active Directory Domain Services. In addition, you can protect tampering and eavesdropping attacks by using SMB Encryption. The encryption algorithm used is AES-CCM, which also provides data integrity validation.

Enabling Storage Spaces Direct Using Windows PowerShell

Storage Spaces Direct is managed using Windows PowerShell, which includes cmdlets for storage and failover clusters.

Some of these cmdlets include the following:

- **Enable-ClusterStorageSpacesDirect:** Configures a cluster for the Storage Spaces Direct feature
- **Enable-ClusterS2D:** Configures a cluster for the Storage Spaces Direct feature for use with Non-Volatile Memory Express (NVMe) devices and SATA SSDs

- **Optimize-StoragePool:** Rebalances storage optimization if a disk or storage node changes
- **Debug-StorageSubsystem:** Displays any faults that are affecting the Storage Spaces Direct feature

The syntax of Enable-ClusterStorageSpacesDirect (and Enable-ClusterS2D) is:

```
Enable-ClusterStorageSpacesDirect [-Autoconfig] [-
CacheMetadataReserveBytes <UInt64> ] [-CachePageSizeKBytes <UInt32>
{8 | 16 | 32 | 64}]
```

The Autoconfig is used to automatically create and configure the pool. AutoConfig is the default value. The –CachePageSizeKBytes specifies the page size used by the Storage Spaces Direct cache. The default value is 16 KB.

Implementing a Hyper-Converged Storage Spaces Direct Scenario in a Cluster

For smaller companies, Storage Spaces Direct can provide local storage as highly available storage. This section shows you how to create a hyper-converged Storage Spaces Direct scenario in a cluster.

CERTIFICATION READY
Implement a hyper-converged Storage Spaces Direct scenario in a cluster
Objective 5.3

The main tasks for this exercise are as follows:

1. Install the Windows Server roles and features.
2. Validate cluster configuration.
3. Create a cluster.
4. Enable the Storage Spaces Direct feature.
5. Create a storage pool.
6. Create a virtual disk.
7. Test high availability for the storage.
8. Create virtual machines.

 IMPLEMENT A HYPER-CONVERGED STORAGE SPACES DIRECT SCENARIO IN A CLUSTER

GET READY. To implement a hyper-converged Storage Spaces Direct scenario in a cluster, perform the following steps.

1. To install the required roles and features on the servers that will be a part of the Storage Spaces Direct cluster, use the following Windows PowerShell command:

   Install-WindowsFeature –Name File-Services, Failover-Clustering –IncludeManagementTools

2. To validate the hardware configuration for Storage Spaces Direct, use the following Windows PowerShell command:

   Test-Cluster-Node <computer names for the nodes in the cluster> –Include "Storage Spaces Direct"

3. To create the cluster without adding any storage, use the following Windows PowerShell command:

   New-Cluster –Name <Cluster name> –Node <computer names for the nodes in the cluster> –NoStorage

   –StaticAddress <IP address>

4. To configure the cluster properties to enable the Software Storage Bus and add storage, use the following Windows PowerShell command:

```
Enable-ClusterStorageSpacesDirect -Cluster S2DCluster
```

As the Storage Spaces Direct cluster is built, all the available disks on each server node will be discovered and claimed into the Storage Spaces Direct pool created.

5. To create the storage pool in the cluster, use the following Windows PowerShell command:

```
New-StoragePool -StorageSubSystemName <Cluster name>
-FriendlyName <Storage Pool name>
```

A new virtual disk is called MultiResilient. Optionally, you can rename the virtual disk to a more meaningful name.

6. To create the volume and add it to the CSVs, use the following Windows Power-Shell command:

```
New-Volume -StoragePoolFriendlyName <Storage Pool name> -
FriendlyName <Friendly name> -FileSystem CSVFS_ReFS -Size <Size
of volume>
```

At this point, you are ready to provision Hyper-V on the cluster to provide fault-tolerant hosts and create virtual machines on the nodes of the hyper-converged Storage Spaces Direct cluster. Remember to store the Hyper-V systems on the CSV namespace.

Implementing a Disaggregated Storage Spaces Direct Scenario in a Cluster

In this section, you will learn how to use disaggregated storage space, which allows you to create a cluster for the disks and then create a Scale-Out File Server that uses Storage Spaces Direct.

CERTIFICATION READY
Implement a disaggregated Storage Spaces Direct scenario in a cluster
Objective 5.3

The steps are nearly identical when creating a disaggregated Storage Spaces Direct system. However, after Storage Spaces Direct is implemented, you create a Scale-Out File Server to provide shared folders. The Scale-Out File Server will be built on the Storage Spaces Direct drives.

The main tasks for this exercise are as follows:

1. Install the Windows Server roles and features.
2. Validate cluster configuration.
3. Create a cluster.
4. Enable the Storage Spaces Direct feature.
5. Create a storage pool.
6. Create a virtual disk.
7. Test high availability for the storage.
8. Create a Scale-Out File Server and file shares.

→ IMPLEMENT A DISAGGREGATED STORAGE SPACES DIRECT SCENARIO IN A CLUSTER

GET READY. To implement a disaggregated Storage Spaces Direct scenario in a cluster, perform the following steps.

1. To install the required roles and features on the servers that will be a part of the Storage Spaces Direct cluster, use the following Windows PowerShell command:

   ```
   Install-WindowsFeature -Name File-Services, Failover-Clustering
   -IncludeManagementTools
   ```

   ```
   Install-WindowsFeature -Name Hyper-V
   ```

   ```
   -IncludeManagementTools
   ```

2. To validate the hardware configuration for Storage Spaces Direct, use the following Windows PowerShell command:

   ```
   Test-Cluster-Node <computer names for the nodes in the cluster>
   -Include "Storage Spaces Direct"
   ```

3. To create the cluster without adding any storage, use the following Windows PowerShell command:

   ```
   New-Cluster -Name <Cluster name> -Node <computer names for the
   nodes in the cluster> -NoStorage -StaticAddress <IP address>
   ```

4. To configure the cluster properties to enable the Software Storage Bus and add storage, use the following Windows PowerShell command:

   ```
   Enable-ClusterStorageSpacesDirect -Cluster S2Dcluster
   ```

5. To create the storage pool in the cluster, use the following Windows PowerShell command:

   ```
   New-StoragePool -StorageSubSystemName <Cluster name>
   -FriendlyName <Storage Pool name>
   ```

6. To create the volume and add it to the CSVs, use the following Windows PowerShell command:

   ```
   New-Volume -StoragePoolFriendlyName <Storage Pool name>
   -FriendlyName <Friendly name> -FileSystem CSVFS_ReFS -Size <Size
   of volume>
   ```

7. To create the Scale-Out File Server on the cluster, use the following Windows PowerShell command:

   ```
   New-StorageFileServer -StorageSubSystemName <Cluster name>
   -FriendlyName <Name of file server in cluster> -HostName
   <Virtual host name> -Protocols SMB
   ```

8. To create a folder on the file server and create a new share, use the following Windows PowerShell commands:

   ```
   md "C:\ClusterStorage\Volume1\<Folder name>"
   ```

   ```
   New-SmbShare -Name <Share name>-Path "C:\ClusterStorage\
   Volume1\<Folder name>" -FullAccess <Users with Full Control>
   ```

   ```
   Set-SmbPathAcl -ShareName <Share name>
   ```

SKILL SUMMARY

IN THIS LESSON YOU LEARNED:

- Storage Spaces Direct uses industry-standard servers with local-attached drives to create highly available, highly scalable, software-defined storage at a fraction of the cost of a traditional SAN or NAS array. It can use the internal disks as nodes in a cluster, or by directly attaching to nodes in a cluster via an enclosure, which can be aggregated to form a virtual disk.

- In the hyper-converged deployment scenario, the Hyper-V and Storage Spaces Direct components are on the same cluster. The virtual machine's files are stored on a Cluster Shared Volume. Once Storage Spaces Direct is configured and the CSV volumes are available, you configure and provision Hyper-V as a failover cluster.

- In the disaggregated deployment scenario, one cluster is for Hyper-V and the other is used as a Scale-Out File Server. This solution gives extra processing power for the virtualization systems, while providing extra storage capacity.

■ Knowledge Assessment

Multiple Choice

Select the correct answer for each of the following questions.

1. Which of the following uses industry-standard servers with local-attached drives to create a highly available, highly scalable, software-defined storage that provides server and storage resilience?
   a. Storage Spaces Direct
   b. Remote Desktop Memory Access
   c. Scale-Out File Server
   d. Hyper-V Replication

2. Which of the following is used in a Storage Spaces Direct hyper-converged deployment scenario to consolidate all volumes into a single namespace, which is accessible through the file system on any cluster node?
   a. SMB
   b. AES
   c. ACL
   d. CSV

3. Which Storage Spaces Direct deployment scenario stores the Hyper-V and Storage Spaces Direct components on the same cluster?
   a. Multi-tenant
   b. Hyper-V Replica files
   c. Hyper-converged deployment
   d. Disaggregated deployment

4. Which Storage Spaces Direct deployment scenario uses one cluster for Hyper-V and another as a Scale-Out File Server?
   a. Multi-tenant
   b. Hyper-V Replica files
   c. Hyper-converged deployment
   d. Disaggregated deployment

5. Which Windows PowerShell cmdlet is used to configure a cluster for Storage Spaces Direct for use with NVMe devices and SATA SSDs?
   a. `Enable-ClusterStorageSpacesDirect`
   b. `Enable-ClusterS2D`
   c. `Enable-StoragePool`
   d. `Enable-StorageSubSystem`

Build a List

1. Specify the correct order of steps necessary to implementing a hyper-converged Storage Spaces Direct scenario.

   _____ Create a cluster.

   _____ Create a virtual disk.

   _____ Validate cluster configuration.

   _____ Test high availability for the storage.

   _____ Create virtual machines.

   _____ Enable the Storage Spaces Direct feature.

   _____ Create a storage pool.

   _____ Install the Windows Server roles and features.

Matching and Identification

1. Match the Windows PowerShell cmdlet with the appropriate description.

   _____ a. `Enable-ClusterStorageSpacesDirect`

   _____ b. `Enable-ClusterS2D`

   _____ c. `Debug-StorageSubSystem`

   _____ d. `Optimize-StoragePool`

   1. Rebalances storage optimization if a disk or storage node changes
   2. Displays any faults that are affecting the Storage Spaces Direct feature
   3. Configures a cluster for the Storage Spaces Direct feature
   4. Configures a cluster for the Storage Spaces Direct feature for use with NVMe devices and SATA SSDs

■ Business Case Scenarios

Scenario 16-1: Building a Resilient Hyper-V Cluster and File System

You are an administrator of a small company that has approximately 150 users and a very small IT budget. Even though it is a small company, you still need to utilize multiple virtual machines that must be available all of the time. Describe a solution that also takes into account your need to manage costs.

Implementing Network Load Balancing (NLB)

70-740 EXAM OBJECTIVE

Objective 5.6 – Implement Network Load Balancing (NLB). This objective may include but is not limited to the following: Install NLB nodes; configure NLB prerequisites; configure affinity; configure port rules; configure cluster operation mode; upgrade an NLB cluster.

LESSON HEADING	EXAM OBJECTIVE
Configuring Network Load Balancing (NLB)	Configure NLB prerequisites
– Configuring NLB Prerequisites	Install NLB nodes
– Installing NLB Nodes	Configure port rules
– Configuring Port Rules	Configure affinity
– Configuring Filtering Mode and Affinity	Configure cluster operation mode
– Configuring Cluster Operation Mode	Upgrade an NLB cluster
– Controlling Hosts in NLB	
– Upgrading an NLB Cluster	

KEY TERMS

affinity

convergence

drainstop

filter mode

heartbeats

Internet Group Management
   Protocol multicast mode

multicast

multicast mode

Network Load Balancing (NLB)

node

port rules

stop action

unicast

unicast mode

■ Configuring Network Load Balancing (NLB)

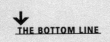

THE BOTTOM LINE

Network Load Balancing (NLB) transparently distributes traffic across multiple servers by using virtual IP addresses and a shared name. With NLB, you gain fault tolerance and enhanced performance. It is often used with mission-critical web servers, but can also be found with other types of servers.

A cluster has two or more servers, known as nodes. Each *node* runs a separate copy of the desired service application, such as a web server, an FTP server, or a Secure Shell (SSH)/ Remote Desktop Server. NLB is a scalable, high-availability feature found in Windows Server 2016. It is considered scalable because you can add more servers to meet increasing demand.

Windows Sever 2016 NLB clusters can have between 2 and 32 nodes. When you create an NLB cluster, you create a virtual network address and adapter that is assigned to the entire cluster. As network requests are sent to the virtual network address, the requests are distributed across the nodes in the cluster. Based on your needs, you can configure the cluster to even out the requests or you can configure one node to be preferred over another node.

All hosts in the NLB cluster receive the incoming traffic. However, only one node in the cluster accepts the traffic and the other nodes drop the traffic. The node that accepts the traffic is determined by the configuration of port rules and affinity settings, which is configured later in this lesson.

If a node fails, the node will no longer be able to accept requests. However, no service is lost because the other nodes are available to accept the request. When the node comes back online, it will start accepting requests and the traffic will be distributed among the nodes.

NLB can detect the failure of cluster nodes by sending packets known as *heartbeats*. NLB cluster heartbeats are transmitted every second between nodes in the cluster. If a node misses five consecutive heartbeats, the node is automatically removed from the NLB cluster.

When a node is added or removed from a cluster, a process known as *convergence* occurs, where the cluster determines its current configuration by building a membership of nodes and mapping client requests based on the available nodes. Convergence can occur only if each node is configured with the same port rules.

Configuring NLB Prerequisites

Although Windows Server 2016 supports NLB and NLB supports running different editions of Windows Server 2016, it is best practice to use computers with similar hardware specifications to run the same edition of the Windows Server 2016 operating system.

CERTIFICATION READY
Configure NLB
prerequisites
Objective 5.6

To support NLB, your systems must use the following requirements:

- All hosts in the cluster must reside on the same subnet.
- Within each cluster, all network adapters must be either multicast or unicast. You cannot have some nodes configured as multicast while other nodes are configured as unicast within a single cluster. We discuss multicast and unicast configuration later in this lesson.
- If unicast mode is used, the network adapter that is used to handle client-to-cluster traffic must support changing its media access control (MAC) address.
- The IP addresses assigned to the nodes must be static.

Although hosts can span multiple geographical areas, to achieve convergence successfully, the latency between nodes cannot exceed 250 milliseconds. If you need geographically dispersed NLB clusters, you should deploy an NLB cluster at each site and then use Domain Name System (DNS) round-robin to distribute traffic between sites.

Installing NLB Nodes

CERTIFICATION READY
Install NLB nodes
Objective 5.6

To install and configure an NLB node, you must first install NLB. Unlike most of the Windows components, the NLB is a feature, and not a role. It is used to enhance other roles such as web services or Remote Desktop Services. After NLB is installed on each machine, you then need to create the node and add each host to the cluster.

TAKE NOTE *

If failover cluster feature has been installed, it must be removed.

To add the NLB feature to a computer running Windows Server 2016, you use Server Manager. After the NLB feature is installed, you can then use the NLB Manager to configure the NLB cluster. Because an NLB cluster is made of multiple computers, you need to install NLB on each server that will be part of the cluster.

⊙ INSTALL THE NETWORK LOAD BALANCING FEATURE

GET READY. To install the Network Load Balancing feature, perform the following steps.

1. Open Server Manager.
2. At the top of Server Manager, click **Manage** and click **Add Roles and Features**. The Add Roles and Feature Wizard opens.
3. On the Before You Begin page, click **Next**.
4. Select **Role-based or feature-based installation** and then click **Next**.
5. On the Select Destination Server page, click **Next**.
6. On the Select Server Roles page, click **Next**.
7. On the Select Features page, click **Network Loading Balancing** and click **Next**.
8. When you are prompted to add features required for NLB, click **Add Features**.
9. On the Select Features page, click **Next**.
10. On the Confirm Installation Selections page, click **Install**.
11. When the installation is complete, click **Close**.

USING POWERSHELL

To install the NLB cluster and the NLB tools using PowerShell, you can use the following cmdlets:

```
Add-WindowsFeature NLB,RSAT-NLB
```

To configure the NLB cluster, you must configure three types of parameters:

- **Host parameters:** Defines what each node can do in an NLB cluster
- **Cluster parameters:** Configures the NLB cluster as a whole
- **Port rules:** Controls which ports the NLB cluster services and how requests are balanced across all servers

CREATE A WINDOWS SERVER 2016 NLB CLUSTER

GET READY. To create a Windows Server 2016 NLB cluster, perform the following steps.

1. Open Server Manager.
2. Click **Tools > Network Load Balancing Manager.** The Network Load Balancing Manager opens, as shown in Figure 17-1.

Figure 17-1

Opening the Network Load Balancing Manager

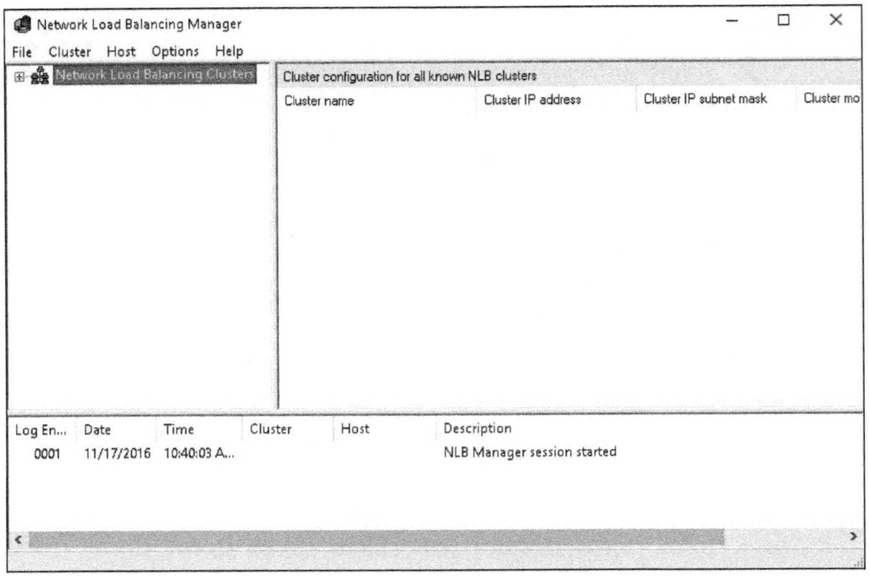

3. Right-click **Network Load Balancing Clusters** and choose **New Cluster.** The New Cluster: Connect Wizard opens, as shown in Figure 17-2.

Figure 17-2

Specifying the host and interface

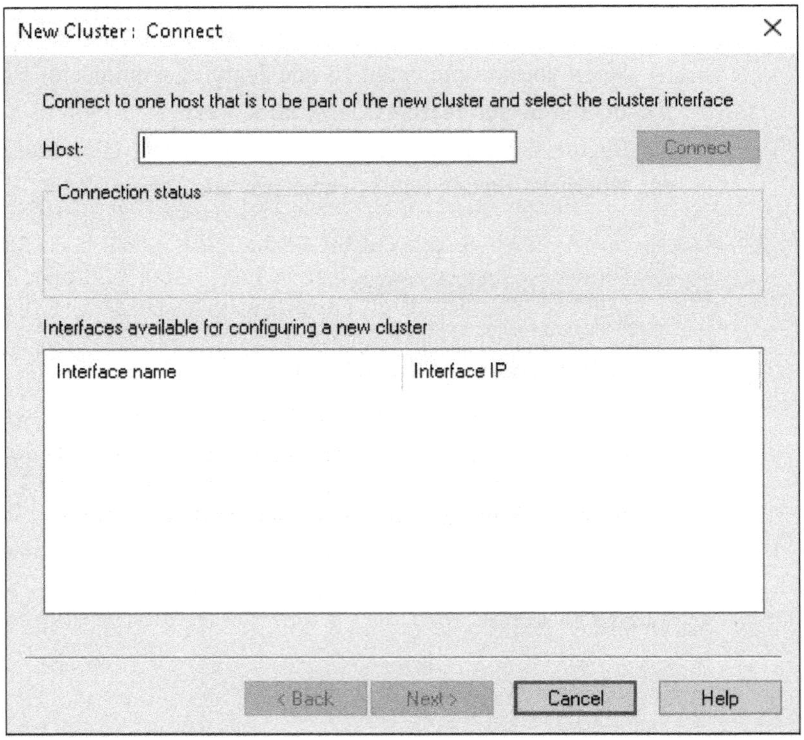

4. In the Host text box, type the name of the current server and click **Connect.**

5. The interface hosts the virtual IP address and receives the client traffic to load balance. Select an interface that you want to use for the cluster and click **Next.**

6. On the New Cluster: Host Parameters page (see Figure 17-3), you select a value in the **Priority (unique host identifier)** drop-down list. The parameter specifies a unique ID for each host. The host with the lowest priority handles all the cluster's network traffic not covered by a port rule.

Figure 17-3

Specifying host priority and dedicated IP addresses

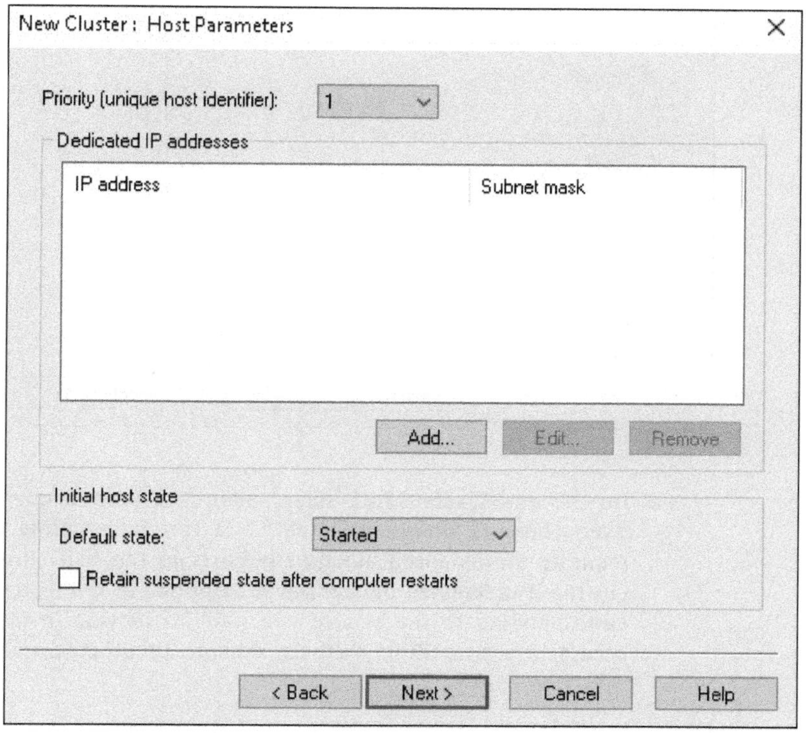

7. In the Dedicated IP addresses section, verify that the dedicated IP address from the chosen interface is visible in the list and click **Next.**

8. On the New Cluster: Cluster IP Addresses page, click **Add** to enter the cluster IP address shared by every host in the cluster. NLB adds this IP address to each selected interface of all hosts chosen to be part of the cluster.

9. In the Add IP Address dialog box, type an IPv4 address and subnet mask to be used for the NLB cluster. Click **OK.**

10. Back on the New Cluster: IP Addresses page, click **Next.**

11. On the New Cluster: Cluster Parameters page (see Figure 17-4), type the full Internet name for the cluster. Then, in the Cluster operation mode section, specify **Unicast, Multicast,** or **IGMP multicast.** Click **Next.**

Figure 17-4

Specifying Full Internet name
and cluster operation mode

Figure 17-4

Specifying Full Internet name
and cluster operation mode

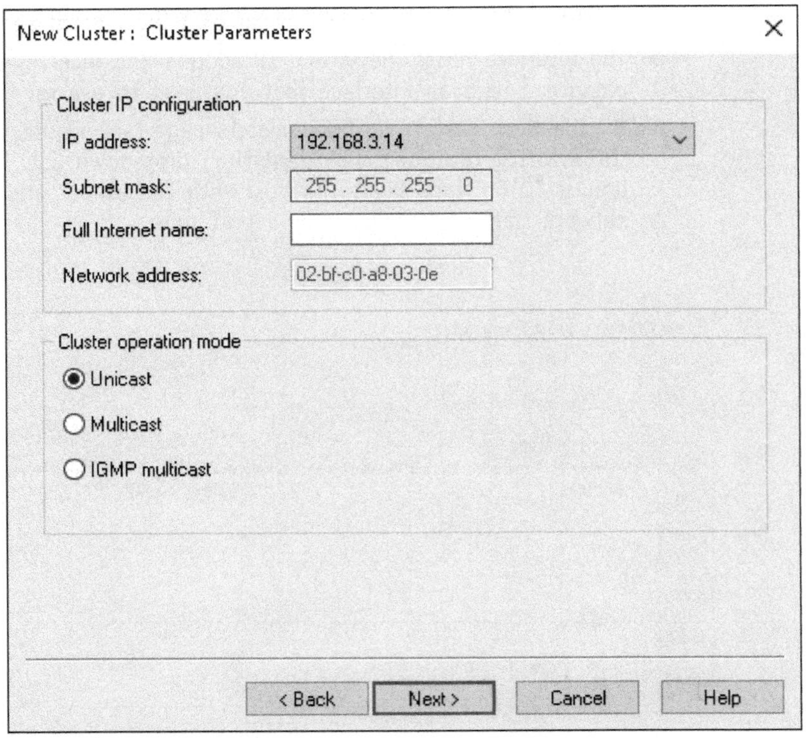

12. On the New Cluster: Port Rules page, click **Edit** to open the Add/Edit Port Rule
    dialog box, as shown in Figure 17-5. Port rules define which incoming TCP/IP
    requests are balanced among the hosts in the NLB cluster. You can specify the
    cluster IP addresses or use the **All** option. In the Port range area, specify a range
    corresponding to the service you want to provide in the NLB cluster. For web
    access, use port 80 or 443. For Remote Desktop Services, use port 3389.

Figure 17-5

Specifying the port rules

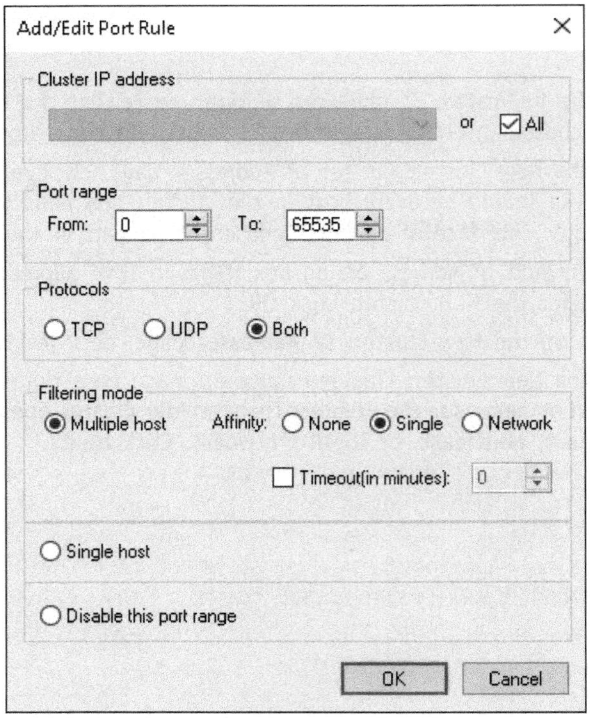

13. In the Filtering mode area, select **Multiple host** if you want multiple hosts in the cluster to handle network traffic for the port rule. If you want a single host to handle the network traffic for the port rule, choose **Single host.**

14. If you choose Multiple host, you can select **None**, **Single**, or **Network**. If you want multiple connections from the same client IP address to be handled by different cluster hosts, select **None**. If you want NLB to direct multiple requests from the same client IP address to the same cluster host, select **Single** (which is the default). If you want NLB to direct multiple requests from the local subnet to the same cluster host, click **Network**. Click **OK** to close the Add/Edit Port Rule dialog box.

15. After you define the port rules, click **Finish.**

To add additional hosts to the cluster, right-click the cluster in Network Load Balancing Manager and choose Add Host to Cluster. You then select an interface for the cluster, configure the unique priority, and define port rules. After a host is added, convergence will occur. When convergence is complete, the host will participate in the cluster (as shown in Figure 17-6).

Figure 17-6

Showing both servers are converged

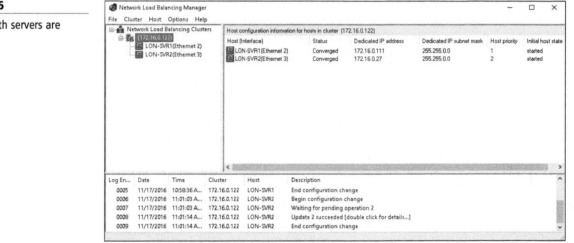

You can configure and manage Networking Loading Balancing using the following cmdlets:

- **Add-NlbClusterNode:** Adds a new node to the NLB cluster
- **Add-NlbClusterNodeDip:** Adds a dedicated IP address to an NLB cluster
- **Add-NlbClusterPortRule:** Adds a new port rule to an NLB cluster
- **Add-NlbClusterVip:** Adds a virtual IP address to an NLB cluster
- **Disable-NlbClusterPortRule:** Disables a port rule on an NLB cluster or on a specific host in the cluster
- **Enable-NlbClusterPortRule:** Enables a port rule on an NLB cluster or on a specific node in the cluster
- **Get-NlbCluster:** Retrieves information about the NLB cluster object that is queried by the caller
- **Get-NlbClusterDriverInfo:** Retrieves information about the NLB driver on the local machine
- **Get-NlbClusterNode:** Retrieves information about the NLB cluster object that is queried by the caller
- **Get-NlbClusterNodeDip:** Retrieves the dedicated IP address that is queried by the caller
- **Get-NlbClusterNodeNetworkInterface:** Retrieves information about interfaces, including information about the NLB driver, on a host

(continued)

- **Get-NlbClusterPortRule:** Retrieves the port rule objects that are queried by the caller
- **Get-NlbClusterVip:** Retrieves virtual IP addresses that are queried by the caller
- **New-NlbCluster:** Creates an NLB cluster on the specified interface that is defined by the node and network adapter name
- **New-NlbClusterIpv6Address:** Generates IPv6 addresses to create cluster virtual IP addresses or node dedicated IP addresses
- **Remove-NlbCluster:** Deletes an NLB cluster
- **Remove-NlbClusterNode:** Removes a node from the NLB cluster
- **Remove-NlbClusterNodeDip:** Removes a dedicated IP address from an NLB cluster
- **Remove-NlbClusterPortRule:** Removes a port rule from an NLB cluster
- **Remove-NlbClusterVip:** Removes a virtual IP address from an NLB cluster
- **Resume-NlbCluster:** Resumes all nodes in an NLB cluster
- **Resume-NlbClusterNode:** Resumes the node in an NLB cluster that was suspended
- **Set-NlbCluster:** Edits the configuration of an NLB cluster
- **Set-NlbClusterNode:** Edits the NLB cluster node settings
- **Set-NlbClusterNodeDip:** Edits the dedicated IP address of an NLB cluster
- **Set-NlbClusterPortRule:** Edits the port rules for an NLB cluster
- **Set-NlbClusterPortRuleNodeHandlingPriority:** Sets the host priority of a port rule for a specific NLB node
- **Set-NlbClusterPortRuleNodeWeight:** Sets the load weight of a port rule for a specific NLB node
- **Set-NlbClusterVip:** Edits the virtual IP address of an NLB cluster
- **Start-NlbCluster:** Starts all nodes in an NLB cluster
- **Start-NlbClusterNode:** Starts a node in an NLB cluster
- **Stop-NlbCluster:** Stops all nodes in an NLB cluster
- **Stop-NlbClusterNode:** Stops a node in an NLB cluster
- **Suspend-NlbCluster:** Suspends all nodes in an NLB cluster
- **Suspend-NlbClusterNode:** Suspends a specific node in an NLB cluster

Examples follow:

To view or get information about nodes in a cluster, use the following command:

```
Get-NlbClusterNode
```

To add LON-SVR2 to the cluster on LON-SVR1, use the following command:

```
Get-NlbCluster LON-SVR1 | Add-NlbClusterNode –NewNodeName LON-SVR2
-NewNodeInterface vlan-1
```

To change or set the primary IP address of the cluster, use the following command:

```
Get-NlbCluster | Set-NlbCluster –ClusterPrimaryIP 172.24.100.100
```

To stop a node in the NLB cluster, use the following command:

```
Stop-NlbClusterNode LON-SVR2
```

For more information about NLB PowerShell commands, visit technet.microsoft.com.

Configuring Port Rules

Often after a cluster is created, you will need to further configure NLB. Most of these options are similar to the configuration that you performed while first creating the cluster. One of the items that you configured previously was the *port rules*, which specify how NLB directs traffic based on the port and protocol.

CERTIFICATION READY
Configure port rules
Objective 5.6

With port rules, you can configure how requests to specific IP addresses and ports are directed by the NLB cluster. For example, you can load-balance web traffic using TCP port 80 across all nodes in an NLB cluster, while directing all requests to TCP port 3389 to a specific host.

When you configure the port rules, you configure the following:

- The virtual IP address that the rule should apply to.
- The TCP or UDP port range that the rule should apply to.
- The protocols that the rule should apply to, including TCP, UDP, or both.
- The filtering mode that specifies how the cluster handles traffic, which is described by the port range and the protocols. Filtering mode is discussed in the next section.

To modify the port rules (including the filter mode and affinity), right-click the cluster in Network Load Balancing Manager and choose Properties. When you click the Port Rules tab, select the defined port rule and click Edit to open the Add/Edit Port Rule dialog box.

CONFIGURE PORT RULES

GET READY. To configure port rules, perform the following steps.

1. Open Server Manager.
2. Click **Tools > Network Load Balancing Manager.**
3. When the Network Load Balancing Manager opens, right-click an NLB cluster and choose **Cluster Parameters.**
4. In the Properties dialog box, click the **Port Rules** tab.
5. To edit a current port rule, click a port rule and click **Edit.** To create a new port rule, click **Add.**
6. In the Add/Edit Port Rule dialog box, you can specify the cluster IP addresses or use the **All** option. In the Port range area, specify a range corresponding to the service you want to provide in the NLB cluster. For web access, use port 80 or 443. For Remote Desktop Services, use port 3389. When done, click **OK.**
7. To close the Properties dialog box, click **OK.**

Configuring Filtering Mode and Affinity

Affinity determines how the servers are going to balance the load. You use affinity settings when you use multiple hosts filter mode.

When you configure port rules, you first select the filter mode. The *filter mode* specifies which hosts can respond to requests. The filter mode includes the following:

- **Multiple hosts:** Permits all cluster hosts to actively respond to client requests. NLB nodes respond according to the weight assigned to each node. Because this allows the customizing of the affinity and load balancing, it is the most common mode used. Multiple hosts filtering increases availability and scalability because you can increase capacity by adding nodes, and the cluster continues to function in the event of node failure.
- **Single host:** Allows only one cluster host (the host with the highest priority) in the cluster to actively respond to client requests. If the host fails, the host with the next highest priority takes over for the failed host. It is usually used to configure one host as the primary server and other hosts as backup servers. Single host rules increase availability, but do not increase scalability.
- **Disable:** Prevents the cluster from responding to a specific type of client traffic.

If you choose the multiple hosts filter mode, you can then configure the affinity. When you configure affinity, you can choose one of three options:

- **None:** Any cluster node responds to any client request, even if the client is reconnecting after an interruption. This option is suitable for stateless application, where the server that is servicing the request does not have to remember the previous events to complete the request. As a result, the client can jump from one server to another within the cluster without problems.

- **Single:** A single cluster node handles all requests from a single client. This option is useful for stateful applications where the status of a process or transaction is maintained through the entire connection, including when using SSL and e-commerce shopping cart applications.

- **Class C:** A single node responds to all requests from a Class C network (a network with a subnet of 255.255.255.0), often found when used with multiple proxy servers. This type of server is often used with cookie-based affinity or when a common database or session state server is used.

Each node in a cluster must have identical port rules. The only exception is the load weight when in multiple hosts filter mode and handling priority in single host filter mode. If the port rules are not identical, the cluster will not converge.

To modify the port rules for an individual host, right-click the host in the left pane and choose Host Properties. Then, click the Port Rules and click Edit to open the Add/Edit Port Rule dialog box. To specify a different load weight while in multiple hosts filter mode, click to deselect the Equal option and then specify the load weight (as shown in Figure 17-7). If you are in single host filter mode, specify the handling priority.

Figure 17-7

Specifying a different load weight

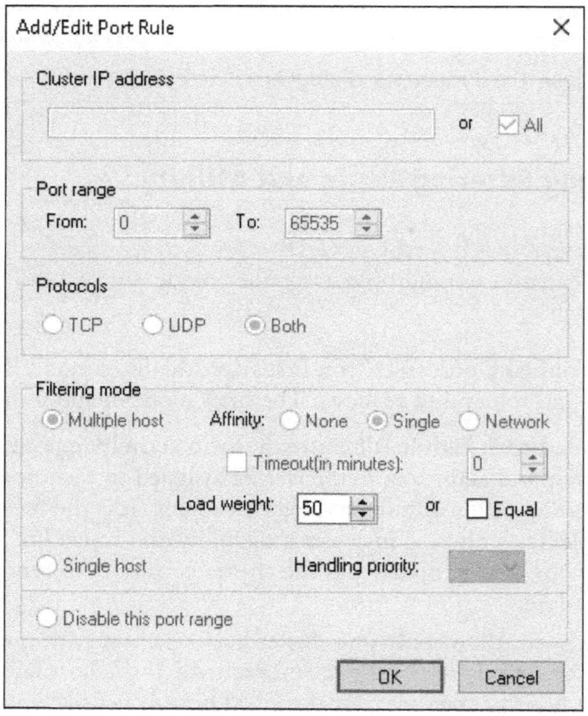

When creating port rules, the number and type of rules must be the same for each host in the cluster. If a host attempts to join the cluster with a different number of rules than the other hosts, it is not accepted as part of the cluster, and the rest of the cluster continues to handle the traffic as before.

Configuring Cluster Operation Mode

> On the Cluster Parameters tab, you configure the virtual IP address, subnet mask, and DNS name that the cluster will use. You also can configure the cluster operation mode, which specifies whether a multicast MAC address should be used for cluster operations.

CERTIFICATION READY
Configure cluster
operation mode
Objective 5.6

When a host communicates with another host, the host uses unicast or multicast packets. When communicating using ***unicast***, each packet is sent to a single network destination identified by a unique address. In other words, a host sends packets to a single computer.

With ***multicast***, packets are sent to multiple computers simultaneously in a single transmission from the source. In other words, when a host sends packets using multicasting, a single set of packets is sent to all computers at once. Copies are automatically created on routers, when the packet needs to go to different subnets. If you have five hosts on the same subnet, and two hosts on another subnet, one set of packets is sent from the source host. When the packets get to a router where the packets need to be sent through two different pathways, the packets are copied and sent to the two separate subnets. When the first set of packets gets sent to the subnet with five hosts, only one set of packets gets sent to all five hosts. The second set of packets gets sent to the subnet with two hosts, and only one set of packets gets sent to the two hosts.

When you configure an NLB cluster to use ***unicast mode***, NLB replaces the network card's original MAC address and all cluster hosts use the same unicast MAC address. When you use unicast mode with a single network adapter on each node, the computer can communicate only with other computers within the same subnet. If you perform management tasks on the computer, you need to perform these tasks on a computer that is on the same TCP/IP subnet as the node, or you have to use a second network adapter and address. Lastly, if you use unicast mode, you can use separate virtual local area networks (VLANs) for cluster traffic and management traffic.

When an NLB host is in ***multicast mode***, each NLB network adapter has two MAC addresses (the original MAC address and the virtual MAC address). However, when using multicast mode, some routers might see a unicast IP address with a multicast MAC address as an invalid packet and reject the update to the ARP table. If this happens, the network administrators might need to manually add ARP entries to the router.

In summary, if your system has two network cards, you should use unicast mode. If a server has only a single network card, you should use multicast mode.

Another mode available is the ***Internet Group Management Protocol multicast mode***, which is a special form of multicast mode that prevents the network switch from flooding with traffic. When you use IGMP multicast mode, traffic is forwarded only through the switch ports that are part of the NLB cluster. However, to use IGMP multicast mode, you need switch hardware that supports IGMP multicast mode.

To modify the cluster operation mode, right-click the cluster in the Network Load Balancing Manager and choose Cluster Properties. On the Cluster Parameters tab, you can modify the cluster IP address, subnet mask, full Internet name, and cluster operation mode.

Controlling Hosts in NLB

> As an administrator, you can manually add or remove nodes from an NLB cluster by using the Network Load Balancing Manager. You can also suspend and resume a cluster node and perform a drainstop.

To remove a node, you can perform a stop or a drainstop action. The **stop action** terminates all existing connections to the cluster node and stops the NLB service. The **drainstop** action blocks all new connections without terminating existing sessions. Therefore, to perform maintenance on an NLB node, which needs to be temporarily removed from the NLB cluster, you should choose drainstop so that connections are not prematurely stopped before the requests are completed. To control the host, you right-click the node, choose Control Host, and select the appropriate option (Start, Stop, Drainstop, Suspend, or Resume), as shown in Figure 17-8.

Figure 17-8

Controlling the host

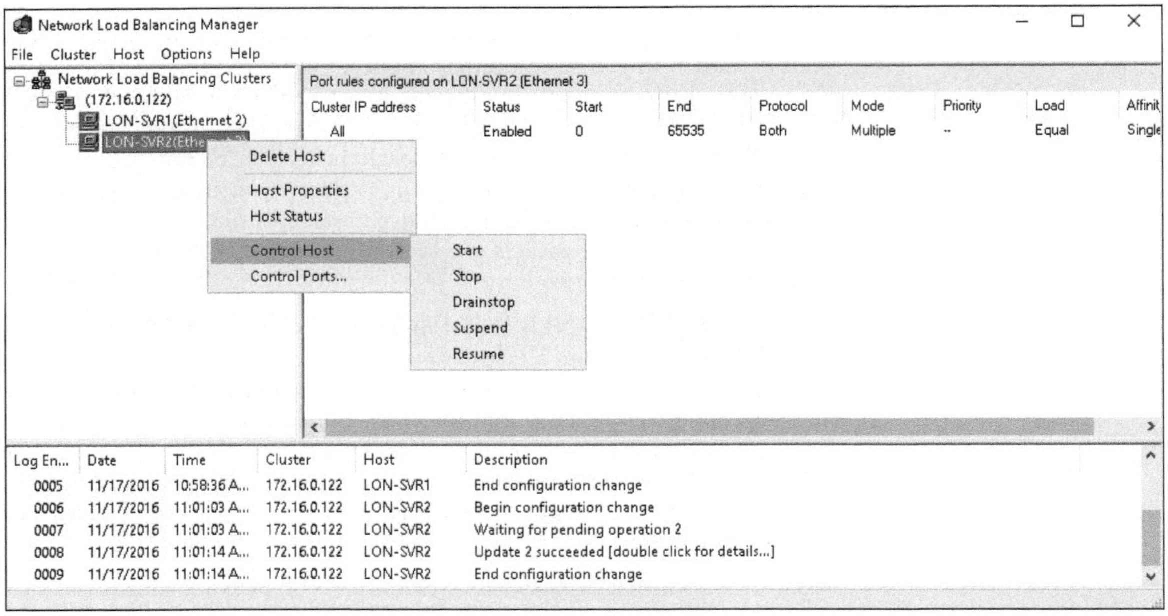

Upgrading an NLB Cluster

There are two ways to upgrade a Windows Server 2012 or Windows Server 2012 R2 NLB cluster to Windows Server 2016. It includes upgrading all the hosts at one time or upgrading each host, one at a time.

CERTIFICATION READY
Upgrade an NLB cluster
Objective 5.6

The quickest upgrade path is to take the entire cluster offline and perform a rolling upgrade. Of course, if you use this method, the cluster is not available. If you require no downtime, you can upgrade each individual cluster host, one at a time. As you upgrade each node, you should first perform a drainstop for the host so that any pending client requests are finished before the upgrade.

SKILL SUMMARY

IN THIS LESSON YOU LEARNED:

- High availability is a system design protocol and associated implementation that ensures a certain degree of operational continuity during a given measurement period.

- A cluster is a group of linked computers that work together as one computer. Based on the technology used, clusters can provide fault tolerance (often referred to as availability), load balancing, or both.

- A load-balancing cluster for the front end provides the web interface to the back-end servers.

- A failover cluster is used for back-end servers, such as a database (such as SQL Server) or mail server (such as Exchange Server).

- Network Load Balancing (NLB) transparently distributes traffic across multiple servers by using virtual IP addresses and a shared name. By using NLB, you gain fault tolerance and enhanced performance.

- A cluster has two or more servers, known as nodes.

- Each node runs a separate copy of the desired service application, such as a web server, an FTP server, or a SSH/Remote Desktop Server.

- NLB is able to detect the failure of cluster nodes by sending packets known as heartbeats.

- When a node is added or removed from a cluster, a process known as convergence occurs, where the cluster determines its current configuration by building a membership of nodes and mapping client requests based on the available nodes.

- To configure the NLB cluster, you must configure three types of parameters: host parameters, cluster parameters, and port rules.

- Port rules specify how NLB directs traffic based on the port and protocol.

- Affinity determines how the servers balance the load. You use affinity settings when you use multiple hosts filter mode.

- For a system with two network cards, you should use unicast mode. If a server has only a single network card, you should use multicast mode.

- The drainstop action blocks all new connections without terminating existing sessions.

- To upgrade an NLB cluster to Windows Server 2016, you can upgrade all the hosts at one time or upgrade each host, one at a time.

■ Knowledge Assessment

Multiple Choice

Select the correct answer for each of the following questions.

1. Which of the following is used to transparently distribute traffic equally across multiple servers by using virtual IP addresses and a shared name?
   a. Network Load Balancing (NLB)
   b. Failover cluster
   c. DFS distribution
   d. Site replication

2. Which of the following uses NLB to provide fault tolerance?
   a. SQL databases
   b. Exchange database
   c. Websites
   d. Shared folders

3. Which of the following is the maximum number of nodes that is supported in a Windows Server 2016 NLB cluster?
   a. 2
   b. 8
   c. 16
   d. 32

4. Which of the following is used to detect the failure of cluster nodes?
   a. Autoconfig
   b. Whoami
   c. Announcements
   d. Heartbeats

5. When adding or removing a node from an NLB cluster, which of the following must happen?
   a. Adaptation
   b. Reset
   c. Convergence
   d. Redefine

6. Which types of parameters configure the NLB cluster? (Choose all that apply.)
   a. Convergence rules
   b. Balance parameters
   c. Cluster parameters
   d. Host parameters
   e. Port rules

7. Which of the following specifies how NLB directs traffic based on the port and protocol?
   a. Convergence rules
   b. Balance parameters
   c. Cluster parameters
   d. Host parameters
   e. Port rules

8. Which of the following determines how servers are balanced with NLB?
   a. Affinity
   b. Drainstop
   c. State sequencing
   d. Convergence

9. Which mode allows an NLB cluster to use two MAC addresses for the NLB network adapter?
   a. Unicast mode
   b. Multicast mode
   c. Internet Group Management Protocol multicast mode
   d. Converging mode

10. Which action blocks all new connections without terminating existing sessions?
    a. Blocking
    b. Suspended
    c. Drainstop
    d. Multimode

11. Typically, port rules would be identical on all nodes on the cluster. What are the exceptions where the port rules don't have to be identical?
    a. Handling priority
    b. TCP, UDP, or both
    c. Load weight
    d. Ports

12. A two-node NLB cluster is intended to provide high availability and load balancing for the Contoso.com website. It has only the default port rule. Which two steps need to be configured for the NLB cluster to accept only HTTP traffic? (Choose all that apply.)
    a. Run the `vlbs disable all` command.
    b. Delete the default port rule.
    c. Create a new Allow rule for TCP port 80.
    d. Change the default port rule to a disabled port range rule.

13. A two-node NLB cluster is intended to provide high availability and load balancing for the Contoso.com website. It has a single port rule that evenly distributes HTTP traffic between LON-SVR1 and LON-SVR2. Which of the following is needed to evenly distribute HTTP traffic while having all HTTPS traffic go to LON-SVR1? (Choose all that apply.)
    a. On LON-SVR2, change the Handling priority option for the TCP 443 port rule to a value of 0.
    b. On LON-SVR1, change the Handling priority option for the TCP 443 port rule to the value of 0.
    c. In the properties for the cluster, create a new port rule for TCP 443 that has a filtering mode option set to a single host.
    d. In the properties for the cluster, create a new port rule for TCP 443 that has the filtering mode option set to multiple hosts and the affinity set to single.

Best Answer

Choose the letter that corresponds to the best answer. More than one answer choice may achieve the goal. Select the BEST answer.

1. Which mode should be used to configure affinity?
    a. Multiple hosts
    b. Single host
    c. Disable
    d. Converging host

2. A server called LON-SVR1 hosts the http://www.contoso.com and https://www.contoso .com websites. An NLB cluster was created using LON-SVR1 and LON-SVR2. Which of the following must be done to ensure that users can connect to the https://www .contoso.com website without any security warnings?
    a. Make sure both servers point to the same enterprise CA.
    b. Create a new digital certificate on LON-SVR2 for www.contoso.com.
    c. Export the SSL certificate from LON-SVR1 and import the SSL certificate to LON-SVR2.
    d. Create an image of the website on LON-SVR1 and import into LON-SVR2.

Matching and Identification

1. Match the description with the appropriate term.
    _____ a. Uses two MAC addresses for a host
    _____ b. Only forwards traffic through the switch ports that are part of the NLB cluster
    _____ c. Gracefully shuts down a node in the NLB cluster
    _____ d. Uses only the host with the highest priority to respond
    _____ e. Replaces the network card's original MAC address with the cluster MAC address
    1. Internet Group Management Protocol multicast mode
    2. Drainstop
    3. Multicast mode
    4. Single host
    5. Unicast mode
    6. Port rule

2. Specify the type of cluster (NLB or Failover) that is used for a particular type of server.

_____ **a.** File server

_____ **b.** DHCP server

_____ **c.** Exchange back-end/mailbox server

_____ **d.** Exchange front-end/CAS server

_____ **e.** Web server

_____ **f.** SQL server

3. Which of the following are prerequisites for NLB?

_____ **a.** The MAC address must be user programmable.

_____ **b.** All network adapters must be multicast or unicast.

_____ **c.** You must use static addresses.

_____ **d.** Servers cannot be geographically dispersed.

_____ **e.** All hosts in the cluster must reside on the same subnet.

Build a List

1. Specify the correct order of steps necessary to creating an NLB cluster in Windows Server 2016. Not all steps will be used.

_____ Specify the priority of the host.

_____ Create port rules.

_____ Configure convergence parameters.

_____ Type the name of the current server and click Connect.

_____ Specify failover options.

_____ Specify a cluster IP address.

_____ Specify the Internet name for the cluster.

■ Business Case Scenarios

Scenario 17-1: Upgrading an NLB Cluster

You are the administrator for several web servers that make up the NLB cluster. They run on servers with Windows Server 2012 R2. Explain the best way to upgrade the NLB cluster to Windows Server 2016 without any downtime.

Scenario 17-2: Creating a Fault-Tolerant Website

You are the administrator for the contoso.com site. Recently, the server hosting the corporate websites had a failure that caused the server to go down for a short period of time while the server was being fixed. In the future, you need to take steps to avoid any hardware failure that would cause the websites to go down. Describe your recommended course of action.

Maintaining Server Installations

70-740 EXAM OBJECTIVE

Objective 6.1 – Maintain server installations. This objective may include but is not limited to the following: Implement Windows Server Update Services (WSUS) solutions; configure WSUS groups; manage patch management in mixed environments; implement an anti-malware solution with Windows Defender; integrate Windows Defender with WSUS and Windows Update; perform backup and restore operations using Windows Server Backup; determine backup strategies for different Windows Server roles and workloads, including Hyper-V Host, Hyper-V Guests, Active Directory, File Servers, and Web Servers using Windows Server 2016 native tools and solutions.

LESSON HEADING	EXAM OBJECTIVE
Configuring and Managing Updates	
• Configuring Update Settings	
• Managing Windows Update Settings with Group Policy	
Implementing Windows Server Update Services Solution	Implement Windows Server Update Services (WSUS) solutions
• Determining a Deployment Strategy	Configure WSUS groups
• Reviewing the Update Services Console	Manage patch management in mixed environments
• Understanding the WSUS Infrastructure	
• Configuring Clients to Use WSUS	
• Configuring WSUS Groups	
• Selecting Server-Side Targeting Versus Client-Side Targeting	
• Managing Patch Management in Mixed Environments	
Implementing an Anti-Malware Solution with Windows Defender	Implement an anti-malware solution with Windows Defender
• Using Windows Defender	Integrate Windows Defender with WSUS and Windows Update
• Integrating Windows Defender with WSUS and Windows Update	

(continued)

LESSON HEADING	EXAM OBJECTIVE
Performing Backup and Restore Operations Using Windows Server Backup	Perform backup and restore operations using Windows Server Backup
• Installing the Windows Server Backup Feature	
• Configuring Windows Server Backups	
Determining Backup Strategies for Different Windows Server Roles and Workloads	Determine backup strategies for different Windows Server roles and workloads, including Hyper-V Host, Hyper-V Guests, Active Directory, File Servers, and Web Servers using Windows Server 2016 native tools and solutions
• Backing Up DHCP and DNS	
• Backing Up Certificate Services	
• Backing Up Active Directory Domain Services	
• Backing Up Web Servers	
• Managing VSS Settings Using VSSAdmin	
• Using Shadow Copies for Shared Volumes	
• Backing Up Hyper-V Hosts and Virtual Machines	

KEY TERMS

autonomous (distribution) mode

Bare Metal Recovery

client-side targeting

critical update

cumulative patch

downstream servers

hotfix

out-of-band patches

Patch Tuesday

replica mode

security update

server-side targeting

service pack

Shadow Copies for Shared Volumes (SCSV)

source volume

storage volume

synchronization

system state

upstream server

Volume Shadow Copy administrative command-line tool (VSSAdmin)

Volume Shadow Copy Service (VSS)

wbadmin

VSS provider

VSS requester

VSS writer

Windows Defender

Windows Server Backup

Windows Server Update Services (WSUS)

Windows Update

■ Configuring and Managing Updates

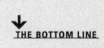

THE BOTTOM LINE

Intruders and some viruses, worms, rootkits, spyware, and adware gain access to a system by exploiting security holes in Windows, Internet Explorer, Microsoft Office, or other software applications. Therefore, the first step you should take to protect yourself against malware is to keep your system up to date with the latest service packs, security patches, and other critical fixes.

Microsoft routinely releases security updates on the second Tuesday of each month, commonly known as *Patch Tuesday*. Although most updates are released on Patch Tuesday, there might be occasional patches (known as *out-of-band patches*) released at other times when the patches are deemed critical or time-sensitive.

Because computers are often used as production systems, you should test any updates to make sure they do not cause problems for you. Although Microsoft performs intensive testing, occasionally problems do occur, either as a bug or as a compatibility issue with third-party software. Therefore, always be sure you have a good backup of your system and data files before you install patches so that you have a back-out plan, if necessary.

Microsoft classifies updates as Important, Recommended, or Optional:

- **Important updates:** These updates offer significant benefits, such as improved security, privacy, and reliability. They should be installed as they become available and can be installed automatically with Windows Update.

- **Recommended updates:** These updates address noncritical problems or help enhance your computing experience. Although these updates do not address fundamental issues with your computer or Windows software, they can offer meaningful improvements.

- **Optional updates:** These include updates, drivers, or new software from Microsoft to enhance your computing experience. You need to install these manually.

Depending on the type of update, Windows Update can deliver the following:

- **Security updates:** A *security update* is a broadly released fix for a product-specific, security-related vulnerability. Security vulnerabilities are rated based on their severity, which is indicated in the Microsoft security bulletin as critical, important, moderate, or low.

- **Critical updates:** A *critical update* is a broadly released fix for a specific problem addressing a critical, non-security-related bug.

- **Service packs:** A *service pack* is a tested, cumulative set of hotfixes, security updates, critical updates, and updates, as well as additional fixes for problems found internally since the release of the product. Service packs might also contain a limited number of customer-requested design changes or features. After an operating system is released, many corporations consider the first service pack as the time when the operating system has matured enough to be used throughout the organization.

Not all updates can be retrieved through Windows Update. Sometimes, Microsoft might offer the fix for a specific problem in the form of a hotfix or cumulative patch that you can install. A *hotfix* is a single, cumulative package that includes one or more files that are used to address a problem in a software product, such as a software bug. Typically, hotfixes are made to address a specific customer situation, and they often have not gone through the same extensive testing as patches retrieved through Windows Update. A *cumulative patch* combines multiple hotfixes into a single package.

Configuring Update Settings

Windows Update provides your Windows 10 and Windows 2016 users with a way to keep their computers current by checking a designated server. The server provides software that patches security issues, installs updates that make Windows and your applications more stable, fixes issues with existing Windows programs, and provides new features. The server can be hosted by Microsoft or it can be set up and managed in your organization by running the Windows Server Update Services (WSUS) or System Center 2016 Configuration Manager.

When you first install Windows Server 2016, you can choose how you want Windows Update to function. On a Windows Server 2016 computer, you can open Settings and click Update & security to open the Windows Update page (see Figure 18-1).

Figure 18-1

The Windows Update page

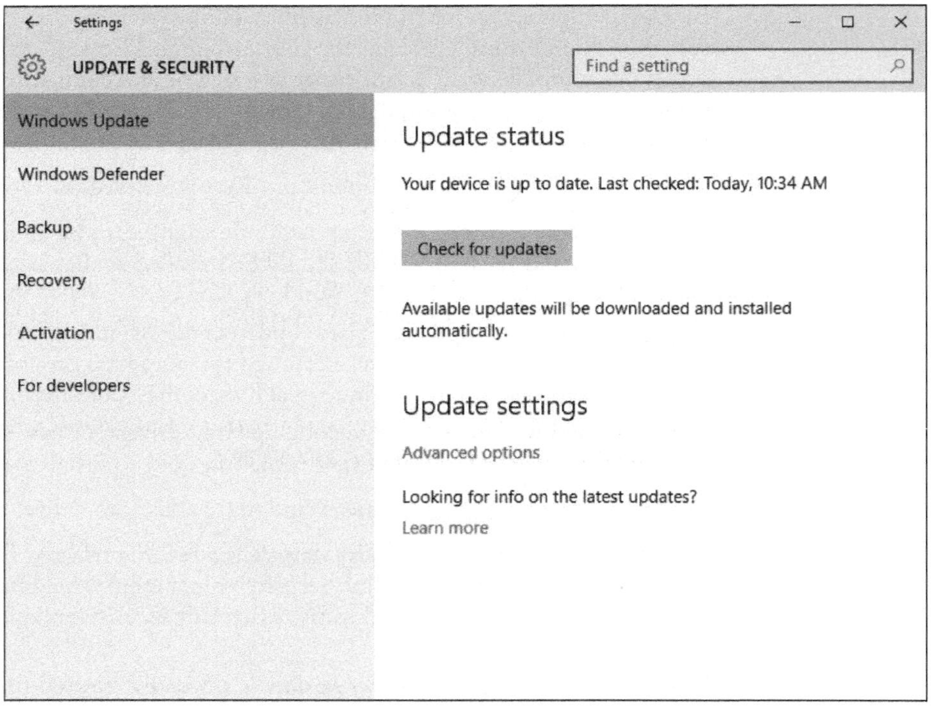

By clicking Advanced options, you can configure for Automatic Updates, give updates for other Microsoft products when Windows is updated, defer upgrades, and view update history (as shown in Figure 18-2).

Figure 18-2

The Windows Update Advanced Options page

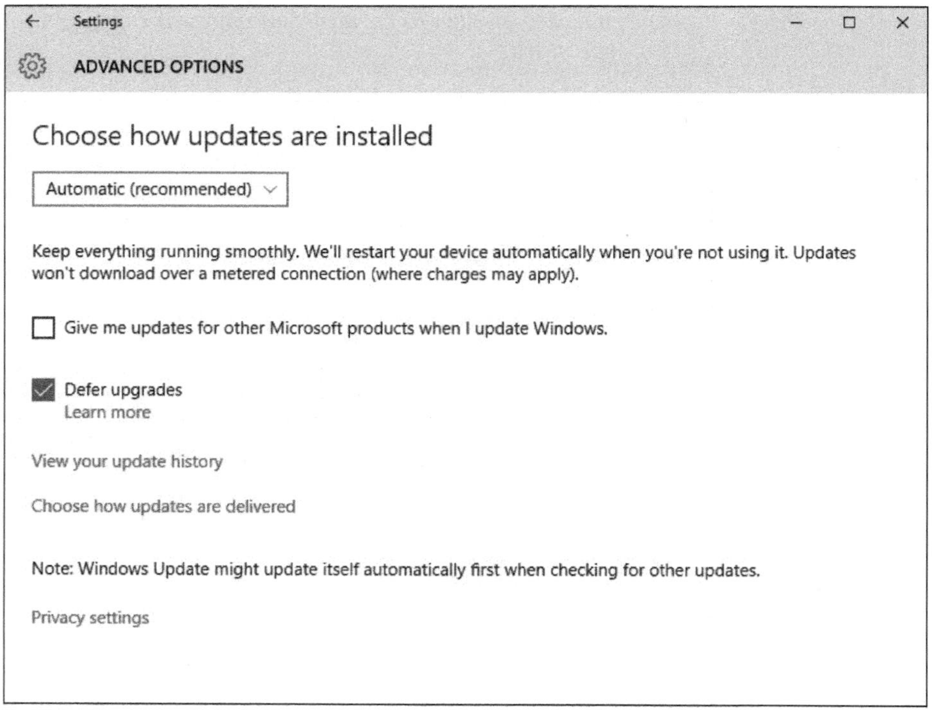

For corporations, you can also use Windows Server Update Services (WSUS) or System Center 2016 Configuration Manager to keep your systems updated. Smaller organizations might use WSUS or cloud-based services such as Microsoft Intune to keep systems up to date. The advantage of using one of these systems is that it allows you to test the patch, schedule the updates, and prioritize client updates. Once you determine a patch is safe, you can enable it for deployment.

Under Advanced options, you can customize how updates are installed. By default, the Choose how updates are installed option is set to Automatic (recommended), which means Windows will pick a time when you don't use your computer to install the updates and reboot the system. Most organizations would prefer the Notify to schedule restart option so that Windows will not reboot your computer when you least expect it.

Windows Server 2016 lets you defer upgrades to your PC. By selecting the Defer upgrades option, new Windows features won't be downloaded or installed for several months. This option is typically used to help avoid problems with an update that might cause problems within your organization.

> **WARNING!** Deferring upgrades does not affect security updates, but it does prevent you from getting the latest Windows features as soon as they are available.

If Windows Update fails to retrieve any updates, you should check your proxy settings in Internet Explorer to see whether the program can get through your proxy server (if any) or firewall. You should also make sure you can access the Internet, such as by going to the Microsoft website.

You can view your update history by opening the Advanced Options and selecting View your update history. On the Update History page, each update, including the KB article number, the version, and the date installed, is shown. If you click *Successfully installed on <date>* for a specific update, it will give a short description of the update.

At the top of the View Your Update History page, you can click *Uninstall updates* to open the Control Panel Installed Updates page, as shown in Figure 18-3. To uninstall or roll back an update, right-click the desired update and choose Uninstall. You will then be prompted to uninstall the update. When you click Yes, the update will be uninstalled.

Figure 18-3

The Control Panel Installed Updates page

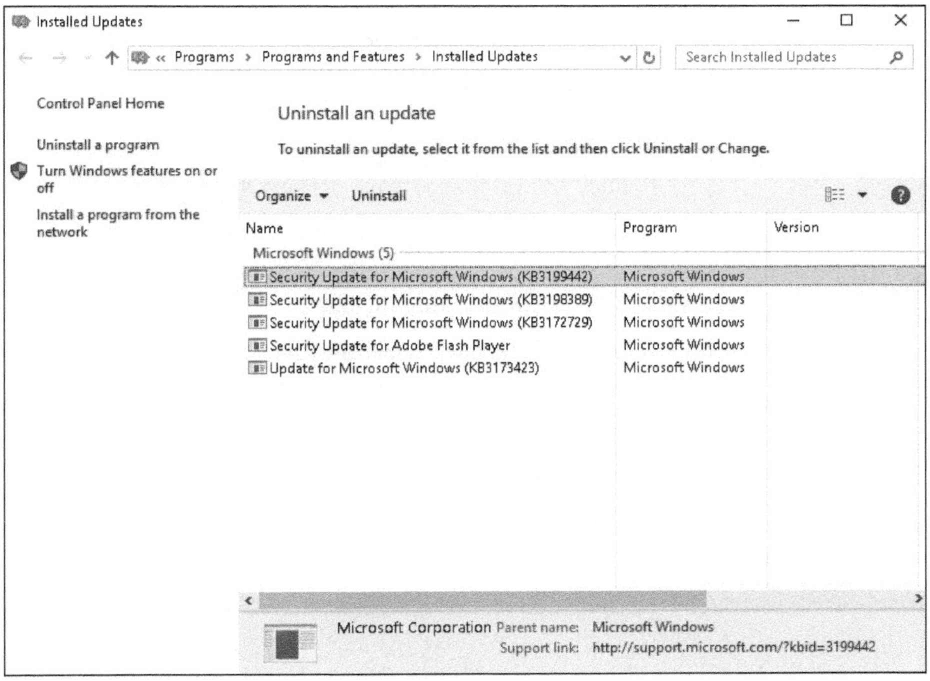

Managing Windows Update Settings with Group Policy

> Group Policy can automatically configure Windows Update settings so that you have better control of when the system gets updates, and when a reboot is performed after updates are installed. These same settings can also be used with other Windows Update platforms, such as WSUS and System Center Configuration Manager.

As with most Windows components, you can also use group policies to automatically configure how Automatic Updates behaves. For example, you can configure for updates to be automatically downloaded and installed or you can configure the user to be notified when updates are available.

➔ CONFIGURE AUTOMATIC UPDATES USING GROUP POLICIES

GET READY. To configure Automatic Updates using group policies, perform the following steps on a domain controller or any computer that has the Group Policy Management Console installed.

1. Open Server Manager.
2. Click **Tools > Group Policy Management**.
3. Using the Group Policy Management Console, open the Group Policy Object Editor for a group policy.
4. In the Group Policy Object Editor, expand **Computer Configuration > Policies > Administrative Templates > Windows Components > Windows Update**.
5. In the details pane, click **Configure Automatic Updates**. The Configure Automatic Updates page appears.
6. Click **Enabled** and then select one of the following options:
   - **Notify for download and notify for install:** Notifies a logged-on administrative user prior to the download and prior to the installation of the updates.
   - **Auto download and notify for install:** Automatically begins downloading updates and then notifies a logged-on administrative user prior to installing the updates.
   - **Auto download and schedule the install:** Automatically downloads the updates and allows the administrator to schedule when to perform the installation. If selected, the administrator must also set the day and time for the recurring scheduled installation.
   - **Allow local admin to choose setting:** Specifies that local administrators are allowed to use Automatic Updates in Control Panel to select a configuration option of their choice.
7. Click **OK** to change your options and close the Configure Automatic Updates page.

Other settings worth noting include the following:

- **Automatic Update Detection Frequency:** Specifies how frequently the Windows Update client checks for new updates. The default is a random time between 17 and 22 hours.
- **Allow Automatic Updates Immediate Installation:** Specifies whether Windows Update will immediately install updates that don't require the computer to be restarted.
- **Turn On Recommended Updates Via Automatic Updates:** Determines whether client computers install both critical and recommended updates.

- **No Auto-Restart for Scheduled Automatic Installations:** Specifies that if a computer needs a restart, it will wait for a user to perform the restart.
- **Re-Prompt for Restart Scheduled Installations:** Specifies how often the Windows Update client prompts the user to restart the computer.
- **Delay Restart for Scheduled Installations:** Specifies how long the Windows Update client waits before automatically restarting.
- **Reschedule Automatic Updates Scheduled Installations:** Specifies how long Windows Update waits after a reboot before continuing with a scheduled installation that was missed previously.
- **Enable Client-Side Targeting:** Specifies which group the computer is a member of.
- **Enables Windows Update Power Management to Automatically Wake Up the System to Install Scheduled Updates:** If a computer supports Wake On LAN, automatically starts up and installs an update at the scheduled time.
- **Allow Signed Updates from an Intranet Microsoft Update Services Location:** Specifies if Windows will install an update that is signed even if the certificate is not from Microsoft.

■ Implementing Windows Server Update Services Solution

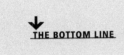

THE BOTTOM LINE

WSUS provides a centralized server that can be used to manage the deployment of updates from Microsoft. Instead of having each of your Windows computers connect to Microsoft to check for updates, consider using *Windows Server Update Services (WSUS)*. WSUS enables you to centrally manage the deployment of updates released through Microsoft, track compliance, and provide basic reporting functions.

CERTIFICATION READY
Implement Windows
Server Update Services
(WSUS) solutions
Objective 6.1

The main components of WSUS are:

- **Windows Server Update Services (WSUS):** This is installed on a Windows server behind your perimeter firewall. This service enables you to manage and distribute updates to WSUS clients. It can also update sources for other WSUS servers.
- **Microsoft Update:** This is the Microsoft website WSUS connects to for updates.
- **Update Services console:** This is the console that can be accessed to manage WSUS.

Setting up WSUS involves the following:

1. Determining a deployment strategy
2. Installing the WSUS server role
3. Specifying an update source for the WSUS server
4. Synchronizing updates to the WSUS server
5. Setting up client computers
6. Approving and installing updates on the client computers

Determining a Deployment Strategy

Determining the appropriate deployment strategy for WSUS ensures that you have the correct servers installed in the appropriate locations based on how your organization is geographically dispersed. It also helps you recognize when and where to place WSUS to reduce needless traffic across your WAN links.

You can deploy a single WSUS server to connect to the Microsoft Update servers and download updates. Figure 18-4 shows an example of a single WSUS deployment in which the clients are connecting to a single server running WSUS. The server connects and downloads updates directly from the Microsoft Update servers. The process of connecting and downloading updates is called *synchronization*. Although a single server option works well in a small office environment, it does not scale very well for companies that have their employees located across branch offices.

Figure 18-4

Deploying a single WSUS server

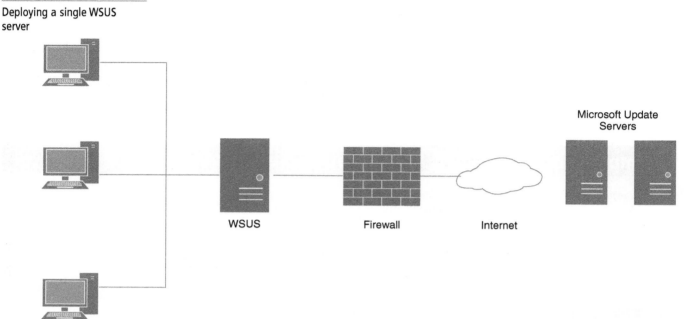

In situations where you need to service a large number of clients or where your computers are dispersed geographically, you should consider implementing more than one WSUS server. The additional WSUS servers can be configured to obtain their updates from the first WSUS server or they can get them directly from the Microsoft Update servers.

When multiple servers are used, the server that provides updates is called the *upstream server*. The server(s) that obtain their updates from the upstream server are called *downstream servers*. If multiple WSUS servers are used, you need to make sure the server-to-server and server-to-client communications use the Secure Sockets Layer (SSL).

Figure 18-5 shows how you might configure multiple WSUS servers when you have a branch office. In this example, the WSUS server at the branch office functions as the downstream server obtaining its updates from the WSUS server (upstream) at the main office either over a VPN or over an intranet connection. The WSUS server at the main office will download the updates from the Microsoft Update servers and distribute them to the downstream WSUS servers. Both the main office and branch office servers can then make the updates available to their clients on their own local network. This utilizes bandwidth more efficiently. In general, Microsoft recommends that you do not create a hierarchy that is more than three levels deep due to propagation issues.

Figure 18-5

Implementing multiple WSUS servers

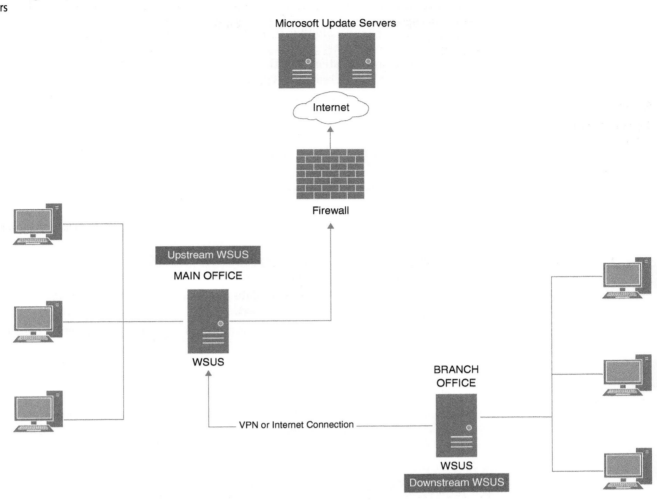

TAKE NOTE * WSUS uses port 8530 for the HTTP protocol and port 8531 for HTTPS to obtain updates from the Microsoft Update servers. In order to communicate with the Microsoft Update servers, make sure you do not block them at your perimeter firewall.

⊙ INSTALL AN UPSTREAM WSUS SERVER

GET READY. To install an upstream WSUS server on a computer running Windows Server 2016, log on with administrative privileges and then perform the following steps.

1. Open Server Manager. Then, click **Manage > Add Roles and Features** and then click **Next.**

2. Select **Role-based or Feature-based installation** and then click **Next.**

3. On the Select Destination Server page, make sure your domain controller is high-lighted and then click **Next.**

4. On the Select Server Roles page, click **Windows Server Update Services.**

5. When you are prompted to install additional features required for WSUS, click **Add Features** and then click **Next.**

6. Click **Next** to continue.

7. On the Select Features page, click **Next** to continue.

8. Read the information about WSUS and then click **Next**.

9. Under Role services, confirm **WID Database** and **WSUS Services** are checked and then click **Next**.

10. On the Content Location Selection page, make sure **Store updates in the following location** is checked, type **C:\WSUSupdates**, and then click **Next**.

    This drive location, which must have at least 6 GB of free disk space, can be used to store updates for client computers to download quickly.

11. Read the information about the Web Server Role (IIS) and then click **Next**.

12. On the Select Role Services page, click **Next** to accept the defaults.

13. Click **Install**.

14. On the Installation Progress page, click **Close** and then wait for the installation to complete.

15. In the Server Manager console, click the **yellow triangle** and then click **Launch Post-Installation tasks**.

    When you see the message *Configuration completed for Windows Server Update Services at <servername>*, you can continue to the next step.

16. Click **Tools > Windows Server Update Services**. In the Windows Server Update Services Configuration Wizard, click **Next**.

    You might need to minimize Server Manager to see the Windows Server Update Services Configuration Wizard.

17. On the Join the Microsoft Update Improvement Program page, deselect the option **Yes, I would like to join the Microsoft Update Improvement Program** and then click **Next**.

18. On the Choose Upstream Server page, click **Next** to choose to synchronize this server with Microsoft Update.

19. On the Specify Proxy Server page, click **Next**.

20. On the Connect to Upstream Server page, click **Start Connecting**.

21. After the server connects, click **Next** to proceed.

22. Click **Download updates only in these languages** and then choose **English**. Click **Next**.

23. Scroll down and deselect **Office**. Continue to scroll until you see *Windows*. Deselect everything except **Windows 10**, **Windows Server 2016**, and **Windows Defender**. Click **Next** to continue.

    This reduces the space and time needed to download updates. If this were a real production server, you would download the application and operating system updates to match your needs.

24. On the Choose Classifications page, Critical Updates, Definition Updates, Security updates, and Upgrades are already selected. Select **Service Packs** and click **Next**.

25. On the Set Sync Schedule page, click **Next** to accept the default setting.

26. Click **Begin initial synchronization** and then click **Next**.

27. Click **Finish**.

28. Your system synchronizes with the Microsoft Update servers in the background.

29. On the Update Services page, you can expand your server name and then click **Synchronizations** to view the progress (see Figure 18-6).

Figure 18-6

Monitoring the progress of the
WSUS synchronization

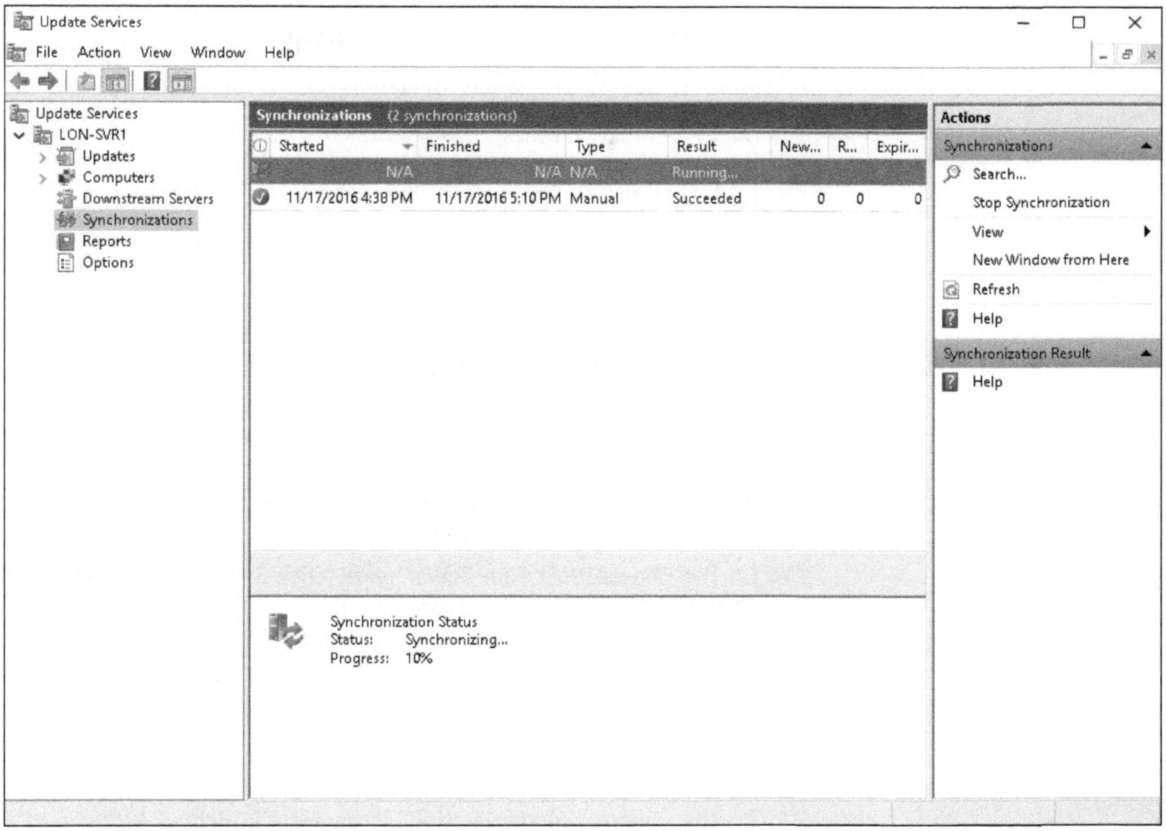

Now that you have your upstream server configured, you can set up a downstream WSUS server on another computer in your domain. In the following exercise, you use a non–domain controller (for example, the member server).

⊕ **INSTALL A DOWNSTREAM WSUS SERVER**

GET READY. To install a downstream WSUS server on a Windows member server, log on with administrative privileges and perform the following steps.

1. Click **Manage > Add Roles and Features** and then click **Next**.
2. Click **Role-based or Feature-based installation** and then click **Next**.
3. On the Select Destination Server page, make sure your member server is highlighted and then click **Next**.
4. On the Select Server Roles page, select **Windows Server Update Services**.
5. When you are prompted to install additional features required for WSUS, click **Add Features** and then click **Next**.
6. Click **Next** to continue.
7. On the Select Features page, click **Next** to continue.
8. Read information about WSUS and then click **Next**.

9. Under Role services, confirm **WID Database** and **WSUS Services** are checked and then click **Next.**

10. On the Content Location Selection page, make sure **Store updates in the following location** is checked, type **c:\WSUSupdates**, and then click **Next.**

    This drive location, which must have at least 6 GB of free disk space, can be used to store updates for client computers to download quickly.

11. Read the information about the Web Server Role (IIS) and then click **Next.**

12. On the Select Role Services page, click **Next** to accept the defaults.

13. Click **Install.**

14. On the Installation Progress page, click **Close** and then wait for the installation to complete.

15. In the Server Manager console, click the **yellow triangle** and then click **Launch Post-Installation tasks.** When you see the message *Configuration completed for Windows Server Update Services at <servername>*, you can continue to the next step.

16. Click **Tools > Windows Server Update Services.** In the Windows Server Update Services Configuration Wizard, click **Next.**

    You might need to minimize the Server Manager to see the Windows Server Update Services Configuration Wizard.

17. On the Choose Upstream Server page, click **Synchronize from another Windows Server Update Services server.** In the Server name field, type the name of the server that you configured in the previous exercise and then click **Next.**

18. On the Specify Proxy Server page, click **Next.**

19. On the Connect to Upstream Server page, click **Start Connecting.** This might take a few minutes.

20. After the server connects, click **Next** to proceed.

21. On the Choose Languages page, to accept the default settings of Download updates only in these languages and English, click **Next.**

22. On the Choose Products page, click **Next.**

23. On the Set Sync Schedule page, click **Next** to accept the default setting.

24. Select **Begin initial synchronization** and then click **Next.**

25. Click **Finish.** Your system synchronizes with the upstream server in the background.

26. On the Update Services page, you can expand your server name and then click **Synchronizations** to view the progress.

When the downstream WSUS server synchronizes with the upstream WSUS server, it downloads updates in the form of metadata and files. The update metadata can be found in the WSUS database. The update files are stored on either the WSUS server or on the Microsoft Update servers. The location is determined when you set up WSUS. In the earlier examples, we configured the WSUS server to store the updates in the *c:\WSUSUpdates* folder.

If the server is a downstream server, the products (Office, Developer Tools, Exchange, Skype, System Center, Windows, and so on) and classifications (critical updates, definition updates, drivers, security updates, and so on) included with the synchronization are set up on the upstream server.

The first time the downstream server synchronizes, it downloads all of the updates you specified. After the first synchronization has completed, the server downloads only updates made since the last synchronization.

Now that you have installed an upstream and a downstream WSUS server, you might wonder which components are installed with WSUS:

- **.NET Framework 4.5:** A software framework that provides core support for running ASP.NET 4.5 stand-alone applications and applications that are integrated with IIS.
- **Remote Server Administration Tools:** A set of tools that includes snap-ins and command-line tools for remotely managing roles and features.
- **Web Server (IIS):** An ASP.NET web service application that requires IIS to deliver access to the services it provides.
- **Windows Internal Database (WID) used by WSUS:** A relational data store used only by Windows roles and features.
- **Windows Process Activation Service:** A software component that generalizes the IIS process model and removes the dependency on HTTP.

Reviewing the Update Services Console

After completing the installation, you can access the Update Services console. In Server Manager, choose Tools > Windows Server Update Services. Figure 18-7 shows the Update Services Options node.

Figure 18-7

Reviewing the folders in the Update Services console

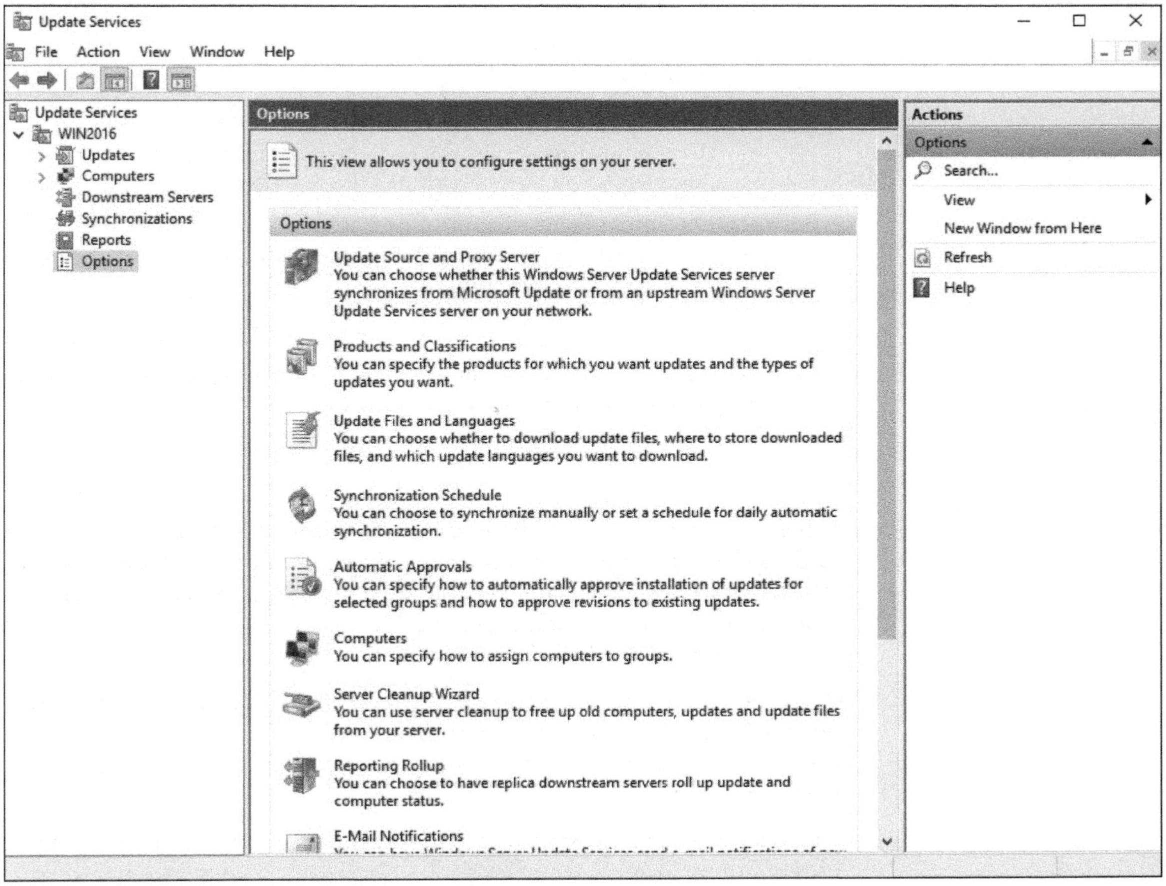

The Update Services console includes the following features:

- **Updates:** Updates, used to repair and/or replace software, consist of metadata (properties of the actual updated data) that allows you to determine its uses and the update files that are required to install the update on a computer. These updates are categorized under the following nodes: All Updates, Critical Updates, Security Updates, and WSUS Updates.
- **Computers:** These groups are created by default during the WSUS installation. Groups enable you to target your updates to specific computers and to stagger your rollout of updates. You do not see any computers in the console until you have configured the clients to use WSUS.
  - **All Computers:** This includes all computers.
  - **Unassigned Computers:** If a computer is not assigned to a group, it is added to this node the first time it contacts the WSUS server.
- **Downstream servers:** This lists the downstream servers that obtain their update files, metadata, and approvals from this WSUS server instead of from Microsoft Update or Windows Update.
- **Synchronizations:** During synchronization, the WSUS server downloads updates in the form of metadata and files from an update source. This can be another WSUS server or from the Microsoft servers and Windows Update servers.
- **Reports:** These reports allow you to monitor updates, computers, and synchronization results. You can also roll up data from downstream servers.
- **Options:** This folder provides access to tools you can use to modify settings on the WSUS server. Using the tools provided, you can specify how you want to approve the installation of updates, change your synchronization schedule, clean up old computers, update files from the server, and choose how data is displayed in the Update Services console.

Understanding the WSUS Infrastructure

When you have both upstream and downstream WSUS servers running on your network, you might want to control how update approvals, settings, computers, and groups are managed. To do this, you must first understand the two modes WSUS can run in: replica and autonomous.

As you learned from setting up the upstream and downstream WSUS servers earlier, you have two options about where you obtained your updates. You can synchronize directly from the Microsoft Update servers or from another WSUS server on your network. The choice you did not have to make at the time was whether or not your downstream WSUS server was going to run in replica or autonomous mode. By default, your downstream WSUS server was automatically set to run in in autonomous (distribution) mode.

In *replica mode*, a WSUS server mirrors update approvals, settings, computers, and groups from the upstream server. In other words, the downstream server cannot be used to approve updates; they must be performed on the upstream server.

If you are operating the WSUS server in *autonomous (distribution) mode*, it enables you to configure separate update approval settings while still retrieving updates from the upstream WSUS server.

Now that you understand the difference between the two, there might come a time when you decide that you want to manage the approval of all updates from the upstream server. This is common in situations where you have a downstream WSUS server at a branch office that has no IT support staff. If that happens, you need to understand how to configure your downstream WSUS server to run in replica mode.

CONFIGURE A DOWNSTREAM WSUS SERVER TO RUN IN REPLICA MODE

GET READY. To assign your downstream WSUS server to run in replica mode, log on to your member server with administrative privileges and then perform the following steps.

1. The Server Manager console opens automatically. If it does not open, on the task-bar, click the **Server Manager** icon.
2. Click **Tools > Windows Server Update Services**.
3. From the pane on the left, click **Options** and then choose **Update Source and Proxy Server**.
4. Click **This server is a replica of the upstream server** and then click **OK**.
5. From the left pane, expand **Updates** and then click the **All Updates** folder.
6. In the middle pane, change the status to **Any** and then click **Refresh** (see Figure 18-8).

Figure 18-8

Reviewing All Updates

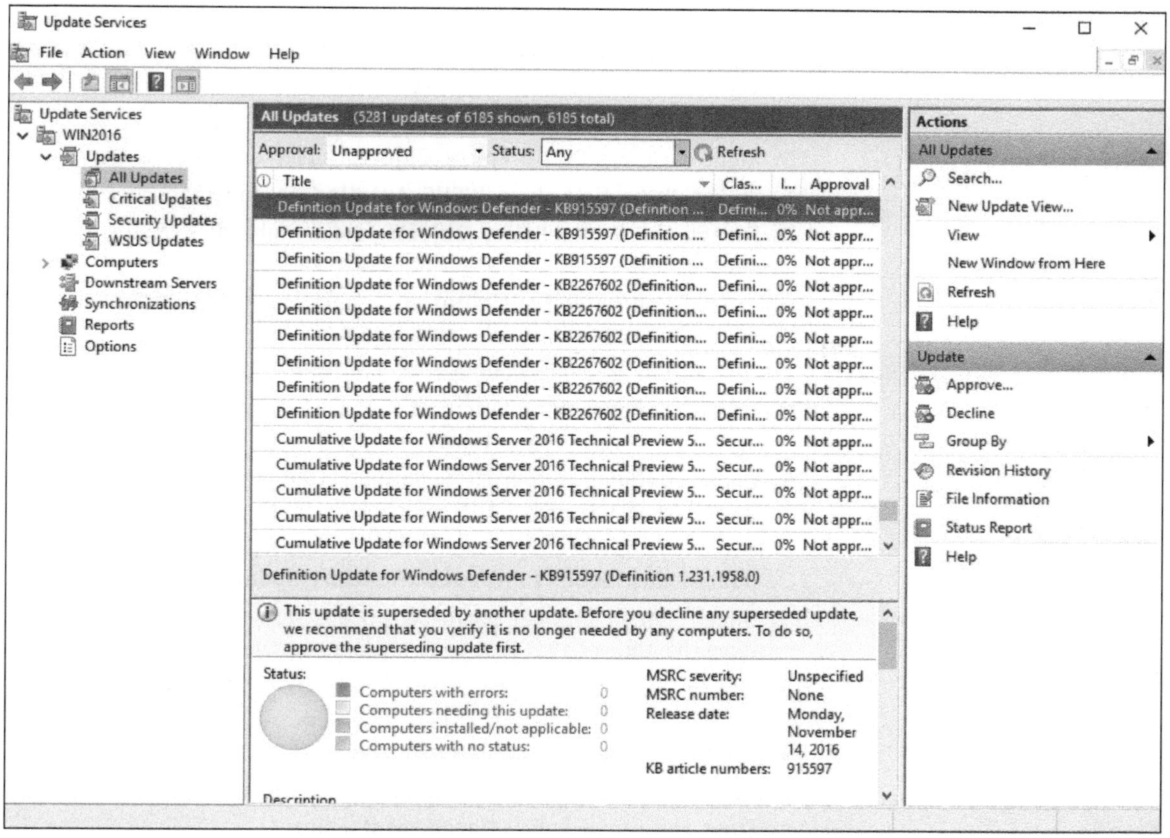

```
Update Services                                                          —  □  ×
File   Action   View   Window   Help                                        _ ᵦ ×
← →  | 🖉 🖬 | 🛛 🖽

Update Services          All Updates   (5281 updates of 6185 shown, 6185 total)    Actions
∨ 🖳 WIN2016                                                                All Updates          ▲
  ∨ 🗐 Updates            Approval: Unapproved    ▾ Status: Any    ▾ ⟳ Refresh    🔎 Search...
    🗐 All Updates        ⓘ  Title                          ▾ Clas... I... Approval ^    🗐 New Update View...
    🗐 Critical Updates   Definition Update for Windows Defender - KB915597 (Definition ... Defini... 0% Not appr...    View                 ▶
    🗐 Security Updates   Definition Update for Windows Defender - KB915597 (Definition ... Defini... 0% Not appr...    New Window from Here
    🗐 WSUS Updates       Definition Update for Windows Defender - KB915597 (Definition ... Defini... 0% Not appr...    🔄 Refresh
  > 💻 Computers          Definition Update for Windows Defender - KB2267602 (Definition... Defini... 0% Not appr...    🛛 Help
    Downstream Servers    Definition Update for Windows Defender - KB2267602 (Definition... Defini... 0% Not appr...
    Synchronizations      Definition Update for Windows Defender - KB2267602 (Definition... Defini... 0% Not appr...    Update               ▲
    Reports               Definition Update for Windows Defender - KB2267602 (Definition... Defini... 0% Not appr...    🖥 Approve...
    Options               Definition Update for Windows Defender - KB2267602 (Definition... Defini... 0% Not appr...    🖥 Decline
                          Cumulative Update for Windows Server 2016 Technical Preview 5... Secur... 0% Not appr...    📑 Group By           ▶
                          Cumulative Update for Windows Server 2016 Technical Preview 5... Secur... 0% Not appr...    Revision History
                          Cumulative Update for Windows Server 2016 Technical Preview 5... Secur... 0% Not appr...    📄 File Information
                          Cumulative Update for Windows Server 2016 Technical Preview 5... Secur... 0% Not appr...    Status Report
                          Cumulative Update for Windows Server 2016 Technical Preview 5... Secur... 0% Not appr... ∨    🛛 Help

                          Definition Update for Windows Defender - KB915597 (Definition 1.231.1958.0)

                          ⓘ This update is superseded by another update. Before you decline any superseded update, ^
                            we recommend that you verify it is no longer needed by any computers. To do so,
                            approve the superseding update first.

                          Status:                          MSRC severity:    Unspecified
                             ⬛ Computers with errors:     0    MSRC number:    None
                             ⬛ Computers needing this update:  0    Release date:   Monday,
                             ⬛ Computers installed/not applicable: 0                 November
                             ⬛ Computers with no status:   0                 14, 2016
                                                           KB article numbers: 915597
                          Description                                                           ∨
```

7. Right-click the first update in the list. In the menu that appears, notice that the option to *Approve* or *Decline* the update is disabled. The downstream server has been configured in replica mode earlier. Updates can be approved only on the upstream server.
8. Close the Update Services console.

Configuring Clients to Use WSUS

For clients to obtain their information from your WSUS servers, you need to first configure them. By default, your computers are configured to communicate directly with the Microsoft Update servers. With an Active Directory domain present, you can create a Group Policy Object to configure your clients.

 CREATE A GPO TO ENABLE AUTOUPDATE FOR CLIENT COMPUTERS

GET READY. To create a GPO to enable AutoUpdate for client computers in an Active Directory domain, log on with administrative credentials, and then on your domain controller, perform the following steps.

> **TAKE NOTE** *
> This can be performed on a Windows 10 client with Administrative Tools or at the domain controller for the domain using the Group Policy Management Console.

1. The Server Manager console opens automatically. If it does not open, on the taskbar, click the **Server Manager** icon.
2. Click **Tools > Group Policy Management**.
3. Right-click the **Group Policy Objects** folder and choose **New**.
4. In the Name field, type **WSUS AutoUpdate** and then click **OK**.
5. Expand the **Group Policy Objects** folder, right-click **WSUS AutoUpdate**, and then choose **Edit**.
6. Expand **Computer Configuration > Policies > Administrative Templates > Windows Components > Windows Update**.
7. In the details pane, double-click **Configure Automatic Updates**.
8. Under Configure Automatic Updates, click **Enabled** and under Configure automatic updating, review the options.
9. Under Configure automatic updating, make sure **3-Auto download and notify for install** is visible. Read the information in the help panel to understand how this setting works. Click **OK** when finished.
10. Double-click **Specify intranet Microsoft update service location**.
11. Under Specify intranet Microsoft update service location, click **Enabled** and then type the URL of the upstream WSUS server you set up earlier. For example, if your domain controller's name is LON-SVR1, type **http://LON-SVR1:8530**. (8530 is the default port used by WSUS.)
12. For the intranet statistics server, type the same information.
13. Click **OK**.
14. Close the Group Policy Management Editor.
15. Right-click the domain container (contoso.com) and choose **Link an existing GPO**.
16. Choose **WSUS AutoUpdate** and then click **OK**.
17. Close the Group Policy Management Console.
18. Restart your Windows 10 or Windows Server 2016 computer and then log on with administrative credentials to the domain.

> **TAKE NOTE** *
> Perform these steps on a Windows 10 or Windows Server 2016 computer that is a member of the Active Directory domain.

19. Click **Start**, type **cmd**, and then press **Enter**.

20. From the Command Prompt window, type **gpresult /r** and then press **Enter.**

The WSUS AutoUpdate GPO should appear under the Computer Settings > Applied Group Policy Objects section of the report. If it does not, type **gpupdate /force** and then try **gpresult /r** again.

21. Type **wuauclt /detectnow** and then press **Enter.** This forces the Windows computer to contact the WSUS server immediately.

22. Open the Update Services console on the domain controller running WSUS (**Server Manager > Tools > Windows Server Update Services**).

23. Expand the **Computers > All Computers** group. You can see the computer under the Unassigned Computers group.

Configuring WSUS Groups

After configuring your clients to use WSUS, organize them into computer groups. This enables you to target specific systems for updates. WSUS comes with two built-in groups: All Computers and Unassigned Computers. If you don't have a need to configure and manage your computers separately, you can stay with these groups. If you want to test the impact the updates will have on your computers and any line-of-business applications before rolling them out to your entire organization, then new groups should be created.

CERTIFICATION READY
Configure WSUS groups
Objective 6.1

Here are a few things to note about computer groups:

- If a computer is not assigned to a specific group, it appears in the Unassigned Computers group in the console.
- A computer can be a member of more than one group and groups can be built in a hierarchical structure.
- If you create a group hierarchy, an update rolled out to a parent group is also distributed to child groups.

 CREATE A GROUP IN WSUS

GET READY. To create a group on your domain controller running WSUS, log on with administrative privileges and then perform the following steps.

1. Open the Update Services console if you closed it earlier (**Server Manager > Tools > Windows Server Update Services**).

2. Expand the **Computers** node, right-click **All Computers**, and then choose **Add Computer Group.**

3. In the Name field, type **IT Staff** and then click **Add.**

4. Confirm the group appears under the All Computers node. Keep the Update Services console open to use in the next exercise.

Selecting Server-Side Targeting Versus Client-Side Targeting

Computers can be assigned to groups using either server-side targeting or client-side targeting. *Server-side targeting* involves moving clients to computer groups using the Update Services console. *Client-side targeting* involves using Group Policy for domain computers or Local Group Policy Editor for non–domain computers. When using client-side targeting, you configure the computers to add themselves automatically to the computer groups by specifying the group in the *Computer Configuration Policies\ Administrative Tools\Windows Components\Windows Update\Enable client-side targeting* policy. Client-side targeting works well when you organize your computers into organizational units based on their configuration or function.

These settings are configured on the WSUS Server via Update Services > Options > Computers.

Selecting the *Use the Update Services console* option uses server-side targeting; computers are automatically added to the Unassigned Computers group. The other option, *Use Group Policy or registry settings on computers*, configures the WSUS server to support client-side targeting.

⊙ USE SERVER-SIDE TARGETING TO MOVE A COMPUTER TO A GROUP

GET READY. To use server-side targeting on your domain controller running WSUS, log on with administrative privileges and then perform the following steps.

1. In the Update Services console, expand **Computers**.
2. In the Unassigned Computers group, right-click the **Windows 10 computer** and choose **Change Membership**.
3. Select **IT Staff** and then click **OK** to add the computer to the group.
4. Click the **IT Staff** group, and in the middle pane, confirm the computer appears. Keep the Update Services console open to use in the next exercise.

Managing Patch Management in Mixed Environments

Most companies have mixed environments, which consist of multiple versions of client operating systems (such as Windows 7, 8.1, and 10) and multiple versions of server operating system (Windows Servers 2012 R2 and Windows Server 2016). When you determine which updates you need to deploy, you need to review updates for all of the Microsoft client, server, and application versions that you have.

CERTIFICATION READY
Manage patch management in mixed environments
Objective 6.1

Updates downloaded to the upstream server will not be distributed to WSUS clients automatically. As the WSUS administrator, you have to approve them first. If you look under Options > Automatic Approval, you can see the following default WSUS settings:

- **Update Rules:** Under this tab, you can specify rules for automatically approving new updates when they are synchronized. The default rule approves security and critical updates for all computers.
- **Advanced tab:** The following options are configured by default under this tab: Automatically approve updates to the WSUS product, Automatically approve new revisions of updates that are already approved, and Automatically decline updates when a new revision causes them to expire.

As the administrator, you can change which updates are automatically detected, which ones are automatically approved, and which groups of computers are targeted to receive the updates.

⊙ APPROVE AND DEPLOY WSUS UPDATES

GET READY. To approve and deploy WSUS updates, on your domain controller running WSUS, log on with administrative privileges and then perform the following steps.

1. In the Update Services console, expand **Updates** and then click **All Updates**.
2. Right-click one of the updates and choose **Approve**.

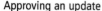

3. In the Approve Updates box, click **IT Staff > Approved for Install.** You should see a green circle with white checkmark check box for IT Staff, as shown in Figure 18-9.

Figure 18-9

Approving an update

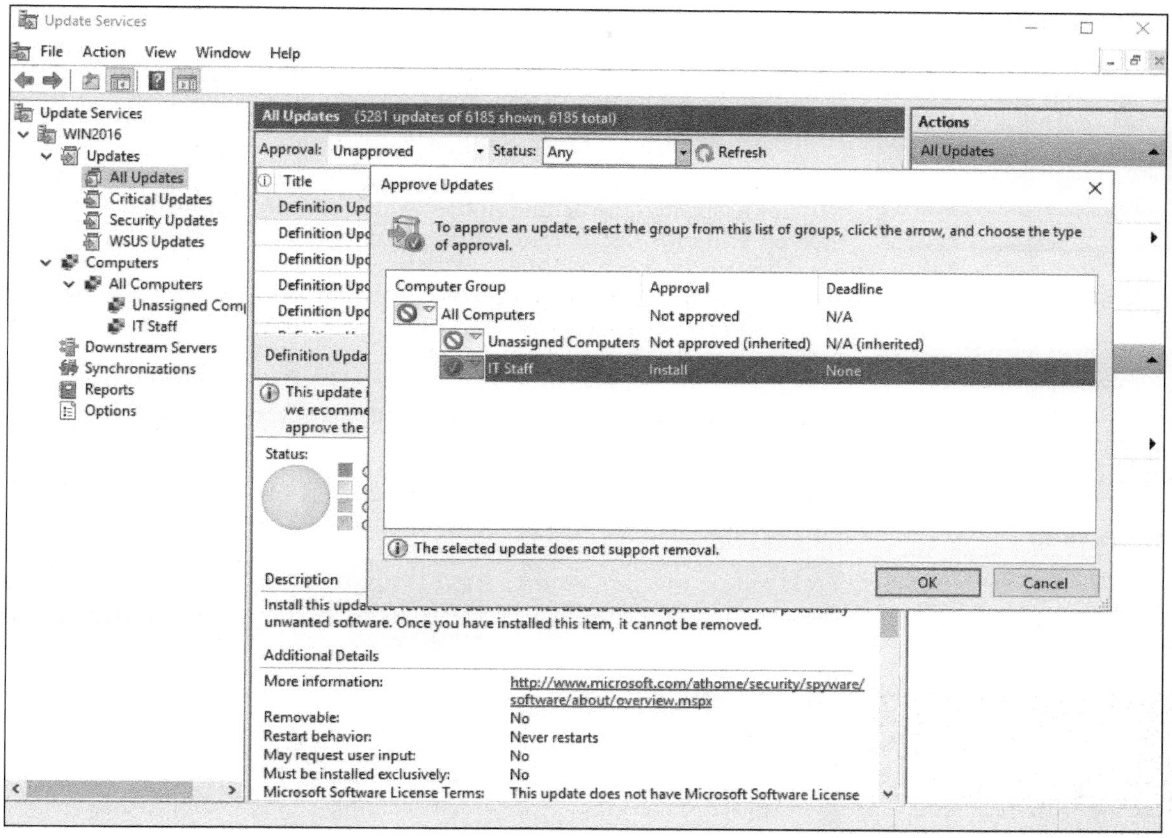

![Screenshot of the Update Services window with the Approve Updates dialog box open. The tree in the left pane shows Update Services > WIN2016 > Updates (All Updates, Critical Updates, Security Updates, WSUS Updates), Computers > All Computers (Unassigned Computers, IT Staff), Downstream Servers, Synchronizations, Reports, Options. The Approve Updates dialog shows a Computer Group table with columns Computer Group, Approval, Deadline: All Computers / Not approved / N/A; Unassigned Computers / Not approved (inherited) / N/A (inherited); IT Staff / Install / None. At the bottom: "The selected update does not support removal." with OK and Cancel buttons.]

4. Click **OK.**

5. When the approval process completes, click **Close.**

   Now, on the Windows Server 2016 system, perform the following steps:

1. Log on to a Windows Server 2016 system that is a member of the domain.

2. Click **Start**, type **cmd**, and then press **Enter.**

3. From the Command Prompt window, type **wuauclt /detectnow** and then press **Enter.** Close the Command Prompt window.

4. This causes the client to detect available updates, automatically queue them for download via Background Intelligent Transfer Service (BITS), and then present a notification to install the updates on the client.

5. Right-click the notification icon and choose **Open Windows Update.**

6. Click **Install Updates.**

7. If you are prompted after the updates are completed, click **Restart now** to complete the installation of the update.

■ Implementing an Anti-Malware Solution with Windows Defender

THE BOTTOM LINE

Windows Defender is designed to protect your computer against viruses, spyware, and other types of malware. It protects against these threats by providing real-time protection in which it notifies you if malware attempts to install itself on your computer or when an application tries to change critical settings.

CERTIFICATION READY
Implement an anti-malware solution with Windows Defender
Objective 6.1

It can also be configured to scan your computer on a regular basis and remove or quarantine malware it finds.

At the heart of Windows Defender are its definition files, which are downloaded from Windows Update. The definition files, which contain information about potential threats, are used by Windows Defender to notify you of potential threats to your system.

TAKE NOTE*

Windows Defender automatically disables itself if you install another antivirus product.

Using Windows Defender

To access Windows Defender, click Start, type Windows Defender, and choose it from the Results. Figure 18-10 shows the Windows Defender Home tab.

Figure 18-10

Viewing the Windows Defender Home tab

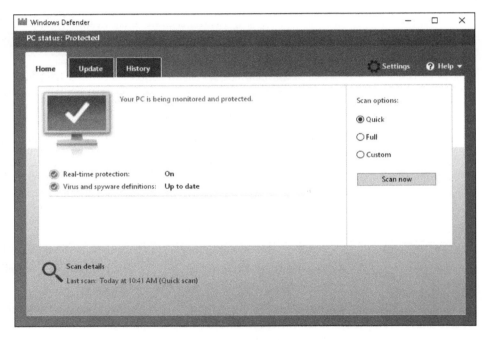

The Home tab allows you to check the status of Windows Defender, including whether Windows Defender is up to date and whether Windows Defender is protecting your system. It also gives you the option to initiate a scan.

When looking at the Home tab, you should always look for a green message indicating *Your PC is being monitored and protected* and you should also make sure your system is up to date. Other components include:

- **Real-time protection:** Real-time protection uses signature detection methodology and heuristics to monitor and catch malware behavior. Signature detection uses a vendor's definition files to detect malicious programs. If the program contains code that matches the signature, the program most likely contains the virus. This works well when the threat has already been identified, but what happens in between the time the virus is released and the definition file is made available? That's where heuristics can help. It is used to monitor for suspicious activity by a program. Suspicious activity includes a program trying to copy itself into another program, a program trying to write to the disk directly, or a program trying to manipulate critical system files required by the operating system. These are indicators of possible malware activity that heuristics can detect.

- **Virus and spyware definitions:** When a new virus is discovered, Microsoft creates a new virus signature/definition update. Each definition file contains a piece of the actual virus code that is used to detect a specific virus or malware. During scans, the content on the computer is compared with information in the definition files. Because new viruses are created every day and existing viruses are modified regularly, it's important to keep your definitions updated.

- **Scan options (Quick, Full, and Custom):** A Quick scan checks the areas that malicious software, including viruses, spyware, and unwanted software, are most likely to infect. A Full scan checks all the files on your disk, including running programs. A Custom scan is designed to check only locations and files you specify.

- **Scan Details:** This area of the Home tab provides information on when the last scan was performed on the computer.

The Update tab provides you with information about your virus and spyware definitions. It is important to keep these current to ensure your computer is protected at all times.

The Update tab provides information about when the definition files were created, the last time you updated them, and the current version numbers for the virus and spyware definitions. Windows Defender updates the definition files automatically, but you can manually check for updates by clicking Update on this tab.

The History tab provides information about items that have been detected in the past and the actions that were taken with them.

The categories of items are as follows:

- **Quarantined Items:** These items were not allowed to run but were not removed from your computer.
- **Allowed Items:** These items were allowed to run on your computer.
- **All Detected Items:** These items provide a list of all items detected on your computer.

➡ REMOVE A QUARANTINED ITEM

GET READY. To remove an item that has been quarantined, perform the following steps.

1. Open Windows Defender.
2. Click the **History** tab.
3. Click **Quarantined Items.**
4. Click **View Details.**
5. Select the detected item and then read the description.
6. Click **Remove.**

The Settings option is where you can fine-tune how Windows Defender works. In Settings (as shown in Figure 18-11), you can:

- Enable or disable real-time protection.
- Enable or disable cloud-based protection, which will send potential security problems to Microsoft.

- Enable or disable automatic sample submission.
- Select the files and folders, file types, and processes to exclude from the scan.

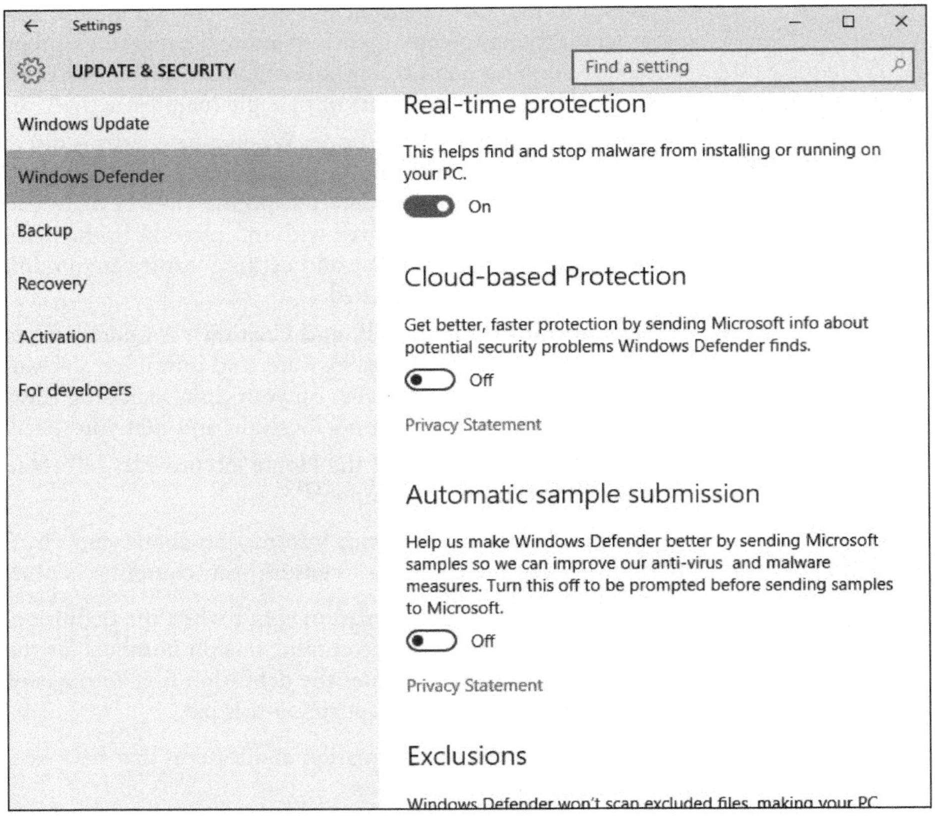

Figure 18-11

Configuring Windows Defender settings

To keep a machine updated, besides keeping Windows Defender and definitions up to date, you should also periodically run a full scan on your system. You can use Task Manager to automatically initiate a full scan.

SCHEDULE A WINDOWS DEFENDER SCAN

GET READY. To schedule a Windows Defender scan, log on with administrative privileges and then perform the following steps.

1. Click **Start**, type **taskschd.msc**, and press **Enter**.
2. In the left pane, expand **Task Scheduler Library > Microsoft > Windows > Windows Defender**.
3. Double-click **Windows Defender Scheduled Scan**.
4. Click the **Triggers** tab and then click **New**.
5. In the Begin the Task field, choose **On a schedule.**
6. Under Settings, select **One time** and in the Start field, change the time to 5 minutes from your current time.
7. Make sure the **Enabled** check box is checked and then click **OK**.
8. To close the Windows Defender Scheduled Scan Properties dialog box, click **OK.**
9. Open Windows Defender to see the status of the scan on the Home tab. Click **Cancel scan.**

Integrating Windows Defender with WSUS and Windows Update

> Because Windows Defender is a Microsoft application, it can be updated with Windows Update, WSUS, and Configuration Manager. Updates include Windows Defender and the definitions that help identify malware.

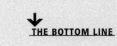

CERTIFICATION READY
Integrate Windows Defender with WSUS and Windows Update
Objective 6.1

When updates are installed using Windows Update, the Windows Update program also updates Windows Defender. However, to update Windows Defender, you must select Windows Defender, so that it will update the program and definitions.

■ Performing Backup and Restore Operations Using Windows Server Backup

↓
THE BOTTOM LINE

> When an organization loses data, the results can range from a loss of productivity to an entire meltdown of the company itself. Having a solid backup strategy along with the systems, processes, and tools to execute the strategy is the key to your ability to recover.

CERTIFICATION READY
Perform backup and restore operations using Windows Server Backup
Objective 6.1

There is an old saying that nothing lasts forever, which means you should live it up, take chances, and never have any regrets. That might be sound advice in some situations, but it's not the approach you want to take when it comes to protecting your data.

If you've been administering servers for any length of time, you most likely have experienced or heard of someone who lost data due to one of the following:

- Hardware failure
- Software failure
- Human error
- Computer virus
- Theft
- Natural disaster (flooding, earthquakes, severe weather, and so on)
- Fire

When an organization loses data, the impact can range from a loss of productivity (employees having to re-create their data or wait for it to be restored) to a complete financial collapse of the company itself. In between these two extremes are costly downtimes that result from restoring or rebuilding your data, delayed responses to customer inquiries, and the overall negative perceptions your customers will have of your organization as a whole.

Unfortunately, most people and companies take backups seriously only after they've experienced the impact of losing their data. It's inevitable; it will happen sooner or later, and you must be prepared by implementing a backup strategy and executing it when the time comes.

Determining what needs to be backed up, the frequency and types of backups, as well as where they are stored (on-site/off-site/cloud) should all be part of your backup strategy. In addition to protecting your data, you must also consider the roles performed by the servers on the network. The role(s) assigned to a server (Active Directory Domain Services, DHCP Server, DNS Server, File and Storage Services, Application Server, Web Server, and so on) can dramatically change its configuration, what you back up, and the frequency with which the backup is performed.

You also need to consider the impact the backups will have on users as well as the ability to keep critical applications running. Users need to get their work done, so critical applications cannot be taken down in order for a backup to be performed. Fortunately, Windows Server utilizes the Volume Shadow Copy Service (VSS) and shadow copies to create point-in-time snapshots, allowing you to keep any downtime to a minimum.

To protect data on your servers, you might have some form of fault tolerance such as RAID or clustering in place. Although these solutions can protect you from single or multiple drive failures, they are not a substitute for performing backups. With these issues in mind, let's take a look at how to protect your data and servers using the tools provided by Windows Server 2016.

Installing the Windows Server Backup Feature

Windows Server Backup, *wbadmin*, and Windows PowerShell cmdlets provide the tools you need to back up and restore your critical data and servers.

To prepare for a server backup, you first need to install the Windows Server Backup feature. Once installed, you have access to the following tools:

- Windows Server Backup Microsoft Management Console (MMC) snap-in
- wbadmin command-line tool (wbadmin.exe)
- Windows PowerShell cmdlets for Windows Server Backup

The Windows Server Backup MMC snap-in is not installed on Windows Server 2016 systems running the Server Core installation option only. To run backups on these systems, you need to use either the command-line tool wbadmin or the Windows PowerShell cmdlets, or manage them remotely from another computer using the Windows Server Backup MMC. You can also use the Windows 10 Remote Server Administration Tools (RSAT).

⊕ INSTALL THE WINDOWS SERVER BACKUP FEATURE

GET READY. To install the Windows Server Backup feature on Server01, perform the following steps.

1. Log on to LON-SVR2 and open Server Manager.
2. In Server Manager, click **Manage > Add Roles and Features**.
3. On the Before You Begin page, click **Next**.
4. On the Installation Type page, click **Next**.
5. On the Server Selection page, select the desired server and click **Next**.
6. On the Server Roles page, click **Next**.
7. Select **Windows Server Backup** and click **Next**.
8. Click **Install** and then click **Close**.

After the installation completes, you can launch the Windows Server Backup Microsoft Management Console (MMC) snap-in by selecting Server Manager > Tools > Windows Server Backup.

To view the list of commands supported by the wbadmin command-line tool (see Figure 18-12), open a command prompt while logged on with administrative rights and use the following command:

```
wbadmin /?
```

Figure 18-12

Reviewing the wbadmin
commands

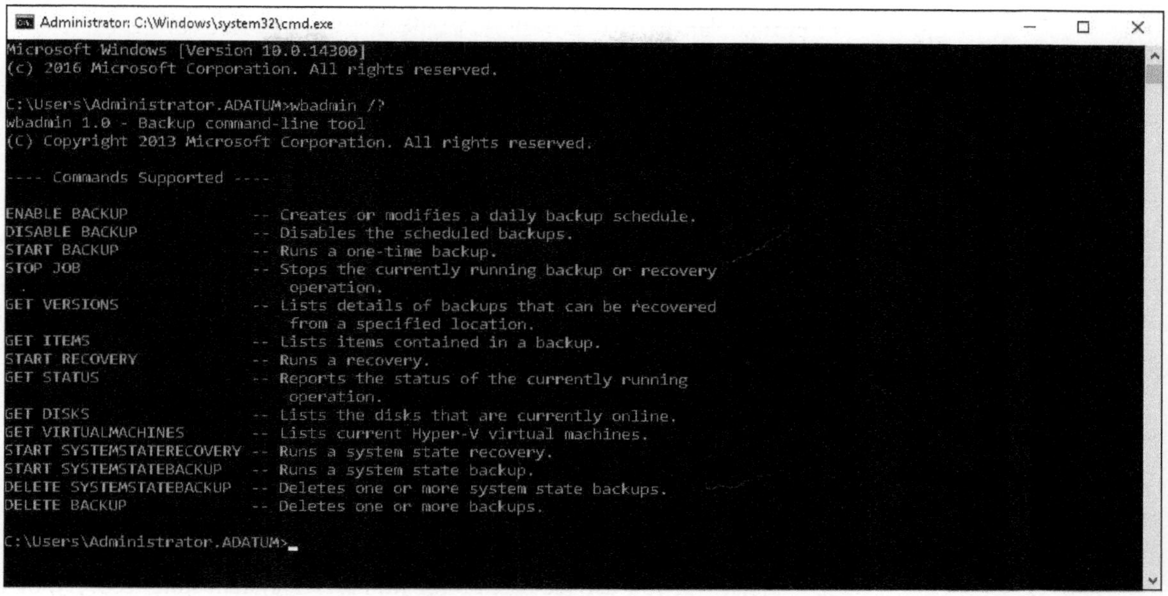

To view the PowerShell cmdlets available for the Windows Server Backup module, use the
following command from within PowerShell:

```
Get-Command –Module WindowsServerBackup

–CommandType Cmdlet
```

→ **INSTALL WINDOWS SERVER BACKUP FEATURES ON A SERVER CORE USING
POWERSHELL (OPTIONAL)**

GET READY. To install the Windows Server Backup features on a Server Core installation,
perform the following steps.

1. Log on to the Server Core installation.
2. Enter the following command from within the command window that appears, and
   then press **Enter** to start a PowerShell session:
   powershell
3. Enter the following command to make the Server Manager features available from
   within the PowerShell session:
   Import-Module Servermanager
4. Enter the following command to add the Windows Server Backup feature:
   Install-WindowsFeature Windows-Server-Backup
5. Enter the following command to confirm the Windows Server Backup feature is
   installed:
   Get-WindowsFeature | where {$_.Name –eq "Windows-Server-Backup"}
6. Type **Exit** to end the PowerShell session and return to the command window.
7. Type **wbadmin /?** and confirm wbadmin tools are installed.

Configuring Windows Server Backups

> The Windows Server Backup feature provides full server, Bare Metal Recovery, system state, system reserve, and local/remote volume backup capabilities.

Once the Windows Server Backup feature is installed, it's time to refer to your backup strategy to answer several key questions. Before we review those questions, there are two important things to consider that will shape your overall strategy:

- The maximum amount of time you will have to bring a system back online before it has a significant impact on your organization. This is called the *Recovery Time Objective (RTO)*.
- The amount of data you can afford to lose before it has a significant impact on your organization. This is called the *Recovery Point Objective (RPO)*.

As you review the following questions, keep the RTO and RPO in mind:

- How often will you perform the backup (hourly, daily, or weekly)?
- When should you perform the backup (which days and times)?
- Where will you store your backups (external hard drive, remote share, or DVD)?
- What will you back up (full server, system state, files, folders, or volumes)?
- What will you use the backup for (full server, system state recovery, or Bare Metal Recovery)?

Here are a few things to keep in mind when working with Windows Server Backup on Windows Server 2016:

- Backing up directly to a tape drive is not supported, although you can still back up to this media if you have System Center 2016 Data Protection Manager (DPM). This works by using a disk-to-disk-to-tape (D2D2T) approach in which data is initially copied to backup storage on a disk, and then copied again to the tape storage system. Third-party backup programs can also be used if you need to back up to tape.
- If your backup strategy incorporates multiple disks, you must have all the disks online when performing the initial setup of the backup. These disks should be dedicated to the backup job, which means they will be formatted and configured as a single New Technology File System (NTFS) volume. NTFS is a proprietary file system developed by Microsoft.
- The system state, which includes the core files and registry settings used by the operating system (boot files, system-protected files, shared system volume [SYSVOL], the COM+ class registration database, and Active Directory files), cannot be backed up to a DVD drive. Active Directory service files and SYSVOL are included as part of the system state on domain controllers.
- Applications can be backed up to attached disks or remote shared folders but not to a DVD, optical disc, or removable media. These disks must be attached and online and should support either USB 2.0 or IEEE 1394 as well as provide at least 1.5 times the storage capacity of the items you are backing up. The additional space allows you to store a couple of backup versions.
- When backing up to folders on a local or remote volume, only one copy of the backup can be stored in the folder. Subsequent backups overwrite the contents from the previous one.
- When using remote shares, you specify the Universal Naming Convention (UNC) path (\\servername\share) to provide the location for storing the backup. If you decide to change this after backups are executed, you will no longer be able to recover your backup data without performing a full restore and creating a new UNC path or resetting the share back to its original configuration.
- Backing up to a folder on a volume where users access data frequently results in a degradation of performance while the backup is in process.

REVIEWING BACKUP CONFIGURATION OPTIONS

When configuring your backup, you select either a full server (recommended) or a custom configuration (see Figure 18-13).

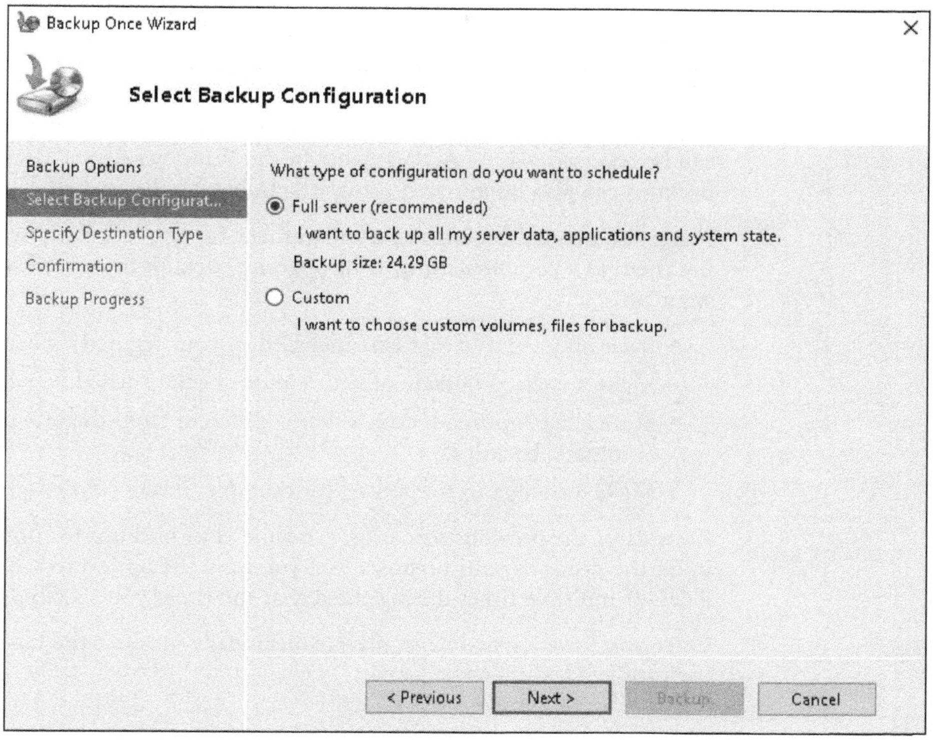

Figure 18-13

Selecting your Backup configuration options

The following provides an overview of the configuration options:

- **Full server (recommended):** This option backs up all hard disk volumes (except for the volume where the backup is stored) as well as any critical data required for recovery. This includes your server data, applications, and system state. Full server backups can be used to recover the Active Directory Domain Services (AD DS), Bare Metal Recovery restores, as well as specific files/folders.
- **Custom:** This option allows you to specify the items you want to include in the backup. The options include:
  - *Bare Metal Recovery:* This option allows you to recover your server from a hard drive failure to a machine running the same/different hardware. It does not support cross-architecture (x86 to x64) and requires Windows Server installation media to start the recovery process. Selecting this option automatically includes system state, system reserved, and the critical volumes that are necessary for the operating system to run. Examples of critical volumes include those that hold the boot files (Bootmgr and the Boot Configuration Data [BCD] store), operating system and registry, SYSVOL, Active Directory database, and Active Directory database log files. When selecting this option as a substitute for a full backup, keep in mind that it will not automatically back up noncritical volumes that contain data you need.
  - *System state:* This option backs up all the files needed to recover Active Directory. The system state includes the registry, boot files, COM+ class registration database, Active Directory database (ntds.dit) and its associated log files, Active Directory Certificate Services database, SYSVOL folder, and system files under the protection of Windows Resource protection. Additional data can be included if the server performs additional roles.

- **System Reserved:** This option contains the Windows Recovery Environment (WinRE) files and can be used to boot the server in situations where the operating system becomes corrupted or fails to boot.
- **Local disk (x:):** This option represents local disks and volumes on the server.

After selecting the backup configuration, your next decision involves determining whether you want to run the backup manually or schedule it to start automatically.

EXPLORING YOUR SCHEDULING OPTIONS

You can run a manual backup (one-time backup) by using the Backup Once Wizard, which can be accessed via the Actions pane in the Windows Server Backup console. These types of backups can also be initiated using wbadmin and PowerShell.

Never use manual backups as a replacement for your regularly scheduled backup. Instead, use them as a complement to your ongoing backups in the following situations when you want to:

- Back up a volume that isn't included in your regularly scheduled backups.
- Make a backup outside of your current backup schedule window.
- Store a backup in a location that is different from the one currently being used by your automatic backups.
- Make a change to the server (for example, install new programs and service packs).

Outside of the previous scenarios, schedule your backups to run automatically. Depending upon the needs of your organization, you have the option to schedule a backup to occur once a day or multiple times during the day at the times you specify (see Figure 18-14).

Once you have a schedule in place, you're ready to select the target location to store your backups.

Figure 18-14

Selecting the Backup schedule options

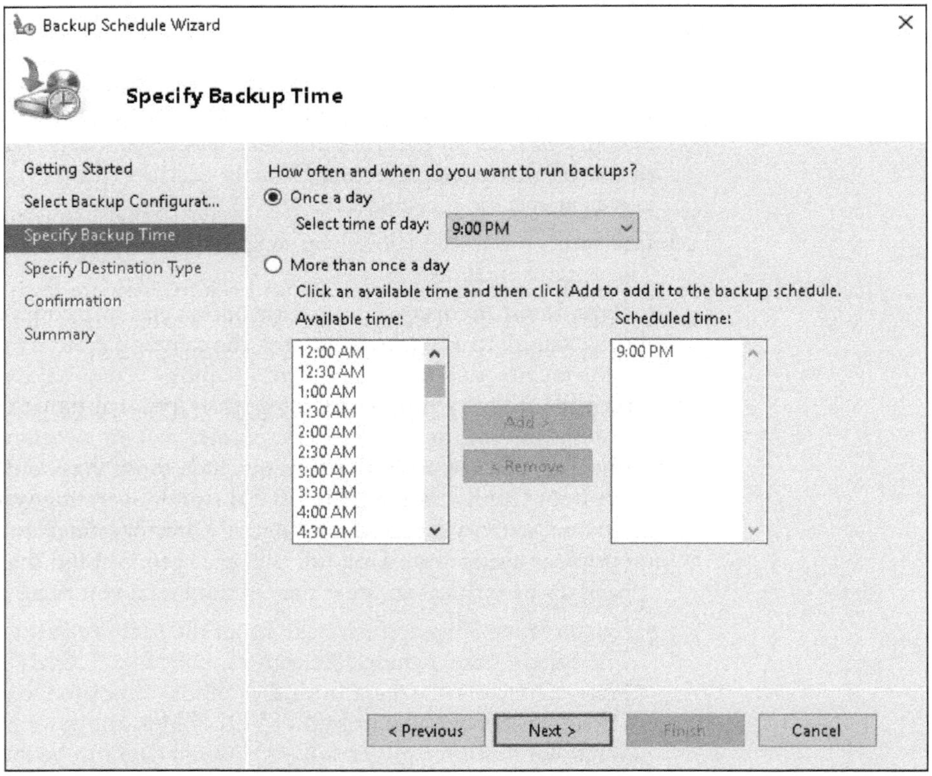

SELECTING WHERE TO STORE YOUR BACKUPS

Windows Server Backup provides three options to select from when deciding where to store your backups. These options include:

- Backing up to hard disk(s) (recommended)
- Backing up to a volume
- Backing up to a shared network folder

The first two options involve storing your backups on the server locally. When backing up to a hard disk, you should dedicate the disks to the Windows Backup program, which means they will be formatted and used exclusively for storing backups and not for holding other data. In other words, you will no longer see them appear in File Explorer, and they will be managed by Windows Server Backup exclusively.

When backing up to hard disks, use multiple external hard disks and then rotate the disks off-site to further aid in disaster recovery. When setting up the backup, Windows Server Backup labels each disk with the server name, the current date and time, and the disk name you assign. To avoid any confusion while rotating disks between sites and when performing a restore, attach a physical label for identification purposes that matches the information provided during their setup.

Because a single NTFS volume is created to span across all the disks, you don't have control over exactly which disks the backup will use in the set. If for some reason you want to back up to a specific disk, you can detach or disable the other disks. The same goes for taking a disk off-site. When the disk is removed, the backup program will use the remaining disks for the next scheduled backup.

If you don't have the disk capacity to back up to a hard disk, you can target your backups to a local volume. Storing your backups on a local volume impacts the volume's performance; therefore, you should not place any additional server data on the volume. Windows Server Backup supports only backing up to a single volume per disk.

The last option, back up to a shared network folder, allows you to store your backups on a remote folder share that will hold only one backup at a time. This means that each time the backup is run, it overwrites the previous backup in the folder. An alternative approach, often used by administrators to avoid overwriting of the remote folder backup, is to create a PowerShell script. The script is used to automate the process of moving the backup on a daily basis to a longer-term storage location. To maintain multiple versions of your backups, consider using dedicated disks. Prior to backing up to a remote share, make sure the appropriate permissions are set on the share and its contents to maintain security and integrity of your backups.

After selecting a storage location for your backups, you are ready to perform the actual backup. Before you do, let's take a quick look at what the folder and file structure of a backup looks like and options for optimizing the backup process.

REVIEWING THE FOLDER AND FILE STRUCTURE CREATED DURING A BACKUP

When your backup starts, Windows Server Backup creates a folder structure in the target location you specified. The parent folder, named *WindowsImageBackup*, includes a subfolder with the name of the server you performed the backup on. If you expand this folder, you can see the following folder/file structure:

- Backup <Date> <ID number>
- Catalog
- Logs
- SPPMetadataCache
- MediaID

These files and folders contain information and details about your backup. For example, the Backup <Date><ID number> folder contains several XML files that provide backup history details along with virtual hard disk (VHD) files that are basically duplicates of your volumes.

The Catalog folder contains information about the volumes backed up and where your backups are stored. The MediaID file contains the identifier tagged to the backup storage location, whereas the Logs folder contains a text file that documents errors that occur during the backup process. The SPPMetadataCache folder contains files used by Metadata Cache Management to store information about metadata caches. You need to keep all of these folders/files together in order to perform a restore.

OPTIMIZING YOUR BACKUPS (FULL VERSUS INCREMENTAL)

After you complete the first full backup, you can then automatically run incremental backups, which saves only the data that has changed from the last backup. By default, Windows Server Backup creates incremental backups that function much like full backups, allowing you to restore from a single backup. In the past, you had to restore a full backup followed by the necessary incremental backup(s) to complete the restore process.

Windows Server Backup also provides performance enhancements by using block-level technology and Volume Shadow Copy Service (VSS). Block-level backup technology increases performance by bypassing the files and file system. In other words, Windows Server Backup reads the blocks in the order they appear on the disk instead of reading them in the order they appear in files, which are usually fragmented across the disk. *Volume Shadow Copy Service (VSS)* takes a snapshot of the volume's current data, which is used by Windows Server Backup to back up the data. The snapshot, or shadow copy, is then deleted when the backup has completed.

If you are backing up full volumes, you have the option to optimize the backup process by selecting *Configure Performance Settings. . .* in the Actions panel in the Windows Server Backup console (see Figure 18-15).

Figure 18-15

Optimizing backup
performance on full volumes

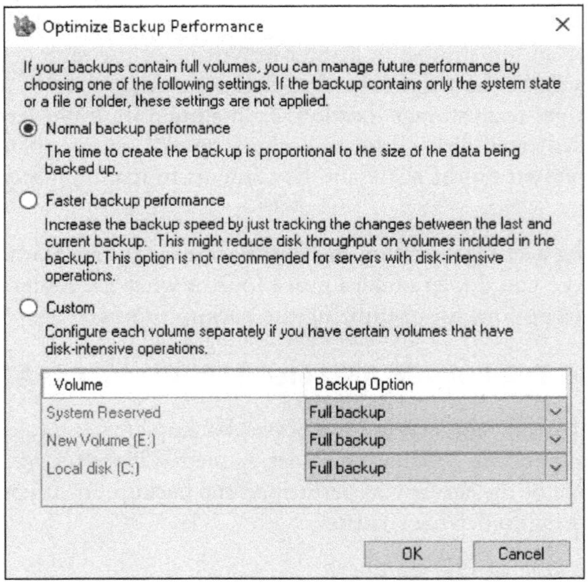

The following provides a brief overview of each option:

- **Normal backup performance (default):** Indicates you are performing full backups and that you want the volume's contents transferred in their entirety.
- **Faster backup performance:** Indicates you are performing incremental backups; therefore, Windows keeps a shadow copy on the source volume, which it will use to track changes. The next time you perform a backup, only the changes made since the last backup will be transferred. This is accomplished by reading from the "diff" area of the shadow copy. The "diff" area is storage space on a volume that is used to maintain a set of information that represents the differences between the current content and the content from a previous point in time. These differences are called *snapshots* and you look at them closer later in this lesson. To protect against data loss, Windows Server Backup still performs a full backup when you reach 14 incremental backups and more than 14 days have passed since the last full backup.
- **Custom:** Allows you to configure each volume separately.

 PERFORM A MANUAL BACKUP OF A LOCAL VOLUME TO A REMOTE SHARE

GET READY. To complete a backup on a volume on Server01 to a remote share on LON-SVR1, perform the following steps.

TAKE NOTE*

A remote share (\\LON-DC1\volbackup) needs to be created on Server02 before starting this exercise, and Server01 needs to have a simple volume named *CorpData* mapped to drive (E:) with a few sample folders and files to include in the backup.

1. Log on to LON-SVR1 and open Server Manager.
2. Click **Tools > Windows Server Backup.**
3. In the Actions panel, select **Backup Once.**
4. When prompted to select a Backup option, select **Different Options** and click **Next.**
5. Select **Custom** for the backup configuration and click **Next.**
6. Select **Add Items,** select the **New Volume (E:)** volume, and then click **OK.**
7. Select **Next** to continue.
8. On the Specify Destination Type screen, select **Remote shared folder** and then click **Next.**
9. Enter the location **\\LON-DC1\volbackup** and click the **More information** link to read and understand the security implications of backing up to a shared folder. Click **OK** and then click **Next** to continue.
10. Review the backup items to confirm your settings and then click **Backup.**
11. Click **Close** after the backup status changes to completed for the Corpdata volume (see Figure 18-16).

Figure 18-16

Completing the backup of the
CorpData volume

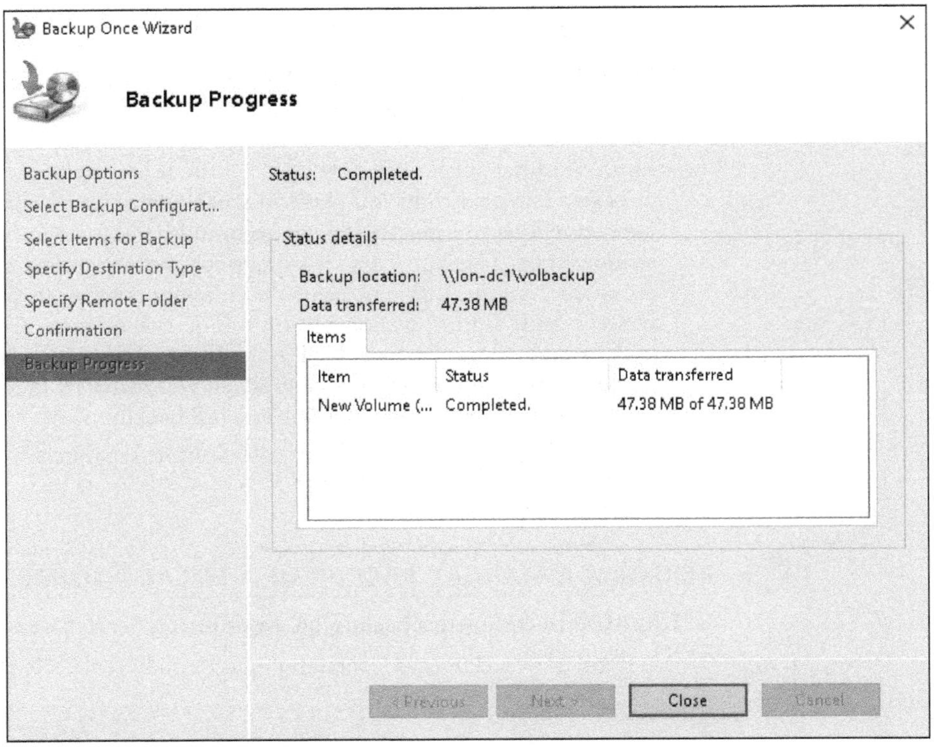

```
Backup Once Wizard                                                    ×

[icon]  Backup Progress

Backup Options              Status:   Completed.
Select Backup Configurat...
Select Items for Backup      Status details
Specify Destination Type        Backup location:   \\lon-dc1\volbackup
Specify Remote Folder           Data transferred:   47.38 MB
Confirmation
Backup Progress                 Items

                                Item          Status         Data transferred
                                New Volume (...  Completed.    47.38 MB of 47.38 MB


                                        < Previous   Next >     Close      Cancel
```

PERFORM A SCHEDULED FULL BACKUP TO A REMOTE SHARE

GET READY. To complete a full backup on Server01 to a remote share on LON-SVR1, perform the following steps.

1. Log on to LON-SVR1 and open Server Manager.
2. Click **Tools > Windows Server Backup**.
3. In the Actions panel, select **Backup Schedule**. In the Getting Started Wizard, click **Next**.
4. Select **Full server (recommended)** and click **Next**.
5. Select **Once a day**, select a time of day that is closest to your current time, and click **Next**.
6. Select **Backup to a shared network folder** and click **Next**.
7. After reading the message that each backup will erase the previous backup when using a remote shared folder as a storage destination, click **OK**.
8. Enter the location for the backup **\\LON-DC1\fullbackup** and then click **Next**.
9. Enter the user name and password to use for scheduling the backup and then click **Next**.
10. Review the settings and click **Finish**.
11. Click **Close**.
12. Confirm the backup was successful by viewing the status in Windows Server Backup after the scheduled time has passed.

TAKE NOTE*

A remote share (\\
LON-DC1\fullbackup)
needs to be created
on Server02 before
starting this exercise.

PERFORM A BARE METAL RECOVERY BACKUP OF A SERVER

GET READY. To complete a Bare Metal Recovery backup on LON-SVR1 to a remote share on LON-DC1, perform the following steps.

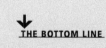

TAKE NOTE[*]

A remote share (\\LON-DC1\ BMbackup) needs to be created on Server02 before starting this exercise.

1. Log on to LON-SVR1 and open Server Manager.
2. Click **Tools > Windows Server Backup.**
3. In the Actions panel, select **Backup Once.**
4. When prompted to select a Backup option, select **Different Options** and click **Next.**
5. Select **Custom** for the backup configuration and click **Next.**
6. Select **Add Items** and select **Bare metal recovery.** Notice that a Bare Metal Recovery includes the system state, system reserved, and C: but not data drives. To restore volumes that include data to a new system, you need to include them as part of the backup. Click **OK.**
7. Click **Next.**
8. Select **Remote shared folder** for the storage location and then click **Next.**
9. Enter the location for the backup **\\LON-DC1\BMbackup** and then click **Next.**
10. Confirm the settings and click **Backup.**
11. After the backup has completed successfully, click **Close.**

■ Determining Backup Strategies for Different Windows Server Roles and Workloads

↓
THE BOTTOM LINE

The roles assigned to a server can dramatically impact its configuration as well as the frequency and type of backup needed to restore it in the future. When determining your backup strategy, you need to consider how often the data changes, whether the data can be replaced if it is lost, and how critical the data is.

CERTIFICATION READY
Determine backup strategies for different Windows Server roles and workloads, including Hyper-V Host, Hyper-V Guests, Active Directory, File Servers, and Web Servers using Windows Server 2016 native tools and solutions
Objective 6.1

As part of your overall backup strategy, take into consideration the roles installed on each of your servers. As you learned, the role performed by the server can have an impact on how you approach the backup and eventually the restore of the server. Let's take a closer look at some of these roles and what can be done to back them up.

Backing Up DHCP and DNS

The Dynamic Host Configuration Protocol (DHCP) database contains information about IP address leases, reservations, scopes, scope options, and DHCP registry key settings. It's backed up automatically at 60-minute intervals to the %systemroot%\ System32\Dhcp\Backup directory. It is also backed up as part of a system state or full backup, and by using the DHCP Manager console.

You can back up DHCP via the DHCP Manager console by performing the following steps:

1. Open the DHCP Manager console.
2. Select the DHCP server that contains the scopes you want to back up.
3. Select Action > Backup.
4. Browse to the folder where you want to store the backup and click OK. By default, this is %systemroot%\Windows\System32\Dhcp\Backup.
5. Click OK.

Active Directory–integrated DNS zone configuration information is stored in the registry; therefore, it's also backed up as part of the system state and during full backups. In situations where you have a corrupted or failing DNS, you can recover it only by restoring the entire system state, which might or might not be what you want to do. An alternative is to use DNSCMD with the /zoneexport switch to export the Active Directory–integrated zones to a file you can back up. This file can be restored as a primary zone file and then converted into an Active Directory–integrated zone, if necessary.

The following command creates a copy of the DNS zone contoso.com in the %systemroot%\system32\dns\backup\contoso.com.dns.bak file:

```
DNSCMD /zoneexport contoso.com \backup\contoso.com.dns.bak
```

The XCOPY command can be used to back up primary and secondary zone files to a backup folder you specify:

```
Example: XCOPY %systemroot%\system32\dns c:\backups\dns /y
```

The command backs up all zone text files into the c:\backups folder.

You can then restore them by using XCOPY to copy the backup to the %systemroot%\system32\Dns folder.

Backing Up Certificate Services

Certificate Services stores a database in the C:\Windows\system32\Certlog location by default. When certificates are issued to users and computers, the associated information is maintained in the Certificate Services database.

If this database becomes corrupted or is accidentally deleted, certificates issued by the server will be considered invalid. Although Certificate Services is backed up as part of a system state and a full backup, you can also back it up via the Certificate Services console by performing the following steps:

1. Open the Certificate Services console.
2. Right-click the server and choose All Tasks >Backup CA . . .
3. Select Next to start the Certification Authority Wizard.
4. Select Private Key and CA Certificate and the Certificate database and certificate database log options.
5. Enter C:\Windows\System32\CABackup and click Next.
6. Click OK to create the directory.
7. Enter and confirm a password to gain access to the private key and the CA certificate file and click Next.
8. Click Finish to back up the Certificate Services.

Backing Up Active Directory Domain Services

Because Active Directory contains the user and computer account for the entire domain and is essential for authentication and authorization for an organization, it is important that you keep Active Directory running smoothly. However, if something goes wrong and you have to restore Active Directory, you will need an Active Directory backup.

Active Directory is backed up as part of system state and full backups. The components included in the system state are as follows:

- **System startup (boot) files:** These files are required to boot Windows.
- **System registry:** This contains registry files that include information about the system hardware, low-level operating system components, and installed programs and their settings.
- **COM+ Class registration database:** The Component Object Model (COM) is a standard for writing component software in a distributed systems environment. COM uses the registry database for storing component registration information. The database supports a VSS writer, allowing VSS requesters to back up the database on a shadow-copied volume.
- **System volume (SYSVOL):** This folder, on a domain controller, contains the net logon shared folders used to host user logon scripts and policy settings for pre-Windows 2000 network clients. The user logon scripts for Active Directory–enabled clients, system policies, Group Policy settings, and the File Replication Service (FRS) directories are used to stage directories and files that must be available and synchronized between domain controllers.
- **Active Directory:** This includes the Active Directory database (ntds.dit), checkpoint file (edb.chk), transaction logs (edb*.log), and reserved transaction logs (Res1.log and Res2.log).

In most Active Directory environments, changes to user passwords, computer accounts, and other domain objects occur on a daily basis. When performing restores, you return the domain controller back to a former state, which can affect authentication and replication; therefore, the more frequently you back up domain controllers, the fewer problems you will encounter after a restore. In general, back up your domain controller at least once per day. In situations where you are upgrading a domain controller or installing a new service pack or hotfix, perform a backup immediately.

Another common mistake regarding Active Directory is the deletion of Active Directory objects by accident. For example, if you delete an organizational unit (OU) by mistake that just happens to contain multiple user accounts, the deletion will be replicated to all other domain controllers. When this happens, you need to perform an authoritative restore to return the OU to its original state. This involves restoring the system state and using the Ntdsutil tool. Fortunately, with the release of Windows Server 2008 R2, there is a more efficient way to handle the restoring of deleted Active Directory objects without having to restore the system state. It's called the *Active Directory Recycle Bin*.

PERFORM A BACKUP OF THE SYSTEM STATE OF AN ACTIVE DIRECTORY DOMAIN CONTROLLER USING WBADMIN

GET READY. To complete a backup of the system state on LON-DC1, perform the following steps.

TAKE NOTE * In this exercise, you back up to a remote share (\\LON-DC1\ADbackup) in which network backups will save only the latest version of the backup. This is used only for training purposes. In a production environment, you back up to attached disks that are rotated off-site to provide additional security and protection. It's also recommend that you perform a scheduled full backup to occur on a daily basis for your domain controllers.

1. Log on to LON-DC1 with administrative privileges.
2. Start PowerShell. Enter the following commands to install Windows Server Backup, pressing **Enter** after each command. If Windows Server Backup is already installed, you can skip this step.
   Add-WindowsFeature Windows-Server-Backup Exit
3. Open a command prompt and type the following to perform a system state backup of the domain controller using wbadmin:
   wbadmin start backup systemstatebackup –backuptarget: \\LON-DC1\ ADbackup –quiet
4. To close the command window after the backup operation successfully completes, type **Exit**.
5. Browse to the share on **\\LON-DC1\ADbackup** to view the files/folders created as part of the system state backup of the domain controller.

Backing Up Web Servers

Windows Server 2016 web services is Internet Information Services (IIS) version 10. By default, the website files are stored in the C:\inetpub\wwwroot folder. The IIS configuration is stored in the c:\Windows\system32\inetsrv. In addition, websites may use SSL digital certificates to provide website security.

To back up IIS and its associated websites, you need to:

- Back up website files.
- Back up/export current IIS certificates.
- Back up IIS configuration (settings).

The configuration can be backed up by opening a command prompt, changing to the c:\ Windows\system32\inetsrv folder, and using the appcmd command:

```
appcmd add backup <name_of_backup>
```

A folder with your backup name appears in c:\Windows\system32\inetsrv\backup, which contains administration.config, application, Host.config, MBSchema.xml, MetaBase.xml, and redirection.config.

To recover the IIS configuration, you would execute the following command:

```
appcmd restore backup <name_of_backup>
```

Managing VSS Settings Using VSSAdmin

Volume Shadow Copy administrative command-line tool (VSSAdmin) can be used to create and delete volume shadow copies/associations, list shadow copy providers and writers, and resize volume shadow storage associations.

The VSSAdmin is used to manage the VSS. Before you take a closer look at this tool and the information it provides, it's important that you have a good understanding of VSS and its components.

The VSS coordinates several components, which allows you to back up your server without impacting running applications or users. It accomplishes this through the use of shadow copies. A shadow copy (also called a *snapshot*) of a volume is a duplicate of the data on the volume at a specific point in time.

The VSS components communicate with each other via the VSS Framework to both create and restore your shadow copies. The following provides a brief overview of the tasks performed by each component:

- *VSS requester:* Requests that a shadow copy be taken. The Windows Server Backup program and the System Center Data Protection Manager are examples of VSS requesters.

- *VSS writer:* Makes sure the data is ready for the shadow copy to be created. The writer is usually provided by the application software itself and each Windows server has one or more writers. Examples of VSS writers include Hyper-V, SQL Server, Exchange Server, Active Directory System Service, Performance Counter Writer, ASR Writers, System Writer, Registry Writer, WINS Jet Writer, DHCP Jet Writer, WMI Writer, Certificate Authority Writer, NTDS Writer, and so on.

- *VSS provider:* Creates and maintains the shadow copies. Examples of VSS providers (file share and system types) include the Microsoft File Share Shadow Copy provider and the Microsoft Software Shadow Copy provider. Hardware vendors also include VSS providers with their storage arrays.

- *Source volume:* Contains the data you want to copy.

- *Storage volume:* Holds the shadow copy storage files for the VSS provider.

The following provides a basic overview of how VSS components interact with each other during a typical backup:

1. When you launch Windows Server Backup (VSS requester), it queries the VSS and asks it to list the VSS writers.

2. Each VSS writer then describes the components and data stores that need to be backed up and provides the information to VSS. VSS provides the information to the VSS requester (for example, Windows Server Backup), which then selects the components to back up.

3. VSS then notifies all VSS writers to prepare their data in order to make a shadow copy. Preparing the data involves completing any open transactions, flushing their caches, and/or rolling any transaction logs. Once the VSS writer has completed its pre-backup tasks, it informs VSS.

4. VSS tells the VSS writers to quiesce (pause) their data and temporarily queue any I/O write requests from applications. This is necessary to ensure a consistent backup and allows VSS to create a shadow copy of the volume. The VSS freezes the file system to ensure its metadata is written in a consistent order.

5. The VSS provider tells VSS to create the shadow copy.

6. After the copy is complete, VSS unfreezes the file system and releases the VSS writers, which allows them to process their queue of I/O write requests.

7. VSS then queries the VSS writers to make sure they held I/O write requests during the time period the snapshot was taken. If they did not, the shadow copy is deleted and Windows Server Backup (VSS requester) is notified. If the VSS writers handled their queues appropriately, VSS provides Windows Server Backup (VSS requester) with information on where it can locate the shadow copy.

When an application attempts to write to the protected sector, VSS makes a copy of the sector before it allows the application to write to it. The copied sector is the one stored in the backup.

Now that you have a better idea of the components that make up VSS and how they interact with each other, you can use the VSSAdmin to view the list of writers and providers on your server, see a list of volume shadow copies on your server, and view how much storage space (currently, in the future, and maximum) is used by shadow copies.

 MANAGE VSS SETTINGS USING VSSADMIN

GET READY. To manage VSS settings using VSSAdmin, perform the following steps.

1. Log on to Server01 with administrative privileges.

2. Open a command prompt.

3. To see a list of commands supported with VSSAdmin, type the following:
   vssadmin /?

4. To see a list of VSS writers on Server01 and their current state, type the following:
   vssadmin list writers

   If this were a server and you noticed one or more of the VSS writers with a state set to Failed, you can most likely fix them with a quick server reboot. In situations where you cannot reboot the server, you can search the registry or the Internet for the Writer ID to identify the service associated with it. You can then restart that specific service and rerun the list writers command to confirm the fix.

5. To see a list of VSS providers on Server01, type the following:
   vssadmin list providers

6. To see a list of existing volume shadow copies, type the following:
   vssadmin list shadows

7. To list the volumes that are eligible for shadow copies, type the following:
   vssadmin list volumes

8. To view used, allocated, and maximum shadow copy storage space, type the following:
   vssadmin list shadowstorage

After running the command, you see the amount of shadow copy storage space being used, the amount allocated for the future, and the maximum space that can be used. If you notice the amount of storage space that is being used is almost as large as the maximum, you might need to move the VSS storage area to another location. This can be accomplished by accessing the computer's volume that is currently used for the volume shadow copy storage area, right-clicking it, and choosing Configure Shadow Copies. Select Settings and then choose another volume to store the shadow copies on.

Using Shadow Copies for Shared Volumes

Shadow Copies for Shared Volumes (SCSV) and Hyper-V snapshots provide you with the ability to return to a specific point in time.

Although Windows client operating systems support the ability to create system restore points, Windows Server 2008 and later operating systems don't. What they do provide is the ability to use Shadow Copies for Shared Volumes (SCSV) as well as Hyper-V snapshots as mechanisms for returning to a specific point in time. You can also utilize the Hyper-V VSS writer and VSS to back up virtual machines (VMs) using Windows Server Backup.

Shadow Copies for Shared Volumes (SCSV) uses the capabilities of VSS to capture and store copies of folders and files (located on shared network resources) at a specific point in time.

When SCSV is implemented on a volume, both end users and administrators can recover accidentally deleted or overwritten files as well as compare different versions of the same file. Because end users can restore their own files, implementing SCSV can dramatically reduce not only the time but the associated costs of having to recover their folders and files via their IT support desk.

You enable SCSV on a per-volume basis by selecting Server Manager > Tools > Computer Management. The volumes must be formatted using NTFS and should not contain any mounted drives or mount points. If the volume has either, their contents will not be included in the shadow copies. The first shadow copy of the volume is a complete copy of the data; subsequent shadow copies include only the changes made since the last shadow copy was created. The source volume is the volume that contains the data you want to copy. The storage volume is where your shadow copies will be located and if possible should be placed on a separate disk from the one that holds the source volume.

You need at least 300 MB of free space to create a shadow copy on the selected volume. By default, a shadow copy is created at 7:00 AM (Monday–Friday) and at 12:00 PM (Monday–Friday). You can modify the schedule by selecting the Settings button. You can also click the Create Now button to take a manual snapshot between scheduled times (see Figure 18-17).

 ENABLE SHADOW COPIES FOR SHARED VOLUMES

GET READY. To enable Shadow Copies for Shared Volumes on LON-SVR2, perform the following steps.

1. Log on to LON-SVR2 with administrative privileges.
2. Create a shared folder called **CorpDocs** on a simple volume (E:) on LON-SVR2 and share the folder so that administrators have full access.
3. Create a file in the CorpDocs folder named **Agenda.txt**, enter sample text, and then save and close.
4. Open Server Manager and select **Tools > Computer Management.**
5. Expand the **Storage** item and select **Disk Management.**
6. Right-click the volume you created the shared folder on and choose **Properties.**
7. Select the **Shadow Copies** tab, as shown in Figure 18-17.
8. Confirm the volume you selected in Step 6 is highlighted and then click **Enabled.**
9. To confirm you want to enable shadow copies on the volume, click **Yes.** A snapshot is taken immediately and the date/time stamp is noted.

Figure 18-17

Enabling Shadow Copy for
a Shared Volume/Taking
snapshot

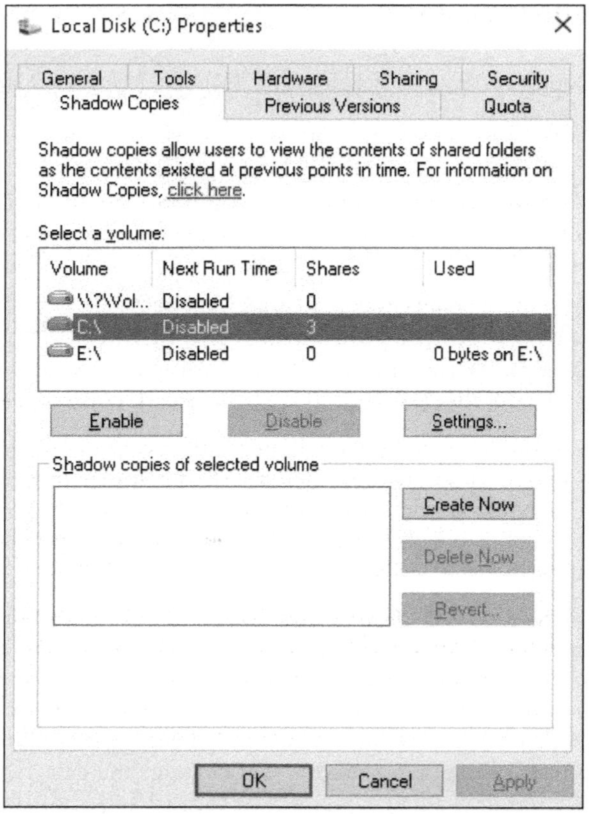

10. To create a second snapshot of the selected volume, click **Create Now** and then
click **OK** to close.

Backing Up Hyper-V Hosts and Virtual Machines

VMs, created by using Hyper-V, are stored as files on your hard disk. These files contain
the VHDs, saved state files, snapshot files, and configuration files. Because these are
stored on a volume on your server, Windows Server Backup can be used to protect them
in combination with the VSS.

TAKE NOTE*

Remember that a
Hyper-V checkpoint
is not a substitute for
backups.

To back up an entire Hyper-V host, it is recommended to perform a full server backup of the
host server. This will back up the configuration of virtual machines, snapshots associated with
the virtual machines, and virtual hard disks used by the virtual machines.

VSS writers are responsible for preparing their data in order to make the shadow copy and are
instructed by VSS to quiesce its associated application to ensure a consistent backup is made.
By using the Microsoft Hyper-V VSS writer, Windows Server Backup can create the snapshots while the VM is running.

Windows Server Backup supports only a volume-based backup for VMs; therefore, you need
to select all volumes that contain your VM files. For example, if you store your VM configuration files on one volume and your VHD files on another, both volumes need to be backed up.

VMs containing dynamic disks need to be backed up offline. Machines running operating
systems that do not support VSS and those that do not have Integration Services installed will
be put in a saved state while the VSS snapshot is created.

SKILL SUMMARY

IN THIS LESSON YOU LEARNED:

- Intruders and some viruses, worms, rootkits, spyware, and adware gain access to a system by exploiting security holes in Windows, Internet Explorer, Microsoft Office, or other software applications. Therefore, the first step you should take to protect yourself against malware is to keep your system up to date with the latest service packs, security patches, and other critical fixes.

- Windows Update provides your Windows Server 2016 users with a way to keep their computers current by checking a designated server. The server provides software that patches security issues, installs updates that make Windows and your applications more stable, fixes issues with existing Windows programs, and provides new features.

- WSUS provides a centralized server that can be used to manage the deployment of updates from Microsoft. Instead of having each of your Windows computers connect to Microsoft to check for updates, consider using Windows Server Update Services (WSUS). WSUS enables you to centrally manage the deployment of updates released through Microsoft, track compliance, and provide basic reporting functions.

- After configuring your clients to use WSUS, organize them into computer groups. This enables you to target specific systems for updates. WSUS comes with two built-in groups: All Computers and Unassigned Computers. If you want to test the impact the updates will have on your computers and any line-of-business applications before rolling them out to your entire organization, then new groups should be created.

- Windows Defender is designed to protect your computer against viruses, spyware, and other types of malware. It protects against these threats by providing real-time protection in which it notifies you if malware attempts to install itself on your computer or when an application tries to change critical settings.

- When an organization loses data, the results can range from a loss of productivity to an entire meltdown of the company itself. Having a solid backup and restore strategy along with the systems, processes, and tools to execute the strategy is the key to your ability to recover.

- Windows Server Backup, wbadmin, and Windows PowerShell cmdlets provide the tools you need to back up and restore your critical data and servers.

- The roles assigned to a server can dramatically impact its configuration as well as the frequency and type of backup needed to restore it in the future. When determining your backup strategy, you will need to consider how often the data changes, whether the data can be replaced if it is lost, and how critical the data is.

◼ Knowledge Assessment

Multiple Choice

Select the correct answer for each of the following questions.

1. Microsoft releases a new code pack that enables viewing RAW camera files. Which category of update does this fall under?
   a. Recommended updates
   b. Important updates
   c. Optional updates
   d. Suggested updates

2. Which of the following is the correct location to configure how Windows Update functions in Windows Server 2016?
   a. Control Panel > System > Windows Update
   b. Control Panel > System and Security > Windows Update
   c. Control Panel > System > Security > Windows Update
   d. Control Panel > Network and Internet > Windows Update

3. Which of the following is true about a replica mode WSUS server? (Choose all that apply.)
   a. It mirrors update approvals, settings, computers, and groups from the upstream server.
   b. It mirrors update approvals, settings, computers, and groups from the downstream server.
   c. It can be used to approve updates.
   d. It cannot be used to approve updates.

4. Which of the following best describes server-side targeting? (Choose all that apply.)
   a. Uses the Update Services console to move computers into computer groups
   b. Uses the Local Group Policy editor to create a group policy designating the computer group to add the computer to
   c. Uses the Group Policy Management Console to create a group policy designating the computer group to add the computer to
   d. Results in computers initially being added to the Unassigned Computers group

5. Which command when run on a Windows 10 and Windows Server 2016 client detects available updates from the WSUS server, queues them, and then presents a notification to install the updates?
   a. wuauclt /detect
   b. wuauclt /detectnow
   c. wuauclt /force
   d. wuauclt /renew

6. Which of the following are scan options available in Windows Defender? (Choose all that apply.)
   a. Quick
   b. Full
   c. Optional
   d. Custom

7. Which tab is the location of the quarantined items Windows Defender finds?
   a. Home tab
   b. History tab
   c. Update tab
   d. Settings tab

8. Which tools are available after installing the Windows Server Backup feature? (Choose all that apply.)
   a. Windows Server Backup MMC snap-in
   b. wbadmin.exe
   c. Windows PowerShell cmdlets for Windows Server Backup
   d. RSAT

9. Which of the following statements best describe Windows Server Backup in Windows Server 2016? (Choose all that apply.)
   a. Backing up to tape drives and attached hard drives is supported.
   b. Applications can be backed up to a DVD drive.
   c. Applications can be backed up to a remote shared folder.
   d. Backing up to folders on a local or remote volume supports only one copy of the backup. Subsequent backups overwrite the contents of the previous backup.

10. Which of the following types of backups will back up all of the files needed to recover Active Directory?

   a. System state

   b. Full backup

   c. Bare Metal Recovery

   d. System reserved

11. Which `wbadmin` command backs up the system state on a domain controller to a remote volume located on Server02 named SysState?

   a. `wbadmin start backup -backuptarget: \\server02\SysState`

   b. `wbadmin start backup -systemstate \\server02\SysState`

   c. `wbadmin start backup -systemstate -backuptarget: \\server02\ SysState`

   d. `wbadmin start backup -systemstate -target: \\server02\SysState`

12. Which Volume Shadow Copy Service (VSS) component is responsible for making sure the data is ready for the shadow copy to be created?

   a. VSS requester

   b. VSS provider

   c. VSS writer

   d. VSS ShadowWriter

13. Which of the following are characteristics of Shared Copies for Shadow Volumes (SCSV)?

   a. It's enabled on a per-volume basis.

   b. By default, shadow copies are taken at 7:00 AM and 12:00 AM (Monday–Friday).

   c. The volumes must be formatted using NTFS.

   d. Mount points are supported.

14. A Bare Metal Recovery backup includes which of the following?

   a. System state

   b. System reserved

   c. Critical volumes

   d. Volumes containing user data files

15. When should a manual backup be performed in place of a regularly scheduled backup? (Choose all that apply.)

   a. The volume isn't included in your regular backups.

   b. The backup needs to be done outside the normally scheduled window.

   c. The backup needs to be stored in a location that is different from the one used for automatic backup.

   d. A change to the server needs to be made (for example, install a new service pack).

16. You select the faster backup performance option via the Windows Server Backup console > Actions panel > Configure Performance Settings. Which of the following describes the impact of making this configuration change on future backups? (Choose all that apply.)

   a. This indicates you are performing incremental backups after the initial full backup.

   b. After you reach 14 incremental backups and more than 14 days have passed, Windows Server Backup will still perform a full backup.

   c. After you reach 21 incremental backups and more than 10 days have passed, Windows Server Backup will still perform a full backup.

   d. After you reach 14 incremental backups and more than 30 days have passed, Windows Server Backup will still perform a full backup.

Best Answer

Choose the letter that corresponds to the best answer. More than one answer choice may achieve the goal. Select the BEST answer.

1. To ensure computers in three branch offices (with no IT support on-site) receive Windows Updates on a regular basis along with those in a main office, which WSUS configuration provides the best solution with the least amount of administrative overhead for the approval and distribution of updates and the least amount of traffic over the WAN link?
    a. Single WSUS server at main office. Branch office PCs configured to use this server.
    b. WSUS server at main office and downstream WSUS servers at each branch office running in autonomous mode. PCs configured to use the local WSUS server.
    c. WSUS server at main office and downstream WSUS servers at each branch office running in replica mode. PCs configured to use the local WSUS server.
    d. WSUS server at main office and downstream WSUS servers at two branch offices running in replica mode and one running in autonomous mode.

2. Which Windows Update option ensures your system receives and uses the most current updates?
    a. Install updates but let me choose whether to install them.
    b. Download updates but let me choose whether to install them.
    c. Check for updates but let me choose whether to download and install them.
    d. Centrally approve and deploy updates using WSUS.

Matching and Identification

1. Match the following terms with the related description or usage.
    _____ a. Application Reputation
    _____ b. Action Center
    _____ c. Autonomous mode
    _____ d. Client-side targeting
    _____ e. Downstream server
    _____ f. Replica mode
    _____ g. Server-side targeting
    _____ h. Synchronization
    _____ i. Upstream server

    1. Uses group policies to configure computers to add themselves automatically to computer groups in the Update Services console.
    2. Provides a central location for viewing notifications regarding problems with your hardware and software. It also provides information related to the security and maintenance of your computer.
    3. WSUS servers that obtain their updates from a WSUS server that has been configured to obtain its updates directly from Microsoft.
    4. Involves moving clients to computer groups using the Update Services console.
    5. The process of connecting and downloading updates.
    6. This WSUS server mode enables you to configure separate update approval settings while still retrieving updates from the upstream WSUS server.
    7. A mode in which the WSUS server mirrors update approvals, settings, computers, and groups from the upstream server.
    8. A WSUS server that obtains its updates directly from Microsoft.
    9. The early warning system that alerts you before running unrecognized applications or downloading files from the Internet during the time between a release of a virus and definitions to protect against it.

Build a List

1. Specify the correct order of steps necessary to setting up a WSUS server.

   _____ Specify an update source for the WSUS server.

   _____ Synchronize updates to the WSUS server.

   _____ Determine a deployment strategy.

   _____ Install the WSUS server role.

   _____ Set up client computers.

   _____ Approve and install updates on client computers.

2. Specify the correct order of steps necessary to creating a computer group in WSUS from the Update Services console.

   _____ Expand the Computers node, right-click All Computers, and choose Add Computer Group.

   _____ Confirm the group appears under the All Computers node.

   _____ Open the Update Services console.

   _____ Type a name and click Add.

   _____ Log on with administrative privileges.

3. Specify the correct order of steps necessary to removing a quarantined item in Windows Defender.

   _____ Select Quarantined Items.

   _____ Open Windows Defender.

   _____ Select the detected item and read its description.

   _____ Click View Details.

   _____ Select the History tab.

   _____ Select Remove.

4. Specify the correct order of steps necessary to backing up the system state using the wbadmin and PowerShell commands on a domain controller without the Windows Server Backup feature installed, by placing the number of the step in the appropriate space. Not all steps will be used.

   _____ Log on to the domain controller with administrative privileges.

   _____ Run `wbadmin /verify` to confirm the backup was successful.

   _____ Open a command prompt and run the following command to back up the system state: `C:\wbadmin start backup -systemstate -backuptarget:\\server02\ADBackup -quiet`

   _____ Start PowerShell and enter the following command: `PS C:\Add-WindowsFeature Windows-Server-Backup`

   _____ Type `Exit` to close the command window after the backup operation completes successfully.

5. Specify the correct order of steps necessary to backing up the DHCP database. Not all steps will be used.

_____ Stop the DHCP service.

_____ Log on to the DHCP Server with administrative privileges.

_____ Open the DHCP Manager console.

_____ Select OK to start the backup.\

_____ Select the DHCP Scope.

_____ Browse to the folder where you want to store the backup.

_____ Select Action > Backup.

■ Business Case Scenarios

Scenario 18-1: Quarantining Files with Windows Defender

After working on a Windows Server 2016 computer running Windows Defender, it maintains quarantined files from the past several months. Is it possible to configure the computer to remove quarantined files on a weekly basis? If so, explain the steps involved.

Scenario 18-2: Configuring WSUS

A WSUS server is set up at a branch office that gets its updates from a WSUS server at the main office. The option to approve updates is not available on the branch office server, yet it receives updates from the WSUS server at the main office on a regular basis. Describe the issue.

Scenario 18-3: Recovering the System State of DNS

You are currently running system state backups on a server that has Active Directory–integrated DNS zones. Will this be sufficient to allow you to restore the DNS zones should they become corrupted? What are the restore implications to consider when using this backup approach?

Monitoring Server Installations

70-740 EXAM OBJECTIVE

Objective 6.2 – Monitor server installations. This objective may include but is not limited to the following: Monitor workloads using Performance Monitor; configure Data Collector Sets; determine appropriate CPU, memory, disk, and networking counters for storage and compute workloads; configure alerts; monitor workloads using Resource Monitor.

LESSON HEADING	EXAM OBJECTIVE
Managing Performance	Monitor workloads using Resource Monitor
• Monitoring Performance Using Task Manager	Monitor workloads using Performance Monitor
• Monitoring Workloads Using Resource Monitor	Determine appropriate CPU, memory, disk, and networking counters for storage and compute workloads
• Monitoring Workloads Using Performance Monitor	
• Determining Appropriate Counters for Storage and Compute Workloads	Configure Data Collector Sets
• Configuring Data Collector Sets	Configure alerts
• Configuring Alerts	
Configuring and Analyzing Event Viewer Logs	
• Understanding Logs and Events	
• Filtering Events	
Managing Services	

KEY TERMS

bottleneck	performance alert	service
Data Collector Sets (DCS)	Performance Monitor	Services console
Event Viewer	process	Task Manager
performance	Resource Monitor	

■ Managing Performance

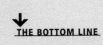

THE BOTTOM LINE

Performance is the overall effectiveness of how data moves through the system. Of course, it is important to select the proper hardware (processor, memory, disk system, and network) to satisfy the expected performance goals. Without the proper hardware, bottlenecks limit the effectiveness of software.

When a component limits overall performance, that component is known as a ***bottleneck***. When you relieve one bottleneck, another bottleneck might be triggered. For example, one of the most common bottlenecks is the amount of memory the system has. By increasing the memory, you can often increase the overall performance of a system (up to a point). However, when you add more RAM, then RAM needs to be fed more data from the disk. Therefore, the disk becomes the bottleneck. So, although the system might become faster, if your performance is still lacking, you will have to look for new bottlenecks.

You usually cannot identify performance problems just by taking a quick look at performance. Instead, you need a baseline. You can get one by analyzing the performance when the system is running normally and within design specifications. Then, when a problem occurs, compare the current performance with your baseline to see what is different. Because performance can also change gradually over time, it is highly recommended that you baseline your computer as early as possible, and regularly thereafter, so that you can chart your performance measures and identify trends. This will give you an idea about when the server needs to be upgraded or replaced or the workload of the server reduced.

There are several tools available with Windows for you to analyze performance. They include:

- Task Manager
- Performance Monitor
- Resource Monitor

Monitoring Performance Using Task Manager

Task Manager gives you a quick glance at performance and provides information about programs and processes running on your computer. A *process* is an instance of a program that is being executed.

Task Manager is one of the handiest programs you can use to take a quick glance at performance to see which programs are using the most system resources on your computer. You can see the status of running programs and of programs that have stopped responding, so you can stop a program running in memory.

To start Task Manager, right-click the empty space on the taskbar and choose Task Manager (or you can open the Security menu by pressing Ctrl+Alt+Del and choosing Task Manager). When Task Manager starts, it displays only the running applications (see Figure 19-1).

Figure 19-1

Using Task Manager

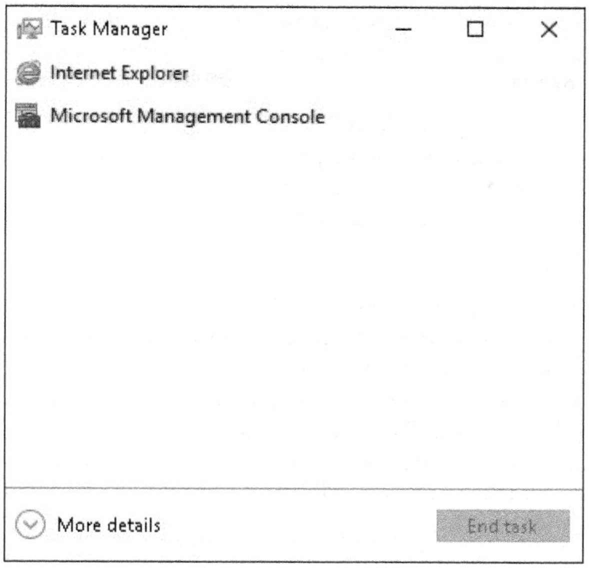

Click the More Details down arrow to show all the available tabs (see Figure 19-2). When you first start Task Manager on a computer running Windows Server 2016, five tabs are opened for Task Manager:

- Processes
- Performance
- Users
- Details
- Services

Figure 19-2

Viewing the Task Manager tabs

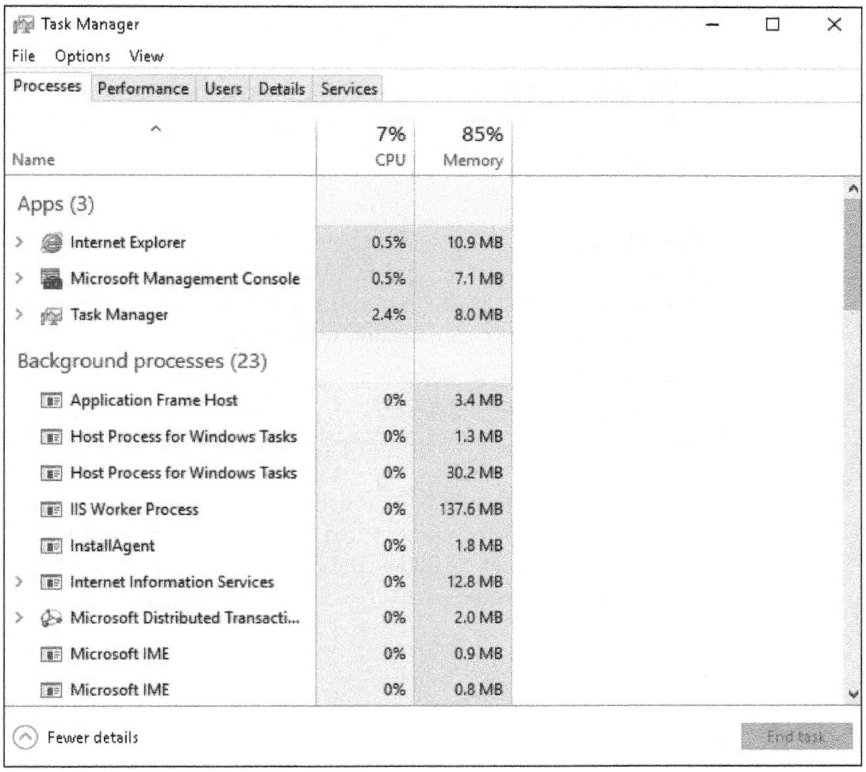

The Processes tab shows all processes running in memory and how much processing and memory each process uses. The processes display applications (as designated by Apps), background processes, and Windows Processes. On the Processes tab, you can perform the following tasks:

- To see the processes that use the highest percentage of CPU utilization, click the CPU column header.
- To stop a process, right-click the process and choose End task.
- To jump to the Details tab for a particular process, right-click the process and choose Go to details.
- If you want to see the executable that is running the processes, right-click the process and choose Open file location.

To add or remove additional columns, right-click a column header and select or deselect the desired column (such as Process Identification (PID) or process name).

The Performance tab (as shown in Figure 19-3) displays the amount of CPU usage, physical Memory usage, and Ethernet throughput. For CPU usage, a high percentage indicates the programs or processes are requiring a lot of CPU resources, which can slow your computer. If the percentage seems frozen at or near 100%, a program might not be responding.

Figure 19-3

Viewing CPU usage

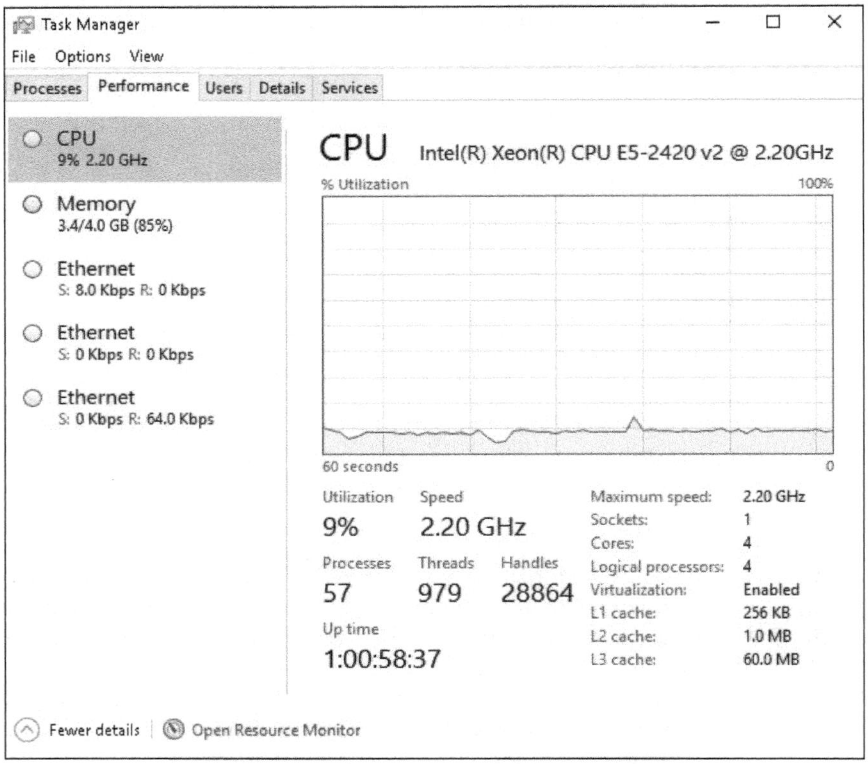

Click Memory to display how much of the paging file is being used (*In use* and *Available*), the amount of Committed and Cached memory, Paged pool, and Non-paged pool. It also shows you the total amount of RAM, the Speed of the RAM, and the number of Slots used for memory on the motherboard.

The Users tab displays the users who are currently logged on, the amount of CPU and memory usage that each user is using, and the processes the users are running. It also gives you the ability to disconnect them.

The Details tab displays a more detailed look at the processes running on the computer, including the Process Identification (PID). The PID is composed of unique numbers that identify a process while it is running. Similarly, you can stop the process and you can increase or decrease the process priority.

If you are an advanced user, you might want to view other advanced memory values on the Details tab. To do so, right-click the column heading and choose Select Columns and then select or deselect values to be displayed or not displayed. While there are nearly 40 columns to display, some of the more useful values include the following:

- **Working set (memory):** Shows the amount of memory in the private working set plus the amount of memory the process is using that can be shared by other processes.
- **Peak working set (memory):** Shows the maximum amount of working set memory used by the process.
- **Working set delta (memory):** Shows the amount of change in working set memory used by the process.
- **Commit Size:** Shows the amount of virtual memory that is reserved for use by a process.
- **Paged pool:** Shows the amount of committed virtual memory for a process that can be written to another storage medium, such as the hard disk.
- **NP pool:** Shows the amount of committed virtual memory for a process that can't be written to another storage medium. (NP is an abbreviation for non-paged.)

The Services tab displays all services on the computer that are running and not running. Similar to the Services console, you can start, stop, or restart services.

Monitoring Workloads Using Resource Monitor

Resource Monitor is a system tool that allows you to view information about the use of hardware (CPU, memory, disk, and network) and software resources (file handlers and modules) in real time. You can filter the results according to specific processes or services that you want to monitor. In addition, you can use Resource Monitor to start, stop, suspend, and resume processes and services, and to troubleshoot when an application does not respond as expected.

CERTIFICATION READY
Monitor workloads using
Resource Monitor
Objective 6.2

Resource Monitor (see Figure 19-4) is a powerful tool for understanding how your system resources are used by processes and services. In addition to monitoring resource usage in real time, Resource Monitor can help you analyze unresponsive processes, identify which applications are using files, and control processes and services. To start Resource Monitor, open Task Manager, click the Performance tab, and click Open Resource Monitor. You can also search for Resource Monitor from the Start page, or you can use a command prompt or Windows PowerShell to execute the `resmon.exe` command.

Resource Monitor includes five tabs:

- Overview
- CPU
- Memory
- Disk
- Network

The Overview tab displays basic system resource usage information; the other tabs display information about each specific resource. Each tab in Resource Monitor includes multiple tables that display detailed information about the resource featured on that respective tab.

The next four exercises cover common tasks for which you might use Resource Monitor. For example, if you want to determine the program (process) that is hogging the processor resources, you can use *Identify the highest current CPU usage*. If a file is locked and you cannot delete it because it is in use, you can use the *Identify the process that is using a file exercise* to see which process has the file open.

IDENTIFY THE HIGHEST CURRENT CPU USAGE

GET READY. To identify a process that is using the highest current CPU usage, perform the following steps.

1. Click **Start** and type **Resource Monitor**. From the search results, click **Resource Monitor**.

2. Click the **CPU** tab.

3. In the Processes section, click **CPU** to sort processes by current CPU resource consumption.

VIEW THE CPU USAGE OF A PROCESS

GET READY. To view the CPU usage for each process, perform the following steps.

1. Click **Start** and type **Resource Monitor**. From the search results, click **Resource Monitor**.

2. Click the **CPU** tab.

3. In the Processes section, in the Image column, select the check box next to the name of the service for which you want to see usage details. You can select multiple services. Selected services are moved to the top of the column.

4. Click the title bar of **Services** to expand the table. Review the data in Services to see the list of processes hosted by the selected services and to view their CPU usage.

 IDENTIFY THE PROCESS THAT IS USING A FILE

GET READY. To identify the process that is using a file, perform the following steps.

1. Click **Start** and type **Resource Monitor**. From the search results, click **Resource Monitor**.

2. Click the **CPU** tab and then click the title bar of **Associated Handles** to expand the table.

3. Click in the **Search Handles** box, type the name of the file you want to search for, and then click **Search**.

 IDENTIFY THE NETWORK ADDRESS TO WHICH A PROCESS IS CONNECTED

GET READY. To identify the network address that a process is connected to, perform the following steps.

1. Click **Start** and type **Resource Monitor**. From the search results, click **Resource Monitor**.

2. Click the **Network** tab and then click the title bar of **TCP Connections** to expand the table.

3. Locate the process whose network connection you want to identify. If there are a large number of entries in the table, you can click **Image** to sort by executable file name.

4. Review the Remote Address column and the Remote Port column to see which network address and port the process is connected to.

Monitoring Workloads Using Performance Monitor

Performance Monitor is an MMC snap-in that provides tools for analyzing system performance. It is included in the Computer Management console and it can be opened as a stand-alone console from Administrative Tools. It can also be started by executing the perfmon command. From a single console, you can monitor application and hardware performance in real time, specify which data you want to collect in logs, define thresholds for alerts and automatic actions, generate reports, and view past performance data in a variety of ways.

CERTIFICATION READY
Monitor workloads using Performance Monitor
Objective 6.2

Performance Monitor (see Figure 19-5) provides a visual display of built-in Windows performance counters, either in real time or as a way to review historical data.

You can add performance counters to Performance Monitor by right-clicking the main pane and choosing Add Counters. Another way to add performance counters is to create and use custom Data Collector Sets. (Data Collector Sets are explained later in this lesson.) Figure 19-6 shows the Add Counters dialog box. You can create custom views that can be exported as Data Collector Sets for use with performance and logging features.

Figure 19-5

Viewing Performance Monitor

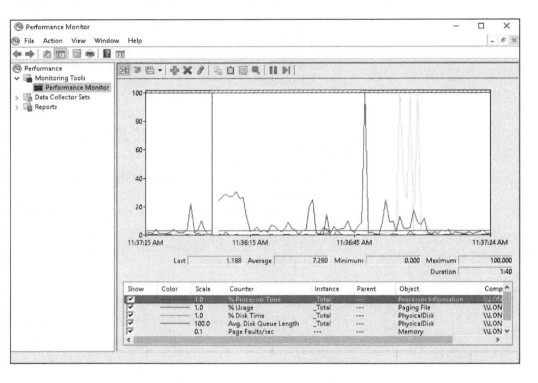

Figure 19-6

Adding counters to Performance Monitor

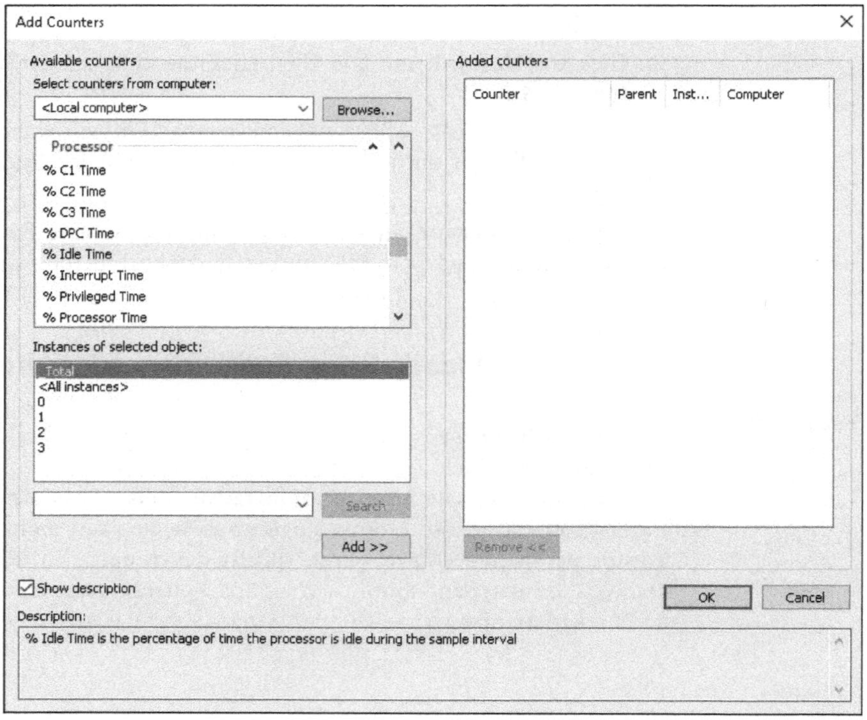

To control how and what is displayed, right-click Performance Monitor and choose Properties. The Performance Monitor Properties dialog box displays the following five tabs:

- **General:** Allows you to adjust the samples, such as how often samples are taken and how much data is displayed on the graph before the graph is redrawn. You can also choose to display the legend, the value bar, and the toolbar.
- **Source:** Allows you to display real-time data or to open a log file that you have saved.
- **Data:** Allows you to choose counters to appear as well as the color and scale of those counters.
- **Graph:** Allows you to configure the available views and if the view starts over or you can scroll to look at previous displayed data. It allows you to display or not display the vertical grid, horizontal grid, vertical scale numbers, time axis labels, as well as determine the maximum scale.
- **Appearance:** Allows you to display the color and fonts used by various components so that you can distinguish one Performance Monitor window from another.

Performance Monitor has multiple graph types that enable you to visually review performance log data. They include:

- **Line:** The default graph type; connects points of data with lines
- **Histogram Bar:** A bar graph showing data
- **Report:** A written description in which values are displayed as text

Performance programs and performance information are not available to everyone. Therefore, if a user needs to use Performance Monitor to view performance information, the user can be added to one of the following groups:

- *Administrators* can access all of the performance tools and data.
- *Performance Monitor Users* can view both real-time and historical data within the Performance Monitor console and can use the Reliability Monitor. However, they cannot create or modify Data Collector Sets or use the Resource View.
- The *Performance Log Users* group can view both real-time data and historical data within the Performance Monitor console. In addition, these users can create or modify Data Collector Sets if they have *Log on as a batch user* rights on the server.

Determining Appropriate Counters for Storage and Compute Workloads

Task Manager, Resource Monitor, and Performance Monitor can be used to view the four primary systems that make up a computer. As previously mentioned, there are hundreds of counters available in Performance Monitor and as you add other services or applications, other counters are made available that allow you to monitor the performance of those applications. Although using all of these counters might take some heavy research, you should always start with some basic performance counters to get a glimpse of how your system is running.

CERTIFICATION READY
Determine appropriate CPU, memory, disk, and networking counters for storage and compute workloads
Objective 6.2

A computer is composed of four primary systems: a processor, memory, disk, and network. For the processor, memory, and disk performance, you should always start with these counters:

- Processor: %Processor Time measures how busy the processor is. Although the processor might jump to 100% processor usage, the processor should not be working at or above 80% capacity most of the time. If it is, you should consider upgrading the processor (using a faster processor or adding additional processors) or move some of the services to other systems. However, high processor utilization may also be caused by not having enough RAM, which causes high drive activity for the drive with the paging file.

- A page fault occurs when a process attempts to access a virtual memory page that is not available in its working set in RAM. If the pages/sec is 1,000 or higher, you should increase the memory.

- Paging File: % Usage shows how much of the paging file is actually being used. If the paging file % usage is above 75%, you might need to increase memory or reduce the server's memory usage.

- Physical Disk: %Disk Time indicates how busy a disk is as measured by the percentage of time that disk was busy. If a disk is consistently approaching 100%, the disk is being overutilized.

- Physical Disk: %Avg. Disk Queue Length is the average number of read requests or write requests queued for the disk in question. A sustained average higher than 2 times the number of spindles (physical hard drives) indicates that the disk is being overutilized.

Configuring Data Collector Sets

Rather than add individual performance counters each time you want to view the performance of a system, you can create *Data Collector Sets (DCS)* that allow you to organize a set of performance counters, event trace data, and system configuration data into a single object that can be reused as needed.

Windows Performance Monitor uses performance counters, event trace data, and configuration information, which can be combined into Data Collector Sets, as follows:

- Performance counters are measurements of system state or activity. They can be included in the operating system or can be part of individual applications. Windows Performance Monitor requests the current value of performance counters at specified time intervals.

- Event trace data is collected from trace providers, which are components of the operating system or of individual applications that report actions or events. Output from multiple trace providers can be combined into a trace session.

- Configuration information is collected from key values in the Windows registry.

Windows Performance Monitor can record the value of a registry key at a specified time or interval as part of a file.

 CREATE AND USE A DATA COLLECTOR SET

GET READY. To create a DCS, perform the following steps.

1. Click **Start** and type **Performance Monitor.** Then, from the results, click **Performance Monitor.**

2. In the left pane, expand **Data Collector Sets.**

3. Right-click the **User Defined** folder and choose **New > Data Collector Set.**

4. On the Create New Data Collector Set page, when you are prompted to create a new Data Collector Set, type a name in the Name text box. Ensure that the **Create from a template (Recommended)** option is selected and then click **Next.**

5. When you are prompted to choose a template, click **System Performance** (see Figure 19-7) and then click **Next.**

Figure 19-7

Selecting a template

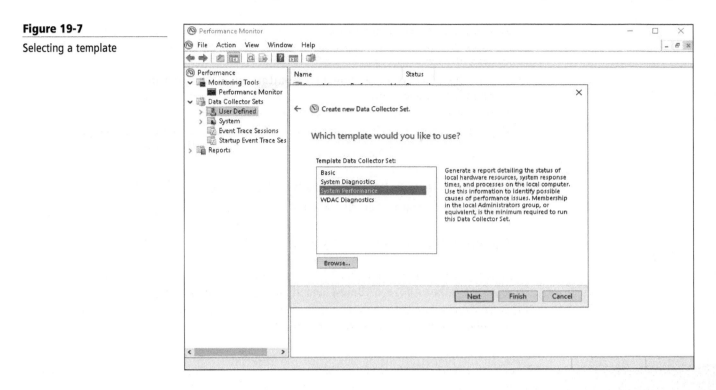

6. When you are prompted to choose where you would like the data to be saved, click **Next**. If you run Performance Monitor to collect data over an extended period, you should change the location to a nonsystem data drive.

7. When you are prompted to create the Data Collector Set, with the **Save and close** option selected, click **Finish**.

8. To start the Data Collector Set, right-click the DCS and choose **Start**.

9. Close Performance Monitor.

Configuring Alerts

In Performance Monitor, a ***performance alert*** is a notification or task that is executed when a performance value is reached. Performance Monitor can also be used to start certain tasks when certain counters reach a particular value. For example, if the processor reaches 90%, you can have Performance Monitor run a command to stop a service or perform some other action in an effort to reduce burden on the processor.

CERTIFICATION READY
Configure alerts
Objective 6.2

When you configure performance alerts, you can perform almost any action that you want. You can send a network message or log events into the application event log. You can configure alerts to start applications and performance logs.

CREATE A PERFORMANCE ALERT

GET READY. To create a performance alert, perform the following steps.

1. Click **Start** and type **Performance Monitor**. Then, from the results, click **Performance Monitor**.

2. In the left pane, expand **Data Collector Sets**.

3. Right-click the **User Defined** folder and choose **New > Data Collector Set**.

4. On the Create New Data Collector Set page, when you are prompted to create a new Data Collector Set, type a name in the Name text box.

5. Select **Create manually (Advanced)** and then click **Next**.

6. Select **Performance Counter Alert** and then click **Next**.

7. When you are prompted to identify the performance counter you would like to monitor, click **Add** to open a dialog box, in which to select the desired counter. When you have added the counter, click **OK**.

8. The limit defines when a performance alert is triggered. For the *Alert when* option, select either **Above** or **Below** and then in the Limit box, type the value. Click **Next**.

9. When you are prompted to create the Data Collector Set, select **Open properties for this data collector set**. Click **Finish**.

10. In the Properties dialog box, click the **Task** tab.

11. In the Run this scheduled task when the data collector set stops text box, type the path of a script or command that you want to execute when the condition is met. If necessary, specify any task arguments in the Task Arguments text box.

12. To specify when the Data Collector Set will run, click the **Schedule** tab.

13. Click **Add.** In the Folder Action dialog box (see Figure 19-8), specify the Beginning date that the task will run, the Expiration date for the task, and the Launch time.

Figure 19-8

Viewing the Schedule tab

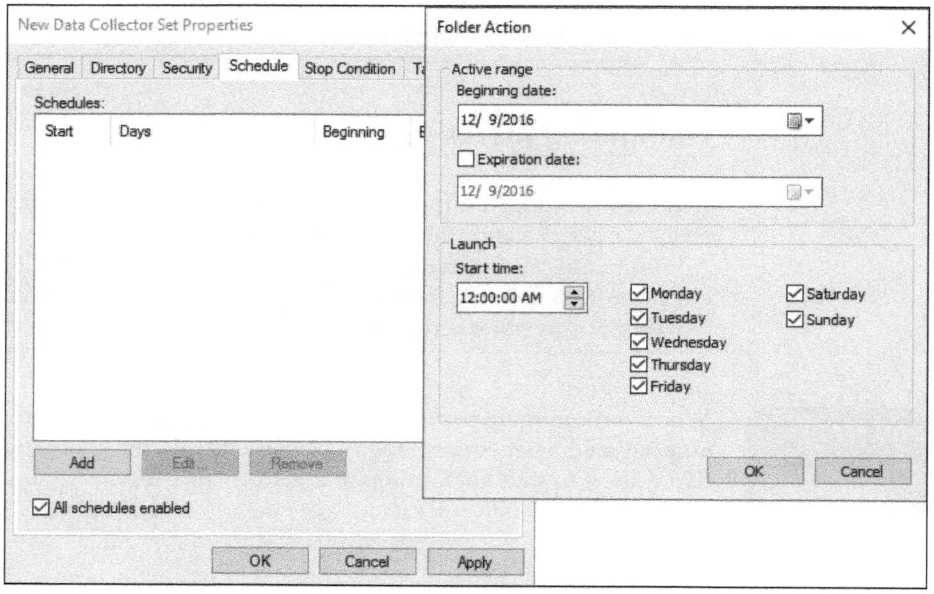

| New Data Collector Set Properties | Folder Action | × |

General | Directory | Security | **Schedule** | Stop Condition | Ta

Schedules:

| Start | Days | | Beginning | B |

Active range
Beginning date:
12/ 9/2016

☐ Expiration date:
12/ 9/2016

Launch
Start time:
12:00:00 AM

☑ Monday   ☑ Saturday
☑ Tuesday   ☑ Sunday
☑ Wednesday
☑ Thursday
☑ Friday

Add   Edit   Remove

☑ All schedules enabled

OK   Cancel

OK   Cancel   Apply

14. Click **OK** to apply your settings and then click **OK** again to close the Properties dialog box.

15. Close Performance Monitor.

■ Configuring and Analyzing Event Viewer Logs

↓
THE BOTTOM LINE
One of the most useful troubleshooting tools is Event Viewer, which is essentially a log viewer. Whenever you have problems, you should look in Event Viewer to see any errors or warnings that might reveal what the problem is.

Event Viewer is an MMC snap-in that enables you to browse and manage event logs. It is included in the Computer Management console and is included in Administrative Tools as a stand-alone console. You can also execute the `eventvwr.msc` command.

Event Viewer enables you to perform the following tasks:

- View events from multiple event logs (see Figure 19-9).
- Save useful event filters as custom views that can be reused.
- Schedule a task to run in response to an event.
- Create and manage event subscriptions.

Figure 19-9

Event Viewer

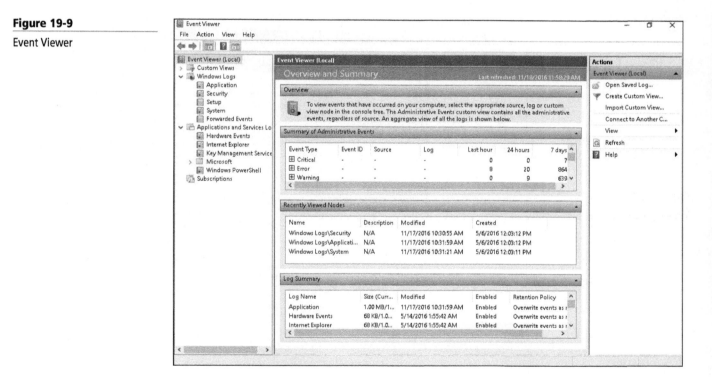

Understanding Logs and Events

To get the best use of Windows logs, you need to understand how the logs are organized and how the events are categorized.

When you examine Event Viewer more closely, you will see the following items:

- **Custom Views:** Allows you to create custom views of events. By default, it includes Administrative Events, which collects Critical, Error, and Warnings from all logs on the server. In addition, you can create your own custom view by right-clicking Custom Views and choosing Create Custom View.

- **Windows Logs:** Includes logs that were available in previous versions of Windows. They include:
  - **Application:** Contains events logged by applications or programs.
  - **Security:** Contains events such as valid and invalid logon attempts and access to designated objects, such as files and folders, printers, and Active Directory objects.
  - **Setup:** Contains events related to application setup.
  - **System** (see Figure 19-10): Contains events logged by Windows system components, including errors displayed by Windows during boot and errors with services.
  - **Forwarded Events:** Stores events collected from remote computers. To collect events from remote computers, you must create an event subscription. It should be noted that Forwarded Events does not work with pre-Windows 7 and Windows Server 2008 operating systems.
- **Applications and Services Logs:** Displays a set of events related to an application or service. Some examples include DHCP, DNS, and Active Directory.

Figure 19-10

Viewing System logs

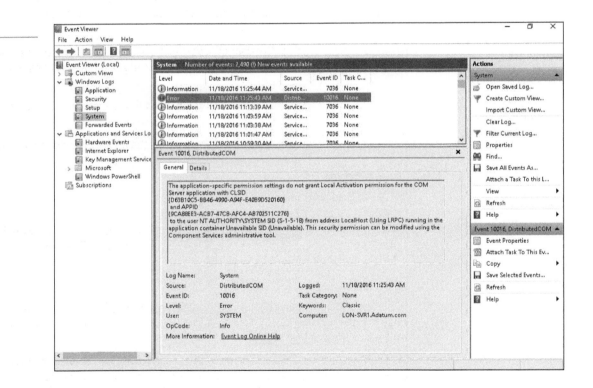

When you open an event, you will see the Log Name, Source, Event ID, Level, User (if applicable), Logged details (date and time), Computer, and other information. Table 19-1 shows the common fields displayed in the Event Viewer logs.

Table 19-1

Common Files Displayed in the Event Viewer Logs

Property Name	Description
Source	The software that logged the event, which can be a program name (such as "SQL Server") or a component of the system or of a large program (such as a driver name)
Event ID	A number identifying the particular event type
Level	A classification of the event severity:
	Information: Indicates that a change in an application or component has occurred (such as an operation has successfully completed, a resource has been created, or a service has started)
	Warning: Indicates that an issue has occurred that can impact service or result in a more serious problem if action is not taken
	Error: Indicates that a problem has occurred that might impact functionality that is external to the application or component that triggered the event
	Critical: Indicates that a failure has occurred from which the application or component that triggered the event cannot automatically recover
	Success Audit: Indicates that the exercise of a user right was successful
	Failure Audit: Indicates that the exercise of a user right has failed

Filtering Events

When looking at the logs shown by Event Viewer, you can be overwhelmed by the number of events. Therefore, you need to know how to filter events so that you can focus on specific information.

When you open any of these logs, particularly the Application, Security, or System logs, they might display thousands of entries. Unfortunately, this means that it might take some time to find what you are looking for.

To begin with, you can sort Event Viewer by clicking the column header. For example, by clicking the Date and Time column header, you can sort the events by date and time. This comes in handy when you know that a problem started at a certain time and you want to view the events that were generated at that time.

To reduce the number of items that are displayed, you can use a filter to reduce the number of entries shown. To filter a log, click Action > Filter Current Log. When the Filter Current Log dialog box opens (see Figure 19-11), you can select when the event was logged, the Event level, Task category, Keywords, User, and Computer(s).

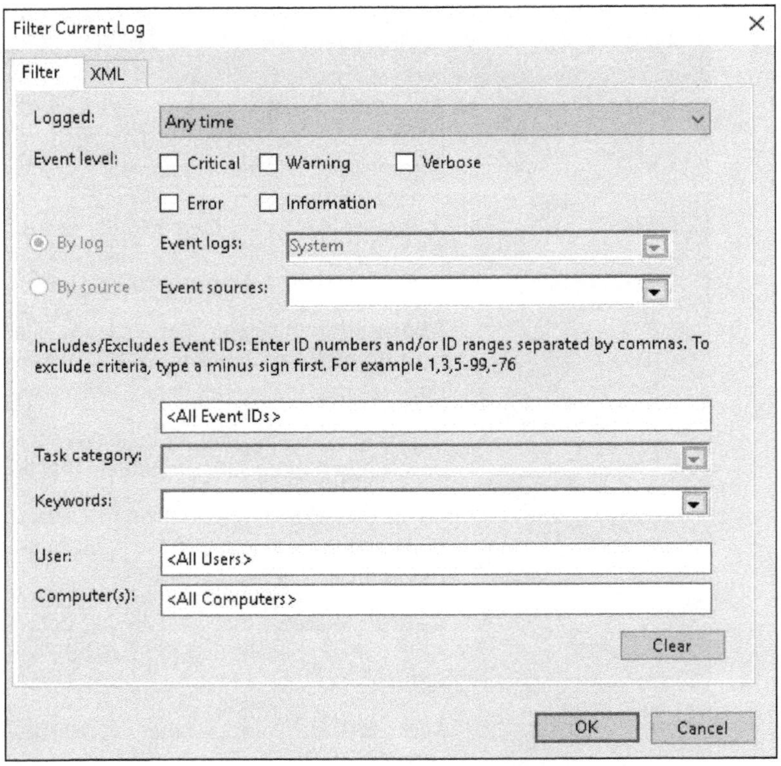

Figure 19-11

Filtering an event log

Filter Current Log ✕

| Filter | XML |

Logged: [Any time ▼]

Event level: ☐ Critical ☐ Warning ☐ Verbose
☐ Error ☐ Information

◉ By log Event logs: [System ▼]

○ By source Event sources: [▼]

Includes/Excludes Event IDs: Enter ID numbers and/or ID ranges separated by commas. To exclude criteria, type a minus sign first. For example 1,3,5-99,-76

[<All Event IDs>]

Task category: [▼]

Keywords: [▼]

User: [<All Users>]

Computer(s): [<All Computers>]

[Clear]

[OK] [Cancel]

→ **VIEW AND MANAGE EVENTS**

GET READY. To view and manage events, perform the following steps.

1. Log on to LON-CL1 as **adatum\administrator** with the password of **Pa$$wOrd**.
2. Right-click **Start** and choose **Event Viewer**.
3. Expand the **Windows Logs** and click **System**.
4. Right-click **System** and choose **Filter Current Log**.
5. In the Filter Current Log dialog box, select **Critical**, **Warning**, and **Error**, and then click **OK**.
6. After you view the listed events, right-click **System** and choose **Filter Current Log**.
7. Deselect **Critical**, **Warning**, and **Error**.
8. In the <All Event IDs> text box, type **8015** and click **OK**.
9. Click the **Application** node. Double-click the first warning or error.
10. In the Event Properties dialog box, click **Close**.
11. Expand the **Applications and Services Logs**, expand **Microsoft**, expand **Windows**, expand **GroupPolicy**, and then click the **Operational** node.
12. Close Event Viewer.

■ Managing Services

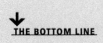
THE BOTTOM LINE

A *service* is a program, routine, or process that performs a specific system function to support other programs or to provide a network service. A service runs in the system background without a user interface. Some examples include World Wide Publishing services, Server services, Workstation services, and Windows Event Log services.

To manage services, use the ***Services console*** located on the Administrative Tools menu. The Services snap-in (see Figure 19-12) is also included in the Computer Management console and the Server Manager console. You can also execute `mmc services.mmc` from a command prompt or Run box.

Figure 19-12

Viewing the Services console

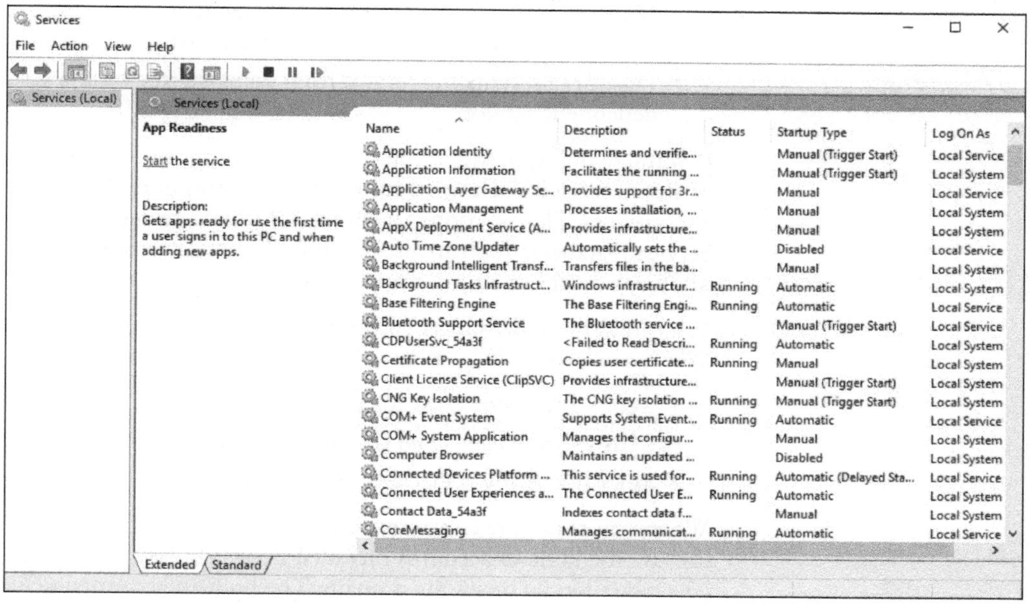

To start, stop, pause, resume, or restart services, right-click the service and choose the desired option. To the left of the service name is a description. To configure a service, right-click the service and choose Properties (or simply double-click the service). Figure 19-13 shows the Services properties.

Figure 19-13

Configuring a service

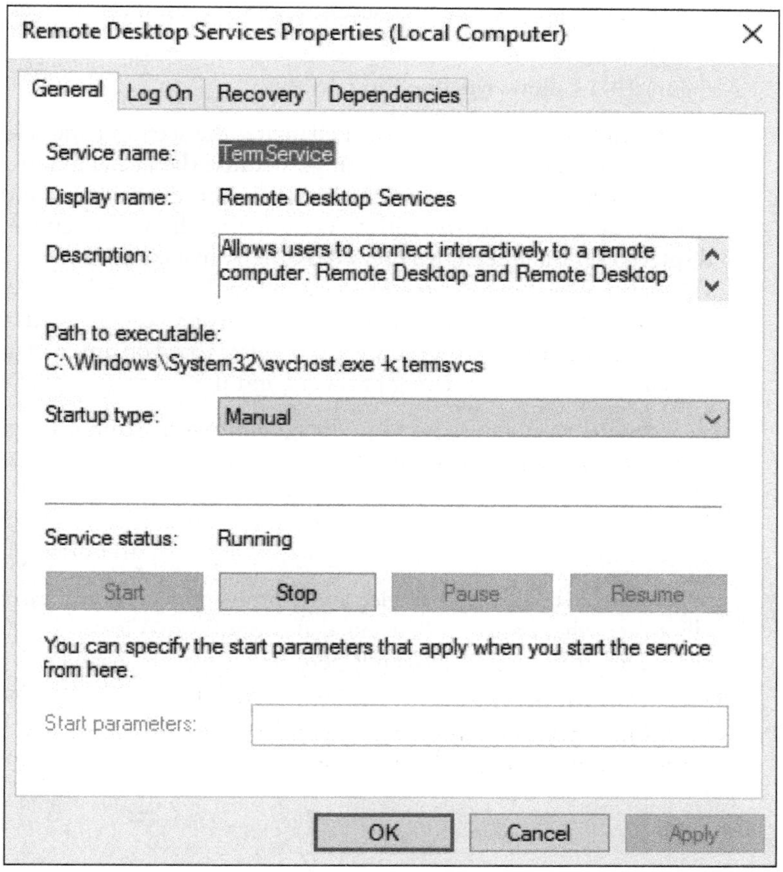

On the General tab, click the Startup type drop-down arrow and choose one of the following:

- **Automatic:** Specifies that the service should start automatically when the system starts.
- **Automatic (Delayed Start):** Specifies that the service should start automatically after the services marked as automatic have started (which is approximately two minutes).
- **Manual:** Specifies that a user or a dependent service can start the service. Services with manual startup do not start automatically when the system starts.
- **Disable:** Prevents the service from being started by the system, a user, or any dependent service.

If you like doing things at the command prompt or you have a need to use a script to start or stop a service, use the sc command to communicate with the Service Control Manager and services. The sc config command is used to modify a service entry in the registry and Service Database. You can also use the net start command to start services and the net stop command to stop services.

You can also use Windows PowerShell to start and stop the services using the following Windows PowerShell cmdlets:

- **Stop-Service:** Used to stop a service
- **Start-Service:** Used to start a service
- **Restart-Service:** Used to restart a service

When you configure a service, you need to configure the account the service runs under. You can use the built-in accounts included with Windows or you can use a service account that you create locally or on the domain. The built-in accounts include:

- **Local System:** Is a highly privileged account that can access most resources on the local computer.
- **NT Authority\LocalService:** Has the same privileges of the local Users group on the computer. When it accesses Network resources, it uses no credentials and a null session.
- **NT Authority\NetworkService:** Has the same level of access as the Users group on the local computer. When it accesses network resources, it does so under the context of the local computer account.

Figure 19-14 shows the Log On tab.

You should always take care when changing the startup parameters for a service, including the *Startup type* and *Log on as* settings, because these changes might prevent key services from running correctly. In addition, Microsoft recommends that you do not change the *Allow service to interact with desktop* setting because this allows the service to access any information displayed on the interactive user's desktop. A malicious user can then take control of the service or attack it from the interactive desktop. If you specify an account that does not have permission to log on as a service, the Services snap-in automatically grants the appropriate permissions to that account on the computer that you are managing. If you use a local or domain account, use a strong password and use a password that does not expire.

As a general rule, you should use the account with minimum rights and permissions for the service to operate. In addition, you should use different service accounts for different services. So if you install Exchange and SQL on a server, you should have a service account for Exchange and a different service account for SQL. SQL and Exchange should be on the same server only for small businesses that have only a handful of employees.

If you enable or disable a service and a problem occurs, you can try to start the service manually to see what happens. You can also check Event Viewer for more information on some of the errors. If the system does not boot because of the enabled or disabled service, you should try to start the computer in Safe mode, which starts only the core services needed to operate, loads only the necessary drivers to operate, and loads in 640 × 480 screen resolution with the minimum number of colors. By using Safe mode, you should have an opportunity to fix the problem.

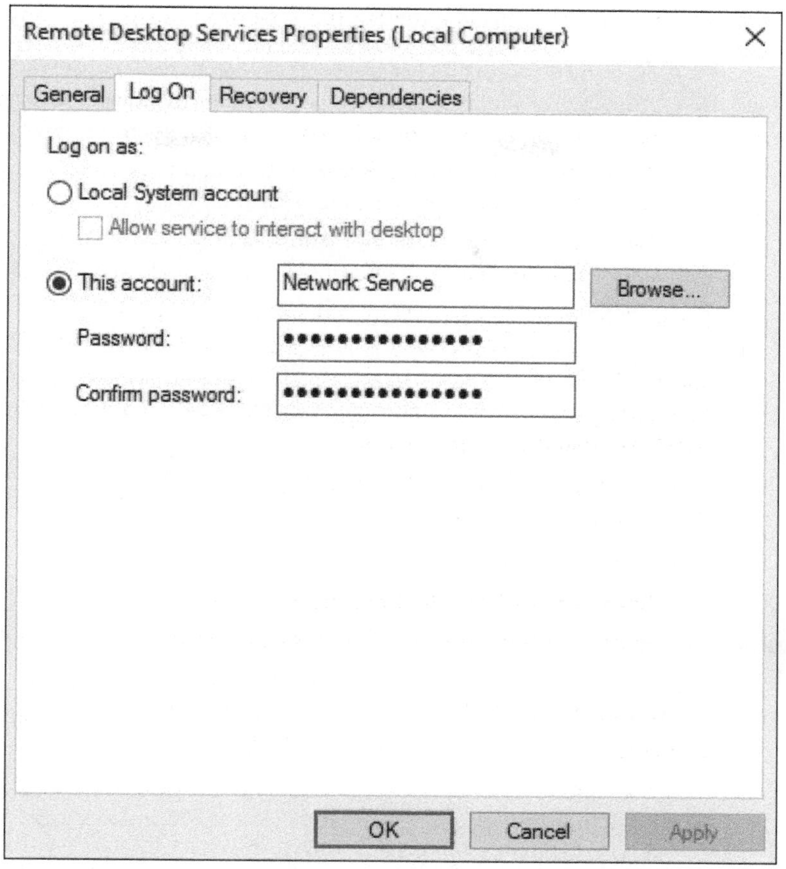

Figure 19-14

Viewing the Log On tab

If you are new to Windows, particularly in administering and configuring Windows, you should click on each service and read the respective description for each service. You will learn that many service names are very descriptive. For now, let's cover two specific services:

- **Server:** Supports file, print, and named-piped sharing over the network. If the Services service is not started, you will not be able to access shared folders, including administrative shares such as C$ and IPC$.

- **Workstation:** Creates and maintains client network connections to remote servers using the SMB protocol. Without this service, you will not be able to access shared folders on other computers.

SKILL SUMMARY

IN THIS LESSON YOU LEARNED:

- Performance is the overall effectiveness of how data moves through the system. Of course, it is important to select the proper hardware (processor, memory, disk system, and network) to satisfy the expected performance goals. Without the proper hardware, bottlenecks limit the effectiveness of software.

- Task Manager gives you a quick glance at performance and provides information about programs and processes running on your computer. A process is an instance of a program that is being executed.

- Resource Monitor is a powerful tool for understanding how your system resources are used by processes and services. In addition to monitoring resource usage in real time, Resource Monitor can help you analyze unresponsive processes, identify which applications are using files, and control processes and services.

- Performance Monitor is an MMC snap-in that provides tools for analyzing system performance. It is included in the Computer Management console and it can be opened as a stand-alone console from Administrative Tools. It can also be started by executing the perfmon command. From a single console, you can monitor application and hardware performance in real time, specify which data you want to collect in logs, define thresholds for alerts and automatic actions, generate reports, and view past performance data in a variety of ways.

- Event Viewer is an MMC snap-in that enables you to browse and manage event logs. It is included in the Computer Management console and is included in Administrative Tools as a stand-alone console. You can also execute the eventvwr.msc command.

■ Knowledge Assessment

Multiple Choice

Select the correct answer for each of the following questions.

1. Which of the following is used to view the Windows logs?
   a. Performance Monitor
   b. Reliability Monitor
   c. System Viewer
   d. Event Viewer

2. When troubleshooting a problem and using Event Viewer, which of the following should be used to help focus on a reduced set of events?
   a. Permissions
   b. Rights
   c. Views
   d. Filters

3. Which program is used to stop a running process?
   a. Performance Monitor
   b. Reliability Monitor
   c. Task Manager
   d. Event Viewer

4. Which program is used to determine what process is using a file?
   a. Performance Monitor
   b. Reliability Monitor
   c. Task Manager
   d. Resource Monitor

5. Which of the following is used to group multiple performance counters so that they can be used over and over in Performance Monitor?
   a. Replay Monitor
   b. Event Viewer
   c. Data Collector Sets
   d. Task Manager

6. After installing a new server (Server1), which is a file and print server, you have received several calls from users who are complaining of slow performance when opening files from the server. Which two tasks determine which application is using the most processing? (Choose all that apply.)
   a. Open Event Viewer and review the Performance logs.
   b. Open Task Manager and view the Processes tab.
   c. Open Resource Monitor and use the Resource View to see the percentage of processor capacity used by each application.
   d. Open Performance Monitor and view the appropriate performance counter.

Best Answer

Choose the letter that corresponds to the best answer. More than one answer choice may achieve the goal. Select the BEST answer.

1. After creating a Data Collector Set, which of the following actions prevents the DCS from logging data when the server has less than 1 GB of available disk space?
   a. Modify the Data Manager settings of the DCS.
   b. Create a passive file screen.
   c. Modify the DCS Actions Properties.
   d. Modify the Disk Redirect option.

Matching and Identification

1. Match each Windows log to the appropriate description or usage.
   _____ 1. Application log
   _____ 2. Security log
   _____ 3. Setup log
   _____ 4. System log
   _____ 5. Forwarded events
   a. Shows boot errors
   b. Shows events collected from remote computers
   c. Shows events generated by applications
   d. Contains events related to the installation of applications
   e. Shows invalid logons and access to audited files

2. Identify the maximum value that will indicate a bottleneck or performance problem for the following performance counters.

   _____ %Processor Time

   _____ Pages/sec

   _____ Paging File:% Usage

   _____ % Avg. Disk Queue Length for each spindle or physical hard drive

■ Business Case Scenarios

Scenario 19-1: Troubleshooting a Performance Problem

You manage several file servers. Several times during the day, the file server performance degrades significantly. Describe how to troubleshoot the problem.

Index

Note: Page numbers followed by "f" and "t" indicates figure and table, respectively.